THE COGNITIVE PSYCHOLOGY OF SCHOOL LEARNING

SECOND EDITION

Ellen D. Gagné
THE CATHOLIC UNIVERSITY OF AMERICA

Carol Walker Yekovich
THE CATHOLIC UNIVERSITY OF AMERICA

Frank R. Yekovich
THE CATHOLIC UNIVERSITY OF AMERICA

HarperCollins*CollegePublishers*

To Robert M. Gagné and John R. Anderson

Besides their far-reaching contributions to theories of cognition and learning, they have inspired us personally with their commitment to both the science of psychology and the improvement of educational practice.

Acquisitions Editor: Chris Jennison
Project Coordination and Text Design: York Production Services
Cover Design: Kay Petronio
Production/Manufacturing: Michael Weinstein/Paula Keller
Compositor: York Production Services
Printer and Binder: R.R. Donnelley & Sons
Cover Printer: The Lehigh Press Inc.

The Cognitive Psychology of School Learning, Second Edition
Copyright © 1993 by Ellen D. Gagné, Carol Walker Yekovich, and Frank R. Yekovich

Library of Congress Cataloging-in-Publication Data

Gagné, Ellen D.
   The cognitive psychology of school learning / Ellen D. Gagné,
Carol Walker Yekovich, Frank R. Yekovich. — 2nd ed.
      p.   cm.
   Includes bibliographical references (p. 476) and indexes.
   ISBN 0-673-46416-4
   1. Learning.   2. Cognition in children.   3. Learning, Psychology
of.   I. Yekovich, Carol Walker.   II. Yekovich, Frank R.
III. Title.
LB1060.G34   1993
370.15′2—dc20   92-38138
                                                       CIP

96 97 98 99 9 8 7 6 5 4

Brief Contents

Detailed Contents

Preface

TO THE STUDENT

This book has two major purposes. The first is to provide you with useful information about cognitive psychology—what cognitive psychology is, how cognitive psychologists go about doing their work, and what they have found that is of relevance to education. The book is intended primarily for graduate students in education who may have little or no background in psychology, but who bring to their reading of the book a wealth of experience as learners, teachers, trainers, curriculum planners, and designers of instruction. We have tried to select ideas and research that

make contact with this rich knowledge base in our readers.

The second purpose of this book is to provide you with a coherent explanatory framework within which you may work to solve teaching and learning problems that are of interest to you. Research on cognition has shown that people who have one or more coherent explanatory frameworks tend to be better equipped to solve problems than are people who lack such frameworks. We have sought to describe a coherent set of ideas about cognition, which we then use throughout the book. Our hope is that readers will become familiar enough with the ideas to be able to use them in solving problems of interest to them. Throughout the book you will find questions and exercises that are intended to make you apply many of the ideas. We encourage you to spend time answering and solving these problems because doing so will increase your chances of developing a better understanding and being better able to use your new-found knowledge more effectively.

In the eight years since the publication of the first edition, much has happened in cognitive psychology and related fields. Neuroscience has begun to develop an understanding of the physiological bases of cognition, so we have included some of this work for interested readers. Motivation researchers have continued to refine their ideas about classroom motivation and this work is included in the motivation chapter. Cognitive psychology—both applied and basic—has continued to develop vigorously. Our revisions incorporate this new work. In the first edition, we were enthusiastic about the insights into educational issues afforded by cognitive psychology and we continue to be in this edition.

TO THE INSTRUCTOR

Several events that have happened since the publication of the first edition of this book have influenced the current edition. Perhaps the most obvious is that there are now three authors rather than one. We decided to collaborate on this edition for a number of reasons. First, we share a belief in the relevance for education of John R. Anderson's cognitive theories, a belief we attempt to articulate in this text. Second, we each have done work in recent years that is relevant to this book's content in different ways. We also have taught different groups of students who might potentially use this book. We believe our varied perspectives enrich the text. Finally, we have argued, discussed, and criticized each other as we worked to reach a consensus on certain

issues, and we believe this discussion benefitted our revisions.

Other changes that have influenced this edition include the continued evolution of Anderson's ideas, the continued evolution of cognitive psychology in general, and the flowering of applied cognitive psychology.

John Anderson's recent writings (e.g., Anderson & Thompson, 1989) have come to include a well-thought out version of schemas as a major form of knowledge representation, and we have therefore added schemas as a major form of knowledge representation in this edition. Too, Anderson addresses the mechanism of learning by analogy, which appears to be an important learning process. We have included learning by analogy in this revision.

Since the publication of the first edition of this text, basic research in cognitive psychology has continued to flesh out the understandings produced by earlier research. Some earlier ideas have been substantially revised while others have been corroborated. A possible new model of cognition called "parallel distributed processing" (e.g., Rumelhart & McClelland, 1986) has been introduced, and we refer to this model in this edition. In general, however, it seems to us that there is more agreement about certain fundamentals than there was several years ago. For example, we think that most cognitive psychologists would agree on the overall distinctions between and among procedural, schematic, and propositional knowledge, and we describe and justify these distinctions in this edition.

The area of applied cognitive psychology—including educational research that is based on or tests cognitive assumptions—has burgeoned in the past decade. Whereas in the first edition it was difficult to find much cognitively based research in the areas of reading, writing, math, and science, for this edition we were overwhelmed with the amount of cognitively based research that was available. Our review of this research satisfied us that the basic models of reading and writing put forward in the first edition were still on the mark, although we added interesting new work on the role of declarative knowledge to Chapters 12 and 13. On the other hand, we were led to make major revisions in the mathematics and teacher-expertise chapters (Chapters 14 and 17) and moderate revisions in the science chapter (Chapter 15). In the latter chapter, we added work on conceptual change theory. Finally, there has been some excellent work in motivation in school settings published recently, some of which we included in a revision of Chapter 16 on motivation.

Many people have given useful feedback on all or part of this book. For the second edition, these individuals include Frank DiVesta, Pennsylvania State University; Shawn Glynn, University of Georgia; Steve Kerst, Catholic University; Mary Lou Koran, University of Florida; Raymond Kulhavy, Arizona State University; Raja Parasuraman, Catholic University; Michael Pressley, University of Maryland; CarolAnne M. Kardash, University of Missouri, Columbia; Judith Sowder, San Diego State University; John R. Surber, University of Wisconsin; and Brent G. Wilson, University of Colorado, Denver. For the first edition, people providing feedback included John Glover, Richard Mayer, John Surber, John R. Anderson, Charles Bethel-Fox, Bruce Britton, Joseph Burns, Patricia Carpenter, Russell Durst, Linnea Ehri, Sarah Freedman, Shawn Glynn, Jill Larkin, Ellen Mandinach,

and John Rickards. The faculty and students at the University of Texas and the Catholic University of America have challenged us to clarify our ideas and to expand our thinking beyond the traditional enterprise known as educational psychology. Because of our associations, we have developed a newfound appreciation for schools, and we hope that is evident here.

We would like to acknowledge those people who have been instrumental in the completion of this book. Our families were patient and supportive. Ellen's husband, William Davis, took on extra tasks at home to ease her load. And her son, Jason, has been eagerly awaiting the time when "mommy's book" would be finished. Carol and Rick's college-age daughters, Ann and Allison, have given us the motivation to prove that not only are we parents, but we're also "real" professors, just like the ones they're taking courses from. Our editor, Christopher Jennison, deserves special credit for his support and patience. We missed our target dates more than once, but he always understood. Thanks also to Shadla Grooms at HarperCollins for her handling of our project, to Maggie Moran at Catholic University of America for her work on the manuscript and the permission requests and to Kirsten Kauffman for shepherding the manuscript through production. Finally, we thank Duffy, Cory, and Buster for their unswerving devotion.

E.D.G.
C.W.Y.
F.R.Y.

The Human Information- Processing System

Our goal in this book is to provide educators with knowledge of current theory and research in cognitive psychology that has bearing on the questions "What shall we teach?" and "How shall we teach?" In order to fully appreciate these ideas, it is useful to put them in context. That is the purpose of the first section of the book, comprised of Chapters 1, 2, and 3.

Cognitive psychology has an interesting history that will be described in Chapter 1. Briefly, early psychologists were interested in studying the mind, but they didn't have reliable methods for doing so. Because of this, they turned to the study of behavior for nearly a century. However, since about 1960, many new and exciting methods for studying mental processes have been developed, leading to the rebirth and flowering of cognitive psychology. We will describe these methods in Chapter 2. As you will find out, many of the methods can be adapted for classroom use.

The research in cognitive psychology since 1960 has given us a good understanding of the nature of the human information-processing system, which we shall describe in Chapter 3. It is a system that excels at recognizing patterns, forming analogies, and building schemas. These strengths account for our ability to adapt to new environments and to solve novel problems.

The level of analysis in cognitive psychology is abstract. It doesn't study neurons and neural circuits, but rather abstract memory structures. However, most cognitive psychologists assume that someday the neural bases of cognition will be determined. Already, there is interesting work in neuropsychology that complements the findings from cognitive psychology. Some of this work will be described in Chapter 3.

We hope that reading these chapters will put you on solid footing for reading the rest of the book. We also hope that you will be infected with our enthusiasm for the progress being made in cognitive psychology and for its clear potential benefits for education.

Chapter
1

History and Models

SUMMARY

1. Cognitive psychology is the scientific study of mental processes.

2. Experimental psychology started out in 1879 with a cognitive orientation, but behaviorism soon became the dominant framework in American psychology. After World War II, there was a rebirth of interest in cognitive psychology, stimulated by both pressure from applied settings and developments in information science.

3. Cognitive psychologists use **information-processing models** to describe psychological events in terms of transformations of information from input to output.

Human learning is a perpetually fascinating topic. Children seem to learn so much in the first few years of life. They learn to walk and to comprehend and use language. By the time they reach school age, they have mastered many of the skills of daily living. During the school years, humans learn to read, write, and compute, and to think and solve problems. In addition, they acquire masses of information about the world as it was in the past and as it is today. In adulthood, people continue to learn. They learn job-related skills and acquire more information. They may refine their reading, writing, and thinking skills. When individuals switch careers, new job-related skills may be learned; when they retire, learning of skills and information related to leisure-time activities takes place.

The great adaptability of our species seems to be one characteristic that sets us apart from other species. We are more able than other animals to live in a variety of environments ranging from the Arctic to the tropics to space. And we live in a variety of cultures from the simple agrarian to the complex technological. Because of these impressive feats of human learning, most people have an intrinsic interest in the topic.

There are also impressive failures of human learning. People labelled "retarded" or "learning disabled" seem to learn slowly or with difficulty in certain areas. Older people often think that they have a more difficult time learning new information than do younger people, although whether or not this is really true remains to be seen. Finally, "unmotivated" students seem unwilling to learn. Knowledge about human learning processes is interesting not only because it explains successes in learning, but because it may help us alleviate or prevent failures.

This book is about human learning. Although it emphasizes the learning of skills and knowledge that typically are learned in school settings, the learning *processes* described are thought to be universal ones. They should apply whether the learner is 2 years old or 100 and whether the situation is an informal parent-child interaction or a more formal teacher-student interaction.

COGNITIVE PSYCHOLOGY

Cognitive psychology is the scientific study of mental events. The "cognitive psychology of school learning" is the scientific study of mental events that take place in learners and teachers during the schooling process. It is a science that sheds light on such questions as why two similar students react differently to the same lesson, what is behind the blank stare of one student or another's flash of insight, and what methods should be used to teach a given topic.

Although cognitive psychology sheds light on these questions, it cannot provide definitive answers to them. Just as physiology and anatomy guide a doctor's thinking about medical problems but do not tell him or her exactly what dosage of what drug to prescribe, so too psychology guides a teacher's thinking about learning problems. It provides a theoretical basis for teacher decision making rather than a set of absolute answers.

All psychologists share the goal of understanding the behavior of individuals. Despite their common goal, however, psychologists differ in (1) their commitment to a particular level of analysis, and (2) the areas of behavior which they study.

Figure 1.1 shows a matrix that results

LEVELS OF ANALYSIS	TYPES OF BEHAVIOR		
	SOCIAL	EMOTIONAL	INTELLECTUAL
Behavioral			
Physiological			
Cognitive			

Figure 1.1 Areas of study within psychology are defined by the type of behavior involved (social, emotional, intellectual) and the level of analysis (behavioral, physiological, cognitive). This book focuses on the cognitive analysis of intellectual behavior.

from crossing three different levels of analysis (behavioral, physiological, and cognitive) with three different areas of behavior (social, emotional, and intellectual). The behavioral level of analysis focuses on identifying relationships between externally observable stimuli and responses. The physiological level tries to explain certain aspects of behavior in terms of physiological causes such as neural pathways or chemical changes. The cognitive level of analysis tries to explain behavior in terms of mental constructs. The area of social behavior includes such topics as how individuals present themselves to others and how people interact. Emotional behavior includes such topics as why different individuals react to the same situation with different feelings or what parental behaviors affect the emotional development of the young. Intellectual behavior includes such topics as how people solve problems and how they learn.

Of course, any given event has social, emotional, and intellectual aspects that can be usefully analyzed at behavioral, physiological, and cognitive levels, but psychology, like other sciences, has found it helpful to divide up the work so that different scientists focus on only one or two cells of the matrix.

A relatively recent trend in psychology is for research teams to look at the interactions of various types of behavior using more than one level of analysis. Borkowski and his colleagues, for example, have integrated emotional, social, and cognitive aspects of motivation (Borkowski, Carr, Rellinger, & Pressley, 1990). And many recent accounts of the attainment of intellectual competence emphasize the social context in which learning occurs (cf., Brown & Palinscar, 1989; Collins, Brown, & Newman, 1989). This trend should benefit educators who do not have the luxury of dividing up their students but rather must deal with students' social, emotional, and intellectual states all at once, using behavioral,

physiological, and cognitive levels of analysis to understand the situation.

In this book, the focus is on a cognitive level of analysis of intellectual behavior, but other levels of analysis and types of behavior are mentioned when they are especially important. We discuss physiological substrates of behavior in Chapter 3. Since school learning is a social enterprise, we mention social facilitators of intellectual functioning in several chapters. And since intellectual functioning can be enhanced or interfered with by emotional states, we consider the interaction of emotional and intellectual behavior, especially in Chapters 11 and 16.

Nonetheless, the questions raised in this book mainly have to do with the mental processes that underlie intellectual performance. What is going on in the learner's head, for example, when he or she is learning a new scientific principle? Or a new mathematical concept? What underlies a student's desire to learn? And his or her learning proficiency? What mental processes support routine and creative problem-solving? We expect that you will find the answers to these questions to be interesting and enlightening. Before delving into these issues, however, we will give a brief history of the science of cognitive psychology and describe the theoretical and methodological tools with which cognitive psychologists work. This information should give you a greater appreciation of the solid foundation upon which cognitive psychology is built.

A BRIEF HISTORY OF COGNITIVE PSYCHOLOGY

Psychology started as an empirical science in 1879, and many of the psychologists of the late 1800s were cognitive psychologists in the sense that they were interested in understanding mental events. Wundt studied the elements of consciousness while Freud tried to understand the unconscious. William

James (1890) defined psychology as "the Science of Mental Life." A predominant method used by many psychologists during this era was introspection (self-observation).

Early in the 20th century, the American psychologist John B. Watson launched an attack on the view that psychology was the science of mental life and instead proposed that it was the science of behavior (Watson, 1914). He argued that introspective data could never be independently verified because they were private. Therefore, such data did not meet the criterion of verifiability demanded by a science. Mental life, in other words, could never be studied objectively. Hence, we should focus our attention on behavior, which could be studied objectively, and about which there was much to be discovered.

From the time of Watson's attack on introspection through World War II, American psychology was predominantly behavioral. It produced the laws of effect and practice (Thorndike, 1913) and the principles of reinforcement (Skinner, 1938). Although these principles were shown to be quite powerful, they did little to explain important intellectual achievements such as learning to read, discovering a theorem, composing a song, or making good decisions under stress. Because behaviorism eschewed references to mental events, complex human performance, which begged for references to mental events, was rarely studied.

During World War II, some psychologists were called into the military to conduct research on the selection and training of skilled military personnel. Because these demands focused their attention on complex tasks—such as flying an airplane—they made some progress in understanding them, and perhaps because of their successes, many of these psychologists continued to study complex tasks following the war when they returned to university settings. Not surprisingly, the study of complex human performance led rapidly to theorizing about mental structures and processes (e.g., Ausubel, 1968; Bruner,

Goodnow, & Austin, 1956; R. Gagné, 1962). These events were partially responsible for the rebirth of cognitive psychology.

Concurrently, a great deal was happening in other fields that facilitated cognitive psychology's renaissance. Information science was developing, starting with a formal definition of a "bit" of information (see Shannon, 1962) and with the publication in 1948 of Weiner's highly influential book, *Cybernetics*. Linguistics was also developing as a formal science, and the linguist Chomsky (1959) challenged Skinner's behavioristic explanation of language development as being woefully inadequate. Both information theory and linguistics provided models of formal analysis, suggesting to some psychologists that formal analysis of mental events and structures might be attempted.

Another event that led to the rebirth of cognitive psychology, an event that was spurred by the growth of information science, was the development of the computer. As we shall see in Chapter 2, the computer is an important tool in the objective measurement of mental process indicators. For example, response latencies can be measured with millisecond accuracy using a computer. This level of accuracy is adequate for detecting subtle differences in thinking processes. The behaviorist argument that there are no objective ways to study mental events may have been valid in 1914, but it is a more difficult argument to make today. In Chapter 2, we will describe modern methods used by cognitive psychologists in some detail. First, however, we will describe what psychologists mean by a "model," as models are prevalent in cognitive psychology.

MODELS

In scientific enterprises, a model is a set of definitions of objects and assumptions about how these objects interact. For example, an early model of the atom defined the nucleus, containing protons and neutrons, and electron orbitals surrounding the nucleus. The assumptions about how the nucleus and electron orbitals interacted included such ideas as that an equal number of protons and electrons were required to keep an atom in equilibrium. In psychology, an early model of psychodynamics was Freud's model of the id, ego, and superego and of how they interacted. Scientists use models of unobservable events and processes to understand observable events and processes. Based on a given model, they make predictions that, if verified by observation, give more credence to the model and, if not verified, lead to a revision of the model or abandonment of the model and development of an alternative.

Models are also used in the application of scientific principles to real-world problems. Thus, when disease was thought to be the result of "bad blood," bloodletting was used to rid the body of bad blood. The contemporary model of bacterial infection and human antibody production is used by doctors when they prescribe antibiotics. In seismology, contemporary models of plate tectonics allow for more accurate predictions of earthquakes than was previously the case, and contemporary models of weather patterns have led to more accurate weather prediction.

Thus, models are useful for scientists and practitioners. They are useful because they provide a way for thinking about a problem that is (1) tractable and (2) supported by empirical evidence. Two types of models used by cognitive psychologists are **information-processing** and **neural-network models.** We will describe these types of models in the next section. It is important for you to become comfortable with such models because they will be used throughout this text.

Information-Processing Models

Human information-processing models attempt to map the flow of information that a human is using in a defined situation. For example, when a second-grader learns a fact for the first time, how is this information processed? These models vary as to how generally they are thought to apply. The model shown in Figure 1.2 is intended to apply to a wide range of situations, while that shown in Figure 1.3 is intended to apply to a rather narrow class of situations—specifically, those in which a teacher (or intelligent tutor) is deciding how to respond to a student's answer to a question.

A General Information-Processing Model. In Figure 1.2, we see four boxes, labelled "receptors," "working memory," "long-term memory," and "effectors." These boxes represent different functions that apply during processing of information. First, something receives the information—for example, eyes receive written information and ears receive spoken information. Second, humans hold new information in awareness (called "working mem-

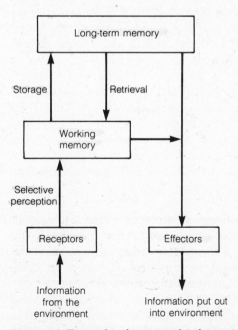

Figure 1.2 Example of a general information-processing model.

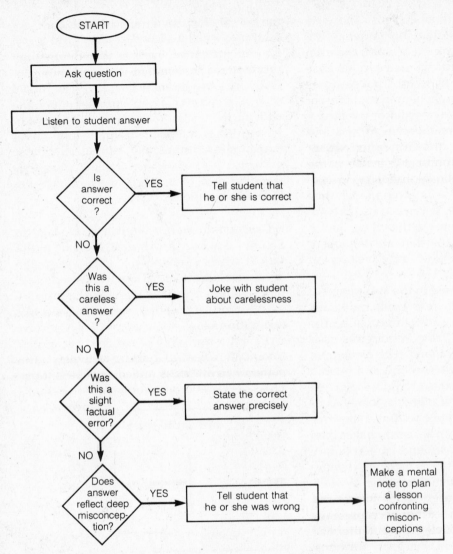

Figure 1.3 Example of a specific information-processing model.

ory") while they "do work" on it. One type of work would be to relate new information to known information; another would be to think about the implications of new information. Third, humans store information in long-term memory. Once it is stored, they are no longer aware of this information, but they may retrieve it when it is needed—for exam-ple, for a test. Finally, humans have ways of communicating information—such as using hands and arms to write down words. In summary, we have described four general functions of the human information-processing system—reception of information, working with information, storing information, and communicating information.

It is important to realize that the boxes in information-processing models don't necessarily correspond to one physical location in the brain. For example, there may not be one location for working memory. That is, boxes in information-processing models represent *functions* rather than physical locations.

The lines in Figure 1.2 have arrows indicating the sequence in which information-processing functions occur. For instance, the function of information reception occurs before the function of working on new information. The lines in general models, such as that in Figure 1.2, are often labelled to indicate a general process. For example, the arrow going from receptors to working memory is labelled "selective perception," which is the process of filtering out a lot of incoming information and selectively focusing on the most important information for our current goals. The arrow from long-term memory to working memory is labelled "retrieval," which is the process of getting information we already know back into awareness. In Chapter 3, we will discuss in more detail a general model of the human information-processing system. Here, we wish only to illustrate what a general information-processing model is like.

A Specific Information-Processing Model. Figure 1.3 shows a more specific information-processing model for a teacher decision-making process. In this model, the input information is a student's answer to a teacher's question. The teacher first determines whether or not the student's answer is correct, and then different activities occur depending upon this determination. If the answer is correct, the teacher does or says something that tells the student he or she is correct. If the answer is wrong, the teacher decides whether or not the wrong answer was due to momentary inattention on the part of the student. Again, different activities occur depending upon this decision. If inattention is seen to be

the reason for the wrong answer, then the teacher does something to get the student to be more attentive, such as humorously observing that the student is daydreaming instead of paying attention.

If inattention is not the problem, then the teacher determines whether the incorrect answer indicates a simple factual mistake or a more deep-rooted misconception. If the former, then the teacher clearly states the correct fact. If the latter, the teacher tells the student that the answer is wrong and that additional lessons will be devoted to explaining the error, and the teacher also makes a mental note to develop lesson materials designed to get the student to confront the misconception.

Note that this model, in contrast to the model in Figure 1.2, is highly specific. It is a description of what happens in a particular event (question answering) in a particular context (a teaching-learning context). The model in Figure 1.2 is intended to be general across a variety of information-processing events—from fact-learning to reasoning to creative problem-solving—and a variety of contexts from social interaction to formal schooling to on-the-job performance. We need both kinds of models. General information-processing models give us an idea of the constraints within which specific information-processing events must occur.

The model in Figure 1.3 contains a diamond-shaped box not used in Figure 1.2. Diamond-shaped boxes are conventionally used to indicate decision points. If one alternative is selected, then subsequent information processing follows one path, while if another is selected, then information processing follows another path. Those of you who have done computer programming may recognize that information-processing models are often written like computer program flowcharts. Diamond-shaped boxes are used to indicate choice points, rectangular boxes indicate operations, and arrows indicate the direction in which information flows. Flowcharts are useful for displaying many ideas compactly. Because cognitive theories tend to be complex, flowcharts are helpful in abstracting their important outlines.

Information-processing models do not necessarily reflect what a person is aware of thinking. In fact, it is sometimes the case that the mental operations proposed take place too rapidly for a person to be aware of each step. This is because the operations are so practiced that they have become highly automatic. Just as many people drive a car without awareness of the motor operations in which they are engaging (e.g., turning the wheel, looking in the mirror, putting on the brakes, etc.), so too people perform many cognitive tasks at an automatic level. For example, we are usually unaware of forming grammatically correct sentences in our native language. Lack of awareness does not invalidate information-processing models; it just suggests that the operations involved take place without conscious attention.

Neural-Network Models

Information-processing models such as those just described are especially useful for forcing the theorist to be specific and detailed about his or her assumptions. Recently, information-processing models have been criticized because they assume a *sequential* flow to cognitive processes that may not always be the case (cf., Rumelhart, Hinton, & McClelland, 1986). More likely, at least some cognitive processes take place *simultaneously* as, for example, when we drive a car and carry on a conversation at the same time. An alternative type of model that is being used more and more frequently is a **neural network** (or "parallel distributed processing") model. This type of model assumes that different cognitive processes may take place simultaneously. This

assumption is consistent with people's subjective sense of many things going on in the mind at once, and it is also consistent with what is known about the operation of neurons in the brain, to be described in more detail in Chapter 3.

Neural-network models assume that there is a set of interconnected processing units and that the level of activation of these units varies. Activation is propagated from one unit to connected units according to various propagation rules. As a specific example of a neural network model, consider Marshall's (1990) work on how students distinguish between and among five types of arithmetic word problems.

Marshall studied the five types of word problems exemplified in Table 1.1. **Change** problems were characterized by a change in state of one quantity. **Group** problems involved situations in which two or more groups could be logically combined into a larger group. **Compare** problems involved contrasting the values associated with two objects. **Restate** problems required rephrasing a verbal description into a different set of quantitative terms. Finally, **Vary** problems depicted direct or indirect variation.

Marshall postulated that through practice and feedback in identifying these five kinds of problems, students begin to form "pattern-recognition" units that map onto problem types. Certain features of the word problems are associated with certain types of problems. For example, comparative phrases like "how much bigger" or "how much more" are almost always associated with Compare problems. Thus, comparative phrases come to be part of the pattern-recognition unit for such problems. These units are said to exist in long-term memory.

After learning, when students read a new problem, they represent its features in working memory. These features then activate the same features coded in long-term memory,

Table 1.1 Examples of five types of arithmetic word problems studied by Marshall (1990)

CHANGE

Jeff loaded his printer with 300 sheets of paper. When he was done there were 35 sheets of paper left. How many sheets of paper did Jeff use?

GROUP

Yesterday, Joe's Pizza Parlor sold 12 cheese pizzas, 15 pepperoni pizzas, and 4 vegetarian pizzas. How many pizzas were sold in all?

COMPARE

Carol can write 10 pages a day and Ellen can write 5 pages a day. Who writes more—Carol or Ellen?

RESTATE

Rick writes twice as fast as Carol. Carol writes 10 pages a day. How fast does Rick write?

VARY

Ellen jogs 1 mile in 8 minutes. How long will it take her to run 5 miles?

and the features coded in long-term memory start to activate the pattern-recognition unit to which they belong. Figure 1.4 shows what happens when a student reads a new word problem. The arrows at the bottom of the figure represent input from the environment (i.e., reading the printed problem statement). The large circle represents working memory, and the elements within this circle represent features of the problem that the student has noted. The dotted lines show connections between these features and pattern-recognition units stored in long-term memory. Notice that elements of three different problem types (Change, Compare, and Restate) have been activated by their connections to the representation of the current problem.

How does the individual decide which of these three problem types is descriptive of the current problem? Usually, more features of one pattern-recognition unit are activated than of any other pattern-recognition unit. The unit with the most activated features is selected as appropriate. In the example in Figure 1.4, the Compare unit has four features activated versus only two and three for the other two units.

What is crucial to notice about this model is that several pattern-recognition units were activated simultaneously. This is a characteristic assumption of neural-network models. Also, notice the importance of **level of activation.** In neural network models, neural units often compete with one another, with the most active unit winning the race.

Summary

Models are important tools for both scientists and practitioners as they try to understand phenomena. In cognitive psychology, information-processing and neural-network models have proven to be useful for understanding mental events and processes. Information-processing models seem to be especially useful when a phenomenon has a sequential character and seems to occur at a conscious level. Neural-network models may be more useful for characterizing parallel processing and mental activities that occur without much attention.

OVERVIEW OF THE BOOK

This book is divided into six sections. The first section introduces some of the major concepts of an information-processing view of human cognition. Following the present chapter, Chapter 2 (Methods Used in Cognitive Psychology) describes some standard methods used by cognitive psychologists. Chapter 3

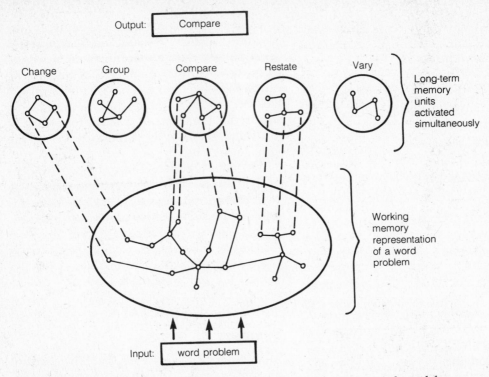

Figure 1.4 A neural-network model of word problem classification (adapted from Marshall, 1990).

(Overview of the Human Information-Processing System) describes some general constraints on the way humans process information. In that chapter, we also discuss the physiological basis of cognition. The second section describes some important types of knowledge representation. Chapters 4 (Representing Declarative Knowledge: Basic Units) and 5 (Representing Declarative Knowledge: Schemas) introduce ideas about the mental structures used to represent factual and conceptual knowledge, respectively. Chapter 6 (Representing Procedural Knowledge) introduces ideas about mental structures used to represent intellectual skills and strategies.

The third section of the book describes how the various types of knowledge are acquired. In Chapter 7 (Acquisition and Retrieval of Propositions: Learning the Basic Units of Meaning), we describe principles of learning and remembering factual information, while in Chapter 8 (Acquisition of Schemas: Schema Formation and Refinement) we describe how conceptual knowledge is acquired. In Chapter 9 (Acquisition of Procedural Knowledge) we describe a model of skill acquisition. The fourth section describes the use of knowledge in problem solving and transfer. In Chapter 10 (Problem Solving and Reasoning) we first describe the nature of expertise in domain-specific problem solving and then discuss issues of general problem-solving strategies. In Chapter 11 (Transfer), we discuss the educationally important issue of transfer, including recent work on transfer that has great promise for practical application.

The fifth section of the book applies the

framework developed in the preceding chapters to specific domains: reading (Chapter 12), writing (Chapter 13), mathematics (Chapter 14), and science (Chapter 15). Finally, in the sixth section of the book we discuss how cognition and motivation interact (Chapter 16) and the cognitive processes of expert teachers (Chapter 17).

CHAPTER SUMMARY AND PREVIEW

This book is about human learning and problem-solving processes. It describes a cognitive framework for viewing human learning and problem solving in the first eleven chapters. It then applies this framework to school subjects and classroom dynamics in the final six chapters. This framework makes clear the incredible complexity of human performance, on the one hand, and the relative simplicity of the principles underlying performance, on the other. It is often the case that the better one understands a phenomenon, the more amazing it seems, and this is certainly true for human learning.

ADDITIONAL READINGS

History
A discussion of the history of psychology can be found in:

Heidbreder, E. (1961). *Seven psychologies*. New York: Appleton-Century-Crofts.

Cognitive Psychology
If you are interested in a general introduction to the field of cognitive psychology, we recommend the following textbook:

Anderson, J. R. (1990). *Cognitive psychology and its implications* (3rd edition). New York: W.H. Freeman & Company.

Neural Networks
Good introductions to neural network models can be found in:

Martindale, C. (1991). *Cognitive psychology: A neural-network approach*. Pacific Grove, CA: Brooks/ Cole Publishing Co.
Bereiter, C. (1991). Implications of connectionism for thinking about rules. *Educational Researcher*, *20*, 10–16.

Chapter
2

Methods Used in Cognitive Psychology

SUMMARY

1. To understand human cognition, psychologists watch people perform cognitively demanding tasks. They collect a variety of data and try to make sense of it. Five types of data that are frequently used are **response latencies, eye fixations, verbal reports, sorting,** and **free recall.**

2. Response latency is the time required for a specific behavior to occur. Response latencies for mental processes tend to be on the order of tens or hundreds of milliseconds—that is, less than half a second.

3. Eye fixations show where an individual is focusing in a stimulus array at any given point in time. Eye-tracking equipment is used to gather eye-fixation data.

4. Verbal reports are of two types—**thinking aloud** and **retrospective reports.** In thinking aloud, the individual says whatever is going through his or her mind while performing a task. In retrospective reports, the individual reports, as soon as the task is completed, what just went through his or her mind.

5. Sorting and free-recall data are used to make inferences about an individual's conceptual understanding.

6. Three types of theory development used by cognitive psychologists are the **subtractive technique, information-processing analysis,** and **computer simulation.**

7. The subtractive technique is used in conjunction with latency data. People perform on two tasks that are identical except for one mental step. Then the time to perform the shorter task is subtracted from the time to perform the longer task to get an estimate of the time needed to perform the mental step that differentiated the two tasks.

8. Information-processing analysis breaks down a complex task into a series of mental operations, often producing a flowchart such as that shown in Chapter 1.

9. Computer simulation involves programming a computer to carry out the steps specified by an information-processing analysis. The simulation tests the internal consistency of the model and allows for making predictions in complex situations.

In Chapter 1, you saw some examples of models developed by cognitive psychologists, such as the "box" model with working memory, long-term memory, and other functions put in boxes. But where do these models come from? Do contemporary psychologists simply introspect about their own mental processes, the way early psychologists did? Do they ask other people to introspect about their mental processes and then attempt to generalize across people? Or have they created methods that are more objective than these just mentioned? As we mentioned in the previous chapter, there have been a variety of innovations in methodology in recent years, many of which we will describe in this chapter.

The effects of the methodological innovations in cognitive psychology may turn out to be as profound for psychology as the effects of methodological improvements in genetics were for the field of biology. Before the 1950s, geneticists were stuck at a fairly global level of description. They knew that certain characteristics of organisms were passed on to offspring in predictable proportions. They called the cause of this predictable event a "factor" or gene, but they didn't know how genes exerted their influence. Then there was a major breakthrough in the methods used to study genes:

the technique of X-ray crystallography was perfected, making it possible to discover the structure of the genetic material DNA. Other techniques such as protein synthesis and radioactive tracing made it possible to crack the genetic code. As many experiments using these new or improved technologies were completed, it became clear that a "factor," or gene, is a segment of a DNA molecule that controls the production of a certain enzyme or other protein and that this enzyme or other protein in turn controls whether a characteristic occurs or not.

Cognitive psychology may be at a point in its development now similar to the point that genetics had reached in the 1950s, when dramatic methodological improvements led to dramatic increases in understanding. If this is so, then we may expect that our understanding of cognitive processes should increase substantially over the next few decades. In fact, this already seems to be happening.

Advances in methodology have come from a variety of sources, but a major source is improvements in computers. Now that microcomputers are relatively inexpensive, many cognitive psychologists and educational researchers use them to conduct experiments. A typical experimental set-up is shown in Figure 2.1. The computer is programmed to display

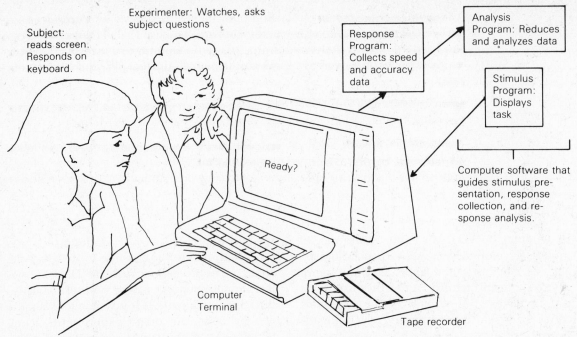

Subject: reads screen. Responds on keyboard.

Experimenter: Watches, asks subject questions

Response Program: Collects speed and accuracy data

Analysis Program: Reduces and analyzes data

Stimulus Program: Displays task

Ready?

Computer software that guides stimulus presentation, response collection, and response analysis.

Computer Terminal

Tape recorder

Figure 2.1 A typical cognitive psychology experimental setup using a computer (adapted from Rumelhart and Norman, 1981).

stimuli on a screen, to record the response made by a subject and the response's latency, and to summarize and analyze the data. Subjects in different conditions of the experiment see different stimuli on the screen. Sometimes the experimenter may sit by the subject and ask her or him questions at various points during task performance. The experimenter's questions and the subject's answers are tape-recorded for subsequent analysis.

In the remainder of this chapter, we will describe eight methods that are often used by cognitive psychologists: five are empirical methods and three are theoretical tools. These are not the only methods used by cognitive psychologists, but they are standard ones, some of which have experienced significant improvements in recent years.

EMPIRICAL METHODS

Latency Data

Psychologists have always been interested in the speed, or **latency,** of responses. However, until fairly recently this type of data was more useful for the study of motor skills than for the study of cognitive skills. Because cognitive operations occur at a very fast rate—anywhere from 1 to 250 milliseconds—it is difficult to measure them accurately. Only recently has the technology for measuring responses with millisecond accuracy become widely available. Now it is typical for psychologists to measure latencies with 15 millisecond accuracy, and an even greater accuracy can be achieved if needed.

One example of the use of latency data comes from a memory experiment conducted by two of the authors of this book (Yekovich & Walker, 1986). The purpose of the experiment was to show how organization of information already stored in long-term memory influences our ability to recall newly learned information.

College students, who were the participants in this experiment, sat before a computer terminal and read several stories, including the following:

> Mary was almost out of food, so she decided to go shopping. She made a shopping list. Then she left for the store. Mary found a parking place right near the door. As she entered, Mary took out her list. She got a shopping cart and started down the first aisle. Mary didn't see the butcher, so she pressed the buzzer on the counter. She went up and down the aisles. Finally, Mary thought she was finished. She checked her list one last time. Then it was time to check out. Mary chose what looked like the fastest line. Mary watched closely as the cashier rang up prices. Mary wrote a check for the total. She asked for some help carrying her groceries out to the car. Mary unlocked the trunk of her car. When they were finished, Mary got in her car and drove home.

Immediately after reading each story, students were asked to decide which of a set of 20 words they had seen *verbatim* in the story. For example, for the above story, the 20 words presented are shown below. Which ones do you think you saw?

prices	speech	cashier	piano
politics	butcher	tattoo	list
luggage	antique	humor	shrubs
cart	aisle	groceries	line
jockey	mask	fence	chess

Each word was presented alone on the screen of the computer terminal and the student was expected to press a "yes" button or a "no" button depending on whether he or she

thought the word had been read. Notice that all of the words that are related to a grocery-shopping theme actually had been seen, while none of the words unrelated to this theme had been seen. The same was true for the other stories—all thematically related words had been seen and all thematically unrelated words had not been seen. When this type of test is given, students typically adopt a "relatedness" strategy for deciding whether or not an item has been seen. That is, they will say "yes" for all items they judge to be theme-relevant and "no" for all items they judge to be theme-irrelevant. When students use this strategy, it should take longer to judge items whose relevance is marginal than items whose relevance is central to a theme because they have to ponder whether a marginally related word is, in fact, relevant. Thus, the prediction was that latency to judge more centrally related words (such as *groceries*) would be shorter than latency to judge marginally related words (such as *line*).

To test this prediction, we measured the student's latency for recognizing (saying "yes" to) words that had occurred in the text. We then looked at latency for the more- and less-central words. We found that the average latency to identify more-central words was 697 milliseconds, while it was 852 milliseconds for the less-central words. Thus, students were 22% faster in judging more-central words.

These results confirmed the prediction that it takes longer to recognize words that are less central to a well-known theme than words that are more central to the theme. This suggests that students do use a relatedness strategy. If they did not, then response latency should not vary as a function of the degree of relatedness.

The results of this study and similar ones have important implications for educational practices that will be discussed elsewhere in this text. The main point for right now is that

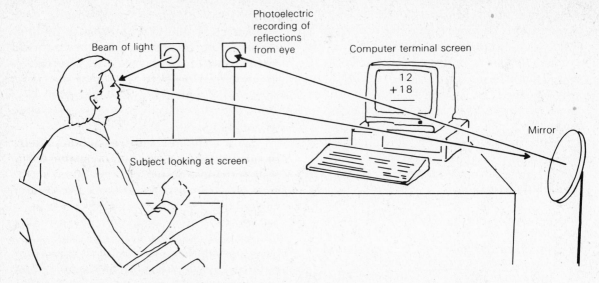

Figure 2.2 An eye-fixation laboratory. A beam of light is directed at the subject's eyes as the subject is performing a task. Reflections of this light from the subject's eyes are deflected by a mirror to a photoelectric recording device.

this study illustrates the use of latency data to make inferences about cognitive structures and processes. Notice that the average difference of less than a fifth of a second (155 milliseconds) was highly significant and meaningful. These small but reliable differences are quite typical of experiments involving cognitive—as opposed to motor—processes, reflecting the great speed with which some cognitive processes occur. This example of the use of latency data is just one of many examples of the use of latency data in understanding human intelligence. You will find other examples throughout the book.

Eye-Fixation Data

Eye fixations are data that show where in a stimulus array a subject fixes his or her gaze at a given point in time. Eye-fixation data are a dense source of data, providing a large number of data points during a subject's performance of even a brief task. As with latencies,

eye fixations have been used as data since the beginnings of experimental psychology. However, in the past, many psychologists were discouraged from using eye-fixation data due to the formidable task of data reduction. Now, however, computers can be programmed to perform the data-reduction task quickly and reliably, so now more and more psychologists are using eye-fixation data.

Figure 2.2 shows a typical eye-fixation laboratory. In it, a subject sits in a chair gazing at a computer terminal. To one side of the terminal is the eye-fixation equipment that beams a light into the subject's eyes. The subject reads or examines the stimulus presented on the screen, and the duration and course of his or her eye fixations on different parts of the stimulus are determined from reflectance patterns. The principle behind eye tracking is that a small but detectable percentage of light hitting the eye is reflected back from various surfaces of the eye, such as the cornea and the front surface of the lens. There-

Item stem:

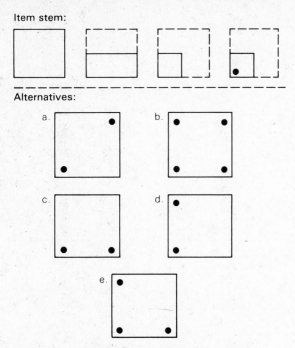

Alternatives:

Figure 2.3 A sample test item from a spatial aptitude test. Subjects are told to assume that the sequence from left to right in the item stem represents a sequence of folds in a piece of paper. Dots represent punches in all the layers of paper that are under the dot. The goal is to choose the alternative that shows what the punched paper would look like after it is unfolded. In this example, **b** is the correct alternative.

fore, measuring eye fixations involves beaming a light (usually a nondistracting infrared light) to the subject's eyes, after which the reflections from various surfaces of the eyes are recorded. A subject's moving his or her head potentially can generate "noise" in the data. However, head movements can be distinguished from eye-fixation changes by different reflectance patterns from various surfaces of the eyes.

Snow (1980) used eye-fixation data to study how people solve test items found on tests of spatial ability. Figure 2.3 shows a

typical test item from a "paper-folding" test. The subject is told that the stem of the item shows a paper being folded and then punched through all of the layers. The alternatives show various possible ways that the paper would look when it is then unfolded. The subject's task is to decide on the correct alternative.

Snow compared the eye-fixation patterns of subjects who scored high on spatial ability tests with those of subjects who scored low on such tests. Figure 2.4 shows the eye-fixation pattern of a typical high-scoring subject and a typical low-scoring subject. The patterns are dramatically different. The high-scoring subject spent 10 seconds examining the stem of the test item before ever looking at the alternatives (top left of Figure 2.4). In particular, she spent 7.2 seconds looking at the final part of the stem. The low-scoring subject, by contrast, spent only .2 seconds looking at the stem initially before looking at one of the alternatives (bottom of Figure 2.4). The low-scoring subject shows a pattern of bouncing back and forth between stem and alternatives while the high-scoring subject, once finished looking at the stem, does not look back at it before she responds.

Snow concluded from these data, in conjunction with subjects' reports, that high scorers use a strategy in which they mentally unfold the paper and then search the alternatives for a match to their mental image. This explains why high scorers spend so much time gazing at the final part of the stem: it is at this point that they are forming a mental image of the unfolded piece of paper. Low scorers, on the other hand, do not form a mental image. Rather, they focus on a perceptual attribute of the stem, such as the placement of a hole, and look for alternatives that somehow match that perceptual attribute. If one perceptual attribute doesn't work, they return to the stem to find another. This, then, explains the low scorer's tendency to bounce

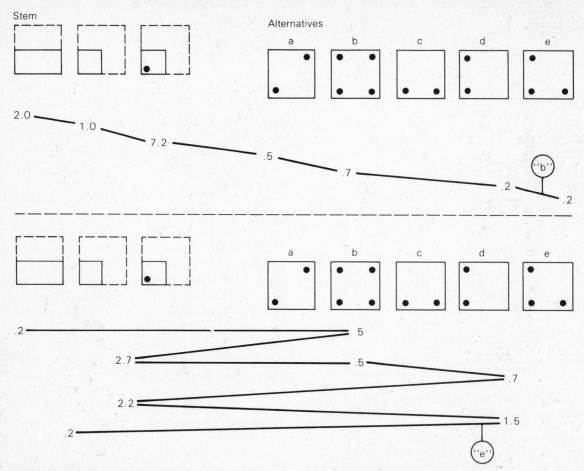

Figure 2.4 Duration and sequence of eye fixations of a typical "good" subject (top) and a typical "poor" subject (bottom) while solving a paper-folding problem. The balloon shows where the subject made a choice. Notice that the subject with high spatial aptitude spends a great deal of time gazing at the last part of the stem and never returns to the stem once she looks at the alternatives. The subject with low spatial aptitude jumps back and forth between stem and alternatives (adapted from Snow, 1980).

back and forth between the stem and the alternatives.

As this example illustrates, the interpretation of eye-fixation data is greatly facilitated by comparing them with some other processing data such as verbal reports. Psychologists who use eye-fixation data generally make the assumption that there is some relationship between where the subject is looking and what he or she is thinking. Since this assumption may not always be correct (as when someone is "daydreaming"), it is useful to have some other measure that validates it.

Verbal Reports

Verbal reports are reports the subject makes before, during, or after performing a task.

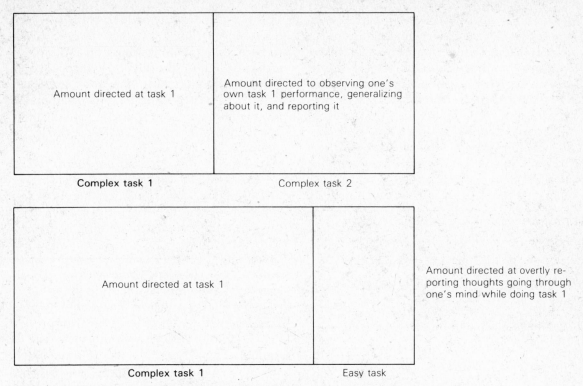

Figure 2.5 The relative amount of attention directed at two complex tasks versus one complex task and one easy task. When one's attention to complex task 1 is severely limited, one may use different strategies to complete the task than when one's attention is less limited.

Such reports were the main data used by introspectionist psychologists at the turn of the century. Because different psychologists got different results, this method fell into disrepute, and for over half a century most American psychologists were unwilling to take seriously any reports made by subjects.

In 1980, Ericsson and Simon proposed a theory of verbal reports that distinguishes the conditions under which reliable and valid subject reports can be obtained from those under which verbal reports may not be valid. Their theory states that the giving of verbal reports is like any other cognitive task in that it can make demands on our limited attention capacity, our unreliable memory, or our faulty reasoning processes. What demands are made depend on the exact nature of the report requested.

For example, if one is asked to explain what one is doing while doing it, this places a great burden on attentional capacity because one has to attend to two complex tasks at once: the task of interest, and the task of explaining what one is doing to perform the task of interest (see Figure 2.5). This heavy demand on attention may lead a subject to use different strategies than would be used when there was not such a demand. Thus, it is not usually very useful to ask people to reflect on what they are doing while they are doing it.

However, as Ericsson and Simon (1980)

demonstrate, there is a valid type of verbal report that can be given while performing a task. This type has become known as "thinking aloud." In thinking aloud, subjects do not explain *how* they are thinking; rather, they report *what* they are thinking. That is, they report whatever thoughts pass through consciousness while performing a task. For example, try this: report whatever goes through your mind as you try to solve the following analogy. (Start out by reading the analogy out loud and then just continue talking out loud):

Washington is to Lincoln as 1 is
   to _____ .

a. 5   b. 12   c. 13   d. 22

Your thoughts may have gone something like this:

"Washington is to Lincoln as 1 is to
   _____ . . .

presidents . . . first, . . . 5, no . . . 22,
no . . . 13."

which would have been a good thinking-aloud protocol. However, if you said something like:

"First, I am comparing Washington
and Lincoln

and asking how they are similar . . ."

you did not state *what* was going through your mind; rather you tried to explain *how* you were thinking. Explaining how you are thinking while you are thinking detracts from the main task. It takes time for subjects to learn not to reflect but simply to say aloud what is going through their minds. Once they are good at it, thinking aloud demands very little attention and, therefore, does not disrupt the main task (as is shown in the bottom part of Figure 2.5).

Just as latency and eye-fixation data provide clues, the data from thinking-aloud protocols provide clues about thinking processes.

In the above-mentioned protocol for solving the analogy, it looks as though the person first recognizes that both Washington and Lincoln are presidents ("presidents"), then realizes that Washington was the first president ("first"), and then scans the possible numbers for the number corresponding to Lincoln's presidency ("5, no . . . 22, no . . . 13"). He eliminates 5 and 22 and settles on 13. By the way, Lincoln was the 16th president, which was not one of the choices. The correct answer to this analogy is 5. Think of money and you will probably figure out why 5 is correct. (You can verify your answer by turning to the end of this chapter.)

Besides overloading attentional resources during a task, there are other sources of invalidity for verbal reports. Specifically, when a researcher asks a *general* question—such as "How do you go about studying your history text?"—the subject can generate an answer in a variety of ways, and the way it is generated affects its validity. For example, a student may try to decide what answer you want and tell you this even if it has nothing to do with what he really does. If you are interested in the question of how history texts are studied, his answer would not be helpful. Or another student may try to remember two or three past occurrences of studying history texts and generalize across them. If her memory is poor or her sample of occasions is somehow biased, then the report will not be valid.

Ericsson and Simon (1980) also argue that a particular kind of retrospective report (report given after a task is completed) can be valid. It is a report that is given *immediately* after the task is completed, so that memory losses are minimal, and it is one that is tied to a specific instance of task performance, so that generalization processes do not come into play. In the example of studying history texts, a good procedure would be to assign a student a chapter in his history text and then, when he indicates that he has finished studying, immediately ask, "Please say what went through your mind while you were studying this page," and repeat the question for each page, allowing the student to look at the page while complying with your request. Answers given can be validated by checking them with other observations. For example, if the subject says, "I thought that this sentence was in conflict with the previous section, so I went back and reread the previous section, and then I saw how the ideas were consistent," and you did not observe him flipping back to the previous section as indicated, then you would have good reason to be suspicious of this subject's reports. Usually, however, retrospective reports about specific tasks have high validity.

Sorting and Free Recall

Latency, eye-fixation, and verbal-report data reveal much about the mental processes the subject is using to solve a particular problem, but they may only give hints about the subject's conceptual understanding of the problem. Sorting and free-recall data are especially useful for drawing inferences about conceptual understanding.

In **sorting** tasks, researchers give participants a set of materials in a domain to sort into as many categories as they wish. The researchers then examine the items that are grouped together. For instance, young children might group all paintings of houses together and all paintings of people together regardless of the artistic style, while an individual with some training in art might group paintings from the same artistic period together regardless of the subject of the painting. This finding would suggest that children have a different understanding of paintings than do trained adults.

In **free-recall** tasks, people recall some material to which they have been exposed previously. The recall is said to be "free" in

that people are not constrained as to the order in which ideas must be recalled. Because of this lack of constraint, the order in which material is recalled can be revealing of the individual's memory structure.

One example of the use of free recall to study people's cognitive processes comes from a study done by Means, Mumaw, Roth, Shlager, McWilliams, Gagné, Rice, Rosenthal, & Heon (1988) on air traffic controllers. In this study, skilled controllers participated in a session of controlling air traffic. Afterwards they were asked to recall all the aircraft that had come up on their radar screens. A naive expectation is that the order of recall might be determined by physical location on the screen—for example, the controller might recall from the left to the right of the screen's image in his or her mind. In fact, controllers recalled together aircraft that were in potential conflict, even though they were from quite different places on the screen. Also, controllers were more likely to omit from recall aircraft for which there was no potential conflict than those for which a conflict existed. In other words, the way controllers conceptualize air traffic patterns is driven by their job-related goal of avoiding traffic conflicts.

Concept mapping is a recent extension of sorting and free-recall methods. In concept mapping, people generate a set of concepts for a domain and show graphically how they perceive these concepts to be related. This technique is described in greater detail in Chapter 14 (Mathematics).

Summary

In summary, latency, eye-fixation, verbal-report, sorting, and free-recall data are frequently used to make inferences about mental processes. While in the past some of these types of data have been difficult to obtain in reliable and valid forms, with current technological and theoretical advances, they can yield valuable information.

METHODS OF THEORY DEVELOPMENT

Concomitant with the improvement in empirical indicators of cognitive processes has been the development of logical analysis techniques that facilitate theorizing about cognitive processes. These techniques include the **subtractive technique, information-processing analysis,** and **computer simulation.**

The Subtractive Technique

The subtractive technique uses latencies as its data source. It is a logical technique used to isolate elementary cognitive processes. The typical experiment involves having subjects perform two slightly different tasks. One of these tasks is thought to involve just one more cognitive operation than the other, and all the other cognitive operations involved in performance on the two tasks are thought to be the same. The average time to perform each task is then measured and the time to perform one task is subtracted from the time to perform the other. The result is an estimate of the time needed to perform the one cognitive operation that is different in the two tasks. The logic of the subtractive technique is shown in Figure 2.6.

An example of a use of the subtractive technique comes from experiments by Hunt and his colleagues, reported in Hunt (1978). These experiments were designed to measure how long it takes individuals to activate highly familiar information stored in memory. Hunt reasoned that activating information required the steps shown in the information-processing model in Figure 2.7. First, an individual physically scans a computer screen (or printed material) containing familiar symbols or words. Then, he or she encodes the salient physical characteristics of the symbols or words. Finally, he or she activates information about the symbols or words—such as their meaning—from memory.

The researchers reasoned further that to estimate the time it takes to activate familiar information stored in memory, they needed to design two tasks—one requiring activation of information and the other, otherwise similar, not requiring activation of information. They could then subtract the average time to perform the latter task from the average time to perform the former to obtain an estimate of time to activate familiar information.

The tasks they used were called "name match" and "identity match." In the identity-match task, subjects had to judge whether or not two letters appearing on a screen were physically the same. For example, C and C are physically the same, but C and c are not. In the name-match task, subjects had to judge whether two letters appearing on the screen represented the same letter, even if they were not physically the same. For example, R and r represent the same letter, though they differ physically, while R and t do not represent the same letter. To perform the identity-match tasks, all subjects have to do is encode the physical stimuli. They don't have to activate information about letter names stored in memory. On the other hand, to perform the name-match task, subjects have to encode the physical stimulus and then activate information about which physical stimuli represent the same letter.

Subjects performed for numerous trials on both of these tasks, and an average reaction time to press a "yes" or "no" key was computed for each subject on each task. Hunt, Lunneborg, & Lewis (1975) were interested in differences between groups of different ages and intellectual levels. Using the subtractive technique, they found that the average activation times were 75, 190, and 310 milliseconds,

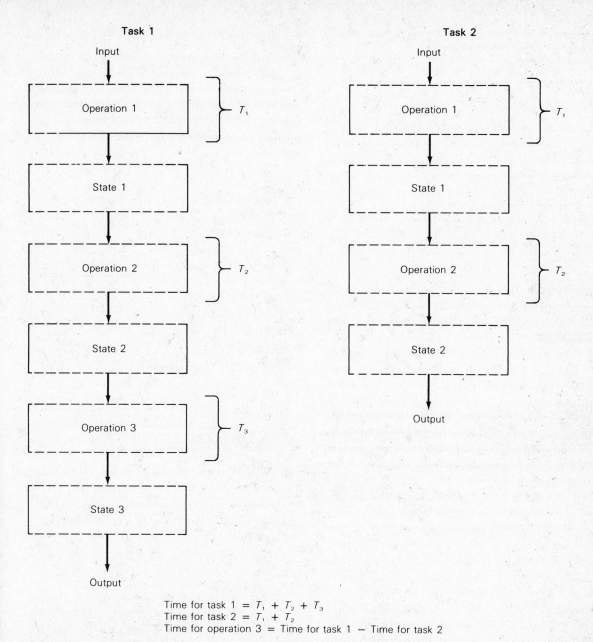

Task 1

Input

Operation 1 $\left.\right\} T_1$

State 1

Operation 2 $\left.\right\} T_2$

State 2

Operation 3 $\left.\right\} T_3$

State 3

Output

Task 2

Input

Operation 1 $\left.\right\} T_1$

State 1

Operation 2 $\left.\right\} T_2$

State 2

Output

Time for task 1 = $T_1 + T_2 + T_3$
Time for task 2 = $T_1 + T_2$
Time for operation 3 = Time for task 1 − Time for task 2

Figure 2.6 A schematic representation of the logic of the subtractive technique.

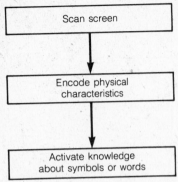

Figure 2.7 Steps needed to activate knowledge in long-term memory when given a cue on a computer screen.

respectively, for college students, normal 10-year-olds, and retarded schoolchildren. Moreover, these differences between groups were statistically significant.

Hunt argued that this basic processing speed difference between groups may partially account for the different levels of academic achievement of the groups. That is, brighter students may learn faster because they activate their knowledge more quickly and therefore can have more opportunity to link new and prior knowledge in any given slice of time.

Of course, we don't know from a study like this how important such processing-speed differences are, relative to other differences. Motivation, general knowledge, and knowledge of strategies all play important roles in academic achievement. Nonetheless, these data suggest that one determinant of academic ability is speed of activation of familiar information stored in memory. We will have more to say about determinants of academic achievement elsewhere in this text. The main point here is simply that the subtractive technique can be used to get estimates of the time it takes to conduct mental processes. As such, it is a very useful technique for cognitive psychologists.

Information-Processing Analysis

Information-processing analysis is the process of analyzing the cognitive elements underlying intellectual performance. The analysis involves identifying the essential processes and mental representations and then specifying the sequence in which the processes occur. The result of this type of analysis is often a flow chart model such as that described in Chapter 1.

As an example of an information-processing analysis, we will return to the study we described when we discussed the use of latency data (Yekovich & Walker, 1986). You will recall that in that study, we were interested in developing a model of how students answer test questions about information just read when they also have prior knowledge related to the newly-read information. We were specifically interested in multiple-choice (or "recognition") types of tests, in which the student's job is to identify studied information from a set of distractors.

Some research shows that having related prior knowledge can interfere with test performance (especially when the test is what students call "picky"), while other research shows that having related prior knowledge can help in test performance (especially when the test doesn't require one to discriminate between newly-learned and old, but relevant, knowledge). In the Yekovich and Walker study, the goal was to develop a model to try to specify what mental processes could account for these results.

The model that was developed is shown in Figure 2.8. In the model, the first step is for the student to decide which strategy to use for answering test questions. If the student determines that the test is such that any theme-related information is correct, then he or she selects the "relatedness" strategy. If, on the other hand, the student determines that the test is such that some theme-related informa-

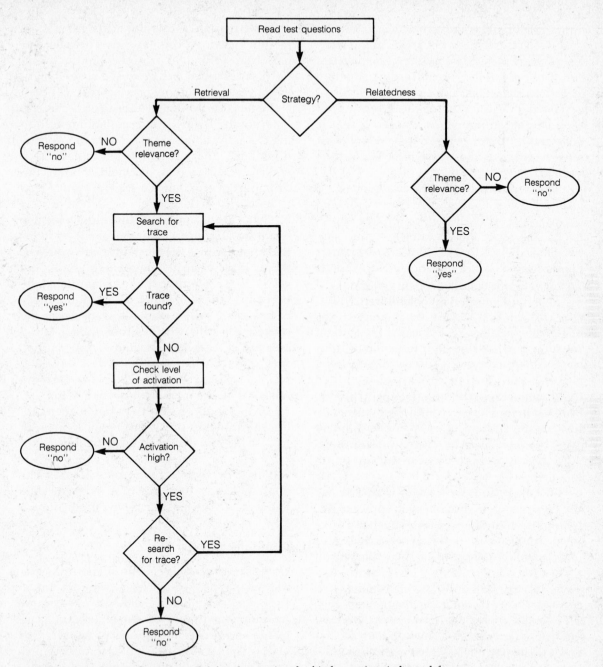

Figure 2.8 A strategy-based model for the retrieval of information (adapted from Yekovich and Walker, 1986).

tion is correct and some is not correct, then he or she selects the more time-consuming strategy of trying to decide if the theme-related test item was read in the recent learning situation or, rather, if it seems familiar simply because it is related to the theme of the recently-read text. This latter strategy is referred to as the "retrieval" strategy because the student must retrieve from memory the information just learned.

The steps involved in the relatedness and retrieval strategies are shown in the right- and left-hand branches of the flow chart, respectively. The relatedness strategy is quite simple: First, the student decides if a test item is theme-related. If it is, then he or she responds "yes," and if it is not, then the response is "no."

The retrieval strategy is more complex, although the first step is the same as in the relatedness strategy. Specifically, the student considers whether or not the test item is related to the theme of the studied material. If it is not, as with the relatedness strategy, then the student responds "no" and goes on to the next test item. However, if the item is theme-related, the student doesn't simply respond "yes," as was the case for the relatedness strategy, but goes on to assess whether or not the item was studied in the recent study event. This is done by searching memory for the recent study event to see if a trace of the test item is stored with this memory. If such a trace is found, then the student responds "yes" and then goes on to the next item. If such a trace is not found, then the student assesses how active the item seems to be in consciousness. If the item is not very active, the student infers that it was not just read because, in general, information that one has just read is more active than other information. In this case, the student responds "no" and then goes on to the next item. If, however, the item seems to be very active, then the student again searches his or her memory of the study event to find a trace of the test item.

Information-processing analysis is a method used by cognitive psychologists to reason about mental processes. In the example just described, we proposed several mental processes, including making a choice about strategies, searching memory for an event, determining theme relevance, and determining the activation level of an item of information. Such analyses allow psychologists to make predictions that, if upheld, tend to confirm the model and, if not upheld, tend to lead to revisions of the model or creation of new models. For example, if the model for the relatedness strategy is correct, then test items that should cause the most difficulty would be those for which theme-relatedness is not clear—that is, items that have a marginal relationship to the theme. In fact, we found this to be the case. When students were using the relatedness strategy, they took longer to decide about marginally-related test items than they did about either unrelated or centrally-related test items, and they also made more mistakes on the marginally-related items.

In summary, cognitive psychologists conduct information-processing analyses in order to develop and elaborate their theories about what is going on in a person's mind while solving a problem or performing a task. The analysis serves to summarize available data and leads to the making of new predictions.

Computer Simulation

Computer simulation is information-processing analysis pushed to its most rigorous limits. In computer simulation, a theory of cognitive operations is translated into a computer language and run as a computer program. (This task is similar to the task of a computer programmer when he or she translates a flowchart into a program.) If the program runs, this tells the theorist that the theory is logically consistent—that is, that there are no undefined or circular terms. More important, if the performance of the computer matches human performance on the same task, then the theory that underlies the computer's performance is a plausible theory of human performance.

One interesting example of computer simulation derives from the work of Kintsch and van Dijk (1978) on language comprehension. A part of their theory has to do with how humans, with their limited-capacity working memory, manage to integrate or put together language inputs. If our working memory were large, we could wait until we had heard many sentences and then inspect them for interrelationships. However, working memory is limited in capacity, so we need some rules for deciding what parts of previously heard sentences to keep in working memory as we listen to new sentences. Naturally, we want to keep those parts that are most likely to be helpful when we are trying to integrate the new sentences with the old. Kintsch and van Dijk proposed that the most *central* and most *recently stated* parts of sentences are the parts that are most likely to be integrated with new sentences. For example, consider the following sentences:

1. The Swazi tribe was at war with a neighboring tribe because of a dispute over some cattle.

2. Among the warriors were two unmarried men, one named Kakra and his younger brother Gum.

The central ideas of the first sentence are that the Swazi tribe was at war with a neighboring tribe. These central ideas connect with the idea of *warrior* in the next sentence.

Or, for example, consider these sentences:

2. Among the warriors were two unmarried men, one named Kakra and his younger brother Gum.

3. Kakra was killed in a battle.

Kakra is the idea that unifies the two sentences. It is also an idea that is from the latter part of the first sentence—and hence from the most recently stated part.

Once the problem of what to keep active in working memory is solved, there is still the problem of how to integrate one's memory for ideas in prior sentences with the ideas in the sentence currently being heard. Kintsch and van Dijk proposed two mechanisms for integration. The first looks for common concept labels in the prior and current sentence and if it finds one, then this is used to tie the two sentences together. *Kakra* is a common concept label in sentences (2) and (3) above. The second mechanism only comes into play if the first doesn't succeed. It tries to infer a relationship between the two sentences based on prior knowledge. There are no common concept labels between sentences (1) and (2) above, so a reader must use his or her prior knowledge about wars and about syntax to infer that the warriors mentioned in sentence (2) were members of the Swazi tribe mentioned in sentence (1). Figure 2.9 shows in flowchart form the process of selection and integration that we have just described.

Kintsch (1979) translated his and van Dijk's ideas into a computer program. The program was then loaded into the computer and sentences (1), (2), and (3) were read into the computer for processing. The processing of each sentence was said to take place on one "cycle." The events that happened during each cycle are shown in Figure 2.10. During the first cycle, the program selected [the Swazi tribe], [was at war with], and [a neighboring tribe] to keep active. It let [because of] and [a dispute over some cattle] become inactive. During the second cycle, the program tried to find a common concept label between the three ideas kept active from the first sentence and the ideas in the second sentence. No common concept label was found, so the program drew the inference that the idea of [the

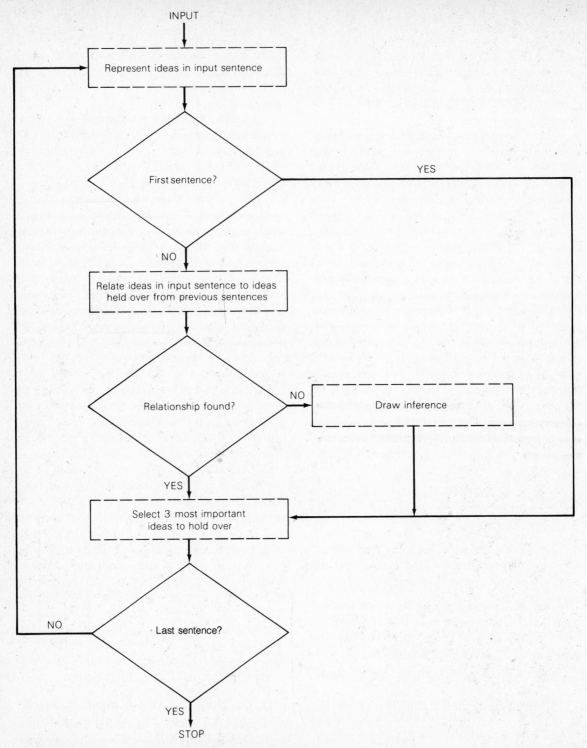

Figure 2.9 An information-processing analysis of some stages in language comprehension.

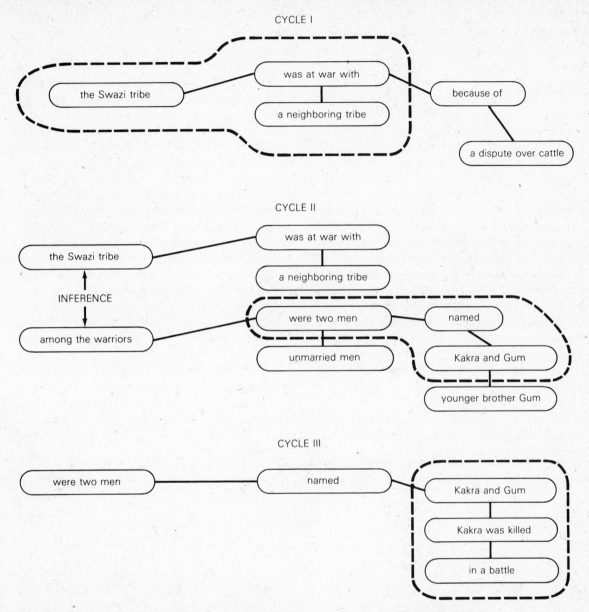

Figure 2.10 The events in a computer simulation of comprehension. The broken lines surround ideas selected for further processing (adapted from Kintsch, 1979).

Swazi tribe] is connected to the idea of [among the warriors] and marked this connection. This is symbolized in Figure 2.10 by the line from [the Swazi tribe] to [among the warriors]. Next, three ideas were selected to keep active. They were [were two men], [named], and [Kakra and Gum]. During the third cycle, the program looked for a common concept label between these three ideas and the new ideas from the third sentence. This time, a common concept label was found. Finally, the connection between the second and third sentences was noted (symbolized by the line between [Kakra and Gum] and [Kakra was killed]).

The important question to ask about this program is does its output somehow correspond to human behavior on this same task? If it does, then this suggests that the theory proposed is a good theory of human comprehension. If it does not, then it rules out this theory as a candidate for explaining comprehension. Kintsch reasoned that if humans use a process similar to that used by the computer program, then they should show better memory for the ideas that the computer worked with on more than one cycle than for the ideas that it worked with on only one cycle. This is because the more operations in which an idea is involved in working memory, the more memorable that idea will be. The computer analog to the number of operations on an idea is the number of cycles in which an idea appears.

Table 2.1 shows the results from a study of 100 college students' recall protocols for the passage shown above, and it compares the recall frequency for each idea to the number of cycles on which this idea occurred in the computer. Idea number two [was at war with], which was recalled by 80 subjects, occurred on two computer cycles, while idea number four [because of], which was recalled by only 46 subjects, occurred on only one cycle. The data from almost all the ideas showed this same pattern: Ideas used on two cycles were recalled by more subjects than were ideas used on only one cycle. (The exceptions are ideas 1 and 13). In general, then, the data are consistent with the theory, and it can therefore be concluded that Kintsch and van Dijk's theory is a plausible one.

Unlike Kintsch and van Dijk's theory, some psychological theories are either vague or circular or both. Such theories may be captivating because of their intuitive appeal, but they really don't do much to forward the generation of new knowledge because they

Table 2.1 Recall of the passage ideas and the number of computer cycles on which the idea occurred. Notice the positive correlation between the number of subjects recalling an idea and the number of cycles in which the idea occurred (from Kintsch, 1979).

IDEA NUMBER		NUMBER OF SUBJECTS (OUT OF 100) RECALLING IDEAS	NUMBER OF CYCLES IN WHICH IDEA OCCURRED
1	The Swazi tribe	45	2
2	was at war with	80	2
3	a neighboring tribe	78	2
4	because	46	1
5	a dispute over some cattle	39	1
6	Among the warriors	42	1
7	were two men	82	2
8	unmarried men	47	1
9	named	79	2
10	Kakra and Gum	81	2
11	younger brother Gum	45	1
12	Kakra was killed	84	2
13	in a battle	17	2

can be bent and molded to account for almost anything and, therefore, can never be refuted. Scientific knowledge is built on the overturning or refinement of theories, and educational practice benefits from the development of new psychological knowledge. So, the development of clear, logically consistent theories is an important goal for cognitive psychology. An advantage of testing a cognitive model as a computer simulation is that the model must be clear and consistent if the program is to run.

Artificial Intelligence.   There is a subfield of computer science called artificial intelligence, which shares some characteristics with computer simulations as practiced by cognitive psychologists. The goal of artificial-intelligence scientists is to design and develop computer systems that mimic some aspect of human intelligence—chess-playing or learning, for example. This goal is one that artificial-intelligence scientists share with cognitive psychologists who design computer simulations of human performance.

The computer scientists, however, are less constrained than the psychologists because they may use any processes they like to achieve intelligent performance. The psychologists may only use processes that are consistent with what is known about human information processing. Chess is a good domain for illustrating this point because many chess programs have been developed by computer scientists (e.g., Greenblatt, Eastlake, & Crocker, 1967). Typical programs consider and evaluate all possible legal moves before deciding on the next move. A human expert does not do this because he or she cannot keep so much information in mind at one time. Rather, the human expert recognizes a huge number of patterns that have become familiar over years of playing chess and retrieves actions that tend to succeed when these patterns occur. Programs that consider all possible legal moves have been successful against rela-

tively expert human chess players (Newell & Simon, 1972), but they do so using processes that are different from those employed by human experts.

It is important to remember the distinction between artificial intelligence and cognitive psychology because similar terms are used in the two fields. If you read about a program that "learns" or "solves problems," try to find out the purpose of the design project and also if the program was designed by a computer scientist or a cognitive psychologist. If you read about this program when you are expecting to learn about human cognition, remember that programs designed by computer scientists may not provide a valid model of human cognition.

Despite the different goals of the two fields, there is much cross-fertilization. For example, machine-learning programs sometimes help psychologists think about learning processes in new ways, thus benefitting the development of psychologically valid simulations.

EDUCATIONAL IMPLICATIONS

Classroom Analogs of Cognitive Psychology Methods

Teachers have always been interested in the minds of their students and have, therefore, been using analogs of cognitive psychology methods ever since there have been students. For example, when a teacher observes that one student is consistently faster than another at solving algebra word problems, he may conclude that the strategy used by the faster student has fewer mental operations than the strategy used by the slower student. This is a form of subtractive technique theorizing. Or if a fourth-grade teacher watches a student's eye fixations while doing "silent reading" and sees that the student spends lots of time looking at the pictures, she may guess that this

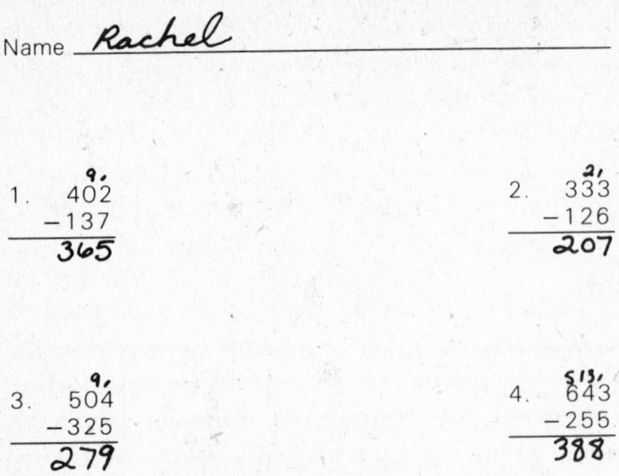

Name *Rachel*

1.　　 9.
　　　402
　　－137
　　　365

2.　　　 2.
　　　333
　　－126
　　　207

3.　　 9.
　　　504
　　－325
　　　279

4.　 5 13.
　　　643
　　－255
　　　388

Figure 2.11 An arithmetic worksheet on which the student has shown her work. Notice that 1 and 3 are wrong. A teacher can quickly figure out that Rachel has an incorrect rule that borrowing from zero affects only the column borrowed from, whereas it really affects the column to the left of the column borrowed from as well. This incorrect rule also suggests that Rachel may not have a good conceptual understanding of the decimal system.

student is forming a mental representation of the story based on pictures rather than on words. This teacher is making use of eye-fixation data to hypothesize about a student's mental processes.

Perhaps the most common educational analog to methods used by cognitive psychologists is the practice of "showing your work" in solving math problems (see Figure 2.11). Showing one's work is like thinking aloud except that one writes rather than states one's thoughts aloud. Arithmetic and math teachers who use this procedure realize that a student may get the wrong numerical answer to a problem yet really be using sound quantitative reasoning. (The wrong answer might be due to misremembering an addition fact.) Also, showing one's work reveals incorrect mental operations and misconceptions. For example, Rachel, the student whose work is shown in Figure 2.11, can borrow correctly except when she runs into a zero. When she

runs into a zero, as can be seen from her notes, she borrows a 10 from it instead of going to the next column to borrow. Once a teacher understands the nature of a student's mental operations, an incorrect operation can be pointed out and the correct operation can be described. This brief procedure sometimes clears up the problem immediately. Deeper misconceptions, such as poor understanding of the decimal system, can also be diagnosed and remediated.

One contribution that cognitive psychology can make to the observational techniques used in the classroom is simply to encourage teachers to use these techniques more. While "showing one's work" is a well-known method in math education, it is used less often in other subject areas. Just as psychologists have hesitated to use verbal reports because of threats to validity, so have teachers hesitated to rely on student's verbal reports. Yet, when the right question is asked at the right time, verbal reports can be quite revealing. For example, in teaching writing, students could be asked to hand in notes, outlines, and drafts, as well as their finished products. Teachers could then try to identify effective and ineffective strategies revealed by these notes. Or in a discussion during a history class, a teacher could ask students not only to answer a question, but to describe the steps in their reasoning that led to the answer. This description could reveal faulty mental operations such as overgeneralization, false deductions, or failure to recognize multiple causes for a given event. These are just a few examples of a much larger set of examples of how verbal reports can be used to find out about students' cognitive processes.

Another contribution that cognitive psychology can make to observational techniques used in the classroom is to make teachers more aware of sources of invalidity. In particular, it appears that asking students general questions about how they solve problems or how they study is not likely to produce informative answers. The students may try to give an answer that they think will please, or they may not know and will therefore invent an answer. Just as it is best for psychologists to collect retrospective reports immediately after a specific event, so too it is best for teachers to ask students about a specific performance soon after that performance.

Finally, with the advent of microcomputers in the classroom, many laboratory techniques may become available to teachers for use in diagnostic testing. Computers can be programmed to detect common error patterns in the responses given by students and then to branch to a variety of instructional procedures depending on the error pattern discerned.

Greater Emphasis on the Teaching of Strategies

Strategies are goal-directed sequences of cognitive operations that lead from the student's comprehension of a question or instructions to the answer or other requested performance. Because strategies are mental, they have been difficult to observe using the traditional method of examining the number of correct solutions to some task. Therefore, little precise knowledge of strategies has been available until relatively recently.

With our increasing ability to observe and model cognitive processes as they take place, we are increasingly able to describe the cognitive strategy differences between skilled and less skilled performance. Presumably, once the strategies used by skilled individuals are known, we will be able to teach them directly to less skilled individuals. For example, Snow's research on spatial ability tests shows that a good strategy to use on such tests is to look at the known shape, imagine the shape going through specified changes, and finally focus attention on the end result, holding that image in working memory while scanning

alternatives for a match. Possibly, these steps could be taught to students who don't use them naturally. Egan (1983) has successfully trained people to use a strategy similar to the one described by Snow.

Greater Emphasis on the Teaching of the Conceptual Basis of Content

As researchers more frequently use concept mapping, sorting, recall, and other methods that reveal the conceptual basis of performance, we are accumulating a better understanding of this basis for a wide variety of subject matter. Moreover, a number of recent studies that compare strategy instruction by itself to strategy instruction coupled with instruction in the conceptual basis of a domain finds much better transfer of learning for the latter type of instruction (cf., Case & McKeough, 1990; Frederiksen & White, 1988). Thus, there is growing evidence that teaching for conceptual understanding is quite fruitful (a point to which we will return in the chapter on transfer). At the same time, we now have some methods by which the nature of conceptual understanding can be revealed in enough detail to be useful for instruction.

CHAPTER SUMMARY

Cognitive psychologists employ a variety of empirical data types and theoretical techniques to gain a better understanding of complex mental processes. The data types include response latencies, eye fixations, verbal reports, sorting, and free recall. The theoretical techniques include the subtractive technique for estimating the time to execute a cognitive process, and information-processing analysis for modelling the various knowledge representations and processes involved in completing a given task. Computer simulation is a rigorous form of information-processing analysis in which a computer is programmed to execute a task in a manner that humans are thought to execute the task. If the trace of the computer's performance somehow matches human performance, then the model programmed into the computer gains credibility as a valid model of human cognitive processing.

The methods used by cognitive psychologists have analogs in the classroom. Many experienced teachers use observations of students' speed, eye fixations, recall, etc. to draw inferences about what the students know. Knowledge of sources of invalidity in these data types can help teachers observe and draw inferences that are more likely to be correct.

Advances in cognitive psychology's methods have led to research on the conceptual and strategic bases of expertise. As we learn more about these bases, we can use this knowledge to reform traditional curriculi.

ADDITIONAL READINGS

Many of the methods described in this chapter have rather technical justifications. If you plan to conduct research using one of these methods, it would be well worth your while to read further before using the method.

Subtractive Technique

Chase, W. G. (1978). Elementary information processes. In W.K. Estes (Ed.), *Handbook of learning and cognitive processes*, Vol. 5. Hillsdale, NJ: Lawrence Erlbaum Associates.

Donders, F. C. (1969). On the speed of mental processes. *Acta Psychologica, 30,* 412–431. (Translated by W. G. Koster from the original in *Onderzoekingen gedaan in het Physiologisch Laboratorium der Utrechtsche Hoogeschool,* 1868, *Tweede reeks, II,* 92–120.)

Sternberg, S. (1969). The discovery of processing stages: Extensions of Donder's method. In W. G. Koster (Ed.), *Attention and performance II. Acta Psychologica,* 1969, *30,* 276–315.

Eye Fixations

Monty, R. A. & Senders, J. W. (Eds.) (1976). *Eye movements and psychological processes.* Hillsdale, NJ: Lawrence Erlbaum Associates.

Rayner, K. (1977). Visual attention in reading: Eye movements reflect cognitive processing. *Memory & Cognition, 4,* 443–448.

Rayner, K. (Ed.) (1983). *Eye movements in reading: Perceptual and language processes.* New York: Academic Press.

Verbal Reports

Ericsson, K. A. & Simon, H. A. (1980). Verbal reports as data. *Psychological Review, 87,* 215–251.

Ericsson, K. A. & Simon, H. A. (1984). *Protocol analysis.* Cambridge, MA: MIT Press.

Computer Simulation

Bower, G. H., & Hilgard, E. R. (1981). Information-processing theories of behavior. In G. H. Bower & E. R. Hilgard, *Theories of learning,* 5th Ed. Englewood Cliffs, NJ: Prentice-Hall.

Artificial Intelligence

Winston, (1984). *Artificial intelligence.* Reading, MA: Addison-Wesley.

Pylyshyn, Z. W. (1986). *Computation and cognition: Toward a foundation for cognitive science.* Cambridge, MA: MIT Press.

Software for Gathering Latency and Other Data

Schneider, W. (1988). Micro experimental laboratory: An integrated system for IBM PC compatibles. *Behavior Research Methods, Instruments, & Computers, 20,* 206–217.

Examples of the Use of Cognitive Psychology in Instructional Practice

Adams, M. J. (1989). *Teaching thinking to Chapter I students.* Center for the Study of Reading, Technical Report #473. Champaign, IL: University of Illinois.

Dillon, R. F., & Sternberg, R. J. (Eds.) (1986). *Cognition and instruction.* New York: Academic Press.

Gallagher, M., & Pearson, P. D. (1989). *Discussion, comprehension, and knowledge acquisition in content area classrooms.* Center for the Study of Reading, Technical Report #480. Champaign, IL: University of Illinois.

Swing, S. R., Stoiber, K. C., & Peterson, P. L. (1988). Thinking skills versus learning time: Effects of alternative classroom-based interventions on student's mathematics problem-solving. *Cognition and Instruction, 5,* 123–191.

Zhu, X. & Simon, H. A. (1987). Learning mathematics from examples and by doing. *Cognition and Instructions, 4,* 137–166.

ANSWER TO ANALOGY

Five is correct because Lincoln's picture is on a five dollar bill; Washington's is on a one dollar bill. (This example comes from R.J. Sternberg, 1979.)

Chapter 3

Overview of the Human Information-Processing System

SUMMARY

1. Information is received by **sensory receptors** and registered in the central nervous system in **immediate memory.**

2. Through **selective perception** processes, a small portion of information registered in immediate memory is selected for additional processing in **working memory.**

3. Information in working memory decays rapidly if not rehearsed or otherwise used. Furthermore, working memory has an extremely limited capacity. It poses a major constraint on the ways humans process information.

4. **Automatic** processes are carried out without demanding much working-memory capacity, while **controlled** processes are highly demanding of limited working-memory capacity.

5. **Storage** processes are used to transfer new information from working memory into **long-term memory.**

6. **Retrieval** processes put information from long-term memory in a form that can be used by current processing activities.

7. **Control** processes control the flow of information that passes through the human information-processing system.

8. The **cerebral cortex** is a highly convoluted sheet of neurons, covering much of the rest of the brain in humans. The interactions of cortical neurons with each other and with subcortical neurons appear to underlie many cognitive processes.

9. In adult humans, highly practiced skills may come to have a specialized locus within the brain.

10. Certain cortical and perhaps subcortical cells are specialized to respond to a particular pattern of input from lower cells; such cells form the basis of selective perception.

11. Working memory appears to be the product of activity in a variety of neurons, distributed throughout the brain, that are interacting during a given cognitive process.

12. The **amygdala** and **hippocampus** are involved in the formation of long-term memory traces, perhaps through the initiation of a binding process in which a higher-level neuron comes to be activated by a certain pattern of lower-level neurons.

THE HUMAN INFORMATION-PROCESSING SYSTEM

Despite the huge variation in human capabilities, all normal humans come equipped with the same information-processing system. Some of the processes used by the system may be performed faster or better by some than by others, but the nature of the system is the same. In this chapter, we will describe some of the fundamental aspects of human information processing. A deep understanding of later chapters depends on your having an understanding of these basics. Also in this chapter, we will contrast humans and computers as information processors because this contrast helps highlight the unique aspects of human cognition. Finally, we will address the intriguing question of what brain mechanisms underlie human information processing.

Figure 3.1 shows some of the more important elements of the human information-processing system. The boxes indicate states of information, which may or may not have unique physical locations in the brain, while the ovals indicate processes that change information from one state to another.

Initial Reception of Information

Information, in the form of some physical energy (light for print, sound for speech, pressure for touch, etc.) is received by **receptors** that are sensitive to that particular form of energy (rods and cones, middle ear bones, proprioceptor cells, etc.). These receptors send signals, in the form of electrochemical impulses, to the brain. Thus, the first transformation of information is from one of several forms of energy to a common form.

From the receptors the nerve impulse goes to the central nervous system, where it is registered in **immediate memory.** There appear to be different immediate memories for visual and auditory information (called **iconic** and **echoic** memory, respectively, by Neisser, 1967), but these memories are similar in that they hold a fairly complete representation of incoming sensory information for an ex-

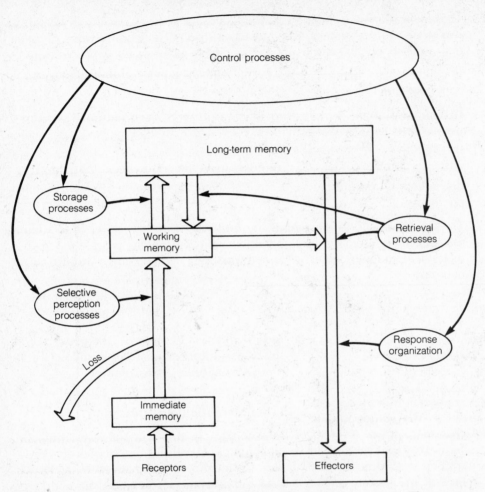

Figure 3.1 Basic elements of the human information-processing system. The system consists of three memory stores (immediate, working, and long-term); processes that transform information between and among input (receptors), output (effectors), and memory stores; and control processes.

tremely brief period of time. Sperling (1960) has estimated that the time a visual stimulus is held in immediate memory before it decays is about a fourth of a second (250 milliseconds). This amount of time is apparently long enough for **selective perception** processes to determine what information should be kept active in **working memory** for further processing. Information not selected is lost to the system.

Selective Perception

Selective perception involves focussing on what is most important in a stimulus array. We are born with a tendency to selectively attend to such stimuli as sudden loud noises, motion, and contrasts of light and dark, presumably because it is adaptive to do so. In addition, we learn to selectively attend to a wide variety of patterns. In fact, one of the hallmarks of being an expert in some domain is the ability to attend to the most important parts of a stimulus (Chi, Glaser, & Farr, 1988). Chess experts, for example, selectively attend to certain patterns of chess pieces while ignoring irrelevant details such as whether the pieces are made of plastic or onyx.

The pattern knowledge that we acquire over a lifetime increases the accuracy of selective perception of items in familiar contexts. One demonstration of contextual enhancement of perception comes from Tulving, Mandler, and Baumal (1964). These researchers asked subjects to identify words presented briefly when these words were either in a context or in isolation. For example, some subjects saw the target word *location*, while other subjects saw a context sentence, "He built his new house in a desirable . . ." prior to seeing the final word, *location*. When *location* was displayed for 60 milliseconds (less than a tenth of a second), the accuracy rate for words identified following a context was 40% greater than for words identified in isolation.

This experiment demonstrates that perception is influenced by what we already know as well as by elements of the stimulus array itself. That is, perception is as much a "top-down" process as it is a "bottom-up" process. Much of the knowledge that makes selective perception a top-down process is stored in schemas, which we will describe in more detail in Chapter 5.

Working Memory

Working memory (WM) corresponds roughly to awareness. That is, what you are aware of at any given moment is said to be in your WM. Information in this memory store decays within about 10 seconds (cf., Murdock, 1961) unless it is rehearsed. When you look up a telephone number, for example, the number gets into your WM. If you don't mentally rehearse this number as you walk from the

telephone book to the telephone, however, you may find that you have forgotten it.

In addition to being of limited duration, WM is of limited capacity. Miller (1956) claims that WM holds 7 ± 2 units of information, while Simon (1974) claims that it holds only about 5 units. Whatever the exact number, the important point for educators is that it is small. Because of its small size, WM is often referred to as the "bottleneck" of the human information-processing system. As we shall see, the small capacity of WM has important implications for instruction.

Working memory functions as a mental workspace. Some people think of it as an internal notepad or blackboard. For example, if you were solving the problem 26×32 mentally, you would hold the intermediate products 52 and 78 in WM and add them together there. Or, if you are imagining the consequences of a particular course of action, the scenario that you imagine is in your WM.

Because of the limited capacity of WM, it is difficult to perform several mental tasks at once. For example, most of us can't dictate a letter and balance a checkbook at the same time or read a technical article and participate in a conversation at the same time. Usually, people are comfortable doing only one cognitively demanding task at once.

One way in which people can do more than one mental task at the same time is by "automating" one of the tasks. Automating, which we will describe in more detail in Chapter 9, means practicing a task until it can be performed with a minimum of awareness. Skilled readers, for instance, decode print without really thinking about it. Beginning readers, on the other hand, use a lot of working memory to "sound out" the words they are reading. Because skilled readers have automated their word-decoding skills, they have more mental capacity (or more "room" in working memory) to devote to understanding what they are reading than do beginning readers.

Schneider and Shiffrin (1977) call processes that are performed without much awareness **automatic** processes and those requiring a lot of attention **controlled** processes. These terms are widely accepted among cognitive psychologists, and we will use them throughout this book.

Storage and Long-Term Memory

Information in working memory may be **stored** in **long-term memory** (LTM). Storage refers to a set of processes by which new information is integrated in various ways with known information. We will describe these processes in more detail in Chapters 7, 8, and 9. The function of LTM is to store information for later use. In contrast to WM, the duration of LTM is long—perhaps as long as a lifetime. There is controversy over whether or not everything that we have ever stored in LTM stays there permanently, but most psychologists agree that much of what we have stored stays with us for quite a long time. The feeling of not being able to remember something is thought to be due more often to a failure to find a good retrieval cue than to a loss of information from LTM.

One study of the relative permanence of memory traces was conducted by Williams and Hollan (1981). These researchers asked subjects who were from 4 to 19 years out of high school to recall as many names as possible of individuals in their high school classes. Using high school yearbooks, the researchers could verify the correctness of the names recalled. You may wish to try this yourself before reading further.

At first, subjects recalled very little. But slowly, over several one-hour sessions, they began to recall more and more. What seemed to lead to ultimate recall of a name was identification of a good retrieval cue. For example, subjects would systematically think about subgroups of students, such as "kids on my block" or "kids in my chemistry class" or "kids in French club." These cues would lead them to generate other cues, until eventually they retrieved in the range of 12 to 35% of possible names of classmates. Since the subjects were from large classes and therefore may not have even known a large percentage of names to begin with, these results are quite impressive and suggest that much of what we know and experience remains in long-term memory.

Retrieval

Retrieval refers to a set of processes that put information stored in long-term memory into a state in which it can be used for current processing. The processes seem to be somewhat different for automatic and controlled processing. This difference is suggested by the separate lines for retrieval in Figure 3.1—one from LTM to WM (controlled processing) and one from LTM directly to effectors (automatic processing).

For controlled processing, retrieval means becoming aware of the previously stored information. This process of re-establishing awareness is often referred to as **activation.** When students take tests in which they must recall factual knowledge, they are said to be activating this knowledge.

When information in LTM is required for use by an automatic process, it is retrieved by means of a **pattern-matching** process. For example, if you are asked to multiply:

$$\begin{array}{r} 26 \\ \times\ 32 \\ \hline \end{array}$$

you might start by multiplying 6 by 2, recording 2 units and "carrying" a ten. Then you might multiply 2 by 2, record the result, and so on. The guide for the sequence of steps you take is automatically retrieved when you recognize the familiar pattern of numbers and multiplication sign.

We will discuss both activation and pattern matching more in later chapters. For now, the main point is that the process of retrieval from LTM differs as a function of whether or not the information being retrieved is being used for automatic or controlled processing.

Response Generation and Effectors

When we wish to respond in some way, the response needs to be sequenced. Physical responses, such as writing or typing, involve specific sequences of actions. When the response involves language production, the message must be generated in a grammatically acceptable form; for example, in English, this usually means having the subject before the verb and the verb before the object.

Response generation refers to activities that organize the sequence of responses and send messages to the appropriate **effectors** to execute this sequence. The effectors include all of our muscles and glands, but, for school tasks, the main effectors are the arms and hands for writing or typing and the voice apparatus for speaking.

Control Processes

The flow of information in the human system is generally organized around achieving some purpose. Whether the purpose be satisfaction of curiosity, solving a problem, aesthetic enjoyment, or mastering a specific skill, information-processing events are not at all random. **Control processes** are the processes that guide and monitor information-processing events. They include goal setting, planning how to achieve goals, monitoring goal attainment, and revising plans.

When we consciously use such processes, we are said to be using **metacognitive** processes ("meta" means above). For example, yesterday my four-year-old was walking towards his father's study repeating to himself, "Fern, Fern, Fern, Fern." When he saw me, he interrupted his repetitions to explain, "I'm going to tell Daddy the name of the girl in *Charlotte's Web* and I'm saying it over and over so I won't forget it." His goal was to remember an unfamiliar name that he had just heard, and he had consciously selected the strategy of repetition. He was using metacognitive processes.

In contrast to consciously deployed control processes, some control processes, either innately or through learning, are deployed automatically. These are not referred to as metacognitive because they do not appear to be "above" the processing event, but rather a part of it. For example, we don't think consciously about how to achieve the goal of multiplying two two-digit numbers—we just do it. In learned, automated skills, the flow of control is embedded in the skill. Nonetheless, the sequence has a control structure.

AN EXAMPLE OF INFORMATION PROCESSING

To make this information-processing model more concrete, let us consider a relatively simple example. Suppose that a second-grade teacher wants Joe to learn the fact that the capital of Texas is Austin. The teacher asks Joe, "What is the capital of Texas?" and Joe says, "I don't know." At the same time he may set up the goal of learning the capital of Texas, and this causes him to pay attention. The teacher then says, "The capital of Texas is Austin." Joe's ears receive this message and also receive other sounds such as the sounds of other pupils' speech and of traffic outside the school.

All of the sounds that Joe hears are translated into electrochemical impulses and sent to immediate memory. The pattern that the capital of Texas is Austin is selected for entry into WM, while other patterns representing the sounds of other pupils' speech are not entered into WM.

Joe may then store the fact that the capital of Texas is Austin by associating it with other facts that he already knows about Austin (e.g., that it is a big city and that he once visited it). This storage process causes the new fact to be entered into LTM. If Joe has already developed special memory strategies, which is somewhat unlikely for a second-grader, his metacognitive processes might direct the storage process to use these special strategies.

The next day, Joe's teacher might ask him, "What is the capital of Texas?" This question would be received in immediate memory and selected for entry into WM. In WM it would provide cues for the activation in LTM of the answer. This activated fact would be used to organize the speech acts that produce the sounds: "Austin is the capital of Texas."

A COMPARISON WITH COMPUTERS

Any system in which information undergoes a series of transformations from input to output can be analyzed from an information-processing perspective. Telephone systems, television systems, and computer systems are all examples of information-processing systems. Computer systems are an especially seductive source of analogies for cognitive psychologists because the behavior of computers sometimes approximates the behavior of humans.

Some people think that it is ridiculous to compare humans and computers because they are so different—after all, computers can't "feel" and can't "be creative." Other people think that the similarities between humans and computers are so great that computers may wrest control from humans. It is important to understand just how computers and humans are alike and different as information-processing systems in order to assess these claims. But before we describe their

similarities and differences, let us describe briefly a simple computer system.

A Computer System

Most computer systems contain at least the following parts: (1) an input device, (2) a central processing unit (CPU), (3) a long-term storage medium, (4) a device for putting information into long-term storage and retrieving it from storage, and (5) an output device. A common input device for a computer is the keyboard. A human sits at a monitor and types information on a keyboard. The information is transmitted to the CPU. The CPU is where the work of a computer gets done. It consists of large numbers of elements, each of which is on or off at any given time. The patterns of on and off are used to represent information, and these patterns change as work is done.

If one desires to save the products of some work that the computer has done, one directs the computer to transfer these products to a storage device. Storage devices are usually either tapes or disks on which information is coded electromagnetically. If one desires to see the products of the work the computer has done, one directs it to output this information, usually by printing it on paper or on a monitor screen.

The Comparison

The parts of a computer system are functionally similar to the parts of the human information-processing system. Humans, like computers, have various ways of receiving input. After receiving input, they do some mental work in working memory, just as computers do work in the CPU. After working with information, humans store it in LTM, just as computers store information on tape or disk. Finally, humans output information through effectors, while computers output information on paper or screen.

Thus, humans and computers are similar in the functional units within their systems. However, at a more detailed level of comparison, the two systems differ a great deal. Table 3.1 shows a comparison of humans and computers.

In terms of size, the size of human WM (5 bits of information) is much smaller than the size of a computer's CPU. Current mainframe computers have up to 800 million bits of information in their CPUs (Slotnick, Butterfield, Colantonio, Kopetzky, & Slotnick, 1986). As was previously mentioned, the small capacity of WM is an extremely important aspect of the human system; now, we see that it is an aspect that clearly distinguishes humans from computers.

In comparison to estimating the size of WM, it is more difficult to estimate the size of human LTM because this estimate depends on one's assumptions about the physiological basis of LTM traces. Whatever assumptions one uses, however, the size is quite large. Kemeny (1955), who assumed (1) that all patterns perceived during waking hours are stored in LTM and (2) that we perceive several patterns per second, estimated the size of LTM to be a billion bits of information. A computer's storage capacity is theoretically unlimited, depending only on the number of tapes and disks that are available. Although human storage capacity is finite and computer storage capacity is theoretically infinite, hu-mans appear never to use up their storage capacity, so this difference between humans and computers is not a crucial one.

When comparing humans and computers for speed, one finds that computer access times are faster than are those of humans. Access time in the CPU refers to the speed with which electricity moves from one area of the CPU to another. Computers are very rapid in this regard, with 15 nanoseconds being possible in large mainframe computers. Humans, as has been determined in experiments done by S. Sternberg (1966), take about 25 milliseconds to shift attention from one part of working memory to another. Access time to information stored on a hard disk in a computer is in the range of 10 to 60 milliseconds (Slotnick et al., 1986), while access time to human LTM is about 200 milliseconds (Sabol & DeRosa, 1976).

Computers thus appear to be more capacious and faster as information-processing systems than are humans. They can have a workspace that is over a millionfold larger than human workspace (WM); their speed of access to information in the workspace is a million times faster than ours; and their speed of access to information in storage is 10 times faster than ours. Clearly, computers have the advantage over humans in the amount of information they can work with and the speed with which they work. This is what makes computers so useful for "number-crunching" problems in which large amounts of data are manipulated in complex ways.

Table 3.1 A comparison of human and computer storage capacities and speed of retrieval of stored information.

	HUMAN	MAINFRAME COMPUTER
Size of WM or CPU	5 bits	800,000,000 bits
Size of LTM	1,000,000,000 bits	unlimited
Speed of access within WM	.025 sec.	.000000015 sec.
Speed of access to LTM	.200 sec.	.020 sec.

However, computers and humans differ in another way that seems to give an advantage to humans. Estes (1980) has suggested that the structure of memory in humans differs from that in computers (see Table 3.2). Human memory is not all-or-none the way computer memory is; rather, we remember partial information. By contrast, in computers, a set of information is either available in its entirety or not at all. Recent physiological data reveal that typical cortical neurons synapse with (connect to) over 1000 other neurons, suggesting that the *interconnectedness* of human memory is much greater than that of computer memory (Anderson, 1990). Human memory capacity and retrieval depend upon the context. In familiar contexts, we seem to be able to deal with much more information, perhaps because of the interconnectedness just mentioned. Computer memory capacity and retrieval, however, are context independent. Human dependency on context allows for learning and adaptation to take place, and our tendency for partial memory allows us to think of novel solutions to problems. In short, the human system has evolved to be adaptive. One adaptation of the human system has been to create fast, capacious machines that perform routine problem-solving tasks.

PHYSIOLOGICAL SUBSTRATES OF COGNITION

The picture of human information processing that we have just painted is an abstract one. It describes characteristics of information processing, such as limited-capacity working memory, but doesn't say anything about the neurological basis of cognition. In this section we will explore the issue of the neurological basis of cognition. First, however, we will review some basic information about the brain upon which neural models depend.

The Brain

Major Subdivisions of the Brain. The brain consists of neurons and supporting cells that are organized into several different structures, shown in Figure 3.2. As you can see, the spinal cord projects up into the **brainstem.** The **cerebellum,** which is involved in motor coordination, straddles the brainstem. Above, and in front of, the brainstem is a set of structures that together look something like a fist. These structures comprise the **forebrain** part of the brain and include the **thalamus, basal ganglia, hippocampus,** and **amygdala.** The thalamus is involved in relaying (and

Table 3.2 A comparison of human and computer memory (from Estes, 1980).

	HUMAN MEMORY	COMPUTER MEMORY
Preferred storage mode	analog; time-oriented	digital; list-oriented
Retention of information	graded	all-or-none
Efficiency (bits/sec.)	low	high
Capacity	dependent on experience	independent of experience
Retrieval		
relative to context	strongly dependent	independent
relative to previous retrievals	dependent	independent
Purpose	general purpose; open set of functions	special or general purpose; closed set of functions

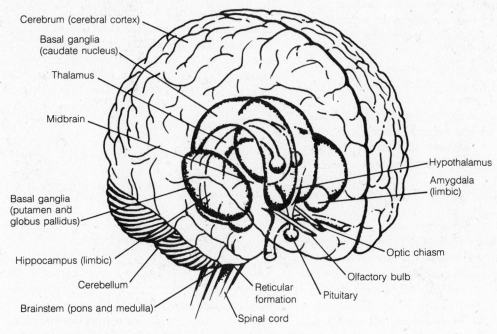

Figure 3.2 The human brain (from R. Thompson, 1985, p. 11).

possibly filtering) stimulus information from sense organs to higher brain locations. The basal ganglia play a role in motor control. The hippocampus and amygdala, as we will discuss shortly, appear to play an important role in the formation of long-term memory traces.

Covering these forebrain structures is the **cerebral cortex,** which in humans is a highly convoluted sheet of neurons. It has been estimated that if this sheet of neurons were stretched flat, it would cover one square meter (Anderson, 1990)! On an evolutionary scale, the cerebral cortex is one of the most recently-evolved brain structures, and it plays a crucial role in complex cognitive processes.

Major Functional Subdivisions within the Cerebral Cortex. Many of the major subdivisions of the brain that we just described are easy to see by visual inspection. The cerebellum, for example, has a unique feathery-like look, and the cortex is characterized by folds. In contrast, we have to look more closely to identify the major subdivisions within the cerebral cortex, tracing pathways of nerve fibers from sense organs such as the eyes to where they project on the cortex. To gain a more complete picture of the functional areas of the cortex, scientists use such techniques as electrical stimulation and recording and CT and PET scans of both brain-damaged and

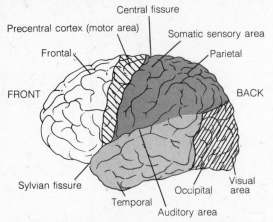

Figure 3.3 Major subdivisions of the cortex (from R. Thompson, 1985, p. 24, after R. Thompson, 1975).

normal individuals. Taking data from all these sources, neuroscientists have developed a fairly complete map of the major functional areas of the cerebral cortex. Figure 3.3 shows this map.

There are three major types of cortical tissue—sensory, motor, and association. The sensory areas receive signals from some type of sense organ. For example, the **occipital** region receives visual signals, the **parietal** region receives signals from the skin and body, and the **auditory** area (buried in a deep fold called the **Sylvian fissure**) receives signals from the ears. The area of the cortex most involved with control of movement is the **motor** or **precentral cortex.** Most of the rest of the cortex, which is a relatively large amount of the cortex in humans, is called the **association cortex.**

As can be seen in Figure 3.4, as one moves up the evolutionary scale for mammals, the size of the cortex increases, especially the amount of cortex involved in association functions. The association cortex appears to be involved in many of the more complex and higher-level cognitive processes that humans perform, although exactly how it is involved is only beginning to be understood.

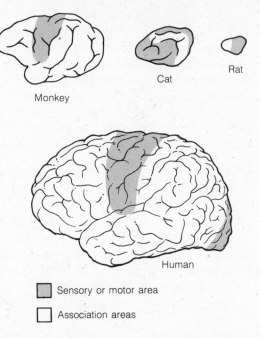

Sensory or motor area

Association areas

Figure 3.4 Cortices of several mammals, showing the increase in the relative and absolute size of the cortex as one moves up the evolutionary scale (from R. Thompson, 1985, p. 26, after R. Thompson, 1975).

The cortex is divided into left and right hemispheres, which are connected by a band of about 200 million fibers called the **corpus callosum.** Studies of individuals who have had their corpus callosi severed (as a treatment for severe epilepsy) show that in the majority of adults, the right hemisphere of the cortex is proficient at spatial processing while the left is proficient at active language processing (the right hemisphere typically can comprehend concrete language, but can't produce it). The notion of hemispheric specialization received much attention in popular educational literature in the 1970s and 80s. Some educators claimed that we were not doing enough to educate the "right side of the brain" and proposed visually-oriented curriculi to stimulate the right side of the brain (for example, Raina, 1984).

While the data from "split-brain" patients show that there is some specialization of functions in the two hemispheres, this does not necessitate drawing the conclusion that we are not doing enough to educate the "spatial" hemisphere. The type of data needed to demonstrate such a conclusion would be data showing that typical students lacked the proficiency in spatial processing needed to function in their environments. To our knowledge, such data have not been presented.

We believe that a better way to look at hemispheric specialization is as an example of a more general principle of brain organization that is beginning to emerge: that there is a tendency for particular areas of the adult brain to show functional specialization. For example, recent studies reveal two separate areas of the cortex involved in two parts of language production. These areas are shown in Figure 3.5. **Broca's area,** in the frontal cortex, seems to be involved in setting up a grammatically correct plan for stating an idea, while **Wernicke's area,** in the temporal lobe, seems to be crucial for the mapping of meaning onto words. Individuals who have brain damage in Broca's area say grammatically correct but rather meaningless things, while those with damage to Wernicke's area say sensible things but in garbled, ungrammatical ways. (Notice that this example of specialization occurs within *one* hemisphere of the cortex.)

Functional specialization seems to progress as humans get older. In comparison to adults, young children who suffer brain damage are much more likely to recover a lost function by recruiting another part of the cortex to perform the function. For example, one patient

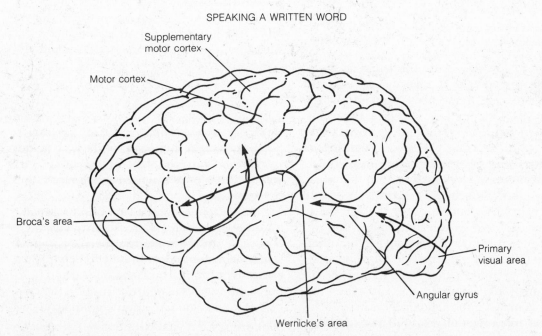

SPEAKING A WRITTEN WORD

Supplementary motor cortex

Motor cortex

Broca's area

Primary visual area

Angular gyrus

Wernicke's area

Figure 3.5 The areas of the brain involved in speaking a written word (from R. Thompson, 1985, p. 310).

who had the corpus callosum severed as an adult had also had damage to the left hemisphere as a child. As a child, this patient's language function had been disrupted for a while, but then recovered. Apparently, both hemispheres developed language abilities because later, after the split-brain operation, both sides of the brain showed good active language ability (described in Thompson, 1985, pp. 315–16).

It is an exciting development that many of the specific functional areas of the brain that are now being identified map onto basic cognitive functions identified in information-processing models. For instance, information-processing models of language processing typically separate out the meaning-interpretation and grammar functions of language. This separation parallels the separation of function found in Wernicke's and Broca's areas of the cortex. The convergence of models from cognitive science and neuroscience is heartening, suggesting that both are on the right track.

Neurons

Anatomy. Signals are transmitted into, around, and out of the brain via neurons, which are cells specialized for conducting electrochemical impulses. A typical neuron is shown in Figure 3.6. This figure shows a **cell body** with one **axon** and several **dendrites.** The dendrites carry information from other neurons into the cell body, and the axon carries information away from the cell body to other neurons. Dendrites and the cell body itself are covered with receptor sites that receive information from the axons of other neurons. Interestingly, cortical neurons typically receive information from thousands of other neurons, suggesting a capability for highly complex information processing.

The area of communication between the axonal end of one neuron and the receptor sites on the next neuron is referred to as a

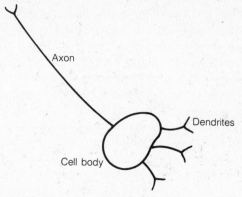

Figure 3.6 A typical neuron.

synapse. As is shown in Figure 3.7, the synapse is composed of a **presynaptic membrane** at the end of the axon, a **synaptic cleft**—or space—between cells, and a **postsynaptic membrane.** In the axon of the presynaptic neuron very close to the presynaptic membrane are **vesicles** containing substances that transmit across the cleft. When the neuron is active, these vesicles merge with the membrane to release their contents into the cleft. Molecules on the postsynaptic membrane receive the transmitter substances, and this causes the postsynaptic neuron to respond.

Types of Neurons. In many areas of the brain there are two different kinds of neurons— large, **principal neurons,** with long axons reaching into other areas of the brain, and smaller **interneurons** whose axons stay within the local area (Thompson, 1985). Apparently, the role of the interneurons is to process information coming into the particular brain area. The principal neuron then sends messages via its long axon to functionally related areas of the brain. These anatomical and functional differences in neurons support the view that at least some parts of the brain achieve a good deal of functional specificity in adults. That is, in order to specialize, the local area would need some neurons that communicate

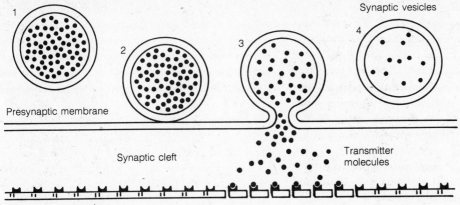

1

2

3

4

Synaptic vesicles

Presynaptic membrane

Synaptic cleft

Transmitter molecules

Postsynaptic membrane

Figure 3.7 The functional elements of a synapse. At the end of the axon (the presynaptic membrane) are synaptic vesicles containing transmitter substances. The transmitter substances cross the synaptic cleft and are received at receptor sites on the postsynaptic membrane of a dendrite or cell body (from R. Thompson, 1985, p. 40, from Stevens, 1979).

information within a small area and some other neurons that communicate output to related areas. Possibly, the pattern-recognition units for arithmetic word problems mentioned in Chapter 1, or the schemas to be described in Chapter 5 have this type of neural basis.

Cognitive Processes

In the previous section, we discussed several points about the nervous system that are relevant to a discussion of physiological substrates of cognition. These included the ideas that the brain is organized into various parts, some of which develop specialized functions; that the brain is also organized so that there is a great deal of communication between and among parts; and that neurons are the basic unit of communication of information, accomplished by an electrochemical process.

Now that we have reviewed some of the basics of the brain and nervous system, we can discuss the neurological basis of some

basic information-processing functions. Specifically, we will discuss selective perception, working memory, and the formation of long-term memory traces.

Selective Perception. You will recall that selective perception is the process whereby certain patterns of stimuli are selected for further processing. Some patterns—such as sharp contrasts—appear to be heeded by infants, and must therefore have an innate substrate, whereas other patterns—such as the sound of one's name—must be learned. Neuroscientists have demonstrated the mechanisms underlying at least some of our innate pattern recognition, and they are beginning to understand the neurological basis of learned pattern recognition as well.

One well-known example of innate pattern recognition comes from the work of Hubel and Weisel (1962) on the visual cortex of cats. These researchers recorded electrical activity from single cells of the cat's visual cortex while simultaneously presenting visual stimuli to the cat. Visual stimuli are received on the retina of the eye where the rod and cone cells convert light energy into neural impulses. These impulses travel along neurons in the optic nerve, through the thalamus, eventually reaching the visual cortex. Each neuron in the optic nerve responds to light coming into a tiny portion of the retina.

Visual cortical cells combine information coming in from several neurons in the optic nerve. For example, cortical cells called **edge detectors** fire when a subset of the optic neurons it synapses with are firing, indicating light, while at the same time another subset from an adjacent area of the retina are not firing, indicating the absence of light. This is exactly the retinal pattern that occurs at the edges of objects where there is a major change in light. Thus, some visual cortical cells respond to simple patterns of stimulation received from a set of cells with which the cortical cell synapses.

Possibly, this neural model of innate pattern recognition will be found to be the basic model for learned pattern recognition as well. That is, the model of a higher-level neuron firing in response to a pattern of input from many lower-level neurons may hold true for learned patterns. Wickelgren (1979) has proposed such a model. While the neural model of innate and learned pattern recognition may be the same, the *location* of the higher-level recognition unit may differ. For example, recent research by LaBerge (1990) suggests that the thalamus is the site of much of our learned pattern-recognition activity.

Working Memory. Earlier writing in physiological psychology hinted that there was a specific brain location for working memory. "Box" models of information processing, such as the one in Figure 3.1 (p. 40), also imply that there is a specific WM location. The current view is that if there is a "location" for WM, it is quite large—consisting at one time or another of most of the cortex. Rather than thinking of a specific location, it seems to be more correct to think of working memory, or consciousness, as an emergent property of the activity of many interacting neurons, especially cortical neurons.

Some people think of consciousness as being limited to the left hemisphere since split-brain patients can't report what is being presented to the right hemisphere. To the extent that WM and consciousness are overlapping concepts, this view suggests that WM is limited to a left-hemisphere location. However, it has been shown that split-brain patients can learn new skills that are presented to the right hemisphere only. Since new learning makes demands on WM capacity, it appears that WM is not located in one hemisphere or another. Rather, it may be "located" in left or right hemispheres or both at any given point in time. It is perhaps best thought of as a dynamic process that emerges from active brain locations.

Formation of Long-Term Memory Traces. You will recall from an earlier section of this chapter that humans receive information and keep it in an active state for a brief time. Active memory for information may be prolonged by repeating the information over and over, as when one repeats a phone number over and over until it is dialed and can be forgotten. Some information in active memory gets processed in a way that allows us to retrieve it later—that is, it gets stored in long-term memory. For example, we hope that you are putting some of the information in this book into your LTM.

Two lines of evidence suggest that the neural structures involved in this storage process are the amygdala and hippocampus. One type of evidence comes from brain-damaged individuals who can remember things they learned or things that happened to them prior to their brain damage, but cannot form any new memory traces. If you introduce yourself to such a person, leave the room, and return in a minute, the person will not remember having seen you. People with this type of disability typically have damaged amygdalas and hippocampi (Thompson, 1985).

The other line of evidence comes from studies of monkeys. Mishkin (1982) trained monkeys to learn to choose the new stimuli in a stimulus array in order to obtain a peanut. For example, if the monkey first saw red and blue boxes, turned upside down, and then saw red and green boxes turned upside down, the peanut would be under the new—or green—box. The monkeys then underwent brain surgery to remove the hippocampus and amygdala. After surgery, they could not remember which stimulus they had seen a minute before, and so they could no longer perform well on this task.

How is it that the hippocampus and amygdala could be involved in creation of long-term memory traces? One effect of activity in the hippocampus is to generate diffuse arousal of the cortical cells. Wickelgren (1979) proposes that if this diffuse arousal is coupled with specific activation of a cortical neuron by input from a particular pattern of cells, a gradual binding of the higher-level cell to the input pattern is initiated. Figure 3.8 shows a schematic representation of this process.

According to this proposal, external stimuli activate some lower-level nodes (for example, edge detectors). These component nodes send concurrent messages to a higher-level chunk node at the same time that the chunk node is receiving diffuse arousal from the hippocampal system. This co-occurrence of events initiates the binding process. As the process continues, some yet-to-be-determined process turns off the diffuse arousal from the hippocampus (as indicated by the minus arrow from node X in Figure 3.8).

Once stimulation from the hippocampus is turned off, node X cannot be recruited for activation by other patterns—that is, interference cannot occur. Since node X can no longer participate in forming other associations, the

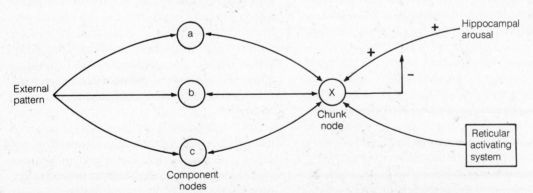

Figure 3.8 The process of binding of a higher-level brain cell (chunk node) to a particular pattern of lower-level activation (component nodes). Hippocampal arousal initiates the binding process, which as it proceeds, turns off the hippocampal arousal (indicated by path with minus sign from chunk node to hippocampal arousal). Later activation of chunk nodes can occur through activation of the component nodes and/or the reticular activating system (from Bower and Hilgard, 1981, p. 503).

association of pattern a, b, and c with node X is preserved. Later activation of node X can occur through activation of node a, b, or c, or through diffuse activation from the reticular activating system. Thus, in Wickelgren's proposal, hippocampal arousal initiates a binding process necessary for formation of a LTM trace, and part of the binding process includes turning off hippocampal arousal so that the trace is preserved.

This model of the role of the hippocampus in formation of LTM traces is consistent with current data, but speculative because there are many unanswered questions. In particular, the nature of the binding process is unknown, as is the mechanism by which hippocampal arousal might be turned off.

Summary

In this section, we have described some of what is known about the neurological substrate of cognition. It appears that the basis of information processing in the brain is transmission of electrochemical messages between and among neurons. The rich interconnections between parts of the brain and the huge numbers of connections on any given cortical neuron form a substrate for complex information processing.

It also appears that, for at least some well-practiced information-processing functions such as language processing, there are localized brain areas involved in these functions in normal adults. Within localized brain areas two types of neurons serve the functions of processing within the local area and communicating the results of processing to functionally related brain areas. Both the capacity for specialization of function and the types of functions that have been identified correspond well with abstract information-processing models.

At a more specific level, the location of some specific cognitive processes is beginning

to be identified—for example the various aspects of language processing. However, locations of many other processes are still unknown, and the details of the neural mechanisms underlying these processes are not known. We expect that the next couple of decades of research on these topics will yield exciting results and do much to integrate the abstract and physiological approaches to cognition.

CHAPTER SUMMARY

In this chapter, we have described in broad outline the three-memory character of the human information-processing system and some basic processes such as selective perception, storage, retrieval, response generation, and control. The three memories are immediate memory, a quite brief but capacious memory store; working memory, a relatively brief and quite limited store; and long-term memory, a large, relatively permanent store. Immediate memory allows enough information to get to the central nervous system for selective perception processes to identify the most important information to retain. Working memory is used in performing conscious mental work. Information is stored in and retrieved from long-term memory, the storehouse of all our accumulated knowledge, skill, and experience. Control processes make information processing a goal-directed set of events.

The computer is another type of information-processing system that, although it has larger workspaces and faster processing systems than humans, does not as yet approach human capabilities in partial pattern matching, creativity, and intuition. Perhaps the next generation of computers will attain such capabilities, but some scholars are skeptical that they ever can (e.g., Searle, 1990; Penrose, 1989).

Work on the neural basis of cognition has

been proceeding rapidly. It now appears that the adult brain is organized so that many highly practiced cognitive functions, such as those involved in language processing, come to have specific areas of brain tissue dedicated to them. Other cognitive functions, such as working memory and novel problem solving, are less localized and can involve activation of a great variety of brain locations.

One theory (Wickelgren, 1979) proposes that cortical cells can function as chunks, or pattern-recognition units. These units interconnect and communicate with a variety of related units in the course of any given information-processing sequence.

ADDITIONAL READINGS

Information Processing

Lindsay, P. H., & Norman, D. A. (1977). *Human information processing.* New York: Academic Press.

Newell, A. (1990). *Unified theories of cognition.* Cambridge, MA: Harvard University Press.

Neuroscience

Martinez, J. L., & Kesner, R. P. (Eds.) (1991). *Learning and memory: A biological view* (2nd edition). New York: Academic Press.

Thompson, R. F. (1985). *The brain: An introduction to neuroscience.* New York: W. H. Freeman & Company.

SECTION
Two

Knowledge Representation

*F*orm and function are beautifully related both in natural creations and in articles made by people. A butterfly's wings are shaped for flight and a duck's webbed feet are made for swimming. Low, sleek automobiles are shaped for speed, boxy pick-up trucks for hauling.

Similarly, the forms that knowledge takes in our minds are related to how that knowledge is to function. If it is to function as a guide to action, it is linked closely to action commands in memory. If, on the other hand, it will serve a variety of purposes, then it has a form that makes it easy to access in a variety of contexts. If it isknowledge that is always used in the same way, it is put in a form that makes few demands on attention. If a set of ideas is frequently used together, then it is tied together in memory.

Over the past twenty years, John R. Anderson has been working on a theory of human intelligence. In his various books, the theory has evolved as he has incorporated new research and new theoretical insights (e.g., *Language, Memory, and Thought* (1976) and *The Architecture of Cognition* (1983). Central to much of his work, however, has been the question of the nature of knowledge representation, its varieties, and their functions. He has been a groundbreaker in elucidating important issues in this area. In this section, we draw on Anderson's work a great deal.

A major purpose of the chapters in this section is to illustrate the relationships between the forms and the functions of knowledge. In Chapter 4, we describe ways that humans represent basic elements of knowledge, such as facts and images. Different types of elements are handy for representing particular aspects of the environment. In Chapter 5, we describe how these basic elements may be linked together in schemas. Finally, in Chapter 6, we describe how basic elements and schemas become linked to action through production rules.

Just as each element of a cell has a discrete function that contributes to the functioning of the whole cell, so too each type of knowledge contributes to the functioning of the cognitive system in an amazing pattern of interactions that we are only beginning to understand. We hope that you get some sense of this amazing system by studying the chapters in this section.

Chapter

4

Representing Declarative Knowledge: Basic Units

SUMMARY

1. **Declarative knowledge** is knowing *that* something is the case. Declarative knowledge is different from **procedural knowledge,** which is knowing *how* to do something.

2. Declarative knowledge is represented mentally in a variety of basic forms, including propositions, images, and linear orderings.

3. A **proposition** is a basic unit of information, corresponding roughly to one idea.

4. Propositions are linked in memory as **propositional networks;** propositions sharing topics are more closely associated than those not sharing topics.

5. **Images** and **linear orderings** are perception-based representations that partially preserve the perceptual structure of the input.

As teachers, we are aware that not all subject matter is taught using the same methods. To take an extreme example, it would be ridiculous to teach volleyball entirely by lecture or even by discussion. The main method most teachers would use would be demonstration, practice, and feedback. Even within a subject we use different methods at different times. History teachers are likely to use discussion when they want students to learn to think and analyze or when a topic is of great importance and they want to be sure that students remember it. They are more likely to use lecturing when they want to cover a lot of material with the hope that students will remember some of it. Science teachers may use labs to help students make complex discriminations and then lecture on information that assumes these discriminations have been made.

While there are several good reasons for varying one's teaching methods (including the motivation and background of the students), one important reason is the type of **knowledge representation** that is the focus of a particular segment of instruction. Knowledge representation refers to how we represent information in long-term and working memory.

Intuitively, most of us are aware of representing some ideas as images and some as "words." We may also realize that some knowledge allows us to do things without much attention—the automatic processing we introduced in the previous chapter. In the chapters in this section, you will learn that different types of knowledge have different mental representations, and you will also learn what is crucial about these different representational types. Once you have a more elaborated understanding of how knowledge is represented mentally, you will be on your way toward being able to tailor your teaching methods for the different types of knowledge representations you hope your students are acquiring.

The most fundamental distinction you will learn is that between **declarative** and **procedural knowledge.** Look at the test items in Table 4.1 and compare the kinds of knowledge needed to answer the questions. Declarative knowledge is knowing *that* something is the case. It is knowledge of facts, theories, events, and objects. Knowledge that one of the causes of the American Civil War was the economic investment of the South in slavery is an example of declarative knowledge. Proce-

Table 4.1 Examples of test items that focus on declarative versus procedural knowledge.

DECLARATIVE KNOWLEDGE
1a. (A test question following a unit on the Civil War):   Describe the major causes of the Civil War.
2a. (First graders, after a lesson on continents): Point to Asia, Europe, and Australia on the globe.

PROCEDURAL KNOWLEDGE
1b. (A paper assignment following a lesson on the use of library sources):   Use three sources from the library to get information about the causes of the Civil War and then write a paper summarizing this information.
2b. (Fourth graders, after a lesson on using the scale of miles to estimate distances on a map):   Using this map, figure out approximately how many miles it is from Pittsburgh, PA, to Denver, CO.

dural knowledge is knowing *how* to do something. It includes motor skills, cognitive skills, and cognitive strategies. Examples of procedural knowledge include knowing how to decide which reference books are useful for a given question and knowing how to read tables of contents and indices in reference books in order to locate desired information quickly.

You can see from these examples not only how the two types of knowledge differ, but how both usually play a role in intellectual performance. For instance, while a teacher may have as her *primary* goal that students learn *how* to use reference books, she may have as the *secondary* goal that they learn *that* a major cause of the Civil War was the South's reliance on slavery for its economic base. It is often the case that the exercise of procedural knowledge produces new declarative knowledge as it does in this example.

You can also see from this example why it is important to distinguish types of knowledge. If the teacher's primary goal is to have students learn the major cause of the Civil War, she should probably *not* send the students to the library. Rather, she should create a meaningful context in which to present information about the causes of the Civil War. Perhaps the students could role-play the important decision makers at the start of the war, using information about what motivated their decisions. Or, the causes of the Civil War could be compared and contrasted with other wars with which the students are familiar. However, since the teacher's primary goal is to have the students learn library skills, her choice of the method of giving an opportunity for practice of these skills is quite appropriate.

To summarize this idea of declarative versus procedural knowledge, look at Figure 4.1. This shows part of the human information-processing system you became familiar with in the last chapter in a slightly new form. Now, instead of one undifferentiated long-term memory, we have two types of long-term memory—declarative memory and procedural memory.

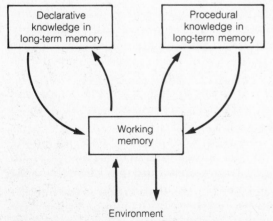

Figure 4.1 The human information-processing system with declarative and procedural long-term memories distinguished.

The distinction between declarative and procedural knowledge was made by the philosopher Ryle (1949) and is a fundamental distinction in Robert Gagné's learning theory (1977; 1985). It is also fundamental to John Anderson's theory of cognition (1976; 1983; and Anderson & Thompson, 1989). Psychologists who distinguish declarative and procedural knowledge believe that the two forms of knowledge are both distinct and interdependent. Recent neurophysiological data also seem to support the distinction (Mishkin & Petri, 1984).

In this chapter and the next, you will learn several ways of representing declarative knowledge. There are exercises for you to do throughout these chapters. Plan to have the time to try the exercises; they are designed to increase your understanding. If you become fluent in thinking in terms of knowledge representations, it may help you in solving your own teaching problems later on.

PROPOSITIONS

A basic unit of declarative knowledge in the human information-processing system is the **proposition.** We call these knowledge units propositions because they express or "propose" relationships among concepts. One propositional unit corresponds roughly to an idea. For example, which of the following two phrases seems to be a complete idea?

the man

the man fixed the tire

Clearly the second phrase is more complete. While the first phrase expresses a concept, the second proposes a way to relate the concepts to express an idea. Although the sentence *The man fixed the tire* contains only one proposition, many sentences contain more than one. For example, *The man fixed the tire and left* contains two ideas (propositions): one is that the man fixed the tire and the other is that he left.

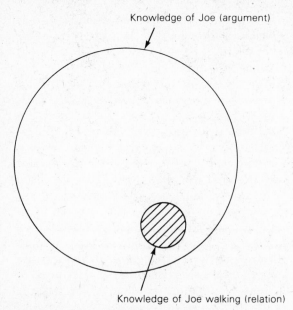

Knowledge of Joe (argument)

Knowledge of Joe walking (relation)

Figure 4.2 The relationship between the relation and argument of a proposition is shown here for the proposition (walk, Joe). Arguments establish general areas of information, and relations narrow the focus within the general areas established by arguments.

A proposition always contains two elements: a **relation** and one or more **arguments**. The arguments are the topics of the proposition, so they tend to be nouns and pronouns (although they can also be verbs and adjectives). The relation of a proposition *constrains* the topics, so relations tend to be verbs, adjectives, and adverbs. For example, in the idea represented by "Joe walked," *Joe* is the topic (argument) and *walked* is what constrains the topic (relation). *Walked* constrains the topic of *Joe* in that it tells us that of all the information we have about Joe, we are attending only to information about Joe walking. Figure 4.2 is a Venn diagram for the argument *Joe* and the relation *walked*. In general, relations narrow focus; *walked* narrows the focus on the topic *Joe* considerably. This aspect of relations makes them the most informative part of the propo-

sition. Table 4.2 shows some other ideas and their arguments and relations. All of these ideas have verbs as relations (*walked, read, swam,* and *gave* for ideas 1, 2, 3, and 4, respectively) because in all of these ideas it is a verb that constrains the topics. Ideas 2 and 3 have not one, but two arguments. That is, they have two topics. Idea 2, that Sandra read a book, has both *Sandra* and *book* as topics. *Read* constrains these topics, telling us that what is happening between Sandra and the book is reading, as opposed, say, to stealing or burning. Idea 3 has the topics (arguments) *Jane* and *shore,* and *swam* tells us that what is going on between Jane and the shore is swimming. Finally, idea 4 has three arguments—*Bill, car,* and *Ellen. Gave* tells us that the relationship among these three arguments has to do with giving, as opposed to, say, "meeting" (as in "Bill met Ellen with the car").

As these examples illustrate, whereas propositions always have only one relation, they may have more than one argument. This is especially true when the relation is a verb, because verbs often set up expectations for more than one argument. For example, the verb *give* leads us to expect information about the giver, the recipient, and the object that was given. The verb *go* leads us to expect information about who did the going, and where he or she went (the goal). Some verbs lead us to expect information about an instrument of action. For example, consider *cut.* If we hear the sentence "Ralph cut his finger," we anticipate finding out what instrument was responsible for the cutting (a razor? a pair of scissors? a knife?).

Because a proposition may have more than one argument, arguments are given different names depending on their role in the proposition. Arguments may be **subjects**, **objects**, **goals** (destinations), **instruments** (means), and **recipients**. Table 4.3 shows some ideas with their arguments labeled according to the role that each plays within the idea.

Table 4.2 Some examples of propositions, showing their relations and arguments. In these examples, all the relations are verbs and all the arguments are nouns.

IDEA	RELATION	ARGUMENT(S)
1. [Joe walked.]	walked	Joe
2. [Sandra read a book.]	read	Sandra, book
3. [Jane swam to shore.]	swam	Jane, shore
4. [Bill give the car to Ellen.]	gave	Bill, car, Ellen

Consider now the sentence "The tall woman played basketball." How many ideas do you think are expressed by this sentence? Clearly, one idea has *played* as its relation. The arguments of *played* include the subject (woman) and the object (basketball). But what about the idea of *tall*? *Tall* constrains the topic of *woman* because it narrows the focus within the topic to a tall woman. Since *tall* constrains the topic of *woman*, it is a relation and *woman* is its argument. Thus, the sentence "The tall woman played basketball" is said to express (or propose) two ideas (propositions): (1) that the woman played basketball and (2) that the woman was tall.

In general, adjectives in sentences form the basis for separate propositions. Unlike verb-based propositions, adjective-based propositions take only one argument—that which is being modified. Thus, *tall woman* expresses a proposition with the relation *tall* and the argument *woman*. The arguments of adjective-based propositions are always nouns.

Now consider the sentence "The tall woman played basketball vigorously." How many ideas does this sentence express? The answer is three. The adverb *vigorously* constrains the verb *played*, narrowing the focus within the concept of play to play that has a vigorous quality. Thus *vigorous* is a relation and its topic, or argument, is *play*. As with adjective-based propositions, adverb-based propositions also have only one argument, which is the subject. Unlike adjective-based propositions, however, the subject of adverb-based propositions is a verb or adjective, rather than a noun or pronoun.

Now it is your turn to try identifying the propositions represented in sentences. For each of the following sentences, list the propositions—relations plus argument(s).

4.1 The wind blew the tall trees.

4.2 The eager teacher selected a microcomputer carefully.

A good way to start is to underline each verb, adjective, and adverb. This will tell you how

Table 4.3 Some examples of propositions that have more than one argument. The arguments are labeled according to their role in the idea being represented.

IDEA	RELATION	ARGUMENTS
[Manuel gave Harry a pencil.]	gave	Manuel (subject), Harry (recipient), pencil (object)
[Carol is going to New York.]	is going	Carol (subject), New York (goal)
[Ralph cut his finger with a paper.]	cut	Ralph (subject), finger (object), paper (instrument)

many propositions the sentence has, because only verbs, adjectives, and adverbs can be relations, and there is only one relation per proposition. After you have identified each relation, list its argument(s). The answers to this exercise are given at the end of the chapter.

Abstractness of Propositions

It is important to distinguish between words, phrases, and sentences, on the one hand, and propositions, on the other. Words, phrases, and sentences represent ways of communicating ideas, whereas propositions represent the ideas themselves.

Research suggests that we store information as propositions, rather than sentences. That is, we generally remember ideas but not necessarily the exact words used to communicate the ideas. Wanner (1968) demonstrated this in a study that used the following sentences:

1. When you score your results, do nothing to correct your answers but mark carefully those answers which are wrong.

2. When you score your results, do nothing to correct your answers but carefully mark those answers which are wrong.

3. When you score your results, do nothing to your correct answers but mark carefully those answers which are wrong.

4. When you score your results, do nothing to your correct answers but carefully mark those answers which are wrong.

Notice that although there are slight wording differences between sentences 1 and 2 ("mark carefully" versus "carefully mark"), the meaning of these two sentences is the same. There are also slight wording differences between sentences 1 and 3 ("correct your" versus "your correct"). However, in this case the wording change drastically alters the meaning. Sentences 3 and 4 are like 1 and 2 in that they differ in wording but not meaning and 2 and 4 are like 1 and 3 in that they differ in both wording and meaning.

The subjects in this study heard one of the four sentences as part of the directions they received at the beginning of the study. Half of the subjects had been warned that they would be asked to recall the wording of the directions and half were not so warned. After hearing one of the sentences, the subjects were told to turn to the next page in their test booklet and mark which of the sentences shown was identical to the last sentence they had heard in their directions. Two sentences were shown. One was the sentence they had heard and the other was one of the other sentences—one that varied in words only or one that varied in both words and meaning.

If people are as sensitive to wording changes as they are to meaning changes, then they should be as good at identifying the correct sentence when the distractor sentence had only a word change as when it had both a word and meaning change. However, the results did not show such an equality, as can be seen in Figure 4.3. Subjects made more errors when the distractor sentence had only a word change than when it had both a word and meaning change. In fact, when they were unwarned about being tested on wording, subjects chose the wrong sentence 50 percent of the time, that is, at a chance level. Thus, it appears that people attend to and store the *meanings* of sentences (propositions) rather than the particular words used.

Propositions in Node-Link Form

Instead of listing a proposition as a relation and one or more arguments, one can draw it in node-link form. For some purposes, such as

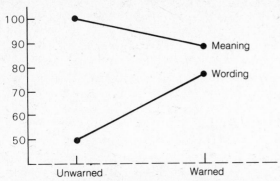

Figure 4.3 Percentage of correct responses when distractor sentence changed the meaning or only the wording of the correct sentence as a function of whether the subjects were warned or not warned that they should pay attention to wording (adapted from Wanner, 1968, as cited in J.R. Anderson, 1990).

when one is describing the relationships among several propositions, a node-link structure is more useful than a listing. Figure 4.4 shows some propositions in node-link form. The nodes, or circles, represent the entire proposition. The links, or arrows, point to each of the elements of the proposition. Each link is labeled to identify the role of the element within a particular proposition. So, for example, in the first proposition *Rachel*, *mowed*, and *lawn* serve as subject, relation, and object, respectively. In the second proposition, *mowed* has a different role than in the first proposition. Whereas *mowed* was the relation in the first proposition, in the second it functions as the subject.

> **4.3** Return now to the propositions you listed for the sentence "The eager teacher selected a microcomputer carefully." Try drawing a node-link structure for each of your propositions. Check your drawings with those shown at the end of the chapter.

Networks

One of the most important characteristics of any given unit of information is its relation-

ship to other units. Our knowledge of such relationships underlies our ability to make analogies and to see other types of connections. Such abilities are important in novel problem-solving situations.

Because the relationships among sets of information are a crucial aspect of intelligence, it is important to have ways of representing them. There are a variety of ways to represent such relationships. One way is in the form of a *network*. Networks have node-link structures in which nodes represent memory units and links specify connections between and among units. When all of the units in a network are propositions, the network is referred to as a **propositional network**.

Figure 4.5 (p. 67) shows two networks for some of the propositions that you have already studied. As you can see, all that was done to generate the networks in Figure 4.5 from the propositions in Figure 4.4 was to identify common elements and then represent these elements only once rather than twice. This brings related propositions closer together than unrelated propositions. For example, *mowed* is a common element in the first two propositions. In Figure 4.4 *mowed* is shown twice, whereas in Figure 4.5 it shows up only once, as a bridge between the two propositions.

A propositional network is a hypothetical construct and should be kept distinct from the notion of a neural network, which is potentially observable. As was mentioned in Chapter 3, we do not yet know in a detailed way how information is represented in a physiological sense. Even when a physiological substrate is found, however, propositional networks should continue to be convenient constructs for helping us think about cognitive processes.

A classic study that supports the notion that information is stored in long-term memory in networks was done by Collins and Quillian (1969). Figure 4.6 (p. 68) shows one of these networks. It has a hierarchical structure

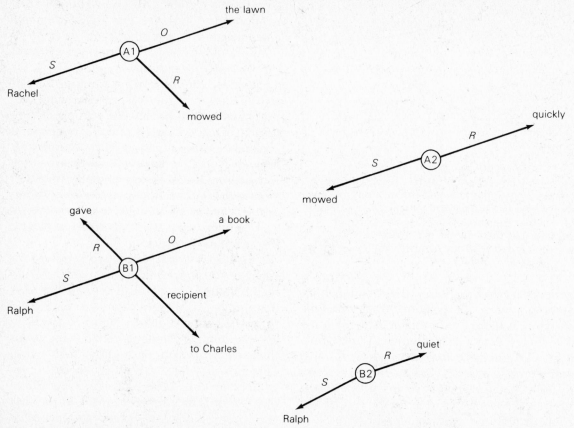

Figure 4.4 Propositions drawn as node-link figures. The nodes (or circles) represent propositions. The links (or lines) point to the elements of the proposition and label them. (S = subject, O = object, R = relation.)

in which facts about certain animals are stored at different levels of generality. For example, the fact that birds have feathers is stored at the level of birds. The fact that birds have skin is not actually stored, but rather is inferred from the fact that animals have skin. In other words, facts are stored at the level of generality where they are used to distinguish among classes of objects. All animals have skin but no rocks have skin, so the idea of skin is useful for distinguishing animals from minerals. On the other hand, only some animals have feathers, so the possession of feathers is not a useful

guide to classifying animals versus minerals. Feather *are* a useful guide to classifying birds versus other small creatures, so the fact that birds have feathers is stored at the level of birds in the knowledge hierarchy.

Collins and Quillian proposed that we store classificatory knowledge in hierarchical networks such as the one shown in Figure 4.6. Further, they proposed a mechanism for verification of facts based on this structure. They argued that when a person is asked to verify a statement such as "Fish have skin," a search starts at the level of fish and looks for the

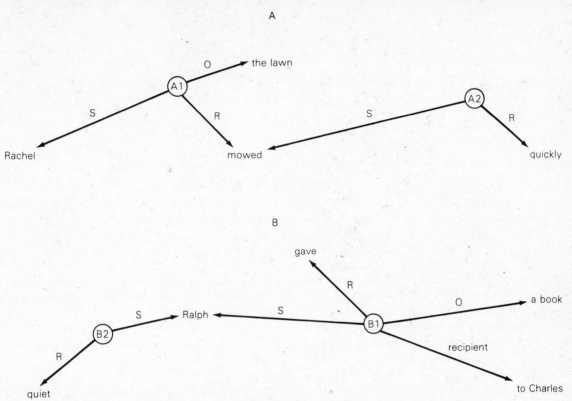

Figure 4.5 Propositional networks show the interrelationships between propositions that share ideas. Network *A* is composed of two propositions that share the element *mowed*. Network *B* is composed of two propositions that share the element *Ralph*.

property of skin. If *skin* is not found at this level, the search moves up a level and again looks for the property of skin. This time *skin* is found. Because of the structure of the hierarchy, all things that are true at the higher levels are also true at the lower levels, so once *skin* is found at a higher level, the subject responds "true."

To test their notion of hierarchical storage of facts, Collins and Quillian predicted that time to verify facts would depend on the distance between the two concepts (e.g., animal and property) in the hierarchy. Thus, it should take longer to verify "Canaries have skin" than to verify "Canaries are yellow,"

because the search from *canaries* to *skin* includes two levels while the search from *canaries* to *yellow* takes place on the same level.

The researchers had subjects sit at a computer terminal and watch the screen. A subject who read a fact such as "Fish have skin" on the screen decided as quickly as possible if the fact was true or false. If it was true, the subject pressed one key on the keyboard and if it was false, another key. The times it took subjects to verify facts with concepts of varying distances from each other in the proposed hierarchy were recorded by the computer.

Figure 4.7 (p. 69) shows the average reaction times to verify true sentences whose con-

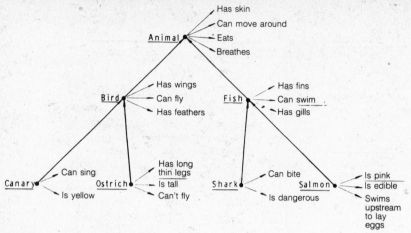

Figure 4.6 A hypothetical memory network for information that is hierarchically organized (from Collins and Quillian, 1969).

cepts spanned 0, 1, or 2 levels in the proposed memory structure. The researchers looked separately at sentences that identified supersets. In both cases the reaction time increased with the distance between the concepts, thus verifying the predictions. While later work was critical of the specifics of the Collins and Quillian model (e.g., Smith, Shobin, & Rips, 1974), the general notion of networks has remained useful.

These results suggest that people organize knowledge into efficient packages. We could store every fact at every level of generality. For example, we could store the fact that birds have skin. Instead, we store the fact that animals have skin and use this to infer that birds have skin when we need such knowledge. In other words, we use our understanding of superordinate-subordinate relationships to reduce the amount of knowledge we need to store directly.

Summary

One form of representing declarative knowledge is the proposition, which is roughly equivalent to one idea. Propositions are not the same as sentences but are more abstract.

Propositions represent *the ideas themselves*, rather than the exact words in which the ideas were communicated.

Propositions that share elements are related in networks. Networks underlie our ability to think of related information at appropriate times. Unlike most computer systems, which store information in arbitrary locations in the central processing unit, propositional networks store related bits of information closer together than unrelated bits. This is important in a system with a limited-capacity working memory because it means that related information that is not active in working memory will be easy to activate because it is closer to what is active than is unrelated information.

By now you should be able to identify the propositions in simple sentences and to identify the relation and argument(s) in any given proposition. Also, you should be able to draw a propositional network structure for sets of related propositions. If you can do these things, you should be able to generate a propositional network for each of the following sentences.

4.4 The very hungry child devoured the hamburger.

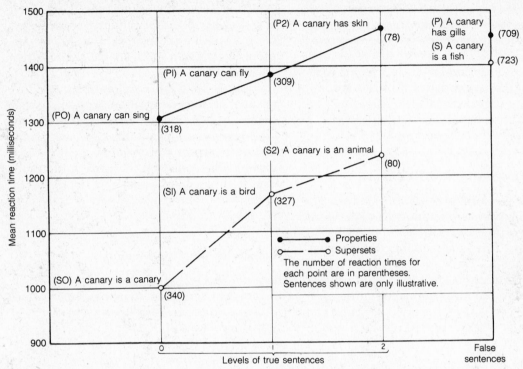

Figure 4.7 Reaction time to verify sentences as a function of distance between concepts in the hierarchical memory structure (from Collins and Quillian, 1969).

4.5 A triangle is a three-sided, closed figure.

To do this, start out by listing each proposition in the sentence. Then draw each proposition as a node-link structure. Finally, look for common elements among the propositions and merge the propositions at the juncture of common elements. Answers are at the end of the chapter.

IMAGES

While in many situations it is useful to think of propositions as the units of declarative knowledge, in other situations it is more useful to think of perceptually-based units such as images and linear orderings. Let's take as an example the statement:

A moose is larger than a lion.

Do you consider this statement to be true? Take a minute to decide. After you have decided, think about your thoughts as you decided. Were you aware of using imagery? Some people, when asked to judge the truth of this statement, check their propositional knowledge base to see if they have stored a proposition describing the relative size of a moose in comparison to a lion. However, most people report that they make judgments of this sort by imagining what a moose looks like and imagining what a lion looks like and then comparing the sizes of the two mental images (Moyer, 1973). This seems to suggest that we have at least two ways of representing declarative knowledge in memory: as abstract meaning-based propositions that don't necessarily preserve perceptual information about concepts, and as perception-based representations that partially preserve the perceptual structure. Anderson (1990) discusses two types of perception-based representations, images and linear orderings. In this section, we will talk about how images represent information in memory. Linear orderings will be considered in the next section.

Images Preserve Spatial Relations

An **image** is a form of declarative knowledge that preserves as continuous dimensions some of the physical attributes of that which it represents. This is something that propositions do not do. Look, for example, at Figure 4.8. This figure shows two alternative ways of representing the ideas contained in the sentence "The book is on the table." Part *A* is an image. It implicitly represents information

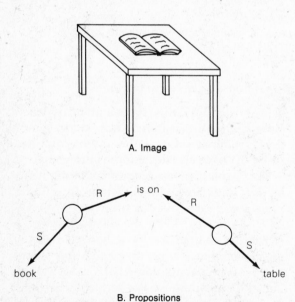

A. Image

B. Propositions

Figure 4.8 Two forms of mental representation of the idea that the book is on the table. Much spatial information implicit in the mental image is lost in the propositional network representation.

about the three-dimensionality of books and tables and about the relative sizes of each. Part *B* is a propositional network. It does not represent information about spatial relationships or size.

Images are analog representations. This means that, in general, they "look like" what they represent. Propositions are discrete, abstract representations. Images are an economical way of representing spatial or continuous information. Although the picture in Figure 4.8 is fairly concrete, images are not necessarily concrete. The crucial aspect of images is that they are continuous.

Imagery in Working Memory

Because of the limited capacity of working memory, images seem to be particularly useful in working-memory representations of spatial information. Recall, for example, the work of Snow that was described in Chapter 2. Snow studied how students solved "paper-folding" test items and concluded that successful students unfold in their minds an image of the punched paper. Suppose for the moment that a particular student could not generate mental images. Instead, assume he or she had to represent all the relevant information as propositions. Table 4.4 shows our guess as to all the propositions that would be needed to solve the paper-folding item shown in Figure 2.3 without using mental imagery. Clearly, these twenty-one propositions go far beyond the limits of working memory's capacity. The mental image of the paper being unfolded does not exceed the limits of working memory, however, because it is a functional unit.

A great deal of evidence suggests that people use mental imagery in tasks for which spatial or visual information is crucial. One task for demonstrating mental imagery is counting the window panes in one's living room. Meudell (1971) asked 62 people to tell

Table 4.4 Propositions needed to solve the paper-folding item shown in Figure 2.3.

[The paper is square.]	[The paper is folded.]
[The paper is folded.]	[It is folded again.]
[It is folded once.]	[The fold is vertical.]
[The fold is horizontal.]	[The fold creates layers.]
[Now there are layers.]	[The layers are four.]
[The layers are of paper.]	[One corner is open.]
[The layers are open.]	[It is the bottom corner.]
[They are open on the bottom.]	[It is the left corner.]
[The layers are closed.]	[A punch goes through corner.]
	[It is the bottom corner.]
[They are closed on the top.]	[It is the left corner.]

him how many window panes they had in their living rooms and recorded the time that it took for them to respond. Figure 4.9 shows the relationship between the speed of response and the number of panes. If people are simply retrieving a proposition from long-term memory, there should be no relationship between speed and number of panes. However, if people are visualizing their living rooms and counting the panes in their mental image, than they should take longer if there are many panes than if there are few panes. As can be seen, people did take longer to respond if there were many panes in their living room than if there were only a few. In addition, most of the participants in the study reported that they did create an image of their living rooms and then count the panes in the windows.

Kosslyn, Ball, and Reiser (1978) demonstrated the analog nature of mental imagery. Figure 4.10 (p. 73) shows the line drawings of faces that they used in their study. Notice that the top three faces have dark eyes and the bottom three have light eyes. Also, notice that

in moving from left to right, the distance between the mouth and the eyes on the faces decreases.

The subjects in this experiment were told to study a given face very carefully. The face was then removed and the subject was told to image the face at either half size, full size, or overflow size. Full size was said to mean the face was seen in the mind's eye as large as possible without losing part of the face from the image. Half size was said to be half of full size. Overflow size was said to mean making the image so large that only the mouth could be seen.

After a subject visualized a face at a given size, he or she was then told to focus on the mouth. When the subject indicated readiness, the word "light" or "dark" was presented. The experimenter then told the subject to "glance up" the image and decide if the color of the eyes agreed or disagreed with the presented color. One or another button was pressed to indicate agreement or disagreement and the reaction time was recorded.

The results are shown in Figure 4.11 (p. 73). As you can see, reaction time increased as a function of the size of the image and also as a function of the distance between the mouth and the eyes in the drawing. These results are in keeping with the notion that mental images preserve distance information in an analog form. Subjects act as if they are scanning an internal image and not as if they are searching a set of propositions formed to describe the pictures that they saw.

One objection to the Kosslyn et al. (1978) study might be that the subjects guessed what the experimenter's hypotheses were because of the directions to "glance up." Wishing to please, they then took longer to respond when they had been shown a picture with a greater distance between the mouth and eyes. However, there are many studies of the use of imagery in working memory in which subjects appear to use an analog representation even when they receive no instruction to use imagery.

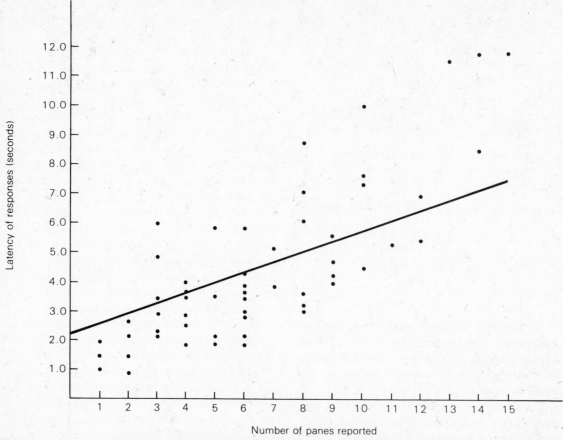

Figure 4.9 Time to respond to the question, "How many window panes are in your living room?" as a function of the actual number of panes (from Meudell, 1971).

A classic example of the spontaneous use of mental imagery is in mental rotation. Subjects are shown stimuli (often letters) that are rotated away from their upright orientation. Some of the stimuli are normal and some are mirror images. The subject's task is to decide if the stimulus is normal or a mirror image, which can be done by first mentally rotating an image of the stimulus to an upright orientation and then comparing it with a normal image. If the two images are identical, then the stimulus is said to be normal. If the two images are the reverse of one another, then the test stimulus is said to be mirror image.

Cooper and Shepard (1973) studied mental rotation of letters such as those shown in Figure 4.12 (p. 74). As you can see, the letters varied in their angle of rotation from the upright and in whether they were normal or a mirror image. Subjects' reaction times to decide if the stimulus letter was normal or a mirror image were recorded. Then they were plotted as a function of the angle of rotation of the letter (Figure 4.13, p. 75).

Reaction time increased from 0 to 180 degrees and then decreased from 180 to 360 (0) degrees. This pattern of results is what one would expect if subjects are mentally rotating

Figure 4.10 Faces that have either dark or light eyes and different distances from the mouth to the eyes (from Kosslyn, Ball, and Reiser, 1978).

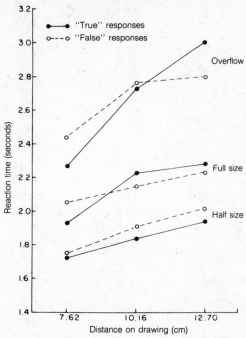

Figure 4.11 Reaction time to focus on eyes when starting at the mouth in an image. Reaction time is longer for larger images and for longer distances between mouth and eyes (from Kosslyn, Ball, and Reiser, 1978).

the test letter and then seeing if it matches the normal letter. The farther the test letter is from the upright, the longer the mental rotation should take, and this is exactly what was found.

Note that in this study, subjects were not told to form a mental image, yet they still behaved as if they had formed one. Thus many people spontaneously use mental imagery when a task requires the spatial manipulation of information.

These studies suggest that for tasks that involve thinking about spatial relationships among concrete objects people construct images of these objects in working memory. If this was the only role that imagery had to play, it would be a highly useful one. People are required to think about spatial relationships among concrete objects almost every day. Spatial relationships are important in judging distances in driving and sports, in planning how to furnish a room, and in finding one's way around in unfamiliar territory. Thus, our ability to use imagery in working memory is an important one.

Imagery in Abstract Reasoning

However, imagery's importance may be even greater than its role in everyday tasks. People may use imagery in thinking about abstract relationships. There are many anecdotal reports of creative artists and scientists who use mental imagery to solve problems. For example, Faraday, one of the most creative physicists of all time, tended to image the abstract concepts with which he worked. As described by Koestler (1964), he

saw the stresses surrounding magnets and electric currents as curves in space, for which he coined the name "lines of forces," and which, in his imagination, were as real as if they consisted of solid matter. He visualized the universe patterned by these lines—or

The six orientations

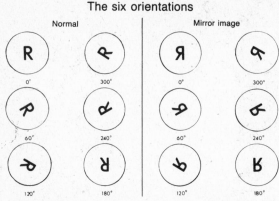

Normal | Mirror image

Figure 4.12 An example of the letter R shown in different rotations from the upright, and in normal and mirror-image position (adapted from Cooper and Shepard, 1973).

rather by narrow tubes through which all forms of "ray-vibrations" or energy-radiations are propagated. The vision of curved tubes which "rose up before him like things" proved of almost incredible fertility: it gave birth to the dynamo and the electric motor; it led Faraday to discard the ether, and to postulate that light was electro-magnetic radiation (p. 170).

Since spatial and distance metrics seem to be useful analogs for thinking about continuous variables and their interactions, mental imagery seems to be useful in abstract reasoning because of its implicit preservation of spatial relationships.

Some studies of mental comparisons suggest that people use imagery to think about abstract dimensions just as they do to think about concrete dimensions. Kerst and Howard (1977), for example, asked students to compare pairs of animals, countries, and cars on the concrete dimension of size and on an appropriate abstract dimension: ferocity for animals, military power for countries, and cost for cars. In a preliminary study, a different group of students rated examples of animals, countries, and cars on size and the appropriate abstract dimension. Table 4.5 (p. 76) shows the results of that study.

The students in the comparison study were shown various pairs of stimuli (e.g., mouse-cow, Mexico-Israel, Toyota-Cadillac) and asked to indicate which one had more of a particular dimension (size, power, cost, or ferocity). Their reaction times to make these comparisons were recorded and later plotted as a function of the distance between stimuli as determined in the preliminary study.

Figure 4.14 (p. 76) shows the findings. The reaction time became slower as the two items being compared got closer. This result makes sense if people are forming mental images. For example, if one images a sheep and a cow, it is more difficult to decide which image is larger than if one images a mouse and a cow, because the sheep and the cow are more similar in size. This difficulty in discrimination is reflected in slower reaction times.

The same pattern of results was observed for the abstract dimensions as for the concrete ones. Since it is not clear what an image of cost or power or ferocity would be, subjects may be using a spatial analogy to represent continuous variation in abstract quantities. Items are arranged in mental space according to how close they are to one another on the abstract dimension. If this is done, then once again it would take longer to discriminate items that are close together than those that are far apart.

Summary

Mental images are analog representations. They are used to represent spatial information. Sometimes, in order to preserve what is important about an event, it is necessary to preserve the perceptual structure as well as the underlying meaning. While propositions don't preserve perceptual structure, images do. Images may also be used to think about abstract dimensions. When perceptual characteristics of an event are important, activat-

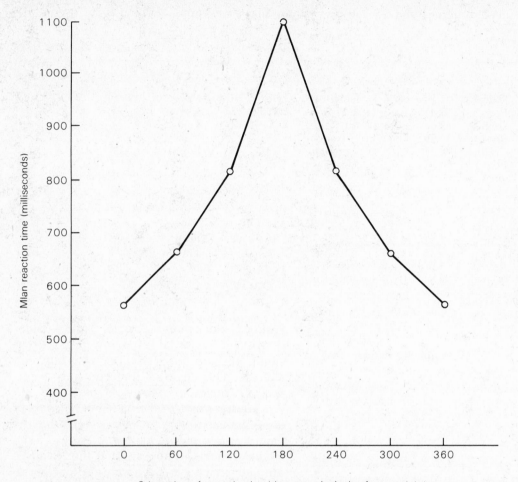

Figure 4.13 Reaction time as a function of angle of rotation of the test letter (adapted from Cooper and Shepard, 1973).

ing an image instead of a propositional representation can save space in working memory.

LINEAR ORDERINGS

A third basic unit of declarative knowledge represents the **linear order** of a set of elements. Sometimes a very important relation among elements in a set is an *ordinal* relation—that is, how are the elements ranked or ordered along some dimension?

Linear orderings are different from propositions in that propositions preserve only the underlying semantic relations among elements and not necessarily the order in which the elements were communicated. Linear orderings are different from images in that images preserve interval information (relative distance between elements) while linear orderings encode only the order from beginning to end, but not necessarily the size of the interval between elements. An example might

Table 4.5 Animals, countries, and cars rated on various dimensions (from Kerst and Howard, 1977).

		MEAN	SD		MEAN	SD		MEAN	SD
	ANIMALS (SIZE)			COUNTRIES (SIZE)			CARS (SIZE)		
Concrete	Mouse	1.22	.85	Israel	1.47	.61	MG	1.09	.30
	Fox	2.41	.53	Japan	2.25	.83	VW	1.91	.57
	Dog	2.66	.51	England	2.53	.71	Toyota	2.31	.54
	Sheep	3.00	.44	Mexico	3.13	.57	Ford	3.41	.46
	Cow	4.25	.62	America	4.25	.57	Pontiac	3.78	.49
	Bear	4.81	.41	Russia	4.97	.14	Cadillac	4.75	.44
	ANIMALS (FEROCIOUSNESS)			COUNTRIES (MILITARY POWER)			CARS (COST)		
Abstract	Mouse	1.44	.79	Mexico	1.81	.69	VW	1.47	.56
	Sheep	1.72	.71	Japan	2.81	.85	Toyota	2.06	.71
	Cow	1.91	.75	Israel	3.16	.82	Ford	2.88	.58
	Dog	3.16	.85	England	3.28	.72	Pontiac	3.34	.56
	Fox	3.69	.66	Russia	4.78	.49	MG	3.59	.94
	Bear	4.94	.20	America	4.94	.20	Cadillac	4.69	.44

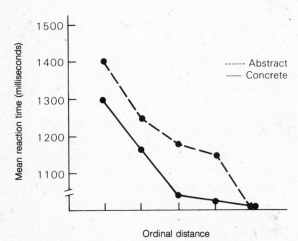

Figure 4.14 Time to compare two stimuli as a function of how close the items are on a particular concrete or abstract dimension (from Kerst and Howard, 1977).

be how you represent the birth order of your siblings if you are from a family of six children. If Ann is the oldest, followed by Mary, Jason, Peter, Sally, and Mark, you could probably verify easily and accurately such assertions as "Mary is older than Mark," or "Ann is older than Peter," without retrieving their current ages and computing age differences between siblings. This suggests that you have direct access to the order of the elements in the set.

When sets of ordered elements are very large, research suggests that we chunk the elements into ordered subsets. For example, in the alphabet, it appears that the 26 letters are clustered into seven subsets that correspond to the sets of letters in the "Alphabet Song": ABCD, EFG, HIJK, LMNOP, QRS, TUV, WXYZ. If subjects are given one letter and asked to produce the next, they are faster when the probe letter is at the beginning of a chunk than at the end (Klahr, Chase, & Lovelace, 1983). For example, subjects are faster to produce M, given L, than they are to produce O, given N. Klahr et al. argued that this is because subjects access each sublist at the beginning of the chunk and proceed to generate each letter in order until they produce the target letter. It is interesting to note that one would not expect this type of finding if the lists were represented as visual images.

In scanning a visual image of a scene, for example, there is not necessarily any "front anchoring" effect such as the one observed by Klahr et al. That is, in scanning a visual image, subjects could scan from top to bottom or right to left as readily as from left to right. No directionality is assumed. This tendency for "front anchoring" in memory for linear orderings is typically interpreted as evidence that linear orderings are not simply one-dimensional visual images, but are a different kind of representational form in memory. To give yourself an even clearer idea of the difference between images and linear orderings, try to hum the tune of the "Alphabet Song" backwards. The impossibility of this task for most people illustrates clearly how your representation of the tune is an ordered representation, not an image you can look at all at once in your mind's eye. If you could "see" the whole ordered representation at once, then presumably you could "read" the tune backwards, assuming you could read music.

Substantial evidence that linear orderings are not represented as propositions comes from the research on judgments of order of elements in an ordered list (e.g., Potts, 1972, 1975; Trabasso & Riley, 1975). These judgments are like the example of sibling birth order we presented earlier. If subjects are asked whether A comes before D in the string ABCDEF, they appear to have direct access to the information about order of elements in the list. Even if subjects are asked to memorize adjacent pairs such as "A comes before B," "B comes before C," "C comes before D," and so on, their judgments about order at test time are *not* faster for memorized pairs than for non-adjacent (and non-studied) pairs such as A-D or B-F. In fact, order judgments are easier to make, the farther apart the elements are in the ordered list, despite the fact that these pairs were not studied prior to test. This finding is interpreted as evidence that the information is stored as an ordered list and not

as propositions representing the relationship of letters in the adjacent pairs.

While substantial work has been done investigating the psychological reality of linear orderings as representational units, there is not a lot of research looking at how linear orderings affect school learning. Potentially, they are important in any school tasks that involves time sequences. However, since research to identify the types of school tasks that are typically represented as linear orders has not been done, this type of representation will not figure prominently in subsequent chapters.

CHAPTER SUMMARY

In this chapter, you have read about the evidence for three basic kinds of knowledge representation. Propositions are basic idea units that preserve the meaning of sentences we hear and read, but not necessarily their surface structure. Propositions are associated with related ideas in a network, making it easy to retrieve related ideas together. Images are units of knowledge about perceptual entities or about the continuously varying characteristics of abstract ideas. They preserve information about spatial relationships. Linear orderings represent sequential or rank order information. Access to linear orderings is best achieved through retrieval of the first element in a sequence.

Different types of knowledge representation are useful in different contexts and for different purposes. Propositions are useful for thinking about abstract ideas and for relating abstract ideas in a network. Images are useful for representing spatial information about concrete entities and also, at times, for thinking about abstract relationships. Linear orders are useful for storing and retrieving order information. It is useful for humans to have a variety of ways to represent knowledge so that they can tailor their representations to their purposes.

Despite the differences among these types of knowledge representation, they share the characteristic of affording economical representation in a limited capacity working memory. Propositional networks reduce the burden on working memory by keeping related knowledge accessible. The result is that when we are thinking about a particular idea, related ideas come easily to mind. Images reduce the burden by implicitly representing spatial information. In comparison to propositions, images can pack more spatial information into working memory without exceeding its capacity. Linear orderings reduce the burden on working memory by keeping sequential information easily accessible. Given that limited capacity working memory is a fundamental aspect of human nature, it is not surprising that we have evolved knowledge representation systems that are compatible with this limitation.

In the next two chapters, you will learn about two additional forms of knowledge representation that build on these fundamental units. These forms are called **schemas** and **productions.** Like the basic forms, they add variety and allow more choices of ways to represent knowledge in a variety of situations. Too, they allow for economical management of knowledge in working memory.

ADDITIONAL READINGS

General

Gagné, R. M. (1984). Learning outcomes and their effects. *American Psychologist, 39,* 377–385.

Rumelhart, D. E. & Norman, D. A. (1988). Representation in memory. In R. C. Atkinson, R. J. Herrnstein, G. Lindzey, & R. D. Luce (Eds.), *Handbook of Experimental Psychology.* New York: John Wiley.

Propositions

Anderson, J. R. (1983). *The architecture of cognition.* Cambridge, MA: Harvard University Press.

Kintsch, W. (1974). *The representation of meaning in memory.* Hillsdale, NJ: Lawrence Erlbaum Associates.

Images

Gentner, D., & Stevens, A. (Eds.) (1983). *Mental models.* Hillsdale, NJ: Lawrence Erlbaum Associates.

Kosslyn, S. M. (1980). *Image and mind.* Cambridge, MA: Harvard University Press.

Richardson, J. T. E. (1980). *Mental imagery and human memory.* London: Macmillan.

ANSWERS TO EXERCISES

4.1 [blew (relation), wind (subject), trees (object)] [tall (relation), trees (subject)]

4.2 [selected (relation), teacher (sub.), microcomputer (obj.)] [eager (relation), teacher (subject)] [carefully (relation), selected (subject)]

4.3

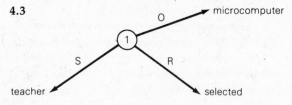

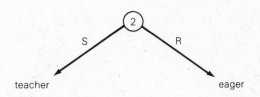

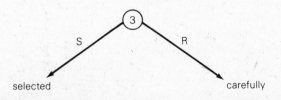

4.4 The very hungry child devoured the hamburger.
1. [The child devoured the hamburger]
2. [The child was hungry]
3. [The hunger was very (extreme)]

4.5 A triangle is a three-sided, closed figure.
1. [A triangle is a figure]
2. [The figure is three-sided]
3. [The figure is closed]

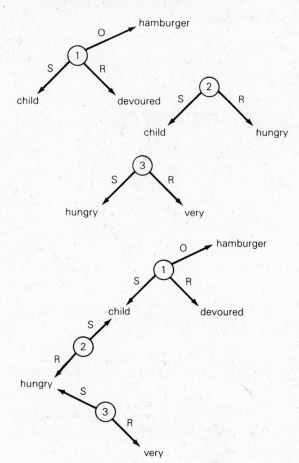

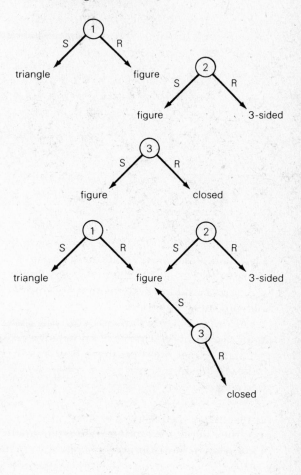

Chapter

5

Representing Declarative Knowledge: Schemas

SUMMARY

1. **Schemas** are integrated units of declarative knowledge. Schemas can incorporate all three basic types of declarative knowledge—propositions, images, and linear orderings.

2. Schemas abstract the regularities in categories—both propositionally and perceptually. The common element in all uses of the term *schema* is some reference to organized knowledge.

3. **Natural categories** are schemas that represent general information about naturally occurring and culturally-defined objects. The **basic** level of category is the level at which distinctions are made most easily.

4. **Event schemas** represent knowledge of typical activities or sequences.

5. **Text schemas** represent various types of text structure such as story structures or expository text structures.

SCHEMAS

In the last chapter, we talked about the representation of declarative knowledge at the level of basic or elementary units. Propositions, images, and linear orderings represent information at the level of a single idea, image, or relation. But often our knowledge about a topic seems to combine images, linear orderings, and propositions. In order to deal with the fact that much of our knowledge seems integrated, psychologists have developed the idea of a **schema.**

Rumelhart and Norman (1983) call this level of representation the "suprasentential" level, indicating that schemas can represent more information than can be expressed in a single sentence. Although most theorists acknowledge a need for representational units at this higher level, it is more difficult to find an agreed-upon definition for a schema than for a proposition. However, the common element in all uses of the term *schema* is some reference to organized knowledge structures. Rumelhart and Norman (1983) define schemas as "data structures for representing the generic concepts stored in memory" (p. 42). Anderson (1990) adds that schemas provide a way "of encoding regularities in categories, whether these regularities are perceptual or propositional" (p. 134). This latter distinction is important because it differentiates schemas from propositional networks, which do not encode perceptual regularities.

Other features that characterize schemas include:

1. Schemas have variables.

2. Schemas may be organized hierarchically and may be embedded, one within another.

3. Schemas facilitate making inferences.

Examples of categories where we might represent information schematically include **natural categories** (like birds, trees, or dogs), **events** (like going to a restaurant, going to the doctor, or checking a book out of the library), and various types of **text** (like stories, newspaper articles, and textbook chapters).

Since schemas are organized knowledge structures that include the concepts, attributes, and relations that *typically* occur in a category member, a schema for a bird would probably include feathers (even though a newly hatched baby bird has no feathers) and the proposition that birds fly (even though some birds, such as penguins, cannot fly). Since we are exposed repeatedly to stimuli that share lots of similar features but are not identical, schemas are a convenient way for us to represent information about these common elements so that when we encounter a new instance of the category, even if it is different in some small way, we can recognize it as having enough features in common with a typical instance that we treat it as a category member, rather than starting from scratch in our processing and classification tasks. Using schemas to simplify classification appears to be an adaptive way to reduce the load on working memory and to allow for variation that occurs naturally in the environment.

Schemas as integrated units can incorporate all three basic types of declarative knowledge: propositions, images, and linear orderings. Schemas abstract the regularities of category membership—both propositionally and perceptually—so they preserve what's *generally* true about category members, what a category member *generally* looks like, and the *general* order of events. To get a feel for what we mean, activate for a moment your "schema" for eating at a fast-food restaurant such as McDonald's. With respect to propositional knowledge, you might activate such information as "prices are relatively low," "service is usually fast," "there's one in my neighborhood," "their fries are good," and so on. In addition to your propositional knowledge, you can also probably form a mental image of McDonald's. If I scan my mental image I see the counter where you go to order your food, the employees in their uniforms, the cash registers with the flat "membrane" keyboards for punching in your order, the rows of paper-wrapped hamburgers and other sandwiches lined up on the stainless steel warming tables, and lots of customers standing in line to order. Your mental image might include some of those same elements, as well as many others. With respect to the order of events, one aspect of the McDonald's experience that might be represented as a linear ordering is the "order, *pay*, *eat*, leave" sequence, which is typical of fast-food restaurants but different from the "order, *eat*, *pay*, leave" sequence, which is standard in *non*-fast-food restaurants.

Figure 5.1 depicts a McDonald's schema in the format we will use throughout this book. Some of the entries represent propositions (e.g., price: relatively low) and some represent linear orderings (e.g., sequence: order, pay, eat, leave). Images are also included. Think back now to our list of features that characterize a schema, and let us review them in the context of the McDonald's example. First, we said that a schema has variables. This means that although there are a number of things about McDonald's that are typically true, such as those we mentioned above, there are also a number of attributes that are free to vary, such as size, number of employees, and seating arrangement within the restaurant. For example, with respect to size, there is a McDonald's restaurant near my home that is

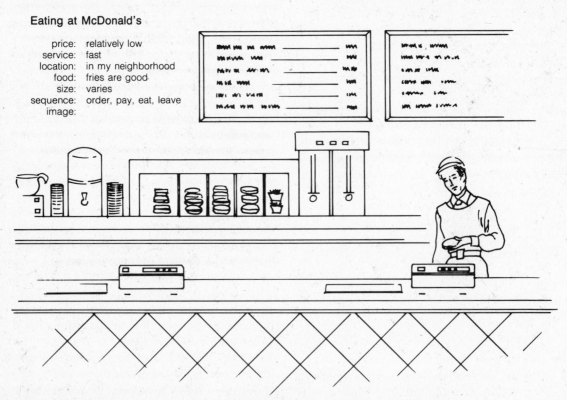

Eating at McDonald's

price:	relatively low
service:	fast
location:	in my neighborhood
food:	fries are good
size:	varies
sequence:	order, pay, eat, leave
image:	

Figure 5.1 A schema for eating at McDonald's. This format for depicting schemas contains propositions, linear orderings, and images that are relevant to the schema.

quite small—probably only 10 or 12 tables. In contrast, there is a large three-story McDonald's in a neighboring town that I would guess has a seating capacity of well over 100 people. Because schemas have slots for variables, my schema for McDonald's can tolerate this variability.

A second feature of schemas is that they are organized hierarchically and can be embedded, one within another. This means that within our schema for eating at McDonald's we can embed a schema for ordering at McDonald's. Also, the schema for eating at McDonald's embeds within a more general schema for eating at restaurants. In other words, schemas can represent knowledge at different levels of abstraction.

Finally, schemas are designed to facilitate making inferences. Although schemas have variables, as we discussed earlier, if the value of a variable is unspecified or unavailable from the current input, we assign a *default value* or an assumed value. Thus, if you are in a strange town and you want french fries, you would assume or infer that you could get some at the local McDonald's, even if you had never been in that particular McDonald's before. Although there are situations where a particular McDonald's restaurant might not be serving french fries (fryer broken? out of cooking oil?), it is much more likely that your inference about french fries would be correct. This quality of facilitating inferences is a very important aspect of schemas as representational units. When we are communicating with other people who have schemas similar to ours, lots of time and effort is saved because our schemas enable both speaker and listener (or writer and reader) to infer information that is typical in the situation, rather than having to communicate all the information explicitly. A danger in relying on schemas, however, is that schemas can encourage the tendency to stereotype, rather than to judge each new instance independently.

The notion that a schema-like construct is an integral part of human learning is not new. For example, Piaget (1952) discussed schemas as representational units in his writings on intelligence in children. However, for many years, schema theory was criticized by experimental psychologists as being too vague and poorly specified (e.g., Thorndyke & Yekovich, 1980). Recently, however, researchers in artificial intelligence have made considerable progress in defining and developing theoretical models of schemas as representational systems (e.g., Minsky, 1975). These highly specified models have made significant contributions to the psychological literature, and have increased the credibility of the schema as a representational construct. Although it is still unclear exactly how a computer schema and a human schema might be similar and different as representational units, there does seem to be considerable evidence to support the psychological reality of the schema in human memory.

In the next three sections, we will review briefly some of the research on three types of schemas that have relevance in a school context: schemas for basic objects in natural categories, schemas for events, and schemas for text.

Schemas for Basic Objects in Natural Categories

Natural categories are categories that include naturally occurring entities such as plants and animals and also culturally generated entities such as crimes and taboos. Such categories often have a somewhat hierarchical structure as, for example, *pears* are an instance of *fruit*, which is an instance of *food*.

Eleanor Rosch and her colleagues have conducted extensive research to learn more about the typical members of categories in hierarchies like the one in the previous chapter (birds and canaries) shown in Figure 4.6.

One assumption of Rosch's work is that categorization schemes are not arbitrary but are based on underlying regularities that occur naturally and typically in category members. A second assumption is that not all the information about features that characterize a category member is represented propositionally—some perceptual information is also represented. A third assumption is that within the overall categorization scheme, there is one level of abstraction, the **basic level**, at which most of the information about category members is stored (Rosch, Mervis, Gray, Johnson, & Boyes-Braem, 1976).

People seem to agree to a large extent about the typical attributes of members of basic categories. For example, when Rosch et al. asked subjects to list all the attributes they could think of to describe basic objects in categories such as trees, fish, birds, chairs, and cars, there was a very high level of agreement among the subjects with respect to the most common features of the basic objects. In the category of birds, for instance, most subjects mentioned feathers, wings, beak, and claws. If people agree about characteristic features, they should also agree about what constitutes a prototypical member of the category, and they do. For example, Rosch (1973) had subjects rate the typicality of various members of basic categories on a scale from 1 (very typical) to 7 (very atypical). In this study, subjects consistently rated certain category members as more typical than other members. In the bird category, subjects rated *robin* (1.1) as more typical than *chicken* (3.8). *Carrots* (1.1) were more typical vegetables than *parsley* (3.8). With respect to crimes, *murder* (1.1) unfortunately was more typical than *vagrancy* (5.3).

Rosch et al. (1976) theorized that if subjects had such high levels of verbal agreement about their prototypical category members, they should have high levels of agreement about the perceptual features of their schemas

as well. They tested this hypothesis in an experiment designed to minimize dependency on linguistic coding, by investigating whether or not subjects could readily identify prototypical category members on the basis of shape. The researchers developed sets of stimuli using as raw materials line drawings like those shown in Figure. 5.2. The line drawings were produced by tracing different pictures of the various objects and adjusting them to comparable size. Once they had four different but comparably sized outlines of each object, they overlapped the outlines using an overhead projector and produced a composite drawing of each object that represented the *average* of the traced outlines. Thus the car outline used in the experiment represented an "average" or prototypical car, the dog outline represented an average or prototypical dog, and so on. Subjects viewed these prototypical drawings of basic level objects (birds, dogs, cars) as well as composites from superordinate categories (animals, vehicles) and subordinate categories (poodles, sports cars). The experiment showed that the basic

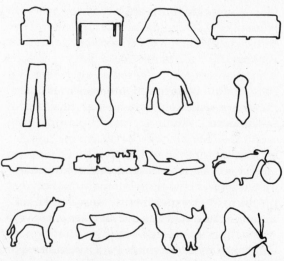

Figure 5.2 Examples of line drawings (from Rosch et al., 1976).

level categories were the most inclusive category level at which category members could be readily identified on the basis of perceptual prototype.

Lack of physical similarity among category members of superordinate categories made identification of superordinate composites very difficult. For example, overlapping images of a chair, a desk, a table, and a couch results in a composite that is too abstract to identify on the basis of shape or visual image. That is, there doesn't appear to be a perceptual composite that corresponds to a prototypical piece of furniture.

At the level of subordinate categories such as breeds of dogs or types of cars, subordinate category members were no more easily identified than were basic-level composites. That is, poodles were not identified as dogs any more easily than the composite dog.

These findings seem to confirm that we categorize objects and store most of the feature information at a level of generality that is most useful and economical. Presumably it is to our benefit to be able to distinguish between a bird and a dog, or a dog and a car, even with only limited information or from a distance, so our schemas for objects in basic-level categories represent information in ways that enable us to make these distinctions. That is, schemas allow for maximal equivalence among category members as well as maximal differentiation between members and non-members. Another way to say this is that schemas for objects in basic-level categories are the most inclusive categories at which information can be coded or represented in a manner concrete enough to be recognized as a visual image.

In further experiments, Rosch et al. also demonstrated that basic-level categories were the first ones learned by small children—before the more inclusive superordinates and before the more specific subordinates. Even with children as young as 3 years old, sorting

tasks at the level of basic categories produced almost perfect performance. When asked to "put together things that go together," 3-year-old children sorted pictures representing basic-level objects correctly 99% of the time. Four-year-old children were perfect at this task. For superordinate categories such as vehicles, 3-year-olds sorted correctly only 55% of the time, but by the age of 4, performance improved to a 96% level. Evidence was presented to suggest that results were not merely a function of familiarity with names of objects in basic categories.

In summary, Rosch et al. suggest that people sort to achieve economy of representation and general usefulness of categories. Their research implies that to some degree, the structure of the world is "given" rather than imposed arbitrarily by those doing the categorizing. Rosch suggests that "the material objects of the world possess highly correlated structures" (p. 428). That is, for given sets of stimuli, certain sets of attributes often co-occur while others rarely combined together. To gain a sense of order and predictability in the world, we seem to form schemas that preserve the underlying regularities while ignoring slight surface irregularities, and we seem to do this consistently and at a very young age.

Schemas for Events

The "Going to McDonald's" example discussed earlier is an example of an event schema. Event schemas represent our organized knowledge about typical activities and sequences of events that we engage in over and over again in our interactions with the world. Schemas for events, like other schemas, can encode information at varying levels of abstraction. So the schema for going to McDonald's is less abstract than the schema for going to a fast-food restaurant, which is less abstract than the overall schema for dining at a restaurant.

An important series of experiments looking at the psychological reality of event schemas was conducted by Bower, Black, and Turner (1979). They asked subjects to generate the typical or most important actions or activities that comprise a number of common events, such as dining at a restaurant, going to the doctor, and checking a book out of the library. Their results were consistent with other results looking at schemas; although there were lots of similarities in subjects' listings of actions, no single action or activity was listed by all subjects. The typical sequence of activities produced in the restaurant script, for example, was *be seated, look at menu, order meal, eat food, pay bill,* and *leave.* These actions were produced by 73% of the 32 subjects tested.

Bower et al. demonstrated that subjects' schemas for typical sequences of events influenced their memory of particular instances. For example, one task in the Bower et al. experiments asked subjects to read a passage describing a hypothetical visit to a restaurant. In this passage some, but not all, of the activities that typically occur in a restaurant were mentioned. Then on a test, subjects were asked to recall the hypothetical account. Their recall protocols included statements from the passage they read as well as statements of actions that typically occur in a restaurant but were not presented in the experimental passage. In a subsequent recognition experiment, subjects also showed a tendency to falsely "recognize" statements that were consistent with their schema but had *not* been presented. Bower et al. argued that when we read or hear new information about a familiar topic, we activate our relevant schema and use this as a guide for processing and remembering the new information. This tendency helps us to construct sensible interpretations of events, even if we are not given all the details. However, as Bower, Black, and Turner demonstrated, this tendency can also account for

errors when we try to remember particulars about stereotypical situations.

Yekovich and Walker (1986) were interested in how the centrality or importance of concepts in situations affected peoples' ability to remember the situation. They investigated subjects' memory of important and less important concepts in several experiments using event schemas similar to the ones used by Bower, Black, and Turner. First, Yekovich and Walker asked subjects to rate concepts in eight contexts to determine their importance or centrality in relation to the event schema. In the "Going to a Restaurant" context, for example, subjects rated concepts like *table, waiter, menu,* and *cocktail* on a scale from 1 (least central) to 7 (most central). Ratings for concepts in the restaurant context are presented in Table 5.1.

After the centrality of the concepts had been determined, a new group of subjects

Table 5.1 Centrality ratings for the concepts in the "Going to a Restaurant" passage used in the Yekovich and Walker (1986) experiments.

CONCEPT	CENTRALITY RATING (1 = NOT IMPORTANT, 7 = IMPORTANT)
Meal	6.76
Dinner	6.29
Cook	6.12
Check	5.88
Waiter	5.83
Menu	5.76
Chef	5.72
Service	5.68
Table	5.36
Plate	5.24
Drink	4.44
Tip	4.16
Napkin	4.04
Wine	4.00
Hostess	3.88
Tablecloth	3.80
Dessert	3.76
Reservation	3.72
Cocktail	3.28
Booth	3.12
Valet	2.64
Coats	1.46

read scripted passages like the one in Table 5.2, where some of the central (average rating = 5.84) and peripheral (average rating = 3.60) concepts were explicitly mentioned in the passage and some were deleted. On a subsequent recognition test, subjects were asked whether particular concepts had been stated in the passage. Subjects responded to central and peripheral concepts differently. For central concepts that had *not* been presented in the passage, subjects responded "Yes" 66% of the time. For peripheral concepts that had *not* been presented, subjects "false alarmed" to only 12% of the items.

Yekovich and Walker argued that when subjects activate a schema, they initially activate only the "top level" or most central and

important aspects. This activation pattern produces a response bias on a subsequent recognition test—subjects will often incorrectly "recognize" these typical but unpresented concepts. For more peripheral or lower-level concepts, subjects can discriminate better between presented concepts and concepts that were not presented but are consistent with the schema. This is because the peripheral or less typical concepts were not automatically activated during reading. Therefore, if they were not encountered in the passage, subjects could correctly reject them at test time.

Based on these studies and on subsequent experiments (Walker & Yekovich, 1987), Yekovich and Walker concluded that schemas for events, like schemas for objects in basic categories, have "basic" levels at which the most prototypical information is stored, and it is this basic-level information that seems to become active immediately upon encountering an instance of the event.

Table 5.2 The "Going to a Restaurant" text passage used by Yekovich and Walker (1986). Test concepts were *table* (central), *meal* (central), *hostess* (peripheral), and *cocktail* (peripheral). Each time a version of the passage was presented to a subject, one sentence containing a central test concept and one sentence containing a peripheral test concept were deleted. Test concepts are italicized here, but they were not during the experiment.

Jack and his girlfriend Chris decided to go out to a nice restaurant. They called to make a reservation and then they drove to the restaurant. When they arrived, Jack opened the door and they went inside. Jack gave his name to the *hostess* at the reservation desk. Since they were a little early, they decided to go in the bar for a *cocktail*. In a few minutes, Jack and Chris went into the dining room. They were seated at a *table* near the window. The waiter introduced himself and gave Jack and Chris their menus. They discussed the menu. When their *meal* was served, Jack and Chris ate leisurely. They talked and admired the view. Later, they decided to order dessert. Jack and Chris ate most of their dessert. It was late, so Jack asked for the check. The service had been good, so they gave the waiter a big tip. They paid the check and got their coats. Jack and Chris walked out of the restaurant. They got their car and drove home.

Schemas for Text

Just as schemas can represent the underlying regularities of basic objects and events, they can also be useful for representing the underlying regularities that occur in different types of text or prose. Journalists and readers of newspaper articles, for example, are very familiar with the "who, what, when, where, why, and how" schema that represents a typical news story. Similarly, textbook chapters, children's stories, and many other kinds of prose have characteristic or typical sections and features that guide our processing and recall of the presented information.

One of the first psychologists to study text schemas was Bartlett (1932). He asked college students to read a passage of text called "The War of the Ghosts" and then tested their memory for the passage over increasing intervals of time. Take a few moments now to read

"The War of the Ghosts," which is presented in Table 5.3.

If you are like Bartlett's students, the ideas in the passage are probably hard for you to organize and remember because you do not have an existing schema that corresponds to the structure of this North American Indian folktale. Consequently, making sense of the passage and remembering it accurately is somewhat problematic. Bartlett deliberately chose this story to investigate what effect a schema (or the lack of one) might have on recall. He found that lack of familiarity with the schema for the folktale led to inaccurate recall and substantial distortion. Students tended to remember only parts of the story and to leave out other parts. Furthermore, they were likely to use a familiar schema to make sense of the parts they included in their versions of the story. For example, students used a naval battle schema or a schema for a fishing expedition. These schemas allowed the students to produce the information in a context that made sense to them. Not surpris-ingly, their versions often included details that were consistent with these familiar schemas but that had not been presented in the passage.

Bartlett pointed out that to understand and remember new information, we have to make it meaningful. If the information presented in the text doesn't appear to have any inherently meaningful structure, readers will use a familiar schema for incorporating the new information. Later, at recall, this schema will be used to guide the reconstruction of the presented text.

Since Bartlett, many researchers have studied the effects of text schemas. For example, Stein and Glenn (1978) have investigated how children use story structures, and Meyer (1975) has looked at many types of schemas for expository texts. This work has important implications for reading instruction and will be considered in some detail when we talk about reading in Chapter 12. For now, simply note that text schemas play an influential role when we perceive, process, and attempt to remember information from text.

Table 5.3 Original version of the story "The War of the Ghosts" (from Bartlett, 1932).

The War of the Ghosts

One night two young men from Egulac went down to the river to hunt seals, and while they were there it became foggy and calm. Then they heard war-cries, and they thought: "Maybe this is a war-party." They escaped to the shore, and hid behind a log. Now canoes came up, and they heard the noise of paddles, and they saw one canoe coming up to them. There were five men in the canoe, and they said:

"What do you think? We wish to take you along. We are going up the river to make war on the people."

One of the young men said: "I have no arrows."

"Arrows are in the canoe," they said.

"I will not go along. I might be killed. My relatives do not know where I have gone. But you," he said, turning to the other, "may go with them."

So one of the young men went, but the other returned home.

And the warriors went on up the river to a town on the other side of Kalama. The people came down to the water, and they began to fight, and many were killed. But presently the young man heard one of the warriors say: "Quick, let us go home: that Indian has been hit." Now he thought: "Oh, they are ghosts." He did not feel sick, but they said he had been shot.

So the canoes went back to Egulac, and the young man went ashore to his house, and made a fire. And he told everybody and said: "Behold I accompanied the ghosts, and we went to fight. Many of our fellows were killed, and many of those who attacked us were killed. They said I was hit, and I did not feel sick."

He told it all, and then he became quiet. When the sun rose he fell down. Something black came out of his mouth. His face became contorted. The people jumped up and cried.

He was dead.

CHAPTER SUMMARY

Schemas are higher-order units of declarative knowledge. They integrate propositional, sequential, and perceptual information about familiar categories, events, texts, or other entities. Schemas contain information both about the crucial or typical characteristics of entities and about other characteristics that may vary. Thus, individuals may use schemas to infer what a newly encountered instance of a schema will be like.

Schemas may be embedded in hierarchies of schemas that represent different levels of generality. For instance, a schema for *apple* may be embedded in a *fruit* schema, which is embedded in a *food* schema. When this is the case, the schema at a middle level of generality often contains the most information. As with simple schemas, hierarchies of schemas are useful for drawing inferences about newly encountered instances. Because of their role in making inferences, schemas are a tremendously important type of knowledge representation.

ADDITIONAL READINGS

General

Anderson, J.R. (1980). Concepts, propositions, and schemata: What are the cognitive units? In J.H. Flowers (Ed.), *Nebraska symposium on motivation* (pp. 121–162). Hillsdale, NJ: Lawrence Erlbaum Associates.

Anderson, R.C. (1977). The notion of schemata and the educational enterprise. In R.C. Anderson, R.J. Spiro, & W.E. Montague (Eds.), *Schooling and the acquisition of knowledge.* Hillsdale, NJ: Lawrence Erlbaum Associates.

Brewer, W.F., & Nakamura, G.V. (1984). The nature and function of schemas. In R.S. Wyer & T.K. Srull (Eds.), *Handbook of social cognition* (pp. 119–160). Hillsdale, NJ: Lawrence Erlbaum Associates.

Rumelhart, D.E. (1980). Schemata: The building blocks of cognition. In R.J. Spiro, B.C. Bruce, & W.F. Brewer (Eds.), *Theoretical issues in reading comprehension* (pp. 33–58). Hillsdale, NJ: Lawrence Erlbaum Associates.

Natural Categories

Rosch, E., & Lloyd, B.B. (Eds.) (1978). *Cognition and categorization.* Hillsdale, NJ: Lawrence Erlbaum Associates.

Event Schemas

Shank, R.C., & Abelson, R.P. (1977). *Scripts, plans, goals and understanding.* Hillsdale, NJ: Lawrence Erlbaum Associates.

Text Schemas

Meyer, B.J.F., Brandt, D.M., & Bluth, G.J. (1980). Use of top-level structure in text: Key for reading comprehension of ninth grade students. *Reading Research Quarterly, 16,* 72–103.

Stein, N.L., & Glenn, C.G. (1978). An analysis of story comprehension in elementary school children. In R. Freedle (Ed.), *Multidisciplinary perspectives in discourse comprehension.* Norwood, NJ: Ablex.

Representing Procedural Knowledge

SUMMARY

1. Procedural knowledge is our knowledge of how to do things. This knowledge is represented in the form of **productions.** Each piece of knowledge is called a production because it "produces" some bit of mental or physical behavior. Each bit of behavior may be thought of as a step in a procedure.

2. Productions are formally represented as IF-THEN contingency statements in which the IF part of the statement contains the **conditions** that must exist for the rule to be applicable and the THEN part contains the **action** that will be executed when the conditions are met. Thus, productions are also known as condition-action pairs.

3. Typically, productions combine to form a set. A **production system,** or set, represents all of the steps in a mental or overt physical procedure. The productions within a set are related to one another by virtue of a **goal structure.** That is, each one contributes in some way to producing a final goal behavior.

4. Productions and production systems vary in their relation to domains. **Domain-general** productions can be applied in more than one domain. Because they are general in nature they are less powerful and are sometimes called weak methods. **Domain-specific** productions apply in only one domain and are ultimately responsible for expertise. They are very powerful pieces of knowledge, but only apply to very specific situations within a domain.

5. Productions also vary in the number of cognitive resources they consume. Some productions are called **automated** (or automatic) because their use is not noticed by

the information-processing system. Other productions are called **controlled** (or conscious or attention-demanding) because their use consumes some or all of the limited capacity of working memory.

6. Skill in a domain is characterized by two kinds of domain-specific production sets. One kind represents automated basic skills for the domain. The second kind represents controlled strategic knowledge of the domain.

7. Productions are an economical way to represent procedural knowledge. Flow of control and automaticity reduce the burden on working memory.

8. Declarative and procedural knowledge differ markedly with respect to four characteristics. Declarative knowledge is knowledge that something is the case. It is considered static, its basic units can be acquired quickly, and the basic units can be modified easily. In contrast, procedural knowledge is knowledge about how to do something. It is considered dynamic, it is acquired slowly, and once automated its basic units (productions) are difficult to modify.

In Chapters 4 and 5 you learned about how we represent our knowledge of the objects, concepts, and situations in the world. Propositions, spatial images, linear orderings, and schemas were the different types of declarative knowledge we discussed. One of the important characteristics of declarative knowledge is that it is static in the sense that it is knowledge "about" things, but it is *not* knowledge about "how to do" things. Consider for a moment your knowledge of a traffic light that is green. You might imagine that part of your declarative knowledge of this object is an image of a rectangular box with three circular openings, one red, another yellow, and the third green. Yet this image, by itself, is unable to express an important feature of human behavior—that under normal circumstances a person will produce a certain behavior when he recognizes that the traffic light is green. If he is walking, he will cross the street, and if he is driving, he will press the accelerator.

Because declarative knowledge does not capture the behavior that people produce, we need another way to represent the knowledge that does produce behavior. This type of knowledge is called **procedural knowledge,** and the current chapter focuses on how this knowledge is represented in memory. Once you have an understanding of how declarative and procedural knowledge are represented, you will be able to see more completely how the human information-processing system works as an integrated whole. At that point, we will be able to take up topics such as how people learn, how they solve problems, how they acquire expertise, and how this model sheds light on areas such as reading, math, and science.

PRODUCTIONS AND THEIR FEATURES

Structural Features

Unlike declarative knowledge which is static, procedural knowledge is represented in an active type of representation called a **production.** A production is a condition-action rule. That is, a production programs a certain action to occur only when the specified condition(s)

Table 6.1 Procedural knowledge represented in production form. Each line in the IF clause specifies a condition that must exist. Each line in the THEN clause specifies an action that will take place when all of the conditions in the IF clause are met.

P_1 REINFORCEMENT

IF ⎧ Goal is to increase child's attending
conditions ⎨   behavior
    ⎩ And child has paid attention slightly
         longer than is typical for this child
action { THEN   Praise child.   *to influence another persons behavior*

P_2 TRIANGLE

IF   Figure is two-dimensional
      And figure is three-sided
      And figure is closed
THEN Classify figure as triangle
      And say "triangle." *classifying an object*

P_3 VIEWING CONTENTS OF A ROOM

IF   Goal is to view contents of a room
      And room is dark
      And I am near light switch
THEN Turn on light switch
      And view contents of the room.
               *perform simple physical act so can
               view room contents.*

---

exist. Table 6.1 shows three sample productions, one for administering reinforcement, one for classifying a triangle, and one for viewing the contents of a room.[1] A production has two parts, an IF portion and a THEN portion. The IF portion specifies the condition or conditions that must exist for a given set of actions to be executed. The THEN portion lists the action or actions that will execute or "fire" when the conditions are met. The individual specifications in the production are called

---

[1]Throughout the book we use simplified forms of productions and production sets. They are meant to illustrate the basic constructs associated with procedural knowledge, but as such are not currently implementable on a computer.

clauses. So, in a production, the number of clauses in the IF portion represents the number of conditions to be satisfied, and the number of clauses in the THEN portion represents the number of actions to be taken. One rough gauge for the complexity of a production rule is the number of clauses it contains. Productions that contain a large number of clauses are more complex than productions containing only a few clauses.

Let's consider these ideas using the productions in Table 6.1. The production labelled P_1: REINFORCEMENT, has two conditions that must be satisfied: (1) someone must want to increase how much the child pays attention, and (2) the child in question must have just shown an above-average amount of attending behavior. If both of these conditions exist simultaneously, the action that will be executed is that the person praises the child. The two conditions plus the single action specified in P_1 produce a total of three clauses for that production. How many condition clauses, action clauses, and total clauses are in P_2: TRIANGLE? Which production, P_1 or P_2, is a more complex rule? The answers to these questions are given at the end of the chapter (Questions 6.1 and 6.2).

Conditions and Actions

The conditions of a production can be either external to the individual or they can be internal, mental conditions. In the REINFORCEMENT production in Table 6.1, the first condition is a personal goal, internal to the individual. It is not necessarily something that others can observe and agree on. By contrast, the second condition exists outside of the individual, and a group of observers (who knew the child's typical attention span) could agree on it.

Just as the conditions of a production can be external or internal, so too can the actions. In the TRIANGLE production, for example, the first action is a mental one. The individual involved has made a mental note (i.e., to classify) that a particular type of figure (i.e., triangle) is being observed. The second action, saying "triangle," is external because the individual has put some information out into the environment.

It is important for you to understand the value and the powerful consequences of the distinction between external and internal conditions and actions. By incorporating this distinction, one can create production rules that contain *only* internal conditions and internal actions. In other words, some production rules can be responsible for unobservable mental behavior. By creating a series of related productions of this type, it becomes possible to model the mental steps that people go through for such cognitive processes as reasoning out a solution to a complex problem or reading a passage with understanding. Thus, productions provide a powerful way to describe the cognitive activities of people. We will return to this issue again later in the chapter.

The Purposive Character of Productions

A final important feature of productions is that they produce *purposive* actions or behavior. This purposive character is built into a production by providing it with a goal as part of the conditions. For example, in P_3 VIEWING CONTENTS OF A ROOM, note that the first condition expresses the goal as wanting to view the contents of a room. This goal constrains the conditions of the production so that it will only apply when the person has this need or desire. In other words, the person will have a purpose in mind. So when the person wants to view the contents, the room is dark, and the person is near enough to find a light switch, then the person will flip the switch to be able to see what is in the room.

Suppose we eliminated the goal clause from P_3. When would this production execute? The answer is that every time the person was in a dark room and was near a light switch, she would flip the switch and look around. This would be odd behavior if the person was getting into bed for the night and happened to walk into a dark room! Or imagine walking into a darkened theater where the light switches were inside the door! The point is that people's behavior is goal-directed, so the knowledge that produces behavior should capture that goal-directedness. As an exercise, can you identify the production in Table 6.1 that would lead to non-directed behavior? What are the behavioral consequences of this production in its present form? Can you add a clause that would make the production goal-based? Check your answers with those at the end of the chapter (Questions 6.3, 6.4, and 6.5).

Exercises in Interpreting Productions

Throughout the rest of the book you will see knowledge represented in production form. Therefore, it is worthwhile to practice interpreting productions. Table 6.2 lists three productions that might underlie the skill of paragraph comprehension. Try answering the following questions about these productions and then check your answers with those given at the end of this chapter.

6.6 Remember that the action(s) of a production take(s) place only if all of the conditions specified in its IF portion are met. Suppose that Barry has the goal of comprehending a paragraph and does not know the meaning of the word *egregious* encountered in the paragraph. Which (if any) of the three productions will execute under these conditions?

6.7 Suppose that Barry understands all the words in a paragraph, but does

Table 6.2 Some productions that underlie the skill of paragraph comprehension.

P_1	IF		Goal is to comprehend paragraph
			And words are known
	THEN		Find topic sentence
			And check to see if other sentences support topic sentence.
P_2	IF		Goal is to comprehend paragraph
			And one or more words are not known
	THEN		Look up unknown words in dictionary
			And find topic sentence
			And check to see if other sentences support topic sentence.
P_3	IF		Goal is to comprehend paragraph
			And other sentences support topic sentence
	THEN		Find topic sentence
			And state topic sentence.

not have the goal of comprehending the paragraph. Which (if any) of the three productions will execute under these conditions?

6.8 In the THEN part of P_3, which action is most clearly an observable (external) action?

6.9 Which production in Table 6.2 is the most complex? Why?

PRODUCTION SYSTEMS

Up to this point, our discussion has centered on individual productions. You may have noticed in the examples that have been given that individual productions tend to represent fairly small pieces of behavior, such as identifying a triangle or praising a child. We have consistently alluded to the actions of individual productions as being single pieces or steps of a behavior. In the real world, people do more than identify a pattern or simply praise a child. For instance, identifying a triangle might be part of the more complex activity of solving a geometry problem. Similarly, praising a child might be a part of a whole sequence

of events designed to modify that child's behavior. These more complex patterns of behavior are what we typically think of as procedural in character. That is, they are comprised of a number of interrelated steps. Let us see now how productions can be used to represent the knowledge that underlies these coordinated series of mental and physical actions.

Interrelating Productions

Recall that in Chapters 4 and 5 we discussed how basic units of declarative knowledge become interrelated (for example, in networks and schemas). Just as something was needed to represent the interrelations among basic declarative units, so too is something needed to interrelate individual productions. For declarative knowledge, the interrelations were produced by common or shared ideas. For productions, the interrelations are produced when the actions of one production create the conditions needed for another production. Put another way, the output of one production becomes part of the input for another production. Consider an example from Table 6.3. Notice that production P_4 has an action to

Table 6.3 A production system that underlies a teacher's skill of dealing with an inattentive student.

P_1	IF	Goal is to get child to pay attention and don't know what reinforces child
	THEN	Set subgoal of determining what reinforces child and set subgoal of reinforcing child for attending.
P_2	IF	Subgoal is to determine what reinforces child
	THEN	Set subgoal to observe conditions under which child misbehaves.
P_3	IF	Subgoal is to observe the conditions under which child misbehaves and child misbehaves when I pay attention to him/her and child doesn't misbehave when I ignore him/her
	THEN	Create proposition that child is reinforced by my attention.
P_4	IF	Subgoal is to observe the conditions under which child misbehaves and child misbehaves when other children pay attention to her/him and child does not misbehave when other children ignore her/him
	THEN	Create proposition that child is reinforced by peer attention
P_5	IF	Subgoal is to reinforce child for attending and child is reinforced by my attention and child has paid attention for longer than average
	THEN	Give child my attention.
P_6	IF	Subgoal is to reinforce child for attending and child is reinforced by peer attention and child has paid attention longer than average
	THEN	Allow child to be with preferred peer.

create the fact that the child is reinforced by peer attention and that P_6 has that same idea as one of its conditions. When P_4 executes, it will in effect create a proposition that will satisfy one of the conditions for P_6. Thus, P_4 and P_6 become interrelated.

The actions of a production create two somewhat distinct types of information. In the example above, P_4 creates a proposition or simple fact, so one type of information a production creates is a simple piece of declarative knowledge. A second type of information that is created is a statement about a subgoal that must satisfied before the overall goal of the task can be achieved. For instance, in a complex task, such as finding the sum of four 3-digit numbers, the goal of finding the sum is achieved by setting a series of subgoals, each of which is tasked with completing a

smaller but integral part of the task. One subgoal involves finding the sum of each column of numbers (starting with the rightmost column). A second subgoal involves finding the sum of the numbers within the column of interest. A third subgoal involves "writing" the result of the summation of each column and if necessary, carrying some value to the next column. The procedural knowledge for doing this type of addition includes some productions whose actions create the above three subgoals. Of course other productions will contain these subgoals as part of their conditions. Thus, the productions for multiple column addition will be interrelated through this goal-subgoal binding.

Consider the example given in Table 6.3 again. In this example, P_1 states a goal as one of the conditions and has actions that form subgoals for achieving that goal. P_2 contains one of the subgoals as its condition and has an action to create yet another subgoal. P_3 and P_4 in turn each contain the subgoal created by P_2 as one of the conditions to be satisfied. Similarly P_5 and P_6 each contain the subgoal created by P_1 as one of the conditions to be satisfied. Finally, notice that every production in the table contains either a goal or a subgoal as one of its conditions, thereby interrelating all of the productions in the set.

Goal Hierarchies and Flow of Control

The use of goals and subgoals in productions creates a **goal hierarchy** that interrelates the productions into an organized set. When productions are interrelated in this way, the result is a **production system** or a **production set.** A production system represents our procedural knowledge for a complex piece of behavior. For instance, the productions in Table 6.3 depict a simple production system for the procedural knowledge that might underlie a teacher's skill of dealing with an inattentive student. You might think of the production set as a package of contingency-based rules that collaborate to govern the teacher's behavior.

The goal hierarchy for the example in Table 6.3 is shown in Figure 6.1. The boxes in the figure depict the goal and the three subgoals and the labelled arrows show how the subgoals are related to one another and to the overall goal. The labels indicate the productions that are responsible for the relations. So, the goal of getting the child to attend (P_1) is achieved by accomplishing two subgoals: determining what reinforces the child (P_2), and providing the appropriate reward when the child is attentive (P_5 or P_6). Similarly, the subgoal of determining what reinforces the child is accomplished by another subgoal that determines when the child misbehaves (see P_2). P_3 and P_4 describe the conditions and the

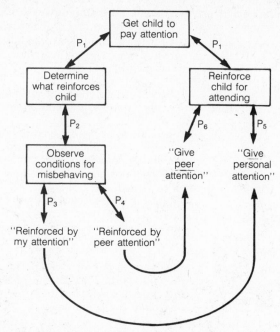

Figure 6.1 The goal hierarchy describing the goal-subgoal relations in the production system for dealing with an inattentive student.

consequent actions that can satisfy the subgoal set by P_2. In other words, those productions actually observe when the child misbehaves and, based on those observations, make inferences about what reinforces the child.

Because of the goal-subgoal relations between and among productions within a set, the control of cognition flows from one production to another within a given production system. At any instant in time, the control of behavior resides with the production whose (sub)goal is active and whose conditions can be satisfied. Once this production executes, control is transferred to another production whose conditions can now be satisfied.

Let us return to the production system given in Table 6.3 to see this flow of control in action. Pretend that you are a teacher in a third grade classroom, and that you have a problem child who is inattentive. Suppose you have the goal of getting the child to pay attention. Suppose also that you do not know what reinforces the child. These two facts together represent the conditions expressed in the first production, P_1, and will enable the production to fire (i.e., the actions will be executed). At this moment in time, the control of your behavior resides in P_1—that production literally determines what your behavior will be because the actions in the THEN portion of the rule are specified explicitly. Assume that P_1 applies. The resulting actions are mental ones, setting the subgoals of finding out what reinforces the child and of reinforcing the child's behavior. The first action creates the one condition necessary for production P_2 to fire. At this point, control moves from P_1 to P_2. Now your behavior is controlled by P_2, so you set the subgoal of observing when the child misbehaves, which is one of the conditions for P_3 and P_4. If the child misbehaves when you pay attention to the misbehavior, but not when you ignore it, then the conditions of P_3 are met. Control moves to P_3 and its action is mentally to classify the child as one who is reinforced by teacher attention. On the other hand, if the child's behavior varies as a function of peer attention, then the conditions of P_4 are met, control transfers to P_4, and the child is classified as one who is reinforced by peer attention.

The knowledge of what reinforces the child allows control to pass to either P_5 or P_6, depending on whether teacher or peer attention reinforces the child. In addition to knowing what reinforces the child, the conditions needed for either of these two productions are that a subgoal of reinforcing the child for paying attention (set by P_1) exists and that the child has paid attention for longer than average. Under these conditions, the action is to reinforce the child in an appropriate manner.

This flow-of-control idea essentially states that in areas where we have acquired procedural knowledge, the control of our overt and cognitive behavior resides within this knowledge. This concept has enormous consequences. One consequence is that the information-processing system does not need a separate executive control mechanism when the control is built directly into our knowledge. This idea contrasts sharply with earlier views of how information processing occurs. A second consequence concerns the process of learning or acquiring a skill. If the control of behavior is literally built into the production systems that represent the various skills, one would hope that the process of acquiring procedural knowledge has some way of insuring that the learned production sets are both correct and safe. Imagine a production set for crossing the street in which the conditions specify the wrong color of the traffic light! These issues will surface again in the chapter on the acquisition of procedural knowledge.

Exercises Concerning Flow of Control

Because an understanding of flow of control is so important, we have created a set of exercises focusing on control. Table 6.4 shows a production system having to do with designing an experiment. The productions in this system have been intentionally mixed up. Try to answer the following questions about this system and then check your answers with those given at the end of the chapter.

6.10 Assume that the starting conditions are having the goal of designing an experiment and knowing the hypothesis, but not knowing explicitly the independent or dependent variables. Which production will apply under these conditions?

6.11 To which production will control transfer when the production in question 6.10 applies?

6.12 Starting with the production you identified in 6.10, trace the flow of

Table 6.4 A mixed-up set of productions that form a production system for the skill of designing experiments.

	IF	Subgoal is to determine dependent variable
P_1	THEN	Find the result in the hypothesis
		And classify the result as the dependent variable.
	IF	Subgoal is to determine independent variable
	THEN	Find the cause in the hypothesis
P_2		And classify the cause as the independent variable
		And set subgoal to determine dependent variable.
	IF	Goal is to design experiment
		And hypothesis is known
		And independent variable is known
P_3		And dependent variable is known
	THEN	Plan a way to manipulate independent variable
		And plan a way to manipulate dependent variable.
	IF	Goal is to design experiment
P_4		And hypothesis is known
	THEN	Subgoal is to determine independent variable.

control from one production to the next until no more productions are available to apply. List the productions in the order in which they take place.

VARIETIES OF PROCEDURAL KNOWLEDGE

Now that you understand how procedural knowledge is represented in memory, it is useful to describe some of the different types of procedural knowledge that exist. In this section we will center our discussions on two important dimensions that describe how procedural knowledge can be differentiated. The first dimension refers to the degree to which procedural knowledge is tied to a specific domain, with the anchor points of the continuum being termed **domain-general** and **domain-specific**. The second dimension classifies procedural knowledge as being more or less automated, with the end points of the continuum being called **automatic** and **con-**trolled (or conscious). The next two subsections are devoted to discussion of these dimensions.

The Domain-General/ Domain-Specific Dimension

In classroom settings, teachers often have dual goals in mind when teaching. On the one hand, teachers attempt to increase students' knowledge about specific disciplines for the purpose of making the students masters or at least competent users of those disciplines. On the other hand, teachers are also concerned with helping students improve their general thinking and problem-solving skills, independent of any particular discipline. Not surprisingly, the knowledge that students acquire in each of these cases can be characterized according to each purpose. In the first case the acquired knowledge is specialized because it is specific to a particular domain. In the second case the acquired knowledge is more general because it is supposed to be applicable across domains.

The dimension that captures this variation in knowledge may be referred to as the degree to which knowledge is domain-specific or domain-general. Domain specificity (or generality) applies to both declarative and procedural knowledge. In this chapter we will concentrate on distinguishing between domain-specific and domain-general *procedural* knowledge. In the chapters that follow this distinction will recur for both declarative and procedural knowledge.

The term *domain* refers to any defined area of content and can vary in its breadth. Sometimes reading and writing are referred to as domains. Often researchers refer to computer programming and physics as domains. Yet the domains of reading and physics differ markedly. Reading is thought to span every topic that can be expressed by our written English symbol system, including the reading of physics. Physics, on the other hand, is a more constrained and well-defined domain with clearer boundaries. Domains like physics are often called "subject-matter areas," while reading and writing are not considered to be subject-matter areas. Some authors have acknowledged this difference by referring to reading and writing as "tool" domains (see Perkins & Salomon, 1989). Since this distinction is useful, we will retain it here.

Domain-General Procedural Knowledge. Some of our procedural knowledge is general in that it is used across domains and in fact is not tied to any particular domain. This type of knowledge is called **domain-general** procedural knowledge and is represented in memory as domain-general production systems. Domain-general procedural knowledge can be thought of as the general methods or approaches that we use. For example, planning ahead, exploring alternatives, and "try, try again" are procedures that can be used in a

wide variety of domains. Take the procedure of planning ahead. Some of the situations in which it can prove useful include taking a vacation, solving a geometry proof, playing chess, having a dinner party, replacing a kitchen sink, and budgeting money.

Interestingly, a production system for planning ahead must be general enough to allow very different pieces of information to satisfy its conditions and thus lead to the execution of the associated actions. How might this disparity be handled? Table 6.5 presents a portion of a hypothetical production system that creates a plan for the different activities listed above. Note first that the production system uses "X" to stand for any of the activities. One way that domain-general productions capture the disparity among various activities is by having variables in them that can stand for different information. Second, note the use of the terms *combination of the factors, factors associated with X,* and *constraints*. These terms are general in that they can take on any number of specific meanings. For planning a vacation a constraint might be money, while for replacing a kitchen sink a constraint might be cabinet size.

What you should be able to see from the example is that the general procedure for planning ahead involves selecting the best plan, which is determined by evaluating alternative possible scenarios. The alternative possibilities in turn are generated by identifying factors that are important for planning the activity and comparing those factors against known constraints. Consider planning ahead for a vacation. The final plan may be a product of having considered several possible vacation alternatives. The criteria for selecting among the alternatives include weighing the factors associated with each possible vacation (e.g., availability of accommodations, geographic location, cost, time of year, mode of transportation) against known constraints (e.g., fi-

ex: preparedness.
listening attentively

Table 6.5 A portion of a hypothetical production system for planning ahead.

P_1	IF	Goal is to create a plan for X
	THEN	Set subgoal to select the best-fitting combination of the factors associated with X.
P_2	IF	Subgoal is to select the best-fitting combination of the factors associated with X
	THEN	Set subgoal of evaluating various combinations of factors associated with X.
P_3	IF	Subgoal is to evaluate various combinations of factors associated with X
	THEN	Set subgoal of creating criteria for evaluation of combinations
		And set subgoal to compare criteria against known constraints
		And set subgoal to generate known constraints.
P_4	IF	Subgoal is to generate known constraints
	THEN	List the constraints in order.
P_5	IF	Subgoal is to create criteria for evaluation of combinations
	THEN	Set subgoal to generate factors associated with X.

nances, amount of time available, number of family members going).

Domain-general procedures are sometimes called "weak methods." They're referred to as weak because although they apply across domains, their application in each situation is often not the most powerful (i.e., foolproof) or the most efficient way to achieve some goal. To illustrate, think about the difference in your own planning for replacing a kitchen sink (assuming you are not a plumbing expert) and the procedure that a master plumber would use. While your own planning might eventually result in the successful replacement of the sink, you might omit several important elements in your planning and consequently find yourself fighting water, lying on your back in the cabinet trying to install the new faucet, and running to the local hardware store four or five times to pick up needed items. Chances are the master plumber's experience with the sink will not be nearly as exasperating!

The reason that the plumber's planning procedure has more foolproof and faster results is that she did not use a domain-general procedure for planning the replacement. Instead, because of her expertise, she used a very plumbing-specific algorithm for planning the sink replacement. This type of procedural knowledge is known as **domain-specific** knowledge.

Domain-Specific Procedural Knowledge. Procedural knowledge that is domain-specific consists of production sets that are capable of being used effectively only in a particular domain. Experts in a domain tend to use domain-specific procedural knowledge to solve routine problems in their area of expertise. Expert teachers, for example, have procedures for introducing new topics, solving discipline problems, monitoring homework assignments, and so on. The details of these procedures are specific to the domain of teaching.

As another example of a domain-specific procedure, consider the production set given in Table 6.6. This production set is a hypothetical procedure for doing multiple-column addition problems such as

614

438

+ 683

Note how the information in the IF and THEN portions contains "math-specific" terms, such as *sum, add, digit,* and *carry.* The production set is so specific in fact that it will not work for anything but addition. About the only leeway is for the number of columns and the number of multi-digit numbers that can be added together.

Domain-specific procedural knowledge, unlike domain-general knowledge, is typically very powerful. That is, its use will lead to fast and foolproof performance. Look at Table 6.6 again, and try to work through the problem given above, applying the productions in the order specified in Figure 6.2 (p. 104). The order in which the productions apply for this problem is listed at the end of the chapter (Ex. 6.13). After working through Exercise 6.13, try making up several addition problems of your own that vary considerably in the number of columns and the size of the numbers. Now use the production system in Table 6.6 to solve your problems. As you work through your problems, you should be able to see that the production set in Table 6.6 will work every time; it is foolproof. Of course, *the specific order in which the productions apply will vary,* depending on the conditions that occur in the problems you generate. For example, sometimes you will need productions whose goal is to "carry," and sometimes you won't. However, all the operations needed to add multi-digit numbers are represented as productions in Table 6.6. The only pieces of knowledge not represented in the set are the math facts that

produce the individual sums (e.g., 7 + 2 = 9). That knowledge resides in declarative memory and is prerequisite. Together the math facts and the production set interact to produce accurate and eventually fast completion of addition problems of the multiple-column sort.

Given this description of the power of domain-specific procedural knowledge, we say that it represents "strong" methods while domain-general knowledge represents "weak" methods. On the other hand, domain-specific procedural knowledge will apply to a rather narrow set of situations whereas domain-general knowledge will apply to many varied situations. The cost-benefit tradeoff for the two types of procedural knowledge is power and speed at the expense of generality of usefulness. Figure 6.3 (p. 105) summarizes the dimension of specificity of application.

Domain-general and domain-specific procedural knowledge are related to each other. Specifically, the former is used to build the latter. The acquisition of domain-specific procedural knowledge is an integral part of what we refer to as becoming "skilled" or "expert." This topic is taken up repeatedly in later chapters. Chapters 7, 8, and 9 describe the learning processes that produce expertise in a domain. Chapters 12 through 15 describe specific examples of these learning processes at work in reading, writing, math, and science.

Automated versus Controlled Procedural Knowledge

There may be an objection to the idea that production systems represent procedural knowledge on the grounds that this type of description implies that a person consciously works through the production set step by step, just as we have worked through the examples thus far. However, just because we have articulated the conditions and actions underlying a sequence of behaviors does not

Table 6.6 A production system for performing addition (from Anderson, 1983).

P₁	IF	the goal is to do an addition problem
	THEN	the subgoal is to iterate through the columns of the problem.

P_1

P_1	IF	the goal is to do an addition problem
	THEN	the subgoal is to iterate through the columns of the problem.
P_2	IF	the goal is to iterate through the columns of an addition problem and the rightmost column has not been processed
	THEN	the subgoal is to iterate through the rows of that rightmost column and set the running total to 0.
P_3	IF	the goal is to iterate through the columns of an addition problem and a column has just been processed and another column is to the left of this column
	THEN	the subgoal is to iterate through the rows of this column to the left and set the running total to the carry.
P_4	IF	the goal is to iterate through the columns of an addition problem and the last column has been processed and there is a carry
	THEN	write out the carry and POP the goal.
P_5	IF	the goal is to iterate through the columns of an addition problem and the last column has been processed and there is no carry
	THEN	POP the goal.
P_6	IF	the goal is to iterate through the rows of a column and the top row has not been processed
	THEN	the subgoal is to add the digit of the top row to the running total.
P_7	IF	the goal is to iterate through the rows of a column and a row has just been processed and another row is below it
	THEN	the subgoal is to add the digit of the lower row to the running total.
P_8	IF	the goal is to iterate through the rows of a column and the last row has been processed and the running total is a digit
	THEN	write the digit and delete the carry and mark the column as processed and POP the goal.
P_9	IF	the goal is to iterate through the rows of a column and the last row has been processed and the running total is of the form "string digit"
	THEN	write the digit and set carry to the string and mark the column as processed and POP the goal.

Table 6.6 (*continued*)

P_{10}	IF	the goal is to add a digit to another digit
		and a sum is the sum of the two digits
	THEN	the result is the sum
		and mark the digit as processed
		and POP the goal.

P_{11}

IF   the goal is to add a digit to a number
and the number is of the form "string digit"
and a sum is the sum of the two digits
and the sum is less than 10
THEN the result is "string sum"
and mark the digit as processed
and POP the goal.

P_{12}

IF   the goal is to add a digit to a number
and the number is of the form "string digit"
and a sum is the sum of the two digits
and the sum is of the form "1 digit*"
and another sum* is the sum of 1 plus string
THEN the result is "sum* digit"
and mark the digit as processed
and POP the goal.

1. Digit is a value 0–9.
2. Number is a sum ≥ 10.
3. "String" is the value of the carry when the carry = 1.
4. Digit* is a value 0–9 that results when summing digits associated with carrying.
5. Sum* is the value of the carry when the carry ≥ 2.

mean that people who possess this knowledge always articulate them as we have. In fact, for a large number of the things we think about and do, people probably do not and cannot articulate the individual sets of conditions and actions. Rather, a good portion of our behavior seems to occur with little or no noticeable effort. Reading the newspaper probably falls into this category. So do things like carrying on a conversation, driving a car, counting out money, writing a letter, and watching TV. The dimension that captures this characteristic depicts some procedural knowledge as being automated and other procedural knowledge as being non-automated. This dimension may be thought of as a continuum labelled "Degree of Automation" with the endpoints being called **automated** and **controlled,** as shown in Figure 6.4 (p. 105). In this section we distinguish between these two characteristics of procedural knowledge.

Automated Procedures. One type of capability that teachers attempt to develop in their students is the skill to perform some school-related tasks quickly, accurately, and with little effort. In the early grades, reading and mastery of basic math are two areas where automated skill is expected. For instance, while young children initially perform simple tasks such as sounding our words and writing their names using conscious and laborious procedures, eventually they are expected to become capable of executing these procedures automatically and without hesitation. What kind of knowledge underlies this form of

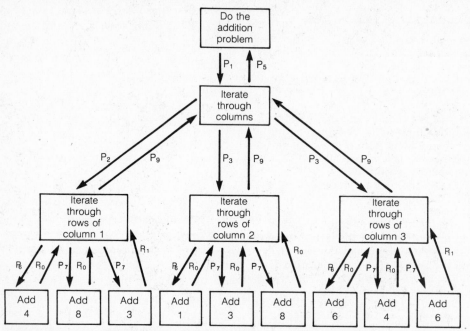

Figure 6.2 A representation of the flow of control of the productions needed to solve the problem, 614 + 438 + 683 = ? from Exercise 6.13. Application of these productions is controlled by the setting of goals. Control starts with the top goal, and the order of application of the productions can be traced by following the arrows up and down as they cycle through the columns, moving from left to right. See the answer to Exercise 6.13 at the end of the chapter (adapted from J.R. Anderson, 1983).

skilled performance? The answer is an automated procedure.

In order to understand what an automated procedure is, we must briefly reconsider the concept of working memory. You will recall from Chapter 3 that working memory was discussed as the part of the information-processing system where the majority of our mental work gets done. Working memory has both processing and holding functions associated with it, and together the processing and holding capacities are thought of as the cognitive resources that are immediately available for completing mental work. You will also recall that the capacities available in working memory are severely limited, and therefore at any instant in time the cognitive

resources available for doing mental work are at a premium. Consequently, the efficient use of these resources is of paramount importance. The possession of some automated procedures that allow us to perform some tasks with little attention is one way that the human information-processing system has evolved to help deal with our limited-capacity working memory. As you will recall from Chapter 3, an **automated** process or procedure is one that consumes none or very few of the cognitive resources of the information-processing system. In other words, this type of procedure actually operates without awareness of it or attention to it.

Many people find the concept of automated procedural knowledge counterintui-

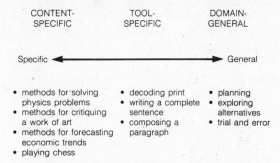

CONTENT- SPECIFIC	TOOL- SPECIFIC	DOMAIN- GENERAL

Specific ⟵⟶ General

- methods for solving physics problems
- methods for critiquing a work of art
- methods for forecasting economic trends
- playing chess

- decoding print
- writing a complete sentence
- composing a paragraph

- planning
- exploring alternatives
- trial and error

Figure 6.3 Domain specificity of procedural knowledge. Procedures vary as to how broadly they apply. Content-specific procedures apply only within a given content area or domain—chess, physics, or art. Tool-specific procedures apply across a variety of content areas, but are tied to a specific tool domain such as reading or writing. Domain-general procedures apply across a large number of domains.

tive—how can a complicated mental or physical procedure be completed without attending to it? Counterintuitive or not, this type of behavior does occur, and a number of examples provide convincing evidence of the existence of automated procedures. Consider first the pejorative comment, "He can't walk and chew gum at the same time." The accused individual supposedly cannot do two natural things at the same time. Yet walking and chewing are both rather complicated motor procedures, and in reality most people not only can walk and chew gum simultaneously,

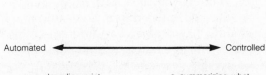

Automated ⟵⟶ Controlled

- decoding print
- mechanics of driving
- disambiguating words in context

- summarizing what one has read
- monitoring traffic and road conditions while driving

Figure 6.4 Degree of automation of procedural knowledge. The amount of attention required for the execution of the procedures varies.

they can also do other things such as talk and watch the scenery while they walk and chew gum. The fact that people routinely engage in these four activities simultaneously is evidence that few cognitive resources are being devoted to any one.

A second example comes from the tool domain of reading. Read the following sentence.

> The soldier drew his weapon and prepared to charge.

Most of you probably experienced little if any difficulty understanding this sentence, and most of you probably didn't even notice any of the things your eyes and mind did to produce that understanding. It's almost as if your eyes simply scanned the line and the meaning magically popped into your consciousness. In truth, however, a very complicated set of procedures was responsible for your successful comprehension. For instance, one set of automated procedures activated and selected the appropriate meanings for the words that have multiple meanings (e.g., *charge* can mean "to move forward in order to attack" or it can mean "to defer payment"). Yet you were unaware that your cognitive system did much mental work to produce the correct interpretation of each of the words in the sentence.

Automated procedures are defined by a number of important characteristics. First, they operate very quickly. In fact, the speed is so fast that a person is literally unaware that the procedure has been used, as in the reading example above. Second, automated procedures are incredibly accurate. They almost always produce the correct or intended behavior. Take the sentence above as an example. Your interpretation of the phrase, *The soldier drew his weapon*, probably did not include the idea of a person in uniform using a pen and paper to sketch a weapon.

A third important characteristic associated with automated procedures is that we typically lack conscious control over them. In other words, we are not able to exert influence over them in a deliberate way. So for instance, we are not really able to consciously control how our mind activates and selects the appropriate meaning of the word *charge* in the sentence above. About all we are conscious of is the result of these processes. That is, we interpret *charge* as "move forward to attack" but we do not notice ourselves choosing that particular meaning from among the possible options.

Fourth, and perhaps most interesting, automated procedures typically cannot be verbalized. Simply put, it is impossible to describe the procedure to someone else. Imagine trying to teach someone to read by describing to her the steps you go through. The description might sound something like, "Well you look at the words one at a time, starting from the leftmost word, and then you, uh, then you know the meanings of the words, uh, . . . and then you group together the words to get the meanings of the ideas, uh. . . ." Needless to say, this description falls far short of exposing what occurs cognitively, and it is a relatively useless form of reading instruction. Fortunately, cognitive psychologists have techniques (such as those described in Chapter 2) for determining the nature of automated skills even though the expert is unable to verbalize them. Thus, we can study what these skills are so that they can be taught to people who lack them.

Procedural knowledge becomes automated over a long period of time and with extensive amounts of use. A baby expends a considerable amount of energy and time becoming a proficient walker. Similarly, a young child develops reading ability over time and with extended practice. The process of acquiring procedural knowledge in various domains and of automating it is a part of learning that is commonly called skill acquisition. Obviously, the development of such skills is a fundamental goal of classroom instruction and deserves detailed discussion. We will take up this topic in detail in Chapter 9.

Controlled Procedures. Teachers spend a moderate amount of classroom time exhorting their students to think an issue through or to deliberate on some topic or to try to reason about a problem. In these instances, teachers are attempting to develop the student's "thinking skills" or strategies. We characterize a "thinking skill" as a set of productions; i.e., as procedural knowledge. The procedural knowledge that underlies deliberate thinking is called **controlled** because it is under the conscious control of the thinker.

Controlled procedures contrast with automated procedures in that controlled procedures use a noticeable number of cognitive resources. That is, controlled procedures take up some or all of the capacity of working memory, and thus are said to occupy our consciousness. Obviously, when working memory is being used in this way, only a limited amount of deliberative thinking can occur at any one time. Typically, multiple controlled procedures cannot be used simultaneously. For instance, a person typically cannot balance his checkbook and carry on a conversation simultaneously. The procedures that govern multiple-column addition and subtraction and the procedures that govern listening and talking all require some conscious effort, and the end result is that most people cannot do all these procedures at once.

Controlled procedures and automated procedures have somewhat different characteristics. First, whereas automated procedures operate very quickly, controlled procedures are typically slower and more serial in nature. Consider your procedural knowledge for doing multiple-column addition. While you are probably relatively fast at completing such problems, still each problem takes a noticeable amount of time, and the problem must be completed in a sequential way (i.e., computing and writing the result one column at a time starting with the rightmost column).

A second characteristic that differentiates controlled procedures from automatic ones is that an individual can consciously monitor the former type of procedure but not the latter. For instance, you can attempt to work through an addition problem at different places. You can also scan the problem and determine that if you do not have to carry, you can work from left to right. The point is that the procedure for addition can be adapted to some degree.

A third characteristic that differentiates controlled procedures from automatic ones is that controlled procedures can more often be described verbally. Whereas you cannot express what goes on in your head when you read a sentence, you can describe somewhat accurately the steps you go through during multiple-column addition.

You might be tempted to conclude that since procedural knowledge of a controlled nature is available to conscious inspection and since it is somewhat describable, educators should be very successful at teaching students about the controlled procedures that govern deliberative thinking. Unfortunately, this conclusion does not always seem to be true. While teachers are quite successful at teaching students how to do multiple-column addition, research indicates that teaching "critical thinking" is not very successful (see Glaser, 1984). Exactly why critical-thinking skills are not very susceptible to instruction remains a mystery. It may be that controlled procedures that are domain-specific (like multiple-column addition) are easier to teach because they are well defined and easy to articulate and do not change much from one situation to the next. In contrast, skills like thinking critically, which can apply in any domain, are harder to teach because the procedures that underlie these skills have so many variables that can change, depending on what domain we are

trying to think critically about. Consequently, procedures for critical thinking are hard to teach because the context in which the procedures can be used keeps changing. We will return to this mystery in Chapter 9 when we discuss the acquisition of controlled procedural knowledge, as well as in Chapters 10 and 11.

Remember that automated procedures and controlled procedures represent the two endpoints of a continuum. Much procedural knowledge falls somewhere in between these two extremes and is partially automated and partially controlled. In fact reading skill is really comprised of numerous sets of complicated procedures, some of which are automated and others of which are more controlled. Further, it is important to remember that the automated-controlled continuum is only one of the ways to characterize procedural knowledge. At least one other way to characterize procedural knowledge is by its tie to a particular domain, as we discussed in the previous section. In the next section, we discuss how procedural knowledge can be characterized using both of these dimensions at the same time.

Before turning to that discussion, however, it is important to assess whether you understand the automated-controlled distinction. For the following examples of procedural knowledge, decide whether each is automated or controlled (for you). Compare your answers with those given at the end of the chapter.

6.14 Writing your name.

6.15 Driving a car.

6.16 Solving a geometry proof.

THE RELATION BETWEEN DOMAIN SPECIFICITY AND AUTOMATICITY

Although we have discussed the dimensions of domain generality/domain specificity and degree of automaticity separately, the two dimensions are in fact related to each other. In this section, we briefly introduce this relation. We will return to it in more detail in our discussion of the acquisition of procedural knowledge in Chapter 9.

Procedural knowledge that is specific to a particular domain can vary in the degree to which it is automated. Some domain-specific procedural knowledge may become automated while other domain-specific procedural knowledge may retain a controlled feature. Consider an expert driver as an illustration. Many of the psychomotor procedures that actually control the vehicle are performed without attention. Use of the accelerator, brake, clutch, and steering wheel are all coordinated without apparent mental effort. In contrast, monitoring the other vehicles and attending to the traffic signs require conscious attention. Further, the degree of attention required is a function of how complicated the surrounding environment becomes. Driving in traffic under bad weather conditions in an unfamiliar location demands much more attention than driving on a deserted street in your own neighborhood on a sunny day.

In this book, domain-specific procedural knowledge that has become automated is referred to as **domain-specific basic skill**. In the domain of driving discussed above, for example, we call the psychomotor behaviors that control the vehicle basic driving skills. In any domain where specialized procedures develop, a portion of the procedural knowledge will consist of automated basic skills. These skills can be invoked automatically to complete the unchanging or routine aspects of problems within the domain.

There are other procedures within a domain that retain a controlled or conscious feature. Such procedures have a more strategic quality than do automated procedures. That is, they do not apply to all similar situations in a domain but apply only when a person has a particular goal and various other conditions are met. For instance, in the driving example, the monitoring of other vehicles and traffic signs is done for the purpose of developing and maintaining a safe driving plan. This plan may be thought of as a strategy for driving safely. Another driving strategy might be figuring out the best way to get to a new place by using a map and considering rush hour traffic patterns. Throughout this book, we will refer to instances of this conscious type of domain-specific procedure as **domain-specific strategies**.

Switching away from procedural knowledge that is specific to a particular domain, let us consider domain-general procedural knowledge. Can this type of procedural knowledge be both automated and controlled? Interestingly, most domain-general (or domain independent) procedural knowledge seems to fall near the controlled or conscious end of the automated-controlled continuum (see Figure 6.5). Consequently, we will often refer to instances of this type of procedural knowledge as **domain-general strategies**. Recall that we also called domain-general procedural knowledge "weak methods." Domain-general strategies are general-purpose approaches that are used in a conscious way to solve novel problems, and they are weak because their use does not guarantee a solution. Our initial attempts to solve problems are characterized by the use of these general-purpose strategies.

In closing this discussion of different types of procedural knowledge, two points are worth reiterating. First, it is important to remember that procedural knowledge varies in degree along the two dimensions of domain specificity and automaticity. Second, not all people possess the same procedural knowledge because the acquisition of procedural knowledge depends upon one's experiences.

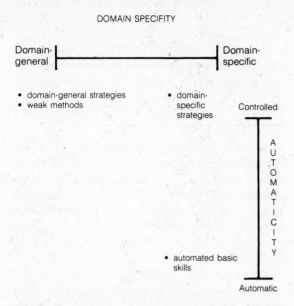

Figure 6.5 Relation between continuum of domain specificity and continuum of automaticity.

Thus, driving skills that have become automated for you (i.e., domain-specific basic skills) may be labor-intensive conscious procedures for a beginning driver.

SIMILARITIES AND DIFFERENCES IN DECLARATIVE AND PROCEDURAL KNOWLEDGE

We have now come to the end of our presentation on the representation of knowledge in long-term memory. In Chapters 4 and 5 we detailed the representational characteristics associated with declarative knowledge and in the current chapter we have discussed how procedural knowledge is represented. Because these chapters are fundamental to the rest of the book, and because they have presented a large amount of new information, it is useful to summarize ways in which declarative and procedural knowledge are the same and different.

Similarity

Although the representational features of declarative and procedural knowledge are quite distinct, both representational systems use economical formats for storing our knowledge and experiences. Declarative knowledge is represented in ways that preserve meaning, temporal order, spatial relations, and/or covariation in the environment. That is, things that often occur together in the environment are often stored together in memory. Procedural knowledge represents the rules that control our behavior. The representations of declarative and procedural knowledge are designed to be economical both in terms of storage in long-term memory and in their flexibility for use within a limited-capacity workspace. In declarative knowledge, for example, networks reduce the burden in working memory by keeping related knowledge accessible. Similarly, images reduce the burden by packing large amounts of spatial information into compact units. Schemas reduce the burden by keeping related perceptual, order, and abstract information together. In procedural knowledge, production systems reduce working memory limitations by (1) controlling the flow of cognition through built-in features and (2) becoming automated. It appears that people have developed ways of representing important information that can function well within the constraints of the human system.

Differences

Form and Function. Although declarative and procedural knowledge are both represented economically, the functions of the representations are quite different, and these different functions lead to unique forms. The function of declarative knowledge is to be available for reflection and for multiple potential uses. Propositions, images, temporal strings, and schemas can be easily manipulated in working memory, allowing for reflection. Moreover, since they provide for close proximity to related information, they facilitate thinking of related ideas, which leads to multiple uses.

The function of procedural knowledge is to provide rapid performance of well-practiced skills. The production form allows for rapid execution of a set of actions under well-specified conditions.

Static versus Dynamic Character. A second characteristic that distinguishes between declarative and procedural knowledge is the dynamic character of procedural knowledge. Declarative knowledge is static in that it cannot be activated until a production fires. Once a production fires, for example a retrieval production, then activity is generated in the declarative knowledge base. This activation spreads until the goal of the production is achieved (i.e., the to-be-retrieved information is found) or until the activity is depleted. Then if a new search is to be initiated, another production must fire to initiate it.

In contrast to declarative knowledge, procedural knowledge is dynamic. It puts "action" into the system. This action can be for the purpose of information retrieval, as we described above, or it can be for the purpose of transforming information. For example, the result of "doing" the problem $286 \div 2$ is 143. The input information ($286 \div 2$) has been transformed to produce an output (143) that looks different from the input. Another example would be the product that results from a series of procedures that a teacher might execute to generate a lesson plan to teach reading. The input information ("I need to get a lesson ready for tomorrow's reading class. The students are having trouble with the 'ch'

sound.") would be transformed to produce an output—a lesson plan—that looks quite different from the input. Thus, procedural knowledge is used to operate on information to transform it. These examples illustrate how the productions that underlie procedural knowledge actually "produce" behavior.

Rate of Acquisition. Declarative and procedural knowledge are acquired at different rates. Basic units of declarative knowledge may be encoded and stored in long-term memory after a single exposure or encounter with the information. Schemas take somewhat longer to develop than do basic units of declarative knowledge, but nonetheless they can be acquired at a fairly rapid rate. In contrast, procedural knowledge is acquired slowly. A student does not learn to do multiple-column addition after attempting one problem. Rather, the algorithm is built over time and usually by incrementally increasing the complexity of the problems. In fact, a number of researchers have suggested that it can take as many as 10,000 practice trials to fully automate complex cognitive procedures, although the rate of improvement diminishes considerably over time (Anderson, 1990). Thus, extended practice and experience govern the acquisition of procedural knowledge.

There are very good reasons why declarative and procedural knowledge are acquired at different rates. Perhaps the most notable is that the two types of knowledge have very different impacts on an individual's survival. Declarative knowledge can be learned quickly because it does not produce or control behavior directly. On the other hand, procedural knowledge does in fact control and produce behavior. Thus, the cognitive system should be cautious in the way it acquires the knowledge that ultimately has control over it. Imagine the different consequences for learning incorrect declarative information versus learning incorrect procedures. Your survival would probably not be jeopardized if you erroneously stored the fact, *George Washington was the third president of the United States.* However, if you automated a production that told you to cross the street when the traffic light is red, you might not be around to correct the erroneous procedure.

Modifiability of Knowledge. The rate of acquisition of knowledge is tied to its modifiability. Since the cost of learning basic units of declarative knowledge is relatively low (i.e., they can be acquired relatively quickly), basic units of declarative knowledge can be modified easily. Thus, propositional information, images, and temporal strings can be added, reorganized, and corrected without too much difficulty. Of course, there are sometimes difficulties with modifying declarative knowledge, once elaborated schemas have been constructed. For example, science teachers report that students are very resistant to modifying or correcting misconceptions of conceptual models.

With respect to procedural knowledge, it is only easy to modify productions in the early stages of acquisition. Once a set of productions has been built by the memory system, it is difficult to modify. Further, once a procedure becomes automated, it is virtually impossible to change. Again, good reasons exist for this difference. Once the cognitive system is ready to relinquish control to a piece of procedural knowledge that has been acquired, the system should not have to change or modify the procedure. Rather, you should be able to count on the fact that this piece of knowledge is correct and will produce the desirable behavior every time. The issues of acquisition rate and modifiability of procedures are important. We will return to them again in Chapter 9 (Acquisition of Procedural Knowledge) and Chapter 10 (Problem Solving and Reasoning).

INTERACTIONS OF DECLARATIVE AND PROCEDURAL KNOWLEDGE

Declarative and procedural knowledge interact in a variety of ways during learning and problem solving. You will encounter many examples of these interactions throughout the rest of this book. Figure 6.6 shows a general model for the interaction of procedural and declarative knowledge.

As can be seen in that figure, working memory is the medium through which the interaction of procedural and declarative knowledge takes place. You are already familiar with the notions of retrieval and storage, the processes whereby declarative knowledge goes in and out of working memory. **Matching,** like the pattern-matching process introduced in Chapter 3, occurs when all of the conditions required by a production are simultaneously active in working memory. This causes the production to **execute,** which often results in changing the contents of working memory, as is signified by the arrow from production memory to working memory.

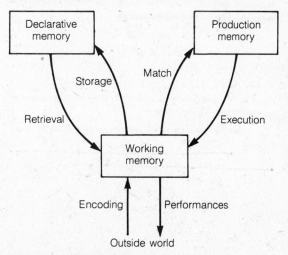

Figure 6.6 The interaction of declarative and procedural knowledge. (adapted from J.R. Anderson, 1983.)

You have already seen several examples in which production sets require some specific pieces of declarative knowledge in order to continue executing. For instance, turn back to Table 6.2, which shows a simple production set for paragraph comprehension. P_2 in that set has one action "find topic sentence." The ideas from the topic sentence of the current paragraph are likely to be represented in propositional form. Thus for P_2 to execute it must find some pieces of declarative knowledge.

Productions typically require data from declarative knowledge to continue executing. This type of interaction occurs in routine problem solving. Two other kinds of interaction between declarative and procedural knowledge occur (1) when declarative knowledge is used to build new productions (which you will learn about in Chapter 9) and (2) when domain-general procedural knowledge such as weak methods are used to build new schemas (which you will learn about in Chapter 8).

CHAPTER SUMMARY

Procedural knowledge is represented in long-term memory by productions. A production is a rule of the IF-THEN form. The clauses in the IF portion of the rule state the conditions that must exist for the rule to apply, and the clauses in the THEN portion state what action(s) to execute when the conditions are met. Thus, a production is sometimes called a condition-action rule.

Productions combine to form sets or systems. A production system represents knowledge of a complex procedure. Productions within a set are interrelated to one another. The actions of one production in the set create the conditions that exist in other productions in the set. In some cases, the action will create a declarative structure. In other cases, the action will create a subgoal that must be achieved. Thus, one fundamental feature of a production system is that it contains a goal-subgoal hierarchy that interrelates all of the productions. Control of cognition flows throughout the productions within a set as the conditions of each production are met.

Procedural knowledge can be classified with regard to at least two dimensions. One dimension describes the degree to which the knowledge is tied to a particular domain or is general across domains. Domain-general procedural knowledge represents general-purpose or weak methods. Domain-specific procedural knowledge applies only in very specific situations. It is very powerful, but it is very constrained in its applicability. The second dimension describes the degree to which procedural knowledge is automated or controlled. Automated procedural knowledge operates without awareness and consumes almost no cognitive resources. Controlled procedural knowledge occupies our consciousness, consumes cognitive resources, and thus operates in a noticeably serial or sequential manner. Domain-specific procedural knowledge can be either automated or controlled. Automated domain-specific procedures are called automated basic skills, whereas controlled domain-specific procedures are referred to as domain-specific strategies. Domain-general procedural knowledge tends to be controlled or conscious in character.

Although declarative and procedural knowledge are both represented economically, the two types of knowledge can be distinguished on the basis of several characteristics. Declarative knowledge is represented as propositions, images, temporal strings, and schemas. It represents knowledge that something is the case. It is static. It is acquired rapidly and thus can be modified relatively easily. In contrast, procedural knowledge is represented as productions. It represents knowledge of how to do something. It is dynamic. It is acquired slowly over time and with extended practice, and once automated it is very difficult to modify.

ADDITIONAL READINGS

The following handbooks have chapters that review production systems:

Barr, A., & Feigenbaum, E.A. (Eds.) (1982). *The handbook of artificial intelligence, vol. 2.* Los Altos, CA: William Kaufmann.

Cohen, P.R., & Feigenbaum, E.A. (Eds.) (1982). *The handbook of artificial intelligence, vol. 3.* Los Altos, CA: William Kaufmann.

Another review of production systems is in:

Waterman, D.A., & Hayes-Roth, F. (Eds.) (1978). *Pattern-directed inference systems.* New York: Academic Press.

A specific example of a production system can be found in:

Anderson, J.R., Kline, P.J., & Lewis, C.H. (1977). A production system model of language processing. In M.A. Just, & P.A. Carpenter (Eds.), *Cognitive processes in comprehension*, (pp. 271–311). Hillsdale, NJ: Lawrence Erlbaum Associates.

ANSWERS TO EXERCISES

6.1 P_2 has three condition clauses, two action clauses, and five total clauses.

6.2 As stated P_2 is more complex because it has more clauses.

6.3 P_2, the TRIANGLE production, leads to non-directed behavior because it lacks a goal clause.

6.4 Any time a person encounters or recognizes a figure consistent with the conditions, the person will make a mental classification and blurt out "triangle." This inappropriate behavior might happen, for example, when a person looks at the roof-line of a house.

6.5 The productions should have a condition clause like:

IF   The goal is to recognize a figure as a triangle

6.6 P_2 because both conditions are satisfied.

6.7 None of the productions will be executed. All of the productions have a condition that states that the reader must have the goal of comprehending. Since Barry does not have that goal, the condition will not be satisfied.

6.8 Stating the topic sentence is most observable.

6.9 P_2 is most complex because it has five clauses.

6.10 P_4 will apply because both conditions are met.

6.11 Control will be transferred to P_2 because the action of P_4 produces the condition required for P_2.

6.12 $P_4 \rightarrow P_2 \rightarrow P_1 \rightarrow P_3$

6.13 $P_1 \rightarrow P_2 \rightarrow P_6 \rightarrow P_{10} \rightarrow P_7 \rightarrow P_{10} \rightarrow P_7$
$P_{11} \rightarrow P_9 \rightarrow P_3 \rightarrow P_6 \rightarrow P_{10} \rightarrow P_7 \rightarrow P_{10}$
$P_7 \rightarrow P_{10} \rightarrow P_9 \rightarrow P_3 \rightarrow P_6 \rightarrow P_{10} \rightarrow P_7$
$P_{10} \rightarrow P_7 \rightarrow P_{11} \rightarrow P_9 \rightarrow P_5 \rightarrow$ Stop.

6.14 For most people, writing a name is fairly automated, especially the spelling, letter formation, and fine motor coordination.

6.15 Driving has automated components (e.g., controlling the speed and direction) and controlled components (e.g., monitoring another driver's car).

6.16 This type of problem-solving is largely controlled.

Knowledge Acquisition

Not much more than a generation ago, many psychologists thought that some unitary process accounted for all of learning, be it learning to press a button, to say one's name, or to use language. Robert M. Gagne was perhaps the first psychologist to make a cogent case for the notion that not all knowledge was learned in the same way, and the first to systematize a diverse range of research on human learning. In the first edition of his ground-breaking book, *The Conditions of Learning* (1965), he identified eight varieties of learning that were distinguished both by the outcome of learning and the conditions required to produce this outcome. In the fourth edition of this book (1985), Gagne described five types of "learned capabilities" and the different conditions required for learning each.

In keeping with the view that different types of knowledge have different conditions for learning, we describe in this section the ways in which propositions, schemas, and procedures are learned. In Chapter 7, we describe the acquisition and recall of propositions. In Chapter 8, we describe the formation and refinement of schemas. And in Chapter 9, we describe the stages in the acquisition of skill.

The educational implications of these chapters are rich. We hope that you will use the information contained herein to reflect on your own learning and teaching and perhaps come up with new insights.

Chapter 7

Acquisition and Retrieval of Propositions: Learning the Basic Units of Meaning

SUMMARY

1. A person's declarative knowledge can be conceptualized as large networks of interrelated basic and integrated units. A basic perceptual unit may be a linear ordering or an image. A basic unit of meaning is a **proposition.** Basic units of all types may integrate to form schemas.

2. Only a few units in the declarative network are active in working memory at any given time. **Spread of activation** is the process whereby activation spreads from an active unit to the units that are closest to it. As activation spreads, the initially active unit becomes inactive.

3. New declarative knowledge units are acquired as a result of **construction** processes. When construction processes are executed, the result is that new knowledge units are stored or deposited in declarative memory.

4. **Elaboration** processes are procedures that generate new ideas that are related to the ideas being received from external sources.

5. **Organization** processes are procedures that divide sets of information into subsets and indicate the relationships among the subsets of knowledge.

6. During **retrieval,** the internal representation of the question activates knowledge related to the question. Activation spreads in the declarative knowledge network until an answer to the question is found.

7. If an answer cannot be retrieved, one can be constructed by bringing inferential processes to bear on activated knowledge so that a plausible answer is generated.

8. Elaborations generated at the time of learning new information can facilitate retrieval by providing alternative pathways for spread of activation. Even if spread of activation fails to find an answer, elaborations generated at the time of learning can still be useful at retrieval because they can facilitate construction by providing more information for inferring an answer.

9. Organization during learning aids in later retrieval of information by providing effective retrieval cues.

In Chapters 4 and 5, you learned that our declarative knowledge is comprised of all the facts, generalizations, and theories that we have ever stored in long-term memory. In addition, it is a record of all the personal events that we have experienced and our personal likes and dislikes. Declarative knowledge is knowledge that something is the case.

You also learned that propositions are a basic form of representation of declarative knowledge and that one proposition corresponds roughly to one idea. In many teaching contexts, a major goal is for students to acquire a new set of propositions. Unfortunately, students sometimes seem to resist acquiring new propositions. They may claim that it is too "theoretical," that it will not help them get jobs, that it is "irrelevant," or that it is just plain boring. This resistance seems to slow down the learning process or give it a cynical quality in the sense that students memorize information for tests and make no attempt to assimilate it meaningfully. In this chapter, one question we will try to answer is: "How do new sets of propositions get into declarative memory?"

Besides the obstacle of the initial learning of information, an even greater obstacle seems to be the later retrieval of information. For example, of all the information you learned in tenth-grade history, how much do you think

you could recall now? Recalling previously learned information becomes increasingly difficult over time. Thus, a second question we will address in this chapter is: "What can teachers do to help students remember information so that they can retrieve it and use it when they need to?"

Both the acquisition and the retrieval of information pose challenges for educators. Near the end of this chapter we will discuss two processes—**elaboration** (adding to information) and **organization** (structuring information)—that have been found to aid both acquisition and retrieval. However, first we must look at some theoretical assumptions about the structure and dynamics of declarative memory and about acquisition and retrieval processes. These assumptions provide a basis for understanding how elaboration and organization processes work.

THE STRUCTURE AND DYNAMICS OF MEMORY

Memory Structure

There are many possible views of how long-term memory is structured. Klatzky (1980) describes a variety of views. The point of view presented here is consistent with a great deal of evidence, and it is at a level of detail that is useful for educators. It is based on J.R. Anderson's (1983) theory.

In this point of view one assumes that all of an individual's declarative knowledge is represented in a network form. We introduced the concept of the propositional network in Chapter 4. Now that you have learned about all the types of declarative knowledge—linear orderings, images, propositions, and schemas—we will generalize the idea of a network to include all of declarative knowledge. As with the propositional network, the declarative knowledge network has a node-link structure. However, now the nodes consist of *any* declarative memory unit, not just concepts or propositions.

Figure 7.1 is a schematic representation of a declarative knowledge network. The small circles represent basic-level units—either a proposition or an image or a linear order. For example, in the figure, the propositions [igneous rocks are hard] and [I hate peas] are highlighted. Also highlighted are an image of a supply and demand curve and a linear order that represents the days of the week. The large circles represent schemas that contain within them several basic-level units. For example, in Figure 7.1, the schema for dog is noted.

The two important points that are illustrated by this figure are (1) all four types of declarative knowledge reside within the network, and (2) all the memory units within the network are linked together. This linking is important for the **spread of activation** principle to operate, and it is to this principle that we now turn. Remember that this image of declarative knowledge is a conceptual convenience. The anatomical basis of memory probably will be found to look quite different from what we have presented here. However, some functional properties of the anatomical system will probably match the functional properties of the conceptual system.

In this chapter, you will learn about how propositions get into memory, and how they are retrieved. Less is known about how basic perceptual units like images get into memory. There is currently an interesting debate in psychology about how people learn to recognize perceptual patterns. Although people are very good at recognizing perceptual patterns (such as faces, for example), it has proved to be extremely difficult to teach a computer to perform this seemingly simple task. The difficulty in simulating this type of human behavior has led cognitive psychologists, brain scientists, and educators to conclude that learning to recognize perceptual patterns is apparently much more complicated than was originally thought. Since the nature of this debate is highly technical, we will not discuss it here (for a summary of the issue, see Bereiter, 1991). Because the acquisition of propositional information is of particular importance to educators, we will discuss this topic in some detail. You will learn about the acquisition and retention of schemas in the next chapter.

Activity Levels in the Declarative Knowledge Network

According to several theories of cognition, nodes and links in a network structure have varying levels of activity (J.R. Anderson, 1983). At any given time the vast majority of nodes and links are inactive. This inactive portion of the network is the declarative knowledge portion of the long-term memory store. The few nodes and links that are active at any specific time are, phenomenally, a portion of what you are thinking about at that moment. They are your old, rather than new, knowledge. For example, if you read the sentence

There are tornado warnings in Ohio today.

the information asserted in this sentence is new. However, as you read the sentence, it may make you think of the meanings of the words in the sentence and of other related

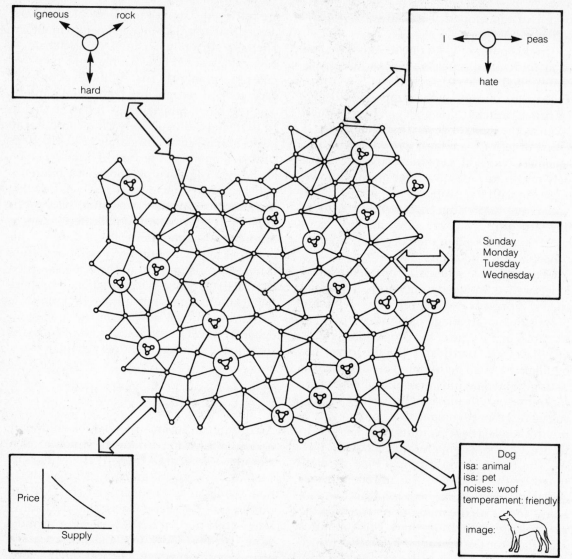

Figure 7.1 The declarative knowledge network. Each memory unit (indicated by a circle) is connected to other memory units. Larger circles represent schemas that embed smaller memory units within them. Smaller circles represent linear orderings, images, and propositions.

information such as that your uncle lives in Ohio. These word meanings and related thoughts are old knowledge. This old knowledge is activated in your declarative network when you read the example sentence.

Working memory is the crucible in which new knowledge is added to old knowledge. Thus one part of working memory (the old knowledge) is comprised of that small part of the network that is active. Another part is new knowledge that is currently being constructed.

Spread of Activation

How is the activity level of nodes and links determined? Before considering a general answer to this question, let us first consider the specific example shown in Figure 7.2. Suppose that at time T_1 you are thinking "I like chocolate pies." That is, the propositions [I like pies] and [the pies are chocolate] are active at T_1 (activity is signified by squiggly lines). Activation spreads along all the links of these propositions to related propositions, such as [pies are made with cream]. (In addition, acti-

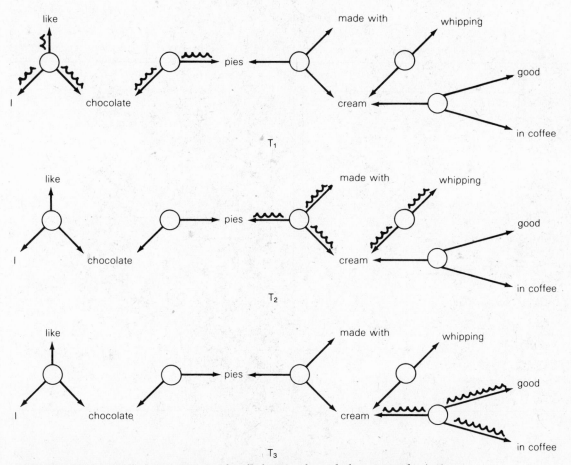

Figure 7.2 The spread of activation in the declarative knowledge network. Active propositions are indicated by squiggly lines along links. At time T_1, the propositions [I like pies] and [pies are chocolate] are active. Activation spreads to related propositions such that at time T_2, the propositions [pies are made with cream] and [cream is whipping cream] are active, and at T_3 [cream is good in coffee] is active. Previously activated propositions become inactive due to limited-capacity working memory.

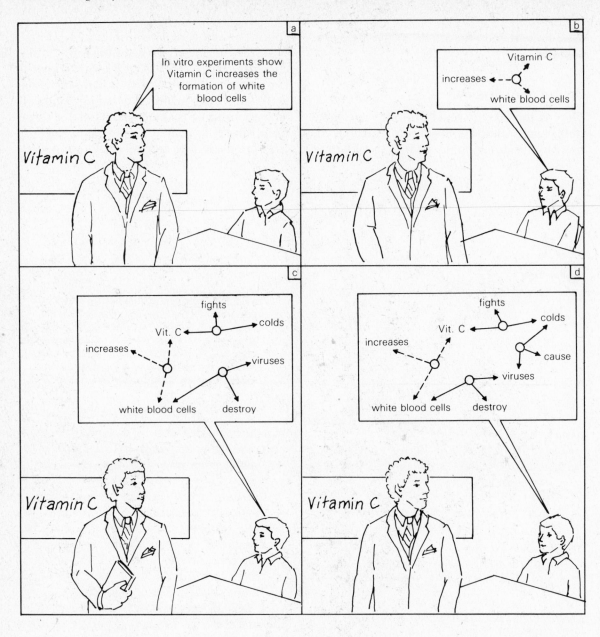

vation spreads to image units representing our perceptual knowledge of pies as well, even though perceptual units or images are not shown in this figure.) Since working memory can hold only a few active units at once, the propositions that were active at T_1 will no longer be active at T_2, but some of the propositions that were inactive at T_1 will now be active. Activation once again spreads along all the links in the active propositions such as

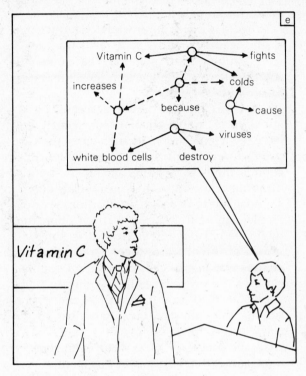

Figure 7.3 The steps in acquisition of new declarative knowledge: (a) New knowledge is presented. (b) It is translated into propositions. (c–d) Related propositions in long-term memory are activated. (e) Elaborations are added. (New propositions are signified by broken lines, and old propositions are signified by solid lines.)

[cream is good in coffee]. At T_3 it is this proposition that is active; the propositions that were active at T_2 have become inactive.

To generalize, spread of activation is the process whereby a given active node-link structure passes activation along to related node-link structures. We are most aware of a spread-of-activation process in free association. However, spread of activation underlies many other thought processes as well.

ACQUISITION OF NEW PROPOSITIONS

The example in Figure 7.2 showed how activation might spread through an existing network as you thought about chocolate pies. However, what happens when you want to add new propositions to the network? New propositions are acquired when they are stored with related units in the knowledge network. They are deposited in the declarative network as a result of the execution of acquisition procedures (productions). Figure 7.3 shows a typical squence of events during acquisition. In panel (a) the teacher states, "In vitro experiments show Vitamin C increases the formation of white blood cells." In panel (b) the student has translated (in working memory) the sounds of the teacher's words into a proposition. This proposition is shown with dashed lines to signify that it is new for the student. The concepts in the proposition (e.g., white blood cells, Vitamin C, etc.) cue the retrieval of related knowledge. That is, activation spreads from *Vitamin C* to the idea that *Vitamin C fights colds* and from *form white blood cells* to the idea that *white blood cells destroy viruses*. This state is shown in panel (c) in which the student has a new proposition and two old propositions active in working memory. In panel (d) spread of activation from *colds* and *viruses* leads to the activation of the proposition that *viruses cause colds*. With this particular set of propositions active in working memory, the student's inference-making processes (stored as sets of productions or procedures) may draw the inference that *Vitamin C fights colds because it increases the formation of white blood cells*. This inference, shown in panel (e), is another new proposition.

This final idea was not an idea from long-term memory or an idea presented by an external stimulus. Rather it resulted from thinking processes. This type of new proposition is called an **elaboration** because it adds information to the incoming information. The elaboration learning process results in the generation of elaborative propositions.

This example illustrates some important principles about acquisition of propositions.

1. New propositions cue the retrieval of related prior knowledge through spread of activation.

2. The new propositions and the prior knowledge may stimulate the student's generation of other new propositions. (This process is called **elaboration**).

3. All the new propositions (both those presented by the environment and those generated by the learner) are stored close to the related prior knowledge that was activated during learning.

Meaningfulness

Notice that the steps in acquisition of propositions make no provision for learning totally meaningless information. This is because a requisite for learning is that some connection (some meaning) be established between new

and prior knowledge. In Figure 7.3, the term *in vitro* did not activate any related knowledge in the learner's network. It also was never stored in long-term memory. That is, its failure to generate a connection led to its being lost from the system.

Yet it is easy to think of cases in which students learn information for which they have few connections. In such cases they are probably connecting the new sequence of sounds they are hearing to known sounds. Thus the propositions they form relate only to sounds, not to conceptual meanings. For example, Figure 7.4 shows a proposition that might be created for *in vitro*. It is simply a record of the fact that a certain sequence of sounds was heard. This proposition is stored close to the procedures for producing these sounds or close to the perceptual unit representing the sound, rather than close to the conceptual knowledge about *in vitro*. As we shall see presently, it is difficult to retrieve information that is stored in this manner.

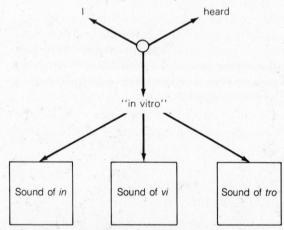

Figure 7.4 A possible propositional representation for information that is conceptually meaningless. The learner records the event of hearing certain sounds in a proposition. This proposition is then connected to productions for each of the sounds.

If all learning of propositions is meaningful (requires connecting new and old knowledge), how do infants store their first proposition? Just as adults store conceptually meaningless ideas by connecting them to sounds, infants store their earliest propositions by connecting them to perceptual units (such as images) and motor procedures. When the perceptual units and motor procedures are activated by input from the environment, they cue the retrieval of these early propositions. When two or more propositions sharing an idea are generated, they will be interconnected, starting the formation of a declarative knowledge network. From then on, although sensations and actions will still cue the retrieval of declarative knowledge, related meaningful knowledge units or propositions will also begin to cue one another.

In summary, meaning is inherent in connections between parts of the knowledge structure. Learning of declarative knowledge is synonymous with the creation of meaning. When no meaning (no connections) can be created, little is learned.

As we shall see later in this chapter, there are many degrees of meaningfulness depending on both the number and type of connections that are formed between new and prior knowledge. And it is true, as most educators well know, that more meaningful information is better learned and better retained.

Knowledge Acquisition and Limited-Capacity Working Memory

The set of procedures that comprise the knowledge acquisition process described earlier, in which new information is connected to old information, takes up space in working memory. This set of procedures also takes time to execute. H. Simon (1974) has estimated that each new bit of information takes ten seconds to process so that it can be stored in long-term memory. These observations

have some interesting implications, including a partial explanation for why even the most conscientious of students seem to forget information that they have just been told.

Consider, in information-processing terms, all that is going on during a lecture. A typical speech rate for lectures is 150 words per minute. Let us assume that an average proposition is formed from five words. Therefore, students are being bombarded with thirty propositions per minute. Of course, some of the units are not crucial, because they are either already known to the learner or simply provide a context for the main ideas in the lecture. So let us assume that only half of the thirty propositions are new and important. Therefore, the hope is that students will store fifteen new knowledge units per minute. But H. Simon's work suggests that the student will store only six new units per minute. Furthermore, if students are actively elaborating on new propositions, this may slow them down to a rate of one unit per minute! Thus it is no wonder that students sometimes seem to forget what a teacher has just stated. In fact, they never stored it to begin with. Sometimes the most thoughtful and creative students seem to forget the most. This may be because their working memories are filled with elaborations to one idea that was presented and hence ideas that follow this one in the lecture are never even represented in their working memories.

RETRIEVAL AND CONSTRUCTION OF PROPOSITIONS

Figure 7.5 shows in flowchart form how retrieval proceeds in the human information-processing system. An episode of retrieval often starts when someone asks us a question or when we read a question (for example, in a test booklet). However, another initiator of retrieval is an internally produced query to ourselves, which may occur when we are

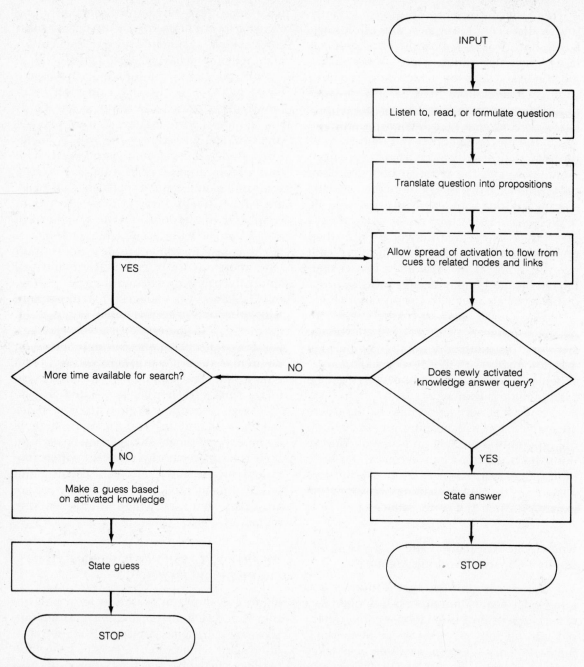

Figure 7.5 An information-processing analysis of retrieval and construction.

solving a problem and need some previously stored information. If the question comes from an external source, it must first be translated into propositions. Once this has been done, the concept labels in the representation will activate associated declarative knowledge. Then the activated knowledge will be examined to see if it answers the question. If it does, it will be translated into speech (or into motor patterns if the answer is written) and output to the environment. If the knowledge does not answer the question, then the search will continue by letting activation spread further until another knowledge unit is activated for consideration as a possible answer. If, on the other hand, there is no time for further search, then the individual may make an "educated" guess that is consistent with the available knowledge. The majority of steps in this process occur unconsciously; awareness is involved primarily at the point at which the activated knowledge is judged to see if it answers the question.

The learning episode shown in Figure 7.3 can be used to illustrate the retrieval process. Panel (e) in that figure shows the learner's knowledge structure at the end of the episode. Suppose that the day after this episode, the teacher asks, "What effect does Vitamin C have on white blood cells?" The retrieval procedure will start as the learner translates the sounds in the question into propositions. The concepts of *white blood cells* and *Vitamin C* will then be activated in the network, and activation will spread from these concepts to related ones. As can be seen in Figure 7.6, the first knowledge that will be activated is the proposition [Vitamin C increases white blood cells]. It will be first because activation is spreading from two sides of the proposition and when it meets in the middle, the entire proposition is active. For other propositions, activation is spreading from only one side; hence it must go twice as far and therefore takes longer to activate the entire proposition. Since [Vitamin C increases white blood cells] is activated first, it will be the first knowledge unit to be judged for its adequacy in answering the question. It does in fact answer the question of how Vitamin C affects white blood cells, so it will be translated into speech sounds and stated.

What happens when a learner either fails to store the fact that is being queried or has difficulty finding it? Quite often she can construct the necessary information from knowledge that was stored (F.C. Bartlett, 1932; Reder, 1979; Spiro, 1977). Suppose, for example, that a learner failed to store the proposition [Vitamin C increases white blood cells]. She did, however, store her elaboration that *Vitamin C cures colds because of its effect on white blood cells*, as is shown in Figure 7.7 (p. 129). When asked what Vitamin C's effect is on white blood cells, spread of activation will lead from *Vitamin C* and *white blood cells* to the propositions: [white blood cells destroy viruses], [Vitamin C fights colds because of its effect on white blood cells], and [colds are caused by viruses]. With this information active in working memory, the learner can use logical procedures to deduce that *Vitamin C must increase white blood cells*.

In summary, retrieval and construction of declarative knowledge both depend on spread of activation. In retrieval, activation spreads from the cues to the to-be-recalled information. In construction, activation spreads from the cues to related information and logical processes operate on this information to generate an answer. Now that we have talked about the structure and dynamics of memory and about the acquisition and retrieval processes, let us look at how two processes—**elaboration** and **organization**—aid acquisition and retrieval.

ELABORATION

Elaboration is the process of adding to the information being learned. The addition could

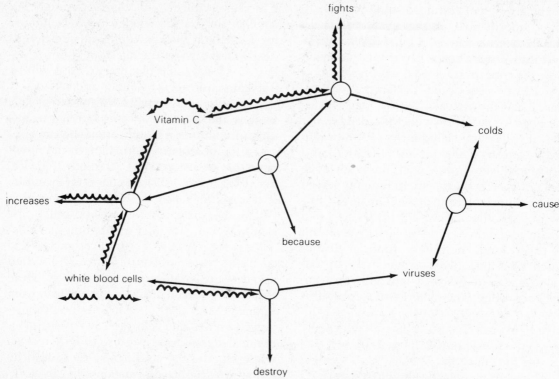

Figure 7.6 Spread of activation during retrieval. With the question, "What effect does Vitamin C have on white blood cells?" *Vitamin C* and *white blood cells* are activated. Activation spreads down all links associated with these concepts, as is indicated by squiggly lines. The first proposition to become fully activated (because activation is spreading to it from two directions) is the proposition that Vitamin C increases white blood cells.

be an inference, a continuation, an example, a detail, an image, or anything else that serves to connect information. Suppose that you were reading a story containing the following sentences:

> *Tim wanted a new model airplane. He saw the change lying on his father's dresser.*

Try to observe your thoughts as you read these sentences. Are you elaborating? Reder's elaborations to those sentences (1976, p. 394) were "Tim is about 8 to 12, has a crew cut; the father's dresser is just at Tim's eye level; the model airplane is silver with chevron decals;

the father is the absent-minded type who would not notice the change missing but who would be furious if he found out his son took it." Some of these elaborations may be represented as propositions in your declarative network, while others may be represented as images.

There is a great deal of evidence that people often generate elaborations for new information that they are learning. One type of evidence is the time it takes to comprehend material that stimulates different amounts of elaboration. For example, these two sentences—"*We checked the picnic supplies. The beer was*

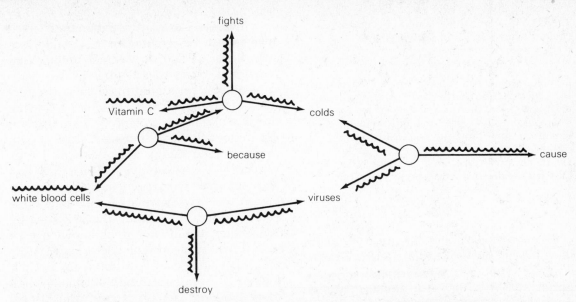

Figure 7.7 Construction of declarative knowledge from partial knowledge. This learner did not store the fact that Vitamin C increases white blood cells. However, when asked, "What is the effect of Vitamin C on white blood cells?" the learner can deduce the answer from related knowledge that is activated. Premise 1: White blood cells destroy viruses that cause colds. Premise 2: Vitamin C fights colds by affecting white blood cells. Conclusion: Vitamin C increases white blood cells.

warm."—stimulate the inference (elaboration) that the beer was among the picnic supplies. By contrast, the two sentences—"*We got some beer out of the car. The beer was warm.*"—do not require production of an inference because the repetition of *beer* in the two sentences makes an explicit connection. Since the formation of elaborations takes time, it should take longer for people to comprehend a pair of sentences that require an elaboration to put them together than to comprehend a pair that doesn't have this requirement.

Haviland and Clark (1974) tested this hypothesis by presenting to research participants pairs of sentences (including those given in the preceding paragraph) that did or did not require "bridging inferences." The participants' task was to press a button when they felt that comprehension of the two sentences was complete. Average comprehen-

sion time for pairs of sentences requiring inferences was 1016 milliseconds, whereas average time to comprehend pairs not requiring inferences was 835 milliseconds. These data suggest that learners elaborate when certain assumptions are left implicit in a text or lecture.

Another type of evidence for elaboration comes from research participants' free recall protocols following the presentation of some new information. Such protocols often include some information that was not presented along with information that was presented. Recall the Bower, Black, and Turner (1979) experiments described in Chapter 5 in the section on event schemas. Bower et al. had students read short stories such as the one shown in Table 7.1 about "Going to the Doctor." All of the stories were about familiar events that clearly are a part of almost every-

Table 7.1 A story with a familiar event sequence (from Bower, Black, and Turner, 1979).

___

THE DOCTOR

John was feeling bad today so he decided to go see the family doctor. He checked in with the doctor's receptionist, and then looked through several medical magazines that were on the table by his chair. Finally the nurse came and asked him to take off his clothes. The doctor was very nice to him. He eventually prescribed some pills for John. Then John left the doctor's office and headed home.

___

one's prior knowledge and hence available for use in elaboration when new related knowledge is encountered. If participants elaborate on the stories as they read them, they may recall these elaborations when asked to recall the story.

When the students in the Bower et al. (1979) study recalled the stories, about 20% of what was recalled were elaborations rather than information explicitly stated in the stories. For example, the "Doctor" story did not state that John entered the doctor's office, nor did it state that the nurse checked John's blood pressure and weight. Yet some students wrote these ideas down in their recall protocols. These data suggest that the students elaborated on the stories as they were reading them and used their own prior knowledge about visits to the doctor to construct a plausible account of John's visit. They used their knowledge of event schemas to generate elaborations.

The Role of Elaboration in Retrieval and Construction

Elaboration facilitates retrieval in two ways. First, it provides alternate retrieval pathways along which activation can spread (J.R. Anderson, 1976; 1983). So if one pathway is somehow blocked, others are available. Sec-

ond, it provides extra information from which answers can be constructed (J.R. Anderson, 1983; Reder, 1982b), as was seen in the "Vitamin C and colds" example described earlier.

Contrast, for example, the memory structures of Student 1 and Student 2 following their reading of the sentence: "Political action committees (PACs) influence Congress with money." (See Figure 7.8.) Student 1 was watching TV while studying. Thus, there was no room in her working memory for elaborating on the new information. She did, however, succeed in encoding the new idea by connecting it with her prior knowledge of what a political action committee is: [a PAC is a group whose goal is to influence policy]. Student 2 was not watching TV. Thus, she had more working memory space available for elaboration. While she read, she activated her prior knowledge of what a political action committee is and, in addition, elaborated on the new information by thinking [The National Rifle Association has a PAC.]. Thus, Student 2's knowledge structure surrounding the new idea in memory is more elaborate than Student 1's.

Now suppose that the following day the teacher of these students asks, "What do political action committees do?" and is expecting the answer: "PACs influence Congress with money." Both students use PAC as a retrieval cue to start spread of activation. For Student 1 there are two pathways by which activation can reach the desired answer; one goes directly to the propositions that [PACs are groups] [whose goal is to influence policy]. Once the concept *influence* is activated, activation spreads to the proposition that [PACs influence Congress with money].

Student 2 has the same two pathways and also a third one moving from *PAC* to the left to the propositions that [NRA has a PAC], [NRA is a group], [the group has the goal of influencing policy], and thence to [PACs influence Congress with money]. Thus Student 2 has

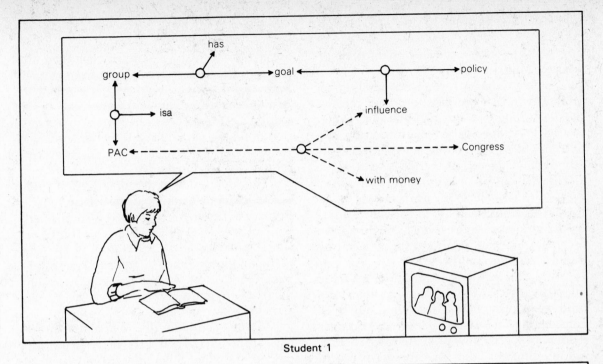

Student 1

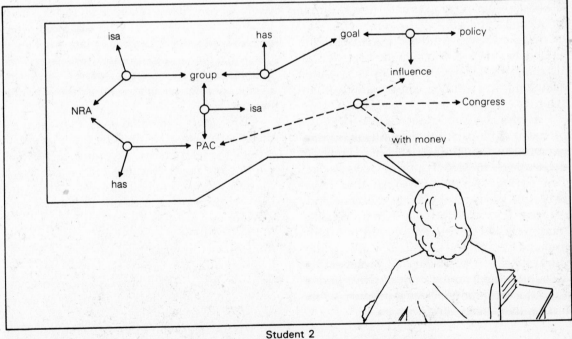

Student 2

Figure 7.8 Encoding of the new proposition that PACs influence Congress with money. (New propositions are indicated by broken lines, old ones by solid lines.) Student 1 attaches the new proposition to relevant prior knowledge, but does not elaborate. Student 2 attaches the new proposition to relevant prior knowledge and also elaborates on it.

three ways to retrieve the desired information whereas Student 1 has only two.

Student 2 has a further advantage over Student 1 in that even if she cannot retrieve the desired answer, she might be able to infer what a PAC does from her elaboration that NRA has a PAC. To do this, she might activate other knowledge about the NRA such as the fact that the NRA tries to influence gun control votes through the lobbying activities of its PAC. This would lead her to guess that PACs try to influence votes, which might be an acceptable answer to the question "What do political action committees do?"

Student 1 has less to go on in trying to guess an answer. She might guess that PACs influence policy, but a teacher might well consider this an unacceptable answer because it does not specify how PACs influence policy. Because Student 1 did not elaborate as much, she has less information to use in constructing an adequate answer.

In summary, Student 2's elaboration helped her in two ways: (1) it provided an alternate retrieval path and (2) it provided useful information for constructing an answer.

A large body of research can be interpreted as demonstrating the value of elaborative processing in the acquisition and recall of declarative knowledge (for reviews see E. Gagne, 1978; Wittrock, 1989.) Another framework that has been applied to the same body of research is called the "depth of processing" framework, a discussion of which can be found in Cermak and Craik (1979). J.R. Anderson and Reder (1979) argue that an elaboration account of the learning of declarative knowledge is more quantifiable and predictive than is a depth-of-processing account.

Types of Elaboration

Although almost any elaborative processing is better than none, elaborations vary, and some are more effective as retrieval cues than are others. Effective elaborations tie together parts of the propositions that one wants to remember or stimulate adequate recall of the learning context. Less effective elaborations do not tie the parts of the to-be-remembered propositions together and do not stimulate recall of the learning context (Reder, 1982a).

This idea was first demonstrated in studies of learning of "paired associates" (e.g., Rohwer & Levin, 1968). Paired associates are pairs of verbal stimuli—either words or nonsense syllables—that are rather arbitrarily paired (e.g., cow-shoe). The research participant's task is to learn the pairs so that given the first item in the pair (cow) as a cue, he can retrieve the second item (shoe).

In one such study (A. Wang, 1983), college students learned lists of twelve noun pairs to the point where they could recall all twelve second items when given the first item in each pair as a cue. The students were encouraged to think of an association between items in a pair and to produce "one word that is related to the picture, story, sentence, rhyme, or relationship" used to associate the items.

The words generated were then used by the experimenters to infer the types of elaborations the learners were forming. For example, for the noun pair *doctor-stone*, the word *gallstone* is related to both the first and second item because it may cause one to think of both a doctor and a stone. The word *Mr.* is related to the first item because it may cause one to think of doctor, while the *Flintstones* is related to the second item because it may cause one to think of stones. The word *movie* is an idiosyncratic elaboration whose relationship to *doctor* and *stone* is not obvious.

According to the number of trials participants took to reach criterion, they were classified as fast, medium, or slow learners. The elaborations produced by the fast and slow groups were then compared. Figure 7.9 shows

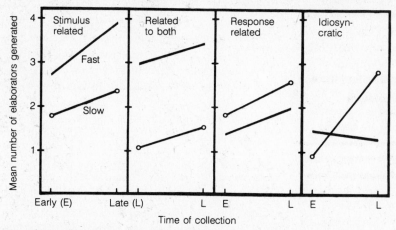

Figure 7.9 The frequency of production of various types of elaborations by fast and slow learners, early and late in learning (from Wang, 1983).

the results. Both early and late in learning, the fast learners produced more elaborations related either to the first item or to both items than did the slow learners, whereas the slow learners produced more elaborations related to the second item, and, late in learning, produced more idiosyncratic elaborations.

The results suggest that some types of elaborations are more effective than others. Specifically, elaborations that either relate the cue word (first item) to the word to be recalled (second item) or relate to the cue word are better than elaborations that relate only to the to-be-recalled word. If an elaboration relates only to the to-be-recalled word, there is no way to get to it from the cue word. Levin, Pressley, McCormick, Miller, and Shriberg (1979) have used these ideas to develop successful programs for learning foreign language vocabulary.

Although elaborations that relate to both a cue and the to-be-remembered item may be effective in learning arbitrary word pairs, we need to ask if the same is true of more meaningful types of material. Bransford and his colleagues have studied the effect of different types of elaborations on recalling sentences.

In one of their studies (Stein et al., 1982) fifth graders were divided into three groups according to success in school based on teacher ratings and achievement test scores. These groups were called "successful," "average," and "less successful." All of the students were given a list of sentences such as "The tall man used the paintbrush" or "The hungry man got into the car." They were told that each sentence referred to a different type of man (e.g., strong, hungry, etc.). Then the children were asked to provide phrases that would help them remember each sentence.

The phrases that the children provided were categorized as being "precise" if they suggested a connection between the action the man was taking and quality that the man possessed. Thus if a child read the sentence and provided the phrase "to paint the ceiling," this phrase was judged to be precise because it connected height (he had to be tall to reach the ceiling) to paintbrush (he needed a paintbrush to paint). Phrases that did not connect the man's quality and action (e.g., "to paint the room") were categorized as imprecise.

The results showed that for any group a student who gave a precise phrase was more likely to correctly recall the sentence than one who gave an imprecise phrase. This suggests that, just as with paired-associate learning, there are better and worse elaborations. The better elaborations are those which interconnect parts of the to-be-recalled information. These results parallel the findings for arbitrary words.

Another interesting finding in the Stein et al. (1982) study was that more successful students were more likely to generate precise elaborations than were less successful students. The successful, average, and less successful students generated, respectively, 70%, 46% and 30% precise phrases. Perhaps successful students do well in school partly because they are more likely to provide good elaborations to new material.

To understand better why precise elaborations are more effective than imprecise ones, let us return to the learning episode involving information about political action committees. Recall that there were two students, one of whom connected the idea *PACs influence Congress with money* to the idea *PACs are groups whose goal is to influence policy*. The other student added an elaboration, *The NRA has a PAC*.

The elaborations generated by a third student are shown in Figure 7.10. This student thinks [oil companies have PACs], [oil companies have money], and [oil companies influence Congress with money]. The structure of Student 3's knowledge is qualitatively different from that of Student 2's, even though both students elaborated on the new information. Student 3's knowledge is more tightly organized around the new idea than is Student 2's. The important effect of this organization is that spread of activation keeps looping back around to the new information for Student 3, whereas for Student 2 spread of activation may just as easily lead away from the new idea as lead toward it. Thus, Student 3 will be more likely to recall the new idea than will Student 2.

Thus, the principle of spread of activation provides an explanation for why precise elab-

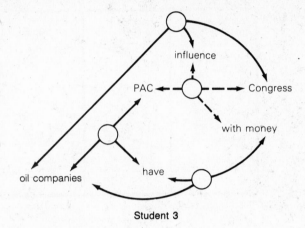

Student 3

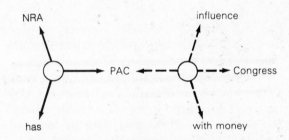

Student 2

Figure 7.10 The elaborations of two students to the new proposition that PACs influence Congress with money. (Elaborations are indicated by solid lines, new propositions by broken lines.) Student 3's elaborations interconnect parts of the new proposition (e.g., *Congress* and *PAC*). Student 2's elaboration does not interconnect parts of the new proposition.

orations are better for recall than are imprecise elaborations. Precise elaborations do not provide as many opportunities for spread of activation to lead away from the to-be-remembered information. This is not to say that imprecise elaborations always have negative effects. For something other than recall of information, such as divergent thinking, imprecise elaborations may be more effective than precise ones. There has not been too much research on the effect of different types of elaborations in divergent thinking situations, although some of Mayer's work (e.g., 1980) can be interpreted as bearing on this question.

ORGANIZATION

Ideal students, given a reading assignment, would elaborate on the information as they read it. That is, they would think of related ideas, examples, images, or details. They would also organize the new information. Organization is the process of dividing an information set into subsets and indicating the relationship among the subsets. In the example of reading about political action committees, one might put the information about PACs in a subset of information about political pressure. Other members of this subset might be voting, demonstrating, and trading votes, since each of these is a distinct way of exerting political pressure. The subset of information about political pressure might be part of a larger set of information about American Gov-

ernment (see Figure 7.11). Other subsets might include: the structure of American government, the Constitution and Bill of Rights, and the role of each branch of government. This example may seem far removed from elementary school, but young children use organizational processes also. For example, a fourth grader may organize her study of American Indians into geographical groups. Or a second grader might design a bulletin board display about the seasons so that information about each season is grouped in one location of the display.

People seem to organize information spontaneously. J. Reitman and Rueter (1980), for example, gave introductory psychology students sixteen words to memorize on their first day of class. They used technical words from psychology with which students were not familiar. The next day the students, using free recall, spoke into a tape recorder the words they had memorized. The experimenters used both the order and the pauses in recall to infer the subsets being used by individual students. They assumed that a pause in

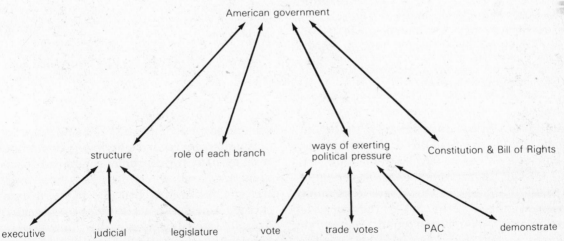

Figure 7.11 A partial knowledge structure for information about American government. Information is divided into subsets, and relationships between subsets are indicated. This structure organizes information.

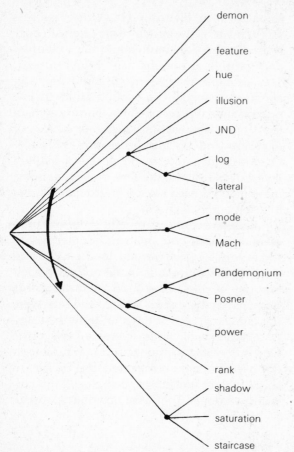

demon
feature
hue
illusion
JND
log
lateral
mode
Mach
Pandemonium
Posner
power
rank
shadow
saturation
staircase

Figure 7.12 A student's alphabetical organization of psychology terms. The branch structure indicates pauses in output. For example, there was a shorter pause between *Pandemonium* and *Posner* than between *Posner* and *power* (from Reitman and Rueter, 1980).

illusion
staircase
rank
mode
log
power
shadow
hue
saturation
feature
demon
Pandemonium
Posner
JND
lateral
Mach

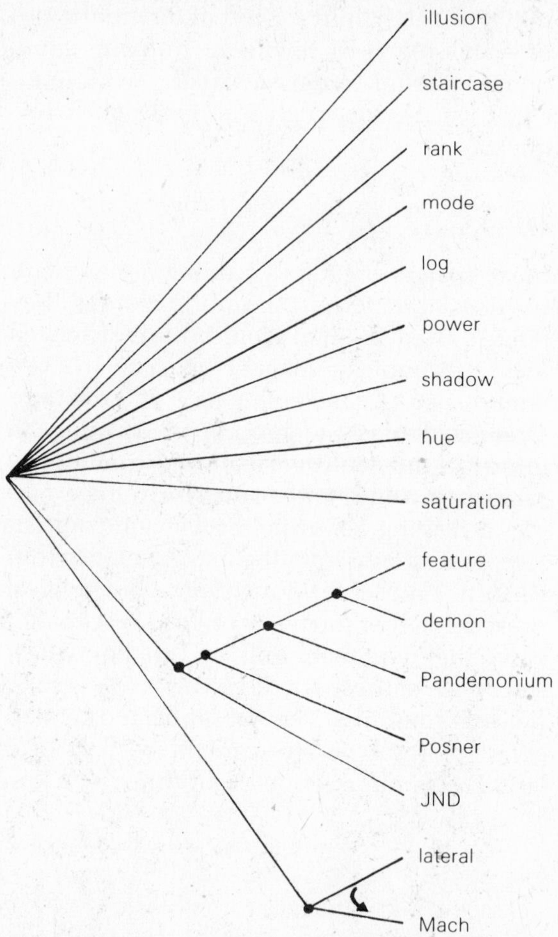

Figure 7.13 A psychology student's attempt at meaningful organization of psychology terms (from Reitman and Rueter, 1980).

output usually indicated a break in the organization of the words in the student's memory structure.

Despite the fact that the words were unfamiliar, the students attempted to organize them. Figures 7.12 and 7.13 show two recall organizations that were found. Figure 7.12 shows an alphabetical organization, and Figure 7.13 shows an attempt to organize by meaning. For example, hue and saturation occur in sequence in Figure 7.13, and these are both concepts that have to do with color perception. Also, feature, demon, and Pandemonium are grouped together, and these three concepts relate to a particular model in psychology. The student who attempted to organize by meaning clearly had more prior knowledge of psychology than did the student who organized alphabetically. However, the important point is that almost all the students tried to organize the words somehow.

The Effect of Organization on Recall

Organization enhances the memorability of material tremendously. Whether the materials are lists of nouns (Bousfield, 1953), narratives (Thorndyke, 1977), or expository text (Frase, 1973; Meyer, 1977), the data show great benefits from organization.

Elementary school students increasingly take advantage of organization to improve their memories over the years of school. The task that has been used most frequently to study this trend is showing children a set of about fifteen pictures of objects and asking them to study the pictures and then recall as many as they can. The set is comprised of subsets such as furniture (e.g., chair, table, lamp), vehicles (bus, truck, car), and animals (cat, dog, cow).

Table 7.2 shows the typical findings in such studies. These particular results are from a study done by Yussen, E. Gagné, Garguilo, and Kunen (1974). As you can see, the amount recalled increases with grade level. Clustering is measured as two or more items from the same subset being recalled consecutively. For example, a child who says, "car, bus, chair, table, cow, dog, cat" gets a higher clustering score than one who says "car, cat, table, bus, cow, chair, dog." Clustering scores range from about 0 to 1. These data suggest that the

older children recall more because they cluster more. Somehow, organizing response output into categories seems to allow for greater recall.

Organization processes improve recall in adults as well as in children. Thorndyke (1977) conducted a study in which he made it increasingly difficult for subjects (college students) to use organizational processes. He postulated that decreased organization would lead to decreased recall. The materials used for this study were two short stories, one of which is shown in Table 7.3.

Well-structured stories (narratives) typically have four main subsets of information (Rumelhart, 1975): setting, theme, plot, and resolution. Narratives usually begin with a setting of the stage (e.g., "Once upon a time in Northern England . . ."). Then they introduce some characters to whom something has happened and who therefore have some goal. This information is the theme of the narrative and motivates the action or plot. That is, the characters do some things to reach their goal. Finally, there is a resolution in which the goal is reached or the characters adjust to failure to reach the goal.

Figure 7.14 shows the structure of the Circle Island story shown in Table 7.3. As you can see, the top level of the structure has the typical subsets of setting, theme, plot, and resolution. The ideas in the narrative that fit into each of these subsets are indicated by numbers. For example, ideas 13 and 14—that

Table 7.2 Increase in recall and clustering across elementary school grade level (adapted from Yussen et al., 1974).

	SCHOOL GRADE				
	1	2	3	4	5
Recall of items	7.13	8.38	9.47	9.41	11.28
Clustering	.16	.21	.28	.22	.38

Table 7.3 A story used to study the role of story organization in recall. The numbers indicate the idea units that are shown in Figure 7.14 (from Thorndyke, 1977).

CIRCLE ISLAND

(1) Circle Island is located in the middle of the Atlantic Ocean, (2) north of Ronald Island. (3) The main occupations on the island are farming and ranching. (4) Circle Island has good soil, (5) but few rivers and (6) hence a shortage of water. (7) The island is run democratically. (8) All issues are decided by a majority vote of the islanders. (9) The governing body is a senate, (10) whose job is to carry out the will of the majority. (11) Recently, an island scientist discovered a cheap method (12) of converting salt water into fresh water. (13) As a result, the island farmers wanted (14) to build a canal across the island, (15) so that they could use water from the canal (16) to cultivate the island's central region. (17) Therefore, the farmers formed a procanal association (18) and persuaded a few senators (19) to join. (20) The procanal association brought the construction idea to a vote. (21) All the islanders voted. (22) The majority voted in favor of construction. (23) The senate, however, decided that (24) the farmers' proposed canal was ecologically unsound. (25) The senators agreed (26) to build a smaller canal (27) that was 2 feet wide and 1 foot deep. (28) After starting construction on the smaller canal, (29) the islanders discovered that (30) no water would flow into it. (31) Thus the project was abandoned. (32) The farmers were angry (33) because of the failure of the canal project. (34) Civil war appeared inevitable.

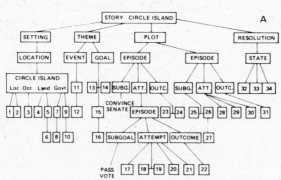

Figure 7.14 The structure of the Circle Island story. The numbers indicate idea units that are numbered in the text of the story shown in Table 7.3 (adapted from Thorndyke, 1977).

the farmers wanted to build a canal across the island—fit into the theme subset. More specifically, they belong to the *goal* part of the theme rather than the *event* part.

Thorndyke progressively degraded the organization of this story by (1) putting the theme statements at the end of the story rather than in their normal position toward the beginning of the story, (2) eliminating the theme statements altogether, and (3) deleting causal connectives in the story so that what was left was a simple description rather than a narrative. He presented four groups of students with the normal story, the story with the theme after, the story with the theme deleted, or the description. In addition, he presented another four groups with randomizations of each of these versions in which the order of sentences varied.

Following presentation of the story, the students wrote down what they could remember and their protocols were scored for the number of ideas recalled. Figure 7.15 shows the percentage recalled by each group. As the stories became less well organized, recall was less good. Overall, the recall difference between the well-structured stories and the random presentations was about 40%. However, in the description version, the difference between the normal and the random condition was only about 10%. These data show the large effect of organization on recall. When the normal cues for organization, such as a theme statement or causal linkages, are absent, it is difficult for people to organize infor-

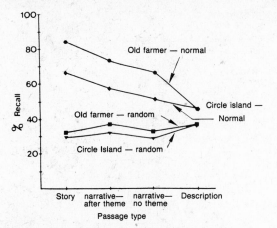

Figure 7.15 Recall of passage ideas as a function of passage organization (adapted from Thorndyke, 1977).

mation, and this in turn affects their ability to recall it later on.

The Mechanisms of Organization

It seems clear that organization greatly enhances recall, but the question remains: How does it enhance recall? There is more than one answer to this question, and it is still an area that is being investigated actively (cf., Yekovich & Thorndyke, 1981).

One possibility is that organization operates in the same way as precise elaborations. It provides tight connections to the to-be-recalled information so that spread of activation will remain in the relevant area of long-term memory rather than spreading away from it.

The other ways that organization may help have to do with the small capacity of working memory. This small capacity causes problems because after retrieving a few items of information, one runs out of space. It would not be a problem in and of itself if to-be-remembered items formed a queue in which as one item became output and left working memory, the next popped up automatically.

However, spread of activation is not very selective about what is represented in working memory: it is just as likely to put an irrelevant item into working memory as a relevant one. Thus, it is the combination of limited-capacity working memory and the nature of spread of activation that creates problems for retrieving information greater than a few bits.

People can use organization strategically to overcome this problem. When information is divided into subsets, the subsets, being fewer than the individual items, provide a way of keeping track of all the information without actually having it all in working memory at once. Computer scientists use the term *pointer* to refer to a tag that points to a given address in a storage device. Subsets serve as pointers in the human system. For example, Figure 7.16 shows the hypothetical long-term and working memories of two children. Here working memory has five slots. Information can be held in these slots or work can be done in them. Child A, who has organized her memory, uses three slots to keep track of three subsets (vehicles, animals, and furniture) and has two slots in which to do mental work (which consists of generating instances of a category and deciding whether or not that instance was in the list just studied). Child B, who has not organized her memory, fills each slot with an individual item from the set of studied items. Because there are no subsets, she has no way of pointing to other items to keep them in mind. Also, there is no space for doing mental work.

In addition to providing pointers to subsets of information, organization can provide a source of internally-produced retrieval cues that guide the spread of activation. For example, the idea *animals* suggests *cat*, *mouse*, and *dog*. Child A, who has slots available for doing mental work, can consider each of these specific animals as they come to mind. If activation from the specific animal and from mem-

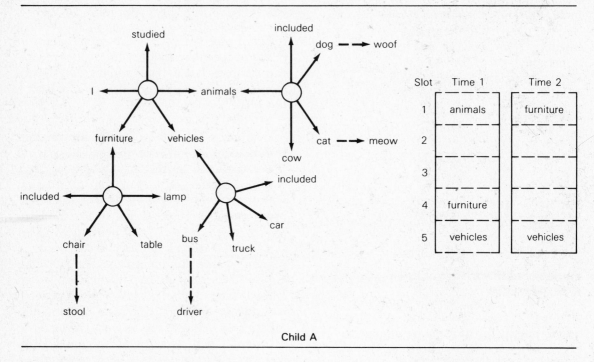

Child A

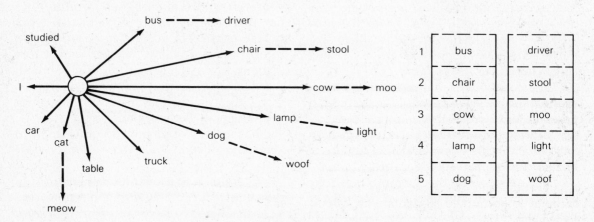

Child B

Figure 7.16 The contents of long-term memory and working memory of two children attempting to retrieve studied items. Organization helps Child A by leaving more space in working memory and by guiding the search.

ory for the study episode intersect (as they would for *cat*) then the child knows that the item was studied. If activation from the animal and the memory of the study episode do not intersect, then the child knows the item was not studied. After Child A has exhausted her knowledge of animals, she can consider furniture, because she still has in working memory a pointer to the furniture subset.

Child B cannot guide the search process by generating her own retrieval cues, because she has not used subsets to organize her memory. For this child, activation will continue spreading in a variety of directions, and the probability of recalling more items than were originally represented in working memory is low.

In summary, organization may influence recall in a variety of ways. It may keep spread of activation in the relevant area of long-term memory, it may provide pointers in working memory to the relevant areas of long-term memory, and it may provide a source of retrieval cues for searching further in memory.

INSTRUCTIONAL SUPPORT FOR ELABORATION AND ORGANIZATION

Since elaboration and organization facilitate learning and recall, it would be useful to increase the probability that these processes occur. As we have seen, individuals differ in the extent to which they spontaneously elaborate on and organize information. Also, some materials stimulate more elaboration or organization than do others. What then, can be done to encourage students who do not always use these processes spontaneously or to improve on materials that do not stimulate these processes?

A great deal can be done through instructions or supplementary materials to increase students' use of elaboration and organization processes. We will describe next some of the studies that demonstrate what can be done. In some of these studies just a few words were needed to stimulate more elaboration. A few carefully chosen and well-timed words can have powerful effects.

Imagery Instructions

Asking students to think of images of what they are studying enhances recall. For example, Kulhavy and Swenson (1975) had 128 fifth and sixth graders read a twenty-paragraph passage called "The Island of Ako and Its People." The passage included a question after each paragraph that required the student to use information in the paragraph just read. These questions were either verbatim from the passage or paraphrases of passage words. For example, for a paragraph about how the people made clothes, the questions were:

Verbatim: The islanders made their clothes from_____ . (palm leaves)

Paraphrase: Garments worn by the natives are made with_____ . (palm leaves)

Some of the students were directed to form mental images of the activities in the paragraph before trying to answer the question. Other students were simply directed to study the passage and questions for a test. Half of the students in each group took a test immediately following their reading of the passage and all of the students took the same test a week later. The test consisted of forty items—twenty verbatim and twenty paraphrase—so each participant had answered twenty of these items during the reading session.

The average numbers correct on the delayed test, as a function of imagery instructions and of whether the immediate test had been taken, are shown in Table 7.4. The students who received imagery instructions performed better, especially on the paraphrase

Table 7.4 Average number of questions correctly answered on a one-week retention test as a function of type of instructions and whether or not an immediate test was taken (adapted from Kulhavy and Swenson, 1975).

	INSTRUCTIONS			
	NO IMAGE		IMAGE	
	VERBATIM	PARAPHRASE	VERBATIM	PARAPHRASE
Received immediate test	11.06	10.89	12.95	14.23
No immediate test	8.94	8.04	8.01	10.93

items. The paraphrase items provided no superficial wording cues to the correct answer. Rather, they had to be answered on the basis of a meaning representation for the passage. Thus it appears that the imagery instructions helped students form a more meaningful representation.

Imagery instructions may not be helpful for all materials or for all students. However, since they are so easy to give, you may want to try them to see what happens.

Presentation of Analogies

Imagery instructions may be particularly helpful with fairly familiar material that suggests images. However, some material that we ask students to learn is so unfamiliar or abstract that it does not evoke images. In situations in which material is fairly unfamiliar, analogies are useful.

D. Hayes and Tierney (1982) demonstrated the effectiveness of analogies in one domain that is fairly unfamiliar to American high school students—the game of cricket. Cricket has many points in common with baseball, so it might be useful to teach the new information about cricket by comparing it to baseball. The comparison could be explicit (specific points about cricket would be compared to specific points about baseball) or implicit (the rules of the game of baseball would be reviewed just before introducing the game of cricket with the hope that students would make comparisons between the two games).

D. Hayes and Tierney (1982) compared both implicit and explicit comparison with no comparison of baseball and cricket. The implicit group read a passage about baseball before reading a passage about cricket. The explicit group also read a passage about baseball before reading one about cricket, and, in addition, the cricket passage made explicit comparisons between baseball and cricket. The no-comparison group read an irrelevant passage before reading the passage about cricket. After reading, all research participants wrote down everything they could remember from the cricket passage. The participants were eleventh and twelfth graders who participated in the experiment during school hours.

Table 7.5 shows the amounts (number of idea units) recalled by the three groups. The researchers counted the idea units in recall that directly matched text units and also the reasonable inferences that were inserted in recall protocols. The explicit-comparison group remembered more from the text itself than did the other two groups, but the implicit group produced the most inferences. This latter result may be due to the fact that readers in the implicit group were drawing comparisons (inferences) between baseball and cricket while reading the cricket passage.

Table 7.5 The amount of information recalled about cricket as a function of whether or not cricket was compared to baseball and, if so, whether or not the comparison was explicit (adapted from Hayes and Tierney, 1982).

	TYPE OF RECALL	
	TEXT STATEMENTS	INFERENCES
Implicit comparison	24.05	6.15
Explicit comparison	27.19	3.43
No comparison	24.90	3.79

If drawing inferences helps recall, why didn't the implicit-comparison group recall any more than the no-comparison group? Since all groups were given the same amount of time to read, and since making comparisons takes time, the implicit group may not have had as much time to encode passage information. The group that was given the comparisons explicitly did have almost as much time as the no-comparison group to encode passage information, and this group showed enhanced recall. If a delayed-retention test had been given, one would predict from elaboration theory that the implicit-comparison group would recall more from the text than the no-comparison group because elaborations become more and more helpful over time.

Of course, for analogies to be effective, the students must be familiar with the analogous domain. Bell (1980) demonstrated this with paragraphs that used a metaphor in their summary sentences. For example, in a paragraph about Beethoven's eccentricity and paranoia, the summary statement was "Beethoven was the Howard Hughes of early 19th-century Vienna." Students read such passages and then answered fill-in-the-blank questions about them. They also were asked a question to assess whether or not the metaphor was understood. The results showed significantly better recall among students who understood the metaphor than among those who did not understand it. In other words, students who do not understand a metaphor cannot use it to elaborate on passage information.

Despite the warning that learners must understand the analogous domain for analogies and metaphors to be effective, we would still suggest that analogies are very powerful learning aids. It is up to the teacher to insure that the analogous domain is one that is familiar to the students. Once that is assured, analogies are highly recommended since the effectiveness of analogies has been demonstrated in several studies (Glynn, 1989; Mayer, 1975; Shustack & Anderson, 1979).

Instructions to Elaborate

One way to get around the problem of selecting an analogy or metaphor that is familiar to all of one's students is to have them generate their own analogies or metaphors. This is exactly what Linden and Wittrock (1981) asked children to do during three days of reading instruction. The children involved were lower-middle-class Hispanic children in the fifth grade.

The researchers compared four methods of instruction for three stories from grade-school reading books. In all methods each story was read and discussed for forty-five minutes before a fifteen-minute test period. The test included multiple-choice items over facts specifically stated in the stories and fill-in-the-blank comprehension items that required the children to draw inferences about the stories. One story was read each day for three consecutive school days.

Two groups of children were instructed to elaborate. The first group, called *imaginal to verbal*, received instructions on day 1 to draw pictures about the story that they had read, on day 2 to write one- or two-sentence summaries for different sections of the story that they had read, and on day 3 to write down analogies or metaphors about the story they had read. In other words, this group's instructions proceeded from imaginal elaboration to verbal elaboration. The second group, called *verbal to imaginal,* received the same instructions over the three days, but in the reverse order: day 1—metaphors, day 2—verbal summaries, and day 3—pictures.

Two other groups of children did not receive instructions to elaborate. The *no-instruction* group had the same teacher as did the two groups that elaborated. Instead of elaborating they answered standard (main idea and phonetic analysis) questions during their reading of the stories. The *classroom teacher* group received instruction from the regular classroom teacher. Her instruction varied a great deal across days: one day she gave the students the test questions ahead of time and told them to read the story with the test questions in mind, another day students read aloud, and a third day they tried to anticipate at different points in the story what would happen next.

Table 7.6 shows the summaries of the test over the three stories. The most striking difference is on the comprehension questions, which the groups who elaborated were much better at answering. They averaged about 30 correct on the comprehension test, whereas the two groups that did not do much elaborating averaged about 19 correct.

The experiments examined the students' elaborations to make sure that they were relevant to the stories (precise). All the elaborations were found to be relevant. The experimenters also correlated the number of elaborations generated by an individual student and that student's score on the comprehension test for the two groups that were instructed to elaborate. The correlations were .57 and .24, respectively, for the imaginal-to-verbal and the verbal-to-imaginal groups. These correlations are consistent with the notion that elaborations improve recall.

Outlining

So far, the instructional manipulations described here have all encouraged elaboration. However, many things can be done to stimulate organization as well. One is to give students an outline before they listen to or read information that fits into the outline. The outline should encourage students to organize their memories.

Glynn and his colleagues (Glynn & DiVesta, 1977; Glynn, Britton, & Muth, 1985) have studied the effects of outlining on acquisition of declarative knowledge. Glynn and DiVesta worked with college students who were studying a fifteen-paragraph passage about the attributes of various kinds of rocks. The hierarchical structure of this passage is reflected in the topical outline shown in Table 7.7. The most general topics discussed were

Table 7.6 Number of correct answers following story reading as a function of what students were asked to do during reading (adapted from Linden and Wittrock, 1981).

	NUMBER OF GENERATIONS	FACT RECALL	COMPREHENSION
Imaginal to verbal	13.0	27.63	28.63
Verbal to imaginal	10.7	23.29	31.28
Traditional	0.0	25.14	17.71
Classroom teacher	1.2	21.57	21.57

Table 7.7 The topics discussed in a passage about stones (adapted from Glynn and DiVesta, 1977).

MINERALS

I. Metals
   A. Rare metals
      Silver
      Gold
   B. Alloys
      Steel
      Brass
II. Stones
   A. Gemstones
      Diamond
      Ruby
   B. Masonry stones
      Granite
      Marble

Table 7.8 The proportion of ideas recalled from the passage about stones as a function of whether or not an outline was studied (adapted from Glynn and DiVesta, 1977).

	PROPORTION OF IDEAS RECALLED FROM PASSAGE	
	GENERAL IDEAS	SPECIFIC IDEAS
Studied outline	.08	.32
Did not study outline	.10	.24

metals and stones. Under metals were two subtopics (rare metals and alloys), and stones also had two subtopics (gemstones and masonry stones). Finally, within each subtopic were two sub-subtopics. For example, within rare metals, silver and gold were discussed.

Some of the students studied the outline of topics before they read the passage. Others simply read the passage. All students read at their own rate. When they were finished, they all were asked to write down what they could remember from the passage.

Table 7.8 shows the results. Both groups recalled about the same proportion of general ideas from the passage. However, the group that studied the outline recalled a higher proportion of the specific details than the group that did not study the outline. This is what one would expect if the outline helps the students search memory.

There are other types of organizational structures besides hierarchical outlines. "Networking" (Holley et al., 1979) and "mapping" (Armbruster and Anderson, 1980) structures have been shown to enhance recall. Fisher and her colleagues (Fisher, 1990) have devel-

oped computer software to aid students in constructing semantic networks and have found positive responses from students who used the software.

Presentation Sequence

In addition to outlining, another factor that influences how learners organize information in memory is the interrelationship of the ideas in the presented material. B. Hayes-Roth and Thorndyke (1979) were interested in the conditions that prompted students to create separate networks in memory when related ideas were presented, as opposed to the conditions that prompted them to create just one integrated network. Figure 7.17 shows two ways that information could be organized and stored in memory if students read the two sentences shown in part (a) of the figure. The middle of the figure shows two networks that can be generated for each sentence separately. As you can see, the networks for the two sentences are almost identical except that for the first sentence it is *Domestic Welfare Agency* that distributes information, whereas for the second sentence it is *computer terminals*. Since the information from the two sentences is partially redundant, it can be combined and represented as shown in Figure 7.17 (c). Here the network represents the idea *the Domestic* (a.) The Domestic Welfare Agency distributes information about professional options.

Information about professional options is distributed by means of computer terminals.

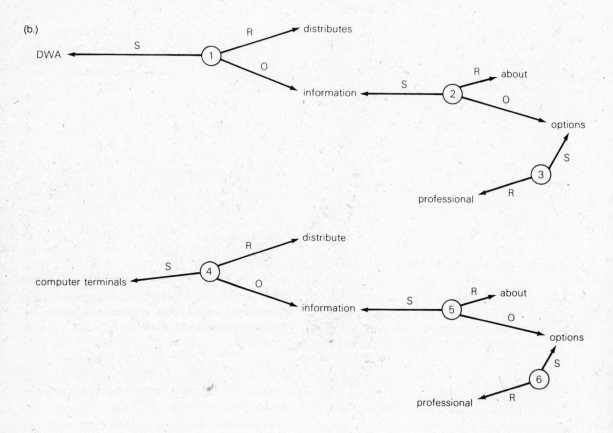

(b.)

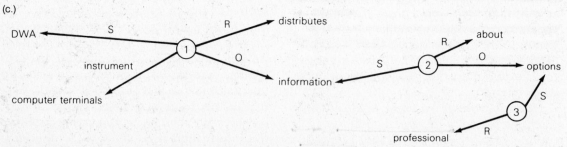

(c.)

Figure 7.17 Part (a) shows two sentences that form the basis of the networks shown in part (b). In part (c) the two propositional networks with redundant information are merged into one (from Hayes-Roth and Thorndyke, 1979).

Table 7.9 Version *A* of a set of three passages about Brownland. There are two italicized sentences that refer to professional options and are separated by sentences and by passage boundaries. In Version *B* (not shown), sentences in the passages were rearranged so that sentences in crucial pairs occurred together (adapted from Hayes-Roth and Thorndyke, 1979).

BROWNLAND 1

In Brownland, the work of the government is divided among several different bureaucratic agencies. Some of the agencies and their responsibilities are given below. The National Intelligence Group collects data regarding the international superpowers. The Navy attacks enemies of Brownland. The Board of Banking studies supply and demand fluctuations in order to prevent fiscal crises. The Royal Knowledge Society monitors scientific investigations in universities. The Internal Guard uses negotiations to deal with civil riots. *The Domestic Welfare Agency distributes information about professional options to all citizens.*

BROWNLAND 2

Government activities in Brownland are undertaken with particular purposes in mind. A representative sample of activities and purposes is given below. The movement of citizens within Brownland is reported to the Statistics Department in order to minimize census-taking difficulties. Spying operations are undertaken primarily to evaluate the likelihood that Brownland will be invaded. The government collects data regarding the interna-

tional superpowers in an effort to anticipate major disruptions. Scientific investigations in universities are monitored so that important findings can be made available to the government. The state keeps track of the wealth of individual citizens in order to facilitate economic planning. County agents maintain permanent files of all violations of the law so that repeat offenders can be punished.

BROWNLAND 3

The Brownland government makes use of various kinds of equipment and personnel in carrying out its functions. Some of these are described below. Social workers are used to insure that children are given adequate home environments in order to promote an egalitarian society. The vice squad uses electronic surveillance equipment to detect crime in the streets at night. Long range missiles are used to attack enemies. Spying operations utilize paratroopers. *Information about professional options is distributed by means of computer terminals.* The state keeps track of the wealth of individual citizens by means of ID cards.

Welfare Agency uses computer terminals to distribute information about professional options.

B. Hayes-Roth and Thorndyke thought that one condition that might be important in determining whether students formed two separate networks or one integrated network was the sequence in which the two sentences were encountered. Specifically, students might be more likely to interrelate two networks if the sentences from which the networks were derived were presented one right after the other than if they were separated by the presentation of several other sentences. This is because when the sentences are encountered one right after the other, their propositional representations are likely to be active in working memory at the same time, leading

to integration. Otherwise, the interrelationship will not be noticed and the two sets will be stored separately in long-term memory.

To test this prediction, B. Hayes-Roth and Thorndyke had two groups of students read different versions of the same set of information about a fictional country called Brownland. In one set (version *A*), as shown in Table 7.9, certain crucial pairs of sentences (such as the pair we described in Figure 7.17) were separated by several sentences and by two paragraph boundaries. In the other set (version *B*), the crucial sentences occurred one right after the other within the same paragraph. Each crucial pair contained a common idea (such as career counseling). Thus, the materials were constructed so that for the group that read version *B*, the two propositions related to a common idea would be active in working memory at the same time, whereas for the group that read version *A*, these two propositions would not be active at the same time.

One way to measure how information is organized in long-term memory is to see if one part of the information cues the other part. In this study if the propositions [the Domestic Welfare Agency distributes information about professional options] and [computer terminals distribute information about professional options] are stored close together, then the cue words *Domestic Welfare Agency* should lead the student to think of computer terminals. If, on the other hand, the propositions are stored separately, then the cue words *Domestic Welfare Agency* should not lead the student to think of computer terminals.

The results showed that when the subjects had read the two crucial sentences one right after the other (version *B*), a cue from one of the sentences led them to produce a related idea from the other sentence 45% of the time. When they were read separately (version *A*), they cued one another only 35% of the time. Thus, the extent to which information is organized into integrated networks in long-term memory depends partly on whether the information was presented close together in time. Another factor that influenced whether the information was organized in separate or integrated networks was the wording of the related pieces of information. B. Hayes-Roth and Thorndyke also showed that when related ideas were worded identically, students were more likely to see the relationship and store the ideas together than when related ideas were worded differently. Apparently, explicit reminders that two pieces of information go together are useful in prompting students to see the relationship and to store the information in an organized and integrated network.

The B. Hayes-Roth and Thorndyke study shows humans behaving as if they stored information in declarative networks. Their study suggests that how well information is integrated in memory depends on whether or not two related bits of information are active in working memory at the same time. This principle is a very important one for teaching. Review, thoughtful organization of material, and reminding students of ideas they know but are not thinking of at the time all help them have related information active in working memory when it can be used to integrate new information. Figure 7.18 shows a teacher who is presenting information in a manner that supports knowledge integration and the formation of organized knowledge structures.

CHAPTER SUMMARY AND CONCLUSIONS

Acquisition of propositions occurs when new information stimulates the activation of relevant prior knowledge, which leads to storing the new propositions with relevant prior knowledge in the declarative knowledge network. Retrieval of declarative knowledge occurs when a retrieval cue activates a particular area of the network and activation thence spreads to related areas until the desired information is activated. If a particular fact cannot be retrieved, logical processes can operate on the activated knowledge in an attempt to infer or construct the desired information.

Elaboration is the process of adding related knowledge to the new knowledge. These additions (elaborations) provide alternate pathways for retrieval and extra information for construction. Elaborations that relate to more than one part of the new knowledge are more effective in enhancing retrieval than are elaborations that relate to only one part of the new information.

Organization is the process of putting declarative knowledge into subsets and indi-

Figure 7.18 This teacher is promoting the integration of knowledge about different ways to identify themes. If he had not reminded the students of what they did yesterday and explicitly related it to what they were about to learn, some students might not have integrated the information learned yesterday with that learned today.

cating the relationships among subsets. It enhances management of limited-capacity working memory during retrieval and also provides effective retrieval cues.

Some procedures that can be used by teachers to encourage elaboration include the use of analogies, instructions to the learners to form images, or instructions to generate elaborations. Two procedures that encourage organization are the provision of outlines and sequencing. Other procedures that should facilitate elaboration and organization include asking students to give examples of new concepts, asking them to fill in a partially completed outline, or using words that cue organization. The list of procedures and questions that stimulate the acquisition of basic units of declarative knowledge is limited only by the imagination of the teacher or designer of instruction.

With so many possibilities, it may be more important to focus on *what not to do* rather than on *what to do* to encourage the acquisition of

basic units of declarative knowledge. Clearly, one should not present new material in a way that reduces its meaningfulness and organization. This is not necessarily an easy task since many instructional materials do not attempt to make new information particularly meaningful and do not organize information in the most effective way. A teacher who takes materials off the shelf and hands them to the student is therefore failing to enhance elaboration and organization. A few words or questions at the start of a lesson that show the student how the new materials relate to something already known can increase learning and recall substantially. A few words or questions throughout a lesson that indicate an organization for the new information can also help substantially.

This chapter started with a problem that is familiar to many teachers—students who appear to resist learning new declarative knowledge. The term "motivation" can be used to label the problem, and this term may imply an *affective* cause, but resistance to learning may have a *cognitive* cause as well. Students naturally seek to elaborate on and organize new information. If they cannot, because the new information does not remind them of anything, then they may become "unmotivated." One solution to this problem is to find out what the students know that can be related to the new information and, as frequently as is needed, to remind them of these connections. Another solution is to encourage students to use elaboration and organization habitually. In Chapter 11 we will look at a program that trained students to elaborate. In Chapter 16 we will explore the topic of motivation in more detail.

ADDITIONAL READINGS

Memory

Anderson, J.R. (1983). *The architecture of cognition.* Cambridge, MA: Harvard University Press.

Klatzky, R.L. (1984). *Memory and awareness: An information processing perpsective.* New York: W.H. Freeman.

Neisser, U. (Ed.) (1982). *Memory observed: Remembering in natural contexts.* San Francisco: W.H. Freeman.

The Acquisition of Declarative Knowledge

Bransford, J.D., Franks, J.J., Vye, N.J., & Sherwood, R.D. (1989). New approaches to instruction: Because wisdom can't be told. In S. Vosniadou & A. Ortony (Eds.), *Similarity and analogical reasoning.* Cambridge, England: Cambridge University Press.

Gagne, R.M. (1985). *The conditions of learning and theory of instruction* (4th edition). New York: Holt, Rinehart and Winston.

Kulhavy, R.W., & Stock, W.A. (1989). Feedback in written instruction: The role of response certitude. *Educational Psychology Review, 1,* 279–308.

Wittrock, M.C. (1989). Generative processes of comprehension. *Educational Psychologist, 24,* 345–376.

Acquisition of Schemas: Schema Formation and Refinement

SUMMARY

1. **Schema formation** involves comparing examples of a schema, identifying similarities, and building a representation of those similarities.

2. Because schema formation uses up a great deal of working memory resources, instruction that provides working memory assistance can speed up schema formation.

3. Because people compare examples of schemas for similarities, it is useful for instructional examples to have only *relevant* similarities. Otherwise, an irrelevant similarity may be incorporated into the schema.

4. **Schema refinement** involves three steps. First, the individual notices that he or she has misapplied a schema. Second, he or she recalls situations in which the schema was applied successfully and compares these with the misapplication to identify crucial differences. Third, the crucial differences are encoded as part of the schema.

5. Schema refinement is supported by arranging situations that cause the learner to be aware of a misapplication of a schema and then ensuring that the examples and non-examples of the schema focus attention on the element of the schema that is causing difficulty for the learner.

6. While students may sometimes acquire schemas from verbal descriptions (without examples), more frequently this form of instruction leads to the learner's having only basic propositions and not the higher-level schemas crucial for flexible access to knowledge.

In the last chapter, you learned about two processes—elaboration and organization—that are especially useful when the goal is to acquire propositions. Often, however, teachers and students are interested in other goals in addition to gaining propositional knowledge. For example, they are interested in having students acquire the larger chunks of knowledge called schemas.

You may recall from Chapter 5 that schemas refer to higher-level units of declarative knowledge that serve to organize lower-level units. Figure 8.1 shows an example of a schema for *saw*. In this example, propositions about the function, categories, and parts of saws and an image of a saw are organized together in memory. By "organized together," we mean that activation of any one of the elements of the schema leads to easy access of other elements.

Some of the functions of schemas that you may recall from Chapter 5 are that schemas allow us to recognize new examples quickly, to draw inferences about new situations based on this initial recognition, and to use knowledge stored in schemas to solve problems. Someone who has a *saw* schema can recognize a new saw even if it looks different from other saws that she has seen (e.g., a table saw with a round blade) and can infer that this new saw could be used to cut wood. An individual without a *saw* schema would have more diffi-

culty figuring out what the round table saw was and how it might be used.

Because schemas are such important outcomes of learning, it is crucial to understand how they are formed and refined. In this chapter we will describe **schema formation** and **refinement** processes and make suggestions for how these processes can be facilitated through instruction. Research on schema formation and refinement is somewhat scanty. The view we present here is based on available relevant research. We also draw on the older concept-learning literature because there are similarities in the functions of concepts and schemas.

SCHEMA FORMATION

Suppose that a little girl is just learning about saws. She accompanies her father to his workshop where he demonstrates for her the use of a standard hand saw and of a coping saw. The girl would represent these events as a set of propositions and images such as is shown in Figure 8.2.

After the girl forms these initial representations, the schema formation process would occur. This process involves noting similarities across examples and forming a representation that encodes these similarities, while leaving out differences. The result would be a schema such as is shown in Figure 8.1, which encodes the similar functions of the two examples (cuts wood), the similar parts (handle, blade, jagged teeth), and an image that abstracts similar aspects of the two concrete images (e.g., shape of the blade). Differences between the two examples, such as their color and the sizes of the blades, are left out of this representation because these attributes are irrelevant.

Since schemas are a form of declarative knowledge and since declarative knowledge is created by actions of productions, the schema formation process can be modelled as

Saw

isa: tool

function: cuts wood

parts: blade, sharp teeth, handle

image:

Figure 8.1 A schema for *saw*. The elements of this schema include propositions and images related to the notion of saw.

It cuts wood. It has a blade.
It has a handle. The blade is large.
The handle is blue. The blade has sharp teeth.

A. Standard hand saw

It cuts wood It has a blade.
It has a handle. The blade is small.
The handle is yellow. The blade has sharp teeth.

B. Coping saw

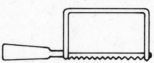

Figure 8.2 Representation of experiences with two instances of saws. Schema formation processes examine these representations for similarities.

a production system. A production model of the formation of category schemas (such as saw) is shown in Table 8.1 and the goal structure for this production model is shown in Figure 8.3. As you can see, the function of the first production (P_1) is to set up some subgoals that achieve intermediate states along the path to formation of a schema. For example, before a schema can be formed, the individual must have a description of the two entities that are being used to induce the schema. This subgoal is what is meant by "set subgoal to describe salient attribute values of entity 1" and "set subgoal to describe salient attribute values of entity 2" in the first production.

The second production (P_2) executes once the subgoal of describing the salient attributes of entity 1 and entity 2 is set by the execution of P_1. When P_2 executes, the individual observes the entity and creates propositions about it. P_2 executes twice—once for entity 1 and once for entity 2. In the example of the saw schema, the result of the execution of P_2 would be the propositions shown in Figure 8.2—for instance, *it has a handle* and *the handle is blue* for the hand saw and *it has a handle* and *the handle is yellow* for the coping saw. The third production (P_3 also executes after the execution of P_1 has set up the subgoal

of creating images for entities 1 and 2. The result of the execution of P_3 would be the images of a hand saw and a coping saw, such as those shown in Figure 8.2.

Production P_4 has as its conditions that the subgoal of comparing attribute values is set, as it has been by the execution of P_1, and that propositions identifying these values exist, which they do now that P_2 has been executed. The action of P_4 is to create propositions for same and different attribute values. These might include:

Function (to cut wood) is the same.

Type of entity (tool) is the same.

Parts of entity (handle, blade, sharp teeth) are the same.

Color of handle is different.

Size of blade is different.

The fifth production (P_5) creates an average image. It executes when the subgoal to create an average image is set and images of each entity exist. When these conditions are met, several steps, summarized by the statement *generate an average image* take place. In the saw example this results in an image such as that shown in Figure 8.1, which is halfway be-

Table 8.1 A set of general productions that induces a schema from inspection of examples.

	IF	the goal is to identify what is common about two entities with the same name,
		and there are no propositions about common attribute values,
		and there is no average image,
P_1 Goal-setting	THEN	set subgoal to describe salient attribute values of entity 1,
		and set subgoal to describe salient attribute values of entity 2,
		and set subgoal to compare attribute values of entities 1 and 2,
		and set subgoal to create image of entity 1,
		and set subgoal to create image of entity 2,
		and set subgoal to create average image.
P_2 Propositional description	IF	the subgoal is to describe the salient attributes of an entity
	THEN	observe the entity,
		and create propositions for each noted attribute value
P_3 Image	IF	the subgoal is to create an image of an entity,
	THEN	observe the entity's shape, size, and color,
		and generate an image.
P_4 Compare propositions	IF	the subgoal is to compare attribute values of entities 1 and 2,
		and propositions identifying these values exist,
	THEN	create propositions for either the sameness or difference of entities 1 and 2 on attributes 1 to n.
P_5 Create average image	IF	the subgoal is to create average image of entities 1 and 2,
		and image of entity 1 exists,
		and image of entity 2 exists,
	THEN	generate average image.
P_6 Create schema	IF	the goal is to identify what is common about two entities with same name,
		and propositions about common attribute values exist,
	THEN	create schema with name *name*,
		and associate with schema a list of common attribute values,
		and associate with schema the average image.

tween the coping saw and the hand saw in size and shape.

After production P_1 through P_5 have executed, the production that actually creates a schema (P_6) can execute. It could not execute before this time because not all of its conditions could be met, until all five other productions had executed. The result of executing P_6 is the formation of a schema, such as the saw schema shown in Figure 8.1.

The schema formation process plays an important role in the formation of all types of schemas—be they category, event, or story schemas. Though the types of schemas being formed differ, the same basic processes are occurring. That is, the learner is trying to develop a knowledge representation that abstracts common elements across a set of instances.

Evidence for Schema Formation

In the description of schema formation that we have just provided, individuals form sche-

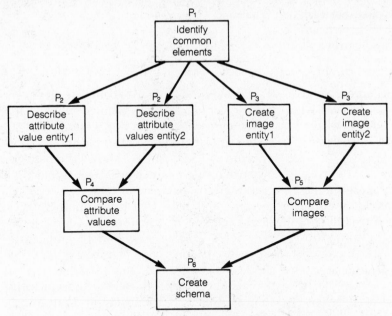

Figure 8.3 The goal structure for the schema induction set shown in Table 8.1. Execution of P_1 creates the conditions needed to execute P_2 and P_3. Execution of P_2 and P_3 creates the conditions needed to execute P_4 and P_5. Execution of P_4 and P_5 creates the conditions needed to execute P_6, which creates the schema.

mas in response to exposure to instances of the schema. While this idea seems intuitively obvious, it was controversial among psychologists not many years ago. The alternative idea was that people form only a propositional or image representation of each instance they experience. According to that notion, when the time comes to identify a new instance of a category, people use their memory of past instances of different categories and find the best match. For example, if an individual who has never seen a mango sees one, then he or she retrieves instances of similar known entities stored in long-term memory—say a carrot and a peach. The carrot is like the mango in that they are both orange, but they don't taste the same—the carrot is not as sweet. The peach is more like the mango in that they are both roundish, yellowish, and sweet. Therefore, the best match is to a fruit rather than a vegetable, so the individual classifies the new instance as a fruit.

Hayes-Roth and Hayes-Roth (1977) designed a clever study that distinguished between these two alternatives—the schema-matching versus instance-matching options. To do this, they used a type of category whose members are defined by their closeness to a prototype rather than by a set of invariant criteria. To the non-scientist, for example, birds are defined by their closeness to a prototypical bird, such as a robin. We can quickly classify a sparrow as a bird because it is similar to a robin. However, we take longer to classify an ostrich as a bird because it looks and acts in ways that are quite different from a robin (Smith, Shoben, & Rips, 1974).

The interesting thing about categories defined by prototypes is that one can form a schema of the most typical instance of the category without having seen this instance. This schema is a natural result of the schema formation processes described in the previous section. Thus, if people are tested with a prototypical instance that they have never seen before and they classify it more quickly than instances that are more like previously-seen instances, this suggests that they have formed a schema and are using it to classify the new instance.

In their study, Hayes-Roth and Hayes-Roth (1977) had subjects study many, many examples of people who belonged to either "Club 1" or "Club 2," but they didn't tell the subjects what typical members of these clubs were like. The examples of club members were displayed on computer terminals and students were told to study each example. A typical sequence might be for a student to read:

Susan Smith, 40 years old, junior high education, married, likes bowling, Club 1

and then to read on the next display:

Jack Brown, 50 years old, senior high education, single, likes to fish, Club 2

and then to read on the next display:

Jane Doe, 50 years old, college education, single, likes to paint, Club 2

When the student reads the description of Jane Doe, the description of Jack Brown is likely to be still active in WM. If the student has the goal of identifying commonalities, then the conditions of P_1 in Table 8.1 are matched, setting in motion the schema-formation production set. The result would be that age (50) and marital status (single) are identified as elements shared in common by two people in Club 2. These elements might be used to begin to construct a schema for Club 2, such as:

Club 2

age: 50

marital status: single

Because the categories being studied were "fuzzy," or not precisely defined, not all Club 2 members were single nor were all age 50. However, a majority were single and a majority were age 50. Table 8.2 shows the patterns of age, education, and marital status that were presented for members of each club. You can see from this table that in addition to being single and age 50, a majority of Club 2 members were college educated. Significantly, however, no one club member was 50 *and* single *and* college educated. That is, none of the instances studied were prototypical instances, none had the most typical value on all relevant attributes.

Looking at Club 1 members, you can see that a majority of people in this club were thirty years old, a majority were married, and a majority had a junior-high level of education. However, as with Club 2, no one member of the club had all of these attributes at once. That is, no one member was thirty and married and junior-high educated—no one instance was a prototypical instance.

The lack of members who had all three of the typical attribute values for the Club to which they belonged was intentional on the part of Hayes-Roth and Hayes-Roth. They did this so that they could differentiate the two theories of classification mentioned above— classification by schema matching versus classification by recalling known examples and matching new examples to known examples. If subjects use schemas to judge new instances, they should be more accurate at recognizing prototypical instances because there would be a perfect match between prototypical instances and the schema. If, on the other hand, subjects are only storing instances, then they should be less accurate at recognizing

Table 8.2 The membership of Club 1 and Club 2 presented to subjects. Notice that the frequency of certain age, education, and marital status patterns varies. For example, ten members of Club 1 were thirty, junior high, and single; while only one member was thirty, senior high, and married. Also, notice that the majority of members of Club 1 were thirty, the majority were junior-high educated and the majority were married. However, no one member of Club 1 was thirty *and* junior-high educated *and* married (adapted from Hayes-Roth and Hayes-Roth, 1977 as described in J.R. Anderson, 1990).

CLUB 1	CLUB 2
A. 10 instances of 30 years, junior high, single	M. 10 instances of 50 years, college, married
B. 10 instances of 30 years, college, married	N. 10 instances of 50 years, junior high, single
C. 10 instances of 50 years, junior high, married	O. 10 instances of 30 years, college, single
D. 1 instance of 30 years, junior high, divorced	P. 1 instance of 50 years, college, divorced
E. 1 instance of 30 years, senior high, married	Q. 1 instance of 50 years, senior high, single
F. 1 instance of 40 years, junior high, married	R. 1 instance of 40 years, college, single
G. 1 instance of 30 years, senior high, divorced	S. 1 instance of 50 years, senior high, divorced
H. 1 instance of 40 years, junior high, divorced	T. 1 instance of 40 years, college, divorced
I. 1 instance of 40 years, senior high, married	U. 1 instance of 40 years, senior high, single
J. 5 instances of 30 years, senior high, single	V. 5 instances of 30 years, senior high, single
K. 5 instances of 40 years, college, married	W. 5 instances of 40 years, college, married
L. 5 instances of 50 years, junior high, divorced	X. 5 instances of 50 years, junior high, divorced

prototypical instances than at recognizing instances that they had previously seen because no stored instances completely match the prototypical instances.

The results showed that subjects were more accurate at recognizing prototypical instances than previously seen instances, demonstrating that people form schemas. Thus, by not presenting prototypical instances during a study period and yet finding that prototypes are more easily recognized than previously seen instances during a test, Hayes-Roth and Hayes-Roth conclusively demonstrated the existence of schemas. This suggests that a schema formation process such as that shown in Table 8.1 occurs naturally when people have the goal of classifying examples.

The Importance of Goals for Schema Formation

In the production set description of schema formation shown in Table 8.1, one of the initiating conditions for these processes is having the goal of finding common elements. This means that if people aren't focusing on the fact that two entities might have something in common, they are unlikely to form a schema.

One study that shows the importance of having the goal of looking for similarities was done by Gick and Holyoak (1983). To better understand this study, try reading the following problem and writing down a solution to it before you read further:

Suppose you are a doctor faced with a patient who has a malignant tumor in his stomach. It is impossible to operate on the patient, but unless the tumor is destroyed the patient will die. There is a kind of ray that can be used to destroy the tumor. If the rays reach the tumor all at once at a sufficiently high intensity, the tumor will be destroyed. Unfortunately, at this intensity the healthy tissue that the rays pass through on the way to the tumor will also be destroyed. At lower

Convergenge Schema

Initial state:　　A threat in one central area.

Goal:　　Use force to overcome the threat.

Resources:　　Sufficiently great force.

Constraint:　　Unable to apply full force along one path.

Solution plan:　　Apply weak forces along multiple paths simultaneously.

Outcome:　　Central threat overcome by force.

Figure 8.4 The convergence schema studied by Gick and Holyoak (from Gick and Holyoak, 1983).

intensities the rays are harmless to healthy tissue, but they will not affect the tumor either.

What type of procedure might be used to destroy the tumor with the rays, and at the same time avoid destroying the healthy tissue?

The answer that Gick and Holyoak sought was to send radiation from a number of different directions simultaneously so that the dosage would be high enough at the site of the tumor to destroy it, but low enough along any one path to prevent the destruction of healthy tissue. Few people can think of this solution to the problem without some preparation, so do not feel badly if you could not solve it. Instead, reflect for a minute on your cognitive processes while trying to solve it and jot these down. Did you activate your knowledge of radiation? of surgery? What other thoughts did you have? What did you do when you got stuck?

Gick and Holyoak (1983) used this problem to study how people form the "convergence" schema shown in Figure 8.4. This schema organizes knowledge about how to solve problems involving the goal of overcoming a threat with force when there is sufficient force to overcome the threat, but it may not all be applied along one path. For example, in a military situation, the enemy may have mined all the roads leading to its location, and heavy loads down any one road would detonate the mines whereas light loads would not. Thus, to destroy the enemy, one must send in troops along several roads so that none of the roads receives so much weight that the mines are detonated. Another example of a problem that can be solved with the convergence schema is the one you just read about in which a tumor is destroyed by small amounts of radiation from several directions rather than a massive amount from one direction, which would destroy healthy tissue along its path.

Gick and Holyoak had college students read either one or two stories that described a problem and a solution using the convergence method. For example, students who read two stories might first read a military story such as the one described above and then read about a fire that was put out using multiple hoses coming from different directions. After reading each story, students wrote a brief summary of it, with the story available for reference. Those students who read both stories were then *asked to write down all the ways in which the two stories were similar,* and they had the stories available to them while they did this activity. Later, the researchers scored student responses according to how well their ideas expressed the convergence schema. Following the story-reading activities, the researchers removed the stories and handed out the tumor problem that you just tried. Students' solutions to this problem were scored as to whether or not they applied the convergence solution.

The results showed that 45% of the students who were asked to compare two stories used the convergence solution to the tumor problem, whereas only 21% of those who only read one story did. Also, 90% of the students in the two-story group whose schemas were rated as good produced the solution whereas only 40% with intermediate-quality schemas and 30% with poor-quality schemas produced the convergence solution to the tumor problem.

These results suggest that it is important for people to consciously look for similarities if a schema is to be formed. Students who were directed to look for similarities were over twice as likely to solve the new problem, which required use of the convergence schema. Of course, the results could also mean that people are more likely to form schemas from two examples than from one, whether or not they have the goal of abstracting similarities. To assess this possibility, one would need to replicate the Gick and Holyoak study using a group that read two stories but did not compare the two.

INSTRUCTIONAL SUPPORT FOR SCHEMA FORMATION

Schema formation is a crucial part of school learning. Teachers and instructional materials can enhance this process by providing working memory support and by selecting appropriate examples for presentation. Also, students can become better independent learners if they know how to seek or generate the right kinds of examples. Each of these instructional variables—working memory support, selec-

tion of examples, and student generation of examples—will be discussed below.

Working Memory Support

If you think for a minute about schema-formation processes, you quickly realize that they put a heavy load on working memory. The individual is trying to hold at least two examples in working memory, put the examples into correspondence with one another, and then note similarities and encode these in a new representation. Thus, anything that can be done to ease the burden on working memory should help.

What might be done to ease the load on working memory? The answer depends on the particular schema being learned, the sophistication of the learners, the availability of resources, and one's other learning goals. However, here are some suggestions that should be widely applicable.

Simultaneous or Nearly Simultaneous Presentation of Examples. For concepts that have a visual component such as types of art work or animal body parts, it should be quite helpful to have at least two examples available for visual inspection simultaneously. This might mean using a split screen in a video display, or having two animal bodies in biology lab, or two pictures on the same page of a book or side-by-side on a bulletin board. When material is so presented, the learner can quickly scan back and forth between the two examples as he attempts to discern similarities.

Of course, some schemas have a sequential nature and cannot be presented simultaneously—for example, the fugue as a musical form or manifest destiny as a cause of historical events. For such schemas, it is best to present examples one right after the other. One might also have tapes that can be replayed or textbook examples that can be reread so that students can focus on one attribute thought to be similar and then compare the two examples with respect to this attribute.

Another way to create nearly simultaneous presentation of examples is to remind students of a previously experienced example when they encounter a new example. Preschool teachers are masters of this technique. For instance, when a preschool teacher reads a story about an elephant, he will remind the children of the elephant they saw last week at the zoo. For some students this has the effect of putting the remembered image of the zoo elephant and the book picture together in working memory so that similarities may be abstracted.

Prompting Students to Compare. Even when examples are presented simultaneously or close together in time, some learners may not perform a comparison process because their working memory is filled up with the details of the examples and associations that have been activated by these details. Thus, it is helpful if teachers ask the students to tell what is similar or to write down similarities as Gick and Holyoak did in their experiment on the convergence schema.

Selection of Examples

In schema formation, the learner is looking for common elements across examples. If the examples presented have elements in common that are *not* part of the schema, the individual may form a schema that is too restricted. For example, an elementary school child who encounters several pictures of construction workers, all of whom are male, may include maleness in her schema for construction workers.

To prevent the formation of schemas that are too restricted, it is important to provide examples that vary widely on irrelevant attributes—such as sex in the above example

(Houtz, Moore, & Davis, 1972; Klausmeier & Feldman, 1975; Tennyson, 1973). Thus, if the child above had encountered an example of a male construction worker followed by an example of a female construction worker, she would not have included maleness in her schema for construction workers.

Tennyson, Woolley, and Merrill (1972) demonstrated the importance of including examples that vary widely on irrelevant attributes when presenting the concept of trochaic meter. Trochaic meter in poetry consists of a stressed syllable followed by an unstressed syllable. For example, the word áp·ple consists of a stressed syllable followed by an unstressed syllable. Other types of meter are an unstressed syllable followed by a stressed syllable (as in a·bóve), a stressed syllable followed by two unstressed syllables (as in "cóme to the"), or two unstressed syllables followed by a stressed syllable (as in "to the séa"). Thus, the crucial attribute values for classifying a line of poetry as trochaic meter are (1) two syllables in each foot, and (2) the sequence of stressed syllable preceding unstressed syllable.

If a teacher presented examples of trochaic meter that were all written by one poet, all from the Romantic period, or all two lines long, the student might form a too-restricted schema such as that shown at the top of Table 8.3. The bottom of Table 8.3 shows the correct schema for trochaic meter. Students who acquire the incorrect schema would fail to correctly classify modern poems that have trochaic meter. In other words, they would undergeneralize.

Tennyson et al. (1972) had college students read through instructional materials on trochaic meter. Different groups were presented with different examples of trochaic meter poetry, but all groups received a definition of trochaic meter at the beginning of instruction. Then some students received examples that did not vary widely on values

Table 8.3 Two examples of trochaic meter schemas. The top schema is too restricted, applying to Victorian poetry only. The bottom schema is correct.

TROCHAIC METER

    isa: rhythm scheme
    context: Victorian poetry
    characteristic: two syllables per foot
    characteristic: stressed syllable precedes
      unstressed
    auditory image: (prototypical sound pattern)

TROCHAIC METER

    isa: rhythm scheme
    context: poetry
    characteristic: two syllables per foot
    characteristic: stressed syllable precedes
      unstressed
    auditory image: (prototypical sound pattern)

given to irrelevant attributes. Two of the examples they saw are shown in Table 8.4. Both are from the Victorian period in British poetry and both are two lines long. Other students received examples that did vary widely on irrelevant attributes, as is shown in Table 8.5. The first example in that table is by an Ameri-

Table 8.4 Examples of trochaic meter that do not vary widely on irrelevant attribute values. Even though the period of poetry and number of lines are irrelevant to the definition of trochaic meter, these two examples have the same values on these irrelevant attributes. They are both from the Victorian period and they both have two lines (adapted from Tennyson, Woolley, and Merrill, 1972).

There they are, my fifty men and women,
Naming me the fifty poems finished!

Wailing, wailing, wailing, the wind over land
  and sea—
                       Tennyson

Table 8.5 Examples of trochaic meter that vary widely on irrelevant attribute values. The first example is by an American poet and is two lines long. The second is by a British poet and is one line long (adapted from Tennyson, Woolley, and Merrill, 1972).

Out of childhood into manhood
Now had grown my Hiawatha
                       Longfellow

Pansies, lilies, kingcups, daisies.
                       Wordsworth

can poet and is two lines long; the second is by a British poet and is only one line long.

After studying several examples, all the students took a test in which they were asked to classify new examples of poetry as having trochaic meter or not. The students who had received a wide variety of examples were much less likely to undergeneralize on the test items than were the students who had received examples that did not vary widely on irrelevant attribute values. Thus, it appears that exposure to examples that vary on irrelevant attribute values is important for the facilitation of schema-formation processes.

This study was done on a well-defined concept in which the students are given the definition along with examples. Elio and Anderson (1981) found a slightly different story for fuzzy categories being learned without any governing rule. In such a situation it appears to be better to start out with a restricted set of examples that are close to the prototype and only later introduce more difficult, less prototypical examples. Since the central tendency in fuzzy categories is more difficult to acquire than in well-defined categories, having widely varying examples may be more distracting than helpful at first. However, it is still important to introduce the entire spectrum of variation eventually.

Student Generation of Examples

So far, we have described ways in which a teacher or instructional designer can sequence and select examples to increase the probability that students will form a schema. Another way to approach the facilitation of learning is to have students become more expert learners. This would involve having them become more aware of their own cognitive processes and of strategies that make learning more efficient and effective. For example, a teacher could help students understand how comparing examples aids schema formation. The teacher might then prompt the students to generate their own examples when new schemas are being presented. Eventually, such understanding and practice might lead the students to habitually generate or seek out their own examples for schemas being formed.

Summary

In summary, instruction to support schema formation should do things to reduce the load on working memory and also to present examples that allow for accurate generalization rather than the formation of too restricted a schema.

The examples of instruction given above amply illustrate the importance of good instruction of details. Of course, some students learn some of the time when instruction directed at schema formation includes one hastily created example. But think about how many more students would learn much more of the time if teachers and instructional designers planned the details of example presentation carefully. Although this is a time-consuming process, it is rewarded with greater student learning and also with less teacher time spent on correcting misconceptions that result from a less thoughtful approach.

Exercises

8.1 A second grade teacher is teaching a unit on bravery. The children have read two stories about brave men— one a soldier and the other a policeman. They have been quite interested in the details of the stories and have enjoyed acting them out. However, the teacher is concerned that the children are missing the main point she is trying to make. What could the teacher say, ask, or have the children do to help them form a schema for bravery?

8.2 The teacher in exercise 8.1 finds that students think that bravery is something that male adults in uniform display. It is as if they have the following schema for bravery:

Bravery
  isa: action in the face of threat

  goal: to help someone

  conditions: grown-up men in
                    uniform

How could the teacher revise this unit so that students form a more general schema for bravery? (Answers to exercises are given at the end of the chapter).

SCHEMA REFINEMENT

Often when schemas are initially formed, they are overly general. We see many examples of overgeneralization in young children; for example, they might incorrectly categorize the first wolf they see as a dog. However, overgeneralization is not so much a characteristic of childhood as it is a *characteristic of being a novice* in a domain, and children just happen to be novices in many domains. Part of learning a domain involves learning to make finer and finer discriminations.

What happens mentally when we learn to make more accurate discriminations? The steps in schema refinement are shown in production form in Table 8.6.

An Example of Schema Refinement

As an example of this process, consider a child who has the following schema for tricycle:

Tricycle
function: transport

power: human pedalling

parts: wheels, handlebars, seat

When this child encounters a bicycle and points to it and says, "Look trike," the caretaker for the child will probably correct the child and say, "No, that's a bicycle," and might go on to add, "Look over there, there's a tricycle. A tricycle has three wheels, and a bicycle has two wheels." This sets the condition for P_1 to fire, creating the goal of determining why the tricycle schema didn't work. This goal sets the condition for P_2 to fire, causing the child to recall examples of tricycles from memory to compare with the bicycle being looked at. The caretaker's words may assist in this reflection or may obstruct it, depending on how the child takes to them,

but let us assume the words help the child focus on exactly what is different about the tricycle and the bicycle. Once this difference is found, the conditions for P_3 are met and the child modifies his tricycle schema:

Tricycle
function: transportation

power: human pedalling

parts: wheels, handlebars, seat

wheels: three

Notice that something has been added to the "tricycle" schema that wasn't there before: the number of wheels. The child noticed that the number of wheels distinguished between successful and unsuccessful application of his schema, so he added this attribute to his representation for tricycle.

In addition to refining an old schema, the schema refinement process may create a new schema that is like the old schema except for the difference that has just been identified. To see how this might occur, replace P_3 in Table 8.6 with:

IF A difference between the situation in which the schema worked and in which the schema didn't work is found,

---

Table 8.6 A production set for schema refinement processes.

P_1	IF	receive information that the schema didn't work,
	THEN	set goal to determine why schema didn't work.
P_2	IF	goal is to determine why schema didn't work,
	THEN	observe current situation in which schema didn't work, and retrieve prior situation in which schema worked, and search for differences in attribute values between the two situations.
P_3	IF	a difference between situation in which schema did and did not work is found,
	THEN	modify schema to include this difference.

THEN   Modify the schema to include the value of the differentiating attribute associated with the schema, And create a new schema by copying the old schema and including the value of the differentiating attribute that is *not* associated with the old schema.

If this version of P_3 fires, then not only is the tricycle schema refined, but also a new bicycle schema is created:

Bicycle
  function: transportation

  power: human pedalling

  parts: wheels, handlebars, seat

  wheels: two

Evidence for Schema Refinement

The way we have just described schema refinement, it appears to be a process that requires conscious mental activity. Specifically, it involves noting that a schema did not work and setting a goal to find out why. In older theories psychologists (cf., Anderson, Kline, & Beasley, 1980) proposed that schema refinement could take place automatically. Perhaps this is true for simple, perceptual schemas, but recent work on complex schemas suggests that conscious processing is crucial.

As an example of this work, consider a study by Lewis and Anderson (1985). These researchers were interested in demonstrating the importance of consciousness in learning to distinguish when to apply the side-angle-side (SAS) and angle-side-angle (ASA) theorems in geometry proof problems. This is a study of schema refinement because the students already have basic problem-solving schemas for SAS and ASA, but have not refined these

schemas so that they recognize quickly when each applies.

Figure 8.5 shows a problem used in this experiment. This problem is solved using the ASA theorem. In one part of this experiment, all of the problems that could be solved using ASA had vertical angles in the problem statement, whereas none of the problems that could be solved using SAS had vertical angles. SAS problems, on the other hand, had other cues associated with them. Experienced teachers know, and researchers have demonstrated (Hinsley, Hayes, & Simon, 1977; Mayer, 1982) that students become sensitive to such cues in problems and use them to decide which problem-solving schema should be applied.

The question posed by Lewis and Anderson (1985) was whether or not students needed to become consciously aware of differences in order to incorporate them into their schemas or whether they might just passively absorb the differences. They answered this question by contrasting the performance of two groups—the "passive" group and the "active" group. Both groups solved twenty geometry proof problems that required either the ASA or SAS theorems. The active group had to explicitly select either ASA or SAS before solving each problem. They then solved the problem but, in contrast to the passive group which had all the necessary

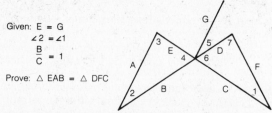

Figure 8.5 A geometry proof problem solved by the ASA theorem. Problems that could be solved using ASA had vertical angles and a ratio of sides as givens (from Lewis and Anderson, 1985).

information, the students in the active group had a crucial piece of information missing from the "givens." These students were told to request the missing information. If they requested information that was consistent with the theorem they chose, then they could go on to the next problem. If they requested information that was inconsistent with the theorem, then they were told to choose a different theorem and try again.

The researchers thought that this procedure would force the active students to consciously correlate problem features and theorems in their minds. In contrast, they thought that the students in the passive group could go through all twenty practice problems without ever consciously considering what distinguished SAS and ASA problems.

Following the practice problems, the students took a test in which they selected a theorem for thirty-two more problems. They also answered a question about any correlations they noticed between problem features and proof theorems. The results showed that students in the active group performed above chance in selecting theorems while those in the passive group performed only at a chance level. Furthermore, of the students in the active group, those who were able to report correlations between problem features and proof theorems chose the correct theorem 75% of the time on the test problems, while those who were unable to report correlations chose the correct theorem only 49% of the time—a chance level of performance.

Thus, it appears that students must be active, conscious processors of information in order for schema refinement to occur. In addition, they must recognize that there is a need for schema refinement because of having experienced situations in which their current schema applies and other situations in which it does not apply.

We will return to the notion of schema refinement in Chapter 15 when we discuss

science. A recent theory in science instruction, called "conceptual change theory" (Posner, Strike, Hewson, & Gertzog, 1982; Hewson & Hewson, 1984) has much in common with the idea of schema refinement. Schema refinement appears to be important in science because people have naive ideas about many scientific phenomena, and these sometimes need to be refined in formal instructional settings.

INSTRUCTIONAL SUPPORT FOR SCHEMA REFINEMENT

During schema formation, the selection and sequencing of *examples* are important for increasing the probability that the learner will form a schema. During schema refinement, it is the selection and sequencing of *non-examples* that are important. A **non-example** is an instance that is not an example of the schema. Thus a particular bicycle is a non-example of the schema for tricycle.

Simultaneous Presentation of an Example and a Non-Example of a Schema

For schema refinement to occur, situations in which schema application was and was not correct need to be active simultaneously in working memory so that the crucial differences between the two can be identified. This simultaneity can be achieved in a variety of ways. The teacher or instructional materials can present an example immediately followed by a non-example. The teacher can list a set of examples and a set of non-examples on an overhead projector. Students can be asked to give examples of a schema. If a student gives a non-example, the teacher can stop soliciting examples and explain why the student's supposed example is really a non-example.

"Microworlds" are computer simulations of various domains which students are free to explore. When students try out various problem-solving schemas within such microworlds, they are often engaging in schema refinement because they encounter examples and non-examples of successful schema application. A thoughtful design of a microworld might include a "clipboard" or other memory device that would allow the student to review past successful applications once she encounters an unsuccessful application.

Selection of Matched Non-Examples

A **matched non-example** is a special kind of non-example that varies in only one way from the example with which it is paired. Specifically, it lacks one of the crucial attribute values for being included in a schema (Houtz, Moore, & Davis, 1972; Markle, 1975). It is matched to its paired example in all other ways. That is, it has all the other crucial attribute values for the schema and also the same irrelevant attribute values as are possessed by the particular example with which it is paired. The use of matched non-examples is particularly helpful for well-defined schemas. Since fuzzy schemas do not have a clearcut set of crucial attribute values, it is not as useful to use matched non-examples with them.

"Minimal contrasts" used in phonics instruction are pairs of examples and matched non-examples. In Figure 8.6, *fate* is paired with *fat* and *rode* is paired with *rod*. The pattern to be learned is that a vowel, consonant, and silent *e* at the end of a word mean that the vowel has a long sound. The matched non-examples (*fat* and *rod*) both have the vowel and consonant, but they lack the silent *e*. Also, they have the same vowel and consonant as the examples with which they are paired. Which vowel and which consonant are in the pattern is irrelevant. However, matched non-examples keep the same irrelevant attribute values as the example with which they are paired.

By holding constant everything between an example and a matched non-example except one crucial attribute, one focuses on this crucial aspect. In schema refinement, one

The long vowel sound

long	short
fate	fat
rode	rod

Figure 8.6 The use of minimal contrasts in phonics instruction is a case of using examples and matched non-examples. The example and its matched non-example differ in only one crucial way—whether the word ends in silent *e* or not.

looks for crucial differences between successful and unsuccessful applications of a schema, and refines the schema to incorporate this difference. If the only difference to be found is a crucial one, then the result of schema refinement will be correct.

Suppose that instead of *fate* and *fat*, one presented *fate* and *fan*. The student might think the crucial condition for a long vowel sound is the absence of the letter *n* at the end of a word. She might form the schema:

Long Vowel
isa: sound

sounds like: letter name

conditions for: no *n* following vowel

By presenting *fate* and *fat*, however, one prevents the student from deriving an incorrect refinement to a schema. Instead, the student would refine her "long vowel" schema to be like:

Long Vowel
isa: sound

sounds like: letter name

conditions for: vowel + consonant +
silent *e*

The non-example *fan* is not as good as the non-example *fat* because it varies in more than one way from its paired example.

Tennyson et al. (1972), in their study of how to help students form a schema for trochaic meter, gave one group of students non-examples that were matched to their paired examples, as shown in Table 8.7. At the top of the table is an example that is a list of four things and is one line long. It is matched with a non-example that is also a list of four things and one line long. The non-example, like the example, has a stressed syllable at the beginning of each foot, but, unlike the example, it has *three* syllables per foot. The second exam-

ple in the table is a two-line fragment by a British poet. Its matched non-example is also a two-line fragment by a British poet. This non-example has two syllables per foot, but the unstressed syllable *precedes* the stressed. Thus, irrelevant attribute values, such as period of poetry, nationality of author, and length are kept constant across an example and a matched non-example. All that varies is the value of one of the crucial attributes. The effect of seeing examples and matched non-examples juxtaposed is to focus attention on crucial attributes.

Table 8.8 shows the type of non-example presented to another group of students. These non-examples sometimes had different irrelevant attribute values than the example with which they were paired—such as different periods of poetry. Also, they sometimes lacked *both* of the crucial attribute values rather than just one. As in the example of minimal contrasts, the use of unmatched non-examples can produce misconception about schemas.

In the classification test that Tennyson et al. (1972) gave following training, the students given unmatched non-examples showed far more misconceptions than did those given matched non-examples. The group given matched non-examples performed quite well. These data, then, support the notion that the provision of examples and matched non-examples facilitates schema refinement.

Creation of a Discrepant Event

You will recall that the first step in schema refinement is one in which the learner realizes that his schema did not apply to a situation as expected—a discrepant event. This motivates the learner to find out why the schema did not apply. In some domains of instruction, this motivational step is rather difficult to achieve

Table 8.7 Two pairs of examples and matched non-examples. In the first pair the main difference between the two is the number of syllables per foot—the non-example has three, the example has two. Both have the stressed syllable preceding the unstressed syllable, both are one line long, and both are a list of four words. In the second pair, the example and non-example share many irrelevant attribute values such as being two lines long, being by a British poet, and ending in an exclamation point. They also have one crucial attribute value in common—having two syllables per foot. However, the non-example lacks the correct sequence of stressed and unstressed syllables (adapted from Tennyson, Woolley, and Merrill, 1972).

PAIR 1

Example: Pán·sies,/ lí·lies,/ kíng·cups,/ dái·sies.

Wordsworth

Matched non-example: Mó·ther·ly,/ Fá·ther·ly,/ Sís·ter·ly,/ Bró·ther·ly!

Unknown

PAIR 2

Example: Máid of/ Ath·ens,/ 'ere we/ párt
Gíve, oh/ gíve me/ báck my/ heárt!

Byron

Matched non-example   Sure só/·la·cér/ of hú/·man cáres,
And swéet/·er hópe,/ when hópe/ de·spaírs!

Bronte

Table 8.8 An example of trochaic meter (top) and an unmatched non-example (bottom). The two differ on the number of syllables per foot, whether the stressed syllable precedes the unstressed syllables in a foot, and the period in which the poem was written.

Thére they/ are, my/ fif·ty/ mén and/ wó·men,
Nám·ing/ mé the/ fif·ty/ pó·ems/ fín·ished!

R. Browning

If the heárt/ of a mán/ is de·préssed/ with cáres,
The míst/ is dis·pélled/ when a wó/ ·man ap·peárs.

Gay

because students come to instruction with schemas that have worked perfectly well for them in their everyday life. Thus they are not very motivated to refine these schemas or to change them in some other way.

How are the barriers to motivation overcome? The main element seems to be getting the learner to actively misapply a schema. In science instruction, one way to create motivation is to have students predict the results of an experiment, then conduct the experiment in a way that dramatically demonstrates that their predictions, based on insufficiently refined schemas, were wrong. In other domains, for example, social science, teachers can use the technique of presenting "counter-examples" (Collins, 1977) that trap students into misapplying a developing schema. Finally, microworld environments on the computer are rich with opportunities to misapply schemas. This is perhaps one reason that well-designed microworld environments seem to be so successful at producing sophisticated conceptual models in learners.

Having learners demonstrate misconceptions in front of their peers can be embarrassing in competitively structured classrooms. One way of dealing with this is to have private means of revealing misconceptions—such as one-on-one interactions with computer microworlds. Alternatively, one can restructure one's entire classroom environment to be more cooperative. If the culture of the classroom is one in which all individuals are valued for their strengths and students realize that learning from "mistakes" is a powerful way of learning, then public commitment to various conceptions becomes valued and students are much more willing to make these commitments. This greatly increases the opportunities that students have to use schema-refinement processes.

Summary

In summary, there are several instructional events that can support schema-refinement processes. At the outset, it is important to get the learner to realize that he has applied a schema incorrectly. Once the learner realizes this and is motivated to refine his schema, then presentation of examples and non-examples simultaneously or in close succession is effective. Also, the use of matched non-examples, which are the same as the example except for one crucial attribute value, is a

highly effective procedure for focusing attention on what needs to be modified in the schema.

Exercises

8.3 Suppose that you are a college teacher and you want your students to acquire the following problem-solving schema:

Positive Reinforcement
isa: event perceived to be pleasant

goal: increase desired behavior

condition: occurs soon after desired behavior

condition: learner perceives the contingency between the behavior and the pleasant outcome

You realize that many students believe that *any* pleasant event is positive reinforcement, whether or not the learner shows the desired behavior. That is, they seem to have the following schema:

Positive Reinforcement
isa: event perceived to be positive

goal: increase desired behavior

What might you do to help students realize that their schema is not always working as expected? That is, how can you create or take advantage of a discrepant event?

8.4 Give an example/matched non-example pair for positive reinforcement that would help the students described in Exercise 8.3 refine their schemas.

(Possible answers to exercises are given at the end of the chapter).

THE ROLE OF SCHOOLING IN SCHEMA FORMATION AND REFINEMENT

In the previous sections, we gave evidence for the notion that schema formation is facilitated by exposure to examples that vary widely on irrelevant attribute values. This prevents an irrelevant attribute value from being encoded as part of the schema. We also presented evidence to support the notion that schema refinement is facilitated by exposure to examples paired with matched non-examples.

Because of the powerful effect of the nature and timing of examples and non-examples, formal schooling can substantially affect the correctness of schemas that people acquire and also how fast they are acquired. Of course, people also acquire schemas through informal interaction with the environment. They do so because newly encountered examples stimulate the retrieval of information about previously encountered examples and hence create the minimal conditions needed for schema formation and refinement processes. However, there is nothing in the "natural" environment to ensure that the new examples and the remembered examples vary widely on irrelevant attribute values or that new non-examples and remembered examples will be matched. In fact, examples are not likely to vary widely because, for many schemas, examples in the real world have correlated irrelevant attribute values (such as male for construction workers). It is also highly unusual for examples and non-examples in the real world to have only one crucial difference between them. Thus, one area in which a teacher or instructional product can make a difference is in careful selection of examples and non-examples.

CAN SCHEMAS BE LEARNED FROM BEING TOLD?

You may have noticed that all of the studies and instructional recommendations in this chapter revolve around providing examples to students. If you noticed this, you may also have wondered why one cannot simply tell students what the schema is, without providing examples. Would this not be much more efficient, since it takes a lot of observation and reflection on the part of the teacher (or instructional designer) to come up with good examples?

Research on this topic suggests that it is difficult to form schemas from an abstract definition. Several studies conducted in the sixties and seventies compared giving students concept definitions with giving them definitions and examples and found that the latter groups did better on concept classification tests (cf., Johnson & Stratton, 1966; Klausmeier & Feldman, 1975). More recently, Gick and Holyoak (1983), in their experiments on the convergence schema, had one group of students simply read the general principle of convergence, rather than reading one or more examples of solving a problem using the convergence schema. This group did much less well on the tumor problem than did the other groups.

While it is not known with certainty why schema acquisition is generally more successful when examples are used, inspection of the production sets for schema formation and refinement in Tables 8.1 and 8.6, respectively, shows that they are consistent with this finding. In both cases, the process of constructing and/or changing schemas is tied to inspection of examples. Without examples, the process simply would not occur, perhaps because the

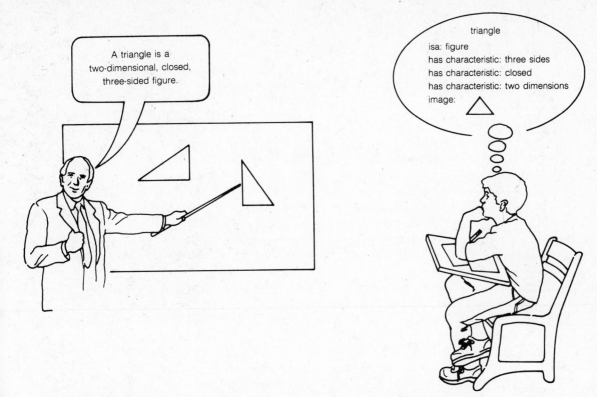

Figure 8.7 An example of instruction in which a verbal description of a schema is combined with presentation of examples. The student combines a prototypical image with propositional information in a schema.

perceptual features of examples often cannot be put into words.

Figures 8.7 and 8.8 show two different teaching procedures for teaching students to recognize triangles and two different representational outcomes. In Figure 8.7, the teacher states the definition of a triangle and gives two examples of a triangle that vary somewhat on irrelevant attribute values. The student in this case is likely to form a schema for triangle that contains both propositional and perceptual information about triangles. Since the student has combined propositional and perceptual information, activation of one

type of knowledge is likely to lead to activation of the other type. Thus, if this student sees a new triangle, the image of a triangle will be activated and this will give access to the label "triangle" and definitional information about triangles.

In contrast, in Figure 8.8, the teacher states the definition of a triangle without giving any examples. The student in this case is likely to form a propositional representation of the information but not go on to incorporate the propositions into a schema. When this individual sees a new instance of a triangle it will not lead to access to propositional infor-

Figure 8.8 An example of instruction in which a verbal description is presented without examples. Such instruction, especially if coupled with tests that can be passed by memorizing, encourage the learner to form propositional representations that are not integrated into a higher-level schema.

mation because perceptual and propositional information are not linked in this student's long-term memory.

The practice of segregating abstract propositional knowledge from situational knowledge leads to the "inert knowledge" problem. When students have inert knowledge, they can access it on verbal definition tests, but are not able to use it in real problem-solving situations.

Increasingly, American education is being criticized for promoting inert knowledge rather than knowledge that is easily transferred. When teachers give too many definitions without examples or require students to

memorize problem-solving steps without learning to recognize when to apply the steps, knowledge becomes inert. Some of the most exciting research on instruction today attempts to identify instructional methods that prevent the formation of inert knowledge (e.g., Bransford, Vye, Adams, & Perfetto, 1989). Sometimes the method involves engaging the learner in problem-solving activities— either in cooperative learning groups or via computer-simulation activities. Sometimes the method involves problem-recognition activities (cf., Cooper & Sweller, 1987), which is more efficient than problem-solving and focuses the learner on refinement of schemas. Some of this research will be described in later chapters.

While it is important to be concerned about the formation of inert knowledge, it is also important not to over-react to this concern by throwing out efficient verbal descriptions when these are appropriate for teaching. In many situations, the great economy of giving verbal descriptions and perhaps just one example is worth it. Students can often retrieve examples from memory, so the teacher does not need to provide them.

CHAPTER SUMMARY

This was the second of two chapters on the acquisition of declarative knowledge. The first of these chapters dealt with acquisition of single ideas, or propositions, and how elaboration and organization are useful for later recall of these ideas. In this chapter, we focused on the acquisition of schemas. The two processes that account for schema acquisition are called schema formation and schema refinement.

Schema formation involves the identification of similarities across examples of a schema and then the formation of a schema that represents a generalized form of these similarities and does not represent irrelevant differences (or irrelevant attributes). Instructional support for schema formation involves supporting working memory by having examples available for inspection and by prompting the learner to compare examples and note similarities. It also involves choosing examples that eventually vary widely on irrelevant attribute values so that the learner forms a correct representation.

Schema refinement involves making a schema more restricted. It is stimulated when the learner encounters a discrepant event to which the schema expected to apply does not apply. The learner then reflects on the difference between this event and previous successful applications of the schema, identifies a difference, and incorporates this difference into the schema. Instructional support for schema refinement involves creating discrepant events in non-competitive settings and choosing examples and matched non-examples that help the learner identify crucial differences.

In the next chapter you will learn about the processes involved in the acquisition of procedures. Recall that procedures allow us to make use of our declarative knowledge. The link is that the conditions for executing procedures often include propositions and schemas. When the propositions or schemas relevant for a particular procedure are active in working memory, the procedure fires and its actions are executed. In this way, declarative and procedural knowledge work together.

Exercise 8.5

Assume that you want a student to develop the following schema for placental mammals:

Placental Mammal
isa: animal

has part: hair

has part: mammary glands

has part: placenta

(For your information, mammals are all animals with both hair and mammary glands. There are two classes of mammals: one—including the majority of mammals—has placentas; the other does not have placentas. The nonplacental class includes the orders **marsupial** and **monotreme**. Marsupials and monotremes, like all other mammals, have hair and mammary glands. However, the monotremes lay eggs, and marsupials give birth to very immature young and have no placentas. Instead, they have external pouches in which they carry the very young animals.)

One thing that would help the student to form the above production would be to present examples that encourage generalization and non-examples that encourage discrimination. Choose from the following list of examples and non-examples of placental mammals:

a. Two examples that vary widely on irrelevant attribute values.

b. An example and a matched non-example.

List of Potential Examples and Non-Examples.

1. An opossum. Small. Long tail. No placenta. Hair. Mammary glands. Eats garbage. Walks on four feet.

2. A human. Large. Walks on two feet. Hair. Mammary glands. Placenta.

3. A koala bear. Medium size. Walks on four feet. Hair. Mammary glands. No placenta.

4. A rat. Small. Long tail. Placenta. Hair. Mammary glands. Eats garbage. Walks on four feet.

5. A whale. Very large. Lives in the water. Hair. Mammary glands. Eats plankton. Placenta.

ANSWERS TO EXERCISES

8.1. He could have them compare the two stories, asking them what was similar about the protagonists in the two stories.

8.2. The teacher could replace one of the stories with a story about a brave girl who saves a friend from drowning. This story varies the age, sex, and uniformed nature of the protagonist, decreasing the chances for the learner to form a schema that is too restricted.

8.3. There are a variety of correct answers to this question. One would be: If you are working with students while they are doing practice teaching, you might catch them when they say, "I used positive reinforcement and it didn't work." You could ask them to describe what they did that was perceived to be pleasant, what behavior they desired the learner to have, and whether the learner displayed this behavior just prior to the pleasant event. If the student says "no" to the final question, you can suggest that positive reinforcement only works when it follows the desired behavior. The main point is to create or take advantage of a discrepant event so that the student becomes motivated to refine her schema.

8.4. Again, there are a variety of correct answers. One would be:
Example: You want a child to raise her hand when she wants to talk in reading group, rather than call out loud. When she raises her hand, you let her speak (pleasant event because she likes attention).
Matched Non-Example: You want a child to raise her hand when she wants to talk in reading group, rather than call out loud. When she speaks without raising her hand you let her speak (pleasant event), hoping that she will remember to raise her hand next time.
Your answer is right if everything (or as much as possible) about the example and non-example is the same, except for one crucial attribute value—occurrence of the desired behavior before the pleasant event.

8.5. a. Whale and rat are the best two examples. They diverge on almost all irrelevant attribute values such as size, where they live, how they locomote, and what they eat.
b. Rat and opossum. Both are small, have long tails, and eat garbage. Both have hair and mammary glands. However, the opossum lacks a placenta.

ADDITIONAL READINGS

For a somewhat different perspective on schema acquisition processes, we suggest that you read:

Rumelhart, D.E., & Norman, D.A. (1978). Accretion, tuning, and restructuring: Three modes of learning. In J.W. Cotton & R. Klatzky (Eds.), *Semantic factors in cognition*. Hillsdale, NJ: Lawrence Erlbaum Associates.

Several chapters in the following volume discuss analogical reasoning as a mechanism for schema formation:

Vosniadou, S., & Ortony, A. (Eds.) (1990). *Similarity and analogical reasoning*. New York: Cambridge University Press.

For a developmental focus on schema acquisition, the following chapter is useful:

Carey, S. (1982). Semantic development: The state of the art. In E. Wanner & L.R. Gleitman (Eds.), *Language acquisition: The state of the art* (pp. 347–389). New York: Cambridge University Press.

For a discussion of the relationships between and among schemas and concepts:

Markman, E. (1989). *Categorization and naming in children: Problems of induction*. Cambridge, MA: MIT Press.

Finally, for a comprehensive instructional approach to teaching well-defined concepts, the following chapter is useful:

Klausmeier, H.J. (1990). Conceptualizing. In B.F. Jones & L. Idol (Eds.). *Dimensions of thinking and cognitive instruction*. Hillsdale, NJ: Lawrence Erlbaum Associates.

Chapter
9

Acquisition of Procedural Knowledge

SUMMARY

1. When people acquire procedural knowledge, they acquire "cognitive skill" or sets of productions. These sets of productions give them the ability to use knowledge to do things such as think, solve problems, and make decisions.

2. Domain-specific procedures can be either basic skills or strategies. **Domain-specific basic skills** can be automated via a three-stage process: the cognitive stage, the associative stage, and the autonomous stage.

3. The **cognitive stage** is often characterized as "guided trial and error." This stage is labor intensive and effortful.

4. During the **associative stage**, small productions are **composed** into larger ones. In addition, **proceduralization** occurs, which means that the declarative cues drop out.

5. In the **autonomous stage**, the skill is fine-tuned to the point where it can run on automatic pilot. This results in a trade-off in which the individual gains speed of execution and accuracy but loses conscious access to the behavior and is often unable to describe or change the procedure.

6. Three important things that teachers can do to help students to automate their basic skills are to encourage mastery of prerequisites by having students practice subskills, to promote composition by showing students the relations among subskills, and to promote proceduralization by having students practice simplified versions of the overall skill right from the beginning.

7. It is not desirable to try to automate **domain-specific strategies** because the conditions in which they apply vary from one situation to the next. Procedural-ization and automation of strategic behaviors can be detrimental and lead to **set effects**. To help learners maintain conscious control over strategic behaviors, provide them with practice in situations where the conditions vary, and provide them with experiences that enable them to see whether their strategies are effective.

8. There is controversy about the degree to which **domain-general procedures** or "weak methods" are acquired or innate.

9. Since domain-general procedures are general enough to apply across domains, they contain variables in their conditions and generalities in their actions.

10. Efforts to teach and modify domain-general procedures have met with only limited success. It appears to be particularly difficult for learners to apply a new domain-general procedure in an unfamiliar domain.

When people acquire procedural knowledge they acquire "cognitive skill" or the ability to use knowledge to do things such as think, solve problems, and make decisions. Since learning to use knowledge to do things is one of the main reasons for going to school, this is a very important chapter for educators.

In this chapter, you will learn the answer to two important questions: "How is proce-dural knowledge acquired?" and "What can teachers do to promote the acquisition of pro-cedural knowledge?" We will address these questions by considering domain-specific pro-cedures and domain-general procedures sep-arately (see Figure 9.1). In the first section, we will consider **domain-specific procedures**. Re-call from Chapter 6 that domain-specific pro-cedures can be either automatic or conscious. Automatic domain-specific procedures are usually called *automated basic skills*. Automated basic skills are methods or tactics or sequences of steps that people learn in order to achieve subgoals in familiar situations. Domain-spe-cific procedures that retain their conscious character are called *domain-specific strategies*. Domain-specific strategies organize proce-

dures in a domain in an optimal way to achieve broad, overall goals.

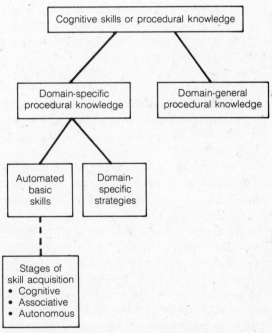

Figure 9.1 Domain-specific and domain-general skills.

Domain-general procedures can apply in any domain. For example, if you tend to be persistent when you are trying to accomplish a goal (whether it is balancing your checkbook, finding a job, or fixing your car), you are probably applying the domain-general procedure "IF at first you don't succeed, THEN try, try again." Domain-general procedural knowledge tends to be controlled or conscious in character.

While acquisition of any of these types of procedural knowledge has certain similarities (for example, they all require practice), we will discuss each in a different section because there are also important differences in the way each type is acquired.

LEARNING DOMAIN-SPECIFIC SKILLS

When we say someone is an expert at performing a skill, we mean two things. First, the expert always seems to know *how* to get the job done. That is, the expert has a method or a sequence of steps that enables her to reach the goal. In addition, the expert always seems to know *when* to apply a particular method to achieve the maximum effect. Thus, a surgeon not only knows how to perform an appendectomy skillfully and competently, she also knows when an appendectomy is the appropriate method for solving the patient's problem, in contrast, say, to a gall bladder operation. Similarly, an expert chess player not only knows how to execute a particular move in accordance with the rules of chess, he also knows when a particular move can be executed to its best advantage. In a school setting, think for a moment of the expert teacher. The domain of classroom teaching is less well defined than medicine or chess, but nevertheless most of us can recognize an expert teacher when we see one and can perhaps remember an expert teacher from our days as students.

And most of us can agree on what characterizes the expert teacher—she knows how to get the job done; that is, she knows her subject matter and how to teach it, and she also knows when to switch methods if necessary to achieve the maximum effect. That is, the expert teacher notices when a particular method is not working for a particular student, and she knows what to try next.

You are probably noticing, by this point, that there are commonalities across all these descriptions of expert performance, namely, that expert behavior is characterized by skillful execution of automated basic skills or methods in a domain as well as skillful strategic behavior in the domain, which enables the expert to know when to execute various skills and how to organize an overall game plan. Thus, we can say that expert performance is characterized by skillful recognition of the demands of problem situations and skillful execution of an appropriate series of steps to solve the problems.

The one major piece of this puzzle that is still missing is this: How did the expert get to be an expert? How did the expert learn to associate so many sets of actions with so many sets of appropriate conditions? And how did the expert learn to organize so many procedures in a strategically optimal way? On the question of whether experts are born or made, the answer seems to be that a lot of what characterizes expert performance is teachable. However, it is also true that expertise in a domain takes a very long time and lots of practice to acquire. So although the problem of inexpert performance often is fixable, there is no quick fix. That is, there is no quick route to expertise or high levels of cognitive skill in any field. According to the late William Chase, who studied expert behavior at Carnegie-Mellon University, two axioms apply in the acquisition of cognitive skill: "No pain, no gain" and "When the going gets tough, the tough get going" (cited in Anderson, 1990).

ACQUISITION OF AUTOMATED BASIC SKILLS

First, let us discuss how **automated basic skills** are acquired. It is typical to divide skill learning into three stages (Anderson, 1983, 1990; Fitts & Posner, 1967), and we will preserve that distinction here. Stage 1 is the **cognitive stage**. In this stage, the learner uses existing general-purpose productions or weak methods to interpret declarative knowledge and to encode an initial declarative representation of the conditions and actions. Stage 2 is the **associative stage**. In this stage, two things happen. First, the declarative representation is transformed into a domain-specific procedure. Second, the connections among the elements of the procedure (i.e., the sequence of conditions and actions) are strengthened. The third stage is the **autonomous stage**. In this stage the procedure is fine-tuned. We will discuss each of these stages in more detail here.

Stage 1: The Cognitive Stage

In the **cognitive stage**, the learner is a novice. The novice uses some existing general-purpose productions to interpret new incoming declarative knowledge in an attempt to carry out some action to achieve a goal. For the most part, humans do not execute random series of actions; our behavior is purposive. So the first step in executing a procedure is deciding what we want to try to do. This means looking at the current situation (set of conditions, information available in the environment, problem) and forming an initial representation of what we think the problem is. Then we attempt to come up with a solution. Often, in a school situation, the teacher

writes the initial representation of a problem on the board, or the student reads it in a textbook.

Consider, for example, what might take place if the teacher put on the board the problem:

$$\tfrac{3}{4} + \tfrac{1}{6} = \underline{}$$

A novice, in the cognitive stage of acquiring the skill of adding fractions, will not have an existing domain-specific production set available in memory to solve this problem effortlessly. So the novice might activate a domain-general production like the following:

> IF   the goal is to achieve a state X
>   and M is a method for
>   achieving state X
>
> THEN   set as a subgoal to apply M

This production would direct the novice to apply some procedure M in an attempt to get the correct answer X. If the teacher reminded the students to look in their textbooks at the rule for adding fractions, the student might find the nine-step rule shown in Table 9.1. Look at that rule now. Notice that while reading the steps in this rule, the student will be creating propositional representations for the steps, some of which are shown at the bottom of Table 9.1. As the student tries to "apply M" as directed in the above domain-general production, he will attempt to interpret domain-specific declarative knowledge (i.e., the rule and known math facts) using a domain-general procedure, with the goal of solving the problem. You can probably predict that the novice math student is going to be straining working memory to the limits at this stage in the skill-acquisition process (see Figure 9.2). During this stage, the student has to concentrate very carefully on each separate step in the procedure as it is being executed. In addition, the student must keep track of

Table 9.1 The steps involved in adding fractions and propositional representations for the first two steps.

1. Find the least common denominator.
2. Divide the denominator of the first fraction into the least common denominator.
3. Multiply the result of step 2 by the numerator of the first fraction.
4. Write the result of step 3 above a line and the least common denominator below that line.
5. Repeat steps 2–4 for the second fraction.
6. Add the numerators of the two fractions written down in step 4.
7. Write the result of step 6 as a numerator.
8. Write the least common denominator as the denominator.
9. If the numerator and denominator have a common factor, divide them by this factor and write the result.

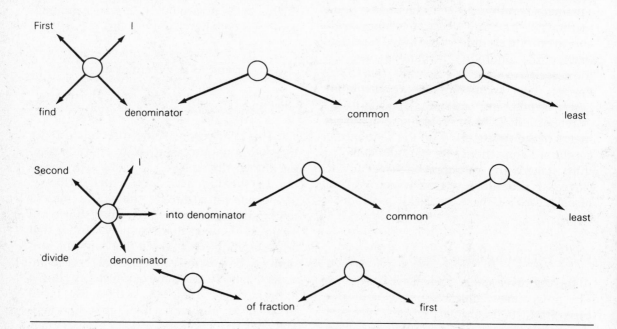

where he is in the overall process by constantly monitoring the results or outcomes of the various steps.

Often at this stage one guides oneself verbally by stating (or thinking) each step and then carrying out that step. Since one is consciously executing all the steps in the procedure at this stage, it is highly resource consuming. However, since one has conscious access to all the steps, one can change or modify the procedure any time it does not seem to work. This stage is often characterized as "guided trial and error," as the student attempts to fill in the missing pieces (i.e., X and M) in the domain-general production shown above. If the student computes the correct answer, he will have reached the goal. However, the cost of achieving the goal will have been lots of mental effort expended and lots of conscious monitoring of the process.

Figure 9.2 Cartoon showing student using domain-general procedure to interpret nine-step rule in attempt to solve problem. In the cognitive stage, the student would be very cognizant of applying procedure step-by-step and attempting to keep track of where he is in the overall procedure, leading to extreme demands on working memory.

The operations used in the cognitive stage are quite inadequate for sustained, skilled performance.

Stage 2: The Associative Stage

The next stage is the **associative stage**. During this stage, the performance of the learner is slowly transformed from a sequence of actions guided by declarative knowledge into a sequence of actions that begins to lose its conscious declarative character. The goal during Stage 2 is to create a "correct" or "bug-free" domain-specific procedural representation of the skill. Table 9.2 shows productions for the

Table 9.2 Production representations for the first three steps in adding fractions shown in Table 9.1.

P_1	IF	My goal is to add fractions and there are two fractions to add
	THEN	Set subgoal to find least common denominator.
P_2	IF	My goal is to add fractions and there are two fractions to add and least common denominator is known
	THEN	Divide denominator of fraction 1 into least common denominator to get result 1.
P_3	IF	My goal is to add fractions and there are two fractions to add and I have result 1
	THEN	Multiply numerator of fraction 1 by result 1.

first three steps in a domain-specific procedure for adding fractions. Anderson (1982) says that the knowledge guiding the behavior is **compiled** during this stage. The term "compiled" suggests an analogy to computers. Computer programs can run in one of two forms—compiled or interpreted. In an interpreted form, each individual line of the program is translated into machine code at the time the program is run; in a compiled form, a program is loaded into the computer in a pretranslated form so that it runs rapidly. Knowledge compilation thus is the process of building a procedural representation for condition-action sequences that leads to smooth and rapid performance. Knowledge compilation is said to be comprised of two subprocesses—composition and proceduralization.

Composition is the collapsing of several procedures into one procedure. During composition, the individual steps of the procedure are combined. In addition, composed steps are associated with each other so that as the actions of one composed production fire, the conditions for the next composed production in the sequence are set up, enabling it to fire. This sets up yet another set of conditions, which are associated with appropriate ac-

tions, and so on and so on. As a sequence is executed over and over, errors are detected and gradually eliminated. As the sequence is executed successfully (i.e., the subgoals and the overall goal are achieved), the associations among the various elements required for successful performance are strengthened to the point that the skill becomes proceduralized (Anderson, 1982, 1983, 1987, 1990).

Proceduralization is the dropping out of cues from declarative knowledge. Once the skill is proceduralized, the learner no longer has to sit for a minute and think about what to do next. Instead, conscious search for the next step turns into an automatic match process. All of these transformations and strengthenings lead to efficient processing that is faster, more accurate, and less effortful.

The most efficient representation for adding fractions might be one large production that had for its conditions (1) the goal of adding fractions, and (2) the existence of fractions to add, and had for its actions the nine steps listed at the top of Table 9.1. Such a representation would be efficient because it would carry out multiple transformations without propositional representation of anything but the intermediate results. Since lots of information is precompiled, the "chunks" of information representing the procedure are large. Therefore, with more of the procedure represented in fewer chunks, less working memory capacity would be taken up with unnecessary memory representations.

Why do we not form precompiled productions initially? If large precompiled productions are so efficient, then why do people not immediately create such productions from declarative knowledge? One reason is limited-capacity working memory. Productions are forged in working memory. When they are forged from propositions, a good deal of working memory's capacity is taken up by the propositions or declarative representation from which the production is being formed. Also, some capacity is taken up by the forging operations or sets of productions used to translate declarative representations into procedural ones. There is simply not enough room to create large productions at first. So, initially, separate small productions are created, often one for each step in a procedure. Later, during composition and proceduralization, larger productions are created from small ones, connections among composed productions are strengthened, and the cues from declarative knowledge drop out.

Another reason, as Anderson (1983) argues, is that it is adaptive for humans to compile procedures gradually. He points out that we are achieving a skillful and effortless level of performance by reducing our conscious access to the declarative representation of the skill. Thus, the end result is a trade-off. We gain a skilled level of performance but we give up conscious control of the process once it is proceduralized. Consequently, it is just as well that we have tried out the procedure a number of times in a variety of settings before we relinquish conscious control of the behavior. Otherwise we might proceduralize a lot of bad habits (that is, incorrect production sets) that would be difficult to modify once we are no longer aware of the conscious steps in performing the behavior.

A final reason we do not form compiled production sets immediately is because of lack of knowledge of all the prerequisite pieces. Almost all procedures refer in their conditions and actions to other procedures that are presumed to be available to the learner. This is somewhat analogous to computer programs that refer to subroutines or to other programs that are supposed to be available in the computer's library. If such subprocedures are not available, then the new complex procedure cannot operate.

One example of reference to other procedures is provided by the first production that was shown in Table 9.2. In that production the action is to set a subgoal of finding the least common denominator. This action, in order to operate, must call up the relevant subprocedure. For example, the production shown in Table 9.3 finds least common denominators. Its actions are (1) multiply all the denominators, (2) identify common factors among the denominators and their product, and (3) di-

Table 9.3 A production for computing the least common denominator.

IF	Goal is to find least common denominator and there is more than one fraction
THEN	Multiply all denominators to get product Identify common factors among denominators and product Divide product by common factors.

vide the product by the common factors. If the production in Table 9.3 were not already known to the person who created production P_1 in Table 9.2, then he would not be able to proceed to the other productions in the sequence because their conditions would not be met. For example, production P_2 has one condition that the least common denominator be known. Since one has no way of knowing in advance the least common denominator for all possible problems, P_2 could not take place unless the lowest common denominator could be computed. Thus, lack of prerequisite procedural knowledge creates another obstacle to compiling new procedures during the initial stages of learning.

Stage 3: The Autonomous Stage

The third stage in the process of skill acquisition is the **autonomous stage**. There is no distinct point in the skill acquisition process when the learner moves from Stage 2 to Stage 3. Rather, the autonomous stage is a continuation of the associative stage. The domain-specific procedure that was forged, composed, and proceduralized in Stage 2 is fine-tuned in Stage 3. Typically, these benefits are accompanied by a further reduction in conscious control of the behavior—in essence, people in the autonomous stage put the skill on automatic pilot. As a result, verbal mediation of the skill may cease entirely. Again, this results in a trade-off—since we no longer need to "talk it through," we also often lose the ability to explain how or why we execute the behavior as we do. This results in the paradox of experts struggling to articulate a procedure as they try to teach novices how to perform basic skills. Often the more expert one becomes in a domain, the harder it is for one to explain how one knows what to do.

This phenomenon is evident when observing the performance of experts attempting to communicate with novices in many domains. When expert medical diagnosticians, expert chess players, expert auto mechanics, and expert teachers are asked how they recognized or diagnosed a problem so quickly and solved it so easily when a number of novices (or interns or apprentices or practice teachers) had been stumped, the expert typically replies, "I don't know how I knew instantly what to do—I just did. It's automatic. I guess it's just based on experience."

Basically, this fine-tuning process in Stage 3 is a discrimination process. That is, experts in a domain come to recognize more and more sets of conditions and the subtle differences among them and to execute finer and finer-grained sequences of actions (either internal cognitive actions or overt external actions) as they hone and automate their basic skills. The speed of execution of the skill becomes faster and the precision of execution more accurate. This gradual improvement in performance that occurs during Stage 3 can continue almost indefinitely. In an early experiment, Blackburn (1936) studied the improvement of two subjects in mental addition over ten thousand practice trials and found that their performance continued to improve as long as they continued to practice. Not surprisingly, the degree of improvement in the skill was greater in the early trials and less dramatic in the later trials as the skill approached an optimal level of performance. More recent studies have confirmed that cognitive skills continue to improve with practice, but that the degree of improvement diminishes in later trials (cf., Neves & Anderson, 1981).

At this point, it is important to stress that what is being fine-tuned in the autonomous stage of skill acquisition is a procedure that associates *schemas* or patterns in the condition clause of the production with appropriate *responses* or subgoals in the action clause. That is, the declarative knowledge that was instantiated in the condition clause in Stage 1 (to enable the learner to recognize a situation) was associated with a particular set of mental or overt actions in Stage 2, and this association between schema and response was automated in Stage 3. So what we are talking about here, in essence, is an extension of the schema refinement process discussed in Chapter 8—by associating schemas with actions and proceduralizing the association, we actually produce complex sequences of behavior. We learn to recognize patterns, we learn to execute actions, and, most importantly, we learn to associate the patterns and the actions together through proceduralization. If you think of schemas in this way, it is easy to see why schemas can have so much influence on our behavior. Of course, a danger in proceduralizing these associations thoughtlessly is that our reactions can become stereotypic and based on misconceptions once a procedure is automated. The importance of retaining conscious control over certain types of procedures will be discussed in later sections of this chapter.

Evidence for the "Stage Theory" of Procedural Learning

As knowledge is transformed from a declarative representation characteristic of Stage 1 to a compiled domain-specific procedure characteristic of Stage 2 to an automated procedural representation characteristic of Stage 3, the performance it underlies speeds up dramatically. Retrieval of propositions is a slow process, relying on conscious search and spread of activation, but retrieval of productions is rapid since the action of one production often creates conditions that directly prompt another production to apply.

Some persuasive evidence demonstrating that procedural learning occurs in stages comes from thinking-aloud protocols produced by students as they acquire new procedures. One example of this is provided by J.R. Anderson (1982). He observed a student reading the side-angle-side (SAS) postulate shown in Figure 9.3 and then attempting to do a problem (shown in Figure 9.4) requiring the use of this postulate. Here is what the student said as he attempted to solve the problem:

> If you looked at the side-angle-side postulate (long pause) well RK and RJ could almost be (long pause) what the missing (long pause) the missing side. I think somehow the side-angle-

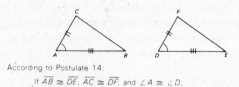

POSTULATE 14 (SAS POSTULATE) If two sides and the included angle of one triangle are congruent to the corresponding parts of another triangle, the triangles are congruent.

According to Postulate 14:

If $\overline{AB} \cong \overline{DE}$, $\overline{AC} \cong \overline{DF}$, and $\angle A \cong \angle D$, then $\triangle ABC \cong \triangle DEF$.

Figure 9.3 The description given for the side-angle-side postulate in the textbook being studied by a high school student. The textbook is *Geometry* by R.C. Jurgensen, A.J. Donnelly, J.E. Maier, and G.R. Rising. Boston, MA: Houghton Mifflin, 1975, p 122. Copyright 1975 by Houghton Mifflin Co. Reprinted by permission (from J.R. Anderson, 1982).

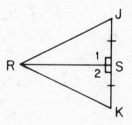

Given: ∠1 and ∠2 are right angles
　　　JS = KS
Prove: △RSJ ≅ △RSK

Figure 9.4 The first problem a student encountered after reading about the side-angle-side postulate (from J.R. Anderson, 1982).

side postulate works its way into here (long pause). Let's see what it says: "two sides and the included angle." What would I have to have to have two sides. JS and KS are one of them. Then you could go back to RS = RS. So that would bring up the side-angle-side postulate (long pause). But where would Angle 1 and Angle 2 are right angles fit in (long pause) wait I see how they work (long pause) JS is congruent to KS (long pause) and with Angle 1 and Angle 2 are right angles that's a little problem (long pause). OK, what does it say—check it one more time: "If two sides and the included angle of one triangle are congruent to the corresponding parts." So I have got to find the two sides and the included angle. With the included angle you get Angle 1 and Angle 2. I suppose (long pause) they are both right angles, which means they are congruent to each other. My first side is JS is to KS. And the next one is RS to RS. So these are the two sides. Yes, I think it is the side-angle-side postulate. (pp. 381–82)

One can see in this protocol several things that are characteristic of Stage 1 in the skill acquisition process. First, there are some false starts. For example, toward the middle of the protocol, it looks as though the student is about to match the SAS postulate. He recognizes the two congruent sides and only has to find that the included angles are congruent. However, what he says at this point is "Angle 1 and Angle 2 are right angles—that's a little problem." Why that is a problem is not clear. This type of false start may be due to the heavy load on working memory. Since the problem is represented as declarative knowledge at this stage, and since only a limited amount of declarative information can be active in working memory at one time, it is very hard for the learner to keep all the relevant factual information active at the same time in order to draw the proper conclusions. As a consequence, he initially misdiagnoses an important piece of the solution (that Angle 1 and Angle 2 are both right angles) as an obstacle to

solving the problem. Another way to explain the false start is to say that the student does not have all the necessary prerequisites proceduralized. If the student had automatically realized that if two angles are right angles, they must necessarily be congruent, then fulfilling the conditions of the SAS postulate would have been easier. Instead the student had to think about the implications of the two angles being right angles, which slowed the process down considerably and sent things off in the wrong direction at first.

Another aspect of Stage 1 that can be seen in the think-aloud protocol is that the learner is constantly having to remind himself of the declarative statement of the overall rule. At two places in the preceding protocol the student goes back to re-read the statement of the SAS postulate in his text. This is an indication that the student is not able to exploit the goal-subgoal structure that relates all the pieces of the task together in a compiled procedural representation. Thus the student keeps "losing his place" in the overall problem-solving process. This is different from not having the prerequisites proceduralized—in that case, you know where you are in the overall operation but you do not automatically execute the subprocedure that is called for. Lots of attention has been paid to the importance of mastering prerequisites in education, while less attention has been given to making sure the learner understands the relationship of various subgoals to the overall goal.

In summary, two main characteristics of Stage 1 in the skill acquisition process are obvious in this protocol. First, the student does not have all the pieces of the skill proceduralized to the level of automaticity, and second, the student continually loses his place in the overall order of operations because he loses sight of the goal. The explicit instantiation of each part of the postulate with declarative information and the explicit reminders of the order of operations suggest that the knowledge guiding the skill is still in declarative form, because once it is in procedural form it will be performed with much less need to verbalize and translate. Once the skill is proceduralized, the student will simply look at a problem and think of SAS automatically. The student whose protocol was just quoted went on to do four more practice problems, two of which involved the use of the SAS postulate and two of which did not. After that he started to work on another problem that involved the use of the SAS postulate. His entire protocol for this problem was:

> Right off the top of my head I am going to take a guess at what I am supposed to do: Angle DCK is congruent to Angle ABK. There is only one of two and the side-angle-side postulate is what they are getting to (J.R. Anderson, 1982, p. 382).

Notice that the student no longer makes false starts, reminds himself of the postulate, or appears to go through a translation process. Rather, he appears to immediately apply the postulate. It seems that his behavior is beginning to emanate from procedural knowledge. With additional practice and feedback, his skill will continue to improve, both in automaticity and accuracy. Eventually, the student will apply SAS automatically when appropriate conditions apply and cease to even consider SAS when the situation indicates another course of action. The effects of practice and feedback on the process of automating basic skills will be discussed in more detail in the next section.

INSTRUCTIONAL SUPPORT FOR LEARNING AUTOMATED BASIC SKILLS

So far in this chapter you have learned that in order to become cognitively skilled or "expert" in any domain, from medicine to reading to teaching, it is necessary to proceduralize and automate lots of domain-specific knowledge. Only then can an individual perform or think accurately and quickly. But we also have acknowledged that to gain this level of expertise takes a long time and lots of practice. Is there anything we who are engaged as teachers can do to make this process easier or faster or even more likely to occur for our students? Are there specific things we can do to help learners proceduralize and automate their cognitive skills?

There are three important things that teachers can do to help students automate their basic cognitive skills in a domain. The first is to help them *automate prerequisite procedures* or subskills. The second is to help them *compose small procedures into larger procedures*. The third is to help them *proceduralize their skills* so that they can exploit the goal-subgoal structure of the procedure without thinking about it. Keep in mind that proceduralization is particularly desirable when the goal is an *automated* basic skill. For strategic behaviors, conscious assess to the conditions and actions of the procedure is often critical in order to avoid misapplication. Later in this chapter, we will mention some cautions about situations in which proceduralization is a liability.

Mastering Subskills or Prerequisite Procedures

When attempting to perform a complex cognitive skill, it is impossible to perform the "whole" process successfully and effortlessly unless one has mastered or automated the execution of the parts. This argument is often provided as the rationale for individualized mastery instruction. Individualized mastery instruction allows each student to proceed at his or her own rate and tests for student mastery of each objective. If an objective is not mastered following instruction, alternative instruction is provided until the objective is mastered. This type of instruction ensures that each student has learned the necessary prior knowledge and subskills required for mastery of a new complex skill. Further, if the objectives and the tests of mastery are appropriately designed, this type of instruction defines mastery as proceduralization to the point where the subskills are automated.

In general, individualized mastery instruction has been found to produce greater achievement gains than traditional instruction (Bloom, 1976; Torshen, 1977), given certain types of learning objectives. In traditional group instruction if an individual fails to master a given objective, instruction proceeds to the next topic anyway. Thus some individuals may not master the prerequisites required for learning new skills. One study compared traditional group instruction to individualized mastery instruction in an introductory college physics course (Moore, Hauck, & Gagné,

1973). Many of the objectives of this course were skill or procedural objectives. Students were randomly assigned to a section that received individualized mastery instruction or traditional lectures. Both groups took the same final exam, which was judged not to be biased in favor of either group. The individualized mastery group received an average of 120 points on the exam; the traditional group averaged 99 points. Probably a major reason for the superior performance of the individualized mastery group was that performance on the skill objectives was facilitated by proceduralization of prerequisites.

We often try to learn procedures without having mastered the prerequisite subskills. In such situations we learn the prerequisites concomitantly with the new procedures. This slows down the learning process. Resnick, Siegel, and Kresh (1971) demonstrated this idea in an experiment in which kindergarten children were taught to classify objects ac-

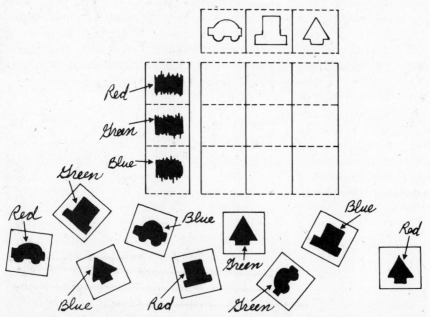

Figure 9.5 The placing task presented to kindergarten children (from a verbal description in Resnick et al., 1971).

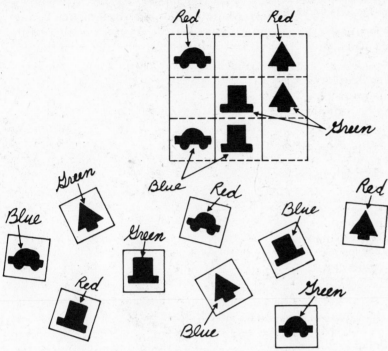

Figure 9.6 The inferring task. Children were directed to select the correct objects to fill each empty cell in the matrix (from a verbal description in Resnick et al., 1971).

cording to attributes. The experimenters focused on the two tasks shown in Figures 9.5 and 9.6.

The task shown in Figure 9.5 was called *placing*. The children were presented with a 3 × 3 matrix of empty cells. Each row in the matrix was associated with a different color, and each column was associated with a different shape. The color was indicated to the left of each row and the shape was indicated at the top of each column. These indicator cells were called "attribute" cells. The children were given nine objects (e.g., blue car) to place correctly in the cells of the matrix.

The task shown in Figure 9.6 was called *inferring*. Children had to infer the attributes associated with each row and column of the matrix before placing the object in its correct cell. The children were given a partially filled

matrix that had no attribute cells. They were also given nine objects. Then they were told to select from the nine objects the object that correctly filled each of the empty cells in the matrix.

Resnick et al. (1971) thought that the inferring task was more complex than the placing task. Moreover, they thought that the inferring task required many of the same procedures as did the placing task, but that it also required more procedures. In other words, the skills used in this placing task were prerequisite to the skills used in the inferring task. One way to represent the relationship between the two tasks is to describe the production sets that would underlie performance on each task and then compare them. Tables 9.4 and 9.5 show these production sets for the placing and inferring tasks, respectively.

Table 9.4 A hypothetical set of productions underlying performance on the placing task.

P_1	IF	Goal is to place object 1 in correct cell
		and attributes of rows and columns are known
	THEN	Set subgoal to identify color of object 1.
P_2	IF	Subgoal is to identify color of object 1
	THEN	Observe object 1
		Let color of object 1 be color 1
		Set subgoal to identify shape of object 1.
P_3	IF	Subgoal is to identify shape of object 1
	THEN	Observe object 1
		Let shape of object be shape 1
		Set subgoal to identify row for color 1.
P_4	IF	Subgoal is to identify row for color 1
	THEN	Scan three attributes for rows
		Find match of attribute and color 1
		Let matching row be row X
		Set subgoal to identify column 1 for shape 1.
P_5	IF	Subgoal is to identify column for shape 1
	THEN	Scan three attributes for columns
		Find match of attribute and shape 1
		Let matching column be column Y
		Set subgoal to find intersection cell.
P_6	IF	Subgoal is to find intersection cell
	THEN	Move finger from start of row X to right
		Move finger from top of column Y down
		Call cell where fingers meet cell 1
		Set subgoal to place object 1.
P_7	IF	Subgoal is to place object 1
	THEN	Place object 1 in cell 1.

Production 1 in each set is similar in that each functions to set the main goal and to identify the starting conditions. In P_1 for placing there are only two conditions, whereas in P_1 for inferring there are three. The first condition is similar for placing and inferring and the second conditions are complements of one another: for placing, the attributes are known, for inferring, they are not known. The actions of the first production in placing and inferring are similar, though not identical. For placing, the action is to set the subgoal of identifying the color of the *object*, whereas for inferring, the action is to set the subgoal of identifying the color associated with the *cell*. If P_1 in placing had been learned before P_1 in inferring, many of the procedures implied by P_1 in inferring would already be proceduralized. For example, the procedure for identifying attributes would be known, as would the procedure for setting up a subgoal to identify color.

Table 9.5 A hypothetical set of productions underlying performance on the inferring task.

P_1	IF	Goal is to identify object that fits in cell 1
		and attributes of rows and columns are not known
		and there are at least two objects in each row and each column
	THEN	Set subgoal to identify color of cell 1.
P_2	IF	Subgoal is to identify color of cell 1
	THEN	Move finger along row to which cell 1 belongs until two objects have been found
		Observe the two objects
		Let color of two objects be color 1
		Set subgoal to identify shape of cell 1.
P_3	IF	Subgoal is to identify shape of cell 1
	THEN	Move finger along column to which cell 1 belongs until two objects have been found
		Observe the two objects
		Let shape of two objects be shape 1
		Set subgoal to find object.
P_4	IF	Subgoal is to find object
	THEN	Scan array of nine objects
		Find object with color 1 and shape 1
		Let object be object 1
		Set subgoal to place object 1.
P_5	IF	Subgoal is to place object 1
	THEN	Place object 1 in cell 1.

A similar analysis of productions 2 and 3 for each task shows a similar relationship between the two tasks. For placing, P_2 and P_3 observe the color and shape of an object, respectively, and assign variable names to the color and shape observed (i.e., color 1 and shape 1). For inferring, P_2 and P_3 perform these same operations for two objects. In addition, they perform the action of moving the finger along a row (P_3) or a column (P_4) in order to identify the two objects to be observed. If placing's P_2 and P_3 had been learned before inferring's P_2 and P_3, then many of the operations in these latter productions would already have been proceduralized.

In general, then, many of the inferring procedures include placing procedures. In that sense, the placing procedures are prerequisite to the inferring procedures. Resnick et al. (1971) hypothesized that children who learned the placing task before they learned the inferring task would learn the inferring task faster than children who learned the inferring task without first learning the placing task. The results confirmed this hypothesis, with children who learned placing before inferring taking an average of 6.86 trials to learn the inferring task and children who learned the inferring task without first learning the placing task taking an average of 8.85 trials to learn the inferring task.

One might argue that the children who learned the placing task first did better on inferring not because they had learned prerequisite procedures but because they were used to matrix problems. If this were the case, then the number of trials to learn both tasks, regardless of the order in which they were learned, should be equal because either task could serve as a warmup for the other. How-

Table 9.6 Four small productions that take place in a sequence in sounding out a word that is unfamiliar in print but is available in a person's aural vocabulary.

P_1	IF THEN	Encounter word that I don't recognize Break word into syllables.
P_2	IF THEN	Word is broken into syllables Pronounce each syllable.
P_3	IF THEN	Each syllable in word has been pronounced Match sounds of syllables to a word I have heard.
P_4	IF THEN	Sounds of syllables are matched to a word I have heard before Say the word that I have heard before.

ever, the children who learned placing first and inferring second learned the two tasks in fewer trials (11.21) than the children who learned inferring before placing (14.23 trials). In other words, learning a complex procedure without first learning some of its components slows down the learning process.

Promoting Composition

A second way in which teachers can help students to automate their basic skills is to provide them with opportunities to combine small procedures into larger ones. As was mentioned previously, the initial productions that are forged during Stage 2 of the proceduralization process are small because working memory does not have room for the direct creation of large productions from declarative knowledge. However, once a set of small productions exists, composition can occur. For composition to take place, a sequence of two productions must be active in working memory at the same time. The system then "notices" that the action of the first production creates the condition for the second production. The result is a new production that has the condition of the first production and the actions of both productions. The condition of

the second production is dropped out as unnecessary information.

Tables 9.6 and 9.7 show an example of composition. Table 9.6 contains four productions that underlie the skill of sounding out unfamiliar printed words. P_1 breaks the word into syllables, P_2 pronounces each syllable, P_3 searches memory for a match between the sounds produced in P_2 and a known word, and P_4 pronounces the known word. Table 9.7 shows two new productions, one composed from P_1 and P_2 in Table 9.6 and one composed from P_3 and P_4. The one composed from P_1 and P_2 keeps the condition of P_1 (encounter a word that I don't recognize), and has as its actions the actions of P_1 and P_2 in that order (break words into syllables, then pronounce syllables). The condition of P_2 (word is broken into syllables) has dropped out.

The two productions shown in Table 9.7 will accomplish the sounding out of a new word more rapidly than will the four in Table 9.6. This is because there is an activation time for each production and also because working memory is less burdened when fewer conditions (chunks) have to be represented. Composition could easily continue to operate on the two productions shown in Table 9.7. The result would be one large pro-

Table 9.7 Two composed productions created from the four small productions shown in Table 9.6. The first production was created from P_1 and P_2 in Table 9.6. The second was created from P_3 and P_4.

IF	Encounter word that I don't recognize
THEN	Break word into syllables and pronounce each syllable.
IF	Each syllable in word has been pronounced
THEN	Match sounds of syllables to a word I have heard
	Say the word I have heard.

duction (shown in Table 9.8) to represent the entire skill.

To help students compose basic skills, practice and feedback are effective. Each practice attempt represents a chance to have two potentially related productions active in working memory simultaneously and hence represents a chance for composition. Suppes and his colleagues (Suppes, Jerman, & Brian, 1968; Suppes & Morningstar, 1972) conducted a large-scale study of the effects of practice and feedback on arithmetic achievement. The procedures that children practiced included those involved in addition, subtraction, fractions, long division, multiplication, percentages, and ratios. They practiced on a computer terminal for about ten minutes a day for an entire school year. The difficulty of the items was adjusted according to how well the student was doing. Immediate feedback was provided.

On a standardized achievement test given at the end of the school year, the students who had practiced did significantly better than students who had not practiced. The improved performance on computational subtests may be due to the fact that the students who practiced had a greater number of composed procedures and hence could get through the timed subtests faster. Moreover, achievement gains on problem-solving subtests may be due to the fact that students with composed computational skills had more room in working memory to think about the problems and to monitor their execution of solutions.

Two characteristics of the practice sessions that appear to be particularly noteworthy include the *spacing* of the practice sessions over an entire school year and the *immediacy* of the feedback. In numerous studies of spaced versus massed practice, spaced practice al-

Table 9.8 One production created from two productions shown in Table 9.7. During composition, intermediate conditions in a sequence of actions are dropped and the entire action sequence is encoded into one production.

IF	Encounter word that I don't recognize
THEN	Break word into syllables
	and pronounce each syllable
	and match sounds of syllables to a word I have heard
	and say the word I have heard.

most always is shown to be more effective than massed practice in promoting skill learning. Cramming lots of practice into a few long sessions typically results in wasted time and effort (e.g., Anderson, 1990, p. 265). *Immediate feedback* is important so that learners can correct their mistakes before the "bugs" or errors in the procedure become an automated part of the compiled basic skill. On the other hand, there are some situations in which a delay of feedback is not harmful for skill acquisition as long as there is feedback. If students are not practicing an incorrect procedure in the interim between performance and feedback, and if they can recall their performance when they receive feedback, they may benefit from it as much as from immediate feedback. For example, there is often a delay between when students write a composition and when they receive written feedback on it. However, since the feedback is often written right on the composition, it is easy for the student to recall the situation and therefore correct an incorrect procedure.

Promoting Proceduralization

During proceduralization conscious or declarative access to the steps in the procedure decreases. This is because a consistent sequence of steps (productions) is executed successfully, over and over, to the point that the execution of the actions in one step sets up the conditions for the next step, which dictates the actions for this second step, which set up the conditions for the third step, and so on. As this sequence of operations is executed successfully (subgoals are achieved) time after time, the associations among the steps are strengthened because the degree of correspondence between the actions for step one and the conditions for step two create a perfect match. This matching cues the sequence of operations to the point where the individual does not have to think about or search for what to do next. The search or thought process is replaced by a match process. Thus, as a skill becomes more proceduralized, the individual becomes more confident about what to do next, but at the same time may become less able to articulate how she knew what to do.

A sequence of productions that underlies a skill is likely to become proceduralized if a consistent (non-varying) sequence of operations is performed over and over. Thus once a student has small productions automated, and has composed small productions into large productions, then a third thing that teachers can do to promote automation of cognitive skills is to make sure students practice the sequence of composed productions as an integrated procedure, rather than in parts. In this way, the connections can be strengthened.

One obstacle to proceduralization is that with so much practice required, students may become bored. Schneider (1985) has several interesting suggestions for enhancing motivation with use of criterion-referenced feedback and/or extrinsic reinforcers for completing a set of practice trials. In Chapter 12 of this book, there is an example of games that were created to motivate low-skill readers to practice phonetic procedures.

Sometimes students learn composed sets of components of various skills but do not know the relation among the skills and when it is appropriate to use them. For example, children may be able to perform addition, subtraction, multiplication, and division rapidly and accurately when told to, but may not know which of these operations to use for a given "story" problem or how to check subtraction problems by adding.

Even composed computational procedures are not fully effective unless they can be activated under all the various conditions and situations in which they are appropriate. For example, one situation for which addition is appropriate has the conditions (1) that there are two quantities, and (2) that one wants to know the quantity that would result from the merging or combining of these two. One situation for which subtraction is appropriate has the conditions (1) that there are two quantities, and (2) that one wants to know the quantity that would result from taking the amount represented by one quantity away from the other quantity.

Learning to recognize the patterns or schemas that are associated with given actions and learning to see the relations among subskills and the relation of composed skills to overall goals involve the same acquisition and refinement processes as those described in the last chapter. Teaching should therefore proceed by giving examples that vary on irrelevant attribute values (e.g., the quantities in word problems could refer to candy, marbles, or inches), by mixing examples with matched non-examples (e.g., an addition problem involving candy followed by a subtraction problem involving candy), and by letting the student practice composed skills in varying combinations instead of in isolation.

Some arithmetic books teach addition, give practice in addition, teach subtraction, give practice in subtraction, teach multiplication, give practice in multiplication, teach division, give practice in division, and then stop. They fail to take the crucial final step of giving mixed sets of "real-world" problems to help students create overall goal-subgoal structures that include the various computational methods associated with appropriate sets of conditions (schemas, patterns) that specify when the methods apply. These types of practice problems help students learn how the execution of a computational method relates to the achievement of a goal. Without practice in relating computational methods to goals, students may learn to execute composed computational procedures flawlessly but fail to use them appropriately because they do not see the relevance of a particular procedure in a particular situation.

Tennyson and Tennyson (1975) examined tenth graders' ability to use two grammatical rules following exposure to instances that varied widely or not so widely on irrelevant attribute values. Students given broad exposure performed 30% better than those given a narrow range of instances. The researchers also compared performance following exposure to matched versus unmatched non-examples of rule use and found 30% better performance among students who had been presented with the matched non-examples. This study demonstrates that actions and rules and methods must become linked to relevant schemas in integrated goal-subgoal structures if they are to be useful. Methods allow the learner to achieve subgoals but are not fully effective unless the learner understands how the methods can be used to achieve meaningful goals. This is analogous to saying that for proceduralized skills to be useful, they should be practiced in context. Practicing parts of an overall skill in a piecemeal fashion may lead to proceduralization of subskills but will not lead to appropriate application of the subskill in context.

John Anderson (1990) recently lamented that "much of education seems to have been designed to decompose a complex skill into independent subcomponents, and to teach each separately" (p. 266). While it is true that many skills in education can be decomposed into subskills and that many subskills need to be practiced in isolation, it is an overstatement to say that the only key to successful curriculum planning is to identify some "correct" hierarchy of subskills and to teach them in order. In recent years, there has been considerable emphasis on learning objectives and on the competency-based approach to curriculum planning. While this approach has yielded some beneficial learning outcomes, it would not seem to be sufficient when students are expected to integrate subskills into complex procedures. To fully understand *when* to use subskills (rather than just *how* to execute them), students must practice subskills in contexts that make the *relations* among them explicit. Practicing comprehensive procedures that incorporate composed subskills enables students to compose small productions into larger production sets and to see and to exploit the relations among the production sets as well.

ACQUISITION OF DOMAIN-SPECIFIC STRATEGIES

In contrast to domain-specific basic skills, it does not appear that domain-specific strategies are acquired in a three-stage process that moves from conscious to automated. This is because strategies, by definition, are never fully automated, due to *variables* in their condition clauses. In essence, this means that since the conditions in which strategies apply change, the process of deciding what strategy to use must be constantly and consciously monitored. Recall the driving example from Chapter 6. A driving skill that could be automated would be coordinating the clutch with the gear shift. Since the conditions for shifting into another gear are similar from one time to the next, it is advantageous to automate this skill. In contrast, monitoring the other vehicles and the traffic signs along the road is (or should be!) a conscious procedure even for the most expert drivers. Because road conditions are constantly changing, these *variables* in the conditions need to be constantly monitored in order to succeed with our strategy of developing and maintaining a safe driving plan.

Strategic learning is concerned with how students organize their solutions to overall problems, and since problems at this level vary a lot in their demands, the strategies appropriate to solving the problems vary a lot also. Expert strategic behavior in a domain depends on recognizing the underlying attributes of the problem situation, even if the surface features change, and then choosing and applying the appropriate actions. In addition, to be a good strategist, one must also be able to solve problems when the problem representation (i.e., the data defining the situation) is incomplete. In these situations it is important to "think consciously" about what the problem is and to "think consciously" about possible methods for achieving a solution. In situations demanding strategic behavior, a common problem is that the learner misdiagnoses the problem and then jumps to a conclusion about how to solve it. What can happen in situations like this is that the learner will execute flawlessly the basic skills chosen for solving the problem, but still be in trouble strategically. Why? Because in essence what happened is that the learner solved the wrong problem. Applying an inappropriate method, overgeneralizing about a situation, undergeneralizing about a situation, and reacting stereotypically are all examples of less-than-optimal strategic behavior.

Thus we might say that Stage 1, the cognitive stage, of skill acquisition could apply to strategic learning. We might also say that part of Stage 2, the composition part, would be useful in learning strategies. If we compose a strategy, that would mean that we would put lots of little pieces of strategic behavior together into an integrated, overall plan that reflects the overall organization and relations that characterize the situation. What we would probably want to avoid would be proceduralizing the strategy—that is, do not get rid of all the declarative or conscious cues that trigger the strategy. And do not automate the strategy. Proceduralization and automation of strategic behaviors can be detrimental and can produce what is called the "set effect" or "Einstellung effect." The set effect (Luchins, 1942) is the situation in which someone applies a less-than-optimal procedure to a new problem because that procedure has become compiled and is activated automatically without conscious appraisal of its appropriateness in the current situation.

Lewis (1978) demonstrated the set effect in college students solving letter-replacement problems. A sample problem is shown in

Table 9.9 A letter replacement problem and two solutions—one with three rules and one with a fourth rule. The goal is to produce a letter string containing the letter G (adapted from Lewis, 1978).

REPLACEMENT RULES

1. If L, replace with D.
2. If both D and M occur, replace with L and O.
3. If two O's occur, replace with G and C.

Start:	Q M X L M
Step 1:	Q M X D M
Step 2:	Q M X L O
Step 3:	Q M X D O
Step 4:	Q L X O O
Step 5:	Q L X G C

ADDITIONAL REPLACEMENT RULE

4. If both M and O occur, replace with G and V.

Start:	Q M X L M
Step 1:	Q M X D M
Step 2:	Q M X L O
Step 3:	Q V X L G

Table 9.10 The individual productions that would result from proceduralization of the replacement rules shown in Table 9.9. After much practice on problems containing L, M, and M, the compiled production would take over control from the individual productions.

INDIVIDUAL PRODUCTIONS

IF	Letterstring contains L
THEN	Replace L with D.

IF	Letterstring contains D and letterstring contains M
THEN	Replace D and M with L and O.

IF	Letterstring contains two O's
THEN	Replace O's with G and C.

COMPILED PRODUCTION

IF	Letterstring contains L, M, and M
THEN	Replace M and M with G and C.

Table 9.9. Here students are given the goal of producing a letter string that contains the letter G. They are also given some rules for letter replacement: (1) if an L occurs, then change it to a D, (2) if both D and M occur, then replace them with L and O, and (3) if two O's occur, then replace them with G and C. Given the starting string Q M X L M, a student can first use rule 1 to produce Q M X D M, then use rule 2 to produce Q M X L O, then use rule 1 to produce Q M X D O, then use rule 2 to produce Q L X O O, and finally use rule 3 to produce a string with the letter G in it: Q L X G C.

At first students may "build" each of the three rules into a separate production and apply each in a stepwise fashion as described previously. Three productions that encode these rules are shown at the top of Table 9.10. However, with extended practice on a set of problems that all contain L, M, and M at the start (e.g., L M X Q M, T M L Q M, and M Q L X M), students may form a compiled production such as the one shown at the bottom of Table 9.10.

If a new replacement rule that reduces the number of steps needed to solve the problem is introduced after extended practice, it may not be heeded. For example, the new rule (rule 4 in Table 9.9)— if both O and M are in the string, replace them with G and V—can shorten the number of steps in problems that contain L, M, and M at the start, such as Q M X L M. First, one applies rule 1 to get Q M X D M, then one applies rule 2 to get Q M X L O, and then one applies rule 4 to get a string with the letter G in it: Q V X L G. This solution took three steps, whereas the solution without the new rule took five. If students are applying rules 1 through 3 in the stepwise fashion they can easily change when rule 4 is introduced because the necessary conditions for rule 4—the presence of O and M—will occur after step 2. However, if students have created a compiled production such as the one shown at the bottom of Table 9.10, then the conditions needed for rule 4 will never occur.

Lewis introduced rule 4 to subjects after no practice with rules 1 through 3, or after twenty practice problems of the type L, M, M, or after fifty practice problems of the type L, M, M. He then gave some new L, M, M problems and observed whether or not students used the new rule (rule 4). He found an increase in resistance to using the new rule as a function of amount of practice without the new rule. Of those with no practice, only 5% failed to use the new rule. Of those with twenty practice trials, 63% failed to use the new rule, and for those with fifty practice trials, 78% failed to use the new rule. These are the results that one would expect if the procedure for solving L, M, M problems had become compiled with practice.

The Lewis study demonstrates how proceduralization—the dropping out of conscious awareness of the declarative cues—can make behavior more rigid. If individuals habitually approach a situation in one way, their procedure for dealing with the situation becomes fully compiled—that is, both composed and proceduralized. Once the procedure is compiled, it is no longer open to conscious inspection and evaluation, and consequently alternative and preferable procedures are rarely or never tried, even if the alternate procedures are in the individual's behavioral repertoire. The reason they are rarely used is because they never enter working memory at the time when the conditions that could trigger the behavior are active. Remember that we said that compilation and automaticity should be approached with caution. Now we would like to say specifically that the criteria for procedures that should be compiled are (1) that the situation is unlikely to change, and (2) that the procedures are used so often that the speed gained in compiling is beneficial. When there is some variability in the situation from one instance to the next, then compilation can

create rigid adherence to inefficient and less-than-optimal ways of doing things. In sum, in situations where there is variability, the principle of set effects suggests that any benefit gained by increased speed in some instances is outweighed by the cost of less-than-optimal procedures in many other instances.

INSTRUCTIONAL SUPPORT FOR LEARNING DOMAIN-SPECIFIC STRATEGIES

How can we help learners to become successful strategists in particular domains? Two good suggestions are: (1) provide the learner with problems that vary a lot with respect to the conditions they present to the learner, and (2) provide the learner with opportunities to practice using strategic behaviors, even in the early stages of learning.

Provide Varied Problems

Since a good strategist needs to be able to diagnose, plan, and execute strategies in a wide variety of situations, practice in real situations that vary is essential. Thus, for example, to promote the development of good reading strategies, students should have opportunities to try out their reading strategies in many different reading situations. Different types of reading opportunities, such as reading stories, reading the newspaper, following written instructions, and doing library research provide students with varied exposure to written materials. If a teacher checks to see if students are monitoring their comprehension (a reading strategy) in all these situations, students get lots of chances to see that as the characteristics of a text change, so too must one's strategy for comprehending. Some situations call for a slower reading pace, re-reading, and lots of note taking, while in other reading situations skimming the text is adequate. Students need to learn to monitor their comprehension and adjust their strategies, depending on whether or not overall reading goals are being achieved. Since a reader's success at comprehending a text may change drastically from one reading situation to the next, it is important to be able to change strategies as the situation changes.

Practice Using Strategies throughout the Learning Process

Our second suggestion, practice using strategies right from the start, derives from the idea that strategic learning involves seeing the effects of the strategies we select on the achievement of the overall goal. Did we make a good decision about how to try to solve the problem? Recall that we said at the beginning of this chapter that experts in a domain not only know how to get the job done, they also seem to know when to apply particular methods in order to achieve overall goals.

One example of this principle can be seen in teacher education programs. Currently, there is increasing emphasis on early field experience, classroom practicum experience, and extensive student teaching experience in teacher preparation programs. This trend indicates the value that teacher educators place on comprehensive "real-life" experiences throughout the teacher education process. Although the early practicum experiences are closely supervised, the novice teachers get the "feel" of the real teaching experience and get to try out their strategies as well as their methods, right from the beginning. This experience allows the learner to begin to identify situations in which particular skills should be applied and to begin to see and experience the dynamics, complexities, and interactions that characterize a classroom situation. Moreover, these early field experiences provide motivation for novice teachers to continue to practice the separate skills and methods that they are learning in their teacher preparation courses.

LEARNING DOMAIN-GENERAL SKILLS

Earlier in this chapter, you learned that domain-specific strategies can be represented as sets of productions in which the conditions may contain variables. The variables allow a person to solve different but related problems within a domain. In the current section, we turn our attention to domain-general procedures. Like domain-specific strategies, domain-general procedures are also represented as sets of productions in which the conditions contain variables. Unlike domain-specific strategies, domain-general procedural knowledge is useful across a wide variety of domains. Thus, the level of generality of this latter type of knowledge is considerably greater.

Domain-general procedural knowledge is thought to underlie our ability to learn, our ability to think critically, and our ability to reason effectively across domains. You may recall that we have also used the term *weak methods* interchangeably with domain-general procedural knowledge. In an earlier section in this chapter, we said that novices use weak methods to interpret declarative knowledge in order to build strong, powerful, domain-specific procedures. In fact, domain-general procedural knowledge was said to be instrumental in the development of domain-specific expertise. Thus far we have had little to say about how people acquire the weak methods that underlie all learning. In this section, we present a distilled version of what is known about the acquisition of domain-general procedural knowledge. Subsequently, we present an example of an instructional program devised to teach domain-general thinking skills.

The truth is that not very much is known about how domain-general procedures are acquired. In fact, considerable controversy exists about whether they are acquired at all.

While most educators have assumed that weak methods can be acquired as easily as all other knowledge, opposition to this view is growing. One position recently put forth is that people start out with one universal weak method to encode information from the environment and use this method as the basis for constructing all subsequent weak methods, as well as all domain-specific procedural knowledge (see Laird & Newell, 1983). A somewhat different position is that weak methods in general are innate or "given" and that these givens are used to produce domain-specific procedural knowledge (Anderson, 1983, 1987).

One fact that has become increasingly clear is that acquiring and modifying general thinking skills appears to be very difficult. This fact has emerged in the arena of curriculum problems that attempt to teach critical thinking and also in research that investigates how students acquire and use general strategies.

A number of courses have been developed for the purpose of teaching general thinking skills (e.g., Feuerstein, 1980; Hayes, 1980). Only a few of these courses have been developed using detailed cognitive theories of learning, and the quality of the curricular efforts has varied. For the most part, these courses have not undergone serious formative or summative evaluation. Thus it is not surprising that these courses have shown mixed results with respect to their effectiveness (see for example, the review by Baker, 1987).

Interestingly, studies aimed at understanding the acquisition of domain-general procedural knowledge have not fared much better than the curricular efforts. A substantial amount of research has investigated whether general strategic behavior can be taught. The general finding has been that while people appear to be able to learn strategic behavior, they do not spontaneously use the acquired strategies in new contexts or domains (Belmont, Butterfield, & Ferretti, 1982). In other words, even though researchers attempt to teach "domain-general" strategies to subjects, the subjects only manage to acquire "context-specific" or "domain-specific" versions of those strategies.

Why should weak methods be so resistant to acquisition and modification? The difficulties underlying the acquisition of domain-general procedural knowledge may be understood by considering more closely their representational features and the ramifications of these features for learning.

Recall from Chapter 6 that domain-general procedural knowledge is comprised of productions that use variables and general concepts in their conditions and actions. An example of such a production is one used earlier in this chapter:

> IF   the goal is to achieve a state X
> and M is a method for
> achieving state X
>
> THEN   set as a subgoal to apply M

Without looking back, can you identify what this domain-general production was concerned with doing? (The answer is that it is a production that a novice might use to add fractions.) If you had trouble remembering, do not feel bad. The production above gives you no hints because the important terms in the conditions and action are the variables *achieve state* X and *apply method* M instead of specific math terms such as *add two fractions* and *find the least common denominator*.

This characteristic of domain-general procedures creates an interesting question: How do people build or form productions that contain variables or generalities? An answer proposed by M.J. Adams (1989b) is that people must form a general schema for thinking processes. This would involve practicing the to-be-learned procedures in a variety of domains and extracting structural similarities from situations that vary widely with respect to surface features. Subsequently, the learners will need to use generalization procedures to create the "rules" or weak methods that contain the perceived generalities (in the form of variables).

The problem is that people have great difficulty recognizing that two very different stimuli may have the same function. In Chapter 6 we used the example of a "Planning Ahead" weak method in which "the size of an opening in a countertop" and "the amount of money available for travel" both functioned as constraints in planning procedures—the former for replacing a kitchen sink and the latter for taking a vacation. You should be able to see that trying to teach someone that "holes" and "money" are the same is a difficult task. What follows is a description of one attempt to achieve this goal.

INSTRUCTIONAL SUPPORT FOR DOMAIN-GENERAL SKILLS: AN EXAMPLE

In the early 1980s, the Minister for the Development of Human Intelligence of the Republic of Venezuela sponsored a collaborative project to develop and test thinking skills curriculum materials on middle school students in Venezuela. The collaboration involved M.J. Adams and some of her colleagues at Bolt, Beranek, and Newman; Harvard University; and the Venezuelan Ministry of Education. The materials were evaluated using hundreds of seventh graders during the 1982–83 school year.

Scope of the Curriculum

Table 9.11 shows the scope and sequence of the lessons in the *Odyssey* program (Adams, 1986), as it came to be called. The first set of lessons, called "Foundations of Reasoning," introduced several processes, such as observation, classification, ordering, and use of analogies, that were then re-introduced and refined in the other lesson sets. For example, in "Understanding Language," students *ordered* words in terms of similarity of meaning, thus using the ordering skills they had learned in the first set of lessons. Or, for example, *ordering* was used in the problem-solving lessons when students constructed tabular representations. The lessons in the first set used rather abstract, non-meaningful material to introduce the basic processes. Later lessons re-introduced the processes in more meaningful contexts such as problem-solving and decision-making situations. Adams (1989b) explains that the reason for starting with non-meaningful material was to help students develop a general representation of the processes rather than one that was bound to a specific context.

Although the major focus of the curriculum was on the processes that are evident from reading the unit descriptions, the program designers also wanted students to acquire a limited set of concepts, strategies, and attitudes. The concepts included explicit versus implicit information, positive versus negative information, and other ideas about information, information sources, and interpretation. The strategies included working backwards, searching for counterexamples, and systematic trial and error. Finally, the attitudes included being willing to criticize one's own beliefs, appreciating the rewards of self-discipline, and being ready to explore and analyze new information.

Instructional Support for Acquiring Procedures

The basic procedures of observing, classifying, ordering, using analogies, and so on were introduced using simple materials. For example, Figure 9.7 shows an early exercise on classification that uses simple figures. The point of the exercise was to demonstrate that

Table 9.11 *Odyssey* lessons (from Adams, 1989b, pp. 50–51).

SERIES AND UNIT TITLES AND DESCRIPTIONS	NUMBER OF LESSONS
LESSON SERIES I: FOUNDATIONS OF REASONING	21
Unit 1: Observation and Classification	6
Using dimensions and characteristics to analyze and organize similarities and differences; discovering the basics of classification and hypothesis-testing.	
Unit 2: Ordering	5
Recognizing and extrapolating different types of sequences; discovering special properties of orderable dimensions.	
Unit 3: Hierarchical Classification	3
Exploring the structure and utility of classification hierarchies.	
Unit 4: Analogies: Discovering Relationships	4
Analyzing the dimensional structure of simple and complex analogies.	
Unit 5: Spatial Reasoning and Strategies	3
Developing strategies to solve problems of resource allocation via tangrams.	
LESSON SERIES II: UNDERSTANDING LANGUAGE	16
Unit 1: Word Relations	6
Appreciating the multidimensional nature of word meanings.	
Unit 2: The Structure of Language	5
Discovering the logic and utility of rhetorical conventions.	
Unit 3: Information and Interpretation	5
Analyzing text for explicit information, implicit information, and point of view.	
LESSON SERIES III: VERBAL REASONING	20
Unit 1: Assertions	10
Exploring the structure and interpretation of simple proportions.	
Unit 2: Arguments	10
Analyzing logical arguments; evaluating and constructing complex arguments.	
LESSON SERIES IV: PROBLEM SOLVING	18
Unit 1: Linear Representations	5
Constructing linear representations to interpret *n*-term series problems.	
Unit 2: Tabular Representations	4
Constructing tabular representations to solve multivariate word problems.	
Unit 3: Representations by Simulation and Enactment	4
Representing and interpreting dynamic problem spaces through simulation and enactment.	
Unit 4: Systematic Trial and Error	2
Developing systematic methods for enumerating all possible solutions; developing efficient methods for selecting among such solutions.	
Unit 5: Thinking Out the Implications	3
Examining the constraints of givens and solutions for problem-solving clues.	
LESSON SERIES V: DECISION MAKING	10
Unit 1: Introduction to Decision Making	3
Identifying and representing alternatives; trading off outcome desirability and likelihood in selecting between alternatives	
Unit 2: Gathering and Evaluating Information to Reduce Uncertainty	5
Appreciating the importance of being thorough in gathering information; evaluating consistency, credibility, and relevance of data.	

Table 9.11 (continued)

SERIES AND UNIT TITLES AND DESCRIPTIONS	NUMBER OF LESSONS
Unit 3: Analyzing Complex Decision Situations Evaluating complex alternatives in terms of the dimensions on which they differ and the relative desirability of their characteristics on each of those dimensions.	2
LESSON SERIES VI: INVENTIVE THINKING	15
Unit 1: Design Analyzing the designs of common objects in terms of functional dimensions; inventing designs from functional criteria.	9
Unit 2: Procedures as Designs Analyzing and inventing procedures in terms of the functional significance of their steps.	6
TOTAL LESSONS PREPARED	100

entities may be classified in more than one way depending on the dimension one focuses on and to give practice in decomposing entities into dimensions and classifying and reclassifying based on these dimensions. Later, in the lessons on word relations, the skill of decomposing and reclassifying is re-introduced. For example, after producing ordered lists of words about temperature (e.g., icy, cold, cool, warm, hot, scalding), students are asked to generate an ordered list of animals. This challenge brings up the multi-dimensionality of animals and allows students to practice recognizing multi-dimensionality, decomposing, and classifying according to dimensions. Soon after this exercise, the students encounter the exercise shown in Figure 9.8. To do this exercise successfully, students need to recognize multi-dimensionality and classify these words based on a dissimilar dimension.

This sequence of lessons, which call on observation of dimensions and flexible classification skills based on this observation, illustrates a general instructional strategy used in the *Odyssey* program. The to-be-learned process is introduced using materials with rela-

tively low meaning so that the students can focus on the process itself. Then students are given many opportunities to practice the process in a variety of contexts. As Adams (1989b) says, it was intended that through the use of the processes "in these other problem domains, the basic processes will themselves become enmeshed, with appropriate elaboration, in an increasing variety of problem types and situations. In this way, we seek to maximize the probability that they will be recalled and applied to whatever amenable challenges the students may encounter beyond the boundaries of this course. This, in other words, is the major mechanism through which we seek to enhance general transfer" (p. 70).

Evaluation

Venezuelan teachers taught over fifty of the program lessons to about 450 seventh graders during the 1982–83 academic year. The experimental classes that used the programs were matched with control classes on students' initial ability and socioeconomic status. Both

Classification

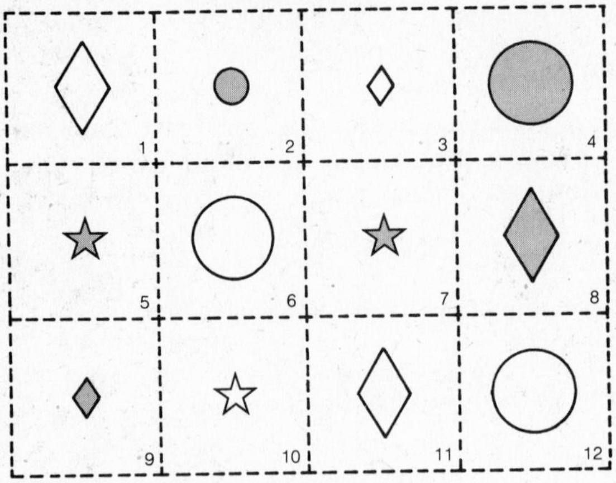

1. Dimension = Color

   Class 1:_____ Class 2:_____

2. Dimension = Shape

   Class 1:_____ Class 2:_____

   Class 3:_____

3. Dimension = Size

   Class 1:_____ Class 2:_____

Figure 9.7 Classification exercise from *Odyssey* (from Adams, Buscaglia, de Sanchez, and Swets, 1986, p. 44).

Not Quite Synonyms

Instructions: Match each pair of words to the description of the difference in their meaning. Write the letter that identifies the description in the blank beside the word pair.

1. ____ jail - cage

   ____ petite - puny

   ____ pig - pork

   ____ boulder - pebble

a) Both are rocks, but the first is very big while the second is very small.

b) The first is for locking up people, while the second is for locking up animals.

c) Both mean small, but the first is kind while the second is insulting.

d) It's the same animal, but you use the first word when it's running around and the second when you're going to eat it.

Figure 9.8 Exercise requiring multi-dimensional thinking (from Herrnstein, Adams, Huggins, and Star, 1986, p. 12).

control and experimental students took a battery of pre- and posttests, including the Otis-Lennon School Ability Test and eight achievement tests. While both groups of students gained significantly on these tests from the beginning to the end of the school year, the experimental students gained more. In terms of percentages, the experimental classes averaged 46% greater gain than control classes on the Otis-Lennon test and 68% greater gain on the achievement tests. (See Herrnstein, Nickerson, deSanchez, & Swets, 1986, for a detailed evaluation.)

Possibly these differences are due to a Hawthorne effect. That is, the experimental classes were receiving novel material and perhaps felt that they were receiving special attention. This feeling might in and of itself have promoted higher motivation and achievement. However, the results are also consistent with the notion that the materials taught transferable thinking skills that the students used in many of their courses, producing the greater gains on achievement tests.

Summary

In summary, *Odyssey* is an ambitious attempt to teach transferable thinking skills. It is also one of the few attempts that has a solid grounding in cognitive theory. It is too early to say whether it has succeeded in its claims although early data look promising. We hope that more research will be conducted on this program and that other programs that incorporate insights from cognitive theory will be developed.

CHAPTER SUMMARY

The problem of how people acquire procedural knowledge has been discussed by considering domain-specific knowledge and domain-general knowledge separately.

Automated basic skills, one type of domain-specific procedures, are acquired in stages. During the cognitive stage, learners initially form declarative representations of procedures and interpret that information using the weak methods that are available in memory. During the associative stage of learning, students build domain-specific procedural representations. This knowledge is the result of composition and proceduralization processes. During the third stage, known as the autonomous phase, learners fine-tune their domain-specific procedures, and with extensive practice this knowledge becomes automated. At this point, the procedures are very hard to modify because the learner has relinquished conscious control. Thus we can say that automated basic skills directly produce behavior.

With respect to domain-specific strategies, the goal is not to automate but to maintain conscious control of the procedure, because of the varying conditions under which strategies apply. Since strategies are important in achieving overall goals, it is important for the learner to practice using strategies under varying conditions and to monitor overall progress and outcomes in order to learn when various domain-specific strategies apply. Inappropriate application of domain-specific strategies results in less-than-optimal behavior. This phenomenon is known as the "set effect."

Since domain-general procedures are general enough to apply in many content areas or domains, they contain variables in their conditions and generalities in their actions. This means that domain-general procedures provide general guidance rather than guaranteed success. For this reason, domain-general procedures are often called "weak methods." Less is known about the acquisition of weak methods than is known about the acquisition of domain-specific procedures. Efforts to teach weak methods have met with only limited success, but there is hope that cognitive research and theory will increase the chances of success in future efforts. We will offer additional perspectives on this problem in the next two chapters.

One commonality across all types of procedural knowledge is that they all appear to require practice and feedback for acquisition. In this way acquisition of procedural knowledge is distinct from acquisition of propositions, which can often be acquired in one trial. Schema acquisition is facilitated by having students practice applying schemas, but the time requirements for practice are generally less than they are for acquisition of procedural knowledge.

ADDITIONAL READINGS

Anderson, J.R. (1982). Acquisition of cognitive skill. *Psychological Review, 89,* 369–406.

Chi, M.T.H., Glaser, R., & Farr, M.J. (Eds.), (1988). *The nature of expertise.* Hillsdale, NJ: Lawrence Erlbaum Associates.

Lesgold, A.M. (1984). Acquiring expertise. In J.R. Anderson & S.M. Kosslyn (Eds.), *Tutorials in learning and memory.* New York: W.H. Freeman and Company.

Schneider, W. (1985). Training high-performance skills: Fallacies and guidelines. *Human Factors, 27,* 285–300.

SECTION FOUR

Use of Knowledge

This section forms a bridge between the basic concepts of cognition that we described in Sections 1 through 3 and their application to areas of curriculum and instruction in Sections 5 and 6. Here we describe in general terms how humans use knowledge to solve problems.

Until quite recently in both psychology and education, chapters on problem solving typically covered *general* problem-solving processes that could apply across domains. Our chapter on problem solving (Chapter 10) does this too. However, in addition, in this chapter we describe what is now known about domain-specific problem-solving processes, as this has been an active research area and one of great interest to educators. It turns out that domain experts in fact do not use *general* problem-solving processes to solve routine problems in their domain because they have acquired domain-specific processes that are more effective. (Of course, when a domain expert encounters a novel problem in his domain, then general problem-solving processes come into play.)

In the chapter on problem solving, we elaborate on a three-point characterization of the knowledge possessed by domain experts. They possess automated basic skills that operate in their domain of expertise, conceptual understanding of their domain, and domain-specific strategies. The automated skills and the strategies are both forms of procedural knowledge, differing as to whether they are deployed automatically or with reflection. Conceptual understanding of a domain is one's declarative knowledge of the domain, largely represented as schemas. When these schemas are active in working, memory they are likely to match the conditions of domain-specific basic skills and strategies, enabling actions to take place.

We like this characterization of expertise, which is implicit in much contemporary work, because it ties together ideas about how knowledge functions in problem solving with how different varieties of knowledge are learned. In education, many curriculum decisions are based in part on the decision-maker's understanding of the role of knowledge in problem solving.

Instructional decisions are based in part on the decision-maker's understanding of how different types of knowledge are acquired. Unfortunately, these two areas of understanding are not very well integrated and neither are curriculum and instructional policies that are based on these understandings. If our understanding of these two areas can be coordinated, then it is likely that educational decisions in the areas of curriculum and instruction will be more coordinated and complementary as well.

In the chapter on transfer (Chapter 11), we continue this three-part characterization of knowledge by examining issues of transfer that are specific to each aspect of expert knowledge: conceptual understanding, basic skills, and strategies. We describe how different issues are salient depending on which type of knowledge is being transferred.

Although many questions remain to be answered, cognitive and educational psychologists have made great strides in understanding how people use knowledge and in understanding the obstacles to its use. Since these are questions of central importance to education, education should reap the benefits of this work.

Chapter 10

Problem Solving
and Reasoning

SUMMARY

1. A problem exists when one has a goal but has not yet determined a means to achieve that goal.

2. Problem-solving processes include **representing** the problem, **searching** through the problem space, and **evaluating** the selected solution.

3. The quality of these problem-solving processes depends upon the solver's domain-specific knowledge.

4. Cognitive psychologists use the **expert-novice paradigm** to study expertise. It involves studying the cognitive processes of domain experts and novices as they solve problems.

5. Using the expert-novice paradigm, cognitive scientists have discovered six consistent differences between experts and novices: size of patterns perceived, size of memory, speed of skill execution, depth of problem representation, time spent developing a problem representation, and degree of self-monitoring.

6. The basis of these differences between experts and novices is that experts have (a) better **conceptual understanding** of their domain, (b) more **automated basic skills** in their domain, and (c) better **domain-specific strategies**. Conceptual understanding is in declarative memory, while basic skills and strategies reside in procedural memory.

7. In domains where individuals lack expertise, they revert to using domain-general strategies to solve problems. Some frequently used methods include **means-ends analysis, working forward, reasoning by analogy**, and **brainstorming**.

8. Courses designed to teach general problem-solving or reasoning strategies have not been very successful at demonstrating transfer of these strategies outside of the course.

9. One reason that such courses are not successful is that they teach strategies that people already use, such as reasoning by analogy. Research shows that even preschool children can reason analogically.

10. Courses that teach formal deductive reasoning may not be successful because people rarely use formal logic in everyday reasoning. Recent research suggests, instead, that we use **pragmatic reasoning schemas** that lead to the same results as formal logic.

11. An exception to the failure of most programs that teach general reasoning are programs designed to improve people's use of probability principles. Apparently these principles map easily onto people's informal statistical reasoning so that they may be easily incorporated into prior knowledge structures.

In Chapter 4, 5, and 6 we talked about how knowledge and skills are *represented* in memory. In Chapters 7, 8, and 9 we discussed how knowledge and skills are *acquired* during the learning process. Now, in this chapter and the next, we focus on the ways people *use* their knowledge and skills to solve problems.

Most educators consider problem solving and reasoning to be two of the most important goals toward which they teach. Science teachers want students to learn not just the content of science courses, but also the manner by which scientists solve problems. English teachers want students to learn not only about the history of literature, but also how to solve their own communication problems effectively. Even most elementary school teachers view reasoning and problem-solving skills as important learning outcomes. Trends in the marketplace tend to support the importance placed by teachers on problem-solving activities. With more and more routine jobs being turned over to robots and other automated devices, the jobs left for humans tend to be less routine—requiring more problem-solving skill for adequate job performance. In essence, a primary goal in education seems to be to enable students to use their declarative and procedural knowledge, once acquired, to solve problems.

From its beginnings, cognitive psychology has had problem solving as a main focus of research. In this chapter, we will summarize what is known about problem solving. Enough is known by now to have significant implications for curriculum and instruction decisions. The perspective to be taken follows from the production system model of cognition that has been developed in previous chapters. Specifically, we will discuss domain-specific and domain-general problem solving separately. The chapter is divided into three major sections. In the first section, we will describe the classical definition of problem solving. In the second section, we consider the topic of domain-specific problem solving and discuss how experts in a domain differ from novices in their problem-solving skills. In the final section, we focus on the case of domain-general problem solving and discuss some obstacles to teaching domain-general reasoning strategies.

PROBLEM SOLVING

Definition of Problem Solving

A problem is said to exist whenever one has a goal and has not yet identified a means for reaching that goal. The problem may be wanting to answer a question, to prove a theorem, to be accepted, or to get a job. In each of these situations, there is a goal and, at least for the moment, the goal has not been reached.

The same problem may be more or less difficult depending on the individual. For example, for you to add 25 and 36 is almost trivial, but for a first grader it is daunting. We recognize in the conditions of the problem a familiar pattern of numbers to be added and this activates procedural knowledge of how to carry out addition. Thus, for literate adults, simple addition problems are problems only for an instant.

The standard information-processing framework for defining problems consists of: (1) a *goal* or end state, (2) an initial or *starting state* which is the given description of the problem, and (3) a number of *intermediate states*, which describe all possible solution paths for reaching the goal. Each solution path is comprised of a number of individual steps that move one away from the starting state and (it is hoped) toward the goal state. Together the initial, intermediate, and goal states comprise the "problem space" (Newell and Simon, 1972).

Figure 10.1 shows several possible problem spaces. In panel (A), there is a goal and there are two solution paths of equal efficiency for reaching the goal. An example of this

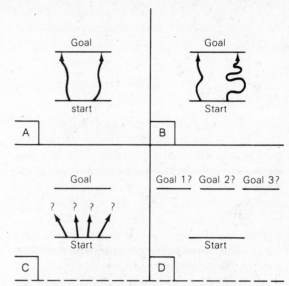

Figure 10.1 A problem consists of a starting state, a goal, and a set of solution paths for reaching the goal. These panels show several types of problem space.

might be performing long division with one of two standard long-division procedures. In panel (B), there is a goal for which one solution path is clearly much more efficient than another. An example of this would be a child's goal of understanding a story. An efficient way to reach this goal is to read the story (assuming, of course, that the child can read). A less efficient way would be to try to find someone to read to her. In panel (C), there are some starting points and a goal at another point and no known path between the starting points and the goal. This is a common situation for people trying to solve novel problems. They can think of actions to try but there is little assurance that what is tried will lead them closer to their goal. Finally, in panel (D), there is a problem in which there are either several possible goals or unclear goals. This situation exists in "ill-defined" problems (W. Reitman, 1964), where the initial step in problem solving is to decide on one's goal.

Once the goal is decided on, such problems then revert to being like those in panels A, B, and C.

Problem-Solving Processes

No matter what the characteristics of the problem space for a given problem, the same processes occur during problem solving. Initially, the solver *forms a representation* of the problem. It may consist of information that is active in working memory and also some external representations such as a diagram on a chalkboard, paper, or computer screen. Typically, this representation contains the "givens" of the problem. For example, when given a word problem in algebra, people read the problem and represent its meaning in working memory, including assigning values to variables. They may also write some equations on paper that represent what they think are the givens in the problem. These representations activate knowledge of word problems stored in long-term memory, such as recognizing what type of word problem it is, which in turn cues associated solution processes. The activated solution process is applied in the current situation. Activation and application of knowledge together are referred to as the problem-solving process of *searching the problem space*. Finally, there is *evaluation* of the success of the solution.

This sequence of processes may occur several times during the solving of a problem. That is, after forming an initial problem representation and activating knowledge that is relevant to that representation, one may find that the knowledge does not apply (i.e., when the solution is evaluated, it turns out that the problem has not been solved). One will then form a new representation and activate different knowledge, which will cue different solution processes, the outcomes of which will then be evaluated. These iterations or cycles

continue until a problem is solved or the solver gives up.

As an example, consider a teacher who wants a student to improve his "C" grade in history. The teacher may initially think such things as "He is bright, so he should be able to do better; therefore, he must be lazy." These thoughts form the initial representation of the problem. The associated solution processes activated by this representation might include ways of motivating "bright, lazy" students— perhaps a challenging assignment. The teacher might apply this idea by having the student do a research project on the causes of World War II. If this fails to produce the intended result (a better grade), the teacher might change her initial problem representation, thinking "Maybe it's not a matter of motivation. Maybe he's not as bright as I thought. He seemed to copy his research paper out of an encyclopedia. Maybe he has poor reading comprehension." The new representation would activate knowledge of how to improve comprehension skills, which would suggest new solution processes, which would be applied and the results evaluated. This dynamic relation among representation, solution, and evaluation would continue until the teacher found a way to solve the problem or changed her goal.

As can be seen, the problem representation is most crucial to the success of problem solving, because the representation determines what knowledge will be activated in long-term memory. People have various ways of developing a good problem representation. Sometimes a problem is familiar and is recognized as such by the solver. In this case, it is relatively easy for the solver to form a good problem representation—it is not necessary to search much through long-term memory for a way to represent the problem, and once a representation is formed there are solutions or ideas for solutions available in long-term memory. That is, the solution may be stored in production rule form. In other cases, the problem is less clear or less familiar to the solver, and then reasoning processes must be used to help the person draw sound conclusions about the information she either has been given or has accessed. These conclusions are then added to the developing problem representation. We will discuss examples of both search and reasoning strategies in later sections of this chapter.

DOMAIN-SPECIFIC PROBLEM SOLVING

So far in this chapter you have learned that the same problem-solving processes—forming a representation, searching the problem space, and evaluating the solution—apply, regardless of the problem to be solved. However, the quality of the representation formed, the difficulty of the search, and the success of the solution all rely not so much on general processing ability as on domain-specific knowledge and strategies. We turn now to a description of what is known about expertise in domain-specific problem solving. This is an important section for you to understand because the framework we develop in this section will be used in the remainder of this book.

The Expert-Novice Paradigm

Cognitive psychologists most often study domain expertise using the **expert-novice paradigm**. In this paradigm, researchers identify a group of experts and a group of novices in a particular domain and give both groups the same set of problems to solve. The study participants may think aloud or give retrospective reports of what they were thinking while solving problems. Researchers may collect latency data and/or eye-fixation data. Often, researchers ask participants to recall the problems they have worked on because what

they recall is revealing of how they represented these problems.

A classic example of the expert-novice paradigm is the work of de Groot (1965, 1966) on chess players. De Groot contrasted chess masters and relatively weak chess players. He showed all participants a series of chess boards with the pieces arranged as they might be at various points in real chess games. The participants studied each chessboard for 5 seconds and then tried to set up pieces on an empty board in the manner just seen. Chess masters were able to correctly place 20 or more pieces, while the novices could only place 4 or 5 correctly. On the other hand, better and less good players were about equal on the number of possible moves considered before making a move during a game. Thus, a major difference between better and less good chess players is the types of patterns they perceive on a chessboard.

This classic example has all the elements of the expert-novice paradigm: (1) selection of experts and novices, (2) presentation of a set of tasks to both experts and novices, and (3) comparison of the two groups as to how they performed the tasks. This method allows cognitive psychologists to come up with good candidates for the cognitive processes and representations that account for domain expertise.

The de Groot study used recall data to study differences between experts and novices. Other studies may use different types of data such as think-aloud protocols. Also, other studies may vary as to how expertise is defined. In the de Groot study, an externally accepted criterion (chess master) was used. Other studies may use test scores, subjective judgments of supervisors, or years of experience. Developmental studies are sometimes cast in an expert-novice framework where younger age groups are seen as novices (for example, in reading) and older age groups are viewed as experts. The common element across all instances of the expert-novice paradigm is a focus on describing differences in problem solving that are associated with level of expertise.

Expert-novice studies are extremely useful for identifying potential cognitive reasons for differences between experts and novices. However, one must remember that such studies are descriptive rather than manipulative. To really determine whether or not the entities uncovered in expert-novice studies are causal, one needs to teach these entities to novices and see if the novices become more expert-like in their performance following instruction. For example, would giving chess novices practice in recognizing typical patterns in chess games increase their skill level? The two types of studies taken together—expert-novice analysis followed by an instructional manipulation—form a powerful research method for determining the cognitive causes of expertise. Ultimately, this knowledge should inform curriculum choices.

Much of what is known about the cognitive processes involved in reading, writing, mathematics, and science competence has been derived from expert-novice studies, and, in some cases, follow-up instructional studies. This research will be described later in this book. Now we turn to a description of domain-specific expertise that emerges when one steps back from a *particular* content or skill domain and asks whether there are some general characteristics of expertise.

Attributes of Domain Expertise

Glaser and Chi (1988) provide a good summary of what is known about the attributes of domain expertise. Their list includes the following: In comparison to novices, domain experts (1) perceive large meaningful patterns in their domain, (2) have superior short- and long-term memory for domain-relevant information, (3) are faster at performing the basic skills of the domain, (4) represent problems at a deep (principled) level, (5) spend a great deal of time analyzing a problem before attempting a solution, and (6) have strong self-monitoring skills. We will discuss each of these elements below.

Perception of Large Meaningful Patterns. The typical way to measure perception of large patterns is to present subjects with information from the domain of interest and ask them to reproduce this information. For example, Chase and Simon (1973) had expert and novice chess players look at chessboards configured in typical game patterns and reproduce these on an empty board, as is shown in Figure 10.2. The researchers measured how many pieces the individual placed before glancing back at the game board. They found that chess masters placed more pieces per glance and the pieces they placed were meaningful patterns such as configurations of pawns that occur in typical games.

The finding that experts perceive large meaningful patterns has been replicated in a wide variety of domains, including air traffic control (Means et al., 1988), radiology (Lesgold, Rubinson, Feltovich, Glaser, Klopfer, & Wang, 1988), and electronics (Egan & Schwartz, 1979). One study of expert recall that is especially interesting is Chi's (1978) work on children who excel at chess. When compared with novices (either adults or children) the expert children showed better memory for meaningful chess patterns. This study demonstrates dramatically that age is not crucial to the ability of experts to recall meaningful patterns, rather it is level of expertise that is important.

Superior Short- and Long-Term Memory. Experts seem to be able to hold more information in short-term memory and to remember more information that they have just heard or read in their domain than do novices. The most

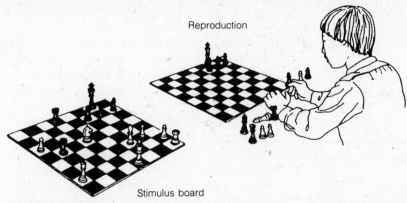

Reproduction

Stimulus board

Figure 10.2 The reproduction task in Chase and Simon (1973). Subjects were to reproduce the configuration of pieces on the reproduction board (from Anderson, 1990, adapted from Klatzky, 1980).

dramatic demonstration of superior memory is a study of an individual who was trained to be an expert in recalling numbers (Chase & Ericsson, 1982). This individual, who happened to be a runner, became quite proficient at recalling a series of randomly presented numbers. His strategy was to use meaningful number patterns from foot races that he had been in or knew about, in order to chunk the incoming digits. While the normal span for holding digits in working memory is roughly 7 digits, this individual came to be able to hold and repeat back 80 recently heard numbers!

In addition, experts have superior long-term recall ability in their domain as well. The expert in the number recall study just mentioned could recognize 80 to 90% of the digit groups presented to him after a week's delay.

The superiority of short- and long-term memory is related to the already mentioned superiority in perception of meaningful patterns. Because experts perceive these meaningful patterns (such as race times or typical chess patterns or typical circuitry), they can use these to organize bits of information into larger groups and thus can retrieve more information overall.

Speed of Skill Execution. Glaser and Chi (1988) point out that there are two ways in which experts are speedier than novices. First, they are speedier in performing the "basic" skills of the domain by dint of many more hours of practice. For example, skilled readers do not "sound out" words in their minds the way beginning readers often do, and hence skilled readers decode printed messages much more quickly. This speed of performing basic skills puts experts at a distinct advantage because it frees up working memory resources to think about the problem at hand rather than about lower-level details that have become automated.

A second way that experts sometimes solve problems more quickly is through "opportunistic" reasoning. Opportunistic reasoning is reasoning that was not part of the initial plan or problem representation, but arises as more information is gathered. For example, expert electronics troubleshooters may not plan every move they make before they start troubleshooting, but during testing of various components they may have an idea that fits with the information they have obtained so far and that leads quickly to a solution (Means et al., 1988). Another example of opportunistic reasoning comes from expert cab drivers who may recognize a shorter route while traveling to their destination (Chase, 1983).

Time Spent Developing a Problem Representation. Whereas experts may be quicker than novices to solve more routine problems in a domain, when a difficult problem is encountered, experts are slower than novices to develop a representation. For ill-defined problems, this slower approach is probably because they have more knowledge to bring to bear in solving the problem and they need to sort through this knowledge in determining what is relevant. For example, Voss and Post (1988) gave Soviet experts and novices a problem to solve that involved developing a policy for increasing productivity in the agricultural sector. For the experts, an average of one-fourth of their solution protocol involved developing the problem representation—for example, using their knowledge of Soviet politics they added constraints on what the solution might be. For novices, an average of only 1% of their protocol involved developing a representation. Rather the novices simply plunged right in to giving a solution.

Even for well-defined problems, experts may take longer to develop the problem representation because they have the skills or knowledge needed to create a meaningful representation. Most mathematics teachers are aware of the fact that good algebra students create a meaningful representation for a problem before solving it, while poorer students just start plugging numbers into formulas without thinking about the meaning.

Depth of Problem Representation. When confronted with a new problem, experts tend to develop a representation in which the essential elements of the problem are laid bare. In contrast, novices tend to get distracted by perceptually salient, but often irrelevant, aspects of the problem.

The standard method for studying depth of problem representation is to ask experts and novices to sort a set of problems into categories of their own choosing and then to determine what features of the problems led to their being grouped together. One example of this is a study of computer programming expertise (Weiser & Schertz, 1983). These researchers found that experts sorted programming problems according to the algorithms that could be used to solve them, while novices sorted them on the basis of what the program should do—for example, generate a list or alphabetize a list. The experts' organization of problems is said to be deeper in the sense that it is based on solution principles.

Self-Monitoring Skills. A final way that experts and novices differ is in terms of self-monitoring. Experts tend to check their solutions to problems more frequently and with better effect than do novices. In the algebra example just discussed, the student with the meaningful representation can use this to check his or her quantitative answer to determine that it "makes sense." In contrast, the student who just does "number plugging" could double-check for computational errors, but could not check to see that the answer made sense.

Summary

In summary, domain experts differ from domain novices in a variety of ways. They are more likely to perceive large meaningful patterns and to use these perceptions to organize memory efficiently. They are faster at executing problem-solution procedures because they have had more practice and because they use opportunistic reasoning. They are slower to develop representations for novel problems, but, once developed, their representations are more likely to be at a deep level, rather than at a superficial level. Finally, experts are better at self-monitoring or checking the success of their own problem-solving strategies.

KNOWLEDGE UNDERLYING DOMAIN-SPECIFIC EXPERTISE

You have just read about a variety of ways in which experts differ from novices. Now that we know how they differ, it is interesting to ask what mental representations and processes account for these differences. The view that is shared in broad outline by many researchers in this area is that experts have (1) more and better **conceptual** or **functional understanding** of the domain, (2) more and better **automated basic skills** in the domain, and (3) more and better **domain-specific strategies**. These elements are shown in Figure 10.3. As can be seen, conceptual understanding is housed in declarative knowledge—images, linear orders, propositions, and schemas. Domain-specific skills and domain-specific strategies are housed in procedural knowledge, with basic skills having more localized elements in their conditions and strategies having more global, goal-directed elements. Note that while conceptual information and conscious strategies and skills occupy space and use resources in working memory, automated skills can execute almost unconsciously when their conditions are met, usurping little or no working memory capacity.

As an illustration, consider expertise in solving algebra problems. Studies involving computer modeling have shown that schemas for different types of algebra problems—conceptual understanding—can account for a great deal of the variance in performance of algebra students (Marshall, 1990). Once good

students access a schema to represent the problem, they then tend to be quicker at performing numerical calculations and legal transformations of equations than are poor students. This speed is due to the fact that these skills have, through practice, come to be performed automatically—that is, speed at calculation and equation transformation are the basic skills involved in algebra. Finally, better algebra students are more likely to check their answers by comparing their numerical answer and quantitative representation of the problem with a qualitative representation of the problem. Such students would recognize, for example, that getting a negative number for a problem involving weight "just doesn't make sense." Poor students overlook the nonsense in certain answers. Thus, we can say that the better students also have a more effective strategy for ensuring that their answers are correct.

Functions of the Three Types of Knowledge

Each of these three types of knowledge—conceptual understanding, automated basic skills, and domain-specific strategies—plays a different role in problem solving. Conceptual understanding helps the solver to develop a meaningful representation of the problem and also to narrow the search for solutions by matching the schema or "conditions" that represent the givens in the problem with a set of "actions" in procedural memory that is most likely to produce satisfactory results. Automated basic skills allow the solver to perform necessary, routine mental operations without thinking much about them. This has the important effect of freeing up working memory space so that the solver can constantly keep her goals in mind while also searching for a solution. Domain-specific strategies help make both the search process

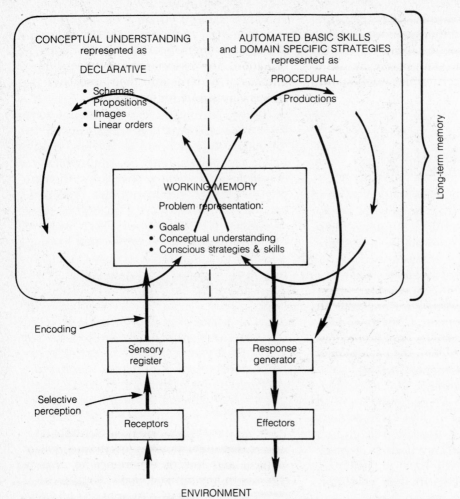

Figure 10.3 The elements of problem-solving expertise (conceptual understanding, domain-specific skills, and domain-specific strategies) and their locations in memory. Conceptual understanding is developed by accessing schemas and other units of declarative knowledge. Domain-specific skills and strategies are in procedural memory and fire when their conditions are matched in working memory.

and the evaluation of the outcome more efficient and effective than would otherwise be the case.

Interactions of the Three Types of Knowledge

During the course of problem-solving, the three types of knowledge interact in a variety of ways. Execution of a basic skill often provides more information to be used in accessing conceptual understanding. For instance, electronics troubleshooters need to take measurements at various points (basic skill) in order to develop their representation (conceptual understanding) of what is wrong (Means et al., 1988). Air traffic controllers need to read flight data information and scan radar screens (basic skills) in order to develop a conceptual understanding of what traffic may cause problems. An algebra student may need to do a few calculations (basic skill) before he has a complete "picture" (conceptual understanding) of the situation.

The execution of strategies also provides a stimulus for access of conceptual knowledge. For example, a strategy that good readers use is called "comprehension monitoring" and involves an almost constant monitoring of whether or not one is understanding what one is reading. When one is not understanding, one interrupts reading and may try to obtain more information to resolve the problem in understanding.

Another beneficial interaction occurs when activation of conceptual knowledge leads quickly to execution of basic skills and/or domain-specific strategies. For example, if an algebra student represents a new problem as being a proportion problem, the basic skill of computing proportions becomes primed for action, as do strategies for short-cut computation of proportions. The mechanism for this priming is the pattern matching we previously described in Chapter 6. Specifically, the conceptual representation in working memory creates the conditions necessary for certain productions to fire, hence enabling the execution of their actions.

Summary

In summary, cognitive psychologists have now studied expertise in a great variety of domains and a consistent picture has emerged from this research. In comparison to novices, experts have more and better conceptual understanding, more and better automated basic skills, and more and better domain-specific strategies. Conceptual understanding is comprised of images, propositions, linear orders, and schemas housed in declarative memory structures. Automated basic skills and domain-specific strategies are comprised of pro-duction rules housed in procedural knowledge memory structures. Since conditions of productions often incorporate schematic information, the associations between these schemas or patterns and their associated actions is very strong for experts.

Possession of better conceptual understanding allows experts to quickly recognize meaningful patterns and to represent problems at a deep level. Possession of automated basic skills gives them greater working memory resources for problem solving. Possession of domain-specific strategies allows them to be more efficient and effective than novices and to engage in opportunistic reasoning.

DOMAIN-GENERAL PROBLEM SOLVING AND REASONING

In the previous section we explained how conceptual understanding, domain-specific basic skills, and domain-specific strategies enable experts to solve problems much more effectively and efficiently than novices in a wide variety of domains. What we failed to stress, however, was that in the vast majority of domains, most of us are novices rather than experts. Recall that it takes lots of time, lots of practice, and lots of experience to acquire expertise in any given domain. Since most of us will acquire expertise in only one or a few domains, what do we do when we are expected to solve problems in domains where we are *inexpert* as opposed to domains where we are *expert?* Furthermore, what do we do when we encounter novel problems even in areas of expertise? The answer is we revert to domain-general problem solving processes, and we do this frequently.

Think, for instance, of an expert accountant who also plays a terrific game of chess. If her checkbook does not balance, she probably knows exactly what to do. However, if her child has a fever and her car will not start, her accounting expertise and her chess expertise will not help her to solve her current problem effectively and efficiently. Instead, she will revert to domain-general problem-solving strategies. Domain-general strategies can be applied to a variety of problems, independent of content, but as is true of other domain-general procedures, their flexibility is also their weakness. Recall from Chapters 6 and 9 that domain-general procedures are called weak methods because they do not guarantee a solution. For example, the strategy of trying to remember an analogous situation can be applied to the problems of how to allocate your study time, how to improve crop yield, or how to smooth over a difficult social situation. Therefore, solving problems by analogy is said to be a general strategy. In the next section, we will describe some domain-general problem-solving strategies.

SOME GENERAL PROBLEM-SOLVING STRATEGIES

As was mentioned previously, search strategies are strategies that assist in accessing long-term memory. Domain-general search strategies are activities that can improve the search for a solution across a wide variety of problems from different domains. Sometimes the search becomes too random; there seem to be too many possible solutions and no way to judge which possibility is most likely to lead to success. In such situations a strategy for *limiting* the search is needed. At other times search seems to be quite impoverished. The solutions that have been thought of do not seem to work. Here a strategy for *expanding* the search is needed.

Limiting Search

Consider a "cryptarithmetic" problem such as the one shown in Table 10.1 (Newell and Simon, 1972). In cryptarithmetic, the goal is to find out what number is represented by each letter. In this problem you are told that D = 5

Table 10.1 A cryptarithmetic problem. The goal is to find what number to assign to each letter such that when added together and translated back to letters, they would produce the name ROBERT (adapted from Newell and Simon, 1972).

$$
\begin{array}{r}
\mathrm{D\,O\,N\,A\,L\,D} \\
+\,\mathrm{G\,E\,R\,A\,L\,D} \\
\hline
\mathrm{R\,O\,B\,E\,R\,T}
\end{array}
$$

Given: D = 5

and your goal is to find what numbers are signified by the other letters, such that the numbers add up to a correct total. Try this problem and think aloud while you do so. The answer may be found at the end of the chapter.

It turns out that there are a third of a million possible answers to this problem (Simon, 1978) because there are 9! ($9 \times 8 \times 7 \times 6 \times 5 \times 4 \times 3 \times 2 \times 1$) possible assignments of nine numbers to nine letters. This is quite a large set of solutions to consider. A large computer might be able to go through it systematically in a reasonable time period, but a human cannot. Although most real-world problems do not have this many possible solutions, they often have more solutions than human working memory can accommodate. Therefore, humans need strategies to limit their search to solutions that are most likely to be correct.

One way to limit search is to "work backwards" from the desired goal. This is what mathematics students are doing when they ask themselves, "What is the unknown?" because the unknown is the desired goal. A powerful form of working backwards is called means-ends analysis. Another way to limit search, which is not as powerful as means-ends analysis, is called working forward and involves performing whatever actions occur to one in response to a given problem.

Means-Ends Analysis. Means-ends analysis involves the following steps:

1. Find the difference between the goal and the current situation.

2. Find an operation that is relevant to that difference.

3. Perform the operation to reduce the difference.

4. Repeat steps 1 through 3 until the problem has been solved.

Consider the problem of a student who shows a great deal of anxiety about speaking in front of his peers. His teacher would like him to be less anxious in this situation. The difference between the goal and the current situation is one of anxiety. The operations that are relevant to reducing anxiety are based on classical conditioning (e.g., systematic desensitization or modeling). The teacher selects systematic desensitization as a procedure. First, she asks the student very easy questions that require short answers, and she asks these when the class has broken up into small groups.

When the student states the answer correctly, she accepts it but does not emphasize the correctness of the answer (it could cause future anxiety if the student learned that being correct had great importance). Gradually the teacher increases the number of students in front of whom she asks questions of the target student; she also increases the length of the required answer and the difficulty of the question. In short, the teacher pairs a relaxed, learning-oriented (as opposed to evaluation-oriented) attitude with the student's speaking aloud in front of peers. Through classical conditioning the student comes to associate speaking aloud in front of peers with positive, relaxed emotions.

This teacher used means-ends analysis. She first thought of the goal (getting the student to relax while speaking in front of peers) and then of a relevant operation to reduce the difference between the student's situation (tenseness) and the goal. Classical conditioning techniques are relevant to problems involving anxiety. Finally the teacher applied these techniques and solved the problem.

Many problems that are solved by means-ends analysis involve several cycles, each of which focuses on a different difference. For example, consider the problem:

John started running at 4:05 and finished at 4:45. He ran 3.5 miles in that time. What is his running speed?

If one uses means-end analysis to solve this problem, one starts out by saying "What is the difference between the current goal (to know speed) and the current situation?" The difference is one to which the operation "speed = distance/time" is relevant. One starts to apply this operation by letting distance = 3.5 miles. But then one realizes that there is no value stated in the problem for time. This leads one to the subgoal of finding a value for time. Again, one asks, "What is the difference between my current goal (to know time) and the current situation?" The difference is one to which the operation of subtraction is relevant. Specifically, if one subtracts the time that John started to run from the time when he stopped running one gets the desired value for time. After performing this operation, one can return to the first goal of solving for speed in the formula speed = distance/time:

speed = 3.5 miles/.67 hour = 5.25 mph

Working Forward. Working forward is much simpler than means-ends analysis. One examines the current situation and performs operations to change it. The operations one selects are not constrained by the goal as they are in means-ends analysis; therefore, they may sometimes lead one in fruitless directions.

In the problem of the anxious student, a teacher who uses a working-forward strategy might say to the student, after he has shown nervousness in speaking, "Don't get so uptight." This statement seems much more direct than the elaborate means-ends analysis. Unfortunately, it is also much less likely to work. It is based on a superficial analysis of the problem: The teacher recognizes the student's anxiety but fails to use knowledge of what reduces anxiety.

In the running speed problem, working forward may work because only a few operations are suggested by the problem statement even when the solver does not keep the goal in mind. The first sentence in the problem almost begs the solver to subtract start time from stop time, which would be the first step performed in working forward. The resulting value could then be brought to bear as the solver reads the second sentence, which would cause him to think of the formula speed = distance/time.

Thus, working forward works when the operations suggested by the current situation are the ones that lead to the goal. If the current situation suggests misleading operations, working forward will not lead to the goal. Then means-ends analysis is more powerful, because it selects only goal-relevant operations.

Means-ends analysis requires more knowledge than does working forward. The crucial step in means-ends analysis is selecting an operation that reduces a functional difference between the current situation and the goal. If one does not possess knowledge of such operations or cannot activate one's knowledge, one cannot use the means-ends strategy. For example, if the teacher in the earlier example had not known the relationship between classical conditioning and anxiety reduction, she could not have applied these principles to the problem. An important aspect of means-ends analysis is that its success depends on the quality of one's content knowledge. If such knowledge is deficient, then one will have difficulty performing means-ends analysis. This is an example of a domain-general strategy which, though it can be applied to a variety of domains, nonetheless requires domain-specific knowledge for use.

Expanding the Search

Means-ends analysis and working forward are strategies for limiting the search for solutions. However, sometimes a problem can be solved best by expanding the search. This is particularly true when known solutions to a problem are inadequate, as is often the case for global and national problems, complex personal problems, scientific and artistic problems, and some teaching problems. Two strategies that may be used in expanding the search for solutions are reasoning by analogy and brainstorming.

Reasoning by Analogy. Reasoning by analogy is often used when people have a problem in a domain for which they have little knowledge. It involves representing the problem, using the representation to access knowledge in a familiar domain relevant to the current situation, and then evaluating the utility of the accessed knowledge. Many examples of reasoning by analogy can be seen when one observes computer-naive adults learning to use a microcomputer for word processing (cf., Rumelhart and Norman, 1981). Such learners solve editing problems as they would on a typewriter and thus they fail to take advantage of the computer's memory. Here analogical reasoning does not lead to effective problem solving.

In other situations, however, an analogy leads to effective solutions to novel problems. For example, when Kekulé was trying to discover the molecular structure of benzene, he dreamed of a snake eating its tail (Glass, Holyoak, and Santa, 1979). This image provided a visual analogy for the ring of carbon atoms in the benzene ring, and led Kekulé to propose that the basic structure of benzene was a ring of carbon atoms. There are many such anecdotes about the use of analogical reasoning in creative problem solving (e.g., Koestler, 1964).

Although analogical reasoning is generally thought to be an important problem-solving strategy, people do not seem particularly good at using it. There is a set of studies in which researchers started out by giving participants a problem that all can solve correctly. They then gave them a second problem that was superficially different, but whose solution process was the same as for the first problem. The results have shown that subjects tend not to see the analogy between the two problems unless it is pointed out to them (Hayes and Simon, 1976; Reed, Ernst, and Banerji, 1974).

All the conditions that favor effective analogical reasoning are not known, but the anecdotes suggest that an important one is the solver's knowledge of both the domain in which the problem exists and the analogous domain. Kekulé knew chemistry and he had visual experience of snakes. On the other hand, the computer-naive adults had little knowledge of the domain of computers. Therefore, they may have formed an inadequate representation of their editing problems. The notion that level of knowledge determines the effectiveness of analogical reasoning needs to be studied experimentally.

Brainstorming. Another strategy for increasing the number and quality of solutions to a problem is called brainstorming (Osborn, 1963). The steps in brainstorming are:

1. Define the problem.

2. Generate, without criticism, as many solutions as possible, however bizarre they may seem at first.

3. Decide on criteria for judging the solutions generated.

4. Use these criteria to select the best solution.

Brainstorming includes elements of both working forward and means-ends analysis and thus has the advantages of both. Step 2 essentially involves working forward: One simply responds to the problem statement with operations that could change the situation. Steps 3 and 4 involve some means-ends analysis: The criteria one develops almost certainly will include that of meeting the desired goal.

If the teacher with the shy student had used brainstorming to solve the problem, she would first have generated a list of possible solutions. For example, she might list these:

1. Tell him to relax.

2. Ask the school counselor to do something.

3. Make him practice speaking out loud every day.

4. Give him tranquilizers.

5. Use systematic desensitization.

6. Have self-confident students model a relaxed attitude.

7. Do not ask him to speak out loud.

After generating a list, she would then think about criteria for a good solution. These might include (1) that it was likely to reach the goal of having the student relax when speaking, (2) that it was feasible, and (3) that it was legal. Solutions 1, 3, and 7 do not have as high a probability of success as do 2, 4, 5, and 6. Solution 2 may not be feasible if the school counselor is already overworked and solution 4 may not be legal. This leaves solutions 5 and 6 as the ones that best meet the criteria.

In this example, one of the solutions selected by brainstorming was also the solution selected by means-ends analysis. However, in many situations brainstorming may lead to a better solution than that reached through means-ends analysis, particularly in situations where the problem solver does not have a well-organized and elaborated knowledge base in the domain. Although studies have not directly compared brainstorming and means-ends analysis strategies, they have compared brainstorming to strategies spontaneously adopted by individuals. These studies sometimes show that brainstorming results in higher-quality solutions than whatever techniques individuals use spontaneously (cf., Parnes and Meadow, 1959). For brainstorming as for analogical reasoning, the quality of solutions seems affected by the amount of relevant knowledge. Parnes (1961), for example, found a correlation between the number of ideas one produces and the originality of the ideas.

Summary

Domain-general problem-solving strategies are used when the solution to a problem is not obvious. They may expand or limit the search for solutions. Some strategies for limiting the search are means-ends analysis and working forward. Means-ends analysis is powerful because it selects only goal-relevant operations. However, the success of means-ends analysis depends on the quality of the problem solver's knowledge of functional relationships. Two strategies for expanding the search are the use of analogies and brainstorming. The success

of both of these techniques also appears to depend on the extent of knowledge that a solver can access.

There are many other procedures for limiting and expanding search and for other aspects of problem solving. These are described in many books and articles, some of which are listed at the end of this chapter. The main point of this discussion is that there are general strategies that work independent of the domain of a problem and that many of these strategies affect the search for solutions.

TEACHING DOMAIN-GENERAL PROBLEM-SOLVING AND REASONING STRATEGIES

At the beginning of this chapter, we mentioned the fact that it is becoming more and more important for people to be able to solve problems on the job because routine jobs are being taken over by robots and other dedicated computers. Educators who wish to improve students' problem-solving skills often try to do so by teaching general strategies such as those just described in courses on general problem-solving. For example, elementary and middle-school gifted education programs frequently train students in brainstorming and other creative problem-solving strategies. Also, many universities offer courses in problem-solving that teach deductive logic or problem-solving heuristics.

People who teach such courses and students who take them attest to their value. The fact is, however, that few such courses have been rigorously evaluated, and, when they are, the typical finding is that there are few if any long-term benefits from the course (cf., Larkin, 1990; Chance, 1986). That is, students did not transfer their newly-learned strategies outside of the course itself. As we will see in the next chapter, one reason for lack of transfer has to do with *how* the strategies are taught. Another reason, which we will discuss here, has to do with *what* is taught.

General problem-solving programs typically teach either general search strategies like those we have discussed (e.g., means-ends analysis or analogical reasoning), or formal reasoning strategies for inductive and deductive reasoning. It turns out that teaching general search strategies does not help because people already have these strategies. Teaching deductive reasoning strategies also is not helpful, not because people already have such strategies, but because most people—even very good reasoners—do not actually use such strategies. Thus, people do not transfer these strategies because they are rarely used in everyday situations. We will elaborate on these conclusions below.

General Search Strategies

Psychologists used to think that preschoolers and even high school students couldn't solve problems because they did not have good search strategies. They did not know how to use means-ends analysis to narrow the search or analogical reasoning to expand a search. Recent research, however, suggests that even young children often are capable of using these strategies.

Brown and her colleagues (Brown, Kane, & Echols, 1986) provide one illustration of preschoolers' use of analogical reasoning in a familiar domain. Children from ages 3 to 5 were presented with the three problems ("stories") shown in Table 10.2 (p. 226). The abstract goal structure for each problem is shown in Table 10.3. In each problem, the solution involved rolling up some paper to perform a task. In Problem 1 (The Genie), the rolled-up paper gave the genie a way to get his jewels into a bottle some distance away without moving his feet, which were stuck. In Problem 2 (The Rabbit), the rolled-up paper allowed the rabbit to get eggs to the other side of the river when there was no boat or bridge and he didn't know how to swim. In Problem 3 (The Farmer), the rolled-up paper allowed the farmer to get cherries from one vehicle to another across a huge tree that had fallen across the road.

The children were randomly assigned to one of three groups—Control, Recall, and Prompted Goal Structure. For children in the Control Group, the researchers simply described each problem and asked them to offer solutions. For children in the Recall Group, the researchers asked them to recall all they could from the story after the children had attempted to solve the problem. For each child in the Prompted Goal Structure Group, the researchers asked four questions that focused attention on the goal structure of the problem just encountered. The four questions were:

1. Who has a problem?

2. What did _____ want to do?

3. What prevented _____ from doing what he wanted to do?

4. How did _____ get his _____ across?

The researchers found that half of the children in the Recall Group spontaneously stated the goal structure of the problem in their recall of the story, while the other half recalled only superficial details. They therefore divided the Recall Group into two subgroups—a Spontaneous Goal Structure Group and a Recall Group. This made four groups for which they examined the results.

Figure 10.4 shows the percent of children in each group who solved the second problem in a manner analogous to the first problem. As you can see, children in the two groups who attended to the goal structure of the first problem were quite likely to solve the second problem by suggesting the use of rolled-up paper. In contrast, children who did not attend to the goal structure of the first problem were unlikely to suggest an analogous solution to the second problem.

Table 10.2 Three analogous problems or stories (adapted from Brown, Kane, and Echols, 1986).

PROBLEM 1. THE GENIE

A magic Genie lived for many years in a field behind a wall. His home was a very pretty bottle where he lived happily and collected a fine set of jewels. But one day an envious witch put a spell on the Genie. He was stuck to the spot, he couldn't move his feet, all his magic powers were gone. If he could move his home to the other side of the wall, he would be out of reach of the spell and his magic would come back. He had found an even prettier, larger bottle on the other side, but he has a problem. How can he get his jewels across the high wall into the new bottle without breaking them and without moving his feet? The Genie has all these treasures to help him [glue, paper, string, tape, etc.]. Can you think of any way the Genie can get his jewels into the new bottle?

PROBLEM 2. THE RABBIT

Here is the Easter Bunny's problem. The Easter Bunny has to deliver all these Easter eggs to all the little children before Easter [tomorrow], but he has been working so hard all week, painting the eggs and hiding them for Easter egg hunts. He would really like to rest and to stay here with his friends and have a picnic. If he stays, he won't have time to finish delivering the eggs. The Easter Bunny has finished delivering all the eggs on this side of the river [*points to picnic side*], but he hasn't started on the other side. The Easter Bunny has a rabbit friend on the other side of the river who has offered to help him [*points to second rabbit waiting with an empty basket on the other side of the river*], but how can the Easter Bunny get the eggs across the river into his friend's basket? The river is big, there are no bridges or boats, and rabbits can't swim and don't like to get wet. What can he do? Can you think of anything he could use to get the eggs to the helpful bunny?

PROBLEM 3. THE FARMER

Farmer Jones is very happy. He has picked a whole bunch of cherries and is taking them to market. When he sells them, he will have enough money to go on vacation with his family. They will go to the seaside. He wants to deliver the load of cherries to the market. That morning there was a great storm, with rain, thunder, and lightning. But he cannot wait to take the cherries to market because the cherries are just ripe now and will go bad. On his way to market, he finds the road blocked by a very big fallen tree knocked over in the storm. What can he do? He must get his cherries to market quickly; otherwise, they will go bad. A friend has driven his tractor up to the other side of the tree and will lend it to Farmer Jones, but how will he get the cherries across the big, big tree? He can't reach over, and he mustn't damage the cherries.

Table 10.3 Common goal structure of scenarios (adapted from Brown, Kane, and Echols, 1986).

SCENARIO	GENIE	RABBIT	FARMER
Protagonist	Genie	Easter Bunny	Farmer Jones
Goal	Transfer jewels across wall into bottle 2	Transfer eggs across river into basket 2	Transfer cherries across tree trunk into vehicle 2
Obstacle	Distance and wall	Distance and river	Distance and tree
Solution	Roll paper	Roll paper	Roll paper

Brown et al. (1986) interpreted these results as showing that preschoolers are capable of analogical reasoning under the right conditions. As with adults, one of the crucial conditions appears to be focusing on the goal structure of the source and target problems.

Other researchers have also demonstrated preschoolers' use of analogical rea-

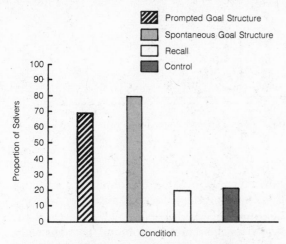

Figure 10.4 Proportion of correct solutions to the first transfer problem as a result of recall conditions (from Brown, Kane, and Echols, 1986).

soning (Holyoak, Junn, & Billman, 1984). Moreover, Klahr (1985) has shown that preschoolers can use means-ends analysis. Because of studies like these, the current view is that the rudiments of general search strategies do not have to be taught in formal schooling. If students do not use such strategies, it is more likely due to lack of the domain knowledge needed to apply the strategy or to incorrect attentional focus than to lack of knowledge of the strategy's steps.

Although it now appears that people know the rudimentary search strategies, they may not know how to use more elaborate strategies such as systematic brainstorming. Thus, it may be worthwhile to teach this elaboration of rudimentary strategies since it (1) is not used spontaneously, and (2) produces more original solutions to problems. (Suggestions about how to teach brainstorming can be found in Hyde & Bizar, 1989). Also, in the next chapter we will discuss ways to teach strategies so as to get transfer, and these suggestions apply to teaching brainstorming.

Reasoning Strategies

Deductive reasoning involves reaching a necessary conclusion from certain first principles that are accepted as true. For example, if it is accepted that all fruits are sweet and that a persimmon is a fruit, then it necessarily follows that a persimmon is sweet. Formal rules of deductive reasoning are described in books on logic. This type of reasoning is called deterministic because it involves complete certainty.

Inductive, or inferential, reasoning involves reaching a reasonable conclusion from examination of a situation. For example, if an entymologist observes twenty zargot moths that are all orange, she may reasonably conclude that all zargot moths are orange. The conclusion in inductive reasoning is not necessarily true, but is likely to be true. Probability and statistics are the formal disciplines that undergird inductive reasoning and, in fact, this type of reasoning is called probabilistic because of its indeterminate nature.

In the following paragraphs, we will discuss what is known about human deductive and inductive reasoning and attempts to train people to improve these reasoning processes. Then we will point out how important it is for people to have adequate domain knowledge if and when they are expected to make reasonable inferences and draw reasonable conclusions in any domain.

Deductive Reasoning. One type of problem that people have great difficulty with is called the "conditional" or "if *a* then *b*" type of problem. Wason (1968) demonstrated this difficulty using a card selection task in which the participants saw four cards, each with one of these letters or numbers drawn on it:

E   K   4   7

Wason showed his research participants the four cards and stated that the cards illustrated

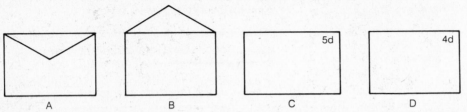

Figure 10.5 Example problem of the type used by Johnson-Laird, Legrenzi, & Legrenzi (1972).

the rule "If a card has a vowel on one side, then it has an even number on the other side."

Wason asked the participants to turn over only the cards necessary to be certain that the rule was correct. You may wish to try your hand at this before reading the answer in the next paragraph.

The correct answer is that the E and 7 cards must be turned over—E to ensure that an even number *is* on the other side and 7 to ensure that a vowel *is not* on the other side. Most people realize that E should be turned over, but few say that the 7 should be turned over. In fact, Wason found that less than 10% of the college students in his study solved this problem correctly! (Another common error is that many people turn the 4 over to see if it has a vowel, but actually that is not necessary. The rule does not say that the *only* time a card can have an even number is when it has a vowel.)

Results such as these suggest that people are not spontaneously good at deductive logic. Since they are not, it seems reasonable to teach them logic as a way of improving logical reasoning. However, a carefully conducted attempt to teach a set of abstract rules was not successful (Cheng, Holyoak, Nisbett, and Oliver, 1986). Also, as mentioned before, college-level courses that teach deductive logic do not appear to benefit everyday logical thinking.

So far, the picture we have painted is gloomy. People do not seem to be logical, nor can they be trained to improve. Other studies, however, seem at first blush to show a brighter picture. Johnson-Laird, Legrenzi, & Legrenzi (1972), for example, gave their research participants a problem that was logically identical to Wason's card-selection problem but embedded in a more meaningful context. Specifically, they showed participants the envelopes shown in Figure 10.5 and said that the rule these envelopes should follow is "If a letter is sealed, then it has a 5d stamp on it." The researchers asked participants to check to be certain the rule was not violated, by turning over any envelopes needed to check the rule. The correct answer was envelope A, which should have a 5d stamp on it, and envelope D, which should not be sealed.

The results were that 81% of the participants got the problem correct, whereas only 15% of them got the correct answer when they were presented with the abstract card-selection problem used by Wason. The result led Johnson-Laird and his colleagues to conclude that people need a familiar context if they are to reach logical conclusions. Possibly, people do not use logical rules at all, but rather use their domain understanding. For example, a person might think:

"Well, I'd better check envelope A to see if there's a 5d stamp on it. B I don't need to check because the rule isn't about unsealed envelopes. I don't need to check C because if it's sealed it's right and if it's unsealed it doesn't matter. It's OK if he paid too much. D, I need to check because if it is sealed, they didn't put enough money on it."

In other words, the person is not thinking "OK, this is a conditional problem so I need to check all cases where the condition occurs and also check to see that if the consequent didn't occur, the condition also didn't occur." Rather, she is using a concrete understanding of postal rules and monetary value to give an answer that appears to be logical. Thus, even though this study shows "logical" answers, psychologists doubted that the answers were reached using formal logical processes.

Once again, we return to a gloomy picture: People can only reach logical conclusions in domains that they are familiar with, and when they do reach logically valid conclusions, it is through a process that will not generalize to other domains.

The most recent chapter in this area of research truly does paint a rosier picture, although the results are so new that we present them here as an exciting prospect rather than a firm conclusion. This newest research shows that (1) people have logical reasoning capabilities that are not content-bound, and (2) these capabilities can be improved through instruction. In contrast to the earlier research, in which people were thought to have something like formal rules of logic in their heads, this recent research assumes that people have informal but domain-general **pragmatic reasoning schemas** (Cheng & Holyoak, 1985) that guide deductive reasoning.

Formal logical rules are defined by syntax—they apply anytime a given logical structure exists (such as "All B are A, X is a B, Therefore X is an A"). On the other hand, pragmatic reasoning schemas are defined by the existence of problem-solving goals. *Causal* pragmatic reasoning schemas apply when the goal is prediction and *permission* pragmatic reasoning schemas apply when the goal is to obtain permission to do something.

Cheng and Holyoak demonstrated the existence of a permission schema by comparing college students' performance on two card-selection problems, one presented in the arbitrary way used in Wason's study and one presented in a manner that should lead students to access their permission schemas. For the latter presentation, the researchers said, "Suppose you are an authority checking whether or not people are obeying certain regulations. The regulations all have the general form, 'If one is to take action A, then one must first satisfy Precondition P.' The cards below contain information on four people: One side of the card indicates whether or not a person has taken action A; the other indicates whether or not the same individual has fulfilled precondition P. In order to check that a certain regulation is being followed, which of the cards below would you turn over? Turn over only those that you need to check to be sure."

The results were that for the problem presented within a permission context, 61% of the participants solved it correctly, whereas in the arbitrary context, the success rate was only 19%. These results imply that people have general pragmatic knowledge about permission situations and they use it to reason deductively if the problem is stated in a way that leads them to activate this knowledge.

In summary, then, people do not use abstract rules of logic to reason about everyday situations and they are not very good at learning to use these rules. Rather, they use both domain-specific knowledge (such as knowledge of postal systems) and domain-general pragmatic knowledge (such as permission schemas) to reach conclusions that are logically valid. This suggests that what we should teach people, if we want them to become better at drawing logical conclusions, are pragmatic reasoning schemas. In fact, Cheng, Holyoak, Nisbett, and Oliver (1986) have tried to do this with success.

Inductive Reasoning. In the previous section on deductive reasoning, we showed that people do not use formal logical rules. The same situation exists for inductive, or inferential, reasoning. If people used formal probabilistic reasoning, then they should come up with sound answers independent of the story line of a problem because such formal rules are domain-general. However, a variety of studies have shown that it is easy to distract people from the statistical basis of many such problems.

As just one example, the "law of large numbers" states that the larger one's sample from a population, the more reliable one's result for this sample. People apply this rule quite well when the story line involves a random device such as drawing a number from a hat, but not so well when the story line involves a less arbitrary scenario such as judging a person's traits. Table 10.4 shows sample problems of these two types studied by Fong, Frantz, and Nisbett (1986). In the top problem, the correct answer is that Joe is not reasoning very soundly because he only had results for a few people so the results may not reflect the actual situation. In the bottom (subjective) problem the correct answer is similar. Gerald is reasoning from a small sample of Timmy's

Table 10.4 Examples of two types of problems—random and subjective—used by Fong et al. to study inductive reasoning.

RANDOM PROBLEM

At Stanbrook University, the Housing Office determines which of the 10,000 students enrolled will be allowed to live on campus the following year. At Stanbrook, the dormitory facilities are excellent, so there is always great demand for on-campus housing. Unfortunately, there are only enough on-campus spaces for 5000 students. The Housing Office determines who will get to live on campus by having a Housing Draw every year; every student picks a number out of a box over a three-day period. These numbers range from 1 to 10,000. If the number is over 5000, the student will not be able to live on campus.

On the first day of the draw, Joe talks to five people who have picked a number. Of these, four people got low numbers. Because of this, Joe suspects that the numbers in the box were not properly mixed, and that the early numbers are more favorable. He rushes over to the Housing Draw and picks a number. He gets a low number. He later talks to four people who drew their numbers on the second or third day of the draw. Three got high numbers. Joe says to himself, "I'm glad that I picked when I did, because it looks like I was right that the numbers were not properly mixed."

What do you think of Joe's reasoning? Explain.

SUBJECTIVE PROBLEM

Gerald M. had a 3-year old son, Timmy. He told a friend: "You know, I've never been much for sports, and I think Timmy will turn out the same. A couple of weeks ago, an older neighbor boy was tossing a ball to him, and he could catch it and throw it all right, but he just didn't seem interested in it. Then, the other day, some kids his age were kicking a little soccer ball around. Timmy could do it as well as the others, but he lost interest very quickly and started playing with some toy cars while the other kids went on kicking the ball around for another 20 or 30 minutes."

Do you agree with Gerald's reasoning that Timmy is likely not to care much for sports? Why or why not?

---

behavior (two cases) that may not reflect Timmy's general tendencies.

Fong et al. (1986) found that the average percent of subjects getting random problems correct was about 65% versus only about 22% for the subjective problems. This finding that people can be easily distracted from the underlying probabilistic nature of a problem has been found for problems involving regression, base rate, and sampling, as well as for the law of large numbers illustrated here (Kahneman, Slovic, & Tversky (1982)). Taken as a whole, the data lead to the conclusion that people do not use abstract rules of probability in drawing inferences.

So far this picture is similar to what we described for deductive reasoning—people are not very good at it. However, in contrast to the dismal results for training in formal logic, training people in formal probability seems to help a good deal. Fong et al. (1986), for example, used a variety of training procedures and a variety of populations and obtained excellent results independent of the particular training procedure or type of subject. This beneficial effect of teaching formal principles suggests that the principles easily map onto the intuitive statistical strategies people have developed for dealing with many everyday problems.

The Importance of Domain Knowledge for Inductive and Deductive Reasoning. The previous section was about problems people have drawing valid inferences of both inductive and deductive types. Perhaps a more basic problem is that of people *failing to even try to draw inferences*. One complaint about today's "lower ability" students is that they simply do not draw inferences. Some believe they do not do so because they have not had practice doing so and that with practice, they will begin to be much better problem solvers (cf., HOTS or Higher Order Thinking Skills, Pogrow, 1990b). While there is probably some

truth to that viewpoint, an equally, or even more important, factor may be lack of domain knowledge. Several recent studies have demonstrated dramatically the importance of domain knowledge for drawing inferences (Walker, 1987; Yekovich, Walker, Ogle, and Thompson, 1990).

As an example of this line of research, consider a study conducted by one of the authors of this text (Walker, 1987). The participants in this study were Army enlisted personnel. Walker tested participants on their knowledge of the game of baseball and divided the group into those with high versus low baseball knowledge. Half of the individuals in each knowledge group were classified as "high-ability" and half "low-ability" as measured by the Army's general ability test. Walker had all participants listen to a description of a half-inning of a fictional baseball game while they followed along with a printed version of the same text. She then asked them to tell what they could remember about the events described and tape-recorded their recountings.

One result that Walker was interested in was the number of correct inferences that were made. Correct inferences were defined as ideas not stated in the description, but consistent with the facts presented. For example, if the game score was 3–0 in favor of the Blue Team and a member of the Blue Team hit a home run with one runner on base, then one can infer that the new score is 5–0.

If drawing inferences is a function of general ability, then the high-ability participants should perform better than the low-ability participants on a measure of correct inferences. Walker did not find this result. If drawing inferences is a function of both ability and domain-specific knowledge, then there should be a difference within the high-knowledge participants between high- and low-ability individuals. Again, this result was not found. If drawing inferences is a function of domain-specific knowledge, then there should be a difference between the high- and low-knowledge groups, which was, in fact, what Walker found. The high-knowledge participants made almost three times as many correct inferences as did the low-knowledge participants, *regardless of overall ability level*. In other words, lack of domain-specific knowledge is a crucial constraint on reasoning processes.

Summary

While there has been great interest in teaching general search and reasoning strategies, many programs designed to do this have not obtained documented success. In the case of search strategies, the lack of success may be due to the fact that most people use such strategies spontaneously, given adequate domain knowledge. In the case of deductive reasoning strategies, lack of success may be due to the fact that almost no one uses such strategies, but rather people use informal knowledge-based strategies that usually lead to the same conclusions as those derived from deductive logic. In the case of inductive reasoning two factors appear to be important. First, training in formal statistical principles underlying inductive reasoning does seem to improve everyday inductive reasoning. Second, possession of domain knowledge is necessary. Without such knowledge, people may have excellent inductive reasoning strategies, but insufficient knowledge to use these strategies.

This analysis suggests four ways in which schools can contribute to the enhancement of general problem-solving skills.

1. Teach elaborated strategies such as brainstorming.

2. Teach pragmatic reasoning knowledge.

3. Teach probability and statistics.

4. Ensure that students have adequate domain knowledge.

CHAPTER SUMMARY

In this chapter, we have described a cognitive psychological perspective on problem solving. Early work by Newell and Simon set a framework for the study of problem solving in which it is viewed as a search through a space of possible solutions. There are several general strategies that guide this search so that it will be more successful than random trial and error. These strategies include means-ends analysis and reasoning by analogy.

Over the past thirty years, cognitive psychologists have accumulated evidence about the nature of expertise in domain-specific problem solving. Whether the domain be chess or electronics, writing or football, experts see patterns missed by novices, use these patterns to develop conceptual representations of problems, and use these representations to quickly access and execute domain-specific skills and strategies. The conceptual knowledge possessed by experts is stored as linear orderings, images, propositions, and schemas in declarative memory, while the domain-specific skills and strategies are stored in procedural memory. Often experts tie their conceptual knowledge to actions by associating a schema with a skill or strategy and by representing this association in the form of productions in procedural memory.

This work on the analysis of expertise holds great promise for education because it suggests that the elements of expertise can be identified, described, and, ultimately, taught. In the past, the perception that problem-solving expertise was more an inherited trait than something that could be acquired had been based on the observation that many students fail to acquire such expertise during twelve or so years of schooling. However, they may have failed to acquire problem-solving expertise not because of lack of ability but because we have been teaching the wrong things. We may have been teaching the wrong things because until now we have not had information about the right things to teach—that is, the mental processes and representations used by experts.

In Section 5 of this book, you will learn about the elements of expertise in reading, writing, science, and math. In each area, the elements include conceptual understanding (declarative) and domain-specific skills and strategies (procedural). You have already learned about the ways in which declarative and procedural knowledge are acquired, and in the next chapter you will learn about knowledge transfer. Once you are armed with an understanding of both the nature of expertise and how it is acquired and transferred, you should be in a good position to design and deliver instruction that promotes the development of expertise.

In recent work on general thinking processes, psychologists have discovered that human reasoning does not follow the dictates of formal deductive and inductive (statistical) models. This result should not be too surprising to you now that you understand some of the constraints on human information processing. For example, the context sensitivity of human memory activation makes it unlikely that humans will use highly context-free reasoning processes. What is most interesting about recent work is the description of processes humans do use to arrive at reasonably valid conclusions. Presumably, these processes could form the basis for future curricular efforts.

ADDITIONAL READINGS

Views of Problem Solving

Chipman, S.F., Segal, J.W., & Glaser, R. (Eds.). (1985). *Thinking and learning skills. Vol. 2: Research and open questions*. Hillsdale, NJ: Lawrence Erlbaum Associates.

Gagné, R.M. (1985). *The conditions of learning and theory of instruction*. (4th edition). New York: Holt, Rinehart, & Winston.

Newell, A., & Simon, H.A. (1972). *Human problem solving*. Englewood Cliffs, NJ: Prentice Hall.

The Role of Domain-Specific Knowledge in Problem Solving

Chi, M.T.H., Glaser, R., & Rees, E. (1982). Expertise in problem solving. In R. Sternberg (Ed.), *Advances in the psychology of human intelligence* (Vol. 1, pp. 7–75). Hillsdale, NJ: Lawrence Erlbaum Associates.

Glaser, R. (1984). Education and thinking: The role of knowledge. *American Psychologist, 39*, 93–104.

Perkins, D.N., & Salomon, A. (1989). Are cognitive skills context-bound? *Educational Researcher, 18*(1), 16–25.

Classroom Applications

Chance, P. (1986). *Thinking in the classroom: A survey of programs*. Teachers College, Columbia University, New York: Teachers College Press.

Glynn, S.M. (1991). Explaining science concepts: A teaching-with-analogies model. In S.M. Glynn, R.H. Yeany, & B.K. Britton (Eds.), *The psychology of learning science* (pp. 219–240). Hillsdale, NJ: Lawrence Erlbaum Associates.

Nisbett, R.E., Fong, G.T., Lehman, D.R., & Cheng, P.W. (1987). Teaching reasoning. *Science, 238*, 625–631.

Segal, J.W., Chipman, S.F., & Glaser, R. (Eds.). (1985). *Thinking and learning skills. Vol. 1: Relating instruction to research*. Hillsdale, NJ: Lawrence Erlbaum Associates.

Chapter
11

Transfer

SUMMARY

1. **Transfer** is the application or use of knowledge learned in one setting to another, different setting.

2. As conceptual understanding increases, the probability of transfer also increases.

3. Even when people have the necessary conceptual knowledge to solve a new problem, they do not always activate it. Instructional programs that seek to increase activation of relevant knowledge focus on teaching the knowledge in a problem-solving context.

4. Transfer of automated basic skills is a function of the degree of overlap of the production sets that underlie the source skills and the target skills. As the degree of overlap increases, transfer also increases.

5. Successful transfer of a strategy depends in large part on a person's *conscious evaluation* of the strategy's effectiveness.

6. Four other factors also affect strategy transfer. The first factor is the degree to which the learner understands the conditions under which the strategy applies. The second factor is whether the learner attributes her successes to her effort and use of strategies. The third factor is whether an individual can screen out irrelevant, distracting thoughts when trying to analyze a new problem. The fourth factor is the degree of relevant declarative knowledge possessed by the learner.

Transfer is the application of knowledge learned in one setting or for one purpose to another setting and/or purpose. As you learned at the beginning of the last chapter, the search stage of problem solving involves searching for knowledge to *transfer* to a new situation. In this chapter, we focus on this one aspect of problem solving because it poses a challenge for educators and researchers alike.

There are many positive examples of transfer related to school learning. A student may learn facts about United States history in order to pass a test and later use these facts to understand historical references in a presidential speech. Another student may learn how to write essays in high school English and later use this skill in writing reports on the job. Examples of transfer abound. Indeed, one of the main assumptions of formal schooling is that knowledge does transfer, and therefore what students learn in schools will be useful outside of the schoolhouse.

Despite the many examples of transfer that one can think of, there are also some notable failures. One area about which you have already learned is the failure of efforts to teach general problem-solving strategies. Another area is the failure of people to realize the relevance of some knowledge they already have when they are trying to solve a novel problem (e.g., Bransford, Vye, Kinzer, & Risko, 1990; Lave, 1988). Sadly, many persons believe that what they learned in high school benefited them very little in later life. In other words, they were not aware of much transfer of knowledge from in- to out-of-school settings (Flanagan, 1978). While some of these failures of transfer may be inherent in the way people think, others may be avoidable by the use of judicious instructional strategies. Throughout this chapter we will suggest some strategies that have a strong research base.

Over the past decade, cognitive and educational psychologists have made progress in understanding and overcoming some of the obstacles to transfer. The picture that is emerging suggests that these obstacles to transfer differ depending on which component of expertise is involved—(1) conceptual understanding, (2) domain-specific basic skills, or (3) domain-specific strategies. Since the factors affecting transfer differ somewhat for these three components of expertise, we will discuss each of these areas separately.

THE ROLE OF CONCEPTUAL UNDERSTANDING IN TRANSFER

Consider two teachers, each of whom has had five years of experience teaching first grade and each of whom has decided to try teaching sixth grade for the first time. After the first week of settling in, each teacher realizes that several students are not paying attention to directions and assigned tasks but instead are acting silly and being noisy. This realization forms their initial representation of their problems (see panel A in Figures 11.1 and 11.2).

Notice, however, that what the representations lead the teachers to recall differs somewhat. The teacher shown in Figure 11.1 recalls that she gave stars to students for being quiet and paying attention. The teacher in Figure 11.2 recalls that she reinforced her students for these behaviors.

These differences in activated knowledge lead to different solutions (shown in panel C of Figures 11.1 and 11.2). The teacher in Figure 11.1 decides to set up a star chart while the one in Figure 11.2 wonders what reinforces sixth graders. Presumably, once she answers this question, she will use these reinforcers in her system.

Which teacher do you think will be more successful in solving the problem of inattentive sixth graders? Most likely, the teacher in Figure 11.2 will be more successful because she is using her understanding that different

Figure 11.1 A teacher trying to solve a sixth-grade discipline problem using her experience with first graders. This teacher has a concrete, rather than conceptual, representation of her first-grade solutions.

events are reinforcing to different people. Sixth graders might consider stars to be babyish but might value having five minutes of class time to socialize with friends. This example illustrates how the quality of one's conceptual understanding affects the probability of successful transfer. By now this principle has been shown in a wide variety of domains, including writing (Case & McKeough, 1990), troubleshooting problems with electrical or mechanical systems (Means & Gott, 1988; Tenney & Kurland, 1988), solving science problems (Bromage & Mayer, 1981), and generating and interpreting computer programs (Mayer, 1975).

Figure 11.2 A teacher trying to solve a sixth-grade discipline problem using her experience with first graders. This teacher has a conceptual representation of her first-grade solutions.

Studies Demonstrating the Role of Conceptual Understanding in Transfer

Mayer (1975) studied the role of conceptual understanding in transfer by giving two groups of students different amounts of conceptual background for the FORTRAN programming language. The group that received more conceptual information was called the *model group*, while the one receiving less conceptual information was called the *rule group*. Students learned about programming by working through self-instructional booklets.

The model booklet started with a diagram (model) of the functional units of a computer and a description of these units. The functions were compared to everyday functional objects with which the students were already familiar. Specifically, the input unit of the computer was likened to a ticket window, the output unit was likened to a message pad, the list of program statements was likened to a shopping list, and the erasable memory was likened to a scoreboard. The seven FORTRAN statements to be learned were introduced after the presentation of the model. They were presented one at a time, with a definition, an example, and an explanation of the statement in terms of the model. For instance, the statement P6 GO TO P4 was explained by saying that the pointer would move from the sixth to the fourth statement on the "list." A3 = 0 was explained by saying that the computer would erase whatever was on its "memory scoreboard" for A3 and write a zero instead.

The rule booklet simply presented each of the seven statements, one at a time. As in the model booklet, each statement was defined and exemplified, but no model was presented and no interpretations of statements in terms of a familiar model were given. Thus, the difference between the two booklets was in whether or not they provided a conceptual underpinning for the computer language.

The model and rule booklets were randomly distributed to students, who read through the booklets at their own rate. When they finished reading, they took a test consisting of two types of problems: (1) a problem in which students were asked to *generate* a program to perform some function, and (2) one in which students were shown some new program statements and asked to *interpret* them. The interpretation problems were considered to be a measure of "far" transfer because they were not as similar to what the students had been exposed to in the booklet as were the generation problems.

Each type of problem was presented at three levels of complexity. The simplest was a one-line statement, which the student was asked to generate or interpret. Of medium complexity were nonlooping programs, and of greatest complexity were looping programs. The looping programs were also considered to demand the farthest transfer because they were least similar to the booklet materials.

Table 11.1 shows the proportion of problems solved correctly by students in the model and rule groups. For generation problems, the two groups performed similarly on questions requiring the generation of one statement. For generating nonlooping programs, the rule group outperformed the model group, whereas for generating looping programs, the model group outperformed the rule group. Mayer (1975) explains that the rule group had a "rote learning set" in which they learned how to use FORTRAN statements in ways that were similar to the examples given during training and the model group had a "meaningful learning set" in which they related new knowledge to prior conceptual knowledge. Thus, the rule group excelled at problems that

Table 11.1 Proportion of problems solved correctly by subjects who read the model and rule booklets (adapted from Mayer, 1975).

	GENERATION			INTERPRETATION		
	STATEMENT	NONLOOPING PROGRAM	LOOPING PROGRAM	STATEMENT	NONLOOPING PROGRAM	LOOPING PROGRAM
Model	.63	.37	.30	.62	.62	.09
Rule	.67	.52	.12	.42	.32	.12

did not require much transfer, but the model group excelled on transfer problems.

The results for the interpretation problems are consistent with this explanation. The model group outperformed the rule group on interpretation of statements and on interpretation of nonlooping programs, but both groups did poorly on looping programs. The model group presumably did better because they could use the conceptual model they had learned to help them interpret new programs.

In the terminology used in this book, Mayer (1975) is arguing that the model group did better on transfer problems because they developed a conceptual understanding relevant to the problems. Although this explanation is plausible, Mayer did not have a direct measure of students' conceptual understanding. In a later study, however, he did (Mayer & Bromage, 1980). In this study, all students were given a conceptual model, but half received it *after* reading about the program statements and half received it before. Those who read about the model after the other material would not have it available to them while they were encoding new information about programming problems, so they would be unlikely to integrate their representation of programming problems with their representation of the conceptual model. Those who read about the model before the programming material, however, would be likely to reflect on it and use it to interpret the new programming information, so that the model and programming knowledge would become integrated.

After the students read through their booklets, instead of solving problems as in the previous study, they were asked to recall the definition and explain each of the statements about which they had learned. Their answers were examined to see if the ideas presented were different for the model-before and model-after groups. The researchers classified the idea units into *technical* information (such as "/ means divide"), *format* information (such as "an address name goes in parentheses"), or *concepts* (such as "an address name is a space in the computer's memory). In addition they categorized instructions in the answers as either *appropriate* (additions that made sense), *inappropriate* (additions that did not make sense), or *model* intrusions (additions based on the model).

Table 11.2 shows the differences that the researchers found. The students who studied the model before learning the programming statements gave more conceptual information, more appropriate intrusions, and more model intrusions. The students who did not study the model first gave more technical and format information and more inappropriate intrusions.

These data provide more direct evidence that students who study a conceptual model before studying programming statements organize their knowledge differently from other students. Specifically, their knowledge seems to be organized around the functional concepts suggested by the model. Thus, the Mayer and Bromage (1980) results lend fur-

Table 11.2 Types of ideas in protocols of subjects given a meaningful model either before or after learning some programming statements (adapted from Mayer and Bromage, 1980).

MODEL	IDEA UNITS			INTRUSIONS		
	TECHNICAL	FORMAT	CONCEPT	APPROPRIATE	INAPPROPRIATE	MODEL
Before	5.0	1.9	6.6	1.2	1.5	3.0
After	5.9	2.8	4.9	.7	2.4	.5

ther support to the notion that breadth of transfer is facilitated by conceptual understanding.

Instructional Implications

Since conceptual understanding seems to play an important role in an individual's ability to transfer knowledge to novel problem situations, it makes sense to ensure that the conceptual basis of a problem area receives adequate attention in one's curriculum. Unfortunately, while it would seem to be easy to do this, it is actually rather difficult. The difficulty lies in the fact that we don't know what the effective conceptual basis of many problem areas is, so we end up teaching *the wrong conceptual information*! Worse, we may feel smug about doing this because the research just described supports the notion of teaching conceptual material.

To take a specific example, a standard approach to training electronics technicians is to start by teaching Ohm's law and other basic physical principles that underlie the conduction of electricity. This is certainly conceptual information. Unfortunately, it is not the conceptual information used by expert electronics troubleshooters (Kieras, 1988). The conceptual basis of electronics maintenance work has to do with functional understanding of the devices and components of the system that one is repairing (Means & Gott, 1988). Thus, what technical schools should be teaching as the conceptual part of their curricula is device knowledge, not physics knowledge.

The most reliable and valid way to get information about the conceptual understanding required for transfer in a problem domain is to perform cognitive analyses of expertise, using the expert-novice paradigm described in Chapter 10. This approach is quite costly, however, so many instructional designers rely on informal interviews with "subject matter experts." In these interviews,

the designer of instruction may ask the expert directly to say what conceptual knowledge is relevant to solving problems in their domain. The expert, perhaps not really understanding what the instructional designer means, often reports using whatever conceptual knowledge he learned in a textbook somewhere, even if this knowledge is not really used during problem solving. Thus, asking experts directly is likely to lead to identification of the wrong conceptual knowledge. It is far better to have the expert think aloud while solving some novel problems and then use the think-aloud protocols to identify relevant conceptual knowledge.

The Problem of Activation of Conceptual Knowledge

Even when students learn the right conceptual knowledge for a given problem-solving domain, they do not always seem to activate it when it would be useful for solving a new problem (e.g., Perfetto, Bransford, & Franks, 1983). This problem of activation is a difficult one that is far from being totally understood. However, progress is being made.

Creating a Problem-Solving Context. Several scholars in this area believe that if one wants students to activate knowledge in problem-solving contexts, then this knowledge should be learned originally in a problem-solving context (Bransford, Vye, Kinzer, & Risko, 1990; Brown, Collins, & Duguid, 1989). This idea is consistent with what we know about spread of activation in the declarative knowledge network—the more the current context provides cues for related knowledge, the more likely that this related knowledge will be activated.

Adams, Kasserman, Yearwood, Perfetto, Bransford, and Franks (1988) tested the importance of a problem-solving context in the following manner. They asked college students to solve a series of verbal problems such as the following (described in Branford, et al., 1990, p. 388):

1. Uriah Fuller, the famous Israeli superpsychic, can tell you the score of any baseball game before the game starts. What is his secret?

2. A man living in a small town in the U.S. married twenty different women in the same town. All are still living, none of them has divorced him, and he has never divorced any of them. Yet, he has broken no law. Can you explain?

The answer to the first problem is 0 to 0 and the answer to the second is that the man is a minister who performs weddings. A study by Perfetto, Bransford, and Franks (1983) showed that, without hints, college students are not very good at solving such problems. Even though they have the required declarative knowledge, they are unlikely to activate it. Moreover, even when students read a list of relevant facts (such as, "Before it starts, the score of a game is 0 to 0") just prior to attempting to solve the problems, they failed to make use of these facts!

Adams et al. (1988) made seemingly slight changes to the list of facts in order to put them in a problem-solving context. For example, instead of "Before it starts, the score of a game is 0 to 0," they said "It is easy to guess the score of any game before it begins; the score is 0 to 0." When students read facts put in such problem contexts, they did quite well at solving the problems. This study, then, demonstrates the idea that people are more likely to recall information relevant to solving a problem if it was previously encoded in a problem context than if it was encoded in an arbitrary manner.

Anchored Instruction. Based on the notion of problem contexts and some related ideas,

Bransford and his colleagues (cf., Bransford et al., 1990) have embarked on a series of development projects in which instruction is *anchored* in a common context that is rich enough to let students explore ideas and identify and solve problems. Perhaps their most ambitious project is the "Young Sherlock" project, designed to teach language arts, science, and social studies to fifth graders. A videodisc version of the movie *Young Sherlock Holmes* provides the common context for classroom activities.

In this project, students engaged in a wide variety of activities stimulated by the Young Sherlock movie over a seven-month period. For example, they played "Sherlock," which gave them the opportunity to practice using Sherlock's vocabulary and problem-solving skills. They checked the details of the Sherlock movie for accuracy, which helped them acquire historical, economic, and geographical information—such as what the Victorian era was like—and gave them skill at using multiple sources for information. After learning about the story using *Young Sherlock Holmes* as an example, they wrote their own mystery stories.

The project developers compared the performance of children in the project classrooms with those in control classrooms. The control classrooms covered the same information, vocabulary, and skill objectives and received excellent instruction, but the instruction was not anchored in one context. The results showed that students in the experimental classrooms retained more vocabulary and factual information and wrote more cohesive stories than did students in control classrooms. While this approach is promising, we do not know the extent of transfer that is attained. Ultimately, one hopes that the knowledge these children acquired transfers to a wide variety of problem contexts. However, it may be that it only transfers to similar contexts.

Cognitive Apprenticeship. Like anchored instruction, cognitive apprenticeship instruction puts learners in a problem-solving context. Initially, the teacher sets problems for the students and models solutions. Gradually, more and more of the responsibility for problem solving is handed over to the learners. This approach to instruction draws on the master-apprentice approach to teaching crafts, in which the apprentice is immersed in a problem-solving context from the start (Collins, Brown, & Newman, 1989).

An example of this type of instruction is described in Lampert (1986). Lampert engaged her fourth graders in solving problems related to money and through skillful problem-solving discussions led them to the point where they understood the conceptual bases of multiplication algorithms and could invent their own computational procedures.

Cognitive apprenticeship has well-documented effects on transfer of strategies (e.g., Palincsar & Brown, 1984), but its effects on improving activation of conceptual knowledge are less well documented. Lampert's work is promising in this regard.

Summary

While it is clear that the possession of appropriate conceptual knowledge is beneficial for transfer in novel problem situations, it is less clear how to identify the appropriate knowledge base for various problem domains. Instructional designers could use the techniques of cognitive psychology to identify implicit elements of expertise, but the cost of doing this is sometimes prohibitive. Perhaps someone will develop less costly but still valid techniques for doing this work in the future.

Even if the practical problem of expensive elicitation techniques is solved, there is still the problem of knowledge activation. We need to do more basic research in this area. For example, we still do not know how people who do activate relevant knowledge differ from those who do not. Do they represent problems differently? Are they more persistent? We also still do not know how effective for transfer are the promising instructional strategies of anchored instruction and cognitive apprenticeship.

TRANSFER OF AUTOMATED BASIC SKILLS

Once the problem solver has identified relevant knowledge to help solve a novel problem, it is often the case that some relevant knowledge may be in the form of automated basic skills, represented in procedural form. Such skills do not have to be re-learned for the new problem. This allows for a great savings in time, as the time-consuming process of proceduralization can be circumvented for a portion of the skills in the new solution.

To return again to our example of the teacher transferring first-grade teaching skills to the sixth grade, there may be a great deal of overlap in the procedural knowledge used to solve first-grade and sixth-grade discipline problems. Figure 11.3 shows the goal structure for the two types of problems. As you can see, the top- and middle-level goals are the same. Only the low-level goals (e.g., "give stars") differ. Thus, many of the cognitive procedures that this teacher already possesses for analyzing problems of this type should transfer easily to the new setting, allowing her to solve the sixth-grade problem almost as quickly as she would solve the first-grade problem. The reason for this easy transfer is the similarity in the representation of the basic skills across the two tasks.

Research on Transfer of Basic Skills

R.M. Gagné (1965, 1970) distinguishes between two types of transfer—**lateral** and **vertical**. In his work, lateral transfer refers to use

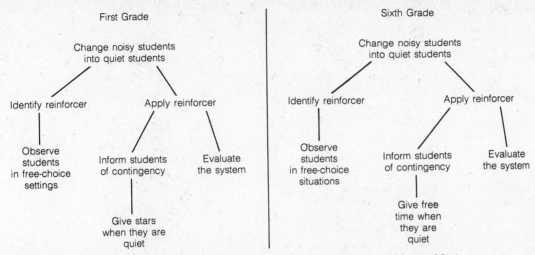

Figure 11.3 The goal structures for first- and sixth-grade discipline problems. Notice that the top- and middle-level goals are identical and that only lower-level goals differ.

of some known knowledge in a new setting but at the same level of complexity as the old setting. For instance, recognizing an unknown animal as a bird is an instance of lateral transfer. So, too, is using elements of printing skill to learn cursive writing. Vertical transfer is the transfer of known knowledge to the acquisition of some more complex knowledge that incorporates the known knowledge. Most often, we think of this type of transfer in a skill acquisition context in which lower-level skills contribute to, and may be prerequisite for, acquisition of a higher-level skill. However, it might apply in the context of schema acquisition where simpler elements of declarative knowledge contribute to the formation of a schema. Thus, while the ideas of lateral and vertical transfer may apply to conceptual knowledge or basic skills or strategies, we will use the distinction here in reference to basic skill acquisition.

In this section, we will describe one of the most important conditions facilitating lateral and vertical transfer of basic skills. In both cases, the *degree of overlap* between the source skill and the target skill is an important condition. The greater the overlap, the greater the transfer will be.

Lateral Transfer

Singley and Anderson (1989) studied the role of skill overlap in lateral transfer among three different text-editing programs. Figure 11.4 shows the top-level goal structure of all of the editing programs studied. The goal given to the research participants was to edit a manuscript, given a marked-up copy showing what to edit. (The participants were experienced secretaries so they were familiar with editorial notation and were fast typists). Given this overall goal, the procedure involved looking at the marked-up copy to find the next edit and then executing the edit. Executing the edit involved finding the location to edit on the computer file of the text and then typing in the necessary commands.

Because of the similar top-level goal structure for the skills involved in using all three programs, Singley and Anderson expected to

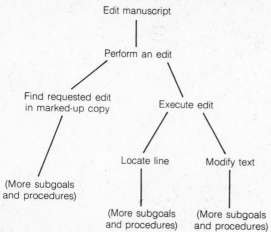

Figure 11.4 Top-level goal structures for text-editing programs studied by Singley and Anderson (1989) (from Singley and Anderson, 1989).

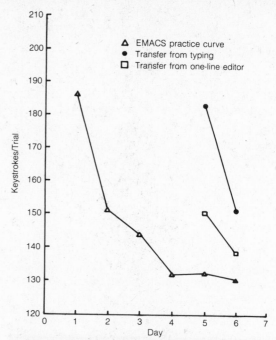

Figure 11.5 Learning the EMACS editor (adapted from Singley and Anderson, 1989).

see a substantial amount of positive transfer between programs. That is, they expected individuals who had already learned one editing program to learn a second program faster than individuals who had not already learned one.

To test their hypothesis, they had some secretaries practice for three hours a day for several days on one editor and then change to another editor. Other secretaries practiced typing the marked-up copy prior to learning an editor. Typing the marked-up copy does not share the goal structure shown in Figure 11.4 and therefore was expected to be less beneficial for learning an editing program than would previously learning another program.

Figure 11.5 shows data for learning the EMACS editor. The measure of improvement was the number of keystrokes per trial. This measure is a measure of the number of errors because more keystrokes are due to the user's making errors and having to retype something. (Since these were experienced typists, the errors were almost always errors in learn-

ing the editor, not typing errors.) A control group practiced on this editor for six days and, as you can see, the efficiency of this group improved dramatically for four days and less dramatically for days 5 and 6.

The top curve in Figure 11.5 shows the degree of transfer from typing practice on the first four days to learning the EMACS editor on the fifth and sixth days. The middle curve shows the degree of transfer from practice on one of the other editors for four days to learning the EMACS editor on the fifth and sixth days. As you can see, transfer from the other editors to EMACS is greater than transfer from typing to EMACS. Singley and Anderson claim that the greater transfer is due to the greater overlap in how the skills are represented mentally—all of the editing programs shared the same top-level goal representation, while the typing task did not.

As a further test of the skill-overlap hypothesis, Singley and Anderson compared transfer from one "line" editor to another line editor versus transfer from a line editor to the "screen" editor. Two of the programs studied—UNIX ED and VMS EDT—were "line editors," while one—UNIX EMACS—was a "screen editor." In line editors, the user must recall the content or number of a line he wishes to edit and use this information to request that that line be put on the screen. Then the user may edit—insert, change, or delete text—within the line on the screen. Screen editors, which are considered to be an improvement over line editors, display a screenful of text. The user moves a cursor around in the text to wherever he wishes to make changes (see Table 11.3 for a summary of the editing commands for the three editors).

Because of this basic difference between line and screen editors, the methods used to solve editing problems differ. For instance, to delete two-thirds of a line using a line editor, it may be most efficient to use the delete line command and then insert the one-third of the line that is not supposed to be deleted. In a screen editor, one moves the cursor to the beginning of the string that one wishes to delete and then uses the command to delete from there to the end of the line. Thus, for solving this type of problem, transfer from one line editor to another should be greater than from a line editor to a screen editor. Almost all that one needs to learn in moving from one line editor to another is the different keystrokes for specific commands. The sequencing of activities (first find the line, then delete, then insert) remains the same. In moving from a line editor to a screen editor, however, one needs to learn a new sequence (find the exact point in the line with the cursor, then delete) as well as new keystrokes for specific commands.

Singley and Anderson compared the percentages of time saved in learning the screen editor given prior learning of a line editor to the percentages of time saved in learning a line editor given prior learning of another line editor. The percentage savings for the former (going from a line to a screen editor) was around 60%. The percentage savings going from one line editor to another, in contrast, was around 95%. Thus, the prediction of greater transfer from one line editor to another was confirmed, again suggesting that the degree of overlap of skills determines the degree of lateral transfer between skills.

As a final test of the degree of overlap hypothesis, the researchers created production rule models of the three text-editing systems and then counted the number of productions that each system shared in common. They used this number to predict the degree of transfer and then compared their prediction with the degree of transfer actually observed. As you can see in Table 11.4, there is reasonable, although certainly not perfect, agreement between the predicted and observed transfer. One assumption that Singley and Anderson made is that it is equally costly to learn any given production. After looking at these data, they now think that some productions may be more costly to learn than others, perhaps because more conditions are involved, or because of some other factor. However, despite the fact that the rather simple model of production overlap they used did not predict the data perfectly, it did predict quite well and, therefore, can be viewed as additional evidence to support the skill-overlap theory.

Earlier Views of Skill Overlap. The skill-overlap hypotheses proposed by Singley and Anderson is similar in some ways to an early theory in the history of psychology called the "identical elements" theory. This theory, proposed by E.L. Thorndike (1906), stated that learning of one skill was facilitated by prior learning of another skill to the extent that the

Table 11.3 Execution of various editing functions in the line and screen editors studied by Singley and Anderson. ED and EDT are line editors and EMACS is a screen editor (adapted from Singley and Anderson, 1989).

COMMAND TYPE	EDITOR	COMMAND	ACTION
Locative	ED	1,$p	Prints all lines of the file
		3p	Prints the third line
		.p	Prints the current line
		.=	Prints the line number of the current line
		CR	Prints the line following the current line
	EDT	t whole	Prints all lines of the file
		t 'dog'	Prints the first line following the current line that contains 'dog'
		t-'dog'	Prints the first line before the current line that contains 'dog'
		t	Prints the current line
		CR	Prints the line following the current line
	EMACS	^f	Moves cursor forward one character
		]f	Moves cursor forward one word
		^b	Moves cursor backward one character
		]b	Moves cursor backward one word
		^a	Moves cursor to beginning of line
		^e	Moves cursor to end of line
		^p	Moves cursor to previous line
		^n	Moves cursor to next line
Mutative	ED	.a	Inserts lines after the current line (type '.' to exit the insert mode)
		.d	Deletes the current line
		.c	Replaces the current line (type '.' to exit the insert mode)
		s/a/b/p	Substitutes the first occurrence of 'a' with 'b' on the current line
	EDT	i	Inserts lines after the current line (type ^z to exit the insert mode)
		d	Deletes the current line
		r	Replaces the current line (type ^z to exit the insert mode)
		s/a/b	Substitutes the first occurrence of 'a' with 'b' on the current line
	EMACS	^d	Deletes the character marked by the cursor
		]d	Deletes the word marked by the cursor
		DEL	Deletes the character to the left of the cursor
		^k	Deletes from the current cursor position to the end of the line
		a	Inserts the character 'a' at the current cursor position (EMACS is in insert mode by default)

Command summary for three editors: ^ denotes a control character and] denotes an escape character.

Table 11.4 Predicted and observed transfer obtained by Singley and Anderson. The rank orders of predicted and observed transfer are the same (adapted from Singley and Anderson, 1989).

COMPONENT	TRAINING EDITOR	TRANSFER EDITOR	PREDICTED TRANSFER	OBSERVED TRANSFER
Line location	ED	EDT	68%	87%
	EDT	ED	75	91
	Line	EMACS	39	61
	Typing	EMACS	19	35
Modify text	ED	EDT	90	105
	EDT	ED	85	99
	Line	EMACS	27	62
	Typing	EMACS	7	29

two skills shared "identical elements." This idea sounds just like Singley and Anderson's idea except for one crucial difference: To Thorndike, an identical element was an observable behavior such as a keystroke or addition facts. To Singley and Anderson, many of the skills that overlap are completely mental—representation of goals and setting of subgoals, for example.

The advantage of being able to include mental operations in one's measure of skill overlap is that one is able to understand why two skills that seem quite different at the behavioral level in fact show transfer between one another. You saw this in the Singley and Anderson study between the two line editors. Thorndike would have predicted very low transfer between the two editors because at the behavioral level of keystrokes, the skills differ. Yet what is obtained is massive positive transfer between the two skills. Thus the modern view of identical elements, in which many of the identical elements are mental, is much more successful at accounting for transfer data than was the earlier view.

Vertical Transfer

As you have just learned, basic skills often provide positive lateral transfer for similar skills. In addition, simple basic skills transfer positively to more complex basic skills that incorporate the simple skills. A classical demonstration of vertical transfer was conducted in 1961 by R.M. Gagné and Paradise. Their demonstration was done in the domain of solving linear algebraic equations such as those shown in Table 11.5. Stop reading here and try solving these problems in order to refresh your memory for the processes involved. Try to observe your own mental processes as you solve the equations. What rules do you think you are using? (Some people collect all the elements containing the same variable on one side of the equation and move all other elements to the other side of the

Table 11.5 Some of the problems solved by students in R.M. Gagné and N.E. Paradise's study of solving linear equations (adapted from R.M. Gagné and N.E. Paradise, 1961).

1. Solve for b:
   $$2b - 3 - 8b - 4 + 3b = 13 - 6 - 3b - 2 - 6b$$
2. Solve for x:
   $$\frac{4x}{2} = 6x - 8$$
3. Solve for x:
   $$7x + 4x = 3a + 3a + 2a - x$$

equation. Another operation is to simplify by reducing fractions to least common denominators).

Gagné and Paradise performed a **rational task analysis** on the task of solving linear equations in order to decide what simpler skills might contribute to later learning of more complex skills. Rational task analysis consists of logically (as opposed to empirically) decomposing an activity into simpler and simpler elements. The result of their analysis is shown in Figure 11.6. Activities lower in this figure are simpler than activities higher in the figure. The simpler activities are related to the more complex activities to which they point. For instance, simplification of fractional expressions is more complex (involves more different kinds of steps) than does recognizing the equivalence of multiplication and division terms or performing multiplication of numbers in sequence, and the latter two activities are related to the former in that they comprise some of the steps in the former.

Gagné and Paradise tested the notion that acquisition of the more complex skills that were higher in the skill hierarchy was dependent on prior knowledge of the lower-level skills. To test this notion they gave about 100 seventh graders a verbal knowledge (intelligence) test and then a programmed instruction unit on solving linear equations. After completing the unit, the students were tested on achievement with equations similar to those they had been asked to solve while completing instruction. Finally, the students answered test items that measured their achievement of each of the lower-level skills identified by the task analysis.

Some of the findings of this study are shown in Table 11.6. Students' knowledge of lower-level skills was highly related to their time to complete the unit of instruction (r = .78) and their overall achievement (r = .82) on the linear equations test. In contrast, their vocabulary knowledge, a measure that correlates highly with intelligence, was only slightly related to learning speed (r = .18) and achievement (r = .22).

These results showed that knowledge of lower-level skills positively transfers to learning related higher-level skills and that it is more important to learning the higher-level skills than is general intelligence. However, Gagné and Paradise were interested in testing an even stronger form of the skill-overlap hypothesis which states that acquisition of lower-level skills in a skill hierarchy is *necessary* for acquisition of higher-level skills, not just facilitative of acquisition. In other words, people who lack the lower-level skills will not be able to acquire the higher-level skills. This contrasts with the prediction for lateral transfer, in which possession of similar skills helps in acquisition of related skills but is not necessary.

To test the necessity of acquisition of lower-level skills, which they called "prerequisite" skills to emphasize this necessary relationship, the researchers examined the data for each individual student. There were four logical combinations of success and failure on subskills that were at adjacent levels in the hierarchy: (1) item testing higher-level skill correct and item testing prerequisite skill correct (++), (2) item testing higher-level skill wrong and item testing prerequisite skill wrong (−−), (3) item testing higher-level skill correct, but item testing prerequisite skill wrong (+−), and (4) item testing higher-level skill wrong and item testing prerequisite skill right (−+). Of these four possibilities, 1, 2, and 4 are consistent with the notion that knowledge of prerequisite skills is necessary for acquisition of higher-level skills. However, the third possibility is not consistent with this notion. That is, if a prerequisite skill is necessary for achievement of a higher-level skill, it should not be possible to fail a test of the prerequisite while passing a test of the higher-level skill.

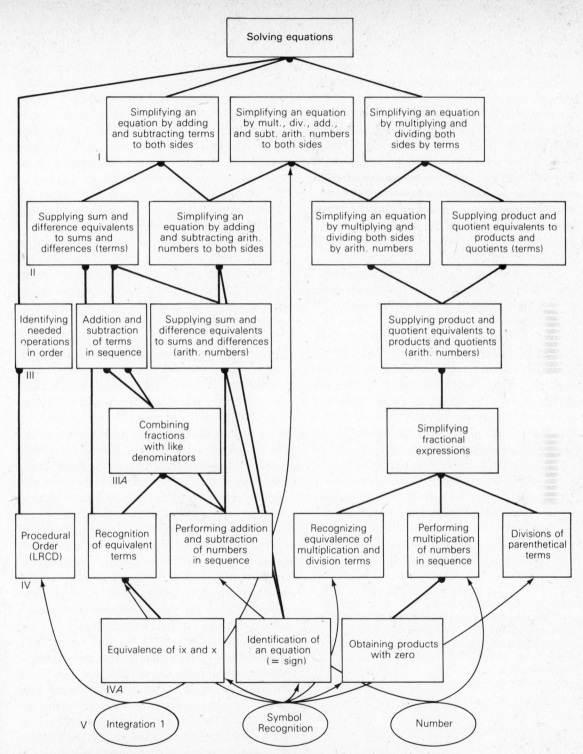

Figure 11.6 Prerequisite subskills identified by a rational task analysis of solving equations (from R.M. Gagné and N.E. Paradise, 1961).

Gagné and Paradise looked at the frequencies with which each of these four patterns occurred in their data. What they found is shown in Table 11.7. The pattern that is inconsistent with the necessity assumption is shown in the third column. In general, there are far fewer entries in this column than in any other column and therefore the notion that the prerequisite skills identified by the task analysis are necessary for acquisition of higher-level learning is supported. More recent research has continued to support this notion (White & R.M. Gagné, 1974, 1978).

It is interesting to represent as a production set some of the skills involved in solving equations, because this representation makes clear the overlap among skills. Table 11.8 shows four production sets, *collect terms, transpose terms, collect numerals,* and *transpose numerals. Collect terms* consists of two productions: $P_{1.1}$ adds like terms and $P_{1.2}$ subtracts like terms. The second set, *transpose terms,* also has two productions: $P_{2.1}$ operates when the largest term for the target variable is on the left side of the equation and $P_{2.2}$ operates when the largest term for the target variable is on the right side of the equation. Production sets 3 and 4 are analogous to 1 and 2 except that they operate on numerals rather than on terms.

To examine an example of the prerequisite relationships implied in production set notation, look at productions 4.1 and 4.2. Notice

Table 11.6 Correlations between vocabulary and prerequisite skill tests and learning speed and achievement on a unit designed to teach students how to solve linear equations (constructed from R.M. Gagné and N.E. Paradise, 1961).

	TIME TO COMPLETE UNIT	ACHIEVEMENT TEST SCORE
Vocabulary test	.18	.22
Prerequisite skills test	.78	.82

that the first condition in both of these productions is that the target variable be represented in only one term. For the variable to be so represented, the student must have already collected like terms and put like terms on one side of the equation. In other words, the skills embodied in *collect terms* and *transpose terms* must already be mastered.

Recent work by Singley and Anderson (1989) in the domain of LISP programming has demonstrated the validity of using production rules as the unit of analysis in problems involving vertical transfer. And, as was the case for lateral transfer, using production rules allows us to think of transfer of unobservable cognitive activity as well as of more observable overt behaviors.

Curriculum Implications. In teaching teachers, we have found that many teachers reject the validity of the notions of "skill hierarchies" and "prerequisite skills." As we have probed to find the source of rejection, most often we have found that its locus is in some of the curricula with which teachers are familiar that seem to draw their basis from hierarchies. Some such curricula seem to teachers to be rigid and boring. They test students on prerequisite skills and give them lessons in a set sequence in an attempt to get students to master the next skills in the hierarchy. The skills are presented in isolation from a meaningful context in which one might use the skills. While some students may derive pleasure from seeing their competence improve, others do not. Also, some students may need less practice than others to master a subskill, yet all students may be required to complete a similar minimum set of practice exercises, which may cause boredom among some students. Finally, some students who enjoy decomposing tasks for themselves may feel that their intelligence is being questioned when they confront materials that have already decomposed the task. Thus, the curriculum ma-

Table 11.7 Pass-fail patterns of achievement between adjacent lower- and higher-level skills (adapted from R.M. Gagné and N.E. Paradise, 1961).

SKILL		FREQUENCY OF PASS-FAIL PATTERN—HIGHER, LOWER			
		++	−−	+−	−+
HIGHER	LOWER	(1)	(2)	(3)	(4)
IV2 from IVA1		110	0	0	8
IV5 from IVA3		113	0	0	5
IIIA1 from IV2, IV3		85	0	7	26
IIIA2 from IV4, IV5, IV6		94	5	10	9
III1 from IV1		45	9	1	63
III2 from IV3, IIIA1		68	30	6	14
III3 from IVA2, IV3		75	25	7	11
III4 from IIIA2		62	40	4	12
II1 from IV2, III2, III3		34	70	3	11
II2 from IVA2, III3		41	60	2	15
II3 from III4		37	72	3	6
II4 from III4		9	85	0	24
I1 from II1, II2		25	78	2	13
I2 from II2, II3		28	80	3	7
I3 from II3, II4		6	104	0	8
	Total	832	658	48	232

terials that seem most clearly related to the idea of the need for mastery of prerequisite skills are found wanting by many teachers for at least some of their students.

Our own opinion is that while we agree that there are curriculum materials that are rigid and boring for both teacher and student, this does not invalidate the wealth of evidence demonstrating the existence of necessary prerequisites in a variety of skill domains. Curriculum materials are designed using a variety of assumptions, and if they do not work any one of these assumptions could be at fault. For example, a curriculum developer may assume that a teacher will take the responsibility for putting basic skill acquisition into a larger meaningful context so that the student sees a reason for acquiring a skill. If this is not done, then this assumption is violated. The materials may not work because the students do not see a reason for learning a skill, and not because the assumption that certain skills are best learned by systematically learning prerequisites first is wrong. Thus, while we think teachers are wise to reject or modify curriculum materials that are not working with their students, we think it unwise for teachers to reject the notion of prerequisite skill relationships.

STRATEGY TRANSFER

While lateral and vertical transfer of basic skills seems to depend a great deal on the amount of skill overlap between the known skill and a new skill, in strategy learning one of the most important factors affecting transfer is the strategy user's *conscious evaluation of strategy effectiveness*.

To return once again to our example of the first-grade turned sixth-grade teachers, let us contrast two teachers who vary in how suc-

Table 11.8 Productions for solving simple linear equations.

<table>
<tr><td colspan="3" align="center">COLLECT TERMS</td></tr>
<tr>
<td>$P_{1.1}$</td>
<td>IF

THEN</td>
<td>More than one like term is on the same side
And like terms are related by addition
Add like terms.</td>
</tr>
<tr>
<td>$P_{1.2}$</td>
<td>IF

THEN</td>
<td>More than one like term is on same side of equation
And like terms are related by substraction
Subtract like terms.</td>
</tr>
<tr><td colspan="3" align="center">TRANSPOSE TERMS</td></tr>
<tr>
<td>$P_{2.1}$</td>
<td>IF

THEN</td>
<td>Only one like term exists on each side of equation
And left side term is more than right side term
Subtract like term on right side from itself
And subtract same from like term on left side.</td>
</tr>
<tr>
<td>$P_{2.2}$</td>
<td>IF

THEN</td>
<td>Only one like term exists on each side of equation
And right side term is more than left side term
Subtract like term on left side from itself
And subtract same from like term on right side.</td>
</tr>
<tr><td colspan="3" align="center">COLLECT NUMERALS</td></tr>
<tr>
<td>$P_{3.1}$</td>
<td>IF

THEN</td>
<td>More than one numeral exists on one side of equation
And numerals are related by addition
Add numerals.</td>
</tr>
<tr>
<td>$P_{3.2}$</td>
<td>IF

THEN</td>
<td>More than one numeral exists on one side of equation
And numerals are related by subtraction
Subtract numerals.</td>
</tr>
<tr><td colspan="3" align="center">TRANSPOSE NUMERALS</td></tr>
<tr>
<td>$P_{4.1}$</td>
<td>IF

THEN</td>
<td>There is only one term in equation
And term and numeral exist on same side of equation
And relationship of numeral to term is subtract
Add numeral to both sides of equation.</td>
</tr>
<tr>
<td>$P_{4.2}$</td>
<td>IF

THEN</td>
<td>There is only one term in equation
And term and numeral exist on same side of equation
And relationship of numeral to term is add
Subtract numeral from both sides of equation.</td>
</tr>
</table>

cessfully they transfer a strategy for identifying what is reinforcing to students. There are several strategies that might be used to find out what reinforces the majority of one's students. First, one might *observe* the students to see what they like to do or play with in their free time, and to see what they are willing to work for. Second, one might *ask students* what activities and objects they like. Third, one might *ask other teachers* of the same type of students what reinforcers they have found to be effective.

In our example, we will assume that both teachers have used the strategy of observation of students as an important source of information about good reinforcers. For instance, both used a star system for eliciting student cooperation and both observed that this system worked. Both have also asked the students what they would like to get as presents and found that some of the things they listed did not turn out to be effective. For example, one child said "crayons" because the children were working with crayons when the teacher asked what the students would like to get. However, when the teacher gave crayons to this student for paying attention, this did not seem to affect his behavior as much as the stars did.

One of the teachers, who was better at evaluating the effectiveness of strategies, noticed that asking students what they preferred seemed less reliable than observing them. She made a mental note to try to use the observation strategy when possible in the future. The other teacher did not really stop to evaluate the difference between the two strategies.

When moving to the sixth grade, the teacher who had remembered the greater reliability of the observation strategy spent some time carefully observing her sixth graders at lunch and on the playground. This led her to conclude that many of her students were powerfully reinforced by attention from their peers. The other teacher, who did not remember the differential effectiveness of the two strategies, selected the strategy of asking students what they like. Unfortunately, she asked some students who were trying to undermine her, so told her they liked to read, even though they did not. This teacher decided to use the reward of a free reading period each week for students who paid attention. She was surprised to find that this reward did not work!

History of Strategy Transfer Research

The early work on training strategies took place in the 1960s and 1970s. Much of the focus of this work was on teaching mentally retarded children to have better memory strategies—for example to use grouping techniques rather than rote rehearsal to remember lists. However, researchers during this time also studied other populations and other strategies. In 1977, Belmont and Butterfield reviewed over 100 studies that attempted to train a variety of types of learners a variety of strategies, none of which were successful in obtaining transfer. They also noted that none of these studies required the students to reflect on the success or non-success of their strategy use. In 1982, Belmont, Butterfield, and Ferretti reviewed seven studies of strategy training that did require students to reflect on the success of their strategies, and in six of the seven, transfer was obtained.

As one example of these studies, Brown, Campione, & Barclay (1979) compared a group of children who were trained to give themselves self-tests to judge whether or not they were ready for a recall test with a group that was not trained to self-test. Both groups were taught an effective rehearsal strategy. The group trained to self-test showed transfer of the strategy to new memory problems a year later while the other group did not.

Since this discovery, many studies have been conducted that confirmed the importance of a learner's self-evaluation process for transfer (cf., Pressley et al., 1984; Palincsar & Brown, 1984; Bereiter & Bird, 1985).

Besides the crucial importance of learner self-evaluation, several other factors appear to play a role in strategy transfer (Pressley, Borkowski, & Schneider, 1987). One is the degree to which the learner understands the conditions under which the strategy applies and the details of how to apply it (cf., Gagné, Weidemann, Bell, & Anders, 1984; O'Sullivan

& Pressley, 1984). There are also two general factors that appear to have an influence. One is whether or not the individual tends to attribute her successes to effort and to use of strategies (Clifford, 1984). Another is whether or not the individual can screen out distracting thoughts when trying to analyze a new problem (Kuhl, 1985). A final important factor is the degree of relevant declarative knowledge possessed by the strategy user (Chi, 1985). Each of the factors that has been shown to affect strategy transfer will be discussed below, beginning with a discussion of the learner's self-evaluation processes.

Self-Evaluation of Strategy Utility

A Study Demonstrating Its Effects on Transfer. Ghatala, Levin, Pressley, and Lodico (1985) worked with second graders and focused on elaboration as a strategy for increasing one's memory for information. The experiment involved three study/test sequences during which the children studied lists of pairs of nouns and then took a recall test. On the first study/test trial, the researchers did not instruct the children to use any particular strategy. The purpose of this trial was to find out if the children in different experimental groups started out at the same level, which they did. On the second study/test trial, half of the children were taught to use elaboration, an effective strategy for recalling information, and half were taught to count the letters in the noun pairs, a very ineffective strategy. On this

trial, the elaboration group recalled much more than did the counting group.

Table 11.9 shows the design for the Ghatala et al. experiment. The two rows show the two strategies—elaboration versus counting—taught prior to Trial 2. The three columns indicate the type of self-evaluation training the child received prior to the first study/test trial. Researchers taught one-third of the children (*strategy utility group*) to evaluate the utility of the strategy used by reflecting on how much they recalled with and without using a particular strategy. The children tried drawing a circle freehand and then using a circular cookie cutter. The researcher then asked which strategy had produced a better circle and why? Also, the researcher asked what strategy the child would select if he were to draw a circle again.

The researchers taught another third (*strategy affect group*) to evaluate whether or not a strategy was "fun" to use. They asked these children whether it was more fun to draw a circle freehand or with a cookie cutter. This was done so that the researchers could determine whether or not *any* evaluation was effective in producing strategy transfer or only evaluation involving the strategy's utility. The final third of the children in each strategy group did not receive any instruction about evaluation (*control group*).

Following self-evaluation training prior to the first study/test trial and strategy training prior to the second study/test trial, all the children received the same instruction for the

Table 11.9 Research design for the Ghatala et al. (1985) study for the role of self-evaluation of strategies in strategy transfer.

	STRATEGY UTILITY	STRATEGY AFFECT	CONTROL
Elaboration strategy			
Counting strategy			

Table 11.10 Average percent recalled by children in each training group (adapted from Ghatala et al., 1985).

| | TRAINING CONDITION | | |
	STRATEGY UTILITY	STRATEGY AFFECT	CONTROL
A. Trial 1			
Elaboration strategy	39.5	37.1	31.9
Counting strategy	36.2	36.2	29.0
B. Trial 2			
Elaboration strategy	98.6	96.7	97.1
Counting strategy	19.0	19.0	9.5
C. Trial 3			
Elaboration strategy	92.4	89.0	79.5
Counting strategy	42.9	29.5	29.0

third trial. Researchers told them that they would once again be asked to recall what they had studied, but they could study the material in any way they wished.

To measure whether or not children maintained strategies on the third trial, the researchers asked the children questions that elicited the strategy used for each noun pair on that trial. To determine the children's awareness of the utility of a given strategy, they asked the children why they selected the strategy. Also, to determine the children's awareness of utility, they showed the children the list of noun pairs from the first two trials and asked them which time they remembered more pairs and why they thought they remembered more pairs that time.

As you can see in Table 11.10, the results for recall of items on the third list showed that children who had used the elaboration strategy on the second trial recalled much more than children who used the counting strategy on that trial. Most children who had used counting on the second trial abandoned it on the third trial, but, since they had not learned the elaboration strategy, their recall was worse than the group that had learned to elaborate. Recall was similar for children in the different self-evaluation groups, so on this

test of immediate, near transfer, the self-evaluation manipulation did not appear to have an effect.

Learning to evaluate a strategy's utility *did*, however affect what children said about their strategy choices after the third trial. Table 11.11 shows the results for the interview that occurred after the third study/test trial. What is most interesting is that the children who had been trained to evaluate strategy utility were much more likely to say that their reason

Table 11.11 Percentage of children giving different reasons for selecting a strategy on the third study-test trial (adapted from Ghatala et al., 1985).

| TRAINING CONDITION | REASON[a] | | |
	MEMORY	FUN	EASY
1. Elaboration strategy			
Strategy-utility	100.0	0.0	0.0
Strategy-affect	0.0	90.5	9.5
Control	0.0	71.4	28.6
2. Counting strategy			
Strategy-utility	76.2	0.0	23.8
Strategy-affect	4.8	52.4	42.8
Control	4.8	28.6	66.7

[a]Based on the subject's most frequently reported strategy (see text for explanation).

for selecting whatever strategy they did on the third trial was that it helped them remember better.

The researchers conducted two tests of delayed transfer to new lists of noun pairs—one at one week after the initial training and one at nine weeks. On these two tests, the strategy-utility group outperformed the strategy-fun and control groups. On the first delayed test, 90% of the strategy-utility children consistently applied the elaboration strategy to the new word pairs versus only about 57% of the other children. On the second delayed test 100% of the strategy-utility children consistently used the elaboration strategy versus 50% of the children in the other two groups.

These results suggest that the careful evaluation of strategy utility done by the strategy-utility children helped them recall this utility information over a long period of time and use it when an analogous situation arose. The children in the other groups, while able to benefit immediately from strategy training, did not store much information about the strategy that they could use later in a transfer setting.

The same type of results have been found for a variety of strategies and a variety of subject populations. There is some indication that adults spontaneously evaluate strategy effectiveness and so need less encouragement to do so (Pressley, Levin, & Ghatala, 1984). However, when adults are resistant to learning a new strategy, then having them evaluate its effectiveness may be appropriate.

Instructional Strategies. There are a variety of ways to encourage learners to self-evaluate. One can have them record results of attempts to reach a goal with and without the use of the strategy and compare the success of the attempts. One can require students to hand in diaries of strategy use over a given time period and ask them to correlate this with perceived success. In computer games, the desire to win the game often encourages the player to evaluate strategies, but some help software could be included to make the evaluation more explicit. Another approach would be to have students try individually to solve a problem, and then have a group discussion that focuses on comparing the strategies used by people who were more or less successful in solving the problem. Of course, this technique will only work if one has developed a cooperative learning atmosphere in which it is OK to admit one's mistakes and in which value is placed on learning from mistakes.

Whatever approach one takes as a teacher, the important elements of self-evaluation include having clear records about when strategies were used and what the outcomes were and then asking students to draw conclusions about these data.

Other Factors Affecting Strategy Transfer

Knowledge of When and How to Use a Strategy. Frequently, in training people to use strategies, the emphasis has been on the mechanics of carrying out the strategy—first this step, then this step, etc. Students are told the steps in the strategy and then they practice using the steps. They receive feedback about whether the steps are done correctly, in the appropriate sequence, and/or fast enough. While this type of instruction is important in learning a new strategy, there is another often omitted element that has to do with recognizing when a given strategy is appropriate. In production systems terms, it is as if training focuses on the *action* side of productions, to the neglect of the equally important *condition* side. One reason that people may fail to transfer strategies is that they do not really know when the strategy should be used.

Besides failing to teach people when to use a strategy, many strategy-training programs do not teach why a strategy works and the details of how to implement a strategy effectively. Pressley and his colleagues refer to all this detailed information about strategies as "specific strategy knowledge" (Pressley, Borkowski, & Schneider, 1987). In our view, knowledge of why and how a strategy works is actually a form of conceptual understanding, where what is being understood is one's own cognitive processes. The more common term for this type of understanding is **metacognition**. At any rate, we believe it forms the conceptual basis for strategy transfer, in the same way that other types of conceptual knowledge form the basis for transfer in other domains.

Tendency to Attribute Success to Effort and Use of Strategies. As we will discuss more in the chapter on motivation, learners vary in their tendency to attribute academic success to effort versus some other factor such as luck or native intelligence. Those who tend to attribute success to effort also tend to be high achievers because they are more likely to persist when the going gets tough. One situation in which the going gets tough is a transfer (novel) situation. Here, the student confronts a new task and does not quite know how to approach it to be most successful. If the student believes that success in novel situations is due to luck, then she is unlikely to put much time and effort into thinking about the task, how it is similar or different to other tasks, and what strategies might be used to perform the task successfully. However, if the student believes that success is due to her effort and use of strategies, then she is likely to persist and try some different strategies to see what works. Therefore, students who have a strong belief in their own role in success are more likely to transfer strategies to new settings.

Tendency to Screen Out Distracting Thoughts. When confronted with a new task, some students have more distracting (usually emotional) thoughts than do others. For example, consider two students in a first-year French class. So far, the instruction has been mostly oral—learning everyday conversation. The only reading has been reading of everyday conversations after the students have practiced them orally. Now their French teacher asks them to read a story in French and answer questions about the story. Both students have experienced a mixture of success and failure in the class so far. When confronted with the novel assignment, they both initially think, "Eek, I can't do this. We haven't learned how to do this yet." However, the student who is better at screening out distracting thoughts stops thinking these thoughts and instead turns to analyzing what is required for the new assignment. This leads him to realize that he has strategies from his first language that he can use in approaching reading in a second language. The student who is less good at screening out distracting thoughts continues to dwell on his lack of experience and his depressed feelings. Because of this, he does not have room in working memory to figure out what strategies might transfer.

The ability to screen out distractions and to take positive mental action has been called "action control" by Kuhl (1985), who has studied this trait extensively. Kuhl's research shows that students with high action control are more strategic in approaching study tasks and ultimately are more successful.

Declarative Knowledge. Declarative knowledge is a final factor that constrains the degree to which at least some strategies transfer. This occurs because many strategies require declarative knowledge for their implementation. For example, in reading, it is almost always helpful to activate one's prior knowledge relevant to what one is reading about. This allows one to form an elaborated memory structure for the new information being read. However, this strategy of knowledge activation cannot be transferred to situations in which one lacks the requisite knowledge (Walker, 1987).

As another example, consider the "split-half" strategy used in electronics troubleshooting. In this strategy, the troubleshooter who understands the pathway that the electrical current takes through a device can divide the pathway in half and measure to see which half of the pathway is having problems. This is much more efficient than starting at one end of the path and taking measurements in sequence all the way to the other end because one can eliminate an entire half of the circuit with just one measurement. Some students in technical school may learn to use this strategy on simple devices and circuits but fail to transfer it to their workplace situations because they lack sufficient declarative knowledge of the complex devices that they are expected to troubleshoot. They do not know where the halfway point in the circuit is because they do not have a functional understanding of the device (Means & Roth, 1988).

In situations such as these, it would not help to have the student evaluate the success of strategy use or to be explicit about the conditions under which a given strategy can be used or to encourage the student to screen out distracting thoughts and feelings. What would help is increasing the student's declarative knowledge.

Summary

The typical situation in which we hope for strategy transfer is some new task that is similar to a task for which the student has already learned to use the strategy. For the student to transfer a strategy, she must represent the new task in a way that stimulates thoughts about appropriate strategies. Several factors seem to influence how the new task is represented.

The first factor is whether or not the student has previously evaluated the utility of the target strategy. If she has, then this utility information is likely to be activated. A second factor is the extent to which the student has a deep understanding of the strategy—why and how it works and the conditions under which it works. A third factor is the student's belief about her role in achieving success. If she believes that success on the new task is contingent on her effort and her application of a good strategy, then she is more likely to take more time in searching for strategies. A fourth factor is the student's ability to screen out distractions. If she can screen out distractions, she has more cognitive capacity available to develop a rich representation of the task.

An Example of Teaching for Strategy Transfer

A study by Gagné et al. (1984) illustrates a strategy training program that attempted to provide for several of the factors that facilitate strategy transfer. The students involved were seventh graders and the strategy involved was the elaboration strategy shown in Figure 11.7. As you can see in that figure, students learned that the strategy was only useful (1) if the goal was to remember some newly learned information, and (2) if the information was understandable. If these two conditions existed, then students learned to generate elaborations and to evaluate the goodness of their elaborations.

Instruction. Table 11.12 shows the sequence of lessons taught to the strategy-training group and the control group. (Students had been randomly assigned to these two groups). Instruction took place during a regularly scheduled study period at the students' school. As you can see from the table, the students in the strategy-training group learned a great deal about the elaboration strategy including what an elaboration is, why

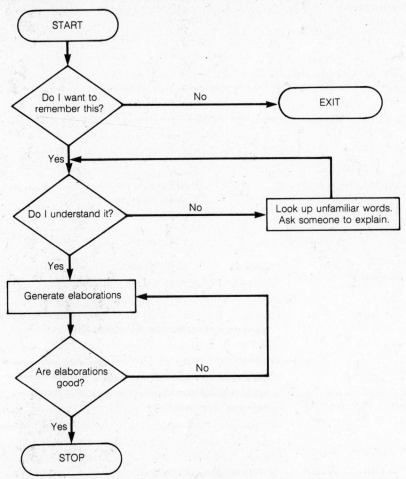

Figure 11.7 The elaboration strategy studied by E.D. Gagné et al. (1984).

it helps us to remember, the difference between good and less good elaborations, recognizing when it should be useful to elaborate, and knowing what to do to activate elaborations during recall. In addition to learning all of this information, this group had a great deal of practice in actually generating elaborations and then trying to recall (the next day) the information for which they had generated elaborations. Table 11.13 shows all of the types of information that students practiced elaborating on.

The control group practiced elaborating on all of the passages and other items on which the strategy-training group practiced. They also attempted to recall the information they had elaborated on the day after they elaborated. The difference between the strategy-training group and the control group during practice was that the strategy-training group was using elaboration consciously— they knew it was supposed to help them recall. Moreover, towards the end of training, they were free to generate and evaluate their

Table 11.12 The sequence of lesson topics for elaboration strategy training and for the control group (adapted from E.D. Gagné et al., 1984).

	TOPIC	
STRATEGY-TRAINING GROUP	CONTROL GROUP	DAY(S)
What is an elaboration?		1
Why use elaborations?		2
Good elaborations generate much information		3,4
Good elaborations organize information		5,6
Good elaborations add to main ideas	Practice Session 1	7
When to elaborate		8
What to do when trying to recall	Practice Session 2	8
Practice in deciding whether to elaborate, elaborating,	Practice Session 3	9
and recalling elaborations	Practice Session 4	10

Table 11.13 The variety of textual materials for which students practiced elaboration.

Passages from students' math text
Passages from students' history text
Passages from students' science text
Passages from students' literature text
A shopping list
Directions for the Heimlich maneuver
A Superman story
An expository passage on the history of the telephone
Eleven sentences
Two one-paragraph passages

own elaborations. The control group responded to questions following each passage they studied, and these questions elicited elaborations from them. However, they were unaware of the purpose of these questions and they never freely generated and evaluated elaborations.

Promoting Schema Formation and Refinement in the Strategy-Training Group. One of the instructional goals was for the students to form a schema for elaborations. The training started out by providing a definition of an elaboration and a variety of examples of elab-

oration. As you learned in Chapter 8, provision of a wide variety of examples facilitates the schema induction process.

The training then moved to helping students refine their elaboration schema. Again, as you recall from Chapter 8, during schema refinement it is helpful to present examples and matched non-examples so that the learner can focus on key elements of a schema that he had not yet heeded. Table 11.14 shows the worksheet the students worked through to assist them in this schema refinement process. Items numbered 2, 5, and 6 are elaborations because they are thoughts that are (1) generated by the learner, and (2) related to the to-be-learned information. Number 3 is not an elaboration because, although it is a thought that is generated by the learner, it is not related to the to-be-learned information. Number 4 is not an elaboration because, although it is a thought related to the to-be-learned information, it is not generated by the learner. Thus, these non-examples each have a different critical attribute missing. This focused the students' attention on each crucial attribute in turn and hence promoted schema refinement.

Another part of the schema that needed to be refined was knowledge of when to use

Table 11.14 An exercise requiring students to discriminate between elaborations and non-elaborations. The students learned that elaborations must be *self*-generated (adapted from E.D. Gagné et al., 1984).

Here are six examples of things that are elaborations and things that are not elaborations. Read each example. In the blank to the left of each example, write E if you think that the example is an elaboration. If you think the example is not an elaboration, write NE in the blank.

E = Elaboration
NE = Not an Elaboration

1. _NE_ A student reads "Columbus discovered America in 1492" and decides she wants to remember it. She repeats in her head, "Columbus discovered America in 1492."
2. _E_ John reads "Columbus was a Spaniard. He sailed to America in 1942." He wants to remember this information, so he thinks, "Columbus most likely sailed West to America because the shortest way to get to America from Spain is to go West."
3. _NE_ Jack reads "Columbus discovered America in 1492. Columbus was a Spaniard." He thinks "I wonder what's for lunch?"
4. _NE_ Susan hears her arithmetic teacher say, "To divide fractions, invert the divisor and multiply." Then the teacher says, "Remember the divisor is what you divide by."
5. _E_ Sally hears her arithmetic teacher say, "To divide fractions, invert the divisor and multiply," and thinks "That's another rule for working with fractions. In the multiplication of fractions, you *don't* invert the divisor, you must multiply."
6. _E_ A student hears his science teacher say, "Molecules are farther apart in gases than in liquids, so gases are lighter." The student thinks "That is like loosely woven cloth is lighter than tightly woven cloth of the same material."

Table 11.15 A workbook exercise to teach discrimination between when one does and does not want to remember something.

For each of the following goals decide whether you should think of elaborations or not. Write *E* if you should think of elaborations and *NE* if you should not think of elaborations.

_NE_ Goal 1: Remember your answer to a math problem the teacher is asking about long enough to raise your hand and say it.
_E_ Goal 2: Remember the rule for dividing fractions so that you can divide fractions when you're 30 years old!
_NE_ Goal 3: Read a space odyssey book for fun. Don't care to remember it.
_E_ Goal 4: Understand the main ideas about how a computer works. Don't know whether you want to remember it or not.
_E_ Goal 5: Remember some information about early humans so that you can use that information in a high school history class.

elaboration. Table 11.15 shows the workbook exercise associated with this topic. As you can see, the point of this exercise was for students to recognize that if they did not want to remember things or did not want to remember something for very long, then the elaboration strategy was not appropriate.

Finally, students received similar types of exercises to help them distinguish between good and less good elaborations.

Promoting Skill Acquisition. As you learned in Chapter 9, the stages in skill acquisition include an initial cognitive phase in which performance of the skill is guided by a declarative (conscious) representation followed by an associative stage in which more and more of the skill comes to be controlled by a procedural representation. A major instructional strategy for skill acquisition is the use of practice and feedback.

The skill being taught in this training program was essentially the skill represented in Figure 11.7. Students in the strategy-training group actually received something quite like this figure as part of their training, and they were encouraged to use it to guide their skill practice initially. After a few practice trials, they tried practicing elaboration without the use of the figure. The hope was that they were moving from a declarative to an associative stage in skill acquisition.

After students attempted recalling information that they had studied and elaborated on the day before, there was a general class discussion in which students shared their elaborations. Students who had found successful elaborations were especially eager to share them with others, and the group was able to figure out why particular elaborations were effective. This method of feedback helped students refine their skills.

Was Instruction Effective? Both the strategy-training and control groups were given a posttest in which they studied new material that they expected to be tested on later, but they were not prompted to use the elaboration strategy. This posttest was given seven days after the training was completed, and for most of the students in each group it was administered by a new researcher who had not administered the training. Also, posttesting occurred in a different location at the school. Having a different room and different person involved should presumably decrease the students' likelihood of thinking of the elaboration strategy.

Immediately after the study period for the posttest, the researchers asked students what

Table 11.16 Percentages of students in the strategy-training and control groups who reported using elaborations while studying on the posttest.

	USE ELABORATIONS	DON'T USE ELABORATIONS
Strategy-training	73%	27%
Control	33%	67%

they did to study. Students in the strategy-training group were much more likely to report elaborations they had generated than were students in the control group. Table 11.16 shows the percentages of students in each group reporting the use of elaboration on the posttest. In addition, when students were tested on recall of posttest material the next day, the strategy-training students recalled significantly more than did the students in the control group.

These results show that the strategy-training program was successful in getting the great majority of students to transfer use of the strategy to a new learning situation.

Factors Supporting Strategy Transfer. The program we have just described included most, but not all, of the factors that research has shown facilitates strategy transfer. Clearly, it included a good amount of practice in strategy evaluation. One form of evaluation was the utility of various types of elaboration. The training workbooks had students compare elaborations that were more and less effective. Another form of evaluation was between use and non-use of elaboration. In fact, the training program started out by having half of the students in the class elaborate on some information and the other half try to remember it some other way. When they recalled the information, it was obvious that the elaboration strategy was more successful.

This type of comparison continued throughout the training program during the group discussions. When a student volunteered an elaboration that she found particularly effective, other students realized that they had not elaborated that particular information and also had not recalled it.

A second factor that was included in this training program was a great deal of strategy information. There was information about what an elaboration is and what it is not, what a good elaboration is and what it is not, why elaborations help recall, and when to use the elaboration strategy. This information helped students form a rich conceptual basis for the strategy.

A third factor that was included was that of declarative knowledge. The students learned that the strategy would not work when they did not understand what they were learning because one cannot elaborate very well on information that one does not understand.

The other factors involved in strategy transfer are more stable dispositional factors—the tendency to attribute success to use of strategies and the ability to screen out distractions—and they were not directly addressed in this training program. However, one can view the program as a partial attempt to promote the attribution of success to use of strategies. The message of the program was that use of a specific strategy helps for a specific goal. Students who received the training experienced increased success at recalling information when they used the elaboration strategy. If these students go on to learn of other strategies that help in other situations, they may begin to develop a tendency to attribute success to the use of strategies.

CHAPTER SUMMARY

Transfer is a matter of great concern to educators. It is also a topic that has generated a great deal of controversy among psychologists. Recent progress in the area has begun to allow us to understand the phenomenon better, although there is still much to be learned.

The emerging picture is that transfer in a novel problem situation is mediated by recall of related declarative knowledge and use of this knowledge to produce a new solution. This process benefits from a deep conceptual understanding of a domain because such understanding will make the knowledge recalled more apt. Once a solution is formulated, any procedural knowledge that applies in both the new and old situations can be easily and quickly transferred to the new situation. This is why the degree of overlap in basic skills is important in transfer.

Strategy transfer benefits from a deep conceptual understanding of one's own cognitive processes. This understanding is promoted both by self-evaluation processes and by direct presentation of information about cognitive processes.

ADDITIONAL READINGS

General Issues

Butterfield, E.C., & Nelson, G.D. (1991). Promoting positive transfer of different types. *Cognition and Instruction, 8,* 69–102.

Voss, J. (1987). Learning and transfer in subject-matter learning: A problem-solving model. *International Journal of Educational Research, 11,* 607–622.

Transfer and Conceptual Understanding

Case, R. & McKeough, A. (1990). Schooling and the development of central conceptual structure: An example from the domain of children's narrative. *International Journal of Educational Research, 13,* 835–855.

Mayer, R. (1989). Models for understanding. *Review of Educational Research, 59,* 43–64.

White, B.Y., & Frederiksen, J.R. (1986). *Progressions of qualitative models as a foundation for intelligent learning environments*. Tech. Rep. #6277, Boston, MA: Bolt, Baranek, & Newman.

Transfer and Basic Skills

Rouse, W.B. (1982). A mixed fidelity approach to technical training. *Journal of Educational Technology Systems, 11,* 103–115.

Singley, M.K., & Anderson, J.R. (1989). *The transfer of cognitive skill.* Cambridge, MA: Harvard University Press.

Transfer and Strategies

Borkowski, J.G., Johnston, M.B., & Reid, M.K. (1985). Metacognition, motivation, and the transfer of control processes. In S.J. Ceci (Ed.), *Handbook of cognitive, social, and neuropsychological aspects of learning disabilities.* Hillsdale, NJ: Lawrence Erlbaum Associates.

Pressley, M., Forrest-Pressley, D.L., Elliott-Faust, D., & Miller, G. (1985). Children's use of cognitive strategies, how to teach strategies, and what to do if they can't be taught. In M. Pressley & C.J. Brainerd (Eds.), *Cognitive learning and memory in children* (pp. 1–47). New York: Springer-Verlag.

Salomon, G., & Perkins, D.N. (1989). Rocky roads to transfer: Rethinking mechanisms of a neglected phenomenon. *Educational Psychologist, 24,* 113–142.

SECTION
FIVE

School Subjects

*I*n the past decade, the ideas and methods of cognitive psychology have come to be used more and more in the study of domains such as reading, writing, and problem solving in math and science. It is becoming evident from this research that expertise in these domains is comprised of conceptual understanding of the domain, automated basic skills, and domain-specific strategies. It is also becoming clear that for some tasks there are multiple areas of conceptual understanding that enable the most sophisticated performance. For example, expert writers have a good understanding not only of rhetorical principles and audience characteristics, but also of the content about which they are writing.

One purpose of this section is to describe models of competence in reading, writing, math, and science that have emerged from careful cognitive analytic studies. In addition, we will describe samples of interventions that take into account these models and that are consistent with the cognitive learning principles described in Sections Three and Four. The number of exemplary instructional studies is delightfully large. We wish we could have described more of them and we hope that you will read more of this work on your own by going to the sources cited at the ends of chapters.

SUMMARY

1. Successful reading comprehension involves both conceptual understanding (declarative knowledge) and skills and strategies (procedural knowledge). The declarative knowledge consists of knowledge about letters, phonemes, morphemes, words, ideas, schemas, and topic or subject matter. The procedural knowledge represents the knowledge of "how to" read and is comprised of numerous component processes.

2. Component reading processes are embodied in production sets and can be divided into **decoding, literal comprehension, inferential comprehension,** and **comprehension monitoring.**

3. **Decoding** involves using the printed word to activate word meanings in memory, either through a direct association of the printed word and its meaning or through the intermediate step of representing letter-sound correspondences.

4. **Literal comprehension** involves putting activated word meanings together to form propositions.

5. **Inferential comprehension** involves going beyond the idea explicitly stated to integrate, summarize, and elaborate on these ideas.

6. **Comprehension monitoring** involves setting a reading goal, checking to see if the goal is being reached, and implementing remedial strategies when one's goal is not being reached.

7. Less skilled and younger readers differ from more skilled and older readers on decoding, literal comprehension, inferential comprehension, and comprehension monitoring skills.

8. Recent evidence suggests that declarative knowledge differences also underlie the observed differences between skilled and less skilled readers.

9. Success in early reading depends on two factors. First, children must develop an awareness of print and its function in everyday life. Second, children must see the value of reading before they will be convinced that reading is an important skill to master.

Reading is a tremendously valuable basic skill. The ability to read opens up the world of jungle animals to an urban six-year-old and the world of sophisticated technology to a ten-year-old villager in Ghana. It allows adults to change careers through independent study. It provides people of all ages with an inexpensive way of finding out about the variety of ideas and social and cultural landscapes that make up our world.

In information-based societies such as our own, reading is not only valuable, it is necessary for adequate functioning. Diehl and Mikulecky (1980) have found that the percentage of time spent reading in various job categories is higher than one might expect: Across a wide sampling of job categories, including both white- and blue-collar jobs, the average time spent reading per day is two hours.

Despite the importance of reading, over 33% of the world's adult population is illiterate (Huss, 1970). In America, 13% of high school graduates are functionally illiterate and another 17% are barely competent (National Commission on Excellence in Education 1983). Overall, 20% of adult Americans are functionally illiterate and the estimates indicate that this number is increasing by 2.3 million people a year (Larrick, 1987, cited in Adams, 1990). Equally disturbing is the fate of the illiterate. Adams (1990) reports:

"According to the Orton Dyslexia Society, illiterate adults account for 75 percent of the unemployed, one-third of the mothers receiving Aid to Families with Dependent Children, 85 percent of the juveniles who appear in court, 60 percent of prison inmates, and nearly 40 percent of minority youth; . . ." (p. 27)

Clearly these statistics suggest that we are failing to impart literacy skills to a substantial segment of our society. What can be done about this problem? Can we reverse the current trends? The answers to these questions rest in part on having a clear understanding of the nature of literacy, and particularly on reading and writing. In this chapter and the next, we consider these two topics in depth. It turns out that recent research on these topics has provided us with greater insights into the component skills that underlie literacy, and consequently educators are now in better position to tackle literacy problems in schools.

How should reading instruction occur in schools? Should "phonics first" be adopted or should one use a "whole language" approach? In other words, how can one know which aspects of reading are most important to spend time on? In order to answer these questions, two prerequisites are needed. First, one must have a conception of the cognitive processes that are responsible for successful reading comprehension. Second, one must tie these cognitive processes to the observed differences between skilled and less skilled readers. Once we understand the differences and what causes them, we can develop instructional methods to enhance reading skill. So, for example, if successful reading involves guessing upcoming words, and if skilled readers are better than less skilled readers at guessing words, then this is probably an important process to teach less skilled readers. If, on the other hand, readers at different levels of skill are equally good at getting word meanings from contexts, then it would be a waste of time to teach this process.

In this chapter, we first describe a model of reading which then serves to organize the information about how skilled and less skilled readers differ. In keeping with the model of cognition developed earlier, (1) the current reading model relies on basic skills, conceptual understanding, and strategies, and (2) reading skill is presumed to be acquired in a stage-like progression. Next, we review current thinking about the ways that skilled and less skilled readers differ. Finally, we discuss the instructional implications and give examples of experimental programs aimed at improving reading skill.

COMPONENT PROCESSES IN SKILLED READING

Successful reading comprehension relies on the three elements of expertise that were described in Chapter 10—conceptual understanding, automated basic skills, and strategies. Conceptual understanding includes knowledge of topics about which one is reading, text schemas, and vocabulary. Automated basic skills include word decoding skills and the ability to construct propositions from strings of words. Strategies include varying one's approach to reading depending upon one's goal and monitoring one's com-

prehension. While the knowledge that forms the basis of conceptual understanding is housed in declarative memory, the underlying skills and strategies are housed in procedural memory. These skills and strategies are really knowledge of "how to" read, and thus the reading processes themselves are embodied as sets of productions. As you can imagine, one consequence of becoming a skilled reader is the automatization of the reading processes.

Skilled reading is a highly complex capability involving many component processes and extensive declarative knowledge. It is, therefore, no wonder that many persons have difficulty learning to read. Problems can occur in any one of the component processes or in some combination of them. Similarly, reading difficulties may stem from a lack of declarative knowledge. Fortunately, however, teachers who understand enough about these sources of difficulty can help solve reading problems.

Reading processes can be broken down into four subgroups: decoding, literal comprehension, inferential comprehension, and comprehension monitoring. At any slice in time during reading, processes included in all of these subgroups are likely to be going on in parallel (Frederiksen, 1982; Just & Carpenter, 1987; Thibadeau, Just, & Carpenter, 1982).

Decoding—Automated Basic Skills

Decoding means cracking a code and this is exactly the function of decoding processes—they crack the code of print to make print meaningful. According to Ehri (1982), there are two main decoding processes. One is *matching*, in which the printed word is matched to a known pattern for the word, which in turn activates the word's meaning in long-term memory. Matching is used in recognizing words in one's sight vocabulary. The other decoding process is *recoding*, which is involved in "sounding out" a word. During recoding, the printed word is translated into sound patterns and then the sound patterns activate the word's meaning in long-term memory.

Matching. All readers acquire a *sight vocabulary*—a set of words that they recognize quickly in print. Words that are in person's sight vocabulary do not need to be sounded out or guessed. Rather, the printed version of the word is directly matched to an internal, declarative representation, with the result being the activation of one's knowledge about the word.

The process of matching can be conceived of in production terms. For example, to recognize the word *cat* in print, a reader may use the production shown in Table 12.1. In this production, there are three conditions. First, the reader must have the goal of identifying the word that he is looking at. Second, there should be an initial *c*, and third the pair of letters *at*. (Since *a* and *t* frequently occur together in English, they are probably recognized as a unit). The actions in the production are activation of the meaning and sound for cat stored in declarative memory.

Matching, then, can be conceived of as the process of matching the condition clauses of word-specific productions. The actions that automatically take place when these condition clauses are satisfied are that both the meaning and the sound of the word are activated. The reason for conceiving of matching in production terms is that procedural knowledge can be automatized, and hence it captures this important aspect of the matching process.

In all the likelihood, the matching process evolves as a person acquires reading skill. Beginning readers do not yet have a sight vocabulary, and consequently the matching process probably operates at the level of letters or features of letters (e.g., lines, rounded shapes). As skill is acquired, the size of the perceptual units increases to bigrams and other sub-words. Eventually, the matching process will operate on entire words. Thus, the declarative knowledge base has information on perceptual features, combinations of features into letters, letter combinations, words, and the meanings, images, and sounds associated with words (cf., Just & Carpenter, 1987). The matching process uses "chunks" that correspond to the largest perceptual patterns a reader knows.

Recoding. In matching, the external print directly activates meaning. In recoding, the print is first translated into a string of sounds and the string of sounds is then used to activate meaning. The recoding process operates when a reader encounters an unfamiliar word or when the length of a word exceeds the eye's perceptual span. The sequence of steps (or procedures involved) in recoding are:

1. Partition the unfamiliar or lengthy word into syllables.

2. Generate a sound pattern for each syllable.

3. String the sounds together.

4. Use the sounds generated in (3) to activate meaning in LTM.

Table 12.1 A production that might underlie the ability to recognize the word *cat* in print.

IF	The goal is to identify the current word, and first letter is *c*, and second and third letters are *a, t*
THEN	Activate concept of cat in declarative memory and activate sound pattern for cat.

For example, if a student did not recognize the word *tiger* through matching, he would first divide the word into two syllables (ti - ger), then generate the sound corresponding to *ti* (ti) and the sound corresponding to *ger* (ger), then string these two sounds together (tiger), and finally use this sound pattern to activate the meaning of tiger stored in declarative memory.

Recoding requires declarative knowledge of sub-word units such as phonemes, syllables, and morphemes. Additionally, one can conceptualize the recoding process itself as being a set of productions that encode the knowledge of letter-sound correspondence of the language being read. One subset of these productions would have to do with syllabification. For example, a production that would correctly segment words such as *letter, runner,* and *jagged* would be:

> IF Goal is to segment current
>   word into syllables
>   and word has six letters
>   and letters 3 and 4 are
>   consonants
>   and letters 3 and 4 are the
>   same
>
> THEN Divide word between letters
>   3 and 4.

Another subset of productions would have to do with what sounds were represented by what letters. For example:

> IF Goal is to determine
>   pronunciation of current
>   word
>
>   and syllable is last in word
>   and syllable begins with
>   vowel
>   and syllable ends with E
>   and consonant is between
>   vowel and E.

> THEN Pronounce long form of
>   vowel
>   and pronounce regular
>   form of consonant
>   and do not pronounce E.

This is a production that encodes the "silent e" rule. Yet a third set of productions would have to do with the blending of sounds. For example, when a *dle* syllable ends a two-syllable word (e.g., *handle, cradle, ladle,* etc.), the *d* is scarcely pronounced. A production representing this knowledge might have the form:

> IF Goal is to determine
>   pronunciation of current
>   word
>   and word has two syllables
>   and second syllable is *dle*
>
> THEN Pronounce first syllable
>   and attenuate D in
>   pronouncing second
>   syllable.

Remember people's productions do not really contain words like "attentuate" or "pronounce." They contain whatever abstract symbol a person uses to produce attenuation or pronunciation. The words used here are chosen to communicate the effect, not the form, of the productions that might underlie recoding skill.

Also, remember that with extensive use, productions represent knowledge of how to act automatically under a given set of conditions. The conditions are recognized and the actions take place without reflection. As it turns out, the decoding processes (i.e., matching and recoding) must be automatized if understanding beyond the word level is to occur.

Literal Comprehension—A Mix of Automated Basic Skills and Conceptual Understanding

The patterns of print or sound that are identified during decoding are part of the input that stimulates literal comprehension processes (the other part comes from higher-level processes such as one's expectations about the passage). The function of literal comprehension is to derive literal meaning from print. It is composed of two processes—*lexical access* and *parsing*.

Lexical Access. During this component process, the meanings of words are identified. The term *lexical access* comes from the notion that humans have mental dictionaries (lexicons) that are accessed during language comprehension. The general consensus is that our declarative knowledge includes this dictionary.

The lexical-access process is a set of productions that uses the products of the decoding process to identify and select the appropriate word meaning. That is, the decoding process activates the word percept in declarative memory, and the lexical-access operations select the right interpretation of the word from all of the knowledge that has been activated. For example, suppose a skilled reader encounters the word *bank* in a text. The decoding processes will locate and activate the reader's declarative knowledge of the concept, "bank." Among the items of information activated will be the knowledge that bank may mean the sides of a river or a place where money is kept or a type of basketball shot. The lexical-access process will select one of these meanings by evaluating the appropriateness of each one for the current situation. If the text is about fishing, the river interpretation will be chosen. Notice that as a skilled reader yourself, you are unaware that this process even occurs. You will recall that that is a sign that lexical occurs automatically.

Exactly what gets activated in long-term memory depends very much on an individual's store of declarative knowledge (or put in other words, it depends on the depth of the individual's conceptual understanding). For example, Figure 12.1 shows two sixth graders' mental dictionaries for the word *oxygen*. As you can see, one student's dictionary has a single entry—"we need it to breathe," while the other's has several entries—"a constituent of air," "a gas," "burns with a blue flame," "combines with hydrogen to make water," and "signified by O." As we shall see presently, a difference in what is activated during the lexical-access process can make a big difference in inferential comprehension.

Parsing. During reading, the meanings of the individual words combine to form larger units of meaning, such as the meaning of a phrase, a clause, or a simple sentence. The ways that word meanings combine are governed by a set of processes known as parsing processes. The parsing processes use the syntactic and linguistic rules of a language for putting words together to form meaningful ideas. For example, in English a common rule is that determiners (e.g., a, the) signal the beginning of a noun phrase (e.g., *The old man . . .*). A production that could parse noun phrases might be:

IF   The goal is to form a phrase
       and a determiner is the
       current word

THEN   Start a new noun phrase
       and expect the phrase to
       end with a noun
       and expect the noun may
       be preceded by modifiers.

You can probably imagine additional productions that parse verb phrases and yet others that combine noun phrases with verb phrases to form complete ideas (see Just & Carpenter, 1987).

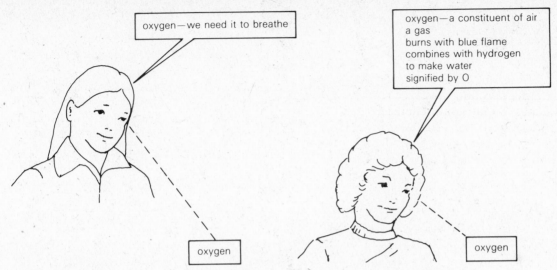

Figure 12.1 A comparison of the mental lexicons of two students who are equally skilled at decoding.

The products of the parsing processes are really propositions—units of declarative knowledge that represent the meaning of the text (see Chapter 4 if you have forgotten what propositions are). Figure 12.2 shows the propositions that are created by parsing the sentences:

John called Sally.

Sally called John.

In these sentences, the parsing processes use cues from word order, word endings, and other sources to decide whether it is John or Sally who is the subject of the sentence. If John occurs first (in an active sentence), he is considered to be the subject; if Sally occurs first (in an active sentence), she is the subject. Without a parsing process, the different relationships in these two sentences could not be distinguished.

Parsing processes can operate on word labels as easily as they can operate on word meanings. Therefore, we can create proposi-

tions for such sentences as Lewis Carroll's famous *Jabberwocky* sentences:

'Twas brillig, and the slithy toves

Did gyre and gimbel in the wabe.

Even though we have no idea what *toves* are, we can recognize that *tove* is a noun (using the noun phrase production from above), that it is plural (by the *s* ending), and that they are the actors in the sentence because they precede the verb (which we detect from the word, *Did*). Thus, we can create a proposition such as that shown in Figure 12.3. The only difference between this proposition and those shown in Figure 12.2 is that the end nodes are word labels rather than word meanings. (This is signified by the quotation marks around the word labels in Figure 12.3).

This example also shows that the various processes can operate independently of one another. While a reader can parse the *Jabberwocky* sentence and gain some level of understanding, she does not have the word mean-

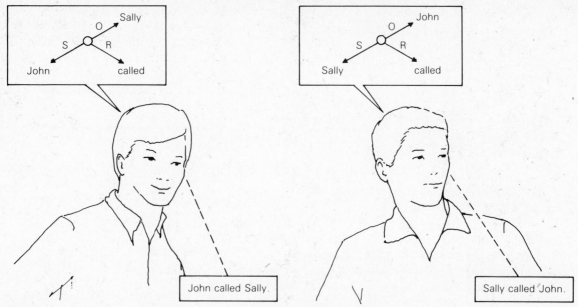

Figure 12.2 Propositional structure for two printed sentences containing the same words.

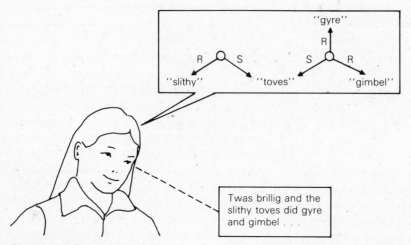

Figure 12.3 Propositional structure for a sentence in which the word meanings are unknown.

ings stored in her lexicon, and consequently lexical access is unsuccessful.

Thus, parsing provides some understanding of sentences by giving us information about the relations between and among words. But the understanding is incomplete. Lexical access provides another type of understanding, i.e., the meanings of the individual words, but it is also incomplete by itself. The two processes working together provide literal comprehension. For the skilled reader, literal comprehension occurs fairly effortlessly.

Inferential Comprehension—A Mix of Automated Skills, Conceptual Understanding, and Strategies

Literal comprehension is sufficient for some tasks that involve reading, such as reading a bus schedule or reading a recipe. However, going beyond the information literally stated in text—inferential comprehension—gives the reader a deeper and broader understanding of the ideas about which he is reading and is therefore an important aspect of reading. The processes involved in inferential comprehension include **integration, summarization,** and **elaboration.**

Integration. Integration processes result in a more coherent declarative representation of the ideas in the text then would otherwise be the case. Suppose, for example, that a third grader reads the sentences:

The bear walked toward John.

He ran.

On the surface, the ideas in these two sentences are not necessarily related. *He* might refer to someone other than John. And the reason for running might be for the fun of it, for participation in a race, or to catch a thief. A skilled reader, however, makes the assumption that the sentences in a text are related to one another. When their relationship is not explicitly stated, the skilled reader often attempts to infer it. In the above example, the skilled reader uses accepted rules of pronominal reference to infer that *He* in sentence 2 refers to *John* in sentence 1. As you can probably imagine, such rules are embodied as pro-

duction sets. Further, the reader uses prior declarative knowledge, such as his schema "reacting to fear," to draw the inference that John ran because the bear was walking toward him. In fact, the final declarative representation of the two sentences might be the inference,

John ran because the bear was walking toward him.

Notice that this combined idea is more coherent than the two separate ideas explicitly communicated by the text because the inference causally links the two ideas to one another (i.e., *because*).

In general, integrative processes connect two or more propositions together. Thus, integration occurs within complex sentences, across sentences, and even across paragraphs. Because the procedural knowledge underlying integration has to be so flexible, not all integration processes operate at an automatic level. Rather, these processes often require cognitive resources. The skilled reader devotes the resources required to integrate text ideas because an integrated representation of a text makes it easier for the reader to remember and reason about the material.

Summarization. The function of summarization is to produce in the reader's declarative memory an overall or "macro" structure that expresses the main ideas of a passage (Kintsch & van Dijk, 1978; van Dijk & Kintsch, 1983). A macrostructure is like a mental outline and can be thought of as a set of hierarchically arranged propositions that capture the main ideas of a passage.

Figure 12.4 shows a paragraph about the climate in Mala (from Rickards, 1976) and a macrostructure for that paragraph, namely that "Mala has a tropical climate." Notice that this idea was not explicitly stated in the paragraph. It is often the case that the idea represented by the macrostructure is not explicitly

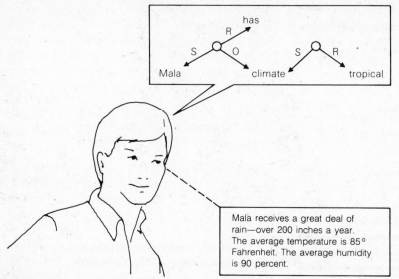

Figure 12.4 A paragraph and the macrostructure developed by the reader for that paragraph.

stated. As with integration, so too with summarization: the mental product is often inferential rather than literal.

The procedural knowledge that underlies the summarization processes are sets of productions that have the goal of extracting the essence from a passage. Often the extraction involves drawing inferences that connect or integrate large amounts of information. In order for this type of summarization process to work, one must have some conceptual understanding of the topic. Return to the example paragraph in Figure 12.4. The summary proposition is really a generalization that has been inferred from the text. Rain, humidity, and temperature are all attributes we associate with "climate." Similarly, 200 inches of rain, 90% humidity, and 85° are indicative of a particular climate, namely "tropical." In order to draw this inferential summary statement, the reader must have this declarative knowledge; otherwise the reader will not recognize the relations among the concepts stated in the paragraph.

The process that finds the relations among the concepts can be conceived of as a production set that identifies the topic concept (i.e., Mala) and then searches through declarative memory for relations or commonalities among the other concepts. Table 12.2 presents a production set that accomplishes this. Essentially it forms a hierarchically arranged set of propositions, spreads activation from the concepts within the propositions, and looks for activation to converge on new concepts. Thus, in the Mala example, activation would spread from rain, humidity, and temperature and would converge on "climate."

Of course, skilled readers possess varied procedural knowledge for summarizing a text. Some of the production sets for summarization resemble strategies. For example, a common summarization strategy is using the first sentence of a paragraph as the "topic" or "summary" statement. Other production sets look for text-based signals, such as words or phrases. Phrases such as "in summary," "in conclusion," and "in general" cue the reader

Table 12.2 A simple production system for extracting the main idea from the Mala passage.

P_1	IF	The goal is to extract main idea and main idea is not given explicitly
	THEN	Set subgoal to identify the topic concept and set subgoal to identify relations among other concepts.
P_2	IF	The subgoal is to identify topic concept
	THEN	Read the passage and note the concept that is referred to or implied most often and mark that concept as the topic.
P_3	IF	The subgoal is to identify relations among other concepts
	THEN	Set subgoal to attempt to form connected propositional representation and set subgoal of determining relations among propositions connected to topic concept.
P_4	IF	Subgoal is to form connected propositional representation
	THEN	Read the passage and form propositional representation of the sentences and include topic concept in propositions in which it is implied and connect any propositions that share a common concept to the proposition that first mentioned the common concept.
P_5	IF	Subgoal is to determine relations among propositions connected to topic concept
	THEN	Activate in declarative memory meanings of concepts within propositions and spread activation in network to neighboring concepts and note activation that converges on a neighboring concept.
P_6	IF	Activation converges on a neighboring concept
	THEN	Use that concept to generate a new proposition about the topic concept and label the new proposition as a summary statement.

that a summary statement is about to be made and trigger productions that create a macrostructure based on this statement.

Other cues for macrostructure come from the skilled reader's schemas for the structure of different types of text. For example, the prototypical structure for stories, discussed in Chapter 5, is a series of episodes with each episode consisting of an exposition about an actor and his goal, actions taken to meet that goal, a complication or obstacle, and a resolution of the complication (Kintsch, 1977).

Expository texts also have typical structures. Meyer (1975) has identified the five structures for expository text that are shown in Table 12.3. The first, **antecedent/consequent,** shows a causal relationship between two topics. For example, eating eggs (antecedent) causes a rise in cholesterol levels in the blood (consequent). The second structure, **comparison,** discusses the similarities and differences of two topics. For example, choosing puppy food and baby food are similar (according to an advertisement) in that they both require a great deal of care. The third structure, **collection,** is a collection of related facts about a topic. For example, a paragraph that lists the various jobs of a cowboy has a collection structure. The fourth structure, **description,** gives details or exam-

Table 12.3 Expository text structures and examples of each.

STRUCTURE	DEFINITION	EXAMPLE
Antecedent/Consequent	Shows a causal relationship between topics.	"If you had two eggs this morning you're already over the daily cholesterol limit; eating the eggs resulted in boosting you over the cholesterol limit."
Comparison	Points out similarities and differences between two or more topics.	"You should be as careful choosing a puppy food as you are in choosing a baby food. Puppies, like babies, have special needs due to their fast growth."
Collection	Shows how ideas are related.	"A cowboy has two jobs. He herds cattle and he brands them."
Description	Gives examples, details, or settings for topic.	"When liquid is heated to its boiling point some of it changes into a gas. An example of this is boiling water."
Response	Presents a problem and solution or question and answer.	"The nation is increasingly confronted with the need for renewable energy sources. One such source is solar energy."

ples about a topic. For example, one could give the example of boiling water as an instance of the general rule that liquids boil when heated. The fifth type of structure for expository text is called **response.** If a passage poses a question and then answers it or presents a problem and a solution, it is said to have a response type of structure. An example of this is a text that starts out by saying that the nation needs renewable sources of energy and then continues by discussing one renewable source—solar energy.

The examples given in Table 12.3 have been condensed into two or three sentences for space-saving reasons. More typically, an entire essay or textbook chapter or section can be classified into one of these five structures for expository text. These structures are stored as schemas and used by skilled readers to form summaries.

Elaboration. Whereas integration and summarization organize new information by building a coherent meaning representation, elaboration adds to this meaning representation by bringing prior knowledge to bear on it. In other words, the main processes involved in inferential comprehension are the same as the main processes involved in learning declarative knowledge (organization and elaboration, discussed in Chapter 7). This makes sense since the most common goal of reading is to acquire new declarative knowledge.

Some types of elaboration are shown in Table 12.4. The first elaboration gives an example of a general class. The second continues a story. The third adds details. And the last is an analogy. In each of these examples, the reader's thoughts are called elaborations because they use pre-existing declarative knowledge to add to the new ideas gleaned from the text. In each example, the processes that produce the elaborations are production-based.

As we saw in Chapter 7, elaborative processes are particularly useful when the reader's goal is to remember or reconstruct

Table 12.4 Some types of elaborations and an example of each.

TYPE	WHAT THE TEXT STATED	WHAT THE READER ADDED (ELABORATION)
Example	"A credenza is a low side cabinet in an office."	"My uncle has a credenza in his office."
Continuation	"And so Tom returned to his home after his trip around the world."	"Tom later became an ambassador due to all his experience in travelling."
Detail	"Jane hit the nail and hung the picture on the wall."	"Jane used a hammer and hit the nail hard."
Analogy	"A credenza is a low side cabinet in an office."	"It's like a bureau because it holds things, but it's in an office, not a house."

information at a later date. By tying new information to something familiar one can more easily retrieve the new information later on. Elaboration also appears to increase the probability of transfer of knowledge (cf., Mayer, 1980; 1987).

Comprehension Monitoring—A Mix of Automated Skills and Strategies

The function of comprehension monitoring is to assure that the reader is meeting her goals effectively and efficiently. The processes involved in comprehension monitoring—**goal-setting, strategy selection, goal-checking,** and **remediation**—are analogous to the executive processes that occur in any situation that involves setting cognitive goals and attempting to meet them in an efficient manner (e.g., such as problem-solving discussed in Chapter 10). This broader set of skills has been called *metacognition* (Baker & Brown, 1984; Flavell, 1979) and refers to one's awareness of one's own cognitive processes. In the current context, this awareness is produced by the reader's procedural knowledge.

Goal-Setting and Strategy Selection. In skilled readers, comprehension monitoring begins at the start of a reading event and continues throughout the event. At the start of reading, the reader sets a goal and selects a reading strategy to use in meeting the goal (this is probably done fairly automatically in skilled readers). The goal might be finding a particular piece of information, in which case the appropriate strategy might be skimming for a key word associated with the desired information. Or, the goal might be getting an overview of a chapter, in which case the appropriate strategy might be skimming the chapter headings.

Goal-Checking and Remediation. The purpose of goal-checking is to assure that the reader's goals are being met. For example, if a goal is to find out when the American Civil War started, a check of the goal would be whether or not the reader could answer the question "When did the American Civil War start?" If, on the other hand, the reader's goal was to pass an essay test on the American Civil War, a test for this goal would be his or her ability to answer potential essay questions.

As reading proceeds, the goal-checking process may disrupt the normal flow, and remediation processes will be activated to deal with whatever caused the break in comprehension. One example of this disruption of reading by goal-checking processes can be observed when a word with two meanings is encountered and the wrong meaning is adopted at first. For example, when people read,

> She was sad. There were tears
> in her brown dress.

they first interpret *tears* to be water from the eyes (Carpenter & Just, 1981; Just & Carpenter, 1987). But when they encounter the word *dress* a signal from the goal-checker is put out indicating lack of understanding. Then the readers disrupt the normal flow of reading and backtrack with their eyes to the word *tear*, this time accessing the other meaning and the other pronunciation of tear (a rip). The sentence now passes the goal-checker and reading proceeds.

The Dynamics of Skilled Reading

It would be useful if teachers knew exactly which component process was taking place during reading at any given time. If a teacher knew, for example, the exact time that a student was decoding the word *somnolent*, he could ask the student questions that would stimulate recoding processes, such as "What is the first letter?" When well timed, such questions would be quite useful. However, what if the student had already successfully decoded the words in the sentence he was reading and was in fact involved in integrating the meaning of the sentence with the meanings of previous sentences? In that case, asking the question "What does the first letter sound like?" would be interfering rather than helpful.

Although it is difficult to know exactly what processes are occurring and when, Just and Carpenter (1980, 1987) have a model of reading dynamics in the skilled reader that provides some good approximations. These researchers had college students read passages from *Scientific American* and measured their average gaze time on each word in the passage. Table 12.5 shows the average number of milliseconds spent looking at each word for two sentences in their study.

There are several interesting observations that can be made about these data. First, there is a large difference between the fixation time on unfamiliar words such as *flywheel* (1566 msec.) and familiar words such as *devices* (767 msec.). This is because it takes a longer time to recode *flywheel* than it does to match *devices*. Another example of recoding is the gaze pattern on the word *contains*. Note how the reader spends time looking at the two syllables in the word. A second observation of interest is that the gaze time on the modifiers within a noun phrase tend to be smaller than the gaze time on the noun itself (e.g., *oldest*—267, *mechanical*—617, *devices*—767). This pattern is evidence for parsing because it sug-

Table 12.5 Average duration of eye fixations (in milliseconds) while reading a text for understanding (adapted from Just and Carpenter, 1980).

1566	267	400	83	267	617	767	450	450	400	616	517

Flywheels are one of the oldest mechanical devices known to man. Every internal combustion

684	250	317	617	1116	367	467	483	450	383	284

engine contains a small flywheel that converts the jerky motion of the pistons into the smooth

383	317	283	533	50	366	566

flow of energy that powers the drive shaft.

gests that readers are sensitive to the different grammatical categories of the words being read. A final observation is that, in general, the fixation time is longer for words at the ends of sentences than for equally or less familiar words in the middles of sentences. For example, *man* is a very familiar word, more familiar than *oldest*. Yet *man*, occurring at the end of sentence 1, is looked at for an average of 450 msec, while *oldest*, occurring in the middle of sentence 1, is looked at for only 267 msec. This suggests that time is taken at the ends of sentences to perform summarization, integration, and elaboration processes.

Thus, these observations suggest that skilled readers decode and parse words as they are fixing them. Further, as the reader's eyes reach the ends of sentences, time is taken to integrate the ideas represented by the sentence with ideas already represented in the reader's mind.

The time spent on various component processes varies depending on the reader's goals. Carpenter and Just (1981), for example, found that readers who expected a test in which they had to write down what they remembered spent more time integrating ideas in the sentences than did readers who expected a multiple-choice test. Readers who are skimming for the main idea may spend little time processing any sentences other than the first and last sentences in each paragraph (see also Graesser & Rhia, 1984).

It is important to realize that the representations in working memory during reading are constantly changing depending on what component processes are taking place. This idea is illustrated in Figure 12.5. The circle around the A in the center of that figure represents Attention. The arrows going out from the circle imply that various intermediate products may be active in working memory at any given point in time. In this example, readers read the sentence *The cat is black* and represent either the visual image of the words in work-

ing memory (matching) or the sound patterns associated with the letters (recoding). Next, the visual or sound representation activates the word meanings (lexical access). For example, the printed word *cat* stimulates the recall of images and/or propositions about cats. After all the word meanings for this sentence have been activated, a proposition is constructed that represents the syntactic and linguistic relations among the word meanings (parsing). At this point, literal comprehension of the sentence *The cat is black* is complete.

When propositions from two or more ideas have been constructed, they are integrated. For example, the idea that the cat is named Mike (obtained from a previous sentence) is connected to the idea that the cat is black because both ideas refer to the same specific cat. Elaboration of the idea that the cat is black may also take place. For example, the reader may use her prior knowledge that cats like to chase birds to generate the elaboration that this particular cat named Mike likes to chase birds. Summarization can also take place, although this process is not shown in Figure 12.5. The propositions developed from parsing, integration, elaboration, and summarization processes are deposited in long-term declarative memory.

Of course, depending on both the goals and the skills of different readers, some of the states represented in Figure 12.5 may be skipped. Also, some processes may occur simultaneously or in a different sequence from the one presented. The main point to be noted is that there are several transitory states and processes that occur as reading proceeds.

PROCEDURAL KNOWLEDGE DIFFERENCES BETWEEN SKILLED AND LESS SKILLED READERS

It would be nice if it could be shown that reading problems were confined to one or two of the component processes described in the

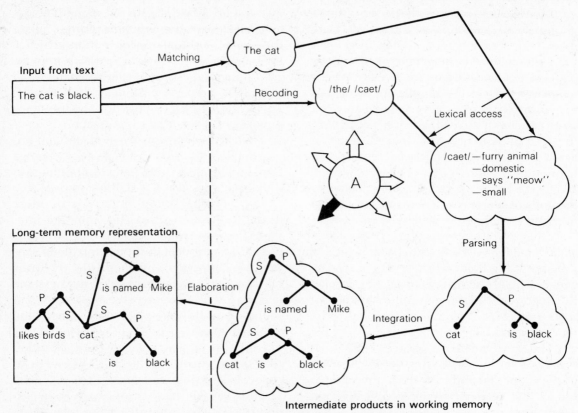

Figure 12.5 A diagram of many of the component processes of reading and the intermediate products they generate in working memory. The *A* in the circle represents attention, which is a limited resource. The dark arrow from attention signifies that attention is currently focused on the ideas that the cat is black and named Mike. (Once a given process is fully automatic, its intermediate products are no longer heeded in working memory.) The arrows represent one logical sequence for the flow of information, but, in reality, there is a flow of information in the other direction as well.

previous sections. Then research and instruction could emphasize these problem areas. Unfortunately, skilled readers appear to be substantially better than less skilled readers in almost all the component reading processes. Additionally, recent research evidence also shows that skilled reading appears to be inextricably tied to one's declarative knowledge. In this section of the chapter, we present some of the evidence that shows how the procedural knowledge of skilled and less skilled readers differs. In the next section we describe some of the evidence that demonstrates that reading skill is also tied to declarative knowledge.

Decoding

Skilled and less skilled readers have been shown to differ in both matching and recoding processes. They do not differ so much in terms of errors as in terms of the speed with which

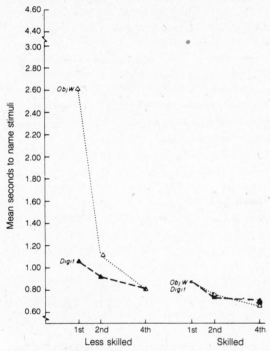

Figure 12.6 Mean number of seconds to identify digits and familiar object words as a function of grade and reading skill (from Ehri and Wilce, 1983).

they typically perform these processes. Speed is important because if it takes a long time to decode a word then one may have forgotten previous words, and therefore it becomes more difficult to generate a meaning representation. In other words, speed is an indicator of the degree to which the processes have become automatized.

Matching. Ehri and Wilce (1983) studied the speed with which skilled and less skilled elementary school children could read familiar printed words such as *hat, boy,* and *car.* They compared this speed with the time it took to read familiar one-digit numbers such as 3, 4, or 8. The results are shown in Figure 12.6. As can be seen, less skilled readers in the first and second grades were substantially slower at

reading words than digits. By fourth grade, however, their word and digit reading times were equal. For skilled readers, there was no difference in word and digit reading time at any grade level. These data imply that, especially in the early years of school, the matching process in poor readers is not as efficient as it is in good readers.

One likely possibility for this difference is that the matching process in poor readers has not yet developed to the same level of sophistication as that of good readers. One of the best predictors of reading skill in the early grades turns out to be the amount of experience with print a child has had prior to entering school (cf., Adams, 1990). Children with a lot of exposure to print (in the form of books, chalkboards, magnetic letters on the refrigerator, etc.) come to school knowing a considerable amount about language in general, and the functions, uses, and conventions of printed language in particular. Thus, when exposed to formal reading instruction, their sight vocabularies develop rapidly. Consequently, the matching process also develops and becomes automatized.

Recoding. By far the most research on differences between skilled and less skilled readers has focused on recoding processes. By now there is ample evidence that skilled readers perform recoding faster and more effortlessly than less skilled readers.

In a typical study of recoding, subjects read aloud words or pronounceable nonsense words (e.g., *noke, pight*). The time between presentation of the stimulus and voice onset (called vocalization latency) is recorded. Shorter vocalization latencies indicate faster, more efficient recoding. Further, since recoding processes are associated with sight-sound correspondence, their efficiency should be especially evident in the reading of pronounceable pseudowords because pseudowords are completely unfamiliar (by definition). In this vein, Frederiksen (1981) found that high school students with very high reading ability were twice as fast at starting to say pseudowords as were students of very low reading ability. Figure 12.7 shows the vocalization latencies for high school students at four levels of reading ability. The lowest ability group took 1.2 seconds on the average to start to say a pseudoword, while the highest ability group took an average of .6 seconds. Other studies have obtained similar results with younger readers (Curtis, 1980; Perfetti & Hogaboam, 1975; Perfetti, Finger, & Hogaboam, 1978).

As discussed earlier, recoding also involves the ability to sequence and blend sounds. This aspect of recoding has been studied by Calfee, Lindamood, and Lindamood (1973). They gave students in grades K–12 a test requiring them to represent sequences of sounds (Subtest I) and blends of sounds (Subtests II and III). Figure 12.8 shows their results. Readers were divided into those

who were in the upper and lower halves of the range of scores for their grade on the Reading and Spelling subtests of the Wide Range Achievement Test. In grades K–4, the less skilled readers were significantly worse than the skilled readers at representing sequences of sounds and, in all grades, the less skilled were worse at representing blends than were the skilled readers.

Are the differences in recoding skill between good and poor readers fixed, or can they be reduced with practice? Venezky and Johnson (1973) have some data that can be used to address this question. These researchers were interested in the development of young children's abilities to pronounce pseudowords that contained either long or short *a* (e.g., *gane* versus *gan*) or hard or soft *c* sound (e.g., *bact* versus *bace*). They grouped first, second, and third graders into three reading ability groups, according to their scores on the Gates-MacGinitie comprehension test. All students were shown pseudowords on flash cards and the correctness of their responses was noted.

Figure 12.9 shows the results for each ability group at each grade level for long and short *a* sounds. You can see that the initially large differences (roughly 45%) between the high- and low-ability groups in the first and second grades substantially decreased (to roughly 25%) by the third grade. These data demonstrate that the differences between ability groups in the letter-sound correspondences for long and short *a* sounds narrows over time.

What about differences in pronunciation of hard and soft *c* sounds? Figure 12.10 shows the percentage correct for high- and low-ability children for these sounds. In contrast to the pattern of data for the *a* sound, these data do not show a consistent reduction of differences between skill levels over time. For the hard *c* sound, the low-ability students lag behind the high-ability students by about 20% in each

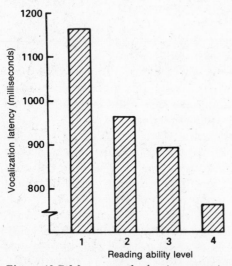

Figure 12.7 Mean speed of voice onset in the pronunciation of pseudowords as a function of reading ability level (1 = lowest ability level, 4 = highest level) (from Frederiksen, 1981).

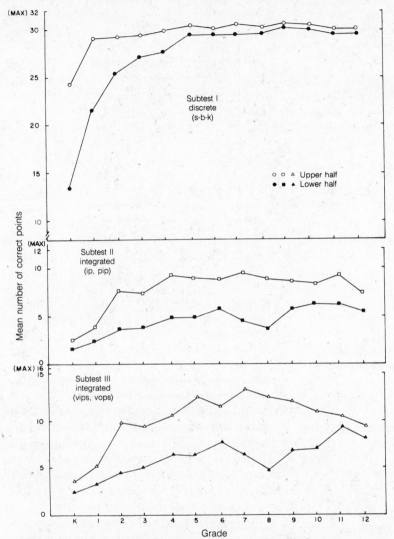

Figure 12.8 Mean number correct on tests of recoding skill as a function of grade and reading skill level (open symbols = above-average skill, closed symbols = below-average skill). Subtest I required students to represent sequences of sounds, whereas Subtests II and III required them to represent blends of sound sequences (from Calfee, Lindamood, and Lindamood, 1973).

grade. For the soft *c* sound, they lag behind high-ability students in the first and third grades, though not in the second. The data for hard and soft *c* sounds, then, suggest that the differences between high- and low-skill students do not decrease over time.

The discrepancy in patterns for the *a* and *c* sound can be explained by differences in (1) the amount of direct instruction given to these children on these various sounds, and (2) the frequency with which words occurred in the children's readers that contained the sounds.

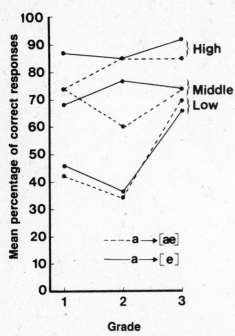

Figure 12.9 Correctness of pronunciation of pseudowords containing long or short *a* sounds as a function of grade and reading ability (from Venezky and Johnson, 1973).

Venezky and Johnson report that in the schools attended by their subjects:

> both long and short *a* correspondences are introduced early in Grade 1 and reinforced frequently. The distinction between the two patterns is pointed out by a variety of mechanisms, including contrastive pairs like *can:cane, at:ate,* and *cap:cape.* (p. 115)

In contrast, they report that for the letter *c,* although the hard *c* sound in the initial position is introduced early in the first grade, the soft *c* sound is often never covered. In addition, few words with soft *c* sounds occur in the beginning reading material of these children. These facts suggest one reason for the decrease in difference between high- and low-ability students on pronunciation of the letter *a:* direct instruction in the letter-sound corre-

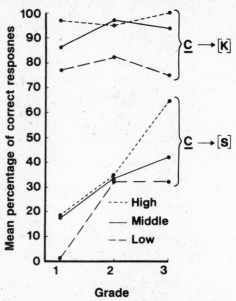

Figure 12.10 Mean correct pronunciation of hard and soft *c* as a function of grade and ability (from Venezky and Johnson, 1973).

spondences benefited the low-ability students more. The lack of such instruction for the soft *c* sound left the low-ability students at their initial disadvantage. Assuming that direct instruction contained many opportunities for practice and feedback, its probable effect was to develop the automated procedural knowledge necessary for recognizing long and short *a* sounds and the hard *c* sound.

The ways in which instruction can improve the performance of students low in reading ability will be discussed more in a later section of this chapter. The important point for now is that there are clear differences between skilled and less skilled readers on recoding ability.

The Relation between Decoding Skills and Comprehension. Some theorists argue that decoding skills are unimportant for skilled reading performance. They say that skilled reading is "conceptually driven"—we use the context and our pre-existing declarative knowledge to predict words. If we do this, then it really does not matter if we think "car" when the book actually says "automobile" because we are getting the correct meaning. Therefore, decoding is unimportant (see Goodman, 1967, or Smith, 1971 for this argument).

While this argument has logical consistency, it is challenged by studies that show a strong relationship between decoding and reading comprehension. Curtis (1980), for example, found an average correlation between word matching (matching) scores and reading comprehension scores of .51. She found an average correlation of .55 across elementary grades between word vocalization speed (recoding) and comprehension. Across grades 1–3, Venezky and Johnson (1973) found an average correlation of .70 between letter-sound (recoding) ability and reading comprehension. Correlations, of course, do not imply causality. These correlations may simply reflect the fact that typical reading programs teach both comprehension and decoding, and good students learn both.

However, besides the correlational data that suggests a relationship between decoding and comprehension skill, a number of large-scale studies of the effectiveness of different types of reading instruction programs consistently support the idea that programs with a strong, systematic emphasis on phonics instruction produce better readers (e.g., Bond & Dykstra, 1967; Chall, 1967, 1983). Thus, a large amount of data, whether correlational, empirical, or evaluative, suggests that children who are taught decoding skills perform better on reading comprehension tests than do children who are not taught decoding (Pflaum et al., 1980). Those who argue that good decoding skills are unnecessary for good comprehension must explain these data.

The emerging view by reading researchers, then, is that decoding skill is an essential prerequisite for successful reading comprehension (see Adams, 1990). Further, the prevailing belief is that decoding processes must be developed to the point of automatization. Readers who spend considerable time and mental effort trying to crack the written code at the word or sub-word level simply do not have enough cognitive resources left to derive the meanings of larger units (i.e., phrases, clauses, sentences, or paragraphs). While this position argues for a strong, systematic phonics component in direct reading instruction, *it does not commit to a particular instructional format* (e.g., whole language or basal). We will return to this point in the last section of the chapter.

Literal Comprehension

We now move on the the question of whether more and less skilled readers differ in literal comprehension. The main literal comprehension skill that has been studied in this regard is lexical access.

Lexical Access. One question that has been examined by cognitive psychologists is whether or not individuals differ in their speed of activation of long-term declarative memory—that is, speed of lexical access. For instance, Hunt, Davidson, and Lansman (1981) studied the relation in college students between lexical access speed and Nelson-Denny reading test scores. Access speed was measured by several tasks, all of which required retrieval of information from declarative memory. In one task, for example, subjects saw two words on a computer screen. One was a superordinate category label (e.g., *furniture*) and the other was an item that 50% of the time was a member of the category specified (e.g., *chair*) and 50% of the time was not a member of the category specified (e.g., *peach*). The subjects responded by pressing response keys labeled *Same* or *Different*, depending upon whether or not the item was a member of the category specified. To decide about category membership, information must be retrieved from declarative memory.

The results were that speed in deciding about category membership correlated about −.30 with the comprehension subtest score for the Nelson-Denny reading test. That is, a weak but significant relation existed between lexical-access speed and reading ability. Quicker access was associated with higher reading ability. Similar results have been found in other studies, using other tasks (e.g., Goldberg, Schwartz, & Steward, 1977; Hunt, Lunneborg, & Lewis, 1975). However, Hogaboam and Pellegrino (1978) failed to find significant correlations between lexical-access speed and comprehension, so some controversy still exists as to the magnitude of this relation (see however, Just & Carpenter, 1987).

Using Context to Speed Lexical Access. Several researchers believe that lexical access can be speeded when the context provides clues that constrain activation to certain parts of long-term declarative memory (e.g., Glucksberg, Kreuz, & Rho, 1986; Sharkey & Mitchell, 1985). As an illustration, try to predict the word that goes in the blank in the following sentences:

> *I reminded her gently that this was something she really wanted to _____ .*

> *Grandmother called the children over to the sofa because she had quite a story to _____ .*

You probably thought of many possibilities for the first sentence (do, buy, take, see, read, try), but only one or two for the second (tell, relate). This is because "wanting to" is appropriate to many contexts and reading *wanting to* therefore does not constrain activation. By contrast, "story" is frequently found in the context of "tell" and therefore *story* will constrain activation to the neighborhood of "tell" in LTM, allowing for quicker processing than if activation were not constrained.

Skilled readers appear to be better than less skilled readers at taking advantage of

context to predict words and therefore speed up literal comprehension. Frederiksen (1981) showed this with high school students. He had the students read sentences with blanks at the ends of them, such as the sentences just shown. When the students had finished reading each sentence, they pressed a button. The word that fit in the blank then appeared and the students pronounced the word as fast as they could. Presumably, if they had already begun activating the word because of the context, they should be able to pronounce it faster than if they were not expecting it.

The first sentence was said to provide a "weak context" whereas the second sentence was said to provide a "strong context." Frederiksen (1981) wondered if good readers capitalized on the strong context more than poor readers. If so, then they should show a greater acceleration in reaction time between weak- and strong-context sentences. Figure 12.11 shows what was found. The high-ability readers showed greater acceleration in reaction time because of having a strong context, and this was especially true for less frequently occurring words. Frederiksen believes that skilled readers automatically activate several word meaning possibilities at once and are ready to pronounce any one of them, while poor readers deliberately search for one word at a time. If it is the wrong word (as would be likely for low-frequency words), they must discard it and search for another one, thus slowing down pronunciation.

Whatever the cause of this difference, it is clear that skilled readers are better able to take advantage of context in speeding up literal comprehension than are less skilled readers.

Inferential Comprehension

Integration. Skilled readers' ability to take advantage of context may be due to their greater ability to integrate propositions both within and between sentences. The Frederiksen (1981) study demonstrated within-sen-

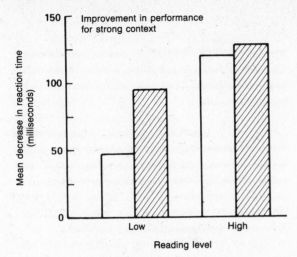

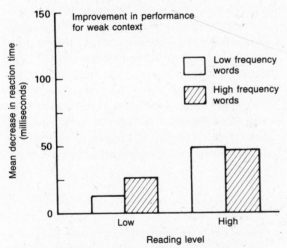

Figure 12.11 Average decrease in reaction time due to context. The high-ability readers show a greater benefit from a strong context than the low-ability readers (from Frederiksen, 1981).

Table 12.6 Percentage of correct predictions of the final word in a sentence as a function of constraint provided by a previous sentence. Notice that skilled readers perform better than less skilled readers in the moderate-constraint condition (adapted from Perfetti and Roth, 1981).

	SKILLED READERS	LESS SKILLED READERS
High constraint	92.9	94.4
Moderate constraint	23.7	15.2
Low constraint	0.2	0.1

scored above the sixtieth percentile. All subjects had average or above average intelligence.

The subjects' task was to listen to pairs of related sentences and predict the last word in the second sentence. By having the subjects listen rather than read, the researchers were able to separate comprehension processes from decoding processes. The first sentence provided either a high constraint, a moderate constraint, or a low constraint for predicting the missing word in the second sentence. For example, two moderate-constraint pairs were:

Lenny wanted to write a letter to his friend.
He opened the drawer and looked for a

_____ .

When I got home from work, I wanted to eat a fruit.
I went to the refrigerator and got a _____ .

Not surprisingly, as can be seen in Table 12.6, the skilled and less skilled readers were equivalent in their performance in high- and low-constraint situations. However, in the moderate-constraint situation, the skilled readers were about 8% more accurate than the less skilled readers. In examining the errors, the researchers noticed that the less skilled readers were more likely to produce words that did not fit with the constraints of the first sentence (e.g., pizza is not a fruit). It was as if the less

tence effects of context. A study conducted by Perfetti and Roth (1981) illustrates between-sentence context effects. In this study, the subjects were eight to ten years old. Less skilled readers scored below the fortieth percentile on the Metropolitan Achievement Test comprehension subtest and skilled readers skilled readers forgot the first sentence as they were making their predictions.

As we discussed previously, one aspect of integration involves pronominal reference— that is, deciding on the referent of a pronoun (e.g., Tom hit Harry. *He* laughed.) How do skilled and less skilled readers compare on this aspect of integration? Frederiksen (1981) has found several interesting differences in high school readers of varying reading levels.

In one study, subjects read text aloud and researchers determined their average reading time per syllable. Some sentences repeated the noun phrase from a previous sentence, others substituted a pronoun reference, and others only indirectly referred to the topic of the previous sentence. If the process of determining the referent of the second sentence is more difficult for a pronoun or an indirect reference than for a repeated noun phrase, this should slow down reading. Frederiksen (1981) found that reading was slowed, especially for the lowest ability group (below the fortieth percentile on the Nelson-Denny reading test). The results are displayed as average differences in reading time for repeated noun phrases versus pronouns (left side of Figure 12.12) and for repeated noun phrases versus indirect references (right side of Figure 12.12). The lowest ability group (Group 1) shows the greatest average difference, and hence the most slowdown, for both pronouns and indirect references.

In a second study, Frederiksen (1981) found that low-skill readers were slowed down much more than high-skill readers by sentences in which the pronoun was not "foregrounded" by an implicit reference in a previous sentence. Thus, in general, less skilled readers appear to be slower at integration processes than are skilled readers.

These studies of integration give the impression that less skilled readers have smaller working memory capacity than do skilled readers. That is, their "hardware" may be deficient in this regard. However, this idea has not received unequivocal support. Some studies show a relationship between WM capacity and reading skill (e.g., Badian, 1977), while others do not (e.g., Guyer & Friedman, 1975). The apparent WM deficit may really occur because less skilled readers perform some of the simpler comprehension operations less automatically and therefore devote

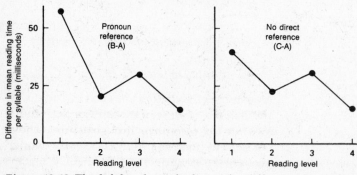

Figure 12.12 The left-hand graph shows the difference in reading time between reading a pronoun referent for a noun phrase and reading the noun phrase repeated. The right-hand graph shows the difference between reading an indirect reference to the noun phrase and reading the noun phrase repeated. The larger the difference, the more the pronominal or indirect reference is slowing down the reader. Poor readers (level I) are slowed down more than good readers (from Frederiksen, 1981).

more room in working memory to them (Daneman & Carpenter, 1980; Just & Carpenter, 1992). In a similar vein, less skilled readers may be using smaller chunks of information for processing (e.g., word meanings instead of propositional meanings) as a result of underdeveloped skills. In either case, this view is a very hopeful one from an educational standpoint. While memory capacity is more or less fixed, automaticity of skills and chunk size of information are quite variable depending on the amount of practice and exposure.

Summarization. Several studies have demonstrated that more competent readers are better at using the structure of a passage to develop a summary of the passage ideas (Bartlett, 1978; Meyer, Brandt, & Bluth, 1980; Taylor, 1980). The typical study in this area presents readers with well-structured text and has them freely recall what they can after reading.

Meyer, Brandt, & Bluth (1980) used this technique with ninth graders. They had the students read two expository passages, one with a comparison structure (see Table 12.3) and one with a problem-solution structure. One of the passages used is shown in Table 12.7. After reading, the students wrote down all they could remember from the passages.

Table 12.8 shows the average number of students who used the same organizational structure as the author's in their recall as a function of reading skill (good, average, and poor readers as measured by the Stanford Achievement Test). About three-fourths of the good readers (i.e., 23.5/32), about one-half of the average readers (16.5/35), and less than one-fourth (6.5/35) of the poor readers used the author's intended structure in recall. Students who did not use this structure tended to list ideas from the passage in a variety of orders. Meyer et al. (1980) also found that the use of the text structure was a substantial predictor of the overall amount recalled. This

Table 12.7 Passage read and recalled by students. The italicized words show the most important ideas (these ideas were not italicized in the student's version) (adapted from Meyer, Brandt, and Bluth, 1980).

SUPERTANKERS

A *problem of vital concern is the prevention of oil spills from supertankers.* A typical supertanker carries a half-million tons of oil and is the size of five football fields. A wrecked supertanker spills oil in the ocean; this oil kills animals, birds, and microscopic plant life. For example, when a tanker crashed off the coast of England, more than 200,000 dead seabirds washed ashore. Oil spills also kill microscopic plant life which provide food for sea life and produce 70 percent of the world's oxygen supply. Most wrecks *result from the lack* of power and steering equipment to handle emergency situations, such as storms. Supertankers have only one boiler to provide power and one propeller to drive the ship.

The solution to the problem is not to immediately halt the use of tankers on the ocean since about 80 percent of the world's oil supply is carried by supertankers. *Instead, the solution lies in the training of officers of supertankers, better building of tankers, and installing ground control stations to guide tankers near shore.* First, *officers of supertankers must get* top *training* in how to run and maneuver their ships. Second, tankers should be *built* with several propellers for extra control and backup boilers for emergency power. Third, *ground control stations should be installed* at places where supertankers come close to shore. These stations would act like airplane control towers, guiding tankers along busy shipping lanes and through dangerous channels.

---

is probably because use of the text structure the encoding and retrieval processes.

The poor readers in the Meyer et al. study seem not to recognize text structure. They may not yet possess the schemas that would be needed to recognize the structure. A study by Brown and Smiley (1977) suggests that there is a developmental sequence in the ability to distinguish important and less important parts of a text's structure (see also Brown & Day, 1983). Thus, some subjects in the

Table 12.8 Average number of students using the structure of the text in their recall protocols (*n* equals the number of students in the group). Average scores on the Stanford Achievement Test (Comprehension Subtest) were 84th, 58th, and 32nd percentile, respectively, for the good, average, and poor comprehenders (adapted from Meyer, Brandt, and Bluth, 1980).

| | STRUCTURE OF RECALL | |
	SAME AS TEXT	DIFFERENT FROM TEXT
Good comprehenders (n = 32)	23.5	8.5
Average comprehenders (n = 35)	16.5	18.5
Poor comprehenders (n = 35)	6.5	28.5

Meyer et al. study may have been developmentally behind others (in terms of formation and refinement of text schemas).

Brown and Smiley (1977) had students in the third, fifth, and seventh grades and college students read unfamiliar folk tales and rate each idea unit in the tales as to how important it was for the overall theme of the passage. They found that college students clearly differentiated among four levels of importance that had been previously established for the ideas. Fifth graders could distinguish the most important ideas, but could not distinguish among ideas at the other three levels. Third graders could not distinguish any levels of importance. Table 12.9 shows these results. Brown and Smiley also found that recall of passage ideas increased with age, suggesting that recall increases because students are learning how to organize or chunk passage information for efficient storage and retrieval. Taken together, the increased recall and the increased ability to discriminate the importance of information in text suggests that the formation and refinement of schemas for text is a developmental phenomenon.

Brown also studied the summarization abilities of both children and adults (Brown & Day, 1983). Essentially, the subjects were asked to write short summaries of texts, and then the researchers classified the summaries for their degree of sophistication (based on a set of linguistic rules for forming summaries). One interesting finding was the presence of a developmental trend where older students used more sophisticated summarization rules than younger students. Another and more interesting result was that when the adults were categorized as poor, average, and good readers, their summaries revealed the same developmental pattern—poor readers used simpler summarization rules, average readers used a mixture of rules, and good readers tended to use more sophisticated rules. Thus, the development of summarization skill is not necessarily age-related. It is probably a function of practice and experience.

In summary, skilled versus less skilled readers differ in their use of text structure in recall and mature versus less mature readers differ in their ability to distinguish the hierarchy of ideas contained in a text. The formation, refinement, and use of schemas for text structure are important for the summarization process to be able to function. If less skilled students could be trained to identify the characteristics of different text structures (i.e., induce the text schemas) and to develop procedures for recognizing and using these schemas, they would probably be able to generate summaries of text using such structures. Then their summarization ability should improve. Bartlett (1978) has demonstrated a successful training program in this area (see also Baumann, 1986).

Elaboration. Elaboration is the reading process during which the reader makes the material meaningful to herself by relating the new ideas being read about to known information. Weinstein (1978) has studied the use of elabo-

Table 12.9 Mean importance ratings for different levels of importance of ideas as a function of the age level of the reader (adapted from A. Brown and Smiley, 1977).

GROUP	IMPORTANCE LEVEL			
	1 (LEAST)	2	3	4 (MOST)
Third grade	2.41	2.52	2.51	2.56
Fifth grade	2.42	2.35	2.46	2.76
Seventh grade	2.02	2.36	2.58	3.05
College	1.61	2.09	2.78	3.52

ration by students who are more and less successful, as measured by grade point average, and by students at various grade levels. She gave students the questionnaire about elaboration shown in Table 12.10. Note that this questionnaire not only asks if a student has used a particular type of elaboration, but also asks for a specific example. If a student can provide a specific example, this is a good sign that her response is valid.

Weinstein (1978) summarizes the results of her studies by saying that "more successful learners, and those with more years of schooling, use meaningful elaboration strategies in preference to more rote, or superficial strate-

gies." While the results do not speak directly to reading skill differences, since reading skill is highly correlated with success in school, it is likely that skilled readers are better at elaborative processing than are less skilled readers.

As discussed earlier, successful elaboration requires procedural knowledge (i.e., algorithms and strategies) and declarative knowledge (i.e., prior knowledge that can be used to "build" a more enriched representation of the text). To date research on elaboration has not concentrated on this distinction, and so it is impossible to determine whether skilled and less skilled readers differ in their processing capabilities or in the knowledge

Table 12.10 Questions asked of students about their elaboration processes (adapted from Weinstein, 1978).

Please try to think of an example of how you would use this method. If you can't, it's OK. Check the method anyway.

_____ A. Think about the purpose or need for the material. Example:
_____ B. Relate it to your experience or characteristics. Example:
_____ C. Relate it to your beliefs or attitudes. Example:
_____ D. Think about your emotional reactions to the content. Example:
_____ E. Relate it to people in general. Example:
_____ F. Think about the ideas that you have as you read it. Example:
_____ G. Think about other people's reactions to the content. Example:
_____ H. Relate it to what you already know. Example:
_____ I. "Free associate" to the topic or ideas. Example:
_____ J. Think about implications of what is stated. Example:
_____ K. Look for common sense or logical relationships. Example:
_____ L. Relate the content to the theme. Example:
_____ M. Relate key words or concepts to ideas. Example:
_____ N. Discussion with other people. Example:

they have available (or both) (see Alexander & Judy, 1988, and Garner, 1990, for relevant discussions).

Comprehension Monitoring

Complex skills that are optimally proceduralized appear to have built-in tests for progress. Since the goal of most reading is comprehension, it is important for readers to assess whether comprehension is occurring. Moreover, when a test indicates noncomprehension, the reader must then use some strategy to remediate the problem, such as re-reading, looking up words in a dictionary, or asking someone for help (T.H. Anderson, 1979). Most of the research on monitoring and remediation has compared readers at different levels of maturity rather than those at the same level of maturity but different skill levels. However, older readers on the average have greater reading skill than do younger readers, so we can use age comparisons to get ideas about reading skill differences. In so doing, we must recognize the possibility that age differences may be due to differences in maturation or general experience rather than skill.

Goal Checking.   More and less mature readers show differential awareness of failure to comprehend (Baker & Brown, 1984; Garner, 1987; Markman, 1979). Harris, Kruithos, Terwogt, and Visser (1981) showed this by having third and sixth grade children read stories, some of which contained an anomalous sentence. Table 12.11 shows a sample of one of the stories used and two different titles for the story. The title, *John at the Dentist*, made the fourth sentence—*He sees his hair getting shorter*—anomalous and was therefore called the *conflicting title*. The title, *John at the Hairdresser's*, made the fourth sentence easy to interpret and was therefore called the *appropriate title*. The titles of stories were counterbal-

Table 12.11 A sample story with a conflicting and an appropriate title. The conflicting title renders sentence 4 anomalous (adapted from Harris et al., 1981).

Appropriate Title: John at the Hairdresser's

Inappropriate Title: John at the Dentist

1. John is waiting
2. There are two people before him.
3. After a while it is his turn.
4. He sees his hair getting shorter.
5. After a while he may get up.
6. He can go home.

---

anced across the two age groups so that story content would not be a confounding variable.

Each child read three stories and his reading time for each sentence was recorded. After all three stories were read, the experimenter asked each child, "Did you notice in one of the stories a line that did not fit in with the rest of the story?" If the answer was yes, the child was asked to recall the line. If he could not recall the line, the experimenter showed the story to the child again and asked the child to point to the line. Finally, for those children who said they had not noticed a problem, the experimenter showed them the story again and asked them to point to a line that did not fit in very well.

The results showed that both age groups were faster at reading a line when the title was appropriate than when it was conflicting. For the appropriate title, the average reading time was 3.3 seconds, whereas for the conflicting title, the average reading time was 4.2 seconds. The two age groups differed, however, in how many children noticed the problem sentence. Even when they were allowed to look back over the stories, 30% of the third graders still could not identify the problem sentence. Only 11% of the sixth graders were unable to identify the problem sentence. Also, 44% of the sixth graders said that they noticed a problem sentence and could recall this sentence without any prompting. Only 11% of the third graders could do this.

The different results for reading time and ability to identify problem sentences suggests that the younger children are producing signals that comprehension is faltering. They lack the ability to monitor these signals. That is, the third graders slowed down while reading a sentence that was incongruent with the story title, and this cued them that their comprehension was failing. However, since third graders frequently could not identify problem sentences, this suggests that they do not monitor the cues available to them. In other words, they have not yet developed procedures that would recognize these cues and trigger some remediation process. Apparently, the sixth graders have acquired these goal-checking procedures.

Remediation. The recognition of problems is prerequisite for their solution. If this is correct, we should find that low-skill readers neither recognize comprehension problems nor have remedial strategies to solve them, whereas medium-skill readers recognize problems but do not yet know how to deal with them, and high-skill readers both recognize and know how to remediate comprehension problems.

Garner and Reis (1981) found just such a pattern when they examined age and reading ability differences in the use of the "lookback" strategy. The look-back strategy involves looking back in a text when one realizes one needs information from preceding pages. It is certainly useful, but apparently not all readers possess it.

The children in this study were good and poor comprehenders in grades 4 through 10. They read passages such as the one shown in Table 12.12 and answered the questions shown. Some of the questions could be answered by referring to the paragraph just read, while others required the reader to look

back to (or possibly remember) information from preceding paragraphs. For example, question 10 could be answered by looking back to the first paragraph, which was on a separate page.

Garner and Reis (1981) counted the number of spontaneous expressions of problems (evidence of goal-checking) and also the number of look-backs to solve the problems. Expressions of problems included such verbalizations (after reading a question) as "hmm" or "let's see" or "I don't know" and also such nonverbal expressions as shrugging or head shaking. Poor comprehenders expressed problems on only 7% of the questions requiring look-backs, whereas good comprehenders expressed problems on 60% of these questions. The good comprehenders looked back on an average of 30% of the look-back questions, whereas the poor comprehenders looked back only 9% of the time. Finally, the six oldest good comprehenders used a look-back strategy almost 80% of the time. Thus, it seems that poor comprehenders neither recognize their problems nor use a look-back strategy very often, whereas younger good comprehenders recognize their problems over half the time and use a look-back strategy about a third of the time. Older good comprehenders consistently recognize comprehension problems and employ strategies to solve them. In a developmental sense, then, problem recognition does precede the acquisition of strategies to solve the problem.

DECLARATIVE KNOWLEDGE DIFFERENCES BETWEEN SKILLED AND LESS SKILLED READERS

We have just described many types of procedural knowledge that differentiate people with higher and lower reading skill. Differences in declarative knowledge can also be a source of reading skill differences. Recall from Chapter 6 that the productions that make up

Table 12.12 Passage and questions used to study the look-back strategy. Each passage and the questions that followed it were printed on a separate page. The questions marked with asterisks are those for which relevant information occurred on a preceding page (adapted from Garner and Reis, 1981).

Bill lived in Maryland, but this summer he was staying at Camp Wildwood in New York. His cabin was Number 11. He shared the cabin with five other boys: Tom from Maine, Sam from Vermont, David from New York, and Richard and Joseph from Pennsylvania. Only Richard and Joseph had known each other before the summer began. Bill enjoyed spending long days outdoors. He especially enjoyed fishing for trout and catfish in Big Bear Lake and for bass in Blue Pond. Bill was the best fisherman in cabin Number 11.

1. Where was Camp Wildwood? _____

2. How many boys were in cabin Number 11? _____

3. What was Bill's favorite camp activity? _____

After one week at Camp Wildwood, nearly everyone had received mail from home. Letters with Vermont, New York, Maryland, and Pennsylvania postmarks arrived almost daily. None of the guys got really homesick. They were too busy. Tom had discovered swimming. Richard had learned how to paddle a canoe. Bill fished from morning until night. One day Bill caught 12 fish in Blue Pond, and the Number 11 group had fresh fish for dinner instead of hamburgers. All six of the boys became close friends.

*4. Which of the boys did not receive mail? _____ (Sect. 1)

5. How many fish did Bill catch for dinner? _____

*6. What kind of fish were they? _____ (Sect. 1)

It finally came time for the boys to leave camp and return home. They were all sad. As parents arrived at camp to pick them up, each boy promised to write to the others. Joseph's mother was not happy when she had to delay her return to Pennsylvania. Her extra rider had decided to take one last canoe trip for the summer. However, by the end of the day, sports equipment was packed away, all the boys were on the road, and cabin Number 11 was closed for the season. Bill had reminded the others that they would all try to get the same cabin next summer at Wildwood.

*7. Which boy made Joseph's mother wait? _____ (Sect. 1 or 2)

8. What had been packed away? _____

9. What was Bill's reminder? _____

*10. Where did Bill fish other than at Blue Pond? _____ (Sect. 1)

our procedural knowledge contain declarative structures in their conditions and actions. In a real sense then, declarative knowledge is a necessary component of any skill. In reading, declarative knowledge must contribute in some way to all of the component processes we have discussed. Until recently, the relation between reading skill and declarative knowledge had not received much study. That situation is beginning to change. In this section, we describe some of this recent work. This section is divided into two parts. First, we briefly review some research that demonstrates that declarative knowledge has facilitative effects on the reading comprehension processes. Then we discuss research that explores the relation between reading skill and declarative knowledge.

Facilitative Effects on Comprehension Processes

Presumably, the more information that one has stored relevant to a word, the more sensitive one's lexical access will be to shades of meaning (Curtis, Collins, Gitomer, & Glaser, 1983). Similarly, the more declarative knowledge a person has, the more that knowledge can aid the component processes responsible for decoding and lexical access. One example of this phenomenon comes from a study by Sharkey and Mitchell (1985). Those researchers investigated how one's scriptal knowledge influences word recognition during reading. Recall from Chapter 5 that scriptal knowledge is declarative knowledge about highly stereotyped event sequences like going to a restaurant, shopping for groceries, and changing a flat tire. Since people typically have a large number of experiences with many of these stereotyped event sequences, our declarative knowledge of these events is very well organized and extensively elaborated (much like expert, declarative knowledge of a domain). Sharkey and Mitchell had subjects read short texts like the following:

> The children's birthday party was going quite well. They all sat around the table prepared to sing.

Immediately after reading each text, a subject was asked to decide whether or not a letter-string presented on a computer screen was a word. The strings were either script-related words (e.g., *candles*), unrelated words (e.g., *rabbits*), or nonwords (e.g., *banfers*). Judgment times were recorded. Among other things, the results showed that script-related words were judged more quickly than unrelated words. Apparently, activating the word meanings from the text led to the activation of the readers' scriptal knowledge, in this case a birthday party script, which in turn made "birthday party" concepts easier to decode and lexically access. So, one's declarative knowledge can apparently foster the decoding and literal comprehension processes.

A study by Walker and Yekovich (1987) investigated how scriptal knowledge affected the integration processes associated with inferential comprehension. In their study, subjects read texts that described scriptal events. An example passage is given in Table 12.13. The passages were presented one sentence at a time on a computer screen and the researchers recorded the sentence reading times in milliseconds. One of the manipulations involved the referential relations that connected adjacent sentences within the passages. For some sentence pairs, a scriptal concept was repeated across the sentences to form an explicit referential tie. In the table, the sentences, *Jack asked for the check. The check came,* represent the explicit condition because of the repetition of *check*. For other sentence pairs, the referential tie was implied. Here the scriptal concept mentioned in the second sentence of a pair had only been implied in the first sentence (*They were seated. Their table was near a window;* the word of interest is *table*). For yet other pairs, no referential tie existed, so readers were forced to construct inferences to connect the two sentences together (e.g., *They decided what they wanted. The waiter took their order;* the word, *waiter*). A second manipulation was that for half of the sentence pairs, the scriptal concept involved in the referential tie was central or important to the script (as determined by normative testing), whereas for the remaining sentence pairs, the scriptal

Table 12.13 Sample of a scriptal passage used by Walker and Yekovich (1987) to investigate the effect of having a large amount of declarative knowledge on inferential comprehension. The scriptal concepts of interest are printed in uppercase letters here though they were not in the original experiment.

Jack and his girlfriend Chris decided to go out to a nice restaurant. They called to make a reservation and then they drove to the restaurant. When they arrived, Jack opened the door and they went inside. Jack gave his name to the hostess at the reservation desk. The hostess said there would be a short wait. Jack and Chris went in the bar. The drinks were prepared by the bartender. Jack and Chris enjoyed the drinks. Soon the hostess called Jack's name. Jack and Chris went into the dining room. They were seated. Their TABLE was near a window. Jack and Chris looked over the menu. They decided what they wanted. The WAITER took their order. While they waited for their meal, Jack and Chris talked and admired the view. Soon their meal arrived. Jack and Chris ate leisurely, savoring every bite. Later, they decided to splurge and order dessert. They finished their dessert. It was getting late. Jack asked for the check. The CHECK came. The service had been good so they left a big tip. Jack paid the check. They were ready to leave. Their coats were given to them. Jack and Chris walked out of the restaurant and drove home.

concept involved was only peripherally related to the script. For instance, *waiters* are more important in restaurants than are *coats*.

You probably have an intuition about what the pattern of reading times for the second sentences of the pairs ought to be. Explicit referential relations should lead to easier integration that implied references, which in turn should lead to easier integration than the no referent condition. Thus, in terms of reading times for the second sentences, explicit should be faster than implied, which should be faster than no referent. (Note the

similarity to the Frederiksen study of pronominal reference discussed earlier in this chapter.)

Table 12.14 presents the results of two different experiments conducted by Walker and Yekovich. In Experiment 1, students read passages like those in Table 12.13. In Experiment 2, the sentence pairs of interest were taken *out* of the passages and presented in isolation (with no surrounding context). Notice first the pattern of results for Experiment 2. In keeping with our intuitions, the reading time patterns showed that as integration diffi-

Table 12.14 The reading times in msec for the second sentences of the pairs containing the scriptal concepts of interest (from Walker and Yekovich, 1987). Experiment 1 presented the sentence pairs in passages. Experiment 2 presented the sentence pairs in isolation.

	TYPE OF REFERENTIAL TIE		
EXPERIMENT/TYPE OF SCRIPTAL CONCEPT	EXPLICIT	IMPLIED	NO REFERENT
Experiment 1			
Central Concepts	1824	1824	1856
Peripheral Concepts	1727	1829	2007
Experiment 2			
Central Concepts	1803	2233	2520
Peripheral Concepts	1766	2056	2667

culty increased, reading time also increased. Further, the pattern was very similar for the central and peripheral concepts. Now look at the results of Experiment 1. The peripheral concepts showed the same pattern as they did in Experiment 2. But the important results are those of the sentences containing central concepts. Notice that reading times did not increase as a function of type of inferential tie (see the first row of reading times in Table 12.14). In fact, the times are uniformly fast. What does this mean? In simplest terms the results show that for the important concepts, text integration was easy, regardless of the referential relations. Thus, the study demonstrates that declarative knowledge can have a facilitative effect on the integrative processes associated with inferential comprehension.

The studies by Sharkey and Mitchell (1985) and Walker and Yekovich (1987) show that having extensive declarative knowledge can have an effect on decoding/lexical-access processes and on integration processes. Have any studies compared the comprehension ability of students who have a large amount of declarative knowledge with those who have less declarative knowledge? This question is important because it tests directly the effects of differing amounts of declarative knowledge.

In a classic investigation, Spilich, Vesonder, Chiesi, and Voss (1979) studied this question by using a text on baseball, a topic about which people have widely differing amounts of declarative knowledge. The text used is shown in Table 12.15. The subjects in this study were divided into groups of high and low declarative knowledge on the basis of a 45-item test of baseball knowledge that included questions about terminology, rules, and procedures of baseball. The high-knowledge group had an average score of 42 on this test whereas the low-knowledge group averaged only 19 correct. The groups were equiv-

alent on the Davis Reading Test, so they did not differ on reading skill.

Subjects listened to the baseball text and wrote down as much as they could remember from the passage. The results showed great quantitative differences in recall, with the high-knowledge subjects recalling an average of 48 propositions and the low-knowledge subjects recalling an average of only 31 propositions. There were also interesting qualitative differences in recall. High-knowledge subjects recalled more information about actions that produced significant changes in the game and they were more likely to recall events in the correct order. Also, they reported larger chunks of information. For example, whereas a low-knowledge subject might state that someone "got a double," a high-knowledge subject would day "the batter lined a double down the left-field line." The high-knowledge subject's chunk contains more information that is significant to the unfolding of the game. These qualitative differences show the important role of declarative knowledge in summarization and integration of text.

The researchers also noted a greater tendency for high-knowledge subjects to elaborate on text information. For example, the text stated that the pitcher struck out many batters and was left-handed. One high-knowledge subject called the pitcher a "big, fastballing lefthander" even though "big" and "fastballing" were not in the text. However, it is a fact that pitchers who get a lot of strikeouts tend to be large and throw fastballs, so the elaboration is quite appropriate.

Here, then, is a situation in which students who have the same reading skill level show large differences in comprehension due to differences in domain knowledge (i.e., baseball). These large differences are particularly noteworthy given that Spilich et al.'s subjects were all college students.

Table 12.15 The baseball text used to study knowledge effects on comprehension (adapted from Spilich et al., 1979).

The Ridgeville Robins are playing the Center City Cougars. The Robins are leading 5–3 with the Cougars at bat in the last half of the fifth inning. The sky is getting darker, and the rain that has started is becoming heavier. The Cougars' first batter, Harvey Jones, is taking his time coming to plate. The umpire steps back from behind the plate and tells him to step into the batter's box.

Jones, the hitter, is left-handed, and has a batting average of .310. Claresen, the pitcher, has allowed only four hits, has walked one, and has struck out six. This performance is about average for Claresen since this left-hander has an earned-run average of 6.00 and typically strikes out quite a few batters.

Claresen now adjusts his cap, touches his knee, begins his windup, and delivers a high fastball that the umpire calls "Ball One." The Robins' catcher, Don Postman, returns the ball, and Claresen takes the sign. The next pitch is swung on and hit to centerfield. Maloney comes in and catches it for the first out.

The next batter is the powerful hitter, Fred Johnson, who leads the league in home runs with 23. Claresen no doubt is glad to face him with no one on base. Claresen is now getting his sign from the catcher, begins his windup, and throws a curveball breaking into a right-hand batter at the knees. The umpire calls it a strike. Claresen is now getting ready again, winds up and throws, and Johnson hits it off to right and into the stands, a foul ball. The count is now 0 and 2. Claresen rubs up the new ball, takes his sign, and throws a fastball which just misses the bill of Johnson's cap. Johnson took one step toward the mound, but then came back. Johnson stepped out of the batter's box, and put some resin on his hands; the bat is no doubt slippery from the rain. Claresen is ready again, winds up and throws a slider which breaks inside, making the count 2–2. Once more Johnson steps out of the batter's box and gets some resin on his hands. He steps back in and Claresen starts his motion and throws. Johnson swings and has a line drive down the left-field line. Ferraro runs over to get the ball as Johnson rounds first and goes toward second. Ferraro's throw is late and Johnson is safe on second with a double.

Beck, the left-handed relief pitcher, is warming up in the bull pen. The next hitter for the Cougars is the right-hand hitting Carl Churniak, a .260 hitter who is known to hit well in the clutch. Claresen takes his sign, delivers, and Churniak takes the pitch for a ball. Claresen again is ready and pitches, and Churniak swings and hits a slow bouncing ball toward the shortstop. Haley comes in, fields it, and throws to first, but too late. Churniak is on first with a single, Johnson stayed on second.

The next batter is Whitcomb, the Cougars' left-fielder. He is a left-hander hitting .255. Claresen wipes his forehead with his sleeve and takes his sign. Claresen looks toward first, where Manfred is holding the runner. He stretches, looks at second, and throws a high fastball for a strike. The catcher returns the ball and Claresen once more gets ready. Claresen throws a low curveball. It bounces into the dirt and past the catcher. Johnson moves to third and Churniak to second before the catcher can retrieve the ball. The ball is returned to Claresen. He gets the sign and winds up, and throws a slider that Whitcomb hits between Manfred and Roberts for a hit. Dulaney comes in and picks up the ball. Johnson has scored, and Churniak is heading for the plate. Here comes the throw, and Churniak is heading for the plate. Here comes the throw, and Churniak is out. Churniak argues, but to no avail. The batter reached second on the throw to the plate.

The next batter is Rob Williams, the Cougars' catcher. He is hitting .230. Claresen is rubbing up the ball and now is ready to pitch. The rain is coming down in sheets. Claresen delivers and Williams takes a curve over the inside corner for a strike. Working rapidly Claresen again delivers and Williams takes a ball, low and outside. Claresen again gets the sign, stretches, and throws a fastball, which Williams swings and misses. The catcher returns the ball and Claresen is ready. The pitch is a curveball which Williams swings at and misses for his third strike.

The umpires now are meeting and they signal that the game is being called.

In summary, declarative knowledge appears to have an impact on the component processes associated with reading comprehension. The magnitude of this impact is only beginning to be understood.

The Relation between Reading Skill and Declarative Knowledge

Is it possible that teachers and standardized tests confuse reading *skill* differences with differences due to *declarative knowledge?* For instance, what if the low-knowledge subjects in the Spilich et al. study had taken a college admissions test for reading comprehension on a series of baseball texts? They might not have been admitted to college! As our school populations become more diverse, it is becoming increasingly important to understand the real source(s) of reading difficulties. Some recent research is beginning to tackle the important issue of how reading skill and declarative knowledge are related.

Walker (1987) completed a study much like the one of Spilich et al., except that she varied the aptitude of her subjects, as well as their amount of baseball knowledge. She used the General Thinking (GT) subtest of the Armed Services Vocational Aptitude Battery (ASVAB) to divide Army enlisted subjects into high-aptitude and low-aptitude groups. The GT subtest is like a measure of intelligence and correlates well with tests of language ability and reading ability. So, low-aptitude translates into poor reading skill and high-aptitude means good reading skill. Walker then divided the aptitude groups, based on their baseball knowledge, to produce four groups—high aptitude/high knowledge, high aptitude/low knowledge, low aptitude/high knowledge, and low aptitude/low knowledge. All subjects saw (and heard) a baseball passage like the one given in Table 12.15, and then told everything they could remember about the passage. The most important find-

ings showed that knowledge about the game of baseball, rather than general aptitude, accounted for most of the differences in recall. In other words, the low-aptitude/high-knowledge group performed as well as the high-aptitude/high-knowledge group and outperformed the high-aptitude/low-knowledge group. Interestingly, the performance level of both high-knowledge groups approximated the level of the college students in the Spilich et al. (1979) study. These results held for recall, inferencing, and elaboration, suggesting that the processes responsible for inferential comprehension were functioning adequately for the subjects categorized as poor readers, as long as they had a large amount of domain knowledge.

Yekovich, Walker, Ogle, and Thompson (1990) took this idea one step farther by testing students' ability to comprehend materials like those on the Scholastic Aptitude Test (SAT). The authors used the Preliminary Scholastic Aptitude Test (PSAT) to identify a group of high-school students who scored at approximately the 10th percentile on the verbal subtest. From this low-aptitude (verbal) group, the researchers identified a subset of students who scored high on a paper-and-pencil test of football knowledge. The researchers selected a set of SAT passages and questions from published SAT preparation materials, and subsequently created a parallel version of each passage on a football-related topic. A sample set of passages and corresponding questions is given in Table 12.16. The students, who were called low aptitude/high knowledge, completed a sort of mock version of the SAT reading comprehension subtest. They read a series of passages and for each passage answered multiple-choice questions. Half of the passages and questions were those from the SAT preparation guides and half were the parallel versions constructed on football-related topics. The most interesting results were found with the multiple-choice

Table 12.16 Samples of the parallel passages and questions used in the Yekovich et al. (1990) study (adapted from Yekovich et al., 1990).

SAT	FOOTBALL

SAT

Lamarck's theory of evolution, although at one time pretty discredited, has now been revived by a number of prominent biologists. According to Lamarck, changes in the animal occur through use and disuse. Organs which are specially exercised become specially developed. The need for this special exercise arises from the conditions in which the animal lives; thus a changing environment, by making different demands on an animal, changes the animal. The giraffe, for instance, has developed its long neck in periods of relative scarcity by endeavoring to browse on higher and higher branches of trees. On the other hand, organs that are never exercised tend to disappear altogether. The eyes of animals that have taken to living in the dark grow smaller and smaller, generation after generation, until the late decendants are born eyeless.

The great assumption made by his theory is that the effects of personal, individual effort are transmitted to the offspring of that individual. This is a doctrine that is very much in dispute among modern biologists.

1. The title below that best expresses the ideas of this passage is
   a. Why Lamarck's Theory Is Valid
   b. A Changing Environment
   c. The Modern Biologist
   d. The Lamarkian Theory
   e. An Attack on Lamarck's Theory

2. The major theme of the passage is
   a. modern evolution
   b. changing animals
   c. a revived theory of evolution
   d. both A and B
   e. none of the above

FOOTBALL

Lombardi's theory of offense, although at one time pretty discredited, has now been revived by a number of prominent coaches. According to Lombardi, changes in the offensive strategy occur through ball placement and time remaining in the game. Plays which have been specially designed for a certain time and ball placement become specially practical in this theory. The need for these special plays arises from the conditions of the game; thus, a changing game situation, by making different demands on the offense, changes the use of plays. The Cowboys, for instance, have developed the shotgun specifically for periods when they are endeavoring to get big yardage late in the game. On the other hand, formations which lead to the sweep are never needed in 2-minute drills and tend not to be used during that time. For a team losing a game, the time-consuming sweeps which were used liberally in the first quarter grow more and more in disuse, quarter after quarter, until late in the game they are not used at all.

The great assumption made by his theory is that time remaining in the game and ball placement dictate the plays to be used. This is a doctrine that is not in very much dispute among modern coaches.

1. The title below that best expresses the ideas of the passage is
   a. Why Lombardi's Theory Is Valid
   b. The Changing Football Scene
   c. The Modern Coach
   d. Lombardi's Theory of Offense
   e. An Attack on Lombardi's Theory

2. The major theme of the passage is
   a. changing rules of football
   b. a summary of plays
   c. a revived theory of offense
   d. both A and B
   e. none of the above.

questions that asked students to identify the title or main idea of the passage (an inferential comprehension type of question). On the real SAT passages, students had on average a 55% rate of correct identification of main ideas. For the "mock" SAT (football) passages, the correct rate jumped to 76%, which represented an almost 40% increase in performance. In other words, students classified as very poor readers performed more like "average" readers when they were asked to read about a topic where they had prior conceptual understanding. So again, declarative knowledge appears to impact on "measured" reading skill.

A final, related study was a dissertation completed by Thompson (1992) under the direction of two of the authors of this text (Frank R. and Carol Walker Yekovich). Thompson identified high- and low-aptitude college students on the basis of SAT-verbal scores, where scores of 650 or higher were defined as high aptitude and scores of 350 or lower were defined as low aptitude. Additionally, she subdivided the groups into high and low football knowledge based on the paper-and-pencil test used by Yekovich et al. (1990). She also used the passages and some of the questions from that study. She had subjects read both SAT and football passages on a computer screen using a method called the "moving window" paradigm (cf., Just, Carpenter, & Wooley, 1982). In this paradigm, an entire passage appears on the screen as a series of dashes (one dash for each letter of each word), with blank spaces separating the words. A press of a button displays the first word, and each subsequent button press displays the next word and simultaneously replaces the previous word with dashes. Since the paragraph is displayed in its entirety, repeated button presses display individual words in a left-to-right fashion that approximates the normal movement of the eyes as a person reads. The paradigm was developed as an alternative to measuring gaze durations since most researchers do not have expensive eye-tracking equipment at their disposal (see Chapter 2). The data consist of the reading time for each word in each passage.

As was discussed in an earlier section of the chapter, good readers spend most of their reading time and "mental energy" on the higher-level processes associated with inferential comprehension, having automatized the lower-level processes associated with decoding and literal comprehension. Poor readers on the other hand, do just the opposite. Most of their time is spent on the lower-level processes. The question in Thompson's study was whether poor readers would shift their allocation of resources to higher-level processes when they were reading passages for which they had the requisite declarative knowledge.

Using sophisticated statistical techniques, Thompson tranformed the reading time for each word into two components—the proportion devoted to lower-level processes (which she called Word Encoding) and the proportion devoted to higher-level processes (which she called Text Integration). These proportions were then used to see which of the two was a more important contributor to the observed reading time on each word.

Thompson's results are displayed in Figure 12.13. The Y-axis displays the degree of importance of the two components, with larger values representing greater importance. The figure is divided into four panels, one for each of the four groups in her study. Notice first the leftmost panel, which displays the results for the high-aptitude/high-knowledge group. In keeping with the prevailing conception of good readers, this group showed that higher-level processes were more important contributors to reading time than lower-level processes, and this pattern obtained for both the SAT passages and the football passages. Next, notice the rightmost panel—the one for low-aptitude/low-knowledge students. Here, the lower-level processes were more important than the higher-level ones, and this pattern persisted across both types of passages. This result is in keeping with the prevailing conception of poor readers. The most important result can be seen in the panel labelled low-aptitude/high-knowledge. Notice that for the SAT passages, the students behaved like poor readers. That is, the lower-level processes were more im-

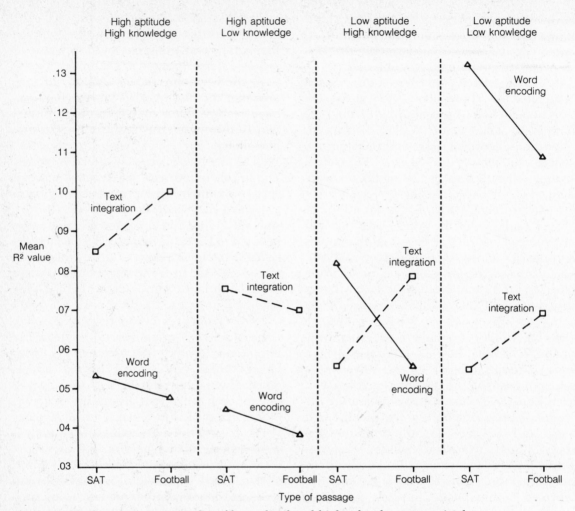

Figure 12.13 The relative importance of lower-level and higher-level processes in the word reading times of skilled and less skilled readers with different amounts of football knowledge for SAT and football passages. Larger R^2 values indicate greater importance (from M.A. Thompson, 1992).

portant contributors to reading time than the higher-level processes. However, this pattern reversed for the football passages. Here, this same group of students looked more like good readers. That is, the higher-level processes became more important contributors to reading time than the lower-level processes. So students considered to have poor reading skills, based on their SAT scores, actually shifted their resources in a way consistent with skilled reading when they encountered material for which they had the requisite declarative knowledge.

The theme that is emerging from this research is that a relation probably exists between declarative knowledge and reading skill. If true, this relation has practical consequences. Teachers, reading specialists, and test developers need to be made aware that reading difficulties may stem from either procedural or declarative knowledge deficits (or both). Instructional interventions, consequently, will have to be designed accordingly. Declarative knowledge deficits need to be handled through enrichment activities. Procedural knowledge deficits, on the other hand, require instruction designed to foster the development and fine-tuning of the productions that form the component processes themselves.

INSTRUCTION

The research on differences between skilled and less skilled readers suggests a variety of reasons for less skilled readers' low performance. Many low-skill individuals (even in the twelfth grade) lack adequate decoding skills. Also, some low-skill individuals are poor at integrating, summarizing, and elaborating on information. Some do not monitor their comprehension and do not have strategies to deal with comprehension problems. Finally, some may lack a rich base of declarative knowledge to use (e.g., in lexical access). One implication for instruction, then, is that reading curricula should *emphasize multiple goals* and should provide diagnostic tests so that each student's strengths and weaknesses can be determined.

In addition to emphasizing multiple goals, instruction should be designed to *increase the probability of reaching a given goal*. For learning declarative knowledge, this means presenting information in organized and meaningful ways, so that students develop organized and elaborated declarative knowledge bases (i.e., conceptual understanding). It also means providing a wide variety of examples to promote generalization, and matched non-examples to promote discrimination, both of which are critical to schema formation and refinement. For learning procedural knowledge, this means providing practice and feedback so that proceduralization, composition, and fine-tuning of the reading processes themselves can occur.

At the beginning of this chapter, it was stated that knowledge of how skilled and less skilled readers differ may help in efforts to improve reading instruction. In this section, this notion is exemplified. First, two training studies will be reported—one that focuses on decoding skills and one that focuses on inferential comprehension and comprehension monitoring skills. Both studies are attempts to train students in skills that have been demonstrated to be lacking in poorer readers. We close the chapter with a brief discussion of the controversy about early reading instruction.

Teaching Decoding Skills

Automaticity of decoding, which seems to be so important for skilled reading (Adams, 1990; LaBerge & Samuels, 1974), is developed through practice and feedback. Some experimental attempts to produce automaticity in less skilled readers have met with some success (Samuels, 1979). Some of these attempts have used microcomputers to present text to readers and give feedback on the readers' increase in speed and accuracy (Carver & Hoffman, 1981; Frederiksen et al., 1983). Microcomputers seem well suited to stimulating the extensive practice needed to automate a skill, on the assumption that the computer environment provides a context for learning and a clear goal to achieve.

Frederiksen and his colleagues (Frederiksen et al., 1983) designed some effective computer games that exemplify how extended practice and feedback can be made interesting. One of the games they developed was designed to improve the speed with which readers recognized common multiletter units (e.g., *un, ism, tion, pro*) within words. This skill is logically prerequisite to recoding since a single sound unit is associated with each of the multiletter units used by Frederiksen et al. This game gave students practice in recognizing sixty of the most frequently occurring multiletter units in the English language. The units were embedded in real words, at different locations within words. For example, for the unit *gen,* some of the words presented to the students were gen*erous,* *re*gency, and *in*dulgen*ce.*

During each "run" of the game, the students focused on only one multiletter unit. They saw many words, some of which contained the unit and some of which did not, and they indicated by pressing a response key whether or not each word contained the target unit. The goal of the game was to increase the speed of responding (the speed of recognizing units) without adversely affecting accuracy.

The game itself had a car race theme. Since subjects were high school males (with decoding deficiencies), this theme was appropriate.

Figure 12.14 shows the types of displays that the student might see during one run of the game. At the start (Panel 1) the student is shown the target unit (*gen*), the initial speed, and the goal speed. An initial speed of "60 per minute" means that the run would start with a presentation rate of sixty words per minute. A run commences with a display such as the one shown in Panel 2. The student sees the target unit at the top of the display and a word (e.g., *gelatinized*) in the box just below the middle of the display. The "error lights" show the number of errors that the student has made so far for a particular run. Up to five errors are permissable. If more than five errors are made, then the display in Panel 4 is shown (a

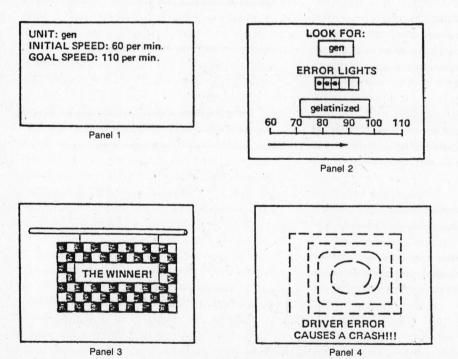

Figure 12.14 Displays seen by students in a microcomputer game designed to teach recognition of common multiletter units (from Frederiksen et al., 1983).

crash that terminates the run). The limitation on number of errors prevents students from responding randomly to increase their speed.

If fewer than five errors have occurred, the run continues for a maximum of 100 words, half of which contain the target unit and half of which do not. Each time a correct response is made within the current presentation speed, the speed is incremented. The increase is shown by the speedometer at the bottom of Panel 2. Thus, throughout the run, the student receives continuous feedback about how near he is to his goal speed and how near he is to crashing. A student who reaches his goal speed within a run sees the display shown in Panel 3. If not, he sees a "Yea, you finished" display.

Later, after runs with other multiletter units, the student repeats runs of any units on which he did not reach the goal. Each repeat run adjusts the initial speed upward somewhat depending on the student's final speed during the first run. Thus, the number of runs depends on the individual. Each performs on as many runs as necessary to get him to the goal speed.

What were the effects of this training? Students were given pre- and posttests on recognition speed for both the sixty trained units and twenty other common multiletter units. The results for recognition speed are shown in Figure 12.15. For both two- and three-letter units, the reaction time decreased by about 75 to 100 milliseconds between the pre- and posttests. Not only did the students' reaction time decrease, but at the end of training, their times were comparable to those of high school students in the top 10% on reading achievement test performance.

It is interesting that the reaction time decreased for untrained units as well as for trained units. This finding suggests that a general attentional skill is being learned. It has been shown that poor readers attend mainly to the initial letters in a word (Harris & Sipay,

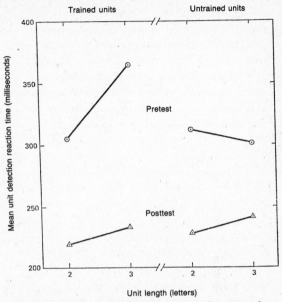

Figure 12.15 Reaction time for identification of multiletter units before and after training (from Frederiksen et al., 1983).

1975). To perform well in this game, however, attention must be distributed across all letters. The students thus learn to allocate attention more effectively.

Besides taking pre- and posttests on multiletter units, students also took pre- and posttests on pseudoword decoding. (You will recall the pseudoword decoding involves pronouncing phonetically regular nonwords). Figures 12.16 and 12.17, respectively, show the students' average reaction times and accuracy on the pseudoword decoding task. As you can see, whereas reaction time decreased from the pre- to the posttest, accuracy increased. These results give empirical support to the logical assumption that multiletter unit detection is prerequisite to recoding skill.

It is probable that the students in this study learned both letter patterns (i.e., declarative knowledge) and sub-word recognition procedures during their thousands of trials at multiletter-unit detection. The letter patterns

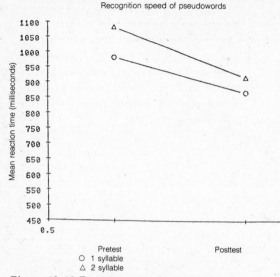

Figure 12.16 Reaction time for pseudoword decoding before and after training (from Frederiksen et al., 1983).

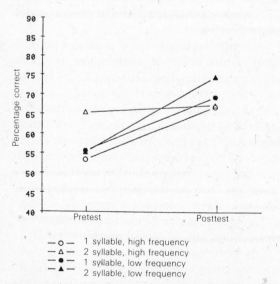

Figure 12.17 Accuracy for pseudoword decoding before and after training (from Frederiksen et al., 1983).

that may have been formed were specific to the sixty trained multiletter units. Conditions were provided that promoted generalization and discrimination. That is, the examples of the units varied widely in that the units were embedded in fifty different words and their position within words varied. This variety should have promoted generalization. Also, many of the distractor words were close to being matched non-examples. For instance, *germane* has two of the three crucial letters of *gen*, forcing attention to the *n* by its absence. Also, *grenadiers* has all three crucial letters, but they do not occur together, forcing attention to the need for the letters in the unit to occur together. Although these words were not completely matched with words in which the target unit appeared, they were similar enough to promote discrimination. It is likely that the resulting declarative structures were like schemas for the subword units.

The procedural knowledge that may have been learned was the development and proceduralization of decoding productions that "perceived" multiletter units. These procedures apparently replaced the less effective procedures that governed focusing on initial letters only or individual letters only. The eventual composition of the productions was probably produced by practice and feedback, with feedback in Frederiksen et al.'s (1983) game including information about both speed and accuracy.

In summary, this study demonstrates the success that can be achieved by using known principles of learning to teach skills that learners are known to lack. It also demonstrates a creative use of microcomputers in reading instruction.

Teaching Inferential Comprehension and Comprehension Monitoring Skills

Recall that skilled readers are better at detecting the main ideas in passages and at monitoring their own comprehension than are less skilled readers. Palincsar and Brown (1984) conducted a series of studies on teaching less skilled readers to detect main ideas and to monitor their own comprehension through making predictions, asking questions, and looking out for unclear portions of text. They worked with middle school students who had good decoding skills but performed poorly on comprehension tests.

In these studies teacher and students took turns being the "teacher." The teacher's role was to ask questions both before and after the group read a segment of expository text. If the segment was at the beginning of a passage, the "teacher" would ask the group to make predictions from the title or to say what the title made them think of. After the group had read a segment, the "teacher" would ask a question about the main point of the segment. If there were unclear phrases, the "teacher" asked the group for clarification.

At the start of each session, the real teacher was responsible for the first reading segment and hence could model good questions before the students took their turns as teacher. Also, the real teacher gave feedback to the students about their responses. Depending on the quality of the response, the real teacher might say "You asked that question well; it was very clear what information you wanted"; "Excellent prediction, let's see if you're right"; or "That was interesting information. It was information that I would call detail in the passage. Can you find more important information?" (Palincsar & Brown, 1984, p. 131). After feedback, the teacher might again model a response and say something like, "A question I might ask would be . . ." or "I would summarize by saying. . . ."

Another feature of instruction was that the students were made aware of the reason for learning to summarize, predict, ask questions, and clarify. The importance of always doing these things when reading was emphasized. The students were given weekly feedback on their improvement on comprehension test questions, which they answered every day after the practice session was over. This feedback lent credibility to the teachers' claims that the skills would help them improve comprehension.

Figure 12.18 shows the results for four different classes of middle school children taught by four different teachers. The first portion of each graph (Baseline) is the performance of the students prior to training. Performance was the percentage correct on comprehension questions over passages that were read silently. As you can see, all groups were averaging 50% or less correct before training. During the training (called "reciprocal teaching"), they gradually improved to about 80% or more correct. This high level of performance was maintained on the days immediately following training and also appeared on comprehension tests given eight weeks later.

The teaching method emphasized modeling followed by a great deal of practice and informative feedback. As was discussed in the chapter on acquisition of procedural knowledge (Chapter 9), modeling, practice, and feedback are important conditions for learning procedures. Another technique that was used in this study was that of calling attention to the reasons for learning the skill and demonstrating the improvements that resulted from learning. Making students aware of why they are learning something, how it will lead to success, and when it will be useful appear to be key elements in obtaining transfer (A.L. Brown, 1978) and in promoting motivation (see Chapter 16).

As with the Frederiksen et al. (1983) study, the Palincsar and Brown (1984) study demonstrates that significant improvements can be made by (1) identifying students who lack skills that have been shown to be possessed by more competent individuals, and (2) facilitating the learning and transfer of these skills by providing appropriate learning conditions. These are demonstration studies, not designed to test hypotheses about specific instructional variables (e.g., amount of prac-

tice). Instead they used a combination of instructional variables that had been shown in other studies to be effective. Thus, these studies demonstrate what creative teachers and instructional designers can do by combining variables in teaching important skills to individuals who lack them.

Literacy and Instruction in Beginning Reading

At the outset we noted that literacy and reading skill are inextricably related. Often people in our society are called illiterate if they are unable to read, although illiteracy more correctly refers to the underdevelopment of language skills and a lack of understanding of the importance of language for success in our culture. Nevertheless, printed language occupies a central role in the development of literacy; consequently, reading and writing skills are essential.

This chapter has focused on a componential description of reading, and it is easy to infer from this description that good reading instruction should involve teaching each of the component skills and then putting them all together. This is the inference made by subskill methods such as the phonics approach. Unfortunately, this inference appears to be incorrect. Recall from the earlier chapters on knowledge acquisition that we have continually referred to the idea that instruction in a skill should include using the entire skill from the outset. The trick is to create simple situations that promote the development of the skill while at the same time not overloading working memory to the point that the learner cannot recover. This approach appears to be more motivating to learners because the end goal toward which they are working is obvious in the learning activities.

In a recent book, Adams (1990) provides extensive treatment of the issues surrounding instruction in beginning reading, and her rec-

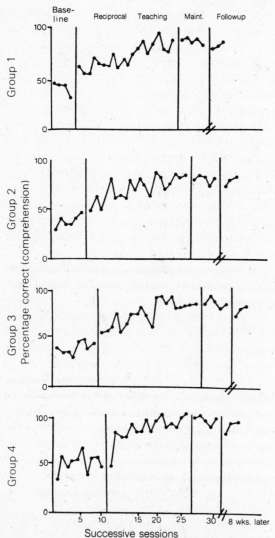

Figure 12.18 Scores on comprehension tests before, during, and after training in four classes. Maint. = maintenance after training stopped (from Palincsar and Brown, 1984).

ommendations fit nicely with the model presented here. We close the chapter by outlining some of her conclusions.

1. Awareness of the functions and use of print are essential and should be developed prior to the age of schooling.

2. Word recognition (i.e., decoding and lexical access) must be developed to the point of automaticity, and consequently systematic phonics instruction should be included in early reading instruction.

3. Children must see the value of reading (i.e., they must come to understand its importance in their own lives), and consequently, the context of instruction is important.

4. As a result of 3, instruction will have to focus on the entire act of reading, rather than on its individual components. Consequently, some of the tenets underlying the whole-language approach are fundamentally correct.

5. Reading instruction should be placed within the larger context of print. Consequently, programs that use writing to teach reading (and vice versa) have substantial value (see Taylor, 1988, for an example of such an approach).

6. Students who come to school without an awareness of print are at a severe disadvantage, and this disadvantage must be remediated early. Remedial programs need to be extensive, such as the Reading Recovery program of Clay and her colleagues (Clay, 1979, discussed in Anderson & Armbruster, 1989).

CHAPTER SUMMARY

Reading is an important skill for adequate functioning in society and for the greatest appreciation of life, yet many people lack this skill. The process model of reading presented in this chapter suggests that problems can occur in one or more component reading skills (i.e., procedural knowledge), and there is evidence that good and poor readers differ on almost all these skills. Several lines of evidence suggest that automaticity of lower-level processes is required in order to carry out higher-level comprehension processes and that poor readers' decoding skills are not as automatic as those of good readers. Declarative knowledge is also important to successful reading, and the research suggests that reading skill differences may sometimes be due to declarative knowledge differences. Readers who have been classified by tests as being less skilled perform more like normal readers when they have the requisite knowledge to understand a text. Instruction to improve procedural knowledge should include practice and feedback because those activities promote proceduralization and composition, which leads to automaticity. In addition, providing support for generalization and discrimination develops and refines declarative knowledge by creating patterns (e.g., words, schemas) that can be used efficiently. Schemas are particularly useful in the processes underlying inferential comprehension and comprehension monitoring. Early reading instruction should focus on the entire act of reading, while including phonics systematically. It should also be embedded in the larger context of print awareness.

ADDITIONAL READINGS

Adams, M.J. (1990). *Beginning to read: Thinking and learning about print*. Cambridge, MA: The MIT Press.

Baker, L., & Brown, A.L. (1984). Metacognitive skills in reading. In D. Pearson (Ed.), *Handbook of reading research* (pp. 353–394). Newark, DE: International Reading Association.

Balota, D.A., d'Arcais, G.B.F., & Rayner, K. (Eds.) (1990). *Comprehension processes in reading*. Hillsdale, NJ: Lawrence Erlbaum Associates.

Britton, B.K., & Glynn, S.M. (Eds.) (1987). *Executive control processes in reading*. Hillsdale, NJ: Lawrence Erlbaum Associates.

Graesser, A.C., & Bower, G.H. (Eds.) (1990). *Inferences in text comprehension. The psychology of learning and motivation: Advances in research and theory*. Vol. 25. San Diego, CA: Academic Press.

Just, M.A., & Carpenter, P.A. (1987). *The psychology of reading and language comprehension*. Newton, MA: Allyn and Bacon.

Lesgold, A.M., & Perfetti, C.A. (Eds.) (1981). *Interactive processes in reading*. Hillsdale, NJ: Lawrence Erlbaum Associates.

Resnick, L.B., & Weaver, P.A. (Eds.) (1979). *Theory and practice of early reading*, (Vols. 1–3). Hillsdale, NJ: Lawrence Erlbaum Associates.

Chapter

13

Writing

SUMMARY

1. The procedural knowledge underlying writing skill can be divided into three major sets of processes: **planning, translating,** and **reviewing.** Each of these is comprised of a number of component processes, some automated and some strategic.

2. The declarative knowledge needed for skilled writing includes conceptual understanding of language and of the topic about which one is writing.

3. The planning and reviewing processes are highly strategic and thus consume many cognitive resources. Since the common goal of skilled writers is to communicate meaning, they spend more of their energy on planning and reviewing than do less skilled writers.

4. The translation process has a large automatic component. Skilled and less skilled writers appear to differ in the degree to which translation has become more or less automatized. As a consequence, less skilled writers focus on avoiding mechanical errors at the expense of communicating meaning.

5. Persons of equal writing skill will vary on the quality of their written products if they possess different degrees of conceptual understanding of the topic about which they are writing.

6. **Conferencing** is a one-on-one instructional technique in which a teacher attempts to identify the sources of a student's writing difficulty and to provide explicit guidance regarding the process of writing and the resulting product. This technique appears to be highly useful for improving the quality of writing.

Writing is the rendering of ideas in the printed symbols of a given language. In some ways it is the complement of reading, which is the comprehension or reception of ideas expressed in the printed symbols of a given language. Writing serves many purposes. On the job it is an important means of communicating and recording what has been communicated. In one's personal life it is a means of expression and a technique for thinking through problems. In intellectual and political arenas writing is a powerful means of persuading others to change their ideas or to take some action. Like other literacy skills, writing is a skill that liberates those who possess it and restricts those who do not.

There has been a great deal of concern over the past two decades that the quality of writing of high school graduates is deteriorating. The National Assessment of Educational Progress, for example, showed a significant decline in the quality of writing for thirteen- and seventeen-year-olds between 1969 and 1974 (R. Brown, 1981). During the 1980s this trend did not reverse. To illustrate this problem, here is a composition written by a college freshman (Perl, 1979):

> All men can't be consider equal in America base on financial situation. Because their are men born in rich families that will never have to worry about financial difficulties. And then theyre are another type of Americans that is born to a poor family. and always may have some kind of fina-difficulty. Especially nowadays in New York city With the bugdit Crisis and all. If he is able To get a job. But are now he lose the job just as easy as he got it. So when he loses his job he'll have to try to get some fina-assistance. Then he'll probley have even more fin-diffuicuty. So right here you can't see that In America, all men are not create equal in the fin-sense.

There are obvious "mechanical" errors in this composition—errors of spelling, punctuation, and agreement. But more grievous than the mechanical errors is the fact that the essay is incoherent.

What can be done to improve students' writing? Applebee (1982) attributes the decline in writing quality to both the nature and the small quantity of writing instruction in grades 1 through 12. One way to increase the quantity of writing required of students is to encourage teachers in almost all subject areas and all grade levels to have students write.

In this chapter we will discuss the components of writing skill. A knowledge of these components will help teachers focus instruction on important aspects of writing that have been neglected. The chapter is organized like the previous chapter on reading. First, we outline a model of writing consistent with our view of cognition and learning. Next we review literature that describes both the procedural and declarative knowledge differences between skilled and less skilled writers. Finally, we present some examples of instructional interventions aimed at improving writing skill.

A MODEL OF WRITING

In school, writing usually begins when a teacher gives her students a writing assignment. Assignments vary in length, amount of originality expected, type of discourse (e.g., description or persuasion), and topic. Variations depend on the age of the student, the subject matter being studied, and the goals of instruction (see Applebee, 1982, for descriptions of writing tasks). Across all this variation, however, some components and dynamics of writing remain constant.

Like reading, writing is a highly complex activity with many component processes. Skilled writing is the result of the acquisition of both declarative and procedural knowledge and of the automatization of the lower-level component processes. Thus, successful writing requires conceptual understanding of the nature and purposes of writing, automated basic writing skills, and strategic knowledge about how to achieve the goal of communicating meaning to an audience.

Components

Flower and Hayes (1981a) have proposed a model for writing, which is shown in Figure 13.1. This model, along with its recent extensions (e.g., Flower, Schriver, Carey, Haas, & Hayes) has been very influential in shaping our understanding of writing, and consequently it serves as a useful reference for describing the writing process. The model has two major parts. The first part is the task environment that exists in the world. This part of the model is comprised of the "rhetorical problem" (i.e., the assignment or task that designates the topic, the audience, and any imposed constraints) and the "text" generated thus far in response to the problem. According to Flower and Hayes, the rhetorical problem and the text generated so far both guide and constrain the writing process.

The second major part of the model is depicted in the box drawn with a broken line and may be thought of as the internal environment or knowledge that is responsible for writing skill. Within this part, two knowledge components exist. On the left side is the writer's declarative memory, which includes knowledge of letters, spellings, words, subject matter, schemas for conventional rhetorical structures, and schemas for addressing audiences. On the right side is the writer's procedural knowledge of how to write. Within the procedural knowledge part resides

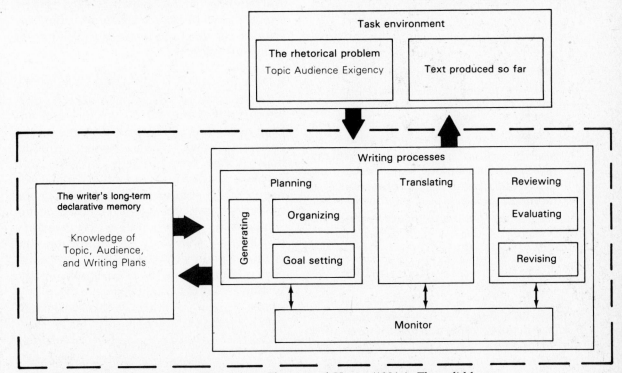

Figure 13.1 A model of writing adapted from Flower and Hayes (1981a). The solid box at the top represents the external world and the broken box represents a person's memory (adapted from Flower and Hayes, 1981a).

the component writing processes. There are three major sets of processes: **planning, translating,** and **reviewing.** Planning refers to the processes of setting goals, generating ideas, and organizing the ideas. Translating refers to the process of tranforming the ideas in one's head into strings of words on a piece of paper or on a computer screen. Reviewing refers to the processes of evaluating what one has written and possibly revising it if deemed necessary.

Planning. Writing is a problem-solving endeavor in which a writer is given a task or assignment that may be thought of as a problem to solve (Carey et al. 1989). In planning, the writer interprets the assignment and sets up in his mind an initial representation (which may change as writing progresses). In building the representation, the writer sets one or more goals aimed at "solving the problem" (i.e., accomplishing the assignment). Once the initial representation of the assignment is in place, the writer begins generating ideas by retrieving information from declarative memory and organizing those ideas according to the constraints of the assignment. Sometimes a writer may adopt the goal of simply recording his stored knowledge on paper (also called "knowledge-telling"; cf., Scardamalia & Bereiter, 1987). Other times one's knowledge must be transformed because of the constraints of the assignment, and thus the writer uses "constructive" planning to accomplish his writing goal (cf., Flower et al., in press).

Planning processes are part of our procedural knowledge. Since planning is usually very deliberative, the procedural knowledge is both conscious (i.e., resource consuming) and strategic (see Chapters 6 and 9). Skilled writers devote proportionally more of their resources to planning activities than do less skilled writers.

Translation. When a writer sets down her thoughts on paper, she engages in transla-

tion. In the most general sense, translation involves selecting words and/or phrases from one's mental lexicon and transcribing those lexical items into print in a syntactically and semantically correct way. In some ways, the translation process in writing can be likened to the decoding and literal comprehension processes in reading. That is, part of the translation process accomplishes many of the lower-level aspects of writing such as the formation of letters, spellings of words, word endings, word order, subject-predicate agreement, punctuation, and sentence formation. As you can imagine, for skilled writers many of these activities are accomplished virtually automatically. That means that translation has a procedural component that must be automatized if the higher-level processes of planning and reviewing are to operate successfully. As you will see later in the chapter, skilled writers devote fewer of their resources to the "mechanics" of the translation process than do less skilled writers.

Reviewing. Reviewing occurs when the writer reads over the generated text to determine whether the overall writing goal has been accomplished. Essentially, the writer evaluates whether the written product matches the current goal (e.g., Does the paragraph persuade a first grader that Santa Claus really exists?). If the evaluation is positive, the written text is accepted as is. If, however, the goal and the written product do not match, revision is undertaken. A production that evaluates whether a paragraph on the existence of Santa Claus matches or satisfies the writing assignment might look like the following:

> IF   The goal is to evaluate
>   whether written text
>   matches writing assignment
>
> THEN   Check constraints of writing
>   assignment

(Constraint 1:
Audience = First
Graders)
(Constraint 2: Rhetorical
Style = Persuasion)
(Constraint 3:
Argument = Santa
Claus exists)
and check written product for
evidence regarding
constraints
(Does text use language
appropriate for first
graders?)
(Does text present
compelling evidence or
examples?)
(Is evidence consistent
with first grade
knowledge of Santa
Claus?)
and compare constraints
against evidence in text
and set subgoal to undertake
revision if necessary

In this example, the writing assignment outlines what the text is to be about and what it is supposed to accomplish (see the Constraints in the production). The evaluation is made by comparing evidence from the generated text with the constraints of the assignment (see the questions in the parentheses).

Further productions would be needed to guide any revision that might be undertaken. Still, the example production shows that our reviewing knowledge is procedural in character, and as such will need to be acquired and refined through practice and feedback. Like planning, the reviewing process also has a deliberative character, and thus our procedural knowledge is both conscious and strategic.

Dynamics

Anyone who has attempted writing knows that it does not proceed in a linear sequence from planning to translating to reviewing. Typically it starts with a brief period of pre-planning, followed by a writing phase in which all the component processes—planning, translating, and reviewing—are used. Plans made before writing may be revised or elaborated in light of what has been written. Detailed plans for achieving cohesion may be formulated during writing rather than before it. Reviewing may occur even before writing starts, as when someone thinks of an idea, then evaluates it and modifies it. Reviewing typically continues throughout writing, as when a writer stops to reread and evaluate what has been written to that point. Thus, as in reading, the component processes in writing may operate in parallel and in collaboration with one another.

To get a feel for the dynamics of writing, it is useful to examine think-aloud protocols, collected as writers are composing. Table 13.1 shows one such protocol in which the writer, a teacher, has been asked to pretend that she is also a freelance writer. Her task is to write an article for *Seventeen* magazine describing her jobs to an audience of teenage girls. The numbers above words in the protocol indicate where the writer paused and the duration of the pause in seconds. Flower and Hayes (1981b) had judges divided this protocol into episodes defined by shifts in attention.

In episode 1 the writer reads the assignment (the words underlined twice) and reacts to it. In episode 2 she tries to solve the problem of writing about a job she is not familiar with (freelance writing). She decides to invent a formula for the job. Episode 3a involves a great deal of translation (the underlined words are those which were written down) in which the plans made in episode 2 are transformed into word strings. Episode 3b involves

Table 13.1 A thinking-aloud protocol as a writer plans and writes. Each episode has a different focus (adapted from Flower and Hayes, 1981b).

Episodes in an Expert Writer's Protocol

Episode 1

My Job for a young—Oh I'm to describe my job for a young thirteen to fourteen year-old teenage female audience—Magazine —Seventeen. -a- My immediate reaction is that it's utterly impossible. I did read Seventeen, though—I guess I wouldn't say I read it -a- I looked at it, especially the ads, so the idea would be to describe what I do to someone like myself when I read— well not like myself, but adjusted for—well twenty years later. -a- Now what I think of doing really is that—until the coffee comes I feel I can't begin, so I will shut the door and feel that I have a little bit more privacy,//

Episode 2

-um- Also the mention of a free-lance writer is something I've —I've no experience in doing and my sense is that it's a—a formula which I'm not sure I know, so I suppose what I have to do is -a- invent what the formula might be, and—and then try to -a- try to include—events or occurrences or attitude or experiences in my own job that would -a- that could be—that

Episode 3a

could be conveyed in formula so let's see -// I suppose one would want to start—by writing something—that would -a- attract the attention of the reader—of that reader and -a- I suppose the most interesting thing about my job would be that it is highly unlikely that it would seem at all interesting to someone of that age—So I might start by saying something like —Can you imagine yourself spending a day—Many days like this—waking up at 4:30 a.m., making a pot of coffee . . . looking around . . . my—looking around your house, letting in your cats . . . -a- walking out—out with coffee and a book and watching the dawn materialize . . . I actually do this . . . although 4:30's a bit early, perhaps I should say 5:30 so it won't seem— although I do get up at 4:30 -a- watching the dawn materialize and starting to work—to work by reading—reading the manuscript—of a Victorian writer . . . with a manuscript of a . . . a Victorian writer . . . a person with a manuscript of a student —Much like yourself—Much like—Much like -a- a student or a book by Aristotle they've heard of Aristotle or—who could

Table 13.1 *(continued)*

	I have it be by—Plato probably When it gets to be—When you've . . . -a- finished your coffee and whatever you had to do (Oh thanks)—whatever—now I've just gotten coffee—finished your coffee (mumbling) . . . when you've finished your coffee 　　3　　　　　　　　2 and -a- foreseen—and -a- ummmmmm—when you've finished your coffee, you dress and drive—about three miles to the university where you spend another—where you spend—you spend hours —you spend about—oh what—four or five—supposed to be four hours—about three hours a day—about three hours teaching— many more hours talking to students—talking to—talking to 　　　　　　　　　6.8
Episode 3b	other teachers . . . Um -/ should I (mumble)—the thing is about saying teachers—the—the teenage girl is going to think teachers like who she has, and professor I always feel is sort of pretentious and a word usually—usually I say teacher, but I 　　2　　　　　　7.6 know that means I . . . It's unfortunate now in society we
Episode 3c	don't—but that that isn't prestige occupation./ Talking to other people like yourselves—that's whoever it may be—other people at your job—other—other people like yourself—uh a lot like yourself but—talking to other people like yourself—going to meetings . . . committee meetings . . . and doing all this for nine months so that the other three . . . and doing all this for three months—okay—nine months . . . If you can imagine that . . .

more planning in light of an audience of teenage girls. The problem being addressed is how these readers will interpret *teacher* versus *professor*. Finally, episode 3c involves further translation activity.

In this example the tempo of writing seems to be to plan some, then write some, then plan some more, then write some more. Long pausing is often associated with the beginning of a planning episode. This protocol was produced by a fairly sophisticated adult writer. Less skilled and younger writers tend not to engage in as much planning activity. However, all writers alternate among the components of writing throughout the course of producing a written document.

DIFFERENCES BETWEEN SKILLED AND LESS SKILLED WRITERS

Just as reading difficulties had different sources, so too writing problems may arise from a lack of either procedural or declarative knowledge. Not surprisingly, research shows that differences in writing skill can be traced to both procedural and declarative knowledge. In this part of the chapter, we describe some of this work.

PROCEDURAL KNOWLEDGE DIFFERENCES

Research shows that individuals differ in their abilities to plan, translate, and review a written product. Since successful writing depends on all three abilities, difficulties in any one (or in combinations) will lead to inferior written products.

Planning: Goal Setting

Planning occurs at many levels. On the one hand, some plans are devised in response to the overall writing task (e.g., How should I go about setting up this paper?). At another level, other plans address more local purposes (e.g., How should I make this particular point? Should I use an example? Should I cite evidence? Should I use an analogy?). The type of planning that goes on at any level depends on the goal that the writer hopes to achieve. The suggestion from recent research is that writers of different skill or maturity levels have varying writing goals and consequently use different planning strategies (Flower et al., in press; Scardamalia & Bereiter, 1987).

One of the most important differences between more and less skilled writers is in the type of goals they set for themselves in writing. Researchers have distinguished at least three types of goals. The goal that is characteristic of skilled writers of any age is to communicate in a meaningful way. Communicating meaning is the most difficult goal to achieve because it requires sensitivity to the demands and constraints of the writing task (see Carey et al., 1989). Consequently the writer must possess a wide array of writing strategies and the flexibility that comes from extensive use of those strategies.

A second goal, which is characteristic of immature writers, occurs in what Bereiter (1980) calls "associative writing" (see also Scardamalia & Bereiter's (1987) discussion of "knowledge-telling"). This goal is simply to dump on paper the contents of one's memory relevant to a given topic. In some writing contexts, the "knowledge-telling" goal might be appropriate, whereas in others it might be inappropriate. For instance, in a writing assignment such as "What I did last summer," a simple memory dump of the facts may suffice. In contrast, using a goal of telling what you know when the assignment requests multiple perspectives on an issue is likely to be inappropriate.

A third goal, which is typical of poor writers at middle, high school, and college levels, is to avoid making errors (cf., Atwell, 1981; Birnbaum, 1982; Perl, 1979). This goal has a parallel in reading, in which poor readers attend to letters, subwords, and/or words, and devote so many resources to the lower processing levels that they miss the meaning. In writing, attending to the mechanics, or worrying about perfect wording and sentences, may result in an incomprehensible text.

A study by Stallard demonstrates nicely a difference in the goals of more and less skilled writers. Stallard (1974) had thirty twelfth graders write on a current news topic, stating their opinion. He compared the retrospective reports of fifteen skilled writers with those of fifteen randomly selected writers. The skilled writers scored at or above the ninetieth percentile on the STEP Essay Writing Test. Stallard found that 93% of the skilled writers versus only 53% of the randomly selected writers reported having thought about the purpose of their essay before starting to write. This is what one would expect if the skilled writers had the goal of conveying meaning and some of the randomly selected writers did not.

Communicating Meaning versus Error Avoidance. Data triangulation, a technique commonly used by writing researchers, is often used to infer a writer's goals. Data triangulation involves collecting several types of data and comparing them for consistency. For example, if subjects' verbal reports match their overt behavior (for example, their writing pauses), the two data sources are said to converge and provide support for an inference about a writer's goal.

Using this technique, Atwell (1981) compared ten college students who were good writers, according to standardized tests, with ten who were in a remedial writing class. She categorized the statements they made in their retrospective reports according to the level of

Table 13.2 Retrospective comments classified according to the level of discourse being heeded (adapted from Atwell, 1981).

	GOOD WRITER	REMEDIAL WRITER
Discourse/structural	50%	30%
Word/surface	27%	51%
Syntax	14%	9%
External/affect	9%	10%

discourse that was being heeded: structural (whole text), syntactic, word, or affect. As Table 13.2 shows, the good writers made 50% of their comments about the whole text (for example, whether or not they had gotten their meaning quite right), whereas only 30% of the remedial writers' comments were at this level. By contrast, 51% of the remedial writers' comments were about word choice or surface considerations such as those of spelling and punctuation; only 27% of the good writers' comments were at this level.

Atwell (1981) also found that the good writers were more likely to interrupt writing at sentence boundaries, whereas remedial writers were more likely to interrupt writing *within* words. Table 13.3 shows these results. Atwell interpreted both sets of results as showing

Table 13.3 Percentage of interruptions of writing that occurred at a sentence boundary, within a word, or at other places in a sentence (adapted from Atwell, 1981).

	GOOD WRITER	REMEDIAL WRITER
Interrupt writing at sentence boundary	29%	21%
Interrupt writing within a word	13%	17%
Interrupt writing at other places	58%	62%

that the better writers were concerned with meaning, whereas the less skilled writers were concerned with penmanship and the surface appearance. In other words, the good writers had the goal of conveying meaning, whereas the remedial writers had the goal of avoiding mechanical errors.

Associative Writing or Knowledge Telling. Young students appear particularly prone to thinking that the goal of writing is to recall all one can about a given topic. This goal is evident in the following composition produced by a ten-year-old when asked to write on the topic, "Should school children be allowed to choose their own subjects?"

> I think children should be able to choose what subjects they have in school. I don't think we should have to do language, and art is a bore a lot. I don't think we should do novel study every week. I really think 4s and 3s should split up for gym. I think we should do a lot of math. I don't think we should do diary. I think we should do French. (Burtis, Bereiter, Scardamalia, & Tetroe, 1983).

From an adult point of view, this young writer does not comply with the assignment. To an adult, the assignment implies, that one should state an opinion and then argue in support of that opinion. In persuasive writing, skilled adult writers adopt the goal of communicating an argument to persuade the reader. This young writer states his opinion but does not support it. Rather, he lists what subjects he would like to take in school. This type of writing appears to be governed by the goal of retrieving information.

Young children are not the only writers who resort to "knowledge telling" or associative writing. Experts in a domain can also fall into that trap. Schriver (1984; cited in Flower et al., in press) gives an example of a computer scientist who was given the task of writing a user's manual for a word processing program that he developed. In complying with the assignment, the scientist "told" about the computer program in a style that only other computer scientists could understand. The intended audience (i.e., secretaries) found the manual virtually incomprehensible. Table 13.4 displays a portion of the text produced by the computer scientist. Part (A) of the table gives the introduction produced by the scientist. Part (B) presents a more comprehensible version written by a professional writer after input from secretaries on the original version. Note the drastic revision. The scientist's version resembles a technical description complete with references whereas the professional writer's version is more "user friendly" and more explicit in its organization. The computer scientist in this example used a knowledge-telling strategy, just like the young child in the previous example, rather than a strategy that communicated effectively to the intended audience.

Associative writing appears to be closer to the goal of communicating meaning than is avoidance of error. This is because associative writing and communicating meaning both focus on *meaning*. Associative writing, however, lacks an emphasis on *communication*. One can imagine that a teaching strategy that encourages young writers to add audience awareness to their meaning-oriented goals might move them toward the goal of communicating meaning.

On the other hand, the writer with the error avoidance goal cares neither for meaning nor for communication. We do not yet know whether the goal of error avoidance is primarily the result of poor translation skills, or whether it is due to one or more sets of rigid rules about the composing process (e.g., The first draft must be nearly perfect). However, in either case, teaching such a writer to adopt the goal of communicating meaning will probably require more extended and complex efforts.

Planning: Idea Generation

People vary in how many ideas they can generate. Young children produce fewer ideas in writing than do older children. For example, when Scardamalia, Bereiter, and Goelman (1982) gave fourth- and sixth-grade children a writing assignment, the sixth graders produced an average of ninety words, whereas the fourth graders produced only fifty-seven words on the average. Average writers in high school produce shorter essays than do highly skilled writers (Stallard, 1974). In college, persons with low verbal SAT scores produce essays with fewer ideas than do persons with average verbal SAT scores (Glynn, Britton, Muth, & Dogan, 1982).

Why do some people produce longer essays than others? There are probably many reasons, including differences in declarative knowledge (Voss, Vesonder, & Spilich, 1980) and differences in management of demands on working memory (Glynn et al., 1982). Another reason that seems to account for the findings of Scardamalia et al. (1982) with young children is that some people do not know how to cue themselves to continue writing. In particular, younger children, being more familiar with conversation than with composition, rely more on external, social cues to continue to produce ideas. In conversation, the listener nods or gives some other cue that gives the speaker "permission" to continue. When young writers are asked to write rather than speak their ideas, they stop after very little production, not because they have run out of ideas, but because they have no one cuing them to keep going. More mature writers have internal cues. For example, they may continue to produce ideas as long as their ideas are cohesive. When cohesion deteriorates, this cues them to stop.

If this argument is correct, then cuing young children to continue should cause them to write more and should also lead to greater

Table 13.4 Introductions written by an expert computer scientist (A) and an experienced writer (B). Note how domain expertise with computers does not guarantee a good written product. Knowing the audience is also important (adapted from Schriver (1984), cited in Flower et al., in press).

(A) A PORTION OF A COMPUTER MANUAL WRITTEN BY A COMPUTER SCIENTIST: THE "BEFORE"

Oil: The Introduction

OIL is yet another text editor. It incorporates features of many previous editors, but is not quite like any of them. The goals of the OIL editor are:

- To fit into the Spice environment. In particular to access the screen through Canvas [Ball 81] and to take advantage of the large virtual storage provided by Accent [Rashid 80].
- To be available quickly, at least in skeletal form. In order for program development under Accent to be possible there must be *some* editor available. The first version of OIL is not meant to be the last word in editors, but was designed to be quickly implementable.
- To be smoothly expandable. The first version of OIL is not the last. Features which are not yet implemented, but which are anticipated include programmability as in Emacs [Gosling 81] interface to MultiScript [Multi 81] and (possibly) multiple character fonts.

This document concentrates on describing the editor as it is now, but there is a section near the end on future plans.

The Basics

OIL is a modeless editor. This means that pressing the same key will always cause the same effect. This statement has to be interpreted somewhat liberally. The ctrl-x key serves as an escape, and changes the meaning of the next key pressed. The ctrl-x and the following key must be interpreted as a single compound stroke.

(B) A PORTION OF A COMPUTER MANUAL WRITTEN BY A PROFESSIONAL WRITER: THE "AFTER"

Oil: The Spice Editor

2.1 Introduction

This chapter is about Oil, the editor that runs on Accent. Many of the Oil commands described in this chapter are similar to EMACS editing commands. Like Pepper (the editor that runs on POS), Oil allows you to position the cursor in two ways: with the pointing device or with the usual keyboard commands. One advantage of using Oil is that it allows you to take advantage of the large storage space provided by Accent.

2.2 The Basics

Read this section through before you use Oil. Then follow the instructions in Exercise 1 on the next page.

2.2.1 Invoking Oil

To create or edit a file   *edit <filename>* RETURN

You may abbreviate the edit command by typing *ed*.
If you are creating a new file, you will need to hit
RETURN a second time in order to use Oil.

After you type the filename and hit RETURN, Oil
gives you a chance to edit the filename. You edit
filenames using the same commands that you would
use to edit text, except that you cannot use commands
that move the cursor between lines of text.

If you do not specify an extension to your file name,
Oil will add one for you (such as .pas, .pasmac, .mss,
.cmd, or .micro).

---

cohesiveness of what is written. That is, if children rely on external cues to continue idea generation, and if such external cues are lacking, they may stop generating ideas before they reach the end of a cohesive chain of ideas. On the other hand, if children rely on their own internal cues, then they should continue producing ideas on their own, whether or not they are cued, until they reach the end of a cohesive chain.

Scardamalia et al. (1982) tested these speculations by cuing fourth- and sixth-graders to continue writing by saying, after a child appeared to be finished writing, "You're doing fine," or "Can you write some more?" Both fourth- and sixth-graders increased the quantity of writing following cuing. However, in terms of coherence and clarity of the product, only the fourth graders' compositions improved from the additional writing. These results support the idea that the fourth graders had ceased writing before they had completed a cohesive chain of ideas. Thus, when they were cued to continue, they completed the chain, causing the ratings of their compositions to improve.

Young writers, then, appear to lack the procedural knowledge that governs the self regulation of idea generation. It would be interesting to see if teachers' modeling of a self-questioning strategy would help young children acquire the procedures that control internal cuing. For example, a teacher could write part of a short composition on the board, then step back and ask herself out loud, "Have I finished? Do I have more to say?" and then add some more. Children viewing this modeling process might well internalize it if they also saw that it led to an improved product.

Planning: Organization

The organization of a written product is important in communicating meaning. Readers expect organization at both local and global levels of discourse. Organization reduces the burden on working memory for the reader (recall the Kintsch and van Dijk model of reading comprehension described in Chapter 3) by grouping related ideas. It also facilitates both comprehension and retrieval of information (cf., Britton, Meyer, Hodge, & Glynn, 1980). In writing, organization is communicated through cohesion (i.e., ties between ideas and sentences) and through coherence (i.e., structuring across paragraphs).

Successfully organizing a written product is accomplished by using both declarative and procedural knowledge. Declarative knowledge provides knowledge about relations between and among concepts and ideas. These relations in turn are used by procedural knowledge that "produces" cohesion at the local level and coherence at the global level of the text.

Cohesion. Cohesive ties are linguistic devices that tie one idea in a text to neighboring ideas. (For a more technical discussion of cohesion, see Halliday & Hasan, 1976.) There are several classes of cohesion, including referential, conjunctive, and lexical. Table 13.5 shows some examples of each of these types. *Referential* cohesion uses pronouns, demonstratives, and definite articles to refer to a previously mentioned item. *Conjunctive* cohesion uses conjunctions such as *and*, and *or* to indicate relationships between ideas. *Lexical* cohesion uses word meanings to establish ties between ideas.

Cohesive ties vary in their dependence on the reader's knowledge. Referential ties that are signaled solely by syntax, such as those conveyed by indefinite and definite articles, do not depend much on declarative knowledge. Even if two sentences have a nonsense word in them, these ties would still signal the relationship between the two occurences of the nonsense word. For example, in the sentences *John saw a jix. The jix cost ten dollars*, the

Table 13.5 Examples of referential, conjunctive, and lexical cohesion.

REFERENTIAL COHESION

John went to the store. *He* bought a newspaper. (Pronomial reference)

It is important to exercise every day. *This* establishes a routine. (Demonstrative reference)

There were two boys at the game, one quite tall, the other of average height. *The* tall boy took the lead. (Definite article)

CONJUNCTIVE COHESION

Jane read about sailing *and* imagined what it would be like. (additive)

Jane read about sailing *but* she couldn't imagine what it would be like. (adversative)

Jane read about sailing *because* she was about to go on her first sailing expedition. (causal)

LEXICAL COHESION

Tony *ran* down the road. He *ran* so fast he missed the turnoff. (repetition)

Tony *sped* down the road. He *ran* so fast he missed the turnoff. (synonyms)

There are several *swimming strokes*. In the *crawl stroke*, the flutter kick is used. (superordinate)

Sandra was *starting at a new school*. She went to the *principal's office* to get her *class schedule*. Then she went to her *homeroom* where the *teacher introduced her to the class*. (collocation)

---

article *The* in the second sentence specifies that the jix being discussed is the same one that is introduced in the first sentence. Without knowing the meaning of jix, the two sentences can be tied to each other by the articles alone.

Many cohesive ties do require some declarative knowledge. Lexical ties, for instance, always depend on the reader's declarative knowledge of word meanings and facts. For example, a synonym of a previously used word is often used to indicate that the same topic is still being discussed (see second example under Lexical Cohesion in Table 13.5).

Similarly, "collocation" ties depend on the reader's organized knowledge structures (i.e., schemas) to tie sentences together. Consider the collocation example shown at the bottom of the Lexical Cohesion section in Table 13.5. A person (say someone from a nonliterate culture) who does not have a "first-day-at-new-school" schema would fail to understand the relationship between going to the principal's office and getting a class schedule or between going to a homeroom and being introduced. The sequence of events would seem arbitrary for such an individual. However, for most people in literate cultures, the description is cohesive because the lexical items occur in a predictable order.

Cohesion in writing is accomplished by a set of procedures that has the goal of finding rule-based ways to connect ideas or sentences together. Since the English language has a variety of linguistic devices available for achieving cohesion, our procedural knowledge must be capable of determining the conditions for the appropriate use of each device, and applying each one accordingly.

Young writers have difficulty writing cohesively. One mistake they make, apparently as a carryover from oral language, is to assume that the reader knows what is being referred to even if the referent has never been specified. Here, for example, are three sentences written by a kindergartener, along with their translations (from King & Rentel, 1981):

Kindergartener's Sentences	Translations
I like Hm	I like him.
Day maj	He did magic.
He jagdo	He juggled.

The referent for *him* and *he* in these sentences is never given. The child seems to assume that the reader will know that she is referring to a juggler she has just seen. King and Rentel found that for kindergarteners and first-graders, 34% of all attempts at cohesive ties made did not specify the referent. By second grade, however, nonspecified referents were down to 5%.

Nonetheless, problems using cohesive ties in a clear way continue throughout the school years. For example, Collins and Williamson (1981) found that weak essays in grades 4, 8, and 12 failed to specify referents twice as often as did strong essays. Looking at all types of cohesion, McCutchen and Perfetti (1982) found that the percentages of unsuccessful cohesive ties were 51, 38, 13, and 18, respectively, in grades 2, 4, 6, and 8.

In college the liberal use of successful cohesive ties results in a higher-quality product. Witte and Faigley (1981) had ninety freshmen write on "Changes in behavior." They then compared the cohesiveness of the five top-rated essays and the five lowest-rated essays. In the best essays, 32% of the words contributed to explicit cohesive ties, whereas only 20% of the words in the worst essays contributed to cohesion. The best essays contained more of almost every type of cohesive tie and a greater variety of subtypes as well. One exception to this finding was that the worst essays contained more cohesive ties that were established by word repetition than did the best essays. Perhaps this is because word repetition, although establishing cohesion, makes for uninteresting reading.

The top-rated essays used collocation three times as often as the lowest-rated essays. This finding suggests that the writers of the best essays may have had more declarative knowledge about the topic than did the writers of the poor essays. For example, students who had taken a high school course in psychology might have some psychology schemas about changes in behavior that could be used by the cohesion productions that govern collocation, whereas students who lacked such schemas would not have this source of input for their procedures.

Coherence. The use of cohesive ties establishes organization at the sentence level. At the level of an entire text, coherent structures create organization. Coherence means the degree to which an entire piece of writing fits together in an organized way.

One example of variation in coherence is shown in the essays in Figures 13.2 and 13.3. These were written in response to the assignment to write an essay that begins with the sentence *There are many things about _____ that make it fun and exciting,* and that ends with the sentence *So while _____ can be fun, there are those dangers that we must watch out for so that the fun is not spoiled.* The topic filling in the blank was selected by the student.

The essay diagrammed in Figure 13.2 is more coherent than the one in Figure 13.3 because the overall structure of the text is tighter. The tightness is due to the fact that most of the sentences have ties to both the previous sentence and the topic sentence, as is indicated by the arrows going from ideas in the left column to ideas in the right column. Most of the sentences in the less coherent essay have ties only to the topic sentence.

Just as there are developmental differences in the establishment of cohesion, so are there development differences in the establishment of coherence. McCutchen and Perfetti (1982) found that only 44% of fourth-graders' essays had the tighter structure shown in Figure 13.2, whereas 67% and 60% of sixth- and eighth-graders' essays, respectively, were tighter in form.

Mastery of coherent form varies with the subject matter and function of writing. Applebee, Durst, and Newell (1984) studied coherence of writing among high school students in "summary" and "analysis" passages written in science and social science classes. A summary passage was one that provided a generic description of a recurrent pattern of events. An analysis passage provided a "generalization or classification related to a situation,

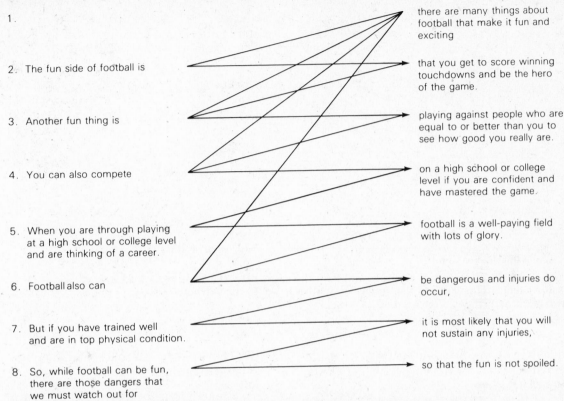

1.

there are many things about football that make it fun and exciting

2. The fun side of football is

that you get to score winning touchdowns and be the hero of the game.

3. Another fun thing is

playing against people who are equal to or better than you to see how good you really are.

4. You can also compete

on a high school or college level if you are confident and have mastered the game.

5. When you are through playing at a high school or college level and are thinking of a career.

football is a well-paying field with lots of glory.

6. Football also can

be dangerous and injuries do occur,

7. But if you have trained well and are in top physical condition.

it is most likely that you will not sustain any injuries,

8. So, while football can be fun, there are those dangers that we must watch out for

so that the fun is not spoiled.

Figure 13.2 An example of a highly coherent essay in which many of the sentences relate back to both the previous and the topic sentences (from McCutchen and Perfetti, 1982).

problem, or theme, with logical or hierarchical relationships among generalizations implicit or explicit."

The coherence scores for student essays were compared with scores given to typical science and social science textbooks. As can be seen in Table 13.6 there is no substantial difference between textbooks' and students' summary passages in either the social sciences or sciences; nor is there much of a difference for analysis passages in the social sciences. However, the textbook analysis passages in science were much more coherent than the student analysis passages.

Figure 13.4 shows coherence graphs for an analysis passage from a typical science

textbook and from a typical science student. The textbook passage has symmetry in describing two alternative types of trees, but the student's passage shows extreme lack of symmetry. The student's passage begins by stating that two alternative types of engines will be discussed, but only one is described in any detail.

Thus, at times, students have difficulty writing in a coherent, organized fashion. This may be due to their lack of procedural knowledge about how to create an organized passage or to their lack of conceptual understanding about the subject being discussed. Later in this chapter we will see how declarative knowledge influences coherence. For the mo-

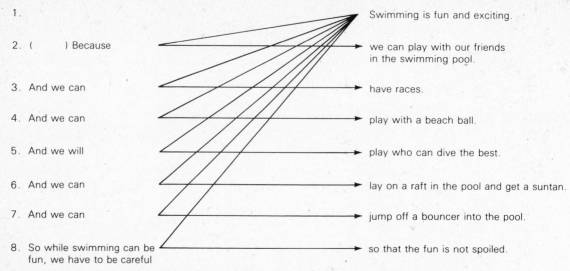

1.   Swimming is fun and exciting.

2. (   ) Because   we can play with our friends
                                                       in the swimming pool.

3. And we can   have races.

4. And we can   play with a beach ball.

5. And we will   play who can dive the best.

6. And we can   lay on a raft in the pool and get a suntan.

7. And we can   jump off a bouncer into the pool.

8. So while swimming can be   so that the fun is not spoiled.
   fun, we have to be careful

Figure 13.3 An essay that is less coherent than the essay shown in Figure 13.2 because each sentence refers back to the topic sentence only, not to the previous sentence (from McCutchen and Perfetti, 1982).

ment let us consider some specific procedural knowledge that might be useful in generating coherent text.

McCutchen and Perfetti (1982) argue that to generate coherent text one must satisfy several constraints at once and that it is the satisfaction of all constraints that leads to the structure of the text fitting together. For example, their subjects were asked to satisfy the following constraints in the compositions they were writing:

1. The topic must be something that is fun.

2. The topic must also be something that is dangerous.

3. Enough must be known about the fun and dangerous components of the topic to support the claims that it is both fun and dangerous.

Once the subjects had identified such a topic in declarative memory, they could produce a coherent text by writing down the contents of memory in a specified order. Thus, the important procedural knowledge is recognizing and applying all constraints. Fourth-graders were

Table 13.6 Average coherence scores for textbook and student passages of two forms (summary and analysis) in the social sciences and sciences (adapted from Applebee, Durst, and Newell, 1984).

	TEXTBOOKS		STUDENTS	
	SUMMARY	ANALYSIS	SUMMARY	ANALYSIS
Social science	72.9	72.9	60.0	61.0
Science	67.2	69.3	69.4	37.9

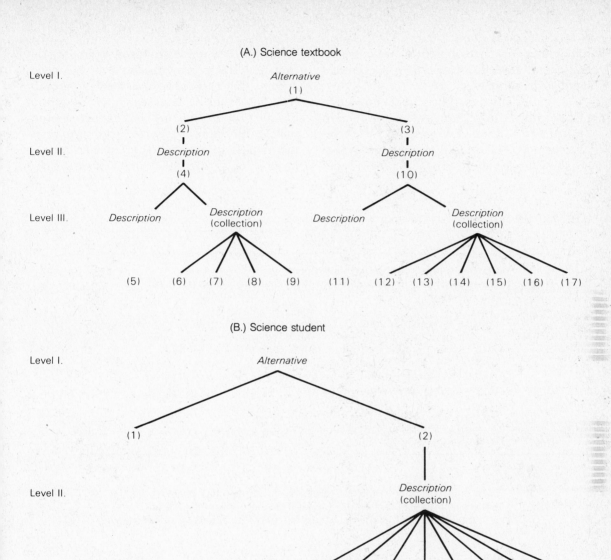

Figure 13.4 The structure of two analysis passages, both starting with an alternative argument. Passage A, from a science text, has a much more balanced structure than does passage B, written by a student (from Applebee, Durst, and Newell, 1984).

not able to write as coherent a text as sixth- and eighth-graders because their procedures were not as complete.

The difference in procedural knowledge just described can be expressed in production system terms. Production systems for a typical fourth-grader and a typical eighth-grader are shown in Table 13.7. The differences begin with how they represent the assignment. The fourth-grader represents the goal as one of arguing that a given topic has a given property (P_1). To do this, he must search for a topic that has the property and also has enough components with the property for supporting arguments to be presented (P_2). Once an area of knowledge is identified that satisfies these

Table 13.7 Production systems for fourth- and eighth-grade text generation.

		FOURTH GRADE	
P_1	IF	Goal is to argue that topic has property A	
	THEN	Set subgoal to search memory for topic that has property A and components.	
P_2	IF	Subgoal is to search memory for topic that has property A and components	
	THEN	Identify node that has property A and two or more components	
		And tag the proposition that node has property A as sentence 1	
		And tag the proposition that component 1 has property A as sentence 2	
		And tag the proposition that component 2 has property A as sentence 3	
		And set subgoal to write argument.	
P_3	IF	Subgoal is to write argument	
		And propositions tagged as sentences exist	
	THEN	Write sentences 1–N.	
		EIGHTH GRADE	
P_4	IF	Goal is to argue that topic has property A but also has property B	
	THEN	Set subgoal to search memory for topic that has property A and components with property A and has property B and components with property B.	
P_5	IF	Subgoal is to search memory for topic that has property A and components with property A and has property B and components with property B	
	THEN	Identify node that has property A and two or more components	
		Identify node that has property B and two or more components	
		Tag the proposition that node has property A as Sentence 1	
		Tag the proposition that component 1 has property A as sentence 2	
		Tag the proposition that component 2 has property A as sentence 3	
		Tag the proposition that node has property B as sentence 4	
		Tag the proposition that component 3 has property B as sentence 5	
		Tag the proposition that component 4 has property B as sentence 6	
		And set subgoal to write argument.	
P_3	IF	Subgoal is to write argument	
		And propositions tagged as sentences exist	
	THEN	Write sentences 1–N.	

constraints, the relevant propositions are tagged (P_2) and the tags are used to guide the process of translating ideas into written form (P_3).

Eighth-graders' procedural knowledge is more elaborate. It has a two-part goal (to argue that a topic has one property and to argue that it also has a contrasting property). To meet the two-part goal, eighth-graders must search their memory for a topic that satisfies four (rather than the fourth-graders' two) constraints; the topic must have (1) property A, (2) some components that have property A,

(3) property B, and (4) some components that have property B (P_5). The relevant propositions are tagged (P_5) and form the basis of writing (P_3).

McCutchen and Perfetti (1982) tested their model of procedural knowledge differences by comparing the output of a computer simulation with the performance of elementary school children. They put into the computer the declarative knowledge representation shown in Figure 13.5. Then they ran a simulation using the model of fourth-graders' procedural knowledge, which ignores some con-

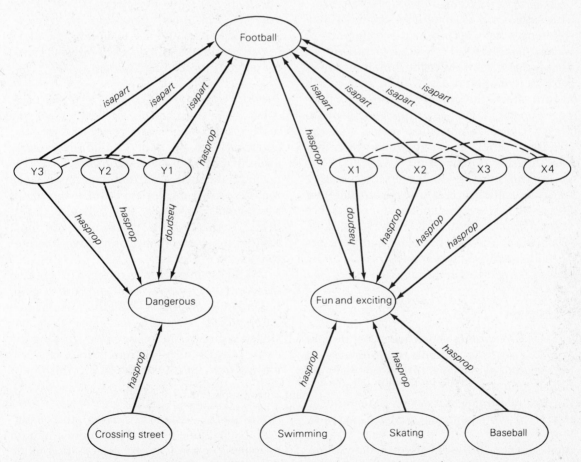

Figure 13.5 Declarative knowledge available to the computer in a simulation of writing skill (from McCutchen and Perfetti, 1982).

straints, and another simulation using the model of eighth-graders' procedural knowledge. (You may wish to think through the simulation by predicting how the production systems shown in Table 13.7 would operate on the knowledge structure shown in Figure 13.5.) The fourth-grade model produced a text with the list-like structure exemplified in Figure 13.3, whereas the eighth-grade model produced a text with the zigzag structure exemplified in Figure 13.2.

An interesting aspect of this model is that the same declarative knowledge representation resulted in qualitatively different essays because of procedural knowledge differences. This suggests that sometimes the individual differences we observe in the coherence of writing are due to variations in procedural knowledge. Specifically, the variations are in the differentiation of the writing goal, which in turn affects the number of constraints imposed on the memory search. Flower et al. (in press) have also presented results that are consistent with this interpretation of coherence differences in writing.

In summary, good writers and mature writers are more successful at organizing their ideas both in sentences and in whole texts. We suspect that procedural knowledge is partly responsible. The superior planning processes of skilled writers apparently include more effective organizational strategies.

Translation

Translation involves the actual generation of text. It starts from a mental representation of the assignment and ends with words on paper or in a computer file. The mental representation may be a goal (or set of goals) and an organized plan for meeting that goal, or it may be a single idea. In either case, the translation processes handle the details of spelling, punctuation, and grammar demanded by the conventions of written language.

Translation can stretch working memory's capacity to its limits. The writer is typically trying to keep many things active in memory at once: the goals and plans for the text, ideas for content, and memory for what has just been written (so that cohesion and coherence can be established and maintained). Just as automatic decoding skills help substantially in reading, so too automatic skills help a great deal in writing. In reading, automatic decoding allows more attention to be devoted to comprehension. In writing, the abilities to spell, to punctuate, to use correct word endings, and to use correct grammar automatically allow more attention to be devoted to continued planning and review. Younger writers and less skilled writers have to pay attention to activities that are automatic for older or more skilled writers.

Attention to Motor Skills. The most basic skills to be automatized in writing are the motor skills of holding a pencil and forming letters with it on paper. Children in early elementary school grades mouth each word as it is written, suggesting that their motor skills require a great deal of attention. After about third grade, however, this behavior disappears, suggesting that by third grade most children have automatic control over the motor aspects of writing.

With the introduction of word processing via computer, typing skill appears to be a second kind of "motor" skill that needs to be automatized. Research indicates that less skilled typists spend more energy finding the correct keys than they do attending to the real writing task. Of course, the lack of this motor skill results in an inferior product.

Attention to Mechanics. Several studies suggest that unskilled writers pay more attention to spelling, grammar, and punctuation while they are translating than do skilled writers (Atwell, 1981; Birnbaum, 1982; Pianko, 1979).

Pianko, for example, found that remedial college writers spent more time writing each word than average college writers and, when asked what they were thinking about during writing, the majority reported thinking about spelling, punctuation, or word choice. The average writers wrote faster, suggesting that they were not consciously spelling out most words as they wrote them. Also, the majority of average writers reported paying attention to style and purpose during pauses in writing. In a previous section, data like these were interpreted as indicating that unskilled writers have a different goal (avoiding errors) than do skilled writers (communicating meaning). These data also suggest that unskilled writers must attend to mechanics because these skills are not yet automatized. It is likely that a person's writing goals are partly driven by his or her cognitive skills. Thus, the goal of avoiding errors derives from the need to devote all of one's cognitive resources to the lower-level mechanics.

External Support for Writing Cohesively. Although cohesion is initiated by organizational processes, it is manifested on paper through translation processses. For less skilled writers, the ability to maintain cohesion during writing is quite fragile. This was demonstrated by Atwell (1981). Atwell had more and less skilled college writers write a personal essay. For the first half of the writing session the students could see what they had written; however, for the second half they used inkless pens. What they wrote was recorded by means of carbon paper, but they were blind to it.

Writing blind caused the compositions of the less skilled writers to lose cohesion, but it had little effect on the cohesiveness of skilled writers. This result is illustrated in Figure 13.6, which shows the propositional structure of a typical essay from (A) the skilled group and (B) the less skilled group. Each circle denotes a proposition, and the lines between circles indicate cohesive ties between propositions. The more lines interconnecting circles, the greater the cohesiveness of the essay. The left half of the figure shows the part of the composition written before writing became blind. Both compositions show cohesiveness there. However, after the blind writing was introduced (right half), cohesion in the less skilled writer's composition breaks down dramatically. Notice the disconnected fragments in the bottom right corner of the figure.

These data demonstrate that less skilled writers need to read what they have just written if they are to maintain cohesion. Skilled writers do not depend as much on this external support. There are several possible reasons for this difference. Perhaps skilled writers generate cohesive text because they have developed cohesive plans prior to writing. Or, because they spell and punctuate automatically, skilled writers have more room in working memory to keep active what they have just written. They can thus check their mental representation for its cohesion, rather than needing to rely on the written text. Less skilled writers, because they must take up space in working memory to make decisions about mechanics, lose their representation of what they have just said. Normally they can look back to see what they have written, but in blind writing they no longer have this external cue.

In summary, although the details of the events of translation are not well known, it is clearly a time when a writer's possession of automatic skills can come in handy. In particular, automatization of motor skills, spelling, punctuation, and grammar seem to free writers to attend to larger issues such as cohesion, coherence, and purpose.

Writer's Block. Other obstacles to translation are getting started and keeping going. At one time or another almost everyone experi-

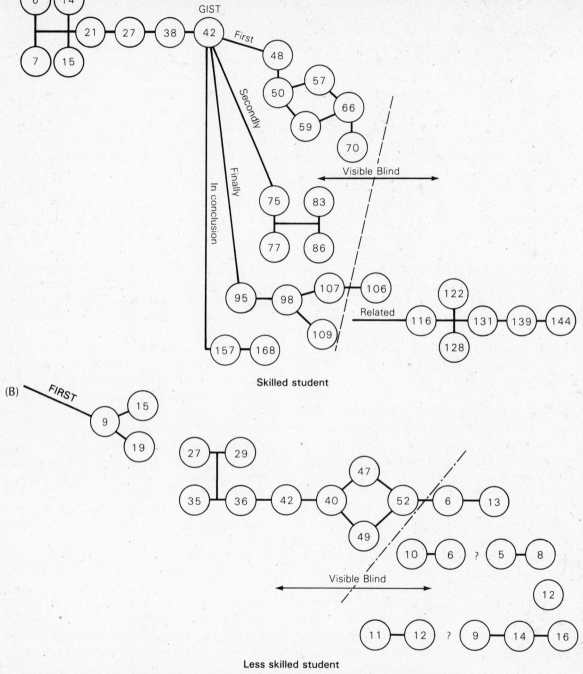

Figure 13.6 Cohesiveness of essays before and after blind writing was introduced. Circles indicate propositions and lines indicate relations between propositions. After blind writing was introduced, the cohesion of the less skilled writer's essay (B) deteriorated (from Atwell, 1981).

ences difficulty getting started with a writing task or completing the task. Sometimes the "block" is due to a need for more knowledge of the topic, in which case more information gathering should alleviate the problem.

Another source of writer's block stems from the rules of thumb that writers acquire to guide their writing. Rose (1980) compared five college students who often experienced writer's block with five who wrote more easily. The students were equivalent in general ability and writing skill. Rose asked the students to report retrospectively what they were thinking while writing. The students who experienced writer's block were using rigid rules (given to them by teachers) to guide their behavior. One, for example, was guided by the rule that a good essay always grabs the reader's attention immediately. With this rule in mind, she had trouble going beyond the first sentence! Another student was using the rule, "You must always make three or more points in an essay, or it won't be a strong essay." When that student had one point to make and elaborate, he felt defeated. Using rules like these can understandably lead to writer's block, since many essays will not fit such exacting standards.

The students who wrote easily used rules that facilitated, rather than blocked, the writing process, such as, "When stuck, write." Also, the rules they used were not stated in such absolute terms—for example, "*Try* to keep your audience in mind," is less absolute then, "You *must* keep your audience in mind." These findings suggest that teachers should think carefully about the rules they explicitly give to students.

Reviewing

Reviewing consists of evaluating what has been written to determine how well it meets one's goals and then remediating unsatisfactory parts of the product.

Young Children's Reviewing Processes. During the elementary school years, children first become proficient at recognizing that their writing has problems (evaluating) and then later at remediating (revising) such problems. Table 13.8, for example, shows data from a study in which children wrote a composition and were asked to evaluate and remediate each sentence as they went along (Scardamalia & Bereiter, 1983). The evaluations and the success of the revision strategies were then judged by expert adult writers. Table 13.8 shows that even fourth graders are fairly good at recognizing when something is wrong (85% success rate). However, only older elementary school children are predictably successful at revising the problem they have recognized. Over 70% of the time fourth graders do not successfully remediate problems they recognize. Table 13.9 shows a similar pattern of results for evaluating and revising ambiguous references in text (E.J. Bartlett, 1982).

This developmental sequence in reviewing is reminiscent of the developmental sequence in comprehension monitoring described in Chapter 12. Recall that for comprehension monitoring, the youngest

Table 13.8 Percentages of children correctly evaluating and revising their compositions as a function of grade level (adapted from Scardamalia and Bereiter, 1983).

	APPROPRIATE EVALUATION	INAPPROPRIATE EVALUATION
Grade 4	85%	15%
Grade 6	93%	7%
Grade 8	100%	0%

	APPROPRIATE REVISION	INAPPROPRIATE REVISION
Grade 4	23%	77%
Grade 6	47%	53%
Grade 8	64%	36%

Table 13.9 Percentage of children correctly evaluating and revising ambiguous references in text (adapted from E.J. Bartlett, 1982).

	ABOVE-AVERAGE WRITERS	BELOW-AVERAGE WRITERS
Correct evaluation		
Grade 5	62%	37%
Grade 6	72%	57%
Grade 7	75%	59%
Correct revision		
Grade 5	17%	6%
Grade 6	32%	17%
Grade 7	36%	21%

children did not even recognize that they had not understood something. Slightly older children realized they were not understanding but did not know what to do about it. Still older children could both recognize and remediate comprehension problems. This correspondence in development of reading and writing skills is expected if one accepts the complementary relation that exists between the two skills.

This developmental sequence also emphasizes the evolutionary character of procedural knowledge. Recall from Chapters 8 and 9 that people must first learn patterns (like schemas) before those schemas can become conditions for productions. Perhaps in writing, young children's schemas for a "good" written product have developed to the point where they can recognize whether a given writing sample matches their internal schemas. This would allow children to recognize that a writing sample needs to be fixed. However, if the schemas have not yet become conditions of revision productions, the children would have no appropriate strategic actions to take and thus would not be able to improve their writing.

This line of reasoning would suggest that if children are provided with strategic help,

their revising behavior should increase. In fact, Bereiter and Scardamalia (1987) have reported just this pattern.

High School and Adult Reviewing Processes. Like young writers, some unskilled older writers fail to recognize problems in what they have written. Perl (1979) had five unskilled college writers think aloud while composing. By comparing what was said with what was written, Perl could identify incidences of reading something that had not actually been written—for example, reading one word when another word had been written or reading a correct word ending when the ending had been left off in the written product. The discrepancies strikingly correlated with the number of unresolved problems in the compositions, suggesting that the problems remained unresolved not because the writer lacked strategies to resolve them but because the writer failed to recognize their existence.

The types of problems that skilled and less skilled writers focus on when they review their writing differ in the same way that their goals differ. Stallard (1974) compared the writing behavior of fifteen high school seniors who scored in the ninetieth percentile on a standardized writing test with that of fifteen randomly selected seniors. Of the revisions made by the top group, 82% were revisions in meaning rather than mechanics, whereas only 41% of the revisions made by the randomly selected group were for meaning. Bridwell (1980) found a similar result.

One type of revision that is strikingly absent from the writing of less skilled writers is that which alters the structure of an entire essay. Faigley and Witte (1981) found that the frequency of such changes was only about one per 1000 words among remedial college writers, whereas among skilled college writers and professional writers the frequency of such changes was about twenty per 1000 words.

Thus, less skilled writers are deficient in re-reading carefully enough to identify problems, and the problems they do find are mechanical. Skilled writers make more meaning-related revisions.

Quantity of Revision. One might expect skilled writers to revise more than unskilled writers. This persistence in revision would then account for the higher quality of the product. On the other hand, one might expect that less skilled writers revise more because they make more errors that need to be remediated. In fact, neither of these expectations is consistently supported by experimental data.

Stallard (1974) had his high school subjects write a persuasive essay, defending their position on a current news topic. His top writers made an average of 12.24 revisions, whereas his randomly selected writers made an average of 4.26 revisions. These data suggest that good writers revise more. However, Bridwell (1980) found no relationship between number of revisions and quality of descriptive essays written by high school students. Perhaps descriptive essays on familiar topics are easier to write, and under such conditions good writers do not revise more than poor writers. However, when the topic is less familiar or the task more demanding, they may revise more. We do know that revision strategies appear to be adjusted for different types of text (cf., Matsuhashi, 1987), although we have not yet identified how this adjustment is mediated by writing skill.

Thus, it seems that sometimes skilled writers revise more than less skilled writers and sometimes there is no difference in the amount of revision. However, less skilled writers do not seem to revise more than skilled writers. For students who think that revision is a sign of lack of skill, it might be useful to inform them that the jury is still out on this question.

DECLARATIVE KNOWLEDGE DIFFERENCES

Recall the study by Spilich et al. (1979) described in Chapter 12, in which it was found that readers of the same skill level differed in their comprehension of a passage about baseball, depending on how much general knowledge they possessed about baseball. Those with much knowledge recalled more from the new passage than did low-knowledge individuals. It seems reasonable to suppose that a similar phenomenon might occur in the domain of writing. That is, people of the same skill level, but with differing amounts of declarative knowledge about the topic of an essay, should produce essays of differing quality.

Voss, Vesonder, and Spilich (1980) examined this hypothesis using college students with equal verbal ability, but different levels of knowledge about baseball. They asked these students to write a fictional account of half an inning of baseball. One result was that the task representation of high- and low-knowledge individuals differed somewhat. All the high-knowledge people successfully complied with the task, but only seven of the ten low-knowledge people did. Of the three who were not successful, one wrote about cricket, one wrote about less than half an inning, and one wrote about more than half an inning. Thus their lack of knowledge led to a misrepresentation of the task.

The compositions of the successful students were analyzed into propositions, and then each proposition was categorized as being about (1) the setting, (2) significant states of the ball game, (3) game actions, (4) auxiliary actions, (5) relevant nongame actions, and (6) irrelevant nongame actions. Game actions were major events in the game that produced changes in the state of the game. For example, *The batter hit a ground ball* is a game action because it changes the status of the game (assuming a fair ball, the batter will either get a hit or make an out, and either result changes the current situation in the game). Auxiliary actions elaborated the game actions. For example, *The batter hit a gound ball that went between the third baseman and the bag and rolled down the left-field line* contains two auxiliary actions about where the ball went. Relevant nongame actions were relevant to the game but did not change the game state (e.g., *The catcher signaled the pitcher*). Irrelevant nongame actions were such things as descriptions of what the fans were doing.

The results of this analysis are shown in Table 13.10. High- and low-knowledge students did not differ in the proportion of setting, significant states, and game action statements written. However, the high-knowledge compositions contained a higher proportion of auxiliary actions (.39 for high-knowledge versus .22 for low-knowledge), and the low-knowledge compositions contained a higher proportion of irrelevant nongame actions (.24 for low-knowledge versus .08 for high-knowledge). Since auxiliary actions provide elaborative detail (whereas irrelevant actions shift the topic), high-knowledge students' compositions were probably more cohesive and coherent than were those of the low-knowledge students.

Table 13.10 Proportion of types of statements written by high- and low-knowledge individuals (adapted from Voss, Vesonder, and Spilich, 1980).

	PROPORTION OF PROPOSITIONS IN CATEGORY	
	HIGH KNOWLEDGE	LOW KNOWLEDGE
Setting	.30	.25
Significant states	.09	.16
Game actions	.10	.09
Auxiliary actions	.39	.22
Relevant nongame	.04	.03
Irrelevant nongame	.08	.24

The role of declarative knowledge in language production was also investigated by Yekovich et al. (1990). Their study used two groups of students who had high football knowledge but differed in verbal aptitude (as measured by the SAT). Because low-ability students tend to write less than high-ability students, the researchers needed another method to capture language production. They devised a task in which the students pretended to be radio broadcasters who commentated a quarter of a professional football game. The data of interest were the "speak aloud" commentaries, which were scored for various aspects of the game (as above), as well as for elaborations and opinions. The most notable finding was that the high- and low-verbal aptitude groups did not differ in any aspect of their commentaries. In other words, knowledge of football was enough to make the groups look indistinguishable in this task. As a check on these findings, the researchers had a small group of football experts listen to excerpts from the tapes and attempt to classify the speakers as high- or low-aptitude. The experts could not tell the difference. While this study did not investigate writing directly, it did investigate a highly related activity, language production. The results are what would be expected if one believes that declarative knowledge is important in idea generation.

It seems, then, that declarative knowledge not only affects the quality of the meaning representation developed in a comprehension task; it also affects the quality of production in a writing task (see also Liebelt, 1980). Inadequate declarative knowledge clearly constrains the effectiveness of procedural knowledge.

INSTRUCTION

So far in this chapter, we have seen that people may differ in many ways in writing skill. These ways include control of mechanics, goals for writing, and focus during revision. They may also differ in possession, access, and organization of relevant declarative knowledge. Writing is not unique in its complexity. We have seen equal complexity in reading, and we will see it again in mathematics. However, since writing is not always included in the core curriculum, variation in writing skill within a group of grade- and ability-level peers may be greater than variation in reading or math skill. Therefore, a major problem in writing instruction is how to handle variation. In this section, we discuss two instructional methods for dealing with this variation, **conferencing** and **teaching revision strategies.**

Conferencing

"Conferencing" refers to a type of writing instruction that includes, as an important component, conferences between the teacher and each student (Duke, 1975; Sperling, 1991). The focus of these conferences is the quality of the student's written product, the processes used by the student, and the relationship between process and product. The teacher questions the student on these topics and gives verbal reinforcement for those ideas expressed by the student that the teacher wishes to encourage. The idea is to diagnose (through questioning) the source of the writing problem (e.g., lack of declarative knowledge, trouble with automated basic skills, or failure to use flexible writing strategies), and to explicitly provide help or guidance.

For example, the following is a verbatim transcript of part of a conference between a teacher and a freshman composition student (Freedman & Swanson-Owens, 1983, p. 23). The student (S) is reading aloud to the teacher (T) a composition that he has written about bus transportation at the university. The teacher has invited him to stop at any point

during reading to comment on both strengths and weaknesses of the composition.

S: [Student finishes reading his paragraph.] That was the second paragraph. It might be a little short in development.

T: Can you think of anything offhand that you would want to develop more? Or, as you read it, when you say, oh, I've left the reader hanging?

S: I think it just touches very lightly on each of the things like too many buses and going one route, and it doesn't say anything about express buses and having and not having enough express buses, and, uh, yeah [unclear].

T: Do you see any other places for development?

S: [long pause] Why the people are discouraged when taking the bus 'cause of the time.

T: How would you develop that?

S: Uh, examples. How long people have to wait and, uh, and how far they have to go to their bus stop, whatever, allowing for transfers and stops.

T: Great, good.

S: And I had those in my one of my drafts, I think, but, uh, I thought I would get overdevelopment. It wouldn't develop the topic sentence if I used all that.

As you can see in the last statement made by the teacher, she strongly praises the student's generation of ideas for how to improve on his written product. The praise informs the student both that the thinking processes he is going through (self-evaluation and remediation) and the details he comes up with to develop his ideas are good. Because feedback is provided when the processes occur, the student learns the processes. Typically, feedback on compositions occurs long after the thinking process and is thus less likely to be informative.

Besides allowing for immediate feedback on composing processes, conferencing allows the teacher to raise questions or give "minilectures" that are intended to get the student to consider alternative writing strategies. For example, in one conference studied by Freedman (1981, p. 83), the following exchange took place:

S: See I saw a lot of things when I was doing the rewrite. But I just couldn't put it down into words.

T: Um, that's interesting. Did you make any, uhm kind of outline on the side trying to get your ideas plugged into an organization?

If this student has never tried using an outline or other organizational strategy during revision, the teacher's suggestion may stimulate her to try it. Since instruction in conferences depends on the learner's needs, it is likely to be heeded.

Conferencing is often combined with classroom instruction on rhetoric and composition, reading of a rhetoric text, writing essays, and receiving peer evaluation of essays in addition to teacher and self-evaluation. If teachers do not have time for out-of-class conferences, they may conduct them during class time while the other students are engaged in in-class writing or peer-group conferences (e.g., Sperling, 1991). Conferencing has been used successsfully in elementary schools (Graves, 1982) as well as high school and colleges, for writing in social science, science, and math classes (cf., Healy, 1981; Marshall, 1984), not just in English classes.

How does this technique help solve the problem of individualization? It does so by helping both the student and teacher focus on problems that are unique to that student. When the student recognizes a problem, she can then seek solutions from the available instructional resources—text, lectures, feedback from peers, and feedback from the teacher. The conference thus sensitizes the student to personal objectives and encourages her to work towards those objectives throughout the course.

One example of this instructional process can be seen in what happened to Cee, a freshman studied by Freedman and her student (1981, 1982; Freedman & Swanson-Owens, 1983). Several changes in Cee's writing and writing behavior occurred during the semester in which she took freshman composition from a teacher who was skilled in conferencing. First, the quality of her writing improved. Two of Cee's compositions, one from the beginning of the semester and one from the end, are shown in the appendix at the end of this chapter. Although the essay written late in the semester has some problems, including a change of focus between the third and fourth paragraphs, it is far more substantial than the essay written at the beginning of the semester.

Cee's self-evaluation also changed. Early in the semester, only one-third of the comments she made during conferences were on the organization and development of her essays. The rest were on mechanics and sentence structure. Late in the semester, however, all of her comments were on organization and development. A final change that was observed was in the extensiveness of Cee's revisions. She spent more time revising at the end of the semester and made many more changes.

Exactly what happened to produce these changes is not clear, but there are hints in the data provided by Freedman on what the teacher did during her conferences with Cee. First, the teacher responded to Cee's concerns about mechanics either neutrally or negatively. A neutral response was one in which she answered Cee's direct question, but did not evaluate Cee's writing in any way. A negative response was one in which the teacher shifted the discussion away from the topic of grammar or spelling that had been raised by Cee. Positive responses occurred when Cee focused on discourse-level concerns, as the following example illustrates:

T: Any other things that offhand you think make the paper good or bad?

S: Let's see. Yeah, I know there was s'posed to be um, one of those things—not a comma . . .

T: Apostrophe?

S: Apostrophe there. And I had a hard time trying to keep track. Uh, I can't think of a correct word for it, but like sometimes I read, go back and say "businesswoman," and then I go on and say "they" when it should have been like "her", so I had to write everything back to plural—to the plural form . . . And let's see . . . And you mentioned something yesterday about how the last paragraph should come together. What I was saying like in the first paragraph of my thesis that it should end with the . . . well, come to a conclusion of what I said earlier. And, I felt that this last paragraph here wasn't what I said up here. And I wasn't too sure about this "male species believe that women, especially ones with children devote more of their time worrying over the family's welfare, welfare, than over the company's." And that sort of left it hanging in a

way. I should have continued it and expanded it more as to why I said that.

T: Okay good . . . Are there any other places where when you went back a little while ago and read, reread the essay, that you felt you should have developed it? You mentioned that you were worried about development. Any other places aside from that place?

S: Let's see . . . in the third paragraph I should have said why, what kind of an assignment that women can handle that men are already handling. That should have been expanded more. And and then needed the I wasn't sure about, uh, the apostrophe on this husband's career. (Freedman & Swanson-Owens, 1983, p. 26)

Even though Cee returned to her concern for apostrophes, she also focused on the discourse level in her self-evaluations. Because her attention was on the discourse level, she probably was open to instruction that helped her with discourse goals. One instructional sequence directed at discourse concerns, which took place during a conference with Cee, is recorded here:

S: But it, it's easier to talk it out than write it down on a piece of paper. [a few lines are deleted here]

T: And start out that way, then you can cross off those extra words. Remember how Trimble suggests that you do that. Just talk. Pretend like you're explaining to a friend.

S: No. it's much more different talking to a friend because you can put in your own ideas. You don't have to watch out too much about the little grammar errors or spelling errors or anything like that. Just say right out or you could maybe exaggerate a little bit more, and everything's just flowing right out. But when you're talking on, to a piece of paper, you're talking, but then you might forget something or you might all of a sudden change it. Because I have a habit of changing everything in mid air. Like I might have an essay al-almost done to type up and then maybe one or two days before it's due, I change the whole essay or go to a new topic because I don't like the form of my essay.

T: Okay. Uhm, the only thing I can say about that is that if if it would help you get ideas on to the paper, to think you were talking, let those grammar errors come out and then when you do your editing you can go back and correct it at a different stage. So the point I just wanted to make for you was that I, that it's possible, maybe, now maybe you're, you're saying that just the speech and putting anything down on paper is really different.

S: Oh yeah.

T: Which it is to a degree, but sometimes if people feel like they're just writing to a friend or they're explaining something to their audience is somebody that's a friend and they're writing out their ideas they can get more out on paper and it flows more smoothly.

S: Like I was writing to a friend recently. And I was telling him about the BART [Bay Area Rapid Transit]. I said I'm crazy about BART. And I was just telling all

these little things and how they're having fights in Daly City and it really came out. So maybe I should pretend that I'm writing to somebody about the M & M's ad.

T: Yeah do. Um, pretend like you and I are, are old buddies and I happen to be in the business now of, producing M & M's and you're the president of another corporation, of an advertising corporation and you're just explaining to me about this ad, and then your editing stage, later, once you get all your ideas out.

S: Yeah.

T: Then go back and look at the grammar, but don't worry about that when you're getting your ideas on the paper.

S: I think that's what I do. I worry too much about the grammar and how it comes out the first time around, and maybe that's the main cause that I worry about that too much, that I don't really worry about how the paper would turn out in the sense of is this the right ideas, will the reader find that she can relate to this ad, can she visualize the picture? (Freedman, 1981, pp. 85–87)

Cee had problems producing ideas as was seen in the brevity of her first essay. In this conference, the teacher attempts to discover why Cee has this problem (she tries to make the first draft perfect and she attends to the mechanics). The teacher suggests pretending that one is talking to a friend as a way of getting ideas down on paper.

There is evidence that this instruction "took," since Cee's compositions are much longer at the end than at the beginning of the quarter. Also, she makes greater changes during revision at the end of the quarter, perhaps because she is no longer trying to make her first draft perfect.

In summary, Cee had unique writing problems that she identified with the help of her teacher. She then found ways to solve these problems and improve her writing as a result. Conferencing allows for individualization within a classroom. Moreover, since students are practicing self-monitoring during conferences, they learn a way to continue improving their writing when the teacher is absent. In the particular case of Cee, she learned that generating ideas and putting them on paper could subsequently be followed by revision and editing. She also seemed to gain an idea about writing to an audience, which will help her planning processes.

Teaching Revision Strategies

As we saw in the section on reviewing, less skilled and younger writers make fewer revisions in their compositions than do more skilled and older writers. In particular, they make fewer meaning-oriented revisions. Because younger writers appear to not revise for meaning, Cohen and Scardamalia (1983) designed a training program to teach young children some revision strategies (see also Bereiter & Scardamalia, 1987).

The children were twenty-one sixth graders who received nine days of instruction (for 45 minutes per day) in revision. Instruction on days 1, 2, 3, 5, and 6 started with having the students write a brief essay on an assigned topic. Then the teacher introduced one or two diagnostic statements to the class as a whole. The entire set of diagnostic statements is shown in Table 13.11. For example, on day 1, one of the diagnostic statements discussed was "Part of the essay does not belong here."

Table 13.11 Diagnostic statements introduced to sixth graders and training day on which each statement was introduced (adapted from Cohen and Scardamalia, 1983).

DAY	DIAGNOSTIC STATEMENT TAUGHT
1	1. Too few ideas.
	2. Part of essay does not belong here.
2	3. Introduction does not explain what the essay is about.
	4. Idea said in a clumsy way.
3	5. Conclusion does not explain ideas.
5	6. Incomplete idea.
	7. Ignored a strong point on other side.
6	8. Weak reason.
	9. Need an example to explain idea.

After introducing each statement, the teacher presented an essay designed to illustrate the problem identified by that statement. The class as a whole judged the essay in light of the statement and suggested revisions. For example, for "Part of the essay does not belong here," students identified a part of the essay that was out of place and then suggested where that part might better fit within the essay. Finally, students were directed to apply the diagnostic statements of that day to the essays they had written at the beginning of class and to revise their essays accordingly.

On day 4, there was a general discussion, and on days 7, 8, and 9 the class as a group practiced revising essays that had been written by some of the students. These practice sessions were directed by students.

The training program was evaluated by having students write and revise an essay before training and then do a second revision of the same essay after training. The essays and revisions I and II were rated globally for quality on a 5-point scale by a person who did not know whether a revision had been produced before or after training. When these ratings were compared statistically, the researchers found that the original essay and revision I (written before training) did not

Table 13.12 Number of changes in revisions I and II (adapted from Cohen and Scardamalia, 1983).

	MECHANICAL	WORD	PHRASE	IDEA	TOTAL
Revision I	4	13	3	5	25
Revision II	8	29	15	47	99

differ in quality. However, revision II (written after training) was better than either the original essay or revision I.

The two revisions were compared for the types of revisions made—mechanical, word, phrase, or idea. Table 13.12 shows that students increased most in their revision of ideas and least in their revision of mechanics. Since the diagnostic statements that formed the core of the training were focused on ideas, it is not surprising that this is where the greatest increase in revisions was found.

Finally, the idea revisions were further divided into those that changed the introduction, clarified an idea, expanded an idea, added more ideas, deleted ideas, or changed the conclusion. Table 13.13 shows the frequency with which each of these subgroups was observed. By far the most frequent revision was the addition of more ideas, a revision that is cued by the diagnostic statement, "Too few ideas."

What is most interesting about these results is that all of these changes are what one would expect if the students used the diagnostic statements to cue their revisions. For example, changes in the introduction would be cued by "Introduction does not explain what the essay is about," and clarification would be cued by "Idea said in a clumsy way."

Taken as a whole, these data suggest that the students learned to recognize problems at the meaning level in their essays and learned ways to remediate these problems. This learning led to higher quality essays. The instruction that facilitated this learning clearly included opportunities for practice and feedback, an important condition for learning procedural knowledge. The instruction probably also included both examples and non-examples of writing problems, and a wide variety of examples. The examples and non-examples probably occurred during the group revision sessions when students proposed that a given part of an essay had a particular problem such as "too few ideas." The teacher presumably gave feedback on the students' proposals. Positive feedback signified an example. Negative feedback signified a non-example. Since the details of this part of training were not described, however, these ideas about examples and non-examples are just speculation. It would be interesting to study more systematically the role of examples and matched non-examples in teaching students to evaluate their own essays.

Table 13.13 Frequency of types of idea change (adapted from Cohen and Scardamalia, 1983).

	INTRODUCE	CLARIFY	EXPAND	ADD	DELETE	CONCLUDE
Revision I	0	1	1	1	0	1
Revision II	3	3	2	28	1	3

SUMMARY AND CONCLUSION

In this chapter, we have seen what is known about cognitive differences between successful and unsuccessful writers. First, successful writers have the goal of communicating meaning. Second, they have enough declarative knowledge to communicate (i.e., they possess conceptual understanding of the topic), and they also possess more schematic knowledge of text structure. Third, they have more of the mechanical and sentence-level cohesion skills under automatic control (i.e., better automated basic skills). Finally, they appear to devote their cognitive resources to planning and reviewing. They apparently possess strategies that result in better organized texts, and they revise for meaning. Thus they are willing to make changes, even drastic changes when such are needed.

What we do not know is precisely how writers' goals determine their strategies. Is each goal automatically associated with a given strategy, or are there a variety of strategies from which the writer selects on the basis of audience, time constraints, and other factors? We also do not know much about the relation between schematic knowledge of text structures and the use of those schemas in generating text. These are just a few of the many questions that remain to be answered through research on writing processes.

ADDITIONAL READINGS

Bereiter, C., & Scardamalia, M. (1987). *The psychology of written comprehension*. Hillsdale, NJ: Lawrence Erlbaum Associates.

Britton, J., Burgess, T., Martin, N., McLoed, A., & Rosen, H. (1975). *The development of writing abilities (11–18)*. London, England: Macmillan.

Dyson, A.H., & Freedman, S.W. (1990). *On teaching writing: A review of the literature* (Occasional Paper No. 20). Berkeley, CA: University of California, National Center for the Study of Writing and Literacy.

Faigley, L., & Skinner, A. (1982). *Writers' processes and writers' knowledge: A review of research* (Tech. Rep. No. 6). Austin, TX: University of Texas, Writing Program Assessment Project.

Fredericksen, C.H., & Dominic, J.F. (Eds.) (1981). *Writing: Process, development, and communication*. Hillsdale, NJ: Lawrence Erlbaum Associates.

Gregg, L., & Steinberg, E. (Eds.) (1980). *Cognitive processes in writing: An interdisciplinary approach*. Hillsdale, NJ: Lawrence Erlbaum Associates.

Hume, A. (1983). Research on the composing process. *Review of Educational Research, 53*, 201–216.

Matsuhashi, A. (Ed.) (1987). *Writing in real time: Modeling production processes*. Norwood, NJ: Ablex.

Nystrand, M. (Ed.) (1982). *What writers know: The language, process, and structure of written discourse*. New York, NY: Academic Press.

Pea, R.D., & Kurland, D.M. (1989). Cognitive technologies for writing. *Review of research in education, 14*, 277–326.

Scardamalia, M., & Bereiter, C. (1985). Written composition. In M. C. Wittrock (Ed.) *Handbook of research on teaching*, Vol. 3.

APPENDIX

CEE'S EARLY WRITING:

A person who believes that time spent in a company or in a trade school will enhance his knowledge in greater than in an university. He will be able to obtain first hand the essentials of his chosen field and learn the ups and downs, the moans and the groans of working in his area. A person is able to learn much quicker what the subject material is about in a work environment. (Freedman & Swanson-Owen, 1983, p. 58)

CEE's LATER WRITING:

SNOOPY

The Peanuts character Snoopy is the best representative for America. Snoopy shows how the American people attitude's are a bit childish. Snoopy's character in the strip tells the public that they are lazy and spoiled.

People in the United States are known to love the easy way of living which is being lazy. People do not particularly like to work but must do so in order to pay for living expenses such as food, clothes, entertainment, and housing payments. If an organization were to do a survey on whether a person likes to work, the company would find that about 66% of the public would prefer to relax and enjoy life as it comes and devote more time to travelling, gardening, visiting friends and relatives, and attending sports events. Snoopy has the same attitudes of the American public because he shows the reader that life should be fun and exciting, not boring like working in a company or going to school. Thus, this is why we never see Snoopy mowing the lawn, fixing his own dinner, or doing homework.

Another reason why Snoopy represents America is that he shows the American people that they are spoiled rotten by throwing tantrums and by not appreciating what they have or what is given to them.

For example, Snoopy throws tantrums when Charlie Brown does not put some type of food decoration such as parsley or croutons in his dinner, and when Charlie Brown does not serve Snoopy his dinner on the patio, otherwise, if Snoopy did not have these "services," he would not eat his dinner until everything is to his satisfaction. Thus, Snoop's attitude reflects the attitude of the people who do not appreciate what they had in the past and what they have now, especially with the current gas crisis. The people did not believe there was a gas crisis until they went to a gas station and found them either closed or with a limited supply. This gas crisis has hit the people right where it hurts the most—in their beloved gas tank.

Hopefully with the current gas crisis, people will use other forms of public transportation such as BART, Muni, AC Transit, Samtrans, and the railroad system and will continue to use these systems when the gas crisis is over. Even if there was no crisis, people are still spoiled by having BART, Muni, and the other public transportations, because other countries and states are not as fortunate as to have these "rides" as the San Francisco-Bay Area. The people who live in San Francisco and the outlying areas take all these services such as public transportations, gas, televisions, for granted until they no longer there to service the people's needs.

In order for a person to get something what he desires, he must appreciate that he is fortunate to have several types of services available to him and that he is lucky to live in the United States as compared to the people in Vietnam who have little or nothing available to them such as public transportation, good food, a house over their head, and gas. As the famous saying goes, "Appreciate what you are lucky to have before it goes out of style or out of order." (Freedman & Swanson-Owens, 1983, pp. 62–63)

Chapter
14

Mathematics

SUMMARY

1. With mathematics, as with other domains, expertise is comprised of **basic skills, conceptual understanding,** and **strategies.**

2. Older students and/or those with more training are faster at retrieving basic number facts and at performing standard algorithms.

3. Older students and/or those with more training have better developed schemas for recognizing various types of math problems. They also have better **number sense** and make greater use of **quantitative concepts.**

4. Conceptual understanding in mathematics influences what is heeded in math problems, what is recalled, and, ultimately, what new ideas are acquired.

5. Students who are more skilled at estimation use the strategies of **reformulation, translation,** and **compensation.**

6. Students who are more skilled at mental calculation use the strategies of **distribution, factoring,** and **direct retrieval** of products of large numbers.

7. Although there is little empirical work on the strategies used in solving novel math problems, scholars agree on a set of strategies that help with problem representation, problem solving, and evaluation of the solution.

8. Extended practice is one form of instruction that helps the development of automated basic skills—such as number fact retrieval—in math.

9. Working with examples of mathematics schemas aids in the formation and refinement of these schemas.

10. Reflective use of math problem-solving strategies assists in accomplishing transfer of these strategies.

Most people agree that reading and writing are essential skills. Fewer agree that competence in mathematics is essential for getting along in our culture. Some would argue that the ubiquitous presence of calculators means that computational skill is unnecessary for daily consumer transactions. Further, they would argue, the need for mathematics beyond the level of blind computation is not pervasive; only a few persons in highly technical engineering and scientific jobs really need it.

The facts, however, refute this argument. Saunders (1980) interviewed persons in 100 job categories representing the entire economic range in our society. He found that knowledge of basic arithmetic was necessary for 62% of these jobs and that knowledge of statistics was essential for 65%. Czepiel and Esty (1980) found that 93% of articles on the front page of *The New York Times* cannot be fully comprehended without fundamental mathematical knowledge. Further, Graziano et al. (1982) found that children's mathematical competence was related to their use of fair play standards: Those who could not divide could not distribute rewards equitably among winners of a game. In general, our knowledge of quantity and space (that is, our knowledge of mathematics) has a pervasive effect on how well we function in society and the number of opportunities open to us.

Unfortunately, American students do not perform as well as one might hope on mathematics tasks. A recent international comparison of mathematics ability in twenty countries showed that American eighth grade students were slightly above the international average on calculation skills, but well below the international average on problem solving (McKnight et al., 1987). This study also found that the performance of American eighth graders had declined since 1964, especially on comprehension and application items. Twelfth grade American students (except for a minority of the most advanced students who were taking calculus classes) also performed well below the international average for twelfth graders. The causes of these differences include differences in the populations of children who attend school and were tested, national differences in the value placed on schooling, differences in the curriculum emphasis on various aspects of mathematics, and differences in instructional strategies. As educators, we have more direct influence over curriculum and instruction than we do over other causes of America's relatively low mathematics achievement. It is a good bet that if curriculum and instruction are improved student competence in mathematics will improve also.

It is well documented that elementary school children spend much less time engaged in arithmetic tasks than they do engaged in reading tasks (Fisher et al., 1978). Elementary school teachers may be less comfortable with mathematics than with reading and may therefore avoid teaching it. Or it may be that elementary school administrators, or even district-wide policy-makers dictate that only a relatively small amount of time be spent on mathematics instruction. For teachers who are uncomfortable with mathematics, however, it might be useful to identify the source of discomfort. Are they uncomfortable because they do not understand certain topics in mathematics themselves? If so, they should seek further training or at least explanations from colleagues who do understand these topics. Are they uncomfortable because they have difficulty communicating mathematics concepts to students? If so, they should seek the reasons for students' difficulties. As one of us has taught elementary school, we do not mean to single out elementary school teachers as villains. Many secondary school teachers of mathematics also feel uncomfortable with math because they were trained in other disciplines. Also, sometimes those who are trained in mathematics feel most frustrated in their attempts to teach it.

In this chapter we will describe some information-processing analyses of mathematical competence. For readers who lack confidence in their own mathematical knowledge, these examples may give you fresh insights into your own cognitive processes. Readers who are discouraged in attempts to teach mathematics may gain new ideas here about students' cognitive processes. Readers who are not primarily involved in teaching mathematics should be stimulated to think more about the commonalities between mathematics competence and competence in other domains.

TYPES OF MATHEMATICS KNOWLEDGE

With mathematics, as with knowledge in other domains, research has uncovered three varieties of knowledge that mutually support one another: automated skills, conceptual understanding, and strategies. Table 14.1 shows problems that emphasize each of these varieties. Problem (a) (assuming that a student has learned and practiced subtraction with borrowing) can be solved by automatically

Table 14.1 Math problems that draw on different varieties of knowledge. Problem (a) draws on the basic skill of subtraction. Problem (b), while using subtraction, draws more centrally on conceptual understanding. Problem (c), if a novel problem, draws on strategies for solving novel problems—such as trying a simpler case.

a. $\begin{array}{r} 72 \\ -13 \end{array}$

b. Lincoln High played and won a basketball game against Washington High. On the same night, Jefferson High played and won a basketball game against Madison High. The next day, the captains of the two winning teams (Lincoln and Jefferson) argued about which team had won by more. It turned out that Jefferson had won by 8 more points than Lincoln had won by. Lincoln scored 65 points. Their opponent, Washington, scored 60 points. Jefferson scored 72 points. How many points did their opponent, Madison, score?

c. There were 9 people in a bowling league. If each person played against every other person once, how many games were played.

moving from one step to the next in the subtraction algorithm—such as starting with the right hand column, subtracting the subtrahend from the minuend in this column, etc. Problem (b) involves this same subtraction problem, but also draws on the individual's conceptual understanding. First, the individual needs some understanding of basketball, but, more importantly, he must understand the idea of comparing differences. Without such understanding, it is difficult for a student to solve this problem (Thompson, 1990). Finally, problem (c) (assuming that the individual is unfamiliar with rules of combinations) draws heavily on strategies for its solution. For example, a solver may use a listing strategy, writing down nine names, pairing them each with every other name, and counting. Alternatively, she may use the strategy of trying a simpler case—say of three people in a bowling league—to see how this problem is solved first.

Notice that the variety of knowledge that is central for the solution of each of these problems depends on the individual's prior knowledge. If a child has not learned a subtraction algorithm, then answering problem (a) would require drawing on conceptual understanding and/or strategies. For problem (b), a student who lacks conceptual understanding of comparison of differences might use a "guess and check" strategy initially and then later develop a better conceptual understanding of the problem. Problem (c), for an individual with a good understanding of combinatorial theory, would not require the use of general problem-solving strategies.

Also notice how the three varieties of knowledge interact in many different ways. To take just one way, a lack of automaticity of basic skills could disrupt problem solving in (b) or (c) because the solver might loose track of her goals or simply become impatient.

In this chapter, we will illustrate each of these types of mathematics knowledge and their interactions. In the final section, we will describe instruction that is focused on improvement in each type of knowledge.

BASIC SKILLS

As with basic skills in other domains, these skills are processes that occur the same way in a variety of contexts and hence are useful to automate. Not being mathematics educators, we will not attempt to list here all of the skills that might be considered basic to various specialties within math. Rather, we will focus on a couple of areas that have been well researched in which automated basic skills distinguish more and less skilled individuals.

Number Facts

The phrase "number facts" refers to those frequently used sums, differences, and products that students are expected to commit to memory (e.g., $4 + 3 = 7$; $7 \times 8 = 56$). It may seem odd that we classify number facts as automated basic skills because they are not skills in the sense of having multiple steps. However, like other automated basic skills, they are most useful when they are retrieved so fast that they seem automatic, which only happens with a good deal of practice. Thus number facts have the same function in problem solving as do other automated basic skills and become automatic in the same way— through practice.

In studies of the development of knowledge of simple addition facts, many studies have shown that young children start by **constructing** these facts rather than **retrieving** them (Groen & Parkman, 1972; Houlihan & Ginsburg, 1981). For example, when a preschooler is asked to add three and five, she may first count out five (using fingers or beans), then three, and finally count all. A kindergartener or first grader may use a slightly more efficient counting strategy called "counting from the maximum." In this strategy, children start with the larger number in the problem and count on from there by the smaller number in the problem to reach the answer. For very familiar facts like $2 + 2$, they may retrieve the answer rather than count. Increasingly, over the early elementary grades, children use counting strategies less and retrieval more. For example, Houlihan and Ginsberg found that second graders retrieve single-digit addition facts 29% of the time, while first graders retrieve them only 4% of the time.

Siegler (1988) studied number fact retrieval differences among first graders. He worked individually with each child, showing

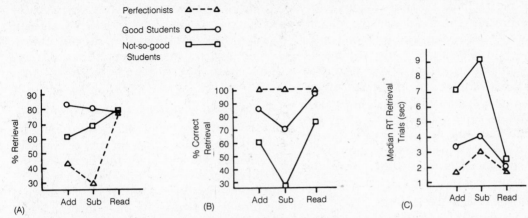

Figure 14.1 The percent of time using retrieval (as opposed to counting) to get addition and subtraction facts (part A), the percent correct retrieval (part B), and the median retrieval speed in seconds (part C), for perfectionists, good students, and not-so-good students (adapted from Siegler, 1988).

him one problem at a time. The sessions were videotaped with a device that printed digital times at the bottom of the taped scene so that retrieval latencies could be determined. In analyzing these tapes, Siegler (1988) discovered three distinct subgroups that he labelled "perfectionists," "good students," and "not-so-good students." Perfectionists tended to use counting strategies to get answers unless they were extremely confident that they could retrieve an answer correctly. Good students were more willing to risk an occasional error to

gain speed by retrieving rather than counting. Not-so-good students also preferred the speedier retrieval over the slow counting process, but, unlike good students, the answers they retrieved were frequently wrong. These results are shown in Figure 14.1.

Siegler (1988) looked at the performance of these groups on a standardized test of mathematics achievement. Table 14.2 shows the results. As you can see, while the perfectionists and good students did not differ much on national percentiles, both groups did sub-

Table 14.2 Achievement test percentile scores of perfectionists, good students, and not-so-good students (adapted from Siegler, 1988).

MEASURE	PERFECTIONIST	GOOD	NOT-SO-GOOD
Total Math	86	81	37
Math Computation	84	68	22
Math Problem Solving	80	80	38

stantially better than the not-so-good students. For instance, in mathematics problem solving, both perfectionists and good students were at the 80th percentile, while not-so-good students were only at the 38th percentile. While there are probably many reasons for the lower achievement of not-so-good students, their inability to correctly retrieve math facts quickly may be one. Just as the slow decoding of words can disrupt comprehension processes in reading, the slow retrieval of number facts can disrupt problem-solving processes in math.

Algorithms

In the standard mathematics curriculum, students learn a variety of **algorithms** for achieving certain goals. An algorithm is a sequence of steps that, if performed correctly, will achieve a desired outcome with 100% accuracy. There are algorithms for addition, subtraction, multiplication, and division of whole numbers and fractions, algorithms for transforming equations in algebra, and so on. Practicing these algorithms so that they can be performed quickly frees the problem solver to attend to the conceptual basis of the problem. Thus, algorithms are best stored in memory as procedural knowledge.

You may recall from the chapter on the acquisition of procedural knowledge (Chapter 9) that there are three stages of acquisition: cognitive, associative, and autonomous. During the cognitive stage, the learner is guiding the execution of a procedure by using a declarative representation. Small productions are being created to represent the skill in procedural form. During the associative stage, errors in the procedural representation of the skill are corrected and larger productions are **composed** from smaller ones. Finally, during the autonomous stage, the skill comes to be performed automatically.

In this section, we will describe two stud-

ies of math algorithms that show learners during the cognitive and associative stages of learning. The first study focuses on identification of incorrect steps in procedures; the second focuses on inefficient procedures.

Incorrect Steps in Subtraction Algorithms. Students seem to be quite good at coming up with incorrect procedures for subtraction with borrowing. For example, the errors on the problems shown in Table 14.3 suggest an incorrect procedure. Stop reading here and see if you can figure out what (incorrect) rule the student is using.

If you hypothesized that the student was subtracting the smallest from the largest number in each column, *independent* of whether the number was on the top or on the bottom, you are probably right. In the first problem, for example, the student correctly subtracts 3 (bottom) from 4 (top) to get 1. Then he *incorrectly* subtracts 3 (top) from 5 (bottom) to get 2. Finally, 1 (bottom) is correctly subtracted from 2 (top) to get 1.

J.S. Brown and R. Burton (1978) found that in a sample of 1325 students in the fourth, fifth, and sixth grades, 54 students (about 4%) consistently used this incorrect procedure. Another 4% used an incorrect rule when borrowing from zero. When confronted with a problem such as 205 − 32, these students

Table 14.3 A hypothetical student's answers to some subtraction problems. The mistakes made are due to the student's use of an incorrect rule.

234 − 153	387 − 124	462 − 234
121	263	232
615 − 351	723 − 258	493 − 289
344	535	216

changed the 0 to 9, but then failed to reduce the number in the next column to the left:

$$\begin{array}{r} 9 \\ 2\cancel{0}5 \\ -\ \ 32 \\ \hline 263 \end{array}$$

Table 14.4 shows fourteen of the incorrect rules discovered by Brown and Burton in their study of children's errors on subtraction problems.

Brown and Burton (1978) refer to students' incorrect rules as "bugs," a term that comes from computer programming. In developing a program, after the initial program is written, it often needs to be "debugged" before it will run. Debugging involves systematically finding the incorrect part of the program code. Brown and Burton believe that if students could learn to think of their errors as being due to some incorrect or incomplete program statement, they could become much more independent in learning new procedures. As they put it, students would begin to "see their own faulty behavior not as being a sign of their stupidity, but as a source of data from which they can understand their own errors" (p. 172).

In order to discover the bugs in children's subtraction procedures, Brown and Burton (1978) first developed a model of competence in subtraction. Their model is a set of interrelated procedures, shown in Figure 14.2. Procedures higher in the figure are composed of procedures lower in the figure. For example, on the left, the SET-UP procedure, which sets up the problems, is composed of two smaller procedures: WRITE TOP (write the top number) and WRITE BOTTOM (write the bottom number). Also, some of the smaller procedures are used by more than one larger procedure. For example, the procedure of focusing on the top digit in a specified column (GET TOP DIGIT) is used by the procedure for deciding if borrowing is needed (BORROW NEEDED) and also by the actual performance of borrowing (DO BORROW). In other words, the skill of focusing on the top digit is a lower-level skill that is integrated into more than one higher-level (more complex) skill.

This set of procedures was translated into a computer program that was capable of performing subtraction problems with 100% accuracy. Then various changes were made in the program in order to mimic the errors made by children. If the altered program made the same pattern of errors as a child made, then it was a good bet that the child had in mind the same incorrect rule as had been written into the program.

This method of diagnosing the reason for errors by matching them with errors that would be produced by a hypothesized underlying faulty procedure may seem to be too detailed and therefore too time-consuming for teachers. However, if classroom microcomputers do the detailed work in the future, then analyses such as these can become a regular part of teaching. A teacher could use diagnostic information produced by a computer analysis of student errors to select the specific remedial instruction needed for a particular student. Some of the waste in education comes from not being able to match instruction to student capabilities. Cognitive analyses such as the one performed by Brown and Burton (1978) on subtraction provide a map for more specific diagnosis of students' faulty procedures and therefore pave the way for more efficient instruction.

Some would criticize the Brown and Burton work because it focuses on procedural knowledge seemingly devoid of a conceptual basis. Such critics would argue that if children really understood the conceptual basis of the decimal system they would not make nonsensical errors. For instance, the children who neglect to reduce the number of elements in the column from which they borrowed are behaving as if they do not understand what it

Table 14.4 Incorrect procedures used by students in solving subtraction problems (from Brown and Burton, 1978).

	THE 14 MOST FREQUENTLY OCCURRING BUGS IN A GROUP OF 1325 STUDENTS

57 students used: BORROW/FROM/ZERO (103 − 45 = 158)

When borrowing from a column whose top digit is 0, the student writes 9, but does not continue borrowing from the column to the left of the 0.

54 students used: SMALLER/FROM/LARGER (253 − 118 = 145)

The student subtracts the smaller digit in a column from the larger digit regardless of which one is on top.

50 students used: BORROW/FROM/ZERO and LEFT/TEN/OK (803 − 508 = 395)

The student changes 0 to 9 without further borrowing unless the 0 is part of a 10 in the left part of the number.

34 students used: DIFF/0 − $N = N$ and MOVE/OVER/ZERO/BORROW

Whenever the top digit in a column is 0, the student writes the bottom digit in the answer, i.e., $0 − N = N$. When the student needs to borrow from a column whose top digit is 0, he skips that column and borrows from the next one.

14 students used: DIFF/0 − $N = N$ and STOPS/BORROW/AT/ZERO

Whenever the top digit in a column is 0, the student writes the bottom digit in the answer; i.e., $0 − N = N$. The student borrows from zero incorrectly. He does not subtract 1 from the 0 although he adds 10 correctly to the top digit of the current column.

13 students used: SMALLER/FROM/LARGER and $0 − N = 0$ (203 − 98 = 205)

The student subtracts the smaller digit in each column from the larger digit regardless of which one is on top. The exception is that when the top digit is 0, a 0 is written as the answer for that column; i.e., $0 − N = 0$.

12 students used: DIFF/0 − $N = 0$ and MOVE/OVER/ZERO/BORROW

Whenever the top digit in a column is 0, the student writes 0 in the answer; i.e., $0 − N = 0$. When the student needs to borrow from a column whose top digit is 0, he skips that column and borrows from the next one.

11 students used: BORROW/FROM/ZERO and DIFF/$N − 0 = 0$

When borrowing from a column whose top digit is 0, the student writes 9, but does not continue borrowing from the column to the left of the 0. Whenever the bottom digit in a column is 0, the student writes 0 in the answer; i.e., $N − 0 = 0$.

10 students used: DIFF/0 − $N = 0$ and $N − 0 = 0$ (302 − 192 = 290)

The student writes 0 in the answer when either the top or the bottom digit is 0.

10 students used: BORROW/FROM/ZERO and DIFF/0 − $N = N$

When borrowing from a column whose top digit is 0, the student writes 9, but does not continue borrowing from the column to the left of the 0. Whenever the top digit in a column is 0, the student writes the bottom digit in the answer; i.e., $0 − N = N$.

10 students used: MOVE/OVER/ZERO/BORROW (304 − 75 = 139)

When the student needs to borrow from a column whose top digit is 0, he skips that column and borrows from the next one.

10 students used: DIFF/$N − 0 = 0$ (403 − 208 = 105)

Whenever the bottom digit in a column is 0, the student writes 0 in the answer; i.e., $N − 0 = 0$.

10 students used: DIFF/0 − $N = N$ (140 − 21 = 121)

Whenever the top digit in a column is 0, the student writes the bottom digit in the answer; i.e., $0 − N = N$.

9 students used: DIFF/0 − $N = N$ and LEFT/TEN/OK (908 − 395 = 693)

When there is a 0 on top, the student writes the bottom digit in the answer. The exception is when the 0 is part of 10 in the left columns of the top number.

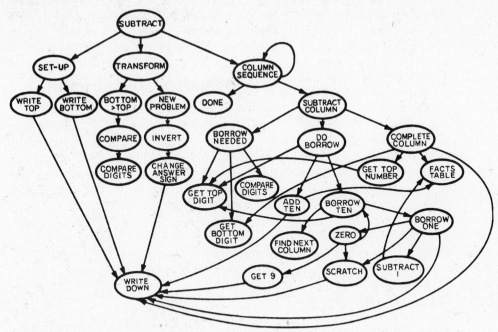

Figure 14.2 A procedural network for subtraction (from Brown and Burton, 1978).

means to borrow within a decimal system. People who argue this way tend to support the idea of radically reforming mathematics instruction to be much more discovery oriented and to emphasize conceptual understanding in every lessson.

A counterargument is that when students correct the "bugs" in their algorithms, there is an opportunity for the teacher (or computer) to point out the conceptual basis of the error. Recall from the chapter on schema acquisition (Chapter 8) that making errors frequently sets the stage for schema refinement. Thus, even though procedural knowledge acquisition may be the focus of a particular lesson, the acquisition of declarative knowledge may be promoted as well. At present, there is simply not enough research of large-scale, longitudinal curriculum projects to state with any certainty what relative mix of conceptual and procedural knowledge instruction is best. We see the two as so interactive that we favor the

view that both are important, as is the third variety of knowledge—strategies.

Inefficient Steps in Linear Algebra. One hallmark of expertise is speed, and one way to speed up skill execution is to practice procedures to the point that several small productions are combined or "composed" into a larger production. If having more composed procedures is one element of faster performance, then experts should show evidence of having more such procedures than novices have. Lewis (1981) reasoned that the number of steps people write down when doing math computations is a clue to the degree to which productions are composed. More steps suggests more small productions with each entity written down being part of the condition required by the next production. He used the domain of solving linear equations to study the question of whether experts write down fewer steps than do novices. His experts were five mathematicians who worked at an IBM research lab, and his novices were ten university students who performed rather poorly on a pretest of skill in solving linear equations.

Lewis gave both groups fourteen new problems to solve and then counted the number of written steps in the correct solutions. The novices wrote down an average of 3.7 steps per correct solution, whereas the experts wrote down an average of 2.7 steps. Lewis took this as evidence that the experts have developed composed procedures in which certain intermediate results never need to be represented in working memory. Of course, the difference in the number of steps written down might reflect differences in WM capacity; mathematicians may have a larger capacity than university students and, therefore, even if both groups are using the same procedures, the mathematicians may have less need to write down intermediate results. Since there is little evidence to support the idea of large differences in absolute working memory capacity, the differences found by Lewis (1981) probably reflect differences in the degree of composition of procedural knowledge.

Summary

In everyday mathematics problem solving it is useful to have some basic skills that are correct and can be performed quickly. We have touched on only a few of these basic skills, including retrieval of number facts, performance of subtraction with borrowing, and solving linear equations. The research we have described demonstrates that better students retrieve number facts faster, possibly allowing them to devote more time and attention to higher-level problem-solving activity. We have also shown how procedural bugs can be identified, smoothing the way for correction of errors. Finally, we have seen that experts' basic skills appear to be stored in

larger productions than are novices', allowing them to be executed faster and with less recourse to writing down intermediate steps.

CONCEPTUAL UNDERSTANDING

With mathematics, as with reading and writing, research shows that better problem solvers have better conceptual understanding (i.e., declarative knowledge) of the domain. In this section, we will describe several studies that demonstrate this point. We will also describe recent work on some important areas of conceptual understanding within mathematics and will review the role that conceptual understanding plays in guiding attention, influencing memory, and affecting the course of learning.

Differences in Conceptual Understanding of Experts and Novices

How does one measure conceptual understanding? You may recall from the chapter on cognitive psychology methods (Chapter 2) that there are a variety of ways to get at conceptual understanding, including analysis of patterns of recall of information and analysis of the ways people group problems together. One of the earliest techniques used for inferring conceptual understanding relied on finding how strongly certain concept labels are associated for a given person—for example, by having her free-associate to the concept label. Try this on yourself by writing down now the first five words that come to your mind when you read *add*. Then write down the first five words that come to your mind when you read *subtract*. Finally, write down the first five words that come to your mind when you read *exponent*.

Figure 14.3 shows Ellen's responses to those three words. Notice that *add* and *subtract* both caused her to think of the other, but neither caused her to think of *exponent*. Also,

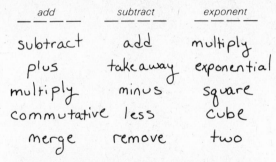

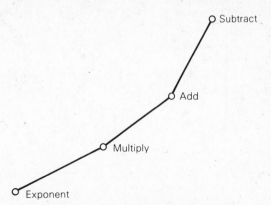

Figure 14.3 Ellen's free associations for *add*, *subtract*, and *multiply*. Concepts whose labels share associations (e.g., *add* and *exponent* share *multiply*) are thought to be closer in memory than concepts whose labels do not share any associations (e.g., *subtract* and *exponent* have no common associations).

Figure 14.4 The arrangement of four mathematical concepts in mental space.

she did not think of *add* or *subtract* in response to *exponent*. With responses such as these from several individuals, psychologists use various statistical techniques to determine how close these words (and, by inference, the concepts to which they refer) are in mental space.

Essentially, the statistical techniques involve counting the frequency with which concept labels of interest are grouped or share some third linking concept label. In Figure 14.3, the lists headed by *add* and *subtract* share two words (*add*, *subtract*), those headed by *add* and *exponent* share one word (*multiply*), and those headed by *subtract* and *exponent* share no words. Thus, the concepts of *add* and *subtract* are said to be closer together in Ellen's mental space than the concepts of *add* and *exponent*, which in turn are closer together than the concepts of *subtract* and *exponent*. A map of these relationships is shown in Figure 14.4. Notice that *add* and *subtract* are directly linked to each other because they cued each other's recall. *Add* and *exponent*, on the other hand, are linked only indirectly through the concept of *multiply* because they did not cue each other's recall, but both cued the recall of *multiply*. In this manner, conceptual understand-

ing is inferred from subjects' associations or groupings of concept labels.

Shavelson, who did some of the early work in developing ways to measure conceptual understanding, used this word-association technique to examine conceptual understanding of eighth graders for the domain of probability. Geeslin and Shavelson (1975a) used the concept labels *probability*, *event*, *independent*, *zero*, *interaction*, *trial*, *experiment*, *mutually exclusive*, and *outcome*. Each student generated associations to these labels three times: immediately before a unit of mathematics instruction (pretest), immediately after the unit (posttest), and two weeks later (retention test). A randomly selected half of the students studied a programmed unit on probability (experimental group), whereas the other half studied a programmed unit on prime numbers (control group). Geeslin and Shavelson predicted that, after instruction, the students who studied the probability unit would arrange probability concepts in their minds in a manner similar to the arrangement reflected in the programmed unit, whereas the other students would not.

The results confirmed their prediction. Figure 14.5 shows the average distance between the organization of concepts found in

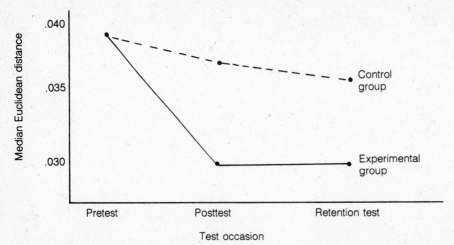

Figure 14.5 Median distances between students' knowledge organization and the organization of the content of instruction (from Geeslin and Shavelson, 1975a).

the instructional material and the organization inferred from the students' responses on the free-association test. On the pretest, both groups showed a similar distance (.04) between their knowledge organization and the content organization. However, on both the posttest and retention test, the experimental group's organizations were significantly closer to the content organization than were the control group's.

The researchers also gave the students a 35-item achievement test on probability concepts and problems. Table 14.5 shows the performance of the two groups on this test. On the pretest, both groups performed equally poorly, but the experimental group performed much better than the control group on the posttest and retention test. Thus the "experts" in probability (those who performed well on the achievement test) had a

Table 14.5 Means and standard deviations of scores on achievement tests for students with different knowledge organization (from Geeslin and Shavelson, 1975a).

TREATMENT GROUP	PRETEST	POSTTEST	RETENTION TEST
Experimental	$\overline{X} = 3.65$ $\sigma = 2.45$ $n = 43$	$\overline{X} = 15.54$ $\sigma = 5.74$ $n = 41$	$\overline{X} = 16.21$ $\sigma = 6.32$ $n = 43$
Control	$\overline{X} = 3.00$ $\sigma = 1.90$ $n = 42$	$\overline{X} = 3.73$ $\sigma = 2.46$ $n = 40$	$\overline{X} = 4.16$ $\sigma = 3.06$ $n = 43$

conceptual understanding different from the "novices" (those who did not perform well on the achievement test). Geeslin and Shavelson (1975b) replicated this study using high school students and obtained similar results.

Middle School Word Problems. Researchers have also studied conceptual understanding of word problems. Silver (1981), for example, studied how seventh graders grouped sixteen word problems that independently varied on content and on the process used to solve the problem. For instance, the following two problems have similar content (farming) but are solved using different processes:

14.1. A farmer is counting the hens and rabbits in his barnyard. He counts a total of 50 heads and 140 feet. How many hens and how many rabbits does the farmer have?

14.2. A farmer is counting the hens and rabbits in his barnyard. He counts 6 coops with 4 hens each, 2 coops with 3 hens each, 5 cages with 6 rabbits each, and 3 cages with 4 rabbits each. How many hens and how many rabbits does the farmer have?

Take a minute to try to solve these two problems. Did you use the same procedures? The solutions are given at the end of the chapter.

Another problem used by Silver (1981) was:

14.3. Bill has a collection of 20 coins that consists entirely of dimes and quarters. If the collection is worth $4.10, how many of each kind of coin are in the collection?

Clearly, this problem has different content from problems 14.1 and 14.2. However, it is solved using the same procedures used to solve problem 14.1.

Silver (1981) asked students to sort sixteen such problems into groups that were "mathematically related." He then asked them to solve twelve of the problems they had sorted. On the basis of their problem-solving performance, he divided the students into good, average, and poor problem solvers. He was most interested in whether or not students sorted problems differently (by content or process) at different levels of expertise in word problems.

Table 14.6 shows the results. If a student is categorizing completely on the basis of one dimension or the other, his problem-sorting score for that dimension would be 24. As you can see, although neither group sorted completely on one dimension, the good problem solvers were more likely to sort by process, whereas the poor problem solvers were more likely to sort by content. These results suggest that the good problem solvers' conceptual understanding of the problems was better than the poor problem solvers'. Research by L. Sowder confirms this interpretation (see Sowder, 1988).

Elementary School Word Problems. Elementary school word problems are perhaps the area of math that has been studied most extensively from a cognitive perspective. Starting with early work on this topic, which demonstrated different difficulty levels for different types of word problems (Carpenter & Moser,

Table 14.6 Categorization of word problems by good, average, and poor problem solvers (adapted from Silver, 1981).

	DIMENSION USED IN SORTING	
	PROCESS	CONTENT
Good problem solver	17.8	0.6
Average problem solver	12.0	3.4
Poor problem solver	6.3	8.9

1982), this work continued with attempts to develop cognitive models to account for the different difficulty levels (cf., Riley, Greeno, & Heller, 1983; Briars & Larkin, 1984; Cummins, Kintsch, Reusser, & Weimer, 1988), and recently with studies that measure the contribution of conceptual understanding to problem difficulty (cf., Dean & Malik, 1986; Morales, Shute & Pelligrino, 1985).

In Table 14.7 you will find examples of the types of word problems that have been studied. They are listed in order of difficulty with *change* problems being easiest, followed by *equalize* problems, followed by *combine* problems, and finally, *compare* problems, which are the most difficult for children to solve. Change problems describe situations in which there is a change in quantity; equalize problems describe situations in which the goal is to equalize quantities; combine problems involve two subsets that are combined to form a superset. Finally, compare problems involve comparing quantities in two sets. Take a moment now to read the examples in Table 14.7 to see if you can explain why change problems are generally easier than compare problems.

The explanations proposed by cognitive psychologists include a lack of requisite procedural and conceptual knowledge (Riley et al., 1983; Briars & Larkin, 1984) and difficulty understanding the linguistic constructions (Cummins, et al. 1988). There is general agreement, however, that developing conceptual understanding plays a central role in the variation in difficulty. The types of understanding that appear to be important include the understanding of part-whole relationships, understanding that processes can be reversed, and possession of problem schemas.

Morales et al. attempted to assess children's problem schemas independent of their problem-solving behavior in order to determine whether or not the two were related. They asked third, fifth, and sixth graders to solve analogs of the sixteen word problems shown in Table 14.7. Three months later the same children sorted the sixteen problems into groups that made sense to them. When the sorting was completed, the researchers asked the children to explain why they had grouped problems as they did.

Table 14.8 shows the proportion of problems correctly answered by grade and by problem type. Within each grade, the easiest problems were Change 1 and 2 (CH1 and CH2) and Equalize 1 (EQ1) and the most difficult problems were Compare 5 and 6 (CP5 and CP6). Also, overall the fifth and sixth graders did better than the third graders. These data are similar to those obtained by others (e.g., Riley et al., 1983).

The new data contributed by Morales et al. (1985) was their analysis of how the children sorted problems. Using cluster analysis, Morales et al. found the pattern of clusters shown in Figure 14.6 (p. 363). In the top panel of that figure, you can see that both grade levels group the change problems (CH1 through CH6) together, suggesting that both have adequate conceptual understanding of change problems. In contrast, the middle panel in that figure shows quite different groupings by third and fifth and sixth graders. Whereas the fifth and sixth graders group the two equalize problems (EQ1 and EQ2) together, the third graders do not. Also, the fifth and sixth graders place the compare problems 1 and 2 (CP1 and CP2) closer together than do the third graders. At a higher level, the fifth and sixth graders group the two equalize problems together with the two easiest compare problems (CP1 and CP2). If you read over these four problems in Table 14.7, you will probably sense that they are quite similar conceptually. Third graders, however, appear not to make this conceptual grouping. Rather, they group together in the middle panel five problems that have a more superficial characteristic in common. Specifically, they all have the same form: X has n objects, Y has m objects.

Table 14.7 Arithmetic word problems in order of increasing difficulty (from Morales et al., 1985).

CHANGE (CH)

Result unknown

1. Pete had 7 marbles
   Then Sam gave him 5 more marbles.
   How many marbles does Pete have now?

2. Terry had 12 marbles.
   Then she gave 4 marbles to Pat.
   How many marbles does Terry have now?

Change Unknown

3. Allen had 9 marbles.
   Then Ken gave him some more marbles.
   Now Allen has 13 marbles.
   How many marbles did Ken give him?

4. Janet had 14 marbles.
   Then she gave some marbles to Sue.
   Now Janet has 6 marbles.
   How many marbles did she give to Sue?

Start Unknown

5. Emily had some marbles.
   Then Ana gave her 8 more marbles.
   Now Emily has 14 marbles.
   How many marbles did Emily have in the beginning?

6. David had some marbles.
   Then he gave 6 marbles to Jim.
   Now David has 9 marbles.
   How many marbles did Divaid have in the beginning?

EQUALIZE (EQ)

1. Rose has 7 marbles.
   Dora has 10 marbles.
   How many marbles must Rose get to have as many as Dora?

2. Nancy has 6 marbles.
   Eve has 3 marbles.
   How many marbles does Nancy need to give away to have as many as Eve?

COMBINE (CB)

Total Set Unknown

1. Fred has 7 marbles.
   John has 5 marbles.
   How many marbles do they have altogether?

Subset Unknown

2. Eddie and Roy have 11 marbles altogether.
   Eddie has 4 marbles.
   How many marbles does Roy have?

COMPARE (CP)

Difference Unknown

1. Jane has 12 marbles.
   Mary has 7 marbles.
   How many marbles does Jane have more than Mary?

2. Jack has 11 marbles.
   Luis has 3 marbles.
   How many marbles does Luis have less than Jack?

Compared Quantity Unknown

3. Bill has 9 marbles.
   James had 7 more marbles than Bill.
   How many marbles does James have?

4. Joe has 12 marbles.
   Tom has 3 marbles less than Joe.
   How many marbles does Bob have?

Referent Unknown

5. Jerry has 10 marbles.
   He has 4 more marbles than Bob.
   How many marbles does Bob have?

6. Tony has 8 marbles.
   He has 5 marbles less than Henry.
   How many marbles does Henry have?

Table 14.8 Proportion of students getting the correct solution as a function of grade level and type of problem (adapted from Morales et al., 1985).

		PROPORTION CORRECT	
		GRADE 3	GRADE 5/6
Change	1 & 2	.63	.88
	3 & 4	.51	.78
	5 & 6	.49	.67
Equalize	1 & 2	.51	.92
Combine	1*	.87	.94
	2	.43	.72
Compare	1 & 2	.54	.86
	3 & 4	.52	.74
	5 & 6	.36	.60

*No significant grade difference ($p > .05$)

Thus, the results show that third graders are less good at solving these types of word problems and also have a weaker conceptual understanding of such problems. The third graders seem to lack adequate problem schemas for equalize, combine, and compare problems.

How might instruction be changed to encourage the development of such schemas? Recall from the chapter about schema acquisition (Chapter 8) that exposure to examples of the schema encourages schema formation, while schema refinement is supported by pairing examples and matched non-examples. One can imagine giving math lessons in which students are not asked to *solve* word problems, but simply to *classify* them. This would focus their attention on the schema rather than on solution procedures (see Sweller & Cooper, 1985, for a similar idea). If this is done, attention should be paid to the sequencing of problems so that the similarity across problems is obvious during the early stages of learning. Later, more variety can be added to encourage formation of an adequately general schema.

Another way to encourage schema formation might be to have small groups of children work on problems together. Yackel, Cobb, & Wood (1991) give some nice examples of schema formation and refinement that occurred in a second grade classroom while using small group problem solving. Schema formation and refinement may occur when children ask each other to explain why they are solving something a certain way. For instance one child may have overlooked a critical attribute that another child can point out. Small group work does not always work well, however. Webb (1991) describes desirable behavior in cooperative learning groups.

Even within the current ways of teaching, giving students exposure to a wider variety of problems and problem types may be beneficial. Stigler, Fuson, Ham, & Kim (1986) found that Russian texts are much more even-handed than American texts in asking students to solve problems of the types shown in Table 14.7, while American texts present the easier problems within each type much more frequently than the harder ones. (Russians, by the way, are noted for their strong mathematics curriculum).

As you can see, there are many ways that conceptual understanding can be encouraged. Perhaps you will try some. Fundamental to this effort, however, is knowledge of what conceptual areas are crucial for mathematics problem solving. We turn to some of these areas now.

Important Areas of Conceptual Understanding within Mathematics

You have just read evidence showing that schemas for different types of math problems are one type of conceptual understanding that is important for expertise in mathematics. Recently, there has been some interesting work on two conceptual areas that cut across problem types—**number sense** (J. Sowder, in

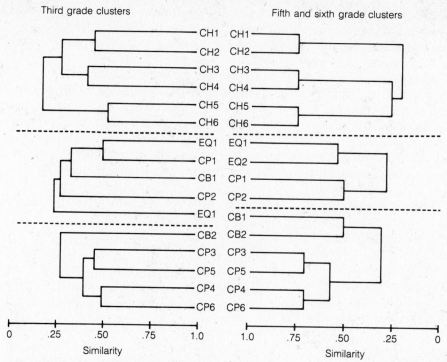

Third grade clusters   Fifth and sixth grade clusters

Figure 14.6 Hierarchical cluster analysis results for sorting patterns of third, fifth and sixth graders (from Morales et al., 1985).

press) and **quantitative concepts** (Thompson, In Press a). In this section, we will describe what is known about these conceptual areas.

Number Sense. Number sense refers to the idea of making numbers and number systems meaningful. A child who wishes to divide 36 cents among 6 people and who thinks of 36 cents as 6 nickels and 6 pennies possesses a meaningful understanding of numbers as used in money systems. A person who thinks of 62 as five tens and 12 ones shows number sense and can use this idea to subtract 38 from 62 in her head. Someone who does not show this facility at regrouping numbers would probably have to write down the 62 − 38 subtraction problem and use borrowing.

According to the National Council of Teachers of Mathematic's standards (1989),

"children with good number sense (1) have well-understood number meanings, (2) have developed multiple relationships among numbers, (3) recognize the relative magnitudes of numbers, (4) know the relative effect of operating on numbers, and (5) develop referents for measures of common objects and situations in their environment." Clearly, number sense is not one schema or one concept, but a whole set of schemas or concepts that develop over years of experience with numbers. Number sense is considered to be extremely important because it forms much of the conceptual basis for reasoning about quantities. As we will see in the section on strategies, number sense is crucial for flexible estimation strategies.

There is currently some concern about number sense among American mathematics teachers because number sense, while being so crucial for conceptual understanding in mathematics, is not taught much in standard math curricula (J. Sowder, in press). Moreover, developmental studies of number sense show that a substantial proportion of children do not have much number sense. For example, J. Sowder asked fourth and sixth graders how many ten-dollar bills could be acquired from $378.00. Only 26% of the fourth graders and 53% of the sixth graders could answer this question correctly. When she asked them how many boxes of 100 candy bars could be packed from 48,638 candy bars, only 2% of fourth graders and 9% of sixth graders could answer her correctly! Sowder and Wheeler (1987) asked students to identify the larger of 5/6 and 5/9. The success rate was 10%, 19%, and 37%, respectively, for fourth, sixth, and eighth graders. Also in that study, the researchers told students that a headline read "Michael Jackson concert a sellout!" and asked them to choose which number of attendees made sense—65,300, 40,000, or 5,000,000. Only 38% of fourth graders chose 40,000 as the most sensible answer. Many other examples of students' apparent lack of understanding of numbers are provided in J. Sowder (in press).

In summary, number sense is a set of schemas that provide an important conceptual basis for reasoning in mathematics, yet appears to be lacking among upper-level elementary and middle school age children. Perhaps as we come to understand the nature of number sense better, we will be better able to include it in our curricula. In the meantime, it is probably worthwhile for teachers to add questions or activities into their current curricula that focus attention on the various meanings of numbers.

Quantitative Concepts. While it is important for children to develop the meaningful understanding of numbers implied by the term "number sense," Thompson (1990) argues

that it is also important for them to develop **quantitative concepts.** Quantitative concepts allow the individual to make sense of situations in terms of the quantities involved and the relationships among quantities.

An important aspect of quantitative concepts is that they are *not* the same as the numbers that are often used to represent them, nor are quantitative relationships the same as the arithmetic operations used to derive a quantity. One example used by Thompson (1990) to illustrate the distinction between quantitative relationships and arithmetic operations is the following:

> Jim is 15 cm taller than Sarah. This difference is five times greater than the difference between Abe's and Sam's heights. What is the difference between Abe's and Sam's heights?

Even though the question asks for a difference, the answer to the problem is found by division (15/5), not subtraction. Difference refers to a **quantity** that expresses how much one entity exceeds another. It does not refer to an operation performed on numbers (such as subtraction). However, children who do not have an understanding of quantity independent of arithmetic operations may try to solve this problem by subtracting 5 from 15.

Thompson (1990) provides a more complex example of the use of quantitative concepts using the following problem:

> I walk from home to school in 30 minutes, and my brother takes 40 minutes. My brother left 6 minutes before I did. In how many minutes will I overtake him?

Try to solve this problem yourself before looking at two possible solution paths shown in Table 14.9. As a hint, try to think about the situation described in terms of the basic quantities involved and their relationships, not in terms of an algebraic formula.

Table 14.9 Two possible solutions to the math problem given in the text. The first solution involves recall of a standard algebraic procedure. The second relies on representing and elaborating the quantitative concepts involved in the problem (from P. Thompson, 1990).

(a) (6 + t) d/40 = t (d/30)

(b) • I take 3/4 as long as brother to walk the same distance, so I walk 4/3 as fast as brother.
   • I imagine him and me walking: What matters is the distance between us and how long it takes for that distance to shrink to zero.
   • The distance between us shrinks at a rate that is the difference of our walking speeds. Since I walk 4/3 as fast as brother, the difference of our speeds is 1/3 of brother's speed.
   • The distance between us shrinks at 1/3 of brother's speed, so the amount of time in which it shrinks to zero is 3 times the amount of time in which brother walked it.
   • Therefore, it will take 18 minutes to overtake brother.

Table 14.9 part (a) shows a standard algebraic solution to this problem. Such a solution could be used by an individual who had had a traditional algebra curriculum and who recognized this problem as a variant of a problem type with which he was familiar. Part (b) shows another way to solve the problem that emphasizes quantitative concepts and their interrelationships. For example, the notion that *I take 3/4 as long as my brother to walk the same distance* represents as a quantity the relationship between my brother's rate and my rate. Also, *What matters is the distance between us and how long it takes for that distance to shrink to zero* represents the important quantities to determine. The solution path given in part (b) does not rely on knowledge of algebra, but relies heavily on understanding of the quantitative relationships involved in this situation.

Thompson (1990) argues that quantitative concepts, if acquired in arithmetic classes, can be used in the transition to algebra because

they form an important part of the conceptual basis of *both* domains. Although research has yet to be conducted to demonstrate this idea, it is a good bet that students who have higher achievement in mathematics make more extensive use of quantitative concepts while solving problems.

The research that has been done on this topic illustrates the utility of quantitative concepts for solving complex arithmetic problems. For example, one of the problems studied by Thompson (in press b) was:

Team 1 played a basketball game against Opponent 1.
Team 2 played a basketball game against Opponent 2.

The captains of Team 1 and Team 2 argued about which team won by more.
The captain of Team 2 won the argument by 8 points.

Team 1 scored 79 points.
Opponent 1 scored 48 points.

Team 2 scored 73 points.
How many points did Opponent 2 score?

The researchers had children think aloud while solving these problems and used clinical interviews to find out how the children were thinking about the problems. They worked with fifth grade children. The two children that we will contrast here will be called "Liz" and "Jill." Liz had average scores in school mathematics, while Jill had high scores.

Liz's drawing of the above problem is shown in Figure 14.7, while Jill's is shown in Figure 14.8. As these drawing suggest, Jill's understanding of the problem was based on an understanding of the quantitative relationships involved, whereas Liz's understanding

Liz's drawing for interview problem 3

Figure 14.7 Student drawing for problem given in text. This drawing reflects minimal quantitative understanding (from P. Thompson, 1990).

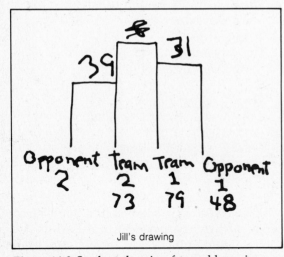

Jill's drawing

Figure 14.8 Student drawing for problem given in text. This drawing shows a grasp of the quantitative concepts involved (from P. Thompson, 1990).

appeared to be dominated by an understanding of basketball and scoreborads in basketball.

Excerpts from the interviews of the two children corroborates the impression that Jill has a better quantitative understanding of the problem than does Liz. First, here is some of the interview with Jill: (I = Interviewer; J = Jill).

I: Could you try to draw a picture?

J: Let's see. (Draws line, labels this Team 2. Draws line, labels this Team 1. Draws line, labels this Opponent 1. Speaking inaudibly throughout. Looks up).

I: Okay, where is Opponent 2 in all of this?

J: Well, Opponent 2 has to be under this. (Points to line Team 2). Wait (inaudible). 48, well, okay, Team 2 scored 79 . . . Team 2 scored 73. Wait. Then this would have to be less than, um, 60. (Shakes head). Wait, 61, okay, because this, um, it is still confusing. (Looks up from paper).

I: Okay, what does the 8 points mean?

J: It means that um, Team 2, um, won by 8 points more than Team 1 did.

I: Alright, what did, could you show me the picture where, how much Team 1 won by?

J: (Draws horizontal line from top of line Team 2 to line Team 1).

I: Who did they play?

J: Oh, they played Opponent 1 (inaudible). This . . . okay, this would have to be, this right here would be more than 8. (Points to the difference between lines Team 2 and Team 1).

I: More than 8?

J: Well, yes. Well, it is, uh, (inaudible), um. (Writes 79 − 48 = 31). 31 points. 31. So you could take 8 away from that, (inaudible) because, this is how much Team 1 won by, (pointing to paper), and they, they argued and Team . . . (pause). Opponent 2 would have to be 30, um, 20, um 27 or less, 27 or less?

I: 27 or less?

J: No, it would have to be . . . it would have to be 38 or more. No, it would have to be 39.

I: 39. Now, what, what does 39 go with?

J: Because, you take 31 plus the 8 . . . (pointing to line Team 1 and the text of the problem).

I: Yeah.

J: . . . and get 39.

I: Yes, that's true. 39 what?

J: 39 points and this. . .

I: (interrupting). Whose points are they?

J: They're, um, they're Team 2's.

I: They're Team 2's points?

J: Uh-huh.

I: Okay.

J: Because they're. . .

I: That's how many points Team 2 scored?

J: No, it's how much more they scored than Opponent 2.

Although Jill is initially confused about where certain quantities go in her drawing (e.g., Opponent 2's score and the quantity 8 representing the difference between the differences), she has enough of the quantitative concepts represented correctly and enough of

a propensity to seek a consistent set of relationships that she reaches a solution to the problem fairly quickly. Contrast this with some of Liz's protocol, which does not show much development of quantitative concepts:

I: Okay. Um, can you draw, a, a picture. . .

L: Um. . .

I: That shows the two teams playing against each other? And, that shows by how much each one won?

L: Um, okay . . . (inaudible) on the basketball hoops. (Begins drawing basketball hoop).

I: Oh, these are basketball hoops?

L: He's trying to, I'm trying to make it. (Continues drawing).

I: Oh, okay, I see . . . (pause). Now, does it, to show that one team beat another, do you have to show basketball hoops and stuff like that?

L: Well, you could, because usually the one thing that is over by, the scoreboard is over by the basketball hoop.

I: Oh, I see.

L: It's going to be right over here (pointing to area in picture near the basketball hoop).

I: Okay.

L: (Draws scoreboard). Um . . . um . . . and Team . . . 73.

I: Okay, I don't see a 65 anyplace up here (pointing to the problem).

L: I know. Well, after I get it here (pointing to subtraction work in which she subtracted 8 from 73).

I: Oh, that's because you said, so this points, this is 8 points up here. (I points to problem as he discusses it. L doesn't watch, continues to draw). Then where it says the captain of Team 2 won the argument by 8 points, you're saying that that then means that Team 2 won by 8 points?

L: Yeah. Kind of. (Ceases drawing).

I: Alright. So, if Team 2 won by 8 points, did they win by more than Team 1? (pointing to the problem).

L: Um. Probably.

I: Can you see a way to, uh, figure that out?

L: Yeah, because it says the captain of Team 2 won the argument by 8 points.

I: How much did Team 1 win by?

L: Um, probably . . . about . . . 31.

I: About 31? And Team 2 won by 8?

L: Uh-huh.

I: So Team 2 won by more?

L: No.

I: But in here (pointing to the problem), doesn't it say that Team 2 won by more? He won the argument about which one, team, won by more?

L: Uh, I don't know.

I: It's getting confusing?

L: Yeah.

Although the interviewer tries to point out the inconsistency in Liz's understanding of the quantities involved, Liz resists recognizing this inconsistency. This resistance may well be due to the fact that she has no alternative conception of the situation that is better than the incorrect one she generated. Thompson (in press b) argues that she lacks the quantitative understanding needed to represent this problem adequately. What she needs, which is what Jill had, was the ability to represent differences as quantities and also *differences of differences* as quantities.

The area of the quantitative conceptual basis of mathematics is just emerging as an important research area. Thompson (In Press a, In Press b), Greeno (1987), and Shalin (1987) have all contributed towards defining what quantitative concepts are. While quantitative concepts appear to be important as a conceptual basis in mathematics performance, the research supporting this claim still needs to be done.

Summary

The available work on the conceptual basis of expertise in mathematics suggests that the possession of problem schemas for various problem types is one important set of concepts. Other concepts include those required for understanding the absolute and relative sizes of numbers and how numbers can be partitioned in various ways that are still consistent with their meaning (number sense). It appears that another set of concepts that may be basic across a wide variety of math domains is that of concepts of quantity. More research is needed to develop this promising area.

THE ROLE OF CONCEPTUAL UNDERSTANDING IN COGNITIVE PROCESSING

The fact that skilled and less skilled persons differ in conceptual understanding for a given mathematics domain might be quite unimportant for performance, just as one's hair color is irrelevant to one's quantitative skill. However, there is growing evidence that conceptual understanding has a pervasive influence on cognitive processing. If influences what is heeded, what is recalled, and therefore, ultimately, what is learned and how problems are solved. In this section we will focus on the role of conceptual understanding in attention, recall, and learning.

The Role of Conceptual Understanding in Attention

Robinson and Hayes (1978) studied the role of conceptual understanding in attention. They reasoned that if students have a good understanding of the concepts that define algebra word problems, they should be able to use it to decide what parts of the problem statement are relevant or irrelevant (that is, to decide what to heed).

One type of word problem commonly found in high school algebra is the "river current" type in which the speed of a boat depends on the rower's strength, the speed of the current, and the direction of the boat with respect to the current. Robinson and Hayes (1978) used an analog of this type of problem involving headwinds and tailwinds rather than current. Their problem is shown Table 14.10.

These researchers had college students who were good algebra students read this problem, segment by segment, and judge which segments of the problem statement were relevant and which were irrelevant to the solution. In fact, only three elements of the statement were essential to finding the solution: (1) "with a 6 m.p.h. tailwind," (2) "back against the same headwind," and (3) "ratio of flying time against the wind to time with the wind is 9:8." If the students are using a schema they have for this type of problem, one would expect them to judge these three elements to be relevant more often than they judged other elements of the problem to be relevant.

Table 14.10 The word problem used by Robinson and Hayes (1978). The question that went along with this problem was, "What was the plane's speed in each direction?"

A crop-dusting plane carries 2,000 pounds of Rotenone dusting compound, 250 pounds of high test fuel, a pilot highly skilled in low-altitude flying, and a duster-machinery operator, the pilot's younger brother. The plane must dust a retangular tobacco field 0.5 miles wide by 0.6 miles long. The dusting compound must be spread with a density of 200 pounds per 0.001 square mile. Further, the compound must be spread between 6 A.M. and 9 A.M., when there is sufficient light and before the morning dew has evaporated, to assure the adherence of the compound to the plants. The plane can dust at 44-foot-wide strip at one time. The plane flies the length of the field with a 6 m.p.h. tailwind and back against the same headwind. With the wind, the plane uses fuel at the rate of 80 pounds per hour. The ratio of flying time against the wind to time with the wind is 9:8. The duster operator must try to spread the compound uniformly on the ground despite varying speed.

The researchers also thought that whether the problem question was seen first (before the statement) or last would influence students' judgments of relevance. The problem question provides a big clue to the type of problem and therefore to what knowledge to activate. Finally, they thought that students' judgments might change from a first to a second reading of the statement, especially if the problem question had been read last.

Table 14.11 shows the results. Overall, the data supported their predictions: the relevant segments were judged to be relevant by a higher proportion of students than were any of the irrelevant segments. Also, the students who had read the problem question first were more likely to judge relevant segments as being relevant on the first reading (.93) than were students who read the problem question last (.84). Improvement in correctly classifying relevant segments on the second reading

Table 14.11 The proportions of students judging each segment in the word problem to be relevant. *Q first* means that the problem question occurred before the problem statements. *Pass 1* and *Pass 2*, refer to the first and second readings of the problem (from Robinson and Hayes, 1987).

	Q FIRST		Q LAST	
	PASS 1	PASS 2	PASS 1	PASS 2
1. Problem-relevant items with a 6 m.p.h. tailwind back against the same headwind ratio of speed w/t against wind is 9:8	.93	.92	.84	.89
2. Space items plane must dust retangular tobacco field .5 miles wide .6 miles long per .001 sq. mile 44 ft. wide strip plane flies length of field	.65	.65	.93	.45
3. Weight items 2000# 60# per hour 250# 80# per hour with a density 200#	.77	.65	.93	.48
Categories 2 and 3 combined	.82 (Pass 1)		.56 (Pass 2)	

4. Irrelevant/other items
a crop-dusting plane
of Rotenone dusting compound
of high test fuel
a pilot
highly skilled in low-altitude flying
a duster-machinery operator
the pilot's younger brother
the compound must be spread between
   6 A.M. and 9 A.M. when there is sufficient light and
   before dew has evaporated to assure adherence of
   compound
the compound must be spread uniformly despite
   varying speed
	.20	.14	.35	.11

(pass 2) was restricted to the students who read the problem question last (they went from .84 correct on Pass 1 to .89 correct on Pass 2).

The Role of Conceptual Understanding in Recall

If people pay attention to information that matches their schemas and ignore other infor-mation, they should be more likely to recall the heeded information. Mayer (1982) exam-ined students' recall of algebra story problems in light of this hypothesis. Some of the prob-lems he used are shown in Table 14.12. His word problems differed in how they had to be solved. For example, the first problem in Table 14.12 is solved by using the formula Distance = Rate × Time, and the second by

Table 14.12 Two of the problems that students studied and recalled (from Mayer, 1982).

---

1. A truck leaves Los Angeles en route to San Francisco at 1 P.M. A second truck leaves San Francisco at 2 P.M. en route to Los Angeles going along the same route. Assume the two cities are 465 miles apart and that the trucks meet at 6 P.M. If the second truck travels 15 m.p.h. faster than the first truck, how fast does each truck go?

2. On a ferry trip, the fare for each adult was 50 cents and for each child was 25 cents. The number of passengers was 30 and the total paid was $12.25. How many adults and how many children were there?

---

setting up some algebraic equations and then solving for each unknown. In all, Mayer studied sixteen problem types. He knew from a previous study (Mayer, 1981) the relative frequencies with which each type occurred in a sample of ten textbooks commonly used in high school algebra classes.

Students in Mayer's (1982) study each read eight story problems for two minutes each. They were directed to read and paraphrase each problem, but not to solve it. After studying the problems, they wrote down what they recalled from each problem. Students who recalled all of the relevant information were said to have recalled the problem. Mayer determined the proportion of students recalling problems of each of the sixteen types and correlated this with the frequency of occurrence of each problem type in textbooks. He found a moderately strong relationship of .66.

These findings can be interpreted in the following way. Students develop schemas for the most frequently occurring story problem types in their textbooks. For example, a schema for a problem like number 2 in Table 14.12 might be:

Money/Combination Problem
has goal: to find how many of two
    different sets

has given: total number of entities
    from both sets

has given: cost of elements in Set 1

has given: cost of elements in Set 2

has given: total cost

When asked to study new problems, students try to match the new problems with one of their problem schemas. If they find a match, it is easier to encode a problem because the relevant aspects of the problem can be heeded and elaborated. This leads to better recall for problems that match students' schemas.

The Role of Conceptual Understanding in Learning

It has long been known that students' prior knowledge plays a crucial role in acquiring new knowledge (e.g., R. Gagné, 1962; Ausubel, 1968), and you have seen that the learning mechanisms described in the early sections of this book rely heavily on prior knowledge. For instance, the initial acquisition of procedural knowledge relies on possession of a declarative representation of the procedure; the way that new propositions are encoded depends on prior related propositions; and schema development depends on prior exposure to examples of the schema.

The influence of prior conceptual understanding is evident throughout the mathematics curriculum. One interesting area where the role of prior knowledge has been studied is learning to interpret decimals. When starting to learn about decimal numbers in elementary school, children frequently misjudge which of two decimal numbers is larger. One type of misjudgment (Rule 1) involves always saying that the decimal number with the greater number of digits is larger—for instance, if asked which is larger, .6 or .123, saying that .123 is larger. One study found that 35% of fifth graders consistently made this type of error (Resnick, Nesher, Leonard, Magone,

Omanson, & Peled, 1989). A second type of misjudgment (Rule 2) that becomes more common and persists in later elementary years is to judge the number with the *smaller* number of digits to always be the larger number (Sackur-Grisvard & Leonard, 1985; Zuker, 1985). For instance, .3 is deemed larger than .45.

Resnick et al. (1989) wanted to understand the conceptual basis for these mistaken rules. They reasoned that Rule 1 comes from treating numbers to the right of the decimal as if they are whole numbers. So, for example, .123 is treated as 123 and .35 as 35. Given this framework, it makes sense to infer that the number with the larger number of digits will be larger because this is true for whole numbers.

When Resnick et al. (1989) examined childrens' reasons for making this type of misjudgment, the most typical reasons they found were like the following:

> 0.5 is less than 0.25 "because 25 is bigger," 4.8 is less than 4.63 "since 63 is bigger than 8" (from Resnick, et al., p. 20).

These reasons clearly suggest that the children are treating the decimal fractions as whole numbers.

What about the second type of misjudgment in which the decimal fraction with the *smaller* number of digits is judged to be larger (Rule 2)? Resnick et al. (1989) speculated that use of Rule 2 reflects a more complete understanding of what decimal fractions really denote than does use of Rule 1. They found that children who made this type of error justified it by saying that since the number with more digits (e.g., 45) represented smaller parts (e.g., hundredths) than the number with less digits (e.g., 3, representing tenths), that it was a smaller amount.

Children who reason in this way appear to be mapping their new understanding of decimal fractions onto their knowledge of common fractions. For instance, when comparing common fractions with like numerators, one determines that the fraction with the larger denominator is smaller (e.g., 1/45 is less that 1/3), so .45 should be less than .3. Whereas Rule 1 users lack the insight that decimal fractions represent fractional parts, Rule 2 users clearly have this understanding and also have an understanding that the size of the fractional parts decreases as one moves to the right of the decimal.

Thus, while both Rule 1 and Rule 2 users make errors in judging the relative sizes of decimal fractions, the knowledge behind their errors is quite different. In a class full of Rule 1 users, a teacher should consider doing work to develop the students' understanding of fractional parts and the meanings of each column. In a class full of Rule 2 users, these basic conceptual understandings are already present, so the teacher could focus attention on translating back and forth between common and decimal fractions so that students come to realize that it is the numerator rather than the denominator of common fractions that is explicitly represented in decimal fractions (the denominator is implicit in the columns). Once Rule 2 users see this, they are likely to abandon their misconception.

Summary

Conceptual understanding plays an important role in new problem-solving and learning situations. It influences what is heeded, what is encoded (and later recalled), and the types of errors that are made while learning new material. Because of its pervasive influence, it is important that students acquire a conceptual basis for mathematics activities.

STRATEGIES

So far in this chapter, we have reviewed some of the automated basic skills (such as number facts and arithmetic operations) and conceptual knowledge (such as problem schemas, number sense, and quantitative concepts) that underlie skilled performance in mathematics. Now we turn to the third element of expertise—strategies. We will describe some specific **estimation** and **mental calculation strategies** and also some **general problem-solving strategies** that are useful for solving novel math problems.

Estimation Strategies

Estimation is a highly valuable mathematics skill because of its role in self-monitoring. Just as **comprehension monitoring** is important in reading and **reviewing** is important in writing, **estimation** is important in math. Like the related skills in reading and writing, an important function of estimation is to help the problem-solver evaluate the success of his efforts. A student who estimates an answer to a problem and then compares this estimate with a calculated answer can detect errors and correct them. A student who does not estimate what a sensible answer would be is less likely to detect errors.

Reys, Rybolt, Bestgen, and Wyatt (1982) studied the strategies used by good estimators. They interviewed 59 students in the seventh through twelfth grades who had been determined to be good estimators. The three most common strategies they found were **reformulation, translation,** and **compensation.**

In **reformulation,** numbers are rounded off to make them more manageable (e.g., 87,236 might be rounded to 87,000). In **translation,** the structure of the problem is changed from the structure suggested by the problem statement. For example, to estimate the answer for the addition problem:

$$504$$
$$492$$
$$+487$$

a good estimator may translate this into a multiplication problem and say, "500 times 3 is 1500, so the answer will be about 1500." Finally, in **compensation,** good estimators compensate for one adjustment by making an equal and opposite adjustment. For example, in the addition problem above, someone using compensation would say, "The answer will be 500 times 3—about 1500—and a little below 1500 because I added more than I subtracted in rounding each number to 500."

Mental Calculation

Mental calculation refers to the ability to perform calculations in one's head rather than on paper. Some of the strategies used by good estimators are also used by good mental calculators—rounding, translating, and compensating—except that here the goal is to obtain a precise answer, not a ball-park estimate.

Hope and Sherrill (1987) studied the differences between skilled and unskilled mental calculators. First, they identified skilled and unskilled eleventh and twelfth graders according to performance on a test of mental calculation. Then they gave each student some new mental multiplication problems to solve, such as the following:

$$25 \times 48$$
$$25 \times 120$$
$$32 \times 32$$
$$8 \times 999$$
$$49 \times 51$$

Try some of these and think about how you solved them. The students in Hope and Sherrill's study tried to solve these without pencil and paper and then explained to a researcher how they had attempted to solve the problem. Hope and Sherrill analyzed these explanations to determine the strategies used.

Table 14.13 shows the four main strategies they found and gives an example of each. The first strategy—**pencil and paper mental analog**—involved performing the algorithm that one would use given pencil and paper. The procedure could be exactly the same as a pencil-and-paper procedure or it could involve the use of some sort of short cut, such as retrieving a partial product rather than computing it (as is done for 96 in the example). What was common to all instances of this strategy is that the problem was set up as a pencil-and-paper multiplication problem would be set up.

The second strategy—**distribution**—involved using the distributive method of calculation. The first step was to transform a factor into a series of sums and differences. Then, additive, subtractive, fractional, or quadratic distribution was used to calculate the answer. An example is shown in Table 14.13.

The third strategy—**factoring**—was similar to distribution in that they both start out by transforming one or more factors. However, in factoring factors are transformed into products or quotients rather than sums and differences. Finally, the fourth strategy was the use of **retrieval** of a numerical equivalent from

Table 14.13 Four mental calculation strategies (adapted from Hope and Sherrill, 1987).

PENCIL-AND-PAPER MENTAL ANALOG

The student sets up and solves the problem in the same way as would be done given pencil and paper.

Example: Calculate 25 × 48

"5 times 48 is . . . 5 times 8 = 40, carry 4, 24, 240. And 2 times 48 is 96. I know that . I think of 96 brought over one. So it's 1200."

DISTRIBUTION

The student transforms one or more factors into a series of sums or differences.

Example: Calculate 8 × 4211

"8 times 4000 is 32000; 8 times 200 is 1600; so it's 33600; 8 times 11 is 88; so the answer is 33688."

FACTORING

The student transforms one or more factors into a series of products or quotients.

Example: Calculate 25 × 48

"5 times 48 is 240 and 5 times 240 is 1200." In other words, this student thought 25 × 48 = (5 × 5) 48.

RETRIEVAL OF A NUMERICAL EQUIVALENT

The student retrieves a product for large numbers from memory.

Example: Calculate 25 × 25

"625—I just know it."

long-term memory. Examples of these strategies are shown in Table 14.13.

Which strategies do you think would be more efficient? Which would be less error-prone? Think about how much of a burden each strategy puts on working memory. In fact, the pencil-and-paper analog puts the greatest burden on working memory because one has to remember several partial products and their relationship to each other. In contrast, retrieval puts the least burden on working memory. Distribution and factoring put intermediate loads on working memory, but much less than does the pencil-and-paper analog. One has to keep track of only one intermediate result because one can keep a running cumulative total.

Given these differences in the effectiveness of strategies, the results obtained by Hope and Sherrill, shown in Table 14.14, are not surprising. They found that unskilled mental calculators relied almost exclusively (86% of the time) on the pencil-and-paper analog. In contrast, the skilled students used that strategy only 22% of the time. They favored the distribution strategy (54%), but also used factoring a significant portion of the time (14%). Finally, the skilled students were far more likely than the unskilled students to directly retrieve a product. For example, most skilled students could retrieve from long-term memory the fact that 25×25 is 625, while many unskilled students could not retrieve this fact.

The distribution and factoring strategies highlight an important theme of this book—basic skills, conceptual understanding, and strategies are interdependent. For example, one student calculated 15×48 in the following way: "10 times 48, 480, and half of 480 is 240, so it's 720." In other words, this student used the distribution strategy to change the problem to:

$$(10 \times 48) + (5 \times 48)$$

To make this change requires understanding that 15 can be regrouped into 10 and 5 and that the distributive law may then be applied without affecting the result. This type of understanding involves both the **number sense** and **quantitative concepts** discussed in the section on conceptual understanding. It is also evident that this student executed basic algorithms, such as multiplying a number by 10, automatically. Clearly, then, carrying out the distribution strategy requires adequate conceptual knowledge and automated basic skills. This example is just one of many in which the three types of knowledge interact.

Table 14.14 Frequency and percent of methods used by skilled and unskilled students to solve mental calculation problems (from Hope and Sherrill, 1987).

METHOD	UNSKILLED ($n = 15$)		SKILLED ($n = 15$)	
	FREQUENCY	%	FREQUENCY	%
Mental pencil-and-paper	387	86.0	101	22.4
Distribution	53	11.8	244	54.2
Factoring	7	1.6	61	13.6
Retrieval, no calculation	2	0.4	44	9.8
Guess	1	0.2	0	0.0

General Problem-Solving Strategies

When a student is confronted with a novel math problem, for which she has no problem schema to help her interpret the problem, what does she do? Do more skilled problem solvers use different strategies than less skilled problem solvers? We could not find any empirical studies of this question, but did find general agreement on some problem-solving strategies that are thought to be effective. Figure 14.9 shows these strategies as they were presented to fifth and seventh graders (Charles & Lester, 1984).

As you can see, some of the strategies help students form a more adequate problem

PROBLEM SOLVING

UNDERSTANDING THE PROBLEM
- Read the problem again.
- Write what you know.
- Look for key phrases.
- Find the important information.
- Tell it in your own words.
- Tell what you are trying to find.

SOLVING THE PROBLEM

TRY THIS
- Look for a pattern.
- Guess and check.
- Write an equation.
- Use reasoning.

WOULD THIS HELP?
- Draw a picture.
- Make an organized list or table.
- Use objects or act out the problem
- Simplify the problem.
- Work backwards.

ANSWERING THE PROBLEM
HAVE YOU
- Used all the important information?
- Checked your work?
- Decided if the answer makes sense?
- Written the answer in a complete sentence?

Figure 14.9 Strategies thought to be generally useful in mathematics problem solving (from Charles and Lester, 1984).

representation ("understanding the problem"). For example, students are encouraged to state the problem in their own words. This should ensure that the individual is activating related prior knowledge that might help solve the problem. Other strategies are designed to help the student **solve** the problem. For example, students are encouraged to work backwards. As you learned in Chapter 10 (Problem Solving), working backwards, or means-ends analysis, is an effective way to constrain the search for solution to areas that are related to the goal state, thus eliminating many false starts. Finally, a set of strategies ("answering the problem") are offered for **monitoring** the solution to ensure that it is correct. For example, students are encouraged to check to see if their answers make sense.

Evidence that use of these strategies helps with math problems comes from a large-scale study done by Charles and Lester (1984). These researchers had fifth and seventh graders receive daily practice in problem-solving strategies for sixteen weeks. On a posttest, the classes that participated in this program outperformed control group classes on almost all measures of problem solving. Moreover, although transfer was not measured directly, many teachers reported anecdotally on such transfer. For instance, one teacher said, "Students didn't understand fractions so they drew pictures" (p. 29).

It is interesting to compare the strategies shown in Figure 14.9 with strategies that have been found to be beneficial in reading or writing, as described in the chapters on reading and writing in this book. There are many similarities across domains. For instance in writing, a prewriting strategy is to write down, without worrying about order or grammar, what one knows about the topic. This activity is similar to writing down what one knows in math problem solving. In both cases, what is written down serves to activate related knowledge and also serves as an external memory aid during the course of problem solving. As another example, writing an equation or drawing a picture in math problem solving are ways of working toward a solution just as is identifying a text structure in reading. Finally, as we have already pointed out, deciding if one's answer makes sense is a way of monitoring, just as is reviewing in writing.

The fact that there are similar problem-solving strategies across domains may lead some to conclude that we should therefore teach problem-solving strategies in a domain-general way. We do not agree with this conclusion for several reasons. First, learning when to apply a strategy means developing schemas for various types of problems for which a strategy may be useful. Schema development proceeds best from a narrow range of examples that only broadens out gradually. Thus, to start out by teaching students to apply a strategy quite broadly would thwart the development of problem schemas. (It might be appropriate to teach a general problem-solving course at the college or other advanced levels when the students already have a great deal of experience with the use of problem-solving strategies in a variety of specific domains.)

A second reason for disagreeing with the idea that we should teach general problem-solving strategies from the start is an empirical one. As we said in Chapter 10 (Problem Solving), there have been very few successful general problem-solving training programs. Most programs successfully teach the strategies, but few achieve transfer of these strategies outside of the program.

Finally, there are contextual and procedural differences in the strategies across the domains. For instance, even though writing an equation and recognizing a text structure are functionally equivalent in that they move the problem solver towards a solution, the need for using these two strategies occurs in quite distinct contexts, and the strategies themselves are executed in quite distinct ways.

Instead of concluding that the functional similarity of problem-solving strategies across domains means that they should be taught at a general level, we conclude that this adds validity to a problem-solving model of human cognition. This model can be used by researchers to gain insights into expertise in domains that have yet to be studied. Early researchers in expertise were not able to capitalize on this general model. Too, the model can be used by teachers and instructional designers as they design instruction. That is, they should design instruction that is compatible with the notion that humans are problem solvers, and they should attempt to enhance the problem-solving capabilities of their learners.

Summary

In this section, we have described what is known about strategies used by people solving math problems. **Estimation** strategies are beneficial because they assist the individual in monitoring his problem-solving activity. Strategies used by good estimators include **reformulation, translation,** and **compensation. Mental calculation** strategies are strategies used to compute without recourse to pencil and paper. Students who are good at mental calculation use **distribution, factoring,** and **direct retrieval,** while students who are poor at mental calculation try to do the pencil-and-paper method in their minds.

While expert and novice math problem solvers have not been compared to see what strategies they use when confronted with novel problems, there is a consensus on a set of strategies that is generally helpful with developing the problem representation, moving the solution forward, and evaluating the success of the solution. These strategies, while different in detail from strategies in other domains, are similar in how they function in the problem-solving process.

INSTRUCTION

In the previous section, you saw that expertise in mathematics is comprised of automated basic skills, conceptual knowledge, and strategies. Knowing this, you know a lot about *what* to teach in mathematics. However, you do not know *how* it should be taught. This section describes some successful ways of teaching students to master these different aspects of mathematics competence.

Since automated basic skills are a form of procedural knowledge, it is a good bet that practice and feedback will be an important part of instruction to promote their development. Conceptual knowledge is declarative knowledge such as schemas and their elements—propositions, images, and linear orderings. Instruction that emphasizes elaboration and organization should promote the growth of the propositional elements of declarative knowledge, while exposure to examples of schemas and practice classifying examples should help with schema formation. Strategic knowledge is procedural and so requires practice, but you learned in Chapter 11 (Transfer) that the biggest problem with strategies is their failure to transfer. **Reflective** practice leads to greater transfer than does **blind** practice. We now turn to some examples of instruction that illustrate many of these points.

Instruction to Promote Automaticity of Basic Skills: Increasing the Speed of Number Fact Retrieval

You may recall from an earlier section in this chapter that in early elementary grades children shift from using counting strategies to retrieval for getting basic number facts. For instance, for the fact:

$$3 + 6 = \underline{\hspace{1cm}}$$

the earliest strategy is the Count All strategy in which the child first counts out 3 objects (fingers), then 6 objects (fingers), then merges these two sets and counts all elements in the superset. The Count from Maximum strategy is a more efficient counting strategy in which the child identifies the larger addend (6), starts with this number, and counts on by the smaller addend (3). Direct retrieval of number facts is even more efficient. By third grade, most normal children use direct retrieval most of the time.

Children who are called "learning disabled for math" typically have normal aptitude test scores but score well below average on math achievement tests. Svenson and Broquist (1975) found that such children are slower than their age-mates to produce answers for addition fact questions. Over the school years, this slowness can cause more and more problems as children attempt work that makes greater demands on working memory.

Goldman, Pelligrino, and Mertz (1988) reasoned that learning disabled (LD) children might benefit from extended practice on addition facts. Such practice might cause them to switch from less to more efficient strategies. To test this idea, they developed a microcomputer program that presented addition facts, accepted the student's answer, and gave feedback on correctness and speed. Each "lesson" was comprised of 40 facts and took an average of only 6 minutes to complete. Math LD students completed about 3 lessons per week for 8 weeks during their regular time in a resource room.

The results showed a significant decrease in time to produce an answer from pre- to posttest. On average, these students took 3.62 seconds to produce answers on the pretest

A

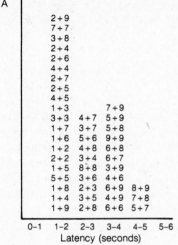

```
        2+9
        7+7
        3+8
        2+4
        2+6
        4+4
        2+7
        2+5
        4+5
        1+3          7+9
        3+3   4+7    5+9
        1+7   3+7    5+8
        1+6   5+6    9+9
        1+2   4+8    6+8
        2+2   3+4    6+7
        1+5   8+8    3+9
        5+5   3+6    4+6
        1+8   2+3    6+9    8+9
        1+4   3+5    4+9    7+8
        1+9   2+8    6+6    5+7
```
0–1   1–2   2–3   3–4   4–5   5–6
        Latency (seconds)

B

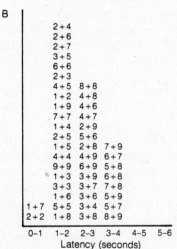

```
        2+4
        2+6
        2+7
        3+5
        6+6
        2+3
        4+5   8+8
        1+2   4+8
        1+9   4+6
        7+7   4+7
        1+4   2+9
        2+5   5+6
        1+5   2+8    7+9
        4+4   4+9    6+7
        9+9   6+9    5+8
        1+3   3+9    6+8
        3+3   3+7    7+8
        1+6   3+6    5+9
1+7     5+5   3+4    5+7
2+2     1+8   3+8    8+9
```
0–1   1–2   2–3   3–4   4–5   5–6
        Latency (seconds)

Figure 14.10 Latency to answer sums before (A) and after (B) extensive practice. The number of sums in the 0–1 and 1–2 second columns, indicating direct retrieval, increased after practice (from Goldman, Pellegrino, and Mertz, 1988).

and 2.97 seconds on the posttest. Goldman et al. (1988) examined data separately for four subgroups. To get an impression of what they found, look at the data for the best group of seven LD students shown in Figure 14.10. This histogram shows the typical speed to respond to different sums. The sums in the 0–1 and 1–2 second columns are likely to be directly retrieved. Sums in the remaining columns reflect use of the Count from Maximum strategy. In this strategy, smaller minimum addends require less counting and therefore should be solved faster. Thus, many of the sums shown in the 2–3 second column have minimum addends of 2, 3, or 4. Those in the 3–4 second column tend to have larger minimum addends. As you can see in this figure, on the posttest a larger number of sums occur in the 0–1 and 1–2 second columns than on the pretest. This suggests that a larger number of facts were directly retrieved on the posttest, due to the effects of practice.

When Goldman et al. (1988) compared the improvements of their subjects with improvements that occur for LD students given a standard curriculum, they concluded that for two-thirds of their subjects "8 weeks of regular practice accomplished what might (and only might) have been accomplished with the continued use of the ongoing curriculum in a 2- to 3-year period." In other words, this rather modest intervention produced improvements that normally took 2 or 3 years to produce without concentrated attention to practice.

This program has some similarities to the microcomputer program of Frederiksen et al. (1983) that we described in the chapter on reading. Both were designed to help students who lacked speed in basic skills. Both were designed to provide extensive practice. And both produced reductions in latency. The programs are quite different, however, in the amount of motivational appeal. The reading program had an exciting game format, while the math program was a straightforward "drill and practice." Yet both programs were successful. The need for highly appealing programs may depend on the context. Frederiksen et al. were working with high school students outside of regular class time. Goldman et al. (1988) were working with elementary school students through their resource teachers during regular school time. Microcomputers may be more novel to elementary school children than to high schoolers and therefore motivating just because they are microcomputers. Also, the resource teachers perhaps had motivational systems intact already.

Instruction to Promote Conceptual Understanding

There have been many studies recently focusing on promoting conceptual understanding of mathematics. They range from highly controlled laboratory studies of small areas of math to large-scale curriculum interventions. They include studying the use of worked examples to enhance schema formation (Cooper & Sweller, 1987), the use of small groups to enhance understanding (Yackel, Cobb, & Wood, 1991; Webb, 1991), and the use of a discovery approach to mathematics (Bednarz & Janvier, 1988; Cobb, Wood, Yackel, Nicholls, Wheatley, Trigatti, & Perlwitz, 1991). There are many exciting developments in this area.

Recall that one area in which many students lack conceptual understanding is number sense. They have trouble selecting the larger of two decimal numbers such as .5 and .42 and have trouble adding decimal numbers such as 2.3 and .62. They act as if they do not understand the meaning of the numbers.

One way to think about knowledge of decimal numbers is as a set of schemas such as:

Tenth
    is a: one tenth part of a whole

    has symbol: .1

    has symbol: 1/10

Hundredth
    is a: one hundredth part of a whole

    has symbol: .01

    has symbol: 1/100

Wearne and Hiebert (1988) designed a unit of instruction for fourth, fifth, and sixth graders that focused on developing schemas for decimal numbers (they called it "semantic analysis"). The unit consisted of nine 25-minute lessons in which students learned to represent decimal numbers with Dienes blocks (see Figure 14.11) and vice versa. The basic form of instruction was practice and feedback with many examples. Later lessons included practice in adding and subtracting decimal numbers first by working with Dienes blocks and then just thinking about the blocks while working with pencil and paper. This type of lesson should promote schema formation and refinement.

The students in the study took pre- and posttests of the ability to represent decimal fractions with Dienes blocks and to solve symbolically presented addition problems such as 5 + .3. They also took a transfer posttest that measured their performance on conceptually related tasks that had not been used during instruction. These tasks included representing with thousandths using Dienes blocks, judging the larger of two decimal fractions, and converting decimal fractions to common fractions.

Table 14.15 shows the number of students who could perform these tasks. Clearly, there is a substantial increase in the students' conceptual understanding from the pre- to the posttest, and this understanding transfers to conceptually related tasks.

Wearne and Hiebert give a vivid example of one student's changes in understanding that typified the group (p. 378):

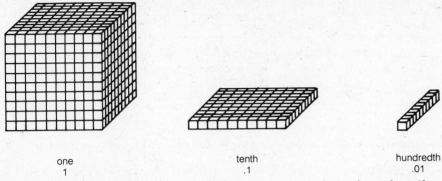

one   tenth   hundredth
1   .1   .01

Figure 14.11 Dienes blocks used by students to represent decimal numbers (from Wearne and Hiebert, 1988).

Table 14.15 Frequency of students (out of 29) who performed task before and after instruction (from Wearne and Hiebert, 1988).

ITEM	BEFORE INSTRUCTION	AFTER INSTRUCTION
Represent 1.503 with blocks	—	27
Represent 1.0623 with blocks	—	19
Choose the larger of .5 and .42	2	13
Write .7 as a common fraction	2	15
Write 6/100 as a decimal fraction	2	12

Before instruction, Barb, a fifth grader, added 1.3 to .25 to get .38 and said, "I just added it up." She wrote .8 as the answer to 5 + .3 and explained that "five plus three is eight, and the point stays right in front of it." After instruction, her processes had changed considerably. She wrote 2.92 as the answer to 2.3 + .62 and said, "There's no wholes, so you put the two down, and then six and three is nine, and nothing added to two is two." (**Interviewer:** "Why did you add the six and the three together?" "Because they're both tenths.")

As promising as this instructional study is, it is unfortunate that the researchers had no control group of any kind. Thus, we cannot say with certainty that the way they taught students or even what was taught caused the change. We hope that future research will clarify these questions.

Strategy Instruction

In the chapter on transfer (Chapter 11), you learned that while it is often easy to teach people the steps in a strategy, it is difficult to get them to use the strategy later when it would be beneficial but no one is prompting them to use it. You also learned that two instructional factors that increase the chances of strategy transfer are (1) getting students to understand the conditions under which a strategy applies, and (2) getting students to consciously evaluate the effectiveness of their strategies.

Table 14.16 General math problem-solving strategies studied by Swing, Stoiber, and Peterson (1988).

DEFINING/DESCRIBING

Mathematical terminology is attached to problem or concept features; a definition or description is attached to a math term.

Example: "How many are in a group" would be your two 10's multiplied together.

COMPARING

Two or more concepts, operations, or problem-solving procedures are described as alike or different.

Example: A line segment has little circles on each end. How is that different from what a ray looks like?

EXPLAINING/EVALUATING

Thinking about why and how to do a mathematics problem. It involves using math facts or rules as a reason or rationale in performing a problem.

Example: The answer can't be correct because the remainder is bigger than the divisor.

SUMMARIZING

Important information from the lesson is repeated or rephrased.

Example: Who can tell me some things we talked about today?

Swing, Stoiber, and Peterson (1988) tried to implement these instructional factors while teaching math problem-solving strategies to fourth graders. The strategies they were interested in are similar to some of the strategies shown in Figure 14.9. Specifically, they were interested in **describing, defining, comparing, explaining,** and **summarizing.** Table 14.16 gives definitions and examples for each of these strategies.

Swing et al. (1988) worked with 29 fourth grade teachers. One group of 14 teachers (the Thinking Skills group) learned to teach the five target strategies during in-service workshops. These workshops emphasized five instructional techniques:

1. Cognitive modeling of the strategy— the teacher "thinks aloud" while solving demonstration problems.

2. Teaching students to ask themselves key questions that stimulate strategy use. For example "What do the math facts mean?" or "Is my answer a good one?"

3. Telling students that the use of the strategy will improve performance in important ways.

4. Instructing students to recognize when the strategy should be applied.

5. Providing practice with a wide variety of problems.

The remaining group of 15 teachers (the Learning Time group) attended workshops in which they learned management strategies for increasing students' time on task. Both groups of teachers received feedback from their peers as they began to implement their new programs.

Children in both Thinking Skills and Learning Time classrooms took pre- and post-tests of math achievement. There were sub-sets for low-level knowledge and skills and high-level understanding and application, and for concepts and computation. Once the teachers had implemented their programs, researchers observed their classes several times to see whether the teachers were actually doing what they had learned about in their workshops. They also observed students and had a sample of students think aloud and give retrospective reports while solving some math problems. The protocols were analyzed for evidence of use of the target strategies.

The researchers found that children in the Thinking Skills classes made greater use of the target strategies than did children in the Learning Time classes. The gains in achievement on higher-level and conceptual subtests were greater for the Thinking Skills classes than for the Learning Time classes, although there were some exceptions to this general finding. Specifically, for the classes that had the lowest average math ability at the start of the program, the Learning Time classes made greater gains than did the Thinking Skills classes. The researchers found that in these low-ability classes, students had trouble following the instruction of the Thinking Skills Teachers.

Within classes that had a higher average math ability at the start of the program, the Thinking Skills program had the greatest benefit on the lower-ability children within the class. The higher-ability students in these classes appeared to already use many of the strategies that were being taught.

Swing et al. (1988) provided the following contrast between a low-ability student from a Learning Time class and one from a Thinking Skills class to show the success of the Thinking Skills program with low-ability students in high-average-ability classes. The problem the students were working on was: "Twenty-nine students went on a field trip. Each van could hold 8 students. How many vans are needed?" The Interviewer is I, the Learning Time student A, and the Thinking Skills student L.

A: You have to multiply 8 × 9 um, um, then you have to multiply 9 and 7. Then you have to multiply um, 8 and 2.

I: Tell me everything you're thinking.

A: Um, then you have to multiply 7 and 2. Then you add 2 um, and you add 6 and 3. Then you add 6 and 2.

I: Okay, are you done? Yes? What do you think the final answer is?

A: 14, 992

I: Okay, what were you thinking about besides the problem?

A: Um, the answer.

L: I'm thinking that I'm timesing it, and I'm seeing which one is closest to 29, like 8 times what is closest to 29. I'd say probably, maybe, 3 to 4, 8 times 4 is 32—that's too high, so I take the 3, and then I'd do this: 8 × 3 is 24, and I'd subtract it, and I'd get 5.

I: Umm hmmmm.

L: You know I'd try to, you know, think about it, like I'd look up on the board, and I'd on the um, read the definitions—see like what the facts are given. There are 29 students who went on a field trip. Each van could hold 8 students. Those are 2 facts.

I: Umm hmmm.

L: And then I'd read all those self-questions, and I would think what I was supposed to do.

I: Tell me everything you are thinking.

L: I'm thinking like maybe I can make a picture and figure out what I could do and make a little van here. I'd put maybe 8, then I'd make like, right here it has 8, 16, 24, that would be um, 3 vans, no 4 vans. (As she speaks, she draws 3 vans and puts 8 marks in each van. Then she draws a fourth van and puts 5 marks in that van.)

I: So your answer is 4 vans? Okay. What were you thinking about besides the problem?

L: Well, I couldn't really answer it really quick so I just tried to figure it out. I couldn't really answer it at first, so I just tried to figure it out. I remembered how to make a picture, so I just tried to make a picture and see how it would work out.

This study provides a nice example of the success that can be achieved with a well-designed instructional program. The students were taught to understand when the strategies were appropriate and they were taught questions to ask themselves as they solved problems. Some of these questions encouraged them to evaluate their answers, which probably had the effect of causing at least some of the students to evaluate the success of the strategies they were using. Finally, the instruction explicitly informed the students of the potential benefits of using the strategies. All of these techniques help ensure that learners will use the strategies they learn in transfer situations.

A CONCLUDING EXAMPLE

Here is a word problem that was given recently to a large national sample of seventeen-year-olds in the National Assessment of Educational Progress (as reported in Mayer, 1982):

Lemonade costs 95 cents for one 56-ounce bottle. At the school fair, Bob sold cups holding 8 ounces for 20 cents each. How much money did he make on each bottle?

Of these students, 71 percent failed this problem (The answer is 45 cents per bottle, assuming no cost for the cups). Yet this type of problem comes up often in personal money-management situations. Some students who fail such problems in test situations may succeed at them in their personal lives, but it is probable that many who fail in test situations also fail to solve such problems in everyday situations.

How can teachers improve students' mathematics competence? In this chapter, we have suggested that automated basic skills, conceptual understanding, and strategies each have a role to play in mathematics competence. We have also suggested that there should be different instructional formats when a given lesson is focused on the development of one or another of these types of knowledge. Too, most lessons will have elements of each type of knowledge, and a teacher who is aware of the different types can make instructional decisions to promote one that is lacking in a given student.

Our purpose in this chapter was to describe the types of knowledge that contribute to the development of mathematical competence. In so doing, we hoped to exemplify the notion that it is important to determine the differences in cognitive representations and processes between skilled and less skilled individuals as a way of understanding what should be taught.

ADDITIONAL READINGS

Instruction

Carpenter, T.P., & Peterson, P.L. (Eds.) (1988). Special issue: Learning mathematics from instruction. *Educational Psychologist, 23,* 1–202.

Hansen, R.S., McCann, J., & Myers, J.L. (1985). Rote versus conceptual emphasis in teaching elementary probability. *Journal for Research in Mathematics Education, 16,* 364–374.

Owen, E., & Sweller, J. (1989). Should problem-solving be used as a learning device in mathematics? *Journal for Research in Mathematics Education, 20,* 322–328.

Peterson, P., & Swing, S. (1988). Elaborative and integrative thought processes in mathematics learning. *Journal of Educational Psychology, 80,* 54–66.

Technology and Mathematics Instruction

Ayers, T., Davis, G., Dubinsky, E., & Lewin, P. (1988). Computer experiences in learning composition of functions. *Journal for Research in Mathematics Education, 19,* 246–259.

Cognition and Technology Group at Vanderbilt University (in press). The Jasper series: A generative approach to improving mathematical thinking. In *This year in school science.* Washington, DC: American Association for the Advancement of Science.

Goldman, S.R., & Pellegrino, J.W. (1987). Information processing and educational microcomputer technology: Where do we go from here? *Journal of Learning Disabilities, 20,* 144–154.

The Role of Instruction in Long-Term Motivation

Nicholls, J.G., Cobb, P., Wood, T., Yackel, E., & Patashnick, M. (1990). Assessing students' theories of success in mathematics: Individual and classroom differences. *Journal for Research in Mathematics Education, 21,* 109–122.

Context and Mathematics Performance

Carraher, T.N., Carraher, D., & Schliemann, A.D. (1985). Mathematics in the streets and in schools. *British Journal of Developmental Psychology, 3,* 21–29.

Saxe, G.B. (1988). Candy selling and math learning. *Educational Researcher, 17,* 14–21.

SOLUTIONS TO WORD PROBLEMS

14.1. x = number of hens; y = number of rabbits

$$x + y = 50, \text{ therefore } x = 50 - y$$
$$2x + 4y = 140$$

$2(50 - y) + 4y = 140$	(substitution)
$100 - 2y + 4y = 140$	(multiply by 2)
$100 + 2y = 140$	(collect terms)
$2y = 40$	(transpose)
$y = 20$	(divide by 2)
$x = 30$	(substitute 20 for y in $x = 50 - y$)

14.2. number of hens = $6(4) + 2(3) =$
$$24 + 6 = 30$$

number of rabbits = $5(6) + 3(4) =$
$$30 + 12 = 42$$

14.3. x = number of dimes; y = number of quarters

$$x + y = 20, \text{ therefore }$$
$$x = 20 - y$$
$$10x + 25y = 410$$

$10(20 - y) + 25y = 410$	(substitution)
$200 - 10y + 25y = 410$	(multiply by 10)
$200 + 15y = 410$	(collect terms)
$15y = 210$	(transpose)
$y = 14$	(divide by 15)
$x = 6$	(substitute 14 for y in $x = 20 - y$)

Chapter
15

Science

SUMMARY

1. As with expertise in other problem-solving domains, expertise in science is comprised of automated domain-specific basic skills, conceptual understanding, and strategies.

2. Lack of basic skills can impede the acquisition of higher-level skills in science.

3. Many studies in science domains have illustrated the ideas that experts have more and better organized conceptual understanding than do novices; older children generally have better conceptual understanding than do younger children; and students after instruction generally have better conceptual understanding of the domain instructed than they had prior to instruction.

4. Conceptual understanding affects how people represent and solve science and social science problems. Novices are more likely to work backwards in solving problems and are less likely to develop a set of constraints to limit their solutions to ill-defined problems.

5. Experts working in technical areas acquire strategies that are effective in speeding up problem solving in their specific contexts.

6. Conceptual-change theory describes the conditions needed to get students to reorganize or even abandon some of their conceptions when confronted with more adequate scientific explanations. Students instructed according to the tenets of this theory show greater conceptual change than do other students.

7. Videodisc and computer technologies appear to be promising adjuncts to promoting conceptual change in science domains.

8. Students can be taught schemas for scientific text structures and strategies for reading text having these various structures.

Science is the study of natural and artificial phenomena through reliable and valid observation. From such study, generalizable knowledge is produced. Science is thus both process and product. Its processes include observation and inductive and deductive reasoning. Its immediate products are the several branches of physical, biological, and social science. At a greater distance, its products include technological developments.

As a society becomes more technological, it is increasingly important for its citizens to understand both the processes and products of science. Without such understanding, people cannot make the choices they need to make about such issues as pollution control, use of pesticides, nuclear waste management, and health care.

This chapter describes what is known about the psychological processes involved in performing the tasks of science. This information should be of interest to teachers of science, of course. But it should also be of interest to teachers with other subject matter expertise since there are many ways that science impinges on other areas. For example, history has been influenced by scientific and technological advances, so students who are informed about science should be better able to appreciate this aspect of history. Also, students with artistic or literary learnings can develop a deeper understanding of the value of art if they understand the value of science as well. Teachers in these areas who are informed about the cognitive components of scientific thought will be better equipped to guide students towards interdisciplinary understanding. In addition, the general information-processing ideas that are developed in this chapter are likely to be relevant to other subject matter domains as well.

COMPONENTS OF SCIENCE EXPERTISE

With science, as with reading, writing, and math, the elements of expertise include basic skills, conceptual understanding, and strategies. The basic skills for a radiologist, for example, include interpreting the basic elements of x-rays and giving dictation (the standard method for reporting results). Conceptual understanding includes having a mental model of normal human anatomy and an understanding of the effects of various diseases, operations, and traumas on anatomical formations. Strategies include attempting to account for as much data as possible with one's diagnosis and attempting to exclude competing hypotheses systematically (Lesgold et al., 1988).

Table 15.1 shows test questions in a basic biology course that emphasize these different types of knowledge. Question 1 tests the basic skill of using a microscope. If the student cannot focus a microscope, then he will not be able to draw the picture. Questions 2 and 3 emphasize declarative knowledge (that is, conceptual understanding). Question 2 could be answered by simply recalling a proposition or image related to xenon's placement on the periodic chart in relation to the placement of metals and halogens. Question 3 tests the adequacy of a "supply and demand" schema.

Table 15.1 Sample science questions that emphasize basic skills (1), conceptual understanding (2 and 3), and strategies (4).

---

1. Draw a picture of what you see under this microscope.

2. Xenon is a member of _____ .

   a. the metals   b. the halogens

3. Using what you know about the relationship of supply, demand, and price, tell which of the following tables is more plausible.

   a. | Year | Supply | Demand | Price |
   |------|--------|--------|-------|
   | 1964 | 4.5 million bushels | .05 bushels/capita | $.20/lb. |
   | 1965 | 5.5 million bushels | .05 bushels/capita | $.15/lb. |
   | 1966 | 3.5 million bushels | .05 bushels/capita | $.25/lb. |

   b. | Year | Supply | Demand | Price |
   |------|--------|--------|-------|
   | 1964 | 4.5 million bushels | .05 bushels/capita | $.20/lb. |
   | 1965 | 5.5 million bushels | .05 bushels/capita | $.25/lb. |
   | 1966 | 3.5 million bushels | .05 bushels/capita | $.15/lb. |

4. A scientist proposes the following theory to explain why "fidgets" (a type of swimming worm) always turn left in their swimming:

   Fidgets turn left due to a gene for left-turning.

   The scientist then deduces that if he removes the suspected gene and the fidgets no longer turn left, that his theory is proved.

   Do you agree or disagree with his conclusion? Why or why not?

Question 4 tests for a general scientific problem strategy of obtaining adequate proof. The fact that the question is about a nonsense domain emphasizes that the interest is in the strategies, not the content.

In this chapter we will discuss research relevant to the declarative and procedural knowledge needed for expertise in science. We will sample some basic skills, conceptual knowledge, and strategies needed in various sub-domains of science, then we will describe some promising approaches to instruction.

BASIC SKILLS

Basic skills are procedures that are performed in a routine manner with minimal attention so that attention to problem-solving goals and solution procedures is not sacrificed. As in mathematics, so too in science the basic skills of any given sub-domain depend on the specifics of that particular sub-domain. Using a microscope is a basic skill required for certain fields of biology but not for chemistry. In chemistry, use of a spectrophotometer might be a basic skill. This specificity of basic skills is somewhat different from what we found for reading and writing, in which the automated basic skills remain the same across sub-domains. For instance, decoding is needed whether one is reading a novel, an income tax form, or a technical article. As you may recall from Chapter 6, we distinguished between "tool" domains and "content" domains, with reading and writing being tool domains. Here we see that one difference between tool and content domains is the degree to which the basic skills apply across the domain or only within specific sub-domains.

There has not been too much work on differences between experts and novices in science on their *speed* of execution of basic skills. However, there are studies of differences in *possession* of basic skills. One illustrative study was done by Okey and R. Gagné (1970). The sub-domain of science that they studied was introductory chemistry. A common type of problem in introductory chemistry classes is predicting whether or not a precipitate (solid matter) will form when two chemicals are mixed together. The answer depends on whether or not the solution is saturated. Once the saturation point is reached, a precipitate will form because a given product can no longer be dissolved.

Figure 15.1 shows a task analysis of the prerequisites needed to solve such problems.

Prerequisites were determined in the same way as for linear algebra problems (see Chapter 11, p. 248). Inspection of this analysis shows that several mathematics skills are needed (skills IIa and IIb and their prerequisites) in addition to several skills specific to chemistry (skill IIc and its prerequisites). Overall, the analysis reveals that many skills are thought to be prerequisite to successful performance. If these skills are performed slowly, or not at all, problem solving will be disrupted.

Okey and Gagné (1970) had high school students work through an instructional program designed to teach the prerequisite skills as well as the final skill of predicting whether or not a mixture would form a precipitate. This instruction took place during science class and

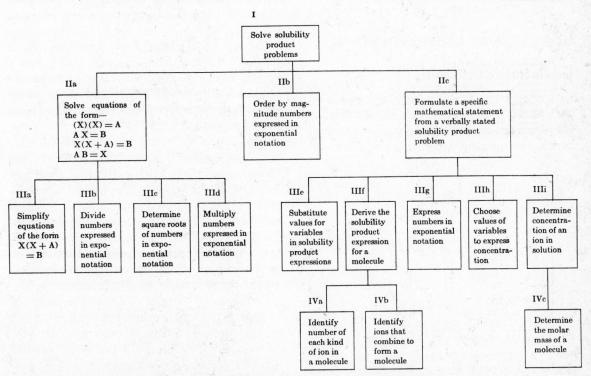

Figure 15.1 A task analysis of the task of solving solubility product problems (from Okey and R.M. Gagné, 1970).

lasted for about a week. They then tested the students on several new prediction problems as well as on their mastery of each prerequisite skill. Figure 15.2 shows what they found out about the relationship between the number of prerequisite skills mastered and successful problem-solving ("criterion test") performance. In general, as the ability to perform basic skills increased, so did performance on the criterion test. Thus, successful problem solving is associated with knowledge of prerequisite skills.

Since work in reading, writing, and math has shown that both knowledge of basic skills and the speed with which these skills are executed are important for problem-solving expertise, it is a good bet that this same finding would hold for science domains. It would be useful to have research data to document this claim.

CONCEPTUAL UNDERSTANDING

Expert-Novice Differences

In Chapter 10 (Problem Solving) you were introduced to the notion that experts analyze problems at a deeper conceptual level than do novices because they have more relevant con-

ceptual knowledge. One example given in that chapter was of expert and novice computer programmers. The expert programmers recalled together lines of program code that fit together to execute a task while the novices recalled together lines of code from different programs that used the same syntax. These data suggested that the experts have schemas for programs and they recall new instances of program code in relation to these schemas. Novices, on the other hand, do not have their knowledge yet organized into conceptual schemas.

In physics, as in programming, differences in the knowledge of experts and novices have been observed. Chi, Feltovich, and Glaser (1981) gave Ph.D. physicists (experts) and students who had had one course in physics (novices) twenty category labels for describing physics problems. These labels had been generated by experts and novices when asked to classify problems. For example, "block on incline" was a typical label generated by a novice, and "Newton's Second Law" was a typical label generated by an expert. Subjects were asked to tell all they could about problems of the type signalled by the label and how these problems might be solved. From the responses, the experimenters created a declarative knowledge network that reflected the ideas described by each subject. If a subject mentioned the conditions under which a given principle should apply, then a box signifying procedural knowledge was added to the declarative knowledge structure. Interestingly, only the experts mentioned conditions of application, which showed greater integration of procedural knowledge and schemas.

Figures 15.3 and 15.4 show the memory structures derived for the label "incline plane" for one novice and one expert, respectively. As you can see, many of the nodes in the novice's structure are descriptive (e.g., "pulley," "angle of incline"). Other nodes are attributes associated with concrete entities

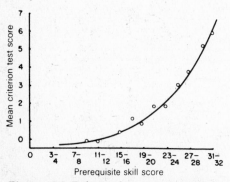

Figure 15.2 Relation between knowledge of prerequisite skills and problem-solving performance (from Okey and R.M. Gagné, 1970).

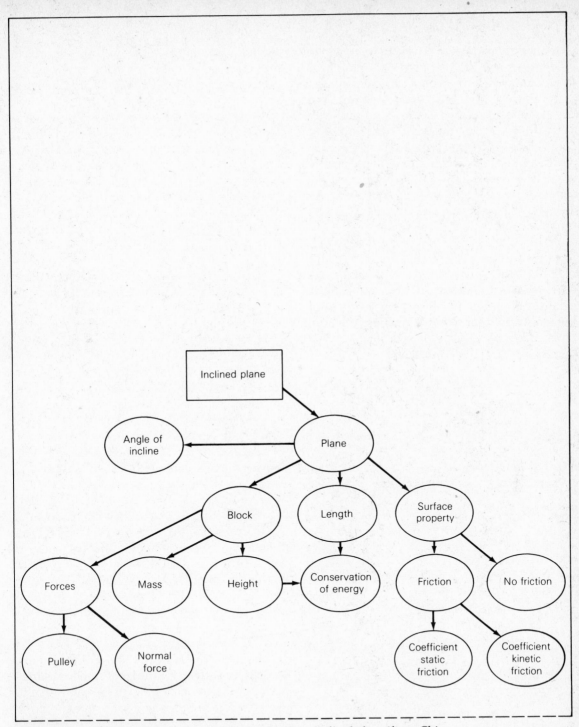

Figure 15.3 A novice's memory structure surrounding *inclined plane* (from Chi, Feltovich, and Glaser, 1981).

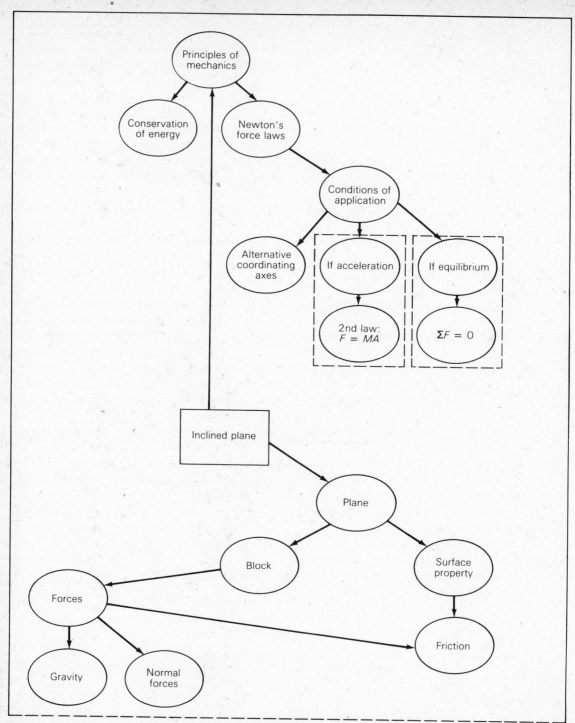

Figure 15.4 An expert's memory structure surrounding *inclined plane* (from Chi, Feltovich, and Glaser, 1981).

(e.g., mass and height are attributes that one associates with blocks). Finally, one node is for a higher-order principle—conservation of energy—but this principle is subordinate in the novice's memory structure.

In contrast, the expert's memory structure contains more fundamental principles (conservation of energy and Newton's force laws) than does the novice's. Also, these principles are not subordinate to more superficial nodes. Finally, the expert's structure contains procedural knowledge for application of Newton's force laws. Thus, the novice and expert memory structures differ in content, organization, and form of knowledge representation.

Bromage and Mayer (1981) have also found a memory content difference between good and poor problem-solvers. The domain that they studied was 35mm cameras and how they work. They had college students (who were unfamiliar with 35mm cameras) read a passage that described (1) how to operate a 35mm camera to achieve various results, and (2) the basic principles that explained why the camera worked the way it did. They then had students recall what they had read and solve some hypothetical problems in camera use. For example, one problem asked the student to describe in writing the adjustments of the camera that would be made to "take a picture of a pole vaulter on a cloudy day."

Students' recall protocols were scored for content. The types of content that Bromage and Mayer were interested in were variables, descriptive relationships, and explanatory relationships. Variables were all those things that could be changed on a camera such as f-stop and shutter speed. Descriptive relationships were empirical summaries of relationships among variables—for example, "If the f-stop is changed you can compensate by changing shutter speed." Explanatory relationships were descriptions of the underlying causes or effects of changing some variable—such as, "If the f-stop is changed, there will be a smaller or larger hole for letting light into the camera." Each student's protocol was scored for the number of variables mentioned and for the numbers of descriptive and explanatory relationships given.

The students were divided into low, intermediate, and high problem solvers according to their scores on the problem-solving test. Then the recall data for these three groups were examined. Table 15.2 shows the average recall of variables, descriptive relationships (d-relations), and explanatory relationships (e-relations) for each group. The average amount of variables and descriptive relationships recalled did not differ significantly across groups, but the high problem solver group recalled more explanatory relationships than did either the intermediate or low groups. In fact, the high group recalled about twice as many explanatory relationships as did the other groups.

Thus, good problem solvers have more access to explanatory principles and to the

Table 15.2 Amount of recall of different types of content from a passage about cameras and problem-solving performance (adapted from Bromage and Mayer, 1981).

PROBLEM-SOLVING ABILITY	RECALL TEST			PROBLEM-SOLVING TEST
	VARIABLES	D-RELATIONS	E-RELATIONS	
Low	9.0	11.0	2.1	6.5
Intermediate	11.1	13.3	2.7	10.5
High	11.0	11.4	5.3	15.0

conditions of application of these principles than do poor problem solvers. Since this study was correlational, we cannot say with certainty that the knowledge differences explain the problem-solving differences. However, we have described studies throughout this book in which knowledge differences were induced and led to problem-solving differences. Moreover, the theoretical framework that we have described elucidates the central role of conceptual knowledge in influencing the direction of attention and also in activating relevant long-term memory structures—be they basic skills or strategies or additional schemas, images, or propositions.

Developmental Studies of Conceptual Knowledge

When one of us was a primary school teacher in West Africa, she was surprised to find that her students believed that the harmless variety of chameleon in the area was poisonous. Similarly, adults are often surprised at the "misconceptions" (from the adult's point of view) that children have about various natural phenomena. Very young children, for example, believe that the earth is flat, and, although older children believe that the earth is a sphere, they also think that all people live on the top of this sphere (Nussbaum, 1979; Sneider & Pulos, 1983).

The Concept of Living Things. One concept that has been studied developmentally in great detail is the concept of *alive*. Siegler and Richards (1983) asked both children and adults a variety of questions that revealed their knowledge of aliveness. For example, they asked them to name some instances of things that were alive, to evaluate whether something (e.g., a car or a tree) was alive or not, and to name the attributes they thought distinguished living from non-living things.

From the answers to these questions, they developed a model of the propositional networks for alive possessed by typical children and adults.

Figures 15.5 and 15.6 show the network representation for four-year-olds and adults, respectively. The propositions connected by solid lines are strong propositions, while those connected by dashed lines are weak. Both the four-year-old and adult have strong propositions representing the ideas that animals are moving things, noisy things, things with eyes, growing things, reproducing things, and that they are alive. Similarly, both have strong propositions for the ideas that plants are growing things, reproducing things, and things with roots. However, only the adult has a proposition for the idea that plants are alive. Also, the adult has stronger propositions than the child for the ideas that reproducing things are alive, and growing things are alive. Finally, the adult has a proposition to represent the idea that moving things are alive in the sense of being lively as distinct from alive in the sense of biological life.

When asked whether a pecan tree is alive, a person can answer this question by retrieving the fact directly (i.e., "trees are alive"), by retrieving some other facts (e.g., "plants are alive," and "pecan trees are plants") and drawing an inference ("therefore pecan trees are alive"), or by determining the amount of overlap between the attributes of living things and the attributes of pecan trees. If there is a substantial amount of overlap, then it is concluded that pecan trees are alive.

Siegler and Richards found that four-year-olds were much less likely to say that a tree is alive than were adults, and we can see why this is so. First, they do not have the fact that trees are alive stored. Second, they do not have all the other facts needed to draw an inference that trees are alive—specifically, they do not have stored the fact that plants are

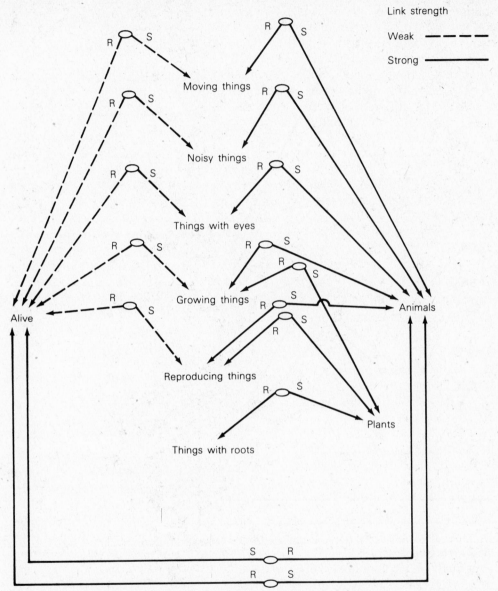

Figure 15.5 A hypothetical propositional network for a four-year-old's concept of *alive*. R = relation, S = subject (adapted from Siegler and Richards, 1983).

alive. Finally, trees have only one of five of the attributes associated with living things—they grow. (Of course, they also reproduce, but this is probably not known to four-year-olds.)

Because there is little overlap for the four-year-old between the attributes of living things and the attributes of trees, she concludes that trees are *not* alive.

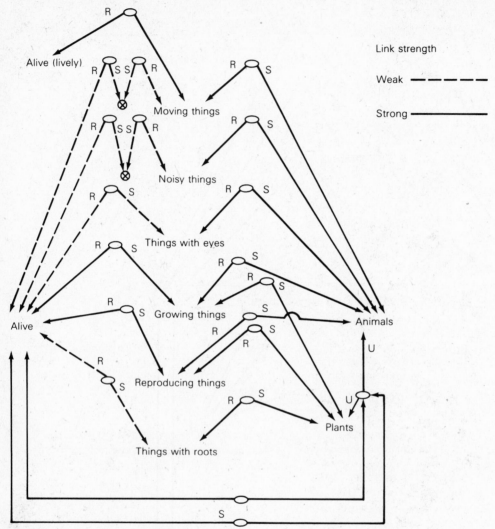

Figure 15.6 A hypothetical propositional network for an adult's concept of alive (adapted from Siegler and Richards, 1983).

In contrast, the adult can deduce that trees are alive from the proposition that plants are alive. Also, for her there is more overlap between attributes of living things and attributes of trees. Besides knowing, as young children do, that trees grow, a typical adult is likely to know that trees reproduce and that they have roots. Thus trees have three attributes of aliveness. Furthermore, two of these attributes are stored as strong propositions, which means they are more likely to be activated than are weak propositions during an attribute comparison process. Thus, the adult's propositional network is much more likely to lead her to conclude that trees are alive.

The Concept of Distance in Balance Beam Problems. Siegler (1976) studied elementary school children's solutions to balance beam problems and found that younger children failed to attend to the distance factor in the problem. Figure 15.7 shows the apparatus used by Siegler, consisting of a balance beam with four pegs placed at equal intervals in each arm. Metal washers could be placed on these pegs, and the arms could move up or down or stay level depending on the arrangement of washers. The experimenter placed washers in various positions while holding the beam steady. He then asked the child to predict what would happen when he released the beam: Would the left arm go up or down, or would the beam not move at all?

Siegler presented each child with six problem types, shown in Figure 15.8. In the **balance** problems, equal numbers of washers were put at equal distances from the fulcrum on each arm, so that the arms should balance. In the **weight** problems, only the weight (number of washers) varied, so that the prediction as to which arm would dip down could be made solely on the basis of weight. Similarly, in the **distance** problems, only the distance of the washers from the fulcrum varied, so the correct answer could be determined solely on the basis of distance. The final three problem types varied both the number of washers and their distance from the fulcrum. In the **conflict-weight** problems, weight was a stronger factor than distance, whereas in the **conflict-distance** problems, distance was the stronger factor. Finally, in **conflict-balance**

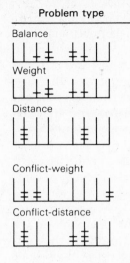

Problem type

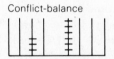

Figure 15.8 The types of problems used to study children's knowledge of factors that influence balance (adapted from Siegler, 1976).

problems, the factors of weight and distance were equal, and the beam would balance.

Table 15.3 shows the percentage of correct answers for different problem types as a function of age. Here all age groups get almost all balance problems correct. Also, the youngest

Table 15.3 Percentage of correct answers for different problem types as a function of age (adapted from Siegler, 1976).

PROBLEM TYPE	AGE			
	5–6	9–11	13–14	16–17
Balance	94	99	99	100
Weight	88	98	98	98
Distance	9	78	81	95
Conflict-weight	86	74	53	51
Conflict-distance	11	32	48	50
Conflict-balance	7	17	26	40

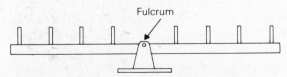

Fulcrum

Figure 15.7 The balance beam used in Siegler's experiments (adapted from Siegler, 1976).

children (5–6) do not do too badly on weight problems and actually do better than older children on conflict-weight problems! For the remaining problem types, there are sizeable increases in success rate across the age groups. The most surprising result is the excellent performance of the five- and six-year-olds on the difficult conflict-weight problems.

Siegler (1976) reasoned that the youngest age group was getting the conflict-weight problems correct not because they were carefully comparing both weight and distance factors, but rather because they were ignoring distance completely. In the terminology we are using in this book, we would say they did not have an understanding yet of the role of distance in affecting balance. The fact that these children did so poorly on distance problems (only 9% correct) supports this explanation. Siegler further suggested that mental representation of distance was needed before children could perform competently across all problem types.

To test this hypothesis, Siegler (1976) placed one balance beam in front of his subjects and one in front of himself. He then placed washers on various pegs on his beam and asked the children to match this on their balance beams. If children are only thinking about weight, they will correctly match the numbers of washers, but not the exact pegs on which these washers are put. On the other hand, if they are thinking about both weight and distance, they will correctly match both the numbers of washers and the exact pegs used by the experimenter. The data showed that five-year-olds were 51% accurate for number of washers, but only 16% correct for peg placement. By contrast, eight-year-olds were 73% and 56% correct, respectively, for number of washers and peg placement. These data confirmed the hypothesis that the five-year-olds were not thinking about distance.

If thinking about distance is important for good performance on balance beam problems,

then training children to think about this dimension should lead to better overall performance. Siegler (1976) trained some five-year-olds to think about distance by using the task in which the children matched on their balance beams what the experimenter had put on his beam. Now, however, the experimenter modeled the process of carefully counting the number of pegs out from the fulcrum. Also, after the child placed her washers, the experimenter gave feedback. Following several training trials, the five-year-olds showed use of the distance factor 51% of the time (compared to 16% with no training). They also improved on their ability to predict what way the balance beam would tilt, especially for problems in which distance was crucial.

In a previous section, we described a correlational study done by Bromage and Mayer (1981) that showed a relationship between conceptual understanding and problem-solving performance. We said that because the study was only correlational we could not firmly conclude that the differences in understanding accounted for the differences in problem solving. In the Siegler study, we have an example in which knowledge was manipulated by helping people acquire the knowledge that was thought to be needed and improvements in problem solving apparently resulted from the increased knowledge. Such instructional studies are a good complement to correlational studies of expertise.

Changes in Conceptual Knowledge Following Instruction

One can imagine that the change from the four-year-old to the adult conception of living things described earlier could occur even in individuals who never take a biology class. Such non-school activities as tending a garden or caring for pets could lead parents to instruct children about the nature of living things. Other studies have documented changes in conceptual understanding that resulted from formal instruction. Shavelson (1972) demonstrated such changes as a result of physics instruction, and Champagne, Klopfer, Desena, and Squires (1981) documented changes that result from geology instruction.

Champagne et al. worked with thirty eighth graders to study changes in knowledge about geology. Prior to instruction, the students were shown thirteen geology concepts written on cards (*granite, igneous, lava, limestone, magma, marble, metamorphic, pumice, rock, sediment, sedimentary, shale,* and *slate*). They were given a large piece of paper and asked to arrange the terms on the paper in a way that showed how they went together. These diagrams were then used to draw inferences about the students' knowledge structures prior to instruction.

Figure 15.9 shows the preinstruction knowledge structure for one student in the study. This student was more advanced than some others in the study in that he already knew that metamorphic, igneous, and sedimentary were different kinds of rock and had ideas about examples of each kind. However, he had no knowledge of the dynamics of rock formation.

After pretesting, the students received four weeks of instruction on types of rocks and how they are formed. Following this, they were again asked to arrange the thirteen geology concepts on a large sheet of paper and indicate the relationships between concepts. Figure 15.10 shows the structure produced after instruction by the student who produced the preinstruction structure shown in Figure 15.9. Notice that to the preinstruction structure has been added new knowledge about how igneous rock forms metamorphic rock and how metamorphic rock forms sedimentary rock. Also, there has been a good amount of rearrangement of examples of each kind of rock. For instance, before instruction this student classified granite as a metamorphic rock, whereas after instruction he classified it as igneous.

Since this study by Champagne et al. (1981) was conducted, science educators have become quite interested in how one best instructs students to help them change or develop their conceptual understanding of natural phenomena. One example of this type of instruction for conceptual change will be given at the end of this chapter.

In sum, a variety of studies have shown that experts, more well-trained students, and older persons all have greater conceptual understanding in science and that increases in understanding are associated with improved

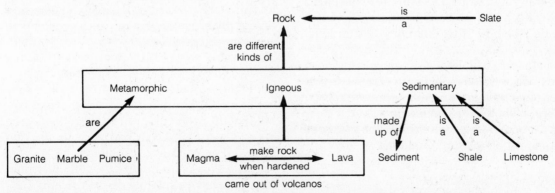

Figure 15.9 Preinstruction knowledge organization of geology knowledge (from Champagne et al., 1981).

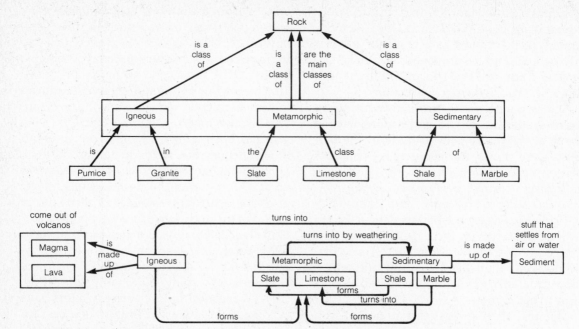

Figure 15.10 Postinstruction knowledge organization of geology knowledge (from Champagne et al., 1981).

problem-solving performance. In the next section we will consider studies that reveal just how increased conceptual understanding influences the problem-solving process.

The Role of Conceptual Understanding in Problem Solving

We may begin to get a feel for how conceptual knowledge and procedural knowledge interact by looking at the different ways in which experts (with more conceptual knowledge) and novices (with less) go about solving problems. The problem-solving process starts with the solver forming a mental representation of the problem in working memory, and it turns out that experts and novices differ a great deal in their problem representations.

Problem Representation

Physical Sciences. Within the physical sciences, problem representation has been most thoroughly studied in physics, usually using dynamics or kinematics problems (Larkin, McDermott, Simon, & Simon, 1980b). One technique for studying problem representation is to ask people to sort problems into categories. The categories can then be used to draw inferences about what aspects of the problem are represented mentally. Chi, Feltovich, and Glaser (1981) gave expert and novice physicists several physics problems to sort into categories in any way they wanted. The experts were Ph.D. physicists while the novices were taking their first course in physics. Figures 15.11 and 15.12 show typical sorting by novices and experts, respectively. Notice that the problems grouped together by the novices were ones that had very similar diagrams. For example, problems 10(11) and 11(39), which were grouped together by novices, both have a rotating disc. Problems 7(23) and 7(35), which were also grouped together by novices, both have an inclined plane. By

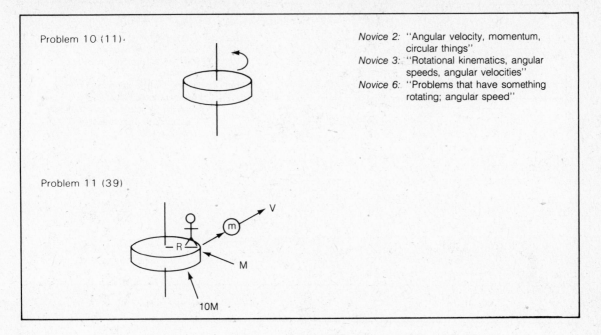

Problem 10 (11).

Novice 2: "Angular velocity, momentum, circular things"
Novice 3: "Rotational kinematics, angular speeds, angular velocities"
Novice 6: "Problems that have something rotating; angular speed"

Problem 11 (39)

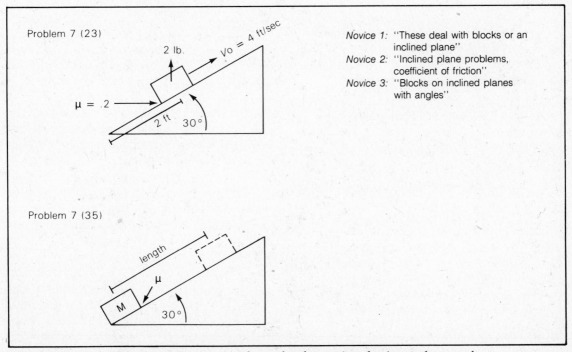

Problem 7 (23)

Novice 1: "These deal with blocks or an inclined plane"
Novice 2: "Inclined plane problems, coefficient of friction"
Novice 3: "Blocks on inclined planes with angles"

Problem 7 (35)

Figure 15.11 Two pairs of problems grouped together by novice physics students and their explanations for the grouping (from Chi, Feltovich, and Glaser, 1981).

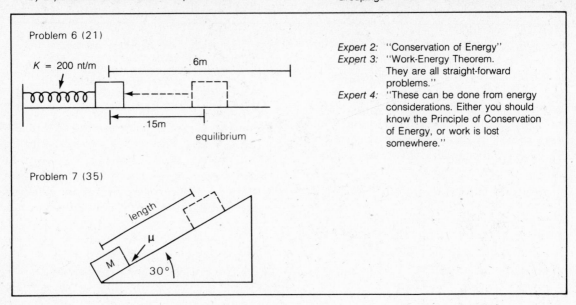

Problem 6 (21)

Problem 7 (35)

Expert 2: "Conservation of Energy"
Expert 3: "Work-Energy Theorem.
They are all straight-forward
problems."
Expert 4: "These can be done from energy
considerations. Either you should
know the Principle of Conservation
of Energy, or work is lost
somewhere."

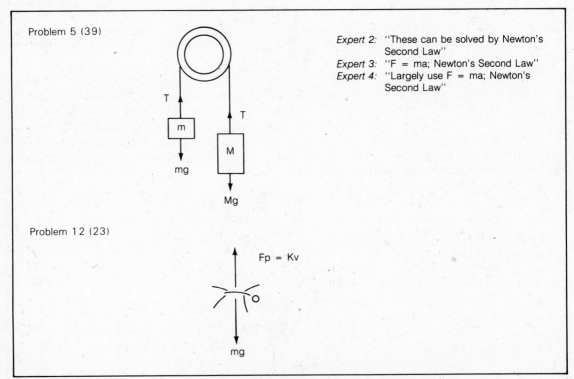

Problem 5 (39)

Problem 12 (23)

Expert 2: "These can be solved by Newton's
Second Law"
Expert 3: "F = ma; Newton's Second Law"
Expert 4: "Largely use F = ma; Newton's
Second Law"

Figure 15.12 Two pairs of problems grouped together by expert physicists and their explanations for why they grouped them (from Chi, Feltovich, and Glaser, 1981).

contrast, the problems grouped together by experts did not necessarily have similar diagrams. Instead, they shared the same underlying solution principle. For example, problems 6(21) and 7(35) in Figure 15.12 are both solved by using the Conservation of Energy principle, while problems 5(39) and 12(23) are both solved by using Newton's Second Law. These results suggest that novices represent more superficial aspects of a problem than do experts.

The novices' and experts' explanations for why they grouped problems together further corroborates the notion that novices represent more superficial aspects of the problem than do experts. For example, novices stated that problems 7(23) and 7(35) go together because they both have inclined planes. On the other hand, experts claimed that they put 6(21) and 7(35) together because they both involved the principle of Conservation of Energy.

Recall that in Silver's study, in the chapter on mathematics, the good problem solvers classified problems according to the solution principle whereas the poor problem solvers classified problems according to their story line, such as farmer stories. Thus, the quality of problem representation appears to be important across problem-solving domains. Another domain in which it appears to be important is social science.

Social Sciences. Like the expert-novice differences in problem representation found for physics, Voss, Tyler, and Yengo (1983) find problem representation differences between experts and novices in the social sciences. These researchers compared thinking-aloud protocols of political scientists whose specialty was Soviet politics and college students taking a Soviet political science course. The problem given to all these individuals was:

Assume you are head of the Soviet Ministry of Agriculture and assume crop productivity has been low over the past several years. You now have the responsibility of increasing crop production. How would you go about doing this?

In comparing the protocols of the Soviet experts and the students, it was found that 24% of the experts' protocol statements were devoted to defining the problem, whereas for the students almost none of their statements had to do with problem definition. What the experts did during problem definition was specify constraints within which they thought the problem had to be solved. For example, Soviet ideology was a constraint, as was the fact that very little of Soviet land is arable. The students failed to further define the problem, but began immediately to spout off a string of possible solutions. Very likely, the students did not have enough declarative knowledge of Soviet economy, geography, and climate to develop constraints on the solution of the problem.

While there are of course great differences between problems confronted in different domains, it is interesting that similarities in the problem-solving behavior of experts and novices can be detected across domains. In political science, the experts clearly represented the problem at a deeper level than did the novices, and in this sense they are similar to experts in physics problem solving. In both cases, the differences in problem representation could be traced at least in part to the differences in the amount of conceptual knowledge possessed by experts versus novices.

Problem Solution Paths

Experts and novices differ not only in the way they represent problems, but also in the way they solve them.

Physics. Recall from Chapter 10 (Problem Solving and Reasoning) that in solving novel problems—that is, any problem for which one does not have a ready solution—a great deal of search is involved in finding the right solution. Various strategies are used to limit search to relevant areas of memory. One of the most powerful of these is means-ends analysis in which one defines one's goal and then retrieves from memory known ways of reaching that goal. In contrast to solving novel problems, solving familiar problems does not involve much search. Rather, the solver acts in a fairly automatic fashion, recognizing a familiar problem schema and carrying out a solution procedure associated with this schema.

Larkin and her colleagues (Larkin, 1981; Larkin et al., 1980b) have found that when experts and novices are confronted with physics problems from introductory level physics, they behave differently. Novice physics problem solvers behave the way people do in general when confronted with novel problems, whereas expert physics problem solvers behave the way people do in general when confronted with familiar problems. That is, novices engage in a lot of search activity while trying to find a solution. Many of them, in fact, use means-ends analysis. For example, they first determine the desired goal of the problem and then try to come up with rules that get them closer to the desired goal.

As an example of this means-ends procedure consider the physics problem shown in Figure 15.13. For those of you who have never had a physics course, we suggest that you read through the problem anyway. Do not worry about the content—just pay attention to the form. The form of the problem is similar to problems in many domains—it has to do with variables and relationships among variables. The goal of this particular problem is to find the block's speed (v) when it reaches the bottom of the plane. The givens are the angle of the plane from the horizontal (θ), the length of the plane (l), the mass of the block (m), and

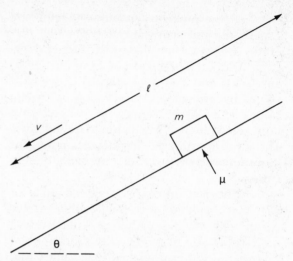

Figure 15.13 A physics problem used to study problem-solution paths (adapted from Larkin et al., 1980b).

the coefficient of friction between the block and the plane (μ).

Larkin et al. had expert and novice physicists think aloud while they solved this problem. From the protocols, they extracted the principles each subject used and the order in which he used them. Table 15.4 shows these data for one expert and one novice. Notice that every step taken by the expert contributes information needed for the solution. The first and second steps determine the two force components that add together to make force (F). The known principle for force is then used to determine the unknown value for acceleration (a) and a is then used to determine the unknown value for time (t). Finally, velocity is determined from the known values for a and t. Clearly, this solution path is a "working-forward" path: it starts with some of the givens in the problem and uses these to generate more information that is needed to determine the unknown velocity.

By contrast, the novice uses a working-backwards solution path. He starts by retrieving a formula that contains the desired un-

Table 15.4 Solution paths for an expert and novice solving the physics problem shown in Figure 15.13 (constructed from information in Larkin et al., 1980b).

	AN EXPERT'S SOLUTION PATH	
STEP	PRINCIPLE APPLIED	QUANTITY COMPUTED
1	$Fg'' = mg \sin \theta$	Finds gravitational force (Fg'')
2	$f = \mu N$	Finds frictional force (f)
3	$F = Fg'' + f = ma$	Finds acceleration (a)
4	$x = v_o + 1/2 \, (at^2)$	Finds time (t) by substituting the known value l for x
5	$v = v_o + at$	Finds velocity (v)

	A NOVICE'S SOLUTION PATH	
STEP	PRINCIPLE APPLIED	GOAL
1	$v = v_o + at$	Tries to solve for velocity
2	$v^2 - v_o^2 + = ax$	Tries to solve for velocity
3	$a(N)$	Tries to solve for acceleration (a), thinking (incorrectly) that a is solely a function of normal force (N)
4	$f = N$	Tries to solve for N

known (v). Then he sees that there are other unknowns in this formula so it cannot be used to solve for v. So he retrieves another formula containing the unknown v. This formula also contains another unknown, but this time, instead of abandoning the formula, he sets a subgoal to find the other unknown (a). He (incorrectly) thinks that a is a function only of normal force (N). Since N is also unknown, he sets the subgoal of finding N. At this point, the novice stops in his attempts to solve the problem.

The important aspect to notice about the novice's protocol is its "working-backwards" character. He starts by identifying the goal (v), then finds a formula that contains v, then works backwards through a series of subgoals to try to solve this formula. The order of application of principles by the novice is almost the exact opposite of the order used by the expert. For example, the first principle used by the novice is the last one used by the expert.

Working backwards is a powerful strategy for a novice to use because it limits the search of memory to areas that have relevance to the goal. If one is lost in a forest, one is better off determining the direction (N, S, E, or W) of one's goal and limiting one's search for a path to this direction than wandering around at random. The difference between the novice and the expert is that the expert is not lost—he knows a path that leads to the goal and follows it.

Although Larkin et al. did not measure conceptual understanding independently, we can speculate that their expert's understanding was organized somewhat like Chi et al.'s expert's—with important principles being the organizing force and with conditions of application of principles being closely tied to general understanding of the principles. In other words, the experts probably had problem schemas for familiar problems. Possession of such schemas led to rapid execution of solution procedures. Novices, lacking this conceptual basis, had to revert to search procedures.

Social Sciences. An example of an expert's solution to the Soviet agriculture problem is

Table 15.5 An expert's thinking-aloud protocol while solving the Soviet agriculture problem (adapted from Voss, Tyler, and Yengo, 1983).

I think that as minister of agriculture, one has to start out with the realization that there are certain kinds of special agriculture constraints within which you are going to work. The first one, the most obvious one, is that by almost every count only 10 percent of the land in the Soviet Union is arable. This is normally what is called the Blackland in the Ukraine and surrounding areas. And secondly, even in that arable 10 percent of the total land surface, you still have climate for instance, problems over which you have no direct control. Okay, so that is sort of the overall parameter in which we are working.

Now we have traditionally in the Soviet Union used three kinds of policies to increase agricultural production. Of course, agricultural production has been our "Achilles' heel" and something that we have inherited from the time the czars freed the serfs. Even before then, the agricultural production was low because historically the aristocracy had no need to fend for itself, as it turned to the czar for its support and hence never, like the English aristocracy for instance, introduced modern methods of fertilization, never went to enclosures or consolidations of lands, never experimented with crop rotation. That was passed on to the peasants and throughout the period when the peasant had been freed to do what he willed with the land, he's responding with the old, rather inefficient ways.

At any rate, we have had three different ways by which we have tried to increase agricultural production. The first one might be labeled exhortation. The Soviet approach to agricultural production is to mount campaigns continually to call for more effort on the part of the peasants and agricultural workers and put more effort into their labor activities for agricultural production. Those things are mounted periodically, quite frankly, I think that they are a waste of time and energy and they really, as minister of agriculture I must say, that they really do nothing more than give the party a sense of false importance because it's normally incumbent upon the party to develop these ideo-

logical indoctrination campaigns and the notion of mind over matter in this case hasn't paid off and it leaves the party with the belief that ideological, and if you'll excuse the term, spiritual policies can overcome objective limitations. So, I wouldn't emphasize very much exhortation.

It seems to me that the second way that we traditionally go about trying to increase agricultural production is through constant reorganization. That leads to confusion, that leads to mismanagement and that has forced a mind set upon the peasant agricultural worker of sort of laying back and waiting because this too will also pass. We've gone through collectives, state farms, and machine tractor stations, the latest attempt at reorganization is through the development of what are called agroindustrialist complexes, which has knocked down, by the way, the number of collectives from about 250,000 to 30,000 in the last five years, in which the former collective farmer becomes a wage earner.

So, I think we're going to have to tend, and I'm going to talk a minute, we have to tend to the nature of agricultural production. I want to say one thing, and I have to recognize that this is clear as day, and that is, that in all of these cases more or less except for stringent ideological periods we've always allowed the private crop to exist even though we take it to be a much more primitive, less historically progressive form of agricultural production. We must realize that in terms of some of our food staples, even until today, roughly 40 percent of the food staples are grown on the private plots.

The third thing that we've done and this is where I'd like to start off in terms of turning around agricultural production, the third thing we've done is we've tried to mechanize, and I want to use that in the broad sense because it is not the word I want, we have tried to mechanize industrial production. Not just mechanize it but also introduce scientific advances in Soviet production.

shown in Table 15.5. The expert begins by adding constraints to the problem, such as the small amount of arable land available in Russia. He then discusses what has been done in the past to solve this problem—exhortation and reorganization—and states why these attempts have failed. Finally, he proposes a solution—mechanization and technological

Table 15.6 A novice's thinking-aloud protocol while solving the Soviet agriculture problem (adapted from Voss, Tyler, and Yengo, 1983).

Old-fashioned methods of farming. So maybe what needs to be done is to introduce newer methods of farming and obviously the people probably need to be educated on how to use these new methods, especially if they introduce new machinery. I remember reading somewhere that on the land that the people own themselves, that crop production is much higher than it was on the state plots. Perhaps if the people could be allocated more benefits from the state land, rather than giving it all to the state, crop production might increase. Maybe the organization of how the crops are planted and harvested is not adequate. Perhaps that should be changed. What kind of system they use to plant the crops, if people from a certain town have to go out to a state plot and plant at a certain time. Maybe if it has to be worked around their own little private ground, perhaps they are planting and harvesting at the wrong times. It seems that just education in general may be a problem, like updating of methods.

[What about their machinery?] I think they would need new machinery. When I think of the machinery they have, they probably have old rusting harvester machinery. And if they got it, they'd probably import their new machinery, and they'd have to educate the people on how to use it, or there would probably be only a handful of people could use it, and if something should break, I doubt there would be very many people who would know how to repair, so maybe something on that line maybe if their machinery is broken down. Maybe soil fertilization methods and maybe their horticulture isn't very good. Maybe the people have been planting crops on this land year in and year out and they never fertilized land and it's just really arid and not fertile.

[What about climate?] I'm not sure about their climate. I know it's very wintery and pretty dry, a short summer. Maybe they're not planting the right crops for the climate. Maybe they're trying to grow the wrong types of plants. Maybe they should study the climate more and what types of crops grow better in that type of climate. They're probably not growing pineapples. Maybe their irrigation is bad. If it's dry maybe they have no irrigation system and the crops all just dry up and wither away, but maybe to have an efficient irrigation system, they would need better engineering. Maybe they don't have that.

That's about it. [Can you think of anything else?] The government is probably very much involved in crop production anyway, but maybe they would really study the problem of why crop production is lower, if they would get more people involved at the lower level where its happening rather than have like a bureaucratic overlook of the thing and maybe have a few foreman-type people supervise them. The people who are doing the planting, and who are deciding what needs to be planted and who are tending the crops—maybe people don't tend the crops, if it is state land. Maybe they're tending their own crops on their own land. Maybe weeds are overcoming them. Maybe there's a way to get the people more incentive. I think that's probably important. If they don't have any incentive, they're not going to take care of the crops very well, if they have to give them all away and have old machinery and no irrigation and dry land and that's about all I can think of.

advancement—that is a good solution within the constraints identified.

An example of a novice's solution is shown in Table 15.6. The novice's entire protocol is devoted to generating solutions. Even in the first paragraph, for example, the novice proposes mechanization, more incentive, reorganization, and education as four possible solutions. This generation of solutions continues throughout the protocol.

Voss et al. (1983) found two major quantitative differences in the protocols of experts and novices. First, the experts backed up any given claim with an average of 8.8 arguments, while the novices used only 2.3 arguments to back up a claim. Second, the experts followed a given line of reasoning for an average of 7.1 ideas, while the novices produced only 2.6 ideas in a given chain of thought. Although they did not have an independent measure of conceptual understanding, it makes a lot of sense to say that these differences in problem solving resulted from such knowledge differences. That is, it is hard to give lots of arguments to back up a claim if one does not have these arguments in memory.

Summary

In this section, we have seen the influence of conceptual understanding on both problem representation and problem-solving processes. Experts, with deeper conceptual understanding, tend to represent problems in terms of this understanding. This shows in how they group problems together and in how they add constraints to ill-defined problems. Too, experts' understanding allows them to recognize familiar problems using problem schemas and to execute the solutions whose conditions are matched by the problem schema. Finally, in ill-defined problems, richer conceptual knowledge leads to more extensive justification of one's proposed solution.

STRATEGIES

The final element of competence in our model of expertise in science is strategies. As was true for math, there are strategies that are specific to particular sub-domains and there are also rather general strategies that apply across many of the sub-domains of science. Since general strategies were discussed in chapters 10 and 11, we will illustrate the notion of strategies here with a specific technological domain: troubleshooting electronics equipment on airplanes.

Strategies for Troubleshooting Electronic Equipment

Means et al. (1988) conducted an analysis of experts and novices in the Air Force whose job was to diagnose electronic problems with aircraft equipment. Their findings illustrate nicely three important points about strategies: (1) that they can be highly context specific, depending on specific equipment for their utility, (2) that they can be dependent on the possession of basic skills, and (3) that they can be dependent for their effectiveness on the degree of conceptual understanding possessed by the problem solver.

Means et al. (1988) found a standard procedure that the technicians use to diagnose equipment failures. First, they receive an aircraft component that was suspected of being faulty. They hook up this component (called the *unit under test* or *UUT*) to automated test equipment. This equipment consists of a computer and banks of electronic relays, switches, and conditioners that simulate flight conditions and record the UUT's reactions to various flight conditions (see Figure 15.14). Depending on the reactions noted, a variety of possible causes of the electrical fault are identified.

Means et al. (1988) discovered that the automated test equipment itself sometimes

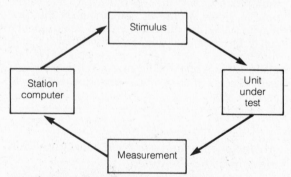

Figure 15.14 An automated test station for diagnosing electronic failures on aircraft equipment. The unit under test is taken off the aircraft and hooked up to the test equipment. The test equipment includes a station computer, stimulus equipment that simulates electrical signals the unit under test would receive in flight, and measurement equipment that measures the unit's reactions to these signals.

had electronic failures and that these failures were even harder to diagnose than were aircraft equipment failures. Only the most expert technicians in a given shop were able to handle these failures.

Because they were interested in how the most expert troubleshooters solved problems, Means et al. used problems involving faults in the automated test equipment itself. They gave these problems to experts and novices and asked them to think aloud while solving. Then they analyzed the protocols to determine the basic skills, conceptual understanding, and strategies that accounted for problem-solving performance.

In a typical problem, both experts and novices started out by running diagnostic software on the automated test equipment. This software often identified probable causes of failure. They then checked the probable causes either by replacing them one by one or by taking measurements to see if they were receiving and putting out the correct amount of current. If these activities failed to identify the failure, then they would trace the circuit in the suspected problem area and take measurements until the fault was localized. Circuit tracing often involved consulting schematic diagrams of circuitry. Because of the size and complexity of the system, schematics for the test equipment were contained in not just one, but several large books.

The researchers identified five strategies. The first—**space splitting**—involved taking measurements at a halfway point in a circuit. For example, look at the circuit in Figure 15.15. There are six devices hooked up in a series, and there is a fault somewhere between the beginning of this series and the end. Someone who uses space splitting will measure the current between the third and fourth device to see if it is as it should be. She can thus eliminate half of the circuit from further investigation. Someone who does not use this strategy might start measuring the input and out-

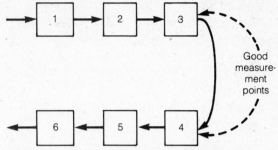

Figure 15.15 A hypothetical electrical circuit showing six devices and input to and output from each device (where measurements can be taken). If it is not known where the fault lies, a good troubleshooter will start by taking measurements near the middle of the circuit (e.g., the output from Device 3 or the input to Device 4). This will allow her to localize the fault faster than would sequential measuring from Device 1 through Device 6. This method is called the space-splitting strategy.

put of each device from one side of the series. If the fault is on the other end, he will take a long time to find it.

The second strategy—**reconfiguration**—involved doing something to make the current go around a suspected faulty area. For example, look at the diagram in Figure 15.16. If element *A* is the suspected faulty element, then a device may be rewired to avoid that element temporarily. If measurements following the reconfiguration are normal, then this confirms that element *A* is the faulty one.

The third strategy was called **historical analysis.** This involved finding out what the system was doing just prior to detection of the fault. Such an analysis can help narrow down the search to areas that are functionally related to whatever was being done just prior to fault detection. For example, if a measurement was being taken by the system when the fault was detected, then the search for a fault might begin in system elements that are related to measurement functions.

The fourth strategy was **use of probability information.** Experienced troubleshooters

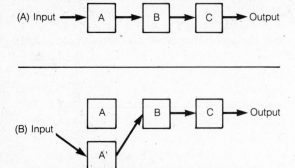

Figure 15.16 (A) A hypothetical circuit involving Device A, and (B) a reconfiguration using A'. Expert troubleshooters, who understand the functions of various system components, use this reconfiguration strategy to localize faults.

knew which devices in the test equipment failed most frequently. If they had a choice between measuring a device that failed frequently and one that failed seldom, they chose the one that failed frequently. Novices who lacked this information often spent time taking measurements or replacing devices that were unlikely to fail.

A final strategy was called **check the probable cause of failure.** This involved checking the device(s) that the computer software identified as being the probable cause of failure.

The researchers found that experts were more likely to use historical analysis, reconfiguration, and probability information than were the novices. Both experts and novices checked the probable cause of failure and both used space-splitting. However, the experts were more successful at space-splitting than were the novices. They were more successful because of their better functional understanding of flow of electricity through the system, so they knew better where real halfway points were. The experts' greater use of historical analysis and reconfiguration was also tied to their better functional understanding. If one does not understand how the components in a system function, then historical analysis does

not help one narrow things down. Moreover, one may not know how the system can be reconfigured. Thus use of several of the strategies required good conceptual understanding of the system.

Strategy use also relied on having automated basic skills. If taking measurements was not done rather automatically, a troubleshooter could forget where he was in a circuit while concentrating on taking a measurement. Reconfiguration was often done via computer code rather than by hands-on rewiring. This required a familiarity with interpreting and using the computer code. Finally, being able to read schematics fairly rapidly was important in implementing space splitting and other strategies.

Thus, we see how strategies that are specific to a sub-domain rely on both basic skills and conceptual understanding for their optimal implementation. Given adequate basic skills and conceptual understanding, the strategies can save the individual a great deal of time and can increase the probability of a successful outcome.

INSTRUCTION

Instruction to Promote Conceptual Understanding

There has been a great deal of interest among science educators in the area of conceptual understanding. Researchers in a number of sub-domains discovered that students had misconceptions about natural phenomena, and they also discovered that both traditional lecture-lab approaches and discovery science approaches did little to get students to abandon or substantially change their misconceptions (for a summary see Roth, 1990). Posner, Strike, Hewson, & Gertzog (1982) and Hewson and Hewson (1984) have proposed theories of conceptual change that address this problem. Posner et al., for example, propose that the following three elements are necessary for students to relinquish misconceptions and create scientifically adequate conceptions of phenomena:

1. The student needs to recognize that there is a conflict between the scientific explanation of a phenomenon and his own explanation.

2. The student needs to realize that his own conceptions are either inadequate to explain or inconsistent with observable evidence.

3. The student needs to believe that the scientific alternative provides a more adequate, consistent, or useful explanation than his own.

To some extent these elements are similar to the elements required for schema refinement, given in Chapter 8. Specifically, for schema refinement, the student needs to see a conflict between his claim for a schema and what others claim for it. Then he needs to have experience with both examples and matched non-examples of the schema that force attention to a distinction that he had not made. Similarly, here, Posner et al. recommend getting students to attend to things that are not adequately explained by the student's conceptions. Then they need to experience an alternative conception and attend to the fact that the alternative provides a more comprehensive or useful explanation of observable events.

However, the goal that Posner et al. are interested in is not *refinement* of a schema, but rather major *reorganization* of a set of schemas and/or *construction* of a new schema. Reorganization is more difficult to achieve than refinement because it may involve more cognitive effort. Therefore, the motivation to do it has to be strong. Also, what is being compared is more complex. In the case of schema refinement, examples and non-examples are being compared for crucial differences. In conceptual change, two whole systems of thinking about phenomena are being compared. Thus, although there are similarities in the need to get the learner to recognize a lack and to compare old and new ways of viewing something, there are differences due to the greater complexity involved in conceptual change.

An Example of Instruction to Promote Conceptual Change. K.J. Roth (1986) studied conceptual change in sixth graders as they dealt with the notions of food and how plants obtain food. Through her own teaching, Roth had found that many students believe that plants get food from the soil, rather than making it in their leaves. Even when they knew that plants made food in their leaves, they still thought that some food came through the soil. These ideas seemed to derive from the everyday notion of food and eating. Humans ingest things and most of these things are called "food." Plants ingest things through their roots, therefore these things they ingest must be food. For example, when asked how a plant gets food, one eighth grade student (typical of others) answered:

> It gets minerals from the soil and water from the soil. It gets sunlight from the sun. It gets . . . that's about it (Roth, 1986, p. 2).

In other words, students had rather strong and well developed ideas about what food is and how plants got food, and they seemed resistant to giving up these ideas.

Roth decided to write an experimental text about photosynthesis, using Posner et al.'s suggestions for how to induce conceptual change. The text presented some experiments that are often presented in units on photosynthesis, but presented them differently. Specifically, this experimental text began by asking students "How do you think plants get their food?" and "How would you define food?" These questions were asked so that students would activate their current understandings, which typically include the misconceptions described above. The text then presented experimental evidence and other information that challenged students' misconceptions. This presentation was done to fulfill the requirements of Step 1 in Posner et al.'s conceptual change model—that of getting students to recognize a problem with their current conceptions. This realization should motivate students to search for new explanations. If soil, water, fertilizer, and sun are not food for plants, then what is?

At this point, the experimental text introduced the idea of photosynthesis. Following this, there was a review of key concepts, then the text posed several application questions to the students—questions that would be answered incorrectly if the students clung to their misconceptions, but correctly if they adopted the more scientifically correct view of how plants get food.

To see if her experimental text was effective in producing conceptual change, Roth compared its effects to the effects of reading one of two alternative texts. The two alternatives were sections of two middle school science texts that dealt with photosynthesis. The alternative texts covered essentially the same material, and the reading levels of all three texts were also similar. However, the commercial texts presented photosynthesis in a more straightforward manner. That is, they did not begin by eliciting students' misconceptions and showing how these misconceptions did not fit with evidence.

Roth used stratified random sampling to assign six middle school students to read each text over a three-day period. In each group, the students' reading abilities ranged from fourth grade to post high school. The students took a pretest two weeks prior to reading the text on photosynthesis and an identical post-

test the day after completing reading of the text. The test included a variety of item formats—from true-false and multiple choice to essay and clinical interview—to probe students' understanding of photosynthesis and food in plants.

On each of the three days of the experiment, the students read a portion of their assigned text and responded to an interview immediately after completing their reading assignment. The interview asked the student to recall what she had just read and to give one or two main ideas. Then the interview probed whether or not the student's conceptions had changed based on the day's reading. Finally, there were questions that attempted to assess the type of reading strategy the student had used—in particular the extent to which the reader relied on prior knowledge versus text-based information.

Table 15.7 shows the six types of reading strategies that Roth identified. The first strategy involved almost completely relying on prior knowledge. The second strategy involved keying in on "big" words in the text as if the goal were to spit back these big words on some test. The third strategy involved memorizing facts from the text. Whereas these first three strategies did not appear to have meaningful learning as a goal, the fourth strategy did. The fourth strategy involved developing a meaningful understanding of text material. Interestingly, it also involved trying to keep one's understanding of the text separate from one's everyday understanding. The fifth strategy had the goal of using the text to confirm one's preconceptions, so it involved a selective reading of information. Only the sixth strategy seemed to have the goal of conceptual change—that is, to make sense of the text ideas and coordinate (and change if necessary) one's prior ideas to be consistent with the new ideas.

Table 15.8 shows the dominant strategy used by each student on each day of the

Table 15.7 Text processing strategies (from Roth, 1986).

	SOURCE OF KNOWLEDGE FOR ANSWERING TEXT-BASED QUESTIONS	SOURCE OF KNOWLEDGE FOR ANSWERING REAL-WORLD QUESTIONS	SCHOOL KNOWLEDGE	READING GOAL
1. Overreliance on prior real-world knowledge	Prior knowledge	Prior knowledge	Prior knowledge can help you answer questions	To finish school task
2. Overreliance on isolated words in text	"Big" words in the text	Prior knowledge	Big words in text are important to use	To finish school task
3. Overreliance on facts in text—additive notion of learning	Facts in the text	Prior knowledge	Learning is memorizing lists of facts	To memorize facts about plants
4. Separating disciplinary knowledge and real-world knowledge as two distinct, equally sensible worlds of knowledge	Disciplinary view presented in the text	Prior knowledge	To make sense of text, you cannot try to relate it to real-world knowledge	To make sense of text view of plants
5. Overreliance on prior knowledge to make "sense" of disciplinary view in the text	Prior knowledge / Disciplinary view presented in the text	Prior knowledge / Disciplinary view presented in the text		To make sure I'm right; to add a few details to what I already know
6. Using text knowledge to change real-world ideas	Disciplinary view presented in the text / Prior knowledge	Disciplinary view presented in the text / Prior knowledge		To make sense of text view of plants and to use text view of plan to change real-world view of plants

experiment. As you can see, on the first day, only one student used the sixth strategy. However, on day two six of seven students who had the experimental text were using this strategy whereas only one other student in the other two groups used it. On day three, all the students who read the experimental text used the conceptual change strategy and again only one other student in the other two groups used it. Thus, the evidence is strong that the

Table 15.8 Strategies used by individual students (from Roth, 1986).

TEXT		READING LEVEL	DOMINANT STRATEGY		
			DAY 1	DAY 2	DAY 3
Modern Science	Linda	4.5	1	1	1
	Tracey	5.6	1	2	1
	Danny	7.1	3	2	3
	Sally	8.4	3	5	5
	Kevin	12.6	5	5	5
	Susan	12.6	5	6	6
Concepts in Science	Jill	4.0	3	2	2
	Maria	4.0	1	1	1
	Myra	6.0	3	3	5
	Phil	6.0	5	5	5
	Deborah	10.0	5	5	5
	Parker	PHS[a]	5	5	5
Experimental	Daryl	3.4	5	6	6
	Evalina	5.6	6	6	6
	Allison	7.6	1	5	6
	Doug	8.1	4	6	6
	Vera	8.6	4	6	6
	James	11.3	4	6	6
	Sheila	PHS[a]	5	6	6

[a]Post high school.

experimental text was successful in changing how students processed textbook information.

How did the changes in processing affect learning outcomes? It had a substantial effect. On three key concepts, all but one of the students who read the experimental text showed that they understood the concepts on the posttest, and for one other key concept all the students in this group showed understanding. In contrast, with the exception of one key concept where four of six students reading one of the commercial texts showed understanding, for all other key concepts only zero, one, or two students showed that they understood the concept on the posttest.

In summary, Roth's experiment shows that one can design instruction that changes how students think about scientific concepts and that has a positive impact on how well students integrate the scientific concepts with their prior knowledge.

Conceptual Change and Computer Technology. Many exciting new developments in science education have to do with using computers and other technologies to speed up and encourage conceptual change in students. Computers can simulate natural events and also can show abstract representations of these simulations in ways that make important distinctions visible. Goldberg and Bendall (1992) have taken advantage of this aspect of computers in their work on optics. Their programs allow students to look at photographs of natural phenomena such as the image of a blade of grass being displaced by water or laboratory phenomena such as experiments with shadows. At the same time, the students can use a mouse to draw vector diagrams right on top of these images to predict and explain visual events. In comparison to students in regular optics classes, students who work with these programs show better conceptual understanding of optical phenomena on transfer tests.

White (1984) used computer games to help students achieve a Newtonian (as opposed to Aristotelian) view of force and motion. The games involved a microworld containing an object, a frictionless environment, and fixed-size impulse forces that can be applied by giving commands via the keyboard. The object was a "spaceship" and the frictionless environment was "outer space." In one game, the goal was to get the spaceship around a corner without having it crash into any walls (see Figure 15.17). Naive students expect that the spaceship will move in the direction opposite where the impulse is applied. That is, they do not take into account the direction the object is already moving. The whole series of games had the effect of calling students' attention to inadequacies in their current ways of thinking. Alternative conceptions were offered, and the students who used these alternatives were more successful at the games. After less than one hour of playing these Newtonian computer games, the students significantly improved their ability to correctly answer force and motion problems.

The computer implementations described above involved using computers to call students' attention to natural phenomena and to have them wrestle with predicting and explaining these phenomena. In contrast, the final implementation we will mention calls students' attention to their developing conceptual understandings, independent of outside reality. This implementation is called "semantic networking" and has been developed by Fisher and a number of her colleagues (e.g., Fisher, 1990). Students who use this software can enter concept names and show relationships among concepts as, for example, is shown in Figure 15.18. In some courses, students work on networks throughout the course and can see how the networks grow and change as their knowledge of the subject matter increases. Instructors who have had their students use this software claim that the students become much more interested in a meaningful—as opposed to rote—approach to learning science. That is, they become much more interested in developing their conceptual understanding.

Teaching Students to Read Scientific Texts

Recall from Chapter 7 that the important conditions for acquiring propositional knowledge are organization and elaboration. Therefore, to help students learn new science information, a teacher should do things that encourage organization and elaboration. Since, at least in high school and college, much of a

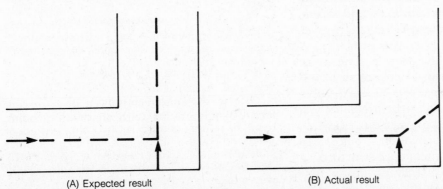

(A) Expected result (B) Actual result

Figure 15.17 The expected and actual results of applying a force to a moving object in White's computer game (from White, 1984).

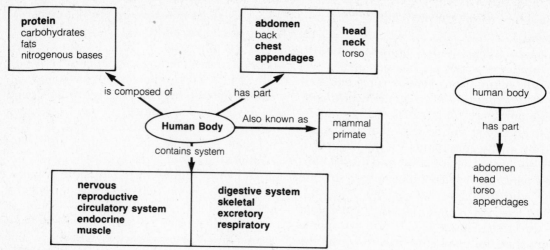

Figure 15.18 Two sample semantic networks (from Fisher, 1990).

student's initial contact with new information comes from texts, it should be useful to teach them how to organize this information. Cook (1983) designed some instructional materials for junior college chemistry students to achieve just this goal.

Cook identified five types of structures commonly used in scientific texts. In her training program, she focused on three of these types: **enumeration, generalization,** and **sequence** (the two other types are **classification** and **compare/contrast**). Enumeration structures give a topic, some subtopics, and several facts related to each subtopic. Table 15.9 gives an example of an enumeration structure. A generalization structure gives a concept or principle and supporting evidence or examples. For instance, the passage shown in Table 15.10 has a generalization structure. Finally, a sequence structure describes a series of events that occur in a particular order. Table 15.11 shows an example of a sequence structure.

Students in Cook's training group first learned to detect these different text struc-

Table 15.9 Passage with an enumeration structure in which there are several subtopics and several facts related to each subtopic (from Cook, 1983).

DNA is unique in three respects. First, it is a very large molecule, having a certain outward uniformity in size, rigidity and shape. Despite this uniformity, however, it has infinite internal variety. Its varied nature gives it the complexity required for information-carrying purposes. One can, indeed, think of the molecule as if it had a chemical alphabet somehow grouped into words which the cell can understand and to which it can respond.

The second characteristic of DNA is its capacity to make copies of itself almost endlessly, and with remarkable exactness. The biologist or chemist would say that such a molecule can replicate, or make a carbon copy of itself, time and again with a very small margin of error.

The third characteristic is its ability to transmit information to other parts of the cell. Depending upon the information transmitted, the behavior of the cell reflects this direction. As we shall see, other molecules play the role of messenger, so that DNA exercises its control of the cell in an indirect manner.

Table 15.10 Passage with a generalization structure in which a concept or principle is defined and then evidence or examples are given to illustrate the general rule (from Cook, 1983).

The human body has an amazing capacity to speed up or slow down physiological processes when changes occur in internal states. This ability is defined as homeostasis. The most sophisticated system in our body which carries on homeostasis is the endocrine system. This is a series of glands in our body which produce hormones. The endocrine system operates on a principle similar to a home heating unit. A thermostat detects the need for heat, turns on the furnace when the temperature is too low, and then turns off the furnace when the temperature is again normal.

One example is the hormone vassopressin, which causes the capillaries to constrict. When the body suffers severe bleeding due to an injury, the amount of this hormone is drastically increased. This helps to slow down blood flow by closing off small blood vessels. Thus, blood flow to the injured area is reduced. The antidiuretic hormone, ADH, helps the body conserve water by directing the kidneys to reabsorb water. A normal amount of ADH tells the kidneys to reabsorb all but about one liter of water daily. However, when the body becomes dehydrated from water loss due to perspiration during hot weather, more ADH is released telling the kidneys to reabsorb more water than usual to make up for that lost.

ated with each subtopic. For generalization passages, the strategy involved identifying the main idea, providing definitions for each word in the main idea, and explaining how the supporting evidence relates to the main idea. For sequence passages, the strategy involved identifying each step, outlining the details of each step, and explaining what was different from one step to the next.

To conduct her study, Cook assigned students in a remedial chemistry course to the strategy training group or the control group. The week of training for the strategy training group was integrated into their regular work for the chemistry course for that week. The assigned reading for the week was a textbook chapter on the electrical properties of atoms. The control group read the textbook in their normal fashion, while the strategy training group read using the new strategies they were learning. For them, the chapter was divided up into nine sections, three each representing enumeration, generalization, and sequence structures.

At the beginning of the week, the strategy training group attended a special lecture designed to motivate them to adopt different reading strategies for different text structures and to teach them to identify the three structures. The motivation was achieved by asking students to state sentences that might occur in two passages—one entitled "Lunch at a Restaurant" and one entitled "The Substantia

tures and then to use a different strategy for reading each type. For enumeration passages, the strategy involved identifying subtopics and then grouping together the facts associ-

Table 15.11 Passage with a sequence structure in which an ordered set of events is described (from Cook, 1983).

ULTRACENTRIFUGATION

The principle behind this is simple. First, a suspension of whole cells in a sugar solution is placed in an ordinary kitchen blender. The solution is mixed in the blender. This causes the cell membrane to break down, and the cell parts are set free in the sugar solution. Then, the mixture is placed in a test tube and the tube spun rapidly for a short time. The most dense parts of the cell, such as the nucleus, are thrown farthest away from the center. They settle in the bottom of the test tube. After these parts are removed, the solution can be spun again at higher speeds. Then the next most dense parts can be removed. Eventually, most of the major parts of the cell can be separated and studied.

Table 15.12 The steps in the reading strategy associated with enumeration passages (from Cook, 1983).

ENUMERATION

Step 1: What is the general topic?
Step 2: Identify the subtopics
   A.
   B.
   C.
   D.
Step 3: Organize and list the details within each subtopic (Do one subtopic at a time, use your own words)
   A.
   B.
   C.
   D.

Nigra." The students were able to generate a complete story for "Lunch at a Restaurant," but virtually nothing for "The Substantia Nigra." This demonstration was used to point out the difference in familiarity between text on everyday topics and scientific text. The lecturer then stated that scientific text did have predictable structures that could be used to help readers organize unfamiliar information and therefore improve learning. Furthermore, they would be learning how to identify and use such structures.

After this motivational segment, the second part of the lecture was devoted to getting the students to distinguish among enumeration, generalization, and sequence passages. This was done by describing the distinguishing criteria for each type of passage and giving an example of each—the minimum needed for schema formation. The examples were segments taken from the students' reading assignment for the previous week. Finally, the steps in each reading strategy (shown in Tables 15.12, 15.13, and 15.14) were demonstrated using the sample passages. At the end of the lecture, the students received a folder containing copies of the reading strategies.

Throughout the week, these students came in at times convenient to them to do their chemistry reading under supervision. They

Table 15.13 The steps in the reading strategy associated with generalization passages (from Cook, 1983).

GENERALIZATION

Step 1: Identify the generalization (main idea)

   List and define key words in the generalization
      Word   Definition

   Restate the generalization in your own words

Step 2: What kind of support is there for the generalization? Does it use examples, illustrations? Does it extend or clarify the generalization?
      Supporting Evidence   Relation to Generalization

Table 15.14 The steps in the reading strategy associated with sequence passages (from Cook, 1983).

SEQUENCE

Step 1: Identify the topic of the passage.
Step 2: Take each step, name it, and then outline the details within each:
        Step 1
        Step 2
        Step 3
        Step 4
Step 3: Discuss (briefly) what is different from one step to the next.
        Step 1 to 2
        Step 2 to 3
        Step 3 to 4

were directed to identify the type of structure used in the chapter segment on which they were working and then to use the reading strategy associated with that particular structure. That is, they were to write down their findings for each of the steps in the strategy. When a student completed a segment, she brought what had been written to the instructor for evaluation. The instructor pointed out any errors and asked the student to correct them. Once the student turned in an error-free worksheet, the instructor gave the student an oral examination over the points covered by the worksheet. The student was not permitted to look at her notes or text during this test.

The purpose of the training program was to get students to learn more from unfamiliar scientific passages by being able to organize the information better. To evaluate the success of the program, students in both the strategy training and control groups took a pre- and posttest. These tests consisted of reading unfamiliar science passages, one each with enumeration, generalization, and sequence structures. After reading, they free recalled information contained in the passages and answered twelve questions over each passage. Eight of the questions were on information directly stated in the passage,

while four questions required the application of text information to novel situations. The highest possible score on the 12 questions across the three passages was 96 points.

Figure 15.19 shows the pre- and posttest results for the twelve questions as a function of training. As you can see, the strategy training group's posttest scores improved by about

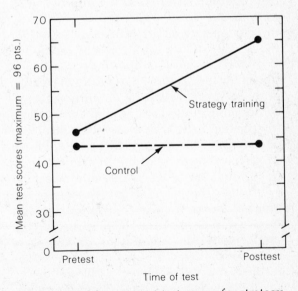

Figure 15.19 Mean correct test scores for strategy training and control groups at pretest and posttest (adapted from Cook, 1983).

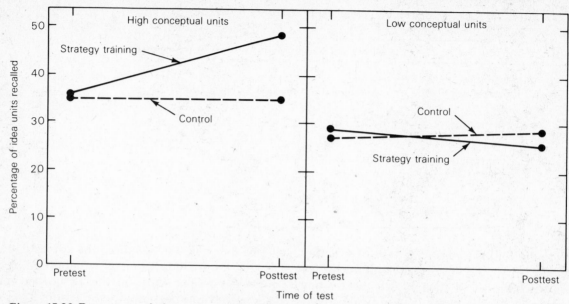

Figure 15.20 Percentage of idea units recalled (high and low) by strategy training and control groups at pre- and posttests (adapted from Cook, 1983).

20 points over their pretest scores, but the control group's scores did not improve at all from the pre- to the posttest.

Students' recall protocols were scored for the number of idea units correctly recalled at high and low levels in the conceptual structure of the text. Figure 15.20 shows the results of this analysis. Following training, the strategy training group became better at recalling information high in the conceptual structure of passages. This suggests that they did learn to organize the passage information better.

Overall, the results of this study are quite promising. They suggest that students can be taught to identify passage organization and then use this organization to structure the propositions that they store in long-term memory. Bartlett (1978) has obtained similar results.

It is interesting to think about the cognitive objectives of Cook's training program. We see her objectives as being a set of three

schemas and three productions, shown in Figure 15.21. Recall that to teach schemas, one must engage the learner's generalization and discrimination processes. In the Cook study, this was done by verbally describing the patterns associated with enumeration, generalization, and sequence structures, which should have called students' attention to the critical attributes for these structures. Then the students practiced identifying each pattern three times and received feedback on their accuracy. During practice, they should have been forming and refining their schemas.

To teach the strategies associated with these schemas, it is important to give students verbal descriptions of steps to follow during the cognitive stage of procedural knowledge acquisition when the procedure is being translated from declarative into procedural form. Cook provided worksheets that described the three reading strategies. For the procedures to

Enumeration Passage
   isa: science passage
   has property: states that there are N elements, where N is greater than 1.
   has property: defines or describes each of N elements

Generalization Passage
   isa: science passage
   has property: states a rule, where rule applies to more than one case
   has property: explains, justifies, or gives evidence for the rule.

Sequence Passage
   isa: science passage
   has property: describes actions or events
   has property: actions or events have a set order

P_1

IF   Goal is to understand passage
       and passage is *enumeration*
THEN   Identify subtopics
       and list details within each subtopic under subtopic heading.

P_2

IF   Goal is to understand passage
       and passage is *generalization*
THEN   Identify main idea
       and list key words in main idea
       and paraphrase main idea
       and list supporting evidence for main idea
       and state relationship between supporting evidence and main idea.

P_3

IF   Goal is to understand passage
       and passage is *sequence*
THEN   Identify topic
       and list each step
       and name each step
       and give details of each step
       and state difference between each pair of steps.

Figure 15.21 Schemas and production rules for organizing information from technical passages.

become composed into larger procedures, practice and feedback are needed. Cook provided three practice and feedback trials for each strategy. Thus, Cook provided the instructional support needed for teaching schemas and procedures.

WHAT WE KNOW AND DO NOT KNOW

A major theme of this chapter has been the fact that there is a relationship between domain-specific knowledge and problem-solving. There is ample evidence that more skilled problem solvers operate from a different knowledge base than do less skilled problem solvers. They have more knowledge of causal principles and their knowledge is more likely to be organized around these causal principles. Furthermore, they have more basic skills and better strategies. It is consistent with the assumptions of information-processing theories that these knowledge differences account, in large part, for the observed problem-solving differences.

Nonetheless, since few training studies have been done to determine whether or not teaching people the types of knowledge described above improves their problem-solving ability, the causal relationship between domain-specific knowledge and problem solving remains an unproven assumption. One type of research that would be beneficial over the coming years would be training research that is designed to validate specific cognitive models. Training research is tremendously expensive and requires a major commitment on the part of school personnel, but the benefits that can accrue from such studies at this point in the development of cognitive models of school tasks are, in our opinion, tremendous.

An important task for cognitive psychologists is to develop more specific theories of how domain-specific knowledge and general reasoning skills affect the problem-solving behavior of individuals. Voss, Tyler, and Yengo (1983) found in their study of political science problem-solving that a majority of Ph.D. chemists who were given the Soviet agriculture problem behaved like the student novices. However, one chemist's protocol looked more like an expert protocol even though he lacked domain-specific knowledge of Soviet politics and economics. Voss et al. suggest that this individual used some general reasoning strategies that he had acquired in the course of his scientific training. If this is the case, why did the other chemists not use such strategies? This is just one example of the complex questions that lie ahead for cognitive research in the area of domain-specific problem solving.

ADDITIONAL READINGS

diSessa, A. (1987). The third revolution in computers and education. *Journal of Research in Science Teaching, 24*(4), 343–367.

Glynn, S., Yeany, R.H., & Britton, B.K. (Eds.) (1991). *The psychology of learning science.* Hillsdale, NJ: Lawrence Erlbaum Associates.

Heller, J.I., & Reif, F. (1984). Prescribing effective human problem-solving processes: Problem description in physics. *Cognition and Instruction, 1,* 177–216.

Perkins, D.N., & Simmons, R. (1988). Patterns of misunderstanding: An integrative model for science, math, and programming. *Review of Educational Research, 58,* 303–326.

Roth, K.J. (1990). Developing meaningful conceptual understanding in science. In B.F. Jones and L. Idol (Eds.), *Dimensions of thinking and cognitive instruction.* Hillsdale, NJ: Lawrence Erlbaum Associates.

SECTION
Six

Schooling

*I*n the previous section, you saw how cognitive principles could illuminate the issues of what should be taught and how students learn best. In this section, we turn to two other crucial aspects of schooling—motivation and teachers.

In the area of motivation, as in the area of cognition, there is a burgeoning of research of relevance to education. Our goal in the chapter on motivation (Chapter 16) is not to survey this research since clearly a whole course could be devoted to the topic. Rather, our goals are to discuss how cognitive processes influence motivation and how motivation influences cognitive processes. We will also suggest how motivational thoughts may be learned in ways that are similar to other thoughts.

In the chapter on teaching expertise (Chapter 17), we return to the theme of a three-part characterization of expertise, but now we put the mirror on ourselves as teachers. Research shows that expert teachers have several types of conceptual understanding—a grasp of the domains they teach, of teaching and learning processes, and of management situations. Expert teachers also have basic tasks such as monitoring homework assignments proceduralized so that they can perform these tasks efficiently. Finally, they have a variety of strategies that apply in different circumstances.

With Chapter 17 we come to the end of this book. We hope that you come away from it with a better understanding of the ways that humans acquire and use knowledge and the ways that different types of knowledge collaborate in problem solving. We hope this understanding will help you in your personal attempts to improve education and learning.

Chapter
16

Motivation

SUMMARY

1. Motivation is that which gives direction and intensity to behavior.

2. A **behavioristic** view of motivation emphasizes the role of external events in determining the direction and intensity of behavior. A **cognitive** view of motivation does not deny the importance of external events but also assigns importance to internal events. These internal events can be thought of as **motivation productions** in procedural memory.

3. Some internal events that have been shown to influence motivation are conceptual conflict, causal attributions and expectations for success, and memories of other people's behavior.

4. **Conceptual conflict** can be created by surprising, novel, incongruous, or uncertain information.

5. People attribute their successes and failures to **luck, effort, ability,** or **task difficulty,** and their attributions affect their persistence.

6. Students can be encouraged to attribute success to effort by giving them individual goals, helping them to focus on strategies for achieving those goals rather than just outcomes, stating effort attributions, and avoiding displays of sympathy for failure.

7. People learn behavioral directions by observing others and then recalling what others did in a given situation.

8. There is growing evidence that the **informational aspect** of feedback is more important for motivation than the **pleasure aspect.** This evidence lends support to the cognitive view of motivation.

Motivation is that which gives direction and intensity to behavior. It is of utmost concern to teachers because the lack of it seems to be a major obstacle to learning. Some students seem to be bored, others anxious, and still others hostile. Yet these same students, outside the classroom, often seems enthusiastic, calm, and friendly. Why are many students unmotivated in the classroom and yet tremendously motivated in out-of-school pursuits?

The focus in this book is on the cognitive aspects of school learning, and this is the intent in this chapter as well. However, a leading opposing view has been a behavioristic one. Thus, to clearly distinguish the two views we will first present a traditional behavioristic view and then contrast it with a cognitive approach to motivation. In the behavioristic model a central theorem is that organisms respond in ways that have been reinforced in the past. Thorndike (1898) first stated this principle, calling it "the law of effect." Later Skinner studied reinforcement extensively and elaborated the view (1938). He described the response patterns that occur under different schedules of reinforcement (e.g., intermittent versus continuous) and also the idea of shaping a response by reinforcing successive approximations to the desired behavior. These ideas form the core of a behavioristic view of motivation.

How can these ideas explain the fact that some students seem motivated for out-of-school pursuits and unmotivated for schoolwork? The explanation is that such students are experiencing reinforcement for out-of-school activities and not for in-school activities. One does not need to look hard to see that videogames or athletics allow more opportu-

nities for success for some students than do classroom assignments or projects.

Although the behavioristic view provides a partial answer to the mysteries of motivation, it is far from complete. A major problem with this view is its failure to explain the wide range of student motivation under apparently similar reinforcement contingencies (both past and present). For example, why would two students of roughly equivalent competence and reinforcement histories behave differently in math class—one patient and persistent in solving homework problems and the other giving up quite quickly? Or, why would two students, again with roughly equal competence and reinforcement histories, choose tasks that vary a great deal in difficulty?

The behavioristic view is incomplete because behaviorists deal only with observable stimuli and observable responses. They do not speculate about what thoughts and emotions might mediate between these observables. By contrast, cognitivists propose that thought influences the direction and intensity of behavior. In recent years there has been a renewed interest in a cognitive view of motivation (cf., Ames, 1990; Borkowski, Carr, Rellinger, & Pressley, 1990; Mook, 1987, pp. 375–416; Weiner, 1980), and it is clear that a cognitive perspective can add precision to the purely behavioristic models.

BEHAVIORISTIC VERSUS COGNITIVE VIEWS OF MOTIVATION

Figure 16.1 shows the behavioristic view of motivation and a more elaborate cognitive view. The elements of the behavioristic view

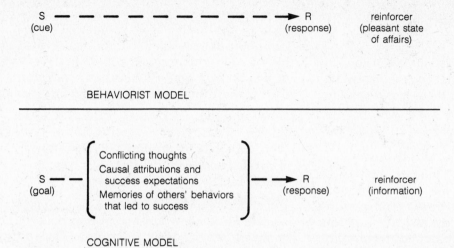

Figure 16.1 Behaviorist and cognitive models of motivation. S = initiating stimulus and R = response. Both models also have a reinforcer. In addition, the cognitive model includes internal events between the S and the R.

are an initiating external stimulus (S), a response (R), and a reinforcer. What occurs between the S and the R is not discussed. In the cognitive view, the stimulus, response, and reinforcer are also present. However, in this view, internal mediating events or "thoughts" are also included.

The first element in both the behavioristic and cognitive views is an initiating stimulus—some event that sets in motion a sequence of responses. However, there are differences in what is meant by "initiating stimulus" in the two views. In the behavioristic view the initiating stimulus is an occurrence in the environment that has been associated with reinforcement following a particular response. For example, a first-grade teacher flicks the light switch to get order in the classroom. The light's flicking is associated with praise for the children if they come to order. In the cognitive view the initiating stimulus is a goal. A goal may be suggested by a teacher ("Do problems 1 through 10 for your homework tonight"), or it may be a self-generated goal ("I'd like to know more about how cars run"). Thus the

initiating stimulus in the cognitive view may come either from the environment or from the learner's own thoughts. It functions not so much as a *cue* for reinforcement opportunity but as a *representation of a problem that includes a goal*.

The reinforcer is also represented differently in the two views. In the behaviorist view, reinforcement is a *pleasant state of affairs*. For the cognitivist, reinforcement can be viewed as *information* that will help the learner find a solution to her problem or achieve her goal. In summary, in the behavioristic view the initiating stimulus directly causes the response, whereas in the cognitive view it activates a variety of internal events, which in turn result in a response.

One way we can think of these internal events, which is consistent with the information-processing view presented in this book, is to represent the internal events as productions. If we think of the initiating stimulus as a representation of a problem with a goal the student wants to reach, it is easy to see how this initiating stimulus could be viewed as the condition clause in a "motivation production" in procedural memory. Similarly, the student's response could be depicted as the action clause of the motivation production. One set of motivation productions representing a learner's motivational thoughts as condition clauses and the learner's response as the action clause is shown in Figure 16.2. Viewing motivational tendencies as production sets sheds new light on the frequently observed teacher's lament that "students' motivational patterns in school are very difficult to change." If we think of these negative motivational patterns as "dysfunctional productions" that have been acquired and proceduralized over long periods of academic frustration, it is easier to understand why these patterns are so resistant to change. (As you may recall, once knowledge is proceduralized it is more difficult to change.)

Whether one thinks of motivation in production rule form or not, several types of internal events seem to play an important role in motivation, including: (1) conflicting thoughts or uncertainty, (2) causal attributions for what led to success (or failure) in reaching goals of interest in the past and expectations about success (or failure) with respect to reaching future goals, and (3) memories of what others did before reaching a goal. Probably other types of internal events contribute to motivation, but those just listed have a good empirical foundation. In the rest of this chapter, we will discuss the role that each of these internal events plays in motivation.

UNCERTAINTY AND CURIOSITY: RESOLVING CONCEPTUAL CONFLICT

Uncertainty is produced when we experience something novel, surprising, incongruous, or complex (Berlyne, 1960). It results in a heightened state of arousal in the central nervous system. For example, when a child goes to school expecting to see the regular fourth grade teacher, and instead finds a substitute teacher, this produces uncertainty about what the teacher is like and what will be expected of the child. If we were to measure the child's physiological responses on discovering the substitute teacher, we might observe an increased heart rate, shallow breathing, or pupil dilation, which are signs of increased nervous system arousal. This moderately aroused state in the face of uncertainty is what Berlyne (1960) calls curiosity (see also Vidler, 1977).

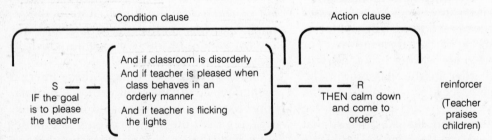

Figure 16.2 A motivation production representing a learner's thoughts as a problem with a goal (condition clause) and a potential solution to the problem (action clause). When this action is executed, the teacher praises the children (reinforcer), which strengthens the production in procedural memory.

Curiosity leads to exploratory behavior directed at reducing uncertainty. For example, the fourth grader might spend a good deal of time looking at the substitute teacher or listening to what he said to other students. Another form of exploration would be to ask the new teacher questions such as "Do we have to have science today?" As one gathers information through exploration, one reduces uncertainty and thus one's arousal level is reduced. According to this theory, reduction in arousal is reinforcing. According to Berlyne, it is reinforcing in much the same way as food is reinforcing to a hungry individual. That is, both hunger and curiosity are seen as having innate physiological bases. Since the reduction of uncertainty should have survival value, it is not surprising that such reduction is innately reinforcing.

Berlyne (1960) distinguished between **perceptual** and **epistemic curiosity.** Perceptual curiosity is caused by novel, incongruous, surprising, or complex *sensory stimuli*. For example, a sudden loud noise causes people to orient in the direction of the noise in order to get more information about it. Epistemic curiosity is caused by discrepant thoughts, beliefs, or attitudes (that is, by *internal stimuli*). Although both perceptual and epistemic curiosity may play a role in classroom learning, epistemic curiosity is the form most clearly related to cognition. Berlyne assumes that discrepant thoughts lead to increased arousal and that the increased arousal leads to exploratory behavior directed at resolving the discrepancy and thus reducing arousal. If we wanted to put this idea into a production system framework, we might say:

IF   My goal is to decrease arousal
      and I feel arousal
      and arousal is due to
         uncertainty over discrepant
         thoughts,

THEN   Explore ways to reduce the
          uncertainty,
       and choose a course of action
          that will resolve the
          discrepancy.

One example of elementary school children attempting to reduce uncertainty comes from a study done by Berlyne and Frommer (1966). These researchers read stories to elementary school children and then invited the children to ask questions about the stories. The stories varied in novelty or uncertainty of outcome. Two that differed in novelty were an Aesop's fable called "The Fox and the Raven" (low novelty) and the same fable using a tayra and an auk in place of the fox and the raven (high novelty). Two stories that differed in uncertainty of outcome were about a little boy who had to make a decision. In the low-uncertainty story there were two possible outcomes, one of which was presented as the likely one. In the high-uncertainty story, there were three possible outcomes, all of which were presented as equally likely. The children in this study asked more questions about the high-novelty and high-uncertainty stories than about the low-novelty and low-uncertainty stories.

According to Berlyne's theory, the novel and uncertain stories produced more **conceptual conflict.** For example, in the novel version of the Aesop's fable, children may have tried to compare a tayra to a more familiar animal, and this comparison would lead to conflicting thoughts. A child may think some aspects of the tayra make it seem like a wolf and others make it seem more like a cow. Asking questions should lead to information that would favor one of these thoughts over the other and thus reduce conflict.

The interesting proposal in Berlyne's theory is that thoughts affect the direction and intensity of behavior; that is, they affect motivation. Piaget (1967; 1980) also postulates an important role for cognitive conflict (disequilibrium) in motivation. Both Berlyne and Piaget argue that the resolution of conceptual ambiguity is adaptive for the species.

What can we add to Berlyne's theory by representing motivational thoughts as productions? An interesting aspect of representing cognitive conflict and its resolution as the conditions and actions of productions is that this way of representing thoughts helps to explain *how* thoughts affect the direction and intensity of behavior. That is, apparently the *conditions* that are present in the learner's mind (initiating stimulus) can have a profound impact on the direction and intensity of the learner's *actions* (response or behavior). Thus, if teachers can create conditions in the classroom where the learner experiences cognitive conflict, then the teacher should be able to expect the learner to take steps to try to reduce that conflict.

What techniques can a teacher use to create cognitive conflict? Setting up debates on political issues in social science classes should create uncertainty about what position is the best. In science, demonstrating an experiment that gives unexpected results produces conceptual conflict and motivates students to understand why the results were different from those expected. In English literature one might create uncertainty by having different students propose interpretations of symbolic stories, thus raising questions about which interpretation is best. This should motivate students to defend their interpretations with specific details and examples.

Entire methods of instruction capitalize on the motivation inherent in conceptual conflict. One of these is "Inquiry Teaching" in science (Suchman, 1962). In this method students are asked questions rather than given answers. Another method, "Socratic Teaching," involves countering students' claims with discrepant information and hence motivating the students to resolve the discrep-

ancy. R.C. Anderson and G.W. Faust (1974) and Collins and Stevens (1982) provide examples of Socratic teaching. Most recently, the work on conceptual-change theory (cf., Hewson & Hewson, 1984) described in Chapter 15 includes conceptual conflict as a crucial motivating condition.

Any teacher who has tried such techniques is aware of the powerful effect they can have. They also require a great deal of preparation and planning to anticipate what types of responses students will give and how one should counter. Other techniques can be used with somewhat less planning. One is simply posing questions rather than always making statements; this method should increase curiosity because the student will experience uncertainty about the answer.

Optimal Level of Arousal

There is a fundamental relationship between arousal and performance that seems to hold not only for humans but for other animals as well. The relationship, the Yerkes-Dodson Law, is shown in Figure 16.3. This figure shows a curvilinear relationship between arousal and performance such that, starting from a very low level of arousal and going to a moderate level, performance increases. Then any further increases in arousal cause performance decrements. Thus there is an optimal level of arousal.

This law has implications for epistemic curiosity, in that it suggests conditions under which a teacher's attempts to induce curiosity might not work. Specifically, the attempts would not work if they generated too much arousal. This might happen, for example, with a student who was very anxious (aroused) about performance in front of a group. A question that produced conceptual conflict would increase this student's arousal level to a nonproductive point. Another situation in which curiosity-inducing procedures

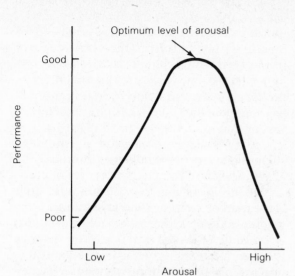

Figure 16.3 The relationship between arousal and performance (Yerkes-Dodson Law, 1908). A low level of arousal produces poor performance, as does a very high level. However, a moderate level of arousal produces good performance.

might not work is when they produce too little arousal. A student who already knows the explanation for a counterintuitive experimental result would not experience conceptual conflict after seeing the experiment and would therefore not be aroused. Thus curiosity-producing techniques will be effective for a particular student only when the techniques generate an optimal arousal level for that student. However, in a classroom situation, achieving optimal arousal levels in all (or even most) students simultaneously will not be an easy task, given the amount of variability in students' conceptual knowledge. Looking at the Yerkes-Dodson Law in the context of a production system theory, it becomes clear that if a teacher is trying to predict the optimal arousal level for each student, she needs to know a great deal about what is going on in each student's mind. Only then can she hope to produce conditions that will result in optimal levels of conceptual conflict for individual students. Given the extreme amount of variability in students' conceptual knowledge, it is not surprising that having a continuing impact on students' motivation levels may be a teacher's greatest challenge.

The Value of Curiosity

Despite the problem of determining optimal arousal levels, curiosity seems to be an important type of motivation to encourage. It is a type that is intrinsic to knowledge, and thus it is cheap and always available. It is also a motivation that learners can use throughout their lives as they acquire new knowledge. Finally, it appears to play a significant role in the lives of inventors, scientists, artists, and other creative individuals (cf., Barron, 1963; Roe, 1960).

Recent work on intrinsic motivation, which includes both curiosity and mastery motives, shows that it has a great many benefits over extrinsic motivation. Lepper (1988) reviews these benefits, while also noting that there are certain situations in which extrinsic motivators are necessary. Other recent work in this area has shown that individuals who have the goal of satisfying their curiosity when completing school tasks tend to use learning strategies that involve more elaborate processing of information than do students who have the goal of performing better than a comparison group (Nolen, 1988).

CAUSAL ATTRIBUTIONS AND SUCCESS EXPECTATIONS

Besides uncertainty, some other types of thought influence motivation: causal attributions and success expectations. **Causal attributions** (within achievement situations) are the explanations people give for why they or others achieved success or failed to achieve it. **Success expectations** are people's subjective estimates of their chances of succeeding at a given task in the future. Both of these classes of thought were studied by Weiner (1979, 1980) as he developed a theory of motivation called **attribution theory.**

Attribution theory, like curiosity theory, gives thought a central role in motivation. However, unlike curiosity theory (in which the important dimension is the *amount* of uncertainty produced by various thoughts, independent of their content), in attribution theory the *content* of thoughts is important. Only thoughts that have to do with causal attributions and success expectations are relevant.

Following Heider (1958), Weiner (1979) postulated that within achievement situations people tend to attribute their failure or success to one of four broad classes of cause: their *ability*, their *luck*, their *effort*, or the *difficulty of the task.* These attributions in turn determine people's feelings about themselves, their predictions of success, and the probability that they will try harder or less hard at the task in the future. For example, if a person attributes her failure to something that she can control (e.g., effort) then she will feel guilty when she fails—she will predict that she can succeed in the future if she exerts more effort, and, in fact, will exert more effort in the future. On the other hand, when someone attributes his failure to low ability, he will feel depressed when he fails—he will predict that he will fail again, and he will use less effort in the future. Thus, attributions are said to affect (1) expectations of success, (2) emotional (affective) reactions, and (3) persistence at achievement-related tasks. We will illustrate each of these links with experimental evidence.

Attributions and Success Expectations

Weiner, Nierenberg, and Goldstein (1976) gave students from zero to five consecutive success experiences on a block-design task. This task involves arranging, in a limited time period, several blocks to match a pattern presented by the experimenter (like a picture puzzle). This task is useful when the experimenter wishes to control the success rate of the subject: by watching the subject and saying when the time is up, the experimenter can produce a *success* situation by letting the subject complete the task, or a *failure* situation by saying time is up before the subject has finished. (Of course, in all such experiments, subjects are carefully debriefed following the experiment.)

In the Weiner et al. (1976) study, after each trial on which success feedback was given, students were asked five questions. First, they were asked to indicate how many of the next ten designs, which were similar to designs already attempted, they felt they would complete successfully. This question measured success expectations. Second, they were asked four questions that determined their success attribution—to luck, task ease, high ability, or effort. The findings revealed that expectancy for success was higher for people who attributed success to either task ease or high ability than for people who attributed success to luck or effort. Task ease and ability are usually considered to be stable characteristics of a situation, whereas luck and effort are usually considered unstable. It makes sense that successful people who thought their success was due to a stable characteristic would be more confident of future success, because they believe the characteristic will continue to exist in the future.

In many situations people perceive effort to be an unstable characteristic, and hence as the Weiner et al. study showed, they do not have high expectations for future success just because they have tried hard in the past. This is unfortunate, since it does not lead to increased effort. If people perceive their effort as a *stable* characteristic, then they should raise their expectations for future success and should also keep putting forth effort.

A study by Rosenbaum (1972; as reported in Weiner, 1980) suggests that when people perceive effort to be stable they are likely to raise their expectations for future success. Rosenbaum gave groups of subjects a story about a boss and his subordinate working together on a project. The success of the project was evaluated, and a causal attribution for the outcome was given. Half of the groups were told that the project succeeded and half were told that the project failed. Crossed with this outcome information was the attributional statement (ability or effort). Within these attributional groups, half the subjects were told that ability and effort were unstable causes, and the other half were told that ability and effort were stable. For example, a success outcome might be attributed to the subordinate's character as "always a hard worker" (stable effort) or to the subordinate's "unusual effort on this occasion" (unstable effort). Or, success might be attributed to the subordinate's "consistent ability to produce high-quality products" (stable ability), or to "a sudden increase in ability to produce" (unstable ability).

A randomly selected set of subjects read each version of the story and then rated how probable they thought it was that the boss and subordinate would succeed on future projects. The results are shown in Figure 16.4. As you can see, what was crucial to the differentiation of expectancy was not whether ability or effort was seen as the cause, but whether the cause was seen to be stable. When either effort or ability was thought to be stable, whatever outcome had already occurred was predicted for the future.

This experiment suggests ways of both encouraging students to attribute their success to effort and increasing their expectancy of success. Assuming this is the teacher's goal, it seems that after a student exerts effort and experiences success, it would be better to say to that student, "You are a hardworking person," than to say, "You really tried hard that time." That is, it may be better to encourage students to see their effort-making propensity as a stable trait (rather than as a temporary

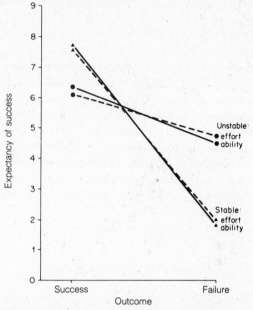

Figure 16.4 Expectancy of future success as a function of type of outcome and stability of outcome (from Rosenbaum, 1972, p. 83, as reported in Weiner, 1980).

state) because this will lead them to have a higher hope of future success. Since expectancy of success causes people to persist longer (James and Rotter, 1958), encouraging students to see their effort-making as a stable trait should increase their persistence. Conversely, if a student's ability level is low and she experiences failure, it would probably be better to say, "You can get better with practice," than to say, "You don't seem to be very good at that." Encouraging students to see their ability level as something that can improve (rather than as a stable trait) should also give students a reason to keep trying.

Recent studies go even further. A number of current theorists suggest that in order to increase success expectations for students low in confidence, it is important to show students *precisely how* they can succeed, rather than just trying to convince them that they have the ability to reach a goal if they try. For example,

Schunk (1989) argues that to bolster children's confidence they should be given practice at reaching short-term goals *and* explicit information about how the strategies they used helped them make progress towards those goals. Similarly, Ames (1990) suggests that if students are taught how to "focus on strategies, rather than outcomes, they are are more likely to 'own' the outcome," (p. 117) and feel responsible for the success. This "ownership of the outcome" or sense of responsibility for the successful achievement is an integral part of empowering students so that they can legitimately expect to succeed (see also Borkowski et al., 1990; McCombs, 1987, 1989).

Attributions and Affective Reactions

Attributions are related not only to expectancy of success, but also to affective (emotional) reactions. One study that demonstrated this idea was conducted by Weiner, Russell, and Lerman (1979). They had subjects retrospect about times when they had succeeded on an exam because of ability, unusual effort, usual effort, help from others, luck, or personality factors. Then they asked the subjects to list three emotions they experienced in the situation. The percentages of respondents listing various emotions for different attributions are shown in Table 16.1.

Happiness was experienced fairly uniformly independent of the perceived cause of success. However, other emotions were correlated with particular attributions. For example, pride was more strongly associated with attributions to ability than with attributions to unusual effort, help, or luck. Satisfaction and relief were associated with unusual effort. For failure outcomes (not shown in Table 16.1), attributions to low ability were associated with resignation and incompetence, and lack of effort was associated with the feeling of guilt.

Attributions and Effort

We have seen that different attributions precede different levels of success expectation and are correlated with different types of affect. Attribution theory also claims that attributions affect

Table 16.1 Emotions reported as being experienced following different attributions for success (from Weiner, Russell, and Lerman, 1979).

| | PERCENTAGE OF EMOTIONAL RECOLLECTION AS A FUNCTION OF THE CAUSAL ATTRIBUTION FOR SUCCESS | | | | | |
AFFECT	ABILITY	UNSTABLE EFFORT	STABLE EFFORT	PERSONALITY	OTHERS	LUCK
Competence	30[a]	12	20	19	5	2
Confidence	20	19	18	19	14	4
Contentment	4	4	12[a]	0	7	2
Excitement	3	9	8	11	16[a]	6
Gratitude	9	1	4	8	43[a]	14
Guilt	1	3	0	3	2	18[a]
Happiness	44	43	43	38	46	48
Pride	39[a]	28	39	43[a]	21	8
Relief	4	28[a]	16	11	13	26[a]
Satisfaction	19	24[a]	16	14	4	52[a]
Surprise	7	16[a]	4	14	0	4
Thankfulness	0	1	0	0	18[a]	4

[a] $p < .01$.

the actual amount of effort people exert in an achievement situation. If people attribute their past failures to lack of effort, they are likely to try harder, whereas if they attribute their failure to lack of ability, they are likely to give up. Similarly, if people attribute a failure to bad luck, they are likely to keep trying because things could change, but if they attribute failure to task difficulty, they are likely to give up when they do not think task difficulty will change.

Meyer (1970; as reported in Weiner, 1980) demonstrated these ideas in a study involving digit-symbol substitution. He created failure by telling subjects their time was up before they had completed the task. He then attributed subjects' failures to bad luck, low ability, task difficulty, lack of effort, or both low ability and task difficulty. After this, the subjects performed on another trial, and the difference in performance speed between trials was measured. Normally one would expect greater speed in the second trial simply because of practice, but as Figure 16.5 reveals,

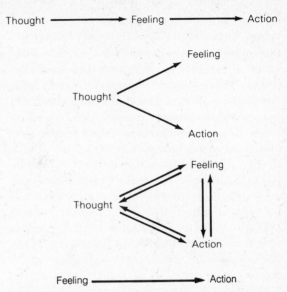

Figure 16.6 Some possible pathways of influence among thought, feeling, and action.

the increase in speed varied a great deal as a function of attributions. Subjects who heard their failure attributed to bad luck or lack of effort increased their speed more than did those who heard their failure attributed to low ability, task difficulty, or both.

Interaction of Thought, Feeling, and Behavior

Attributions have been shown to influence expectations for success, to be correlated with affective responses, and to influence effort. A question that has received considerable attention, and one that will probably continue to receive attention for some time to come, is: Just how *do* the cognitive, emotional, and behavioral consequences of attributions interact? Do thoughts cause feelings, which cause actions, or do thoughts concomitantly cause actions and feelings, or are they all quite interactive? A number of possible pathways of influence are depicted in Figure 16.6. In the 1980s, several theoretical positions were put

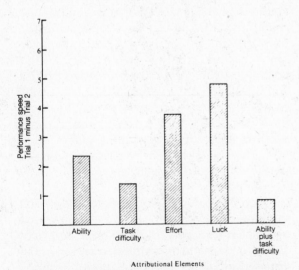

Figure 16.5 Amount of speed up in performance (in seconds) from Trial 1 to Trial 2 as a function of attribution for prior failures (adapted from Meyer, 1970, as reported in Weiner, 1980).

forward on the interaction of affect and cognition. One position is that thoughts cause feelings which cause actions (cf., Bower, 1981; Fiske, 1981); that is, "schemas trigger affect" (Fiske, 1982, cited in Mook, 1987, p. 383). Another position is that elaborative cognitive operations do not necessarily precede emotions (Zajonc, 1980; 1984). According to Zajonc, "preferences need no inferences" (1980, p. 151). A third position is that "strategy-based actions directly influence self-concept, attitudes about learning, and attributional beliefs about personal control. In turn, these personal-motivational states determine the course of new strategy acquisition and, more importantly, the likelihood of strategy transfer and the quality of self-understanding about the nature and function of mental processes" (Borkowski et al., 1990, p. 3). Although the question continues to generate interest (see Borkowski, Johnston, & Reid 1987; Clarke and Fiske, 1982; Fiske and Taylor, 1984; Mook, 1987; Wilson, 1985), the issue of how thought, feeling, and behavior relate is a complex one and a straightforward answer is not likely to be immediately forthcoming.

On the more specific question of how cognition, affect, and behavior interact within achievement settings, Weiner's (1980) position is shown in Figure 16.7. Recall that in his view, the outcome of a task (success or failure) may lead a person to try to infer the cause of the success or failure. These attributions then lead to feelings such as pride or guilt and further thoughts about the future chances of success. If one acts on the basis of these thoughts, then both feelings and expectations can be said to have influenced behavior. One example of how this sequence might operate in the classroom is when a student who thinks she has low ability in math experiences success on her first algebra test. She might infer (since success could not be due to her ability) that it was due to an easy test, and hence she would experience relief (see Table 16.1). She would increase her expectation for future success, because the difficulty level of tests is a stable aspect of the situation. (It is stable because teachers are perceived to maintain a consistent level of difficulty across their tests.) The attribution of success to task ease would not lead to much increase in effort, since effort is not seen to be a cause of success.

Now suppose that this student does well on a second test and meanwhile finds that half the class flunked. This information might cause her to change her attribution of success from task ease to effort or ability. Then she would experience feelings of competence and pride, and think that if she keeps trying she may continue to succeed. The result would be that she would continue to exert effort. Alternatively, she might do well on the second test and find out that everyone got an A. She would not feel proud and would begin to think her chances of success even without exerting much effort were good. In this situation there would be neither emotional nor cognitive reasons to exert much effort, and she would stop trying.

The most depressing cycle that one can think of, using Weiner's (1980) model, is that in which a student attributes failure to lack of ability. This leads to depression and resignation and predictions of more failure. Resignation leads to lack of effort, as does the thought that failure is a certain outcome. Most teachers have had students who show signs of possess-

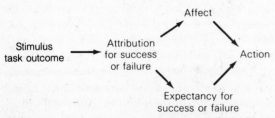

Figure 16.7 The flow of causation of Weiner's attributional model of achievement behavior (adapted from Weiner, 1980, p. 388).

ing this negative motivation cycle. These students do not try hard and believe (whether they are willing to admit it or not) that they are not capable of academic success. There is evidence that children of lower socioeconomic status are more likely to be victims of this cycle (Falbo, 1973; Raviv, Bar-Tal, Raviv, and Bar-Tal, 1980).

Figure 16.8 shows production set models of the interaction of thoughts, feelings, and behaviors. These particular examples follow Weiner's model (Figure 16.7) in that a performance outcome leads to an attribution, which leads to both feelings and success expectations, which lead to action. The set at the top of the table shows a positive motivation pattern associated with an individual's participation in football. In P_1, if the person wants to do

better than others in football and has a setback (say misses several passes that he should not have missed), he automatically thinks that he just had a bad day. This thought creates the condition for P_2 to fire, causing feelings of calm and high expectations for future success. These feelings and expectations then create the conditions for P_3 to fire, resulting in increased concentration and effort.

In contrast to the positive cycle shown at the top of Figure 16.8, the bottom shows a negative pattern. As in the former pattern, the latter is initiated by the desire to do better than others (this time in math) and the experience of a setback (perhaps difficulty with homework problems). However, unlike the events in the positive pattern, in this pattern, these conditions lead to the thought that the person's ability is low. This thought then creates the condition for P_2 to fire, leading to depressed feelings and a low expectation for future success. The depressed feelings and low expectations create the conditions for P_3 to fire, resulting in the individual's ceasing effort.

This analysis in terms of production rules shows how thought, feelings, and action can be linked in mental representations and suggests that there are a variety of ways to disrupt a negative pattern. For example, one could make the goal of "doing better than others" less salient. If this were done, then P_1 would not fire. Dweck (1989) recommends this approach. She argues that classrooms in which students have the goal of learning or improving competence have fewer individuals who show negative motivational patterns than do classrooms in which students have the goal of beating out their peers. In fact, students with learning goals spend less time analyzing failures and making attributions and more time planning and implementing strategies for achieving goals.

Another way to disrupt this type of negative motivational pattern is to change stu-

Football Setting

P_1 IF   My goal is to do better than others in football and I experience a setback,
  THEN   Create proposition that setback was due to a bad day.

P_2 IF   Setback was due to a bad day,
  THEN   Feel calm,
  and create proposition that "tomorrow will be better."

P_3 IF   Feel calm
  and expect that "tomorrow will be better."
  THEN   Try hard,
  and concentrate.

Math Setting

P_1 IF   My goal is to do better than others in math, and I experience a setback,
  THEN   Create proposition that setback was due to low ability.

P_2 IF   Setback was due to low ability,
  THEN   Feel depressed,
  and create proposition that "I'll never succeed."

P_3 IF   Feel depressed,
  and expect to not succeed.
  THEN   Give up.

Figure 16.8 Two production sets representing a student's schema for success in football and his associated responses and the same student's schema for failure in math and his associated responses.

dents' understanding of the concept of ability. A number of researchers have found that some children have an "incremental" theory of ability in which it is assumed that ability is something that can be increased through learning. Other children have an "entity" theory in which ability is seen as a fixed phenomenon that cannot be changed through learning (cf., Harari & Covington, 1981; Stipek, 1981). Production P_2 in the bottom half of Figure 16.8 is logical given an entity theory but illogical given an incremental theory. That is, if one sees one's ability as something that can be improved, then one need not predict failure in the future. Several studies described by Dweck (1989) have found that incremental theorists are more likely to choose challenging tasks than are entity theorists, probably because they are not as likely to have discouraging thoughts and affect when pursuing challenging tasks.

Although there are ways to intervene in negative motivational patterns, by inducing students to change their goals and/or their views of ability, we can also see that if these patterns are indeed proceduralized, as they might be by the high school years, then a teacher's challenge is formidable. Since students at the high school level have had years and years of experiences in which they built, modified, and fine-tuned their motivation productions in various domains, it is clear why it will take time and energy both on the part of the teacher and on the part of the student to make significant changes in these attitudes.

Looking at motivation and attribution theory in a production theory context also emphasizes the extraordinary importance of early childhood experiences. Children build their motivational schemas and skills and strategies by experiencing success and failure, and by explaining their experiences in ways that make sense to them (Mook, 1987, Ch. 11). If their early experiences are positive and they receive appropriate guidance, then they are likely to try hard to achieve success and to attribute their success to self-direction and effort, which in turn maximizes self-worth and self-esteem (Borkowski et al., 1990; McCombs, 1987, 1989). In contrast, if early experiences are negative or confusing, then children are likely to develop low self-esteem and misconceptions about the causes and effects of their attempts to achieve (cf., Ames, 1990; Borkowski, et al., 1990). This is likely to result in the development of what we might call "maladaptive motivation productions" (misconceptions that trigger inappropriate responses) that will be very resistant to change in the future.

In summary, we began this section by posing the question, "How do the cognitive, emotional, and behavioral consequences of attributions interact?" While we cannot provide a definitive answer to this question, we can argue that cognition and affect are "intimately interrelated" (Mook, 1987, p. 504) and that motivational *behavior* in achievement situations is strongly influenced by attributional beliefs, regardless of whether these attributional beliefs are classified as "cognitive" or "affective" by researchers and theorists (and regardless of which came first, the schema or the affect). From the perspective of the educator, it is useful to know how and why motivational conditions (both cognitive *and* affective) influence motivational actions, and why both are hard to modify (see also Ames, 1990; Borkowski, et al., 1990). With this knowledge and a lot of patience, teachers can attempt to help students restructure unproductive motivational patterns and behaviors.

Attribution Training Programs

In the last few sections, we have presented a lot of arguments explaining how students' attributions influence their behavior in achievement situations, and we have summarized the ideas of a number of theorists. Now that we know something about attribution theory and something about the interaction among cognition, affect, and behavior, it seems reasonable to ask: Can students who attribute their failure to low ability learn to change their attribution productions? Specifically, can they learn to attribute failure to lack of effort and success to adequate effort? If so, their affective reactions to failure should change from resignation to guilt, and guilt should lead to action rather than inaction. Furthermore, their thoughts about future success would change from "I can't succeed; I'm too dumb" to "If I try hard, I might succeed," which should also encourage action.

Several studies suggest that students can learn to change their attributions and that changes in attributions are paralleled by changes in persistence (Andrews and Debus, 1978; Borkowski, et al., (Study 2), 1990; Chapin and Dyck, 1976; Dweck, 1975; Schunk, 1989). Andrews and Debus (1978), for example, identified forty-two sixth grade boys who did *not* tend to attribute their failures to lack of effort. They then had two-thirds of these boys perform a block-design task. The trainer controlled the success or failure outcome by giving time limits that were either very liberal or too strict. The pupils were allowed to experience success on half the trials.

After each trial the student indicated what he attributed his success or failure to—luck, task difficulty, effort, or ability. Whenever the pupil attributed success to effort or failure to lack of effort, the trainer reinforced that attribution by saying such things as "That's good!" or "Very good!" or "OK!" If the pupil attributed success or failure to something other than effort, the trainer simply said, "Here's your next design," and did not look directly at the pupil. The pupils were trained until they made effort attributions 80% of the time or for sixty trials, whichever came first.

After training, the pupils performed on two other tasks and were asked to give their attributions for success and failure on these (another block-design task and an anagrams task). They also performed a third (insolvable) task, and their persistence (amount of time spent trying to solve this task) was measured. The third of the boys who did not receive training (control group) also performed on these three tasks. The pupils who received attribution training were much more likely than the control group pupils to attribute both success and failure to effort and to persist at an insolvable task. Furthermore, another test given a week later showed the same results.

A strict behaviorist would say these results were due to establishing a history of partial reinforcement in the training group and not in the control group. That is, for the training group the 50% success rate became a cue that success would be forthcoming, and so they persisted. Chapin and Dyck (1976), however, independently varied partial reinforcement and attribution training and found that, although partial reinforcement had a positive effect on persistence, attribution training caused more persistence than did partial reinforcement alone. Thus there is good evidence that causal attributions mediate motivation.

Because these training studies directly manipulate attributions, they provide strong evidence for the causal role of attributions in motivation. Most studies of attributions simply observe attributions and effort and determine the correlation between them. As has been stated previously, correlations can be used to suggest causal relationships, but experimental manipulation is needed to verify that the suggested factor does play a causal role.

It is worth noting that in the Andrews and Debus (1978) study, the trainer asked the pupil to make the attribution and then selectively reinforced effort attributions. In the Chapin and Dyck (1976) and Dweck (1975) studies, however, the trainer made the attribution for the pupil (e.g., "You must have really tried hard"). Either procedure appears to work. In the Borkowski et al. (1990) Study 2, students were given explicit instruction in strategy training as well as attribution training, and this combination appeared to be more beneficial than either strategy training or attribution training alone. In all cases, the students showed evidence that they appeared to be in the early stages of building motivation productions that attributed success to effort. However, it would require additional observations of many pupils in many different situations over long periods of time in order to determine if these motivation productions would generalize to other achievement situations and to see if the productions would become proceduralized to the point where they would automatically produce sustained effort in difficult task situations.

The studies described above indicate why teachers who attempt to change student attributions must be both careful and patient. Care is needed to select tasks at which the student can succeed with effort. Following the behavioristic principle of shaping, it may be better to start with tasks that require only a small (but perceptible) amount of effort and then, as the student shows a greater willingness to exert effort, increase the amount needed for success. If the teacher selects tasks that require no effort and then attributes the student's success to effort, the teacher will lose credibility. In addition, cognitive principles suggest that the students need to understand what strategies they used to achieve success and why these strategies worked in the current situation (Ames, 1990; Borkowski et al., 1990).

Patience is needed because people tend to cling to their self-concepts, whatever they are (see Ames, Ames, and Garrison, 1977). This is not surprising, given the "stubbornness" of schemas (Mook, 1987), the automated nature of productions, and the fact that attributional

beliefs appear to be deeply rooted in cultural and familial contexts (Kurtz, Schneider, Carr, Borkowski, and Turner, in press, cited in Borkowski et al.). Thus people with low-ability self-concepts do not seem willing to give them up. For example, suppose that a teacher arranges for a student who believes he has low ability to succeed at a task after some effort. To the student, this success is a surprising event and surprising events tend to be attributed to unstable causes such as luck or task ease (Simon and Feather, 1973; Valle and Frieze, 1976). Attributing the current event to an unstable cause allows the student to "make sense" of the discrepant event (i.e., understand the current situation) without giving up an old schema or attempting to modify an entrenched production. It seems to take many trials before a student with a low self-concept is willing to attribute success to effort. In fact, a teacher may patiently spend an entire year in trying to change a student's attributions without seeing any change. The teachers who have the student the following year, however, will reap the rewards of the former teacher's patience.

In summary, looking at these phenomena from the perspective of cognitive theory—that is, adopting the view that attributions are schemas and schemas function as condition clauses in automated productions—helps to explain why it can be so hard to change a student's perceptions and a student's behaviors. The view taken here is that attributions become part of procedural knowledge, and as we have argued throughout this book, procedural knowledge takes a long time to acquire, and once acquired and automated, it is very hard to consciously reflect on these procedures and even harder to change them. Note also that if a student develops maladaptive schemas and productions that are *domain-independent* (i.e., general motivation productions that apply across academic subject matter areas), they will be particularly hard to change (i.e., "I don't see myself as being very good at anything" will be even harder to change than "I just don't see myself as being good at math"). Fortunately, we typically do not form attributions of ability at a general level; instead, we make attributions about our abilities and assign expectations about future capabilities in a task- or situation-specific manner (Ames, 1990).

Classroom Goals and Attributions

There is growing evidence that competitive goals cause children to be more ability-focused in their causal attributions whereas individualistic goals cause them to be more effort-focused (see Ames, 1984a; 1990). One study that demonstrates this relationship was done by C. Ames (1984b). In this study, fifth and sixth graders were asked to trace two sets of line-drawn puzzles. Half of the children were told to try to be the winner (competitive goal) and half were told to try to solve as many puzzles as they could and to try to solve more puzzles on the second set (individualized goal).

After performing on the second set of puzzles, children were asked about their attributions for success or failure and about instructions they had given themselves. The results revealed that children given the individualized goal selected more effort-related attributions than did children given the competitive goal. Conversely, children given the competitive goal selected more ability-related attributions than did children given the individualized goal. The children given the individualized goal also gave themselves more facilitative instructions such as "I will work carefully," "I will take my time," or "I will make a plan." That is, they seemed to think about the details of strategies that would help them reach their goals.

More recent classroom-based research shows that children's goals can be changed in real class settings. Nicholls et al. (1990) measured students' goal orientations in experimental and control second grade classes at the end of the school year. The experimental class, to which students had been randomly assigned at the beginning of the year, had received problem-centered, conceptually-oriented mathematics instruction for the entire year. In this classroom, students frequently worked in pairs to solve challenging math problems, the results of which were then discussed by the whole class. Students in the experimental classroom showed a significantly higher learning orientation than did students in the control classes, whereas students in the control classes showed a significantly higher competitive orientation.

Thus, teachers may be able to encourage both effort attributions and facilitative self-instructions by focusing students on individual or cooperative learning goals and self-improvement. A major obstacle to doing this is that it requires a good deal of planning, organization, and management to individualize instruction effectively or to teach students how to function well in cooperative groups. However, the rewards in terms of student motivation may be worth it. M. Wang and her colleagues have demonstrated one way of managing the task of individualization, by teaching students to take more and more responsibility for goal setting and planning of instructional sequences (Wang, 1974). It may also help, as Ames (1990) has argued, to give children choices among tasks and activities in the classroom in order to foster a sense of personal involvement.

Teacher Behavior and Attributions

One very powerful constellation of cues about student ability comes from the teacher. Some teachers treat high- and low-ability students quite differently. For example, they ask high-ability students more challenging questions and follow up on these students' answers, but they give low-ability students more help and praise for mediocre work. If students in fact perceive this differential treatment, they may use it to infer ability differences. The work of R.S. Weinstein and others (reviewed by R.S. Weinstein, 1983) suggests that children do perceive such differential treatment.

In one study (Weinstein, Marshall, Brattesani, and Middlestadt, 1982), fourth through sixth grade children were questioned about how their teachers would treat hypothetical high- and low-ability children. Some teachers were not perceived to give much differential treatment, but those who were perceived to give differential treatment were said to give high achieving students more opportunities and choices and higher expectations, and to give low achievers more negative feedback, more directions, and more work and rule statements.

Besides differential teacher behavior towards students (praise, types of assignments, etc.), another cue for attributions is differential teacher affect. Graham and Weiner (1987) have shown that children as young as six years of age can distinguish between teacher pity and teacher anger. Furthermore children infer from a teacher's pity that the student being pitied could not control the outcome (was of low ability) whereas they infer from a teacher's anger than the student could control the outcome (did not try hard).

Graham (1982; reported in Graham and Weiner, 1987) conducted an experiment with sixth grade children in which the children were given four trials on a novel puzzle task. After each trial they received failure feedback. The "teacher" accompanied the failure feedback with both verbal and non-verbal affective cues. For the sympathy group, the teacher said, "I feel sorry for you," and for the angry group she said, "I'm angry with you." A control group did not receive any cues about the teacher's emotions.

After receiving these different affective cues for five trials, the students were asked to state why they thought they were doing poorly at the task and to predict their chances for success in the future. Figures 16.9 and 16.10 show the results for attributions and predictions, respectively. The children who received anger cues were most likely to attribute their failure to lack of effort, and the children who received sympathy cues were most likely to attribute their failure to lack of ability (Figure 16.9). The children who received anger cues maintained a higher level of expectation for success than did the children who received sympathy cues. This is especially evident on the fifth trial (Figure 16.10). Since other studies have shown that a very low expectation of success leads to a lessening of effort, it is likely that the children who received sympathy would decrease their effort over trials.

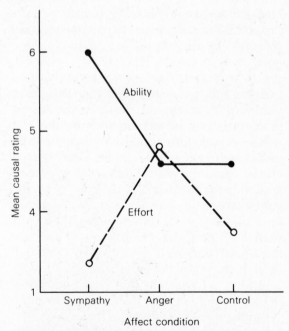

Figure 16.9 Children's causal attributions as a function of the teacher's affect (from Graham and Weiner, 1987).

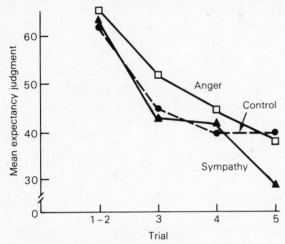

Figure 16.10 Children's changes in success expectations given different teacher affect following the children's failures (from Graham and Weiner, 1987).

Summary

Students' thoughts about the causes of success and failure influence their motivation. In particular, if students think that their failures are due to lack of effort and their successes are due to effort, and if they see themselves as hardworking, they will persist longer in achievement situations. Teachers can play a role in encouraging such effort-related attributions by calling attention (when appropriate) to success due to effort, by emphasizing individual improvement rather than competition, and by being aware of the effect of their own behavior and emotions on students' perceptions of ability. Teachers who attempt to change student attributions must be both careful and patient.

MEMORIES OF HOW OTHERS ACHIEVED SUCCESS: OBSERVATIONAL LEARNING

Besides the influence on motivation of conflicting thoughts and of attributions, thought influences motivation in another way. This is through retrieved thoughts about prior events that an individual has observed. Specifically, people sometimes choose a particular course of action because they remember that this choice brought positive results for some other person. This process is called "observational learning" and is described in Bandura's social learning theory (Bandura, 1977).

Figure 16.11 shows a typical sequence of events in observational learning. First, someone other than the learner (M for Model) responds in a particular way (raises his hand). While M is responding, the learner (O for Observer) is paying attention and creating propositions and schemas that describe what is happening. The model's response is followed by something that the observer considers to be rewarding (teacher calls on Sam). At this point, the observer may build a production that says, "IF I would like to receive a similar reward, THEN I should emit a similar response when I am in that situation." Some time later, when the observer is in the same situation as the model, she will recall the model's response in that situation and the pleasant consequence. This recollection will prompt O to make the same response. If she then receives reinforcement, this condition-action sequence will be strengthened.

In the sequence of events shown in Figure 16.11, the observer chose to do something (raise her hand) that had resulted in reinforcement to someone else in the past. This form of observational learning is called *vicarious reinforcement*. In another form of observational learning, the observer may choose *not* to do something because it was observed in the past to be followed by negative consequences to someone else. This process is called *vicarious punishment*. Studies of aggression, for example, have shown that children are less likely to engage in aggressive behaviors if they have observed another being punished for aggression (Rosenkrans, and Hartup, 1967).

Figure 16.11 An example of observational learning. O = observer, M = model.

People often imitate models even when they do not observe the model receiving reinforcement (Harris, 1970). This seems to be especially true when the model is respected or is someone with whom the observer identifies. One example of this type of observational learning is given in a study by Lippett, Polansky, and Rosen (1952). These researchers observed the frequency with which children imitated the actions of other children at a summer camp. They found that a few boys who had a lot of power were the most frequently imitated. Imitation occurred whether or not the observed action was seen to be directly reinforced. Apparently, people believe that the behaviors of respected others are likely to receive reinforcement, and this belief is enough to lead them to imitate their behaviors.

Instructional Implications of Observational Learning

What are the implications of observational learning for classroom motivation? One is that students learn from the behavior of their teachers. In the classroom they may choose to work at problems longer if they have first observed their teacher taking time with a difficult sample problem and persisting until it is solved. Too, if a teacher tells his students about out-of-school activities that he pursues (e.g., "Last night, I read in the newspaper that . . ."), then the students may be inclined to imitate these activities. Of course, the tendency for students to learn from teachers' behaviors depends on how well liked and respected the teacher is. Thus, it is important for teachers to do things, particularly at the beginning of the year, to create an atmosphere of warmth and mutual respect.

Another implication is that other students can serve as models of desirable classroom behavior. Teachers can call students' attention to the successful behavior of a classmate. For example, a teacher might have a session in which students discussed how they had come up with their ideas for a composition they had just completed. One student might report that she tried writing down her free associations first and that she thought this had helped her find a focus. Hearing this, other students might try it for the next composition.

As high school teachers know, for many adolescents the most imitated person in the classroom is neither the teacher nor the most academically successful student; it is the most popular student. Popular students are perceived as having lots of power in the high school culture, so it is not surprising that other students often accord them a great deal of respect. If a popular student is not motivated to do schoolwork, many other students may imitate his lack of motivation. Thus, it behooves teachers of adolescents to determine early in the year which students are most popular and then seek to get them academically involved. Once they show positive academic motivation, the rest of the class is likely to as well.

In conclusion, students observe the extent to which teachers, parents, and friends persist in learning and problem solving, and they observe the positive or negative consequences of such persistence. They also observe others' learning strategies and whether or not such strategies appeared to pay off. Finally, they observe the activities respected others choose as careers and as recreation. Later, when they must decide whether or not to persist, the decision will be influenced by memories of these observations. When they must decide what learning strategy to use, the decision will be influenced by memories of effective strategies. And when they must decide what elective to take or whether or not to go to college, the decision will be influenced by their observation of the consequences of others' choices. Memories of the behaviors of others, then, play an important role in human motivation.

THE REINFORCER

In Figure 16.1, you saw a contrast between a behavioristic and a cognitive view of motivation. So far in this chapter the two models have been contrasted in terms of how the initiating stimulus is conceptualized (either as a cue or as a goal) and in terms of the role played by mediating thoughts and affect (either the role is excluded from consideration or it is given a prominent place). Now let us turn to the final element in both types of models—the reinforcer.

Strictly speaking, for behaviorists a reinforcer is anything that increases the probability of the response it follows. However, many practitioners with a behaviorist bent consider a reinforcer to be something that brings about pleasant feelings. Praise is reinforcing because it makes people "feel good," avoidance of pain is reinforcing because of a feeling of relief, and candy is reinforcing because it tastes good. Indeed, Thorndike (1913), who first described the "law of effect," explained that it worked because it brought about a satisfying state of affairs. Thus, many people hold the theory that reinforcers work because they *are pleasing*.

An alternative conception of reinforcers is that they work because they *provide information*. This view is consistent with the information-processing framework presented throughout this book. In this view, people tend to repeat a behavior that has previously led to a positive state of affairs because they have formed a *rule* that such behavior has desirable consequences and so far, their rule has worked. That is, they think they know *why* their behavior led to desirable consequences, so when they receive reinforcing information after a response (i.e., confirmation that their rule is working as they expected), they repeat the behavior because the reinforcing information tells them that their rule is still valid. The important aspect of the consequence is thus its informativeness (in terms of validating the person's predictions), not just its pleasantness.

Can we separate the "pleasure" aspect of reinforcers from the rule-affirming or "information" aspect, in order to test this hypothesis? Can we tell if the pleasure aspect or the informational aspect of reinforcers accounts for increases in responding? Historically, this was a difficult question to answer because, for a long time, no one could think of a way to vary the pleasure and informational aspects of reinforcement independently. Nonetheless, the question continued to be of great interest to researchers and teachers because it bears directly on the role of feedback in learning. If feedback works because it provides a satisfying state of affairs, then teachers should avoid critical feedback, because it will make an individual feel bad. However, if feedback works because it provides information, then teachers should use critical feedback if it is specific and therefore informative, and allows the individual to understand the rules of the world.

In the 1970s researchers came up with some clever ways to separate the pleasure and informational aspects of feedback (Estes, 1972; Guthrie, 1971; Surber and Anderson, 1975). For example, in Estes's (1972) experiment, subjects were asked to pretend that they were traffic-control workers for an airline. They were seated in front of computer terminals on which they viewed a set of arrows that indicated an airplane (see Figure 16.12). Their job was to choose a command (one of two keys) to give the pilot. If they chose the correct command, the word SAFE appeared on the screen, indicating that the plane had avoided a collision. If they chose the wrong command, the word FAIL appeared on the screen, indicating a collision. The subject had to learn which key of the pair communicated the correct information, because on later trials (following some trials for other pairs of keys) she would see again this same pair of keys and be asked to choose.

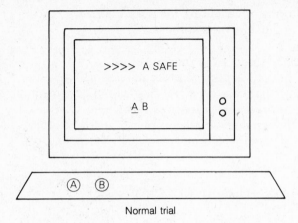

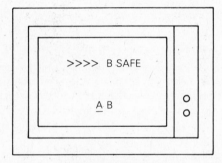

Figure 16.12 Displays for normal and conflicting feedback trials in the Estes (1972) experiment. On a normal trial the "pilot" received the message sent. On a conflicting feedback trial the pilot received a different message from the one sent (adapted from Estes, 1972).

In a normal situation a SAFE trial produced a display such as that shown at the top of Figure 16.12. At the bottom of the screen are shown the choices of two keys (A or B). The line under the A indicates that A was selected by the subject. At the top of the screen are the arrows, depicting the airplane, a letter stating what message (A or B) was received by the pilot, and the result (in this case, SAFE). Thus, in the normal situation the message sent by the subject was the message received by the pilot.

On some trials, however, the pilot received a different message from the one sent by the subject. These were called "conflicting feedback" trials. An example of one such trial is shown at the bottom of Figure 16.12. In this example the subject selected A, but the pilot received B. Subjects had been warned that sometimes there was noise in the radio communication between ground control and the airplane, so that sometimes the pilot would receive a different message than the one sent. In this example the pilot was SAFE only because he received the message *not* selected by the subject.

Thus, on conflicting feedback trials the pleasure and information aspects of feedback were uncorrelated. The pleasure the subject received because the pilot avoided a collision should lead to an increase in responding the *same* way (e.g., an increase in selecting A in the example at the bottom of Figure 16.12). However, the information the subject received told her that the key *not* selected (B, in this example) is actually the key that leads to a safe outcome most of the time. Thus the information aspect of feedback should lead to an increase in selecting the nonselected key in the future.

What did subjects actually do following conflicting feedback trials? On the average there was a *decrease* in responding with the previously selected key following such trials. This was in contrast to the increase in responding with the previously selected key following normal trials. In other words, subjects did not respond in the manner that had led to a pleasant outcome most recently; rather they responded in a manner that they *expected* would lead to a pleasant outcome in the future, based on information received during feedback.

Thus, although in most reinforcement situations behavioristic and cognitive views lead to the same predictions, under some conditions, predictions differ. When they do, the cognitive framework accounts for the data better. People appear to be seekers of information more than seekers of immediate pleasure. This orientation is adaptive for our species, because it leads us to explore new environments in an attempt to understand them and ultimately to learn to exist in new environments. If we had sought pleasure at the expense of information for the past four million years, it is doubtful that we would have survived as a species.

CONCLUSIONS AND DIRECTIONS FOR FUTURE RESEARCH

The theme of this chapter has been that internal events play an important role in motivation. This has been demonstrated for conflicting thoughts, attributions and predictions of success, and memories for what others did to achieve a goal. The effects of thought on motivation help explain why similar reinforcement histories do not necessarily lead to similar levels of motivation in two people. One needs to know *how* a person interprets his successes and failures and what he recalls about the successes and failures of others in order to make accurate predictions about the effects of reinforcement on that person.

It appears that students whose motivational patterns are negative and self-defeating can be encouraged to attribute success to effort and to put forth effort. In order for students to attribute success to effort it is important for teachers (1) to give individual learning goals rather than competitive goals, (2) to help students to focus on strategies, (3) to state effort attributions, and (4) to avoid displays of sympathy for failure. Borkowski et al. (1990) provide a clear summary of the arguments:

> In short, children need to be "convinced" that it is possible for them someday to perform life's many functions competently, and that a key ingredient for success is here-and-now learning of the strategies and knowledge presented

in school. If children can be led to believe that they are acquiring powerful and important tools, self-esteem and self-confidence should also increase. Given the many real-world reinforcements for literacy and numerical competence, motivation to learn new skills should be heightened. And so it goes, competent strategy use affects motivation and self-esteem which jointly fuel additional strategy learning, transfer and modification of strategies (p. 46).

ADDITIONAL READINGS

Ames, R., & Ames, C. (Eds.) (1984). *Research on motivation in education, Vol. 1.* New York, NY: Academic Press.

Bandura, A. (1977). *Social learning theory.* Englewood Cliffs, NJ: Prentice-Hall.

Borkowski, J.G., Carr, M., Rellinger, E., & Pressley, M. (1990). Self-regulated cognition: Interdependence of metacognition, attributions, and self-esteem. In B.F. Jones & L. Idol (Eds.), *Dimensions of thinking and cognitive instruction,* pp. 53–92. Hillsdale, NJ: Lawrence Erlbaum Associates.

Clarke, M.S., & Fiske, S.T. (1982). *Affect and cognition: The seventeenth annual Carnegie Symposium on Cognition.* Hillsdale, NJ: Lawrence Erlbaum Associates.

Covington, M.V., & Berry, R.G. (1976). *Self-worth and school learning.* New York, NY: Holt, Rinehart, & Winston.

Keller, J.M. (1983). Motivational design of instruction. In C.M. Reigeluth (Ed.), *Instructional-design theories and models: An overview of their current status.* Hillsdale, NJ: Lawrence Erlbaum Associates.

Kulhavy, R.W., & Stock, W.A. (1989). Feedback in written instruction: The place of response certitude. *Educational Psychology Review, 1,* 279–308.

Lepper, M.R. (1988). Motivational considerations in the study of instruction. *Cognition and Instruction, 5,* 289–309.

McCombs, B.L. (1991). Motivation and life-long learning. *Educational Psychologist, 26*(2), 117–127.

Weiner, B. (1980). *Human motivation.* New York, NY: Holt, Rinehart, and Winston.

Chapter

17

The Cognitive Psychology of School Teaching: How Do We Characterize Expert Teachers?

SUMMARY

1. **Expert teachers** are like expert problem solvers in other fields—they have highly organized and elaborated sets of *conceptual knowledge* in their domain; they have *sets of automated basic skills* that they execute smoothly and seemingly without effort; and they have well-developed but flexible and adaptive sets of *strategic knowledge* that they use for planning, for working towards their pedagogical goals, and for evaluating their progress and modifying their actions.

2. **Conceptual knowledge** for teachers includes knowledge about subject matter, knowledge about students, knowledge about teaching, and knowledge about the context or situation in which the teaching and learning are taking place. Much of the current literature in teacher education characterizes teachers' conceptual knowledge as *schematic* in form.

3. Expert teachers have streamlined and automated their procedures for managing the classroom. **Automating basic skills** enables expert teachers to allocate their conscious cognitive resources to other relevant aspects of teaching and learning.

4. Expert teachers are effective classroom managers from the very first day of school. Basic management routines used by expert teachers include being well organized, setting up rules, having students practice appropriate behavior, and removing rewards for inappropriate behavior.

5. The **strategic knowledge** or instructional strategies used by expert teachers to facilitate learning include communicating objectives; giving directions; presenting

content clearly; adapting instruction to students' ability levels and interests; explaining to students *why* they are learning particular material; explicitly *connecting* new material to previously studied concepts; giving students opportunities to respond, practice, and solve problems; and giving specific, informative feedback.

6. During instruction, experienced teachers attend more to student performance relative to the goal of instruction than do inexperienced teachers.

7. Attempts to train teachers to use the management routines and instructional strategies used by expert teachers have been successful, but further research is needed.

Teaching is a complex problem-solving activity, the goal of which is to facilitate student learning. The "teacher" may be a designer of instructional software, a writer of textbooks, a producer of educational videotapes, an industrial trainer, or a classroom instructor. Each of these people has a goal of increasing student learning.

Of these teacher roles, that of classroom instructor is probably the most difficult, because it involves the attempt to reach many goals with limited resources. A typical classroom teacher has twenty-five to thirty-five individuals to teach in a limited time period. Since each student has a different configuration of prior declarative and procedural knowledge and different motivational tendencies, each should be given different learning goals. In pursuit of this ideal a few school systems have changed to individualized instruction. However, for many teachers, individualized instruction is not feasible. In such cases the problem of classroom teaching becomes one of optimizing the learning of individuals rather than maximizing it. In this chapter we will see how successful teachers solve the problem of optimizing instruction.

Some people believe that teachers do not make a difference in school learning. However, studies done over the last twenty-five years have shown that teachers do make a

difference. Chall and Feldmann (1966), for example, found that in reading achievement the curriculum materials used were not as important as the teacher. Inman (1977) estimated that 25% of the variance in student achievement is accounted for by the teacher's actions, and for children of low socioeconomic status, the importance of teachers is even greater. What, then, differentiates effective teachers from less effective teachers?

For years, most research on teaching focused on teacher behaviors and student outcomes rather than on teachers' cognitive processes. Westerman (1991) recently made this point when she reported that the 1973 edition of the *Handbook of Research on Teaching* "did not contain a single reference to teachers' thought processes" (Westerman, 1991, p. 292). However, that situation is changing. A review of current publications in the fields of educational psychology and teacher education yields numerous articles on such topics as teacher cognition, teacher decision making, teacher thinking, teacher knowledge, and cognitive differences in expert and novice teachers.

What can we learn from all these studies on teacher cognition? Is there consensus among these researchers on "the cognitive psychology of school teaching"? Can the findings from these studies be interpreted within the context of the cognitive framework presented in this book? All the articles we discuss in this chapter view teaching and learning from a cognitive perspective. However, none of the authors whose work we report uses a declarative-procedural distinction to interpret teacher thoughts and behaviors. Presumably, for many researchers in teacher education, the goals of the work and the level of analysis are somewhat different from the focus here. However, the arguments advanced in the articles about teacher expertise, and the findings reported in the articles about cognitive differences in expert and novice teachers, can be interpreted as consistent with the position taken in this book.

Basically, the picture that is emerging indicates that **expert teachers** appear to be **expert problem solvers,** as are experts in other fields such as medicine or chess. Expertise in teaching, like expertise in other domains, seems to be characterized by three things: (1) a highly organized and elaborated declarative knowledge base that provides the expert problem solver with a sophisticated *conceptual understanding* of the principles and relationships in the domain; (2) *highly automated sets of basic skills* that enable the expert teacher to execute basic routines smoothly, efficiently, and without apparent effort; and (3) well-developed but flexible and adaptable sets of *teaching strategies* that enable the expert teacher to plan, teach, and evaluate lessons in successful and imaginative ways.

In this chapter we will describe the conceptual knowledge, automated basic skills, and sophisticated strategies used by expert teachers as they solve classroom problems. We will also provide examples to show how these elements contribute to expert teaching. Then, in the last section, we will discuss the dynamics of instruction. In that discussion we will attempt to show how the aspects of teacher cognition interact during instruction.

CONCEPTUAL KNOWLEDGE

A basic assumption is that one cannot teach what one does not know. That is, we would assume that it is necessary to have a well-developed knowledge base in the subject-matter area(s) to be taught before one can teach. While on the surface this appears to be a straightforward assumption, it has been surprisingly difficult for educators to specify (1) what is meant by "knowing," (2) precisely what the subject matter is that teachers need to know, and (3) how well they need to know it.

Traditionally, "what teachers needed to know" was content knowledge in their subject-matter disciplines. At the level of university teaching, for example, it was assumed (and may still be assumed) that knowledge in a discipline is necessary and *sufficient* for teaching in that discipline. According to Shulman (1986), both "master" and "doctor"—the words that we use to designate persons with advanced levels of "knowledge"—are derived from words for "teacher." Thus traditionally there was no sharp distinction between "knowledge" and "pedagogy." Knowing *what* to teach and knowing *how* to teach were not separated. Even today, it is well known that most university professors were prepared for their careers as teachers by taking lots of courses in their subject-matter discipline, but few if any courses in how to teach. And to a large degree, this assumption has paid off at the university level. While there is currently a renewed interest in the improvement of university teaching at the undergraduate level, American universities have been and still are touted as the best part of the American educational system. Despite all the criticism of education in the United States, "Americans have the most successful system of higher education [in the world], especially postgraduate programs" (*Newsweek*, December 2, 1991, p. 51).

What about teacher knowledge at the level of the elementary school teacher? According to Shulman (1986), the situation for elementary school teachers used to be parallel to the one described in the preceding paragraph. That is, the "knowledge" thought to be needed for teaching elementary school 100 years ago was primarily subject-matter knowledge. Shulman used the California State Board Examination for elementary school teachers from 1875 as an example. On that Board Exam, elementary teachers were tested on the following categories:

1. Written Arithmetic
2. Mental Arithmetic
3. Written Grammar
4. Oral Grammar
5. Geography
6. History of the United States
7. Theory and Practice of Teaching
8. Algebra
9. Physiology
10. Natural Philosophy (Physics)
11. Constitution of the United States and California
12. School Law of California
13. Penmanship
14. Natural History (Biology)
15. Composition
16. Reading
17. Orthography
18. Defining (Word Analysis and Vocabulary)
19. Vocal Music
20. Industrial Drawing

As Shulman argues, this is certainly an impressive list of "knowledge categories." And further, note that out of the twenty categories on the test, only one—Theory and Practice of Teaching—is what we might classify today as a "pedagogical" category.

In contrast to 1875, recent emphasis on most teacher certification exams seems to have shifted to "assessment of capacity to teach" (Shulman, 1986, p. 5). Shulman cites as an example a list of competencies recently prepared by a state that was planning for state-wide evaluation of teachers. The list included the following categories:

1. Organization in preparing and presenting instructional plans
2. Evaluation
3. Recognition of individual differences
4. Cultural awareness
5. Understanding youth
6. Management
7. Educational policies and procedures

Certainly the shift in emphasis is dramatic. As Shulman asks, "Where did the subject matter go? What happened to the content?" (p. 5).

There are a number of related factors that have led to the shift in emphasis. One is the acknowledgement of the fact that knowledge of content alone often is *not* sufficient for expert pedagogy. That is, just knowing a lot about a subject-matter domain does not necessarily mean you will be expert at teaching in that domain. In fact, many researchers who study experts and novices in various domains remark on the "paradox" of the expert—namely that if you become "too expert" in a domain then your expertise becomes "too automated," and you cannot communicate effectively with nonexperts because so much of your knowledge is tacit or implicit that you cannot consciously articulate what you know.

This results in the phenomenon we described in Chapter 9, where an expert when asked how she knew what to do in a difficult problem-solving situation replied, "I don't know *how* I knew, I just knew. It was obvious based on my experience." Subject-matter expertise in a situation like this may enable the expert to solve a problem but it does not enable the expert to teach others to solve similar problems. Perhaps you remember classes where it was clear that the professor was "brilliant" but you could not understand a word that the professor said! In such classes, despite the subject-matter expertise of the teacher, very little learning will occur on the part of the students. Recognition of this phenomenon was one factor that led to an emphasis on "how to teach" as well as "what to teach." Other factors include research in teacher effectiveness, growing emphasis on teacher accountability for student failure, and attempts to simplify the teacher assessment process.

In summary, it appears that we have moved from the position of saying that knowledge alone is sufficient for teaching to the position of almost ignoring knowledge, and in doing so, we have traded one set of problems for another. Simply acknowledging that subject-matter knowledge alone is insufficient as a teacher knowledge base does not tell us what teachers *do* need to know in order to be effective teachers. Researchers have begun to ask questions about the characteristics of the knowledge bases of effective teachers, such as these, proposed by Shulman (1986):

- Where do teacher explanations come from?

- How do teachers decide what to teach, how to represent it, how to question students about it, and how to deal with problems of misunderstanding?

- What are the sources of teacher knowledge?

- What does a teacher know and when did he or she come to know it?

- How is new knowledge acquired, old knowledge retrieved, and both combined to form a new knowledge base?

Shulman argued that questions like these must be asked and answered in order to understand knowledge growth in teaching. It only makes sense that research on teachers should focus on issues like these, since research on learners has "focused almost exclusively on such questions in recent years" (Shulman, 1986, p. 8). As a starting point for research and discussion, Shulman proposed the following categories of "teacher knowledge" within what he calls the "domain of content knowledge in teaching."

Shulman's Categories

Content Knowledge. Content knowledge is defined as the subject matter knowledge and its organization. Shulman stresses that content knowledge goes beyond just concepts to the organizational and relational structures that connect concepts as well. Content knowledge includes both substantive and syntactic structures (see Schwab, 1978), and seems to be similar to the idea of "content structure" described by Meyer (1975) in her work on the organization of text. A key idea here is that the knowledge base must enable the "knower" to understand *that* something is so and also to understand *why* it is so. This emphasis on relations among concepts is often described as "schematic" (see, for example, Borko & Livingston, 1989; Shavelson, 1986; Westerman, 1991), as researchers in education continue to adopt and apply the terminology of cognitive psychology.

Pedagogical Content Knowledge. This type of content knowledge "embodies the aspects of content most germane to its teachability" (Shulman, 1986, p. 9). Distinct from "pure" content knowledge, pedagogical content knowledge enables effective teachers to understand which aspects of a particular subject-matter area are hard or easy to understand, and why. Pedagogical content knowledge includes conscious knowledge of examples, ideas, analogies, illustrations, explanations, and demonstrations that enable the teacher to make the content comprehensible to others.

Presumably, this type of knowledge would also include knowledge of who the "others" are and what they know, as well as knowledge of how to "connect" the new content to what the learners know already. Pedagogical content knowledge, when defined in this way, seems to contextualize or situate or personalize the content for the learner, because the teacher has knowledge of the learner and the context, as well as knowledge of the content in an abstract sense. This type of knowledge would seem to be particularly important in helping to correct the preconceptions and misperceptions that many learners bring to the teaching-learning situation (see, for example, Brown, Collins, and Duguid, 1989).

Curricular Knowledge. The curriculum is the range of instructional programs and materials for teaching various subjects to various learners at various levels. So, curricular knowledge is knowledge of the curricular or "instructional" alternatives that can be "prescribed," depending on how the teacher "diagnoses" the instructional problem. Shulman likens curricular knowledge to medical "pharmacopeia" (p. 10)—treatments or interventions that are appropriate, depending on the situation at hand.

In the framework used in this book, *content knowledge, pedagogical content knowledge,* and *curricular knowledge* would be composed of propositions, images, and linear orderings, and all these would relate schematically in the teacher's declarative knowledge base (see Figure 17.1). In addition, in order to connect these schemas or conceptual knowledge units to teacher actions and teacher behaviors, the content schemas would also combine to form conditions of productions in procedural knowledge (see Figure 17.2). That is, effective teachers would not only associate related concepts to each other in schematic networks in declarative memory, they would also associate conceptual information with appropriate actions in procedural memory. The conceptual information would comprise the "situation" or "conditions" of the production, and the teacher's thoughts about what to do and the teacher's behaviors would comprise the "actions" of the production. This depiction helps to explain how effective teachers use their information-rich schemas to "drive" their internal and external actions and behaviors in problem-solving situations. For the effective, experienced teacher, knowledge of the content, knowledge of how to communicate the content to the learners, and knowledge of curricular alternatives all combine to enable the teacher to set goals, formulate plans, execute plans, and evaluate progress. All the types of knowledge work together to enable strategic planning and appropriate action. According to this view, if teachers are lacking any of the types of content knowledge, their ability to plan and execute plans would be impaired.

Does Lack of Conceptual Knowledge Affect Practice?

Is there evidence in the research on teaching to support this view? What happens in the classroom if a teacher's content knowledge, pedagogical content knowledge, or curricular knowledge is incomplete, poorly organized, or otherwise lacking? Can you tell the difference between a teacher who has these types of knowledge and one who does not?

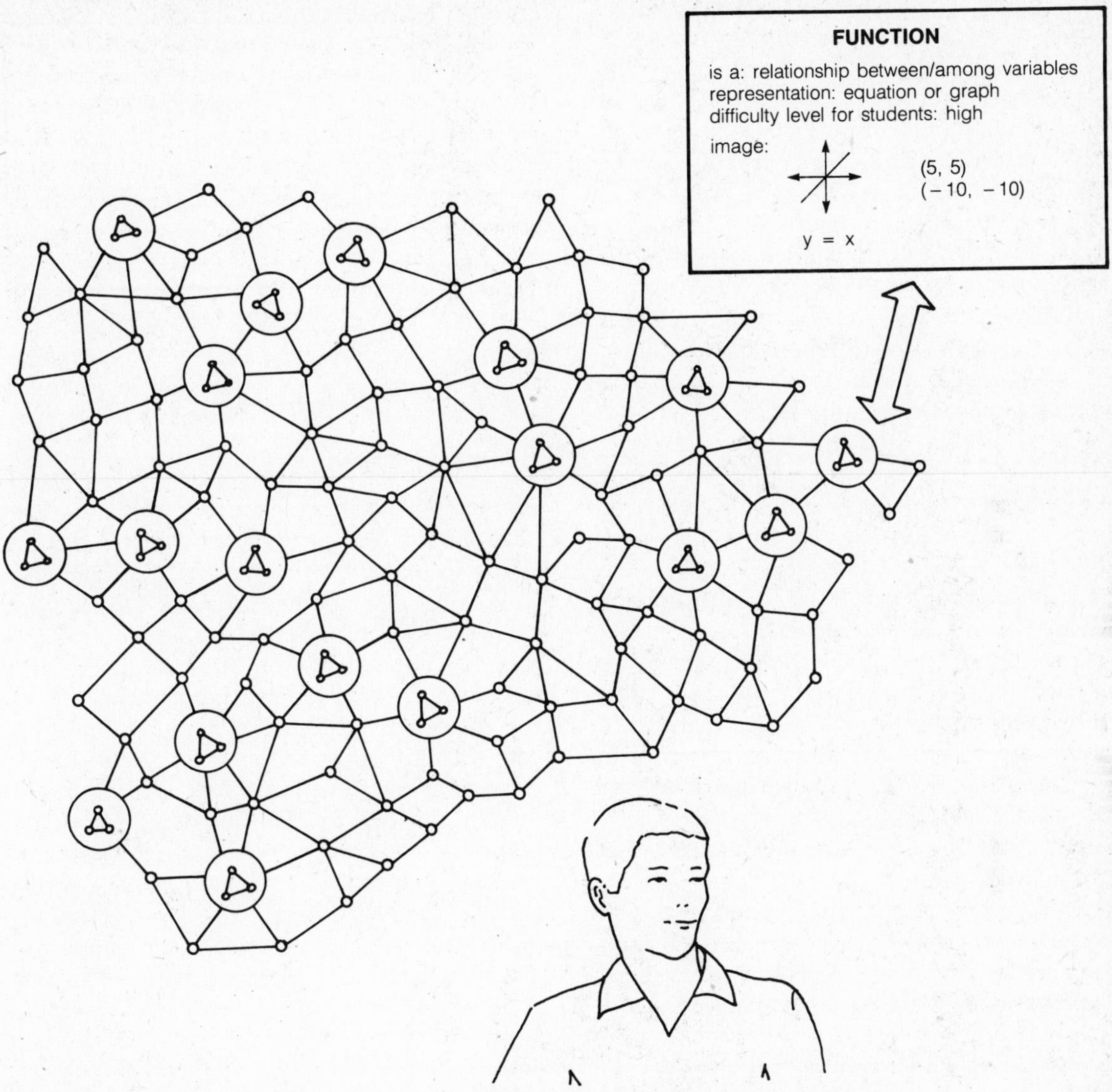

FUNCTION

is a: relationship between/among variables
representation: equation or graph
difficulty level for students: high

image:

(5, 5)
(−10, −10)

$y = x$

Figure 17.1 Schematic representation of content knowledge, pedagogical content knowledge, and curricular knowledge in a teacher's declarative knowledge base. The teacher is thinking, "Today, I'll teach the function $y = x$," and since his knowledge base is organized and elaborated, activation spreads to related content knowledge, pedagogical content knowledge, and curricular knowledge. Content consists of the equation $y = x$ and the graphic representation of the function represented as an image. Pedagogical content might include "It's hard for the kids to see the relation between the equation and the graph," and perhaps some examples of ordered pairs that represent the function. Curricular knowledge might include activities the teacher would "prescribe" for teaching the concept. All the knowledge is related schematically.

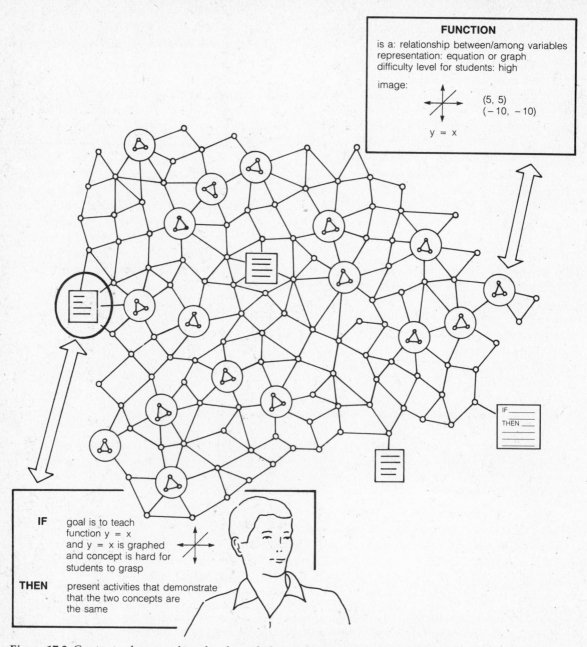

FUNCTION

is a: relationship between/among variables
representation: equation or graph
difficulty level for students: high

image:

(5, 5)
(−10, −10)

y = x

IF _____
THEN _____

IF goal is to teach
function y = x
and y = x is graphed
and concept is hard for
students to grasp

THEN present activities that demonstrate
that the two concepts are
the same

Figure 17.2 Content schemas of teacher knowledge are also represented as the conditions of productions in the teacher's procedural knowledge. This representation shows how effective teachers are able to utilize their information-rich schemas to "drive" their internal and external actions and behaviors in problem-solving situations.

A recent study reported by Stein, Baxter, and Leinhardt (1990) looked at the relationship between teacher subject matter knowledge and instructional practice in elementary math. An experienced fifth grade teacher was videotaped as he taught a lesson sequence on functions and graphing. In addition to the videotaping, the teacher was also interviewed about his subject matter knowledge and asked to sort some cards representing concepts in graphing and functions. The purpose of the sorting task was to get some insight into how the teacher "mapped" or organized these concepts in memory. Also, a mathematics educator was interviewed about functions and graphing and was asked to sort the cards. The interviews and the sorting results of the fifth grade teacher and the math educator were compared. The results suggested that the fifth grade teacher's knowledge of functions and graphing was lacking some key math concepts. Further, the teacher's knowledge was not organized in a way that related key ideas to each other.

For example, when the fifth grade teacher, Mr. Gene (a pseudonym), was asked why functions and graphing needed to be taught in the same unit, he replied that they did not really need to be taught together. Specifically, he said:

> I think you can teach graphing separate from functions and maybe do a better job of just teaching them how to make graphs and how to interpret graphs (p. 651).

> The graphing part of it, I just think it's a bonus. Graphing is neat for kids. But I'm not really convinced that it's critical for most children. I mean how many people in the real world, outside of a few business people who are interested in marketing or statistics or something like that, really make a whole lot of use of graphs? We need to be able to interpret graphs because they come out in newspapers and magazines and things like that periodically, but we don't make a lot of graphs or whatever. And I think if I weren't a school teacher, if I worked in some other line of work, I probably would not be making a lot of graphs (p. 647).

He made only one comment to suggest why functions and graphing might be taught in the same unit—because graphs can be used to check the answers to function problems. This seems to emphasize the importance of "getting the right answer," rather than the importance of the conceptual relationship between functions and graphing. In contrast, the math educator emphasized that graphs are "alternate representations" of the information expressed in algebraic functions. That is, she stressed that the two—graphs and functions—both represent the same relationship between variables; they just express the relationship in different ways. The function is a *statement* of the relationship and the graph is a *picture* of the relationship.

The ways in which Mr. Gene and the math educator sorted the concept cards also revealed the differences in their knowledge organization. When Mr. Gene sorted the cards, he put all the graphs (pictures) together and all the equations (statements) together (see Figure 17.3). He seemed to sort the cards into groups based on their surface or superficial similarities—that is, based on the way the information was represented. In contrast, the math educator separated the functions from the nonfunctions (see Figure 17.4, p. 459), and within these groups, sorted the cards so that equations *and* graphs that represented the same functional relationship were together. So, for example, the equation $y = x$ and the graphic representation of this function and the ordered pairs representing this function (i.e., (5,5), and (-53, -53) and (0,0)) were all grouped together (see the group on the left in the middle row in Figure 17.4). This type of arrangement indicates an organizational scheme based on the functional similarities of the cards rather than on the surface similarities—that is, the math educator sorted the

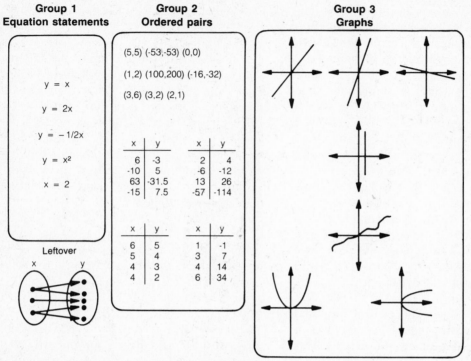

Group 1
Equation statements

$y = x$

$y = 2x$

$y = -1/2x$

$y = x^2$

$x = 2$

Leftover

x   y

Group 2
Ordered pairs

(5,5) (-53,-53) (0,0)

(1,2) (100,200) (-16,-32)

(3,6) (3,2) (2,1)

x	y		x	y
6	-3		2	4
-10	5		-6	-12
63	-31.5		13	26
-15	7.5		-57	-114

x	y		x	y
6	5		1	-1
5	4		3	7
4	3		4	14
4	2		6	34

Group 3
Graphs

Figure 17.3 Groups into which Mr. Gene sorted the cards representing concepts in the graphing and functions unit (from Stein, Baxter, and Leinhardt, 1990).

cards on the basis of what they meant rather than the way they looked.

Based on the results of this sorting task, it would appear that the math educator's schema for a particular function includes propositional information ($y = x$), spatial information (the image or graph of this function), and order information (the ordered pairs), all related in a way that preserves the underlying functional relationships of the information. Mr. Gene, on the other hand, did not indicate the same level of conceptual understanding in his organizational scheme.

Did the organization of Mr. Gene's schemas influence his teaching behavior? When Mr. Gene taught a lesson, was it apparent how his conceptual understanding of the subject matter "drove" his decisions and actions in the classroom? To attempt to answer this question, Stein et al. videotaped Mr. Gene during a 25-unit lesson on functions and graphing and looked for evidence of how his knowledge influenced his teaching. They found that Mr. Gene's knowledge limitations narrowed his instruction in three ways. First, he sometimes neglected to provide groundwork for future learning. Second, he sometimes overemphasized the importance and utility of rules that had only limited application. And third, he missed opportunities to point out meaningful connections between key concepts.

Take, for example, the second limitation, "overemphasis of limited truths." One rule that Mr. Gene taught the children was that there are three parts to a function problem— the input, the function rule, and the output. So, if the *input* is "3" and the *function rule* is

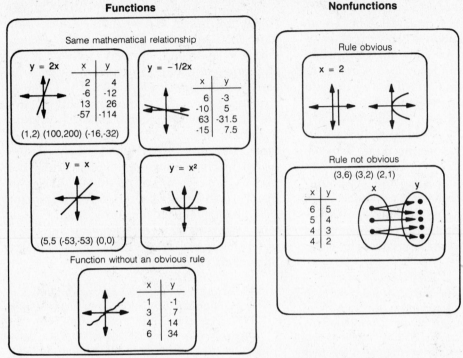

Figure 17.4 Groups into which the math educator sorted the cards. This arrangement groups concepts on the basis of what they mean rather than on the basis of their surface similarities (from Stein, Baxter, and Leinhardt, 1990).

"times 2," then the *output* is "6" (i.e., $3 \times 2 = 6$). Or if the *input* is "4" and the *function of our operation* is "to square," then the *output* is "16." He taught the rule by using an analogy to a computer, which has input, program, and output, and he explained to the students that in a function problem they would be given two of the parts and be asked to solve for the missing part. In describing the lesson, we quote from Stein et al.:

After he worked through several examples of finding the missing input, the missing function rule, or the missing output, Mr. Gene presented a generalized rule to the students: *If one knows two out of the three pieces of information, one can find the third missing piece* (pp. 652–653).

Stein et al. noted that while it is probably true that the *"two-out-of-three rule"* will serve

the students well for the remainder of the fifth-grade unit, from a mathematical perspective this rule is not always true. That is, if you know the input and the function you can find the output, but if you know the input and the output you cannot always find the function. For example, if the input = 3 and the output = 6, the function could be either "plus 3" or "times 2." Similarly, if you know the function and the output, there can be more than one possible input. That is, if the function is "to square" and the output is 25, the input could be either +5 or −5. Thus, the student using the "two-out-of-three" rule could probably solve most of the math function problems required in fifth grade, but at the deepest conceptual level, this rule misrepresents functions as *always* having a "one-to-one" correspondence, when in fact functions can sometimes have a "several-to-one" or even a "many-to-one" correspondence. This somewhat skewed conception is likely to perseverate in the student's math knowledge base and at a later date to undermine the student's math problem solving and the way the student understands math relationships.

With respect to the third limitation in Mr. Gene's instruction, "missed opportunities for fostering meaningful connections between key concepts," Stein et al. noted how Mr. Gene's belief that "functions" and "graphing" could be taught separately was passed on to his students through his teaching. In describing a part of Mr. Gene's lesson where he could have related these two key concepts, Stein et al. reported:

> Although Mr. Gene linked ordered pairs to functions and ordered pairs to graphs, he never directly united the two representations of functions and graphs. Rather, functions and graphs had the sense of being glued together by the ordered pairs representation; that is, the ordered pairs served as the only bridge between functions and graphs. Indeed the students seemed to lose sight of the fact that they were *graphing functions.* The intermediary link of ordered pairs overwhelmed the much more significant connection between graphs and functions (p. 657).

Stein et al. concluded that he failed in his lessons to draw students' attention

> to the fact that the lines are indeed graphs of functions (not simply finite sets of connected points on a line). In essence, the students could have been helped to step back and "see the forest instead of the trees." Instead, Mr. Gene only focused on whether or not each individual line was straight. The more significant connection between the graph and the function was lost (or never established). Mr. Gene even chose to label the graphs according to their problem numbers instead of by their functions (p. 659).

In summary, Stein, Baxter, and Leinhardt (1990) concluded that in math, which they have studied, there appears to be a very strong relationship between teacher knowledge and mathematics instruction, even at the early elementary grade levels. They argued that "different ways of knowing mathematics are reflected in how elementary teachers communicate their subjects" (p. 641). Further, Stein et al. pointed out that connections between teacher knowledge and instructional practice have been suggested by studies in history (Wilson, 1988), English (Grossman, 1987), biology (Hashweh, 1987), science (Hollon, Anderson, & Roth, in press), and computer science (Baxter, 1987). In summary, Stein et al. argued that:

> These and other studies (e.g., Gudmundsdottir & Shulman, 1987; McGraw, 1987; Marks, 1987; Peterson, Fennema, & Carpenter, in press) have provided evidence that teachers' knowledge affects both the content and the processes of their instruction, influencing both what they teach and how they teach. In general, teachers with more explicit and better organized knowledge tend to provide instruction that features conceptual connections, appropriate and varied representations, and active and meaningful student discourse. On the other hand, teachers with limited knowledge have been found to portray the subject as a collection of static facts; to provide impoverished or inappropriate examples, analogies, and/or representations; and to emphasize seatwork assignments and/or routinized student input as opposed to meaningful dialogue (p. 641).

Their work helps to document how schematic knowledge influences behavior, and seems to agree with the position we have taken in this book. Stein et al. argue that there is a need for "fine-grained" work to complement the existing studies, in order to build a "robust picture" of the role of teacher knowledge in instruction. We would certainly agree.

AUTOMATED BASIC SKILLS

In addition to knowing the subject matter that they want to teach, teachers also need to know how to keep students engaged in the instructional process. Even the most knowledgeable content experts will not be expert teachers if they cannot keep the students engaged. For effective teachers, "classroom management routines" often have become second nature, and they are proceduralized in the form of automated basic skills. The ability to manage the classroom in an efficient and effective manner seems to be another way to distinguish experts from novices. The schemas in classroom management routines can be described as "pedagogical knowledge of teaching" (Shulman, 1986). By embedding this knowledge in the conditions of productions, we can refer to classroom management as "pedagogical knowledge in action."

Differences in effective and ineffective classroom managers have been studied at both the middle school (Moskowitz and Hayman, 1976) and elementary school levels (Emmer, 1982; Emmer, Evertson, and Anderson, 1980; Evertson and Anderson, 1978) with similar results.

Management during the First Few Weeks

Emmer, Evertson, and Anderson (1980) studied fourteen third-grade teachers, seven of whom were effective managers and seven of whom were ineffective. The students in effective and ineffective managers' classes did not differ at the beginning of the year on aptitude or achievement test scores. However, throughout the school year the students in the effective managers' classrooms showed more on-task behavior and, by the end of the year, they showed greater achievement gains than did the students in the ineffective managers' classrooms. The researchers were particularly interested in how these effective and ineffec-

tive teachers differed during the first few weeks of class, so they made extensive observations at this time. Since they did not know at the time of observation which teachers would fall into the effective and ineffective manager categories, their observations were unbiased.

The results showed how effective and ineffective managers differed. The typical effective teacher started out the first day by greeting students, giving them assignments, and informing the class about such things as where to put their personal belongings and rules about going to the bathroom and water fountain. If a parent or school administrator tried to interrupt, the effective teacher resisted these attempts and refused to leave the classroom on this crucial first day. The typical ineffective teacher (who was often a beginning teacher) started the first day in a less organized fashion. He did not have rules for going to the bathroom or drinking fountain or for lining up. No name tags were handed out, and the children were not given activities to work on while waiting for other students, so they wandered about most of the time. If a parent or administrator called on the teacher, the teacher left the room and the children were left unsupervised.

Besides acting more organized on the first day of school, the effective teachers were persistent in teaching classroom rules during the first few weeks of school. Routines, such as lining up to sharpen pencils, were rehearsed, and their rationale was explained. Any transgressions were stopped quickly with a reminder to the transgressor about the rule. The initial "seatwork" done by students was relatively easy so that students could learn the routines for doing seatwork without being confused by difficult material at the same time. Ineffective teachers, on the other hand, did not teach rules to their students, or if they did, the rules were taught ineffectively. One ineffective teacher gave a rule that was too vague for children to follow: "Be in the right place at the right time." Another teacher did not follow up on enforcing a stated rule. She told the children that one bell ring meant for them to stop talking and two bell rings meant for them to pay attention, but when the students did not immediately follow these rules, she abandoned them. The effective teachers seemed to have an implicit or explicit understanding that rules about classroom behavior, just like rules about addition and subtraction, were skills to be learned through the use of practice and feedback. The ineffective teachers seemed to lack this insight.

Table 17.1 shows other ways in which the effective and ineffective managers differed during the first three weeks of instruction. The scores ranged from 1, which indicated that the teacher exhibited very little of this characteristic, to 7, which indicated a high frequency. One interesting observation is how the effective managers dealt with disruptive behavior (item 5). Some textbooks advise teachers to "ignore disruptive behavior and praise correct behavior." Yet the effective managers were more likely to stop quickly when disruptive behavior occurred and do something about it, whereas the less effective managers were more likely to ignore the disruptive behavior (item 6). The idea of ignoring disruptive behavior may be based on the idea

that pleasure is the most important aspect of reinforcement. That is, one should not criticize students for being disruptive because criticism is unpleasant. However, if one thinks of the information aspect of reinforcement discussed in Chapter 16, then calling attention (in a constructive manner) to unacceptable behavior is highly informative. Like any other matched non-example, it helps students make discriminations.

One of the most interesting findings of the Emmer, Evertson, and Anderson (1980) study was the extent to which behavior during the first few weeks of class determined the discipline and achievement in the class for the whole year. This finding supports what many experienced teachers know about the importance of "getting things off to a good start." This is not to say that a class that gets off to a bad start can never be turned around. However, starting school in an organized manner and teaching classroom procedures early seems to help a great deal in keeping students "on task."

Homework

In middle school, if not before, students start to receive homework assignments. The collection and correction of homework are tasks that

Table 17.1 Differences between effective and ineffective classroom managers. Values range from 1 (teacher exhibited very little of this characteristic) to 7 (teacher exhibited a lot of this characteristic) (adapted from Emmer, Evertson, and Anderson, 1980).

VARIABLE	MORE EFFECTIVE MANAGERS	LESS EFFECTIVE MANAGERS
1. Variety of rewards	4.3	3.1
2. Signals appropriate behavior	5.4	3.8
3. Eye contact	6.1	4.9
4. States desired attitudes	5.5	3.9
5. Stops if disruptive behavior	4.9	3.5
6. Ignores disruptive behavior	2.9	3.6

can be managed more and less effectively. Leinhardt (1983) observed expert and novice math teachers' homework-checking behavior and found large differences between them. A typical expert started class by calling the roll. Students responded "yes" if they had done their homework and "no" if they had not. The students who responded "no" put their names on the blackboard. This procedure gave the teacher information about how many people had done their homework and who had not. The information would not be forgotten, because it was on the board, and it was obtained efficiently, since while a student wrote his or her name on the board, the teacher continued the roll call.

After the roll call the teacher asked for choral answers to each homework problem. When the chorus weakened, the teacher tagged the problem as being difficult. The students marked their own problems and after all answers had been given, the teacher tallied how many students got each problem correct by calling out each number and asking students to raise a hand if they got that problem right. This tally gave the teacher a summary of how the class was doing and of which problems were difficult. The summary was used in adapting the day's lesson if students had not done well on their homework. The entire homework-checking procedure took about two minutes.

In contrast to the expert, one typical novice teacher took six minutes to check homework. She started out by asking the group, "Who doesn't have their homework?" Some students responded by holding up their papers, others walked up to the teacher to tell her that they either did or did not have their homework, and still others called out that they did not have it. The teacher then marked down who had and had not completed homework. Unlike the expert teacher, the novice did not end up with a visible tally of those who had not completed homework. Next the nov-

ice teacher asked the slowest child in the class to give the answers to problems 1 through 10. The child answered very slowly because she was unprepared and was trying to do the problems (unsuccessfully) on the spot. The students checked their work but the teacher did not collect a tally at the end, so she did not know how many children had missed each problem.

The difference between the expert and novice here seems to be that the expert had a smooth action sequence that the novice lacked. The novice was on the way to acquiring such a sequence, but some of the steps in the sequence (such as calling on the slowest student) disrupted the flow. With experience, the novice is likely to develop a better procedure, and to automate the procedure so it can be executed with less effort.

Summary

With respect to management, expert teachers differ from inexpert teachers in several ways. Expert managers are more organized on the first day of school, and they have routines for teaching students the norms for their classrooms. They also have efficient methods of checking homework, such as having students check their own work, getting a summary of how well the class did, and then using this summary to adjust the lesson plan. In short, these routines or automated basic skills seem to make the teacher's life easier and to increase the amount of time and energy that can be spent on teaching and learning. Since the conditions that precipitate these routines do not vary (e.g., roll always needs to be taken), automating these skills is appropriate.

STRATEGIC KNOWLEDGE

In addition to conceptual understanding and automated management routines, what else do effective teachers have that ineffective teachers appear to lack? Are there other ways that a production system framework can help to explain the relation between teacher cognitions and teacher behavior? In the previous section, we discussed how teachers can automate particular routines or basic skills to help them manage the classroom. However, automating procedures is appropriate only when there is very little variability in the situation from one time to the next, such as in taking roll or checking to see who has done homework. And it is clear to any observer of classroom activity that most situations in the classroom are far from routine. A number of researchers have remarked on the complexity of the classroom environment and on the fact that teaching and teacher decision making are complex and cognitively demanding activities (cf., Westerman, 1991). How do expert and less expert teachers differ in the multitude of cases where the problem or situation is complex and sophisticated use of strategic knowledge is required in order to solve the problem?

This question has also been studied at both elementary and middle school levels, with some fairly consistent findings emerging from the data (see for example, Borko and Livingston, 1989; Borko, Livingston, and Shavelson, 1990; Emmer, Evertson, and Anderson, 1980; Evertson, Emmer, and Brophy, 1980; Good and Grouws, 1979; Housner and Griffey, 1983; Leinhardt, 1989; Westerman, 1991). In general, it appears that expert teachers use a variety of instructional strategies appropriate to the situation. A partial list includes:

1. Communicate objectives, give directions, and present content *clearly*

2. *Adapt* instruction to students' ability levels

3. *Explain* to students *why* they are learning particular material

4. Explicitly *connect* new material to previously studied concepts

5. Give students opportunities to respond, practice, and *solve problems*

6. Give specific, informative *feedback*

Clarity, Adaptability, and Providing a Rationale

Table 17.2 shows some additional findings from the Emmer et al. (1980) study that was

Table 17.2 Instructional strategies of more and less effective teachers (adapted from Emmer, Evertson, and Anderson, 1980).

TEACHER BEHAVIOR	MORE EFFECTIVE TEACHERS	LESS EFFECTIVE TEACHERS
1. Describes objectives clearly	5.1	3.1
2. Uses a variety of materials	5.6	3.7
3. Materials are ready	6.2	4.4
4. Materials support instruction	6.0	4.3
5. Clear directions	5.2	3.8
6. Clear presentation	5.8	4.1
7. Provides/seeks rationale or analysis	4.9	3.4
8. Attention spans considered in lesson design	5.2	2.8
9. High degree of pupil success	5.5	3.9
10. Content related to pupil interests	5.2	3.6
11. Reasonable work standards	5.8	4.6

described in the previous section. At the end of the year the most and least effective teachers were identified using pupil achievement tests. As you can see in Table 17.2, the more effective teachers differed from less effective ones in several ways with respect to how successful they were in communicating the information so the students could understand it. The more effective teachers communicated objectives, directions, and content (items 1, 5, and 6) more clearly. They also seemed to adapt their instruction to the students' interests, skill levels, and attention spans (items 8, 9, and 10). Finally, they explained to students *why* they were learning particular material (item 7). The ineffective teachers gave vague directions for seatwork, failed to give a rationale for such work, and failed to check to see that the children understood directions. Thus, being clear, monitoring students, and adapting instruction all appear to be important instructional strategies used by effective teachers.

Feedback

Students' questions, comments, and responses are crucial to learning, for both declarative and procedural knowledge. This is because they provide a means for teachers to give informative feedback (Kulhavy, 1977), so the student can find out what to do differently next time and why.

For learning declarative knowledge, feedback should enhance the organization of information and stimulate students to elaborate on the information. This will help students to construct expert-like schemas, as we suggested in Chapter 8.

Since schemas also function as the conditions of productions, feedback should also be given to help students distinguish examples from non-examples, so that students can learn when different *conditions* call for different *actions*. And, for learning to execute the actions

in production sets, feedback should remind the student of the relations among the steps or the pieces in the procedure, so that small procedures will be compiled into larger procedures (see also Chapter 9 on the acquisition of procedures).

Do more and less effective teachers differ on how they respond to students? The answer is yes, although investigators have not yet looked at whether teachers give different feedback for the different types of knowledge just mentioned. Nonetheless, the results are suggestive. Evertson, Emmer, and Brophy (1980), for example, found several differences between more and less effective middle school math teachers on the feedback they gave to student responses. Table 17.3 (p. 466) shows some of their findings.

The first two items in Table 17.3 indicated that the more effective teachers asked more questions than did the less effective teachers. By asking questions they were initiating opportunities for students to obtain feedback and increasing the probability that students would learn accurately. Item 4 shows that effective teachers were far more likely than ineffective teachers to follow up a correct answer with another question to the same student, thereby rewarding that student and encouraging her to think further. For wrong answers the differences between effective and ineffective teachers are not very large, but the effective teachers did ask another question of the same student or give process feedback more often. (In process feedback, the teacher identifies what step in the process produced the wrong answer, rather than just saying that the answer was wrong.) Finally, effective teachers were four times as likely as ineffective teachers to follow up with feedback when students initiated comments (item 11). Thus, although we cannot tell from these data whether teachers adjusted their feedback strategies for different types of knowledge, we can tell that the effective teachers gave

Table 17.3 Differences in feedback strategies by more and less effective teachers. Numbers indicate the average frequency in a fifty-minute period (adapted from Emmer, Evertson, and Anderson, 1980).

VARIABLE	MORE EFFECTIVE	LESS EFFECTIVE
1. Process questions	5.91	1.29
2. Product questions	17.42	6.95
3. Correct answer praised by teacher	4.26	.32
4. New question after correct answer	2.93	.25
5. Correct answer integrated into discussion	3.25	.60
6. Correct answer — no feedback	.38	.06
7. Wrong answer — teacher criticizes	.01	.01
8. Wrong answer — new teacher question	.41	.07
9. Wrong answer — process feedback	.28	.09
10. Wrong answer — teacher gives answer	.72	.27
11. Student-initiated comments given feedback	1.00	.28

students more opportunities to get feedback and were more likely to be clear and specific in the feedback they gave. Clear and specific feedback is important for any type of knowledge.

Review of Prerequisite Knowledge

In Chapter 9 we saw how important a student's ability to recall prerequisites was for acquiring more complex skills (see also Chapter 14–Mathematics). Effective math teachers appear to be aware of the importance of recalling prerequisites. Evertson et al. (1980) found that the more effective teachers in their study spent significantly more time than less effective teachers reviewing whole-number operations and fractions before teaching decimals, percentages, and algebra topics. This finding held up even when all the items relevant to whole-number operations and fractions were eliminated from the achievement test used to judge effectiveness. Thus, effective teachers seem to know when reviews are needed. How do they know? Recall the discussion of Mr. Gene's conceptual knowledge and the math educator's conceptual knowledge earlier in this chapter. If teachers have a clear understanding of the conceptual relations in the subject they are teaching, they are likely to know when explicit connections among concepts should be pointed out. In addition, it is likely that they will review the earlier concept if they think there is any chance that the students have forgotten it.

TEACHING INSTRUCTIONAL STRATEGIES TO TEACHERS

So far we have seen that classroom teaching involves optimizing the learning of all students in the class. This difficult problem is solved partially through lots of conceptual knowledge, partially through good management routines, and partially through good instructional strategies. Effective teachers appear to have many instructional strategies that are *conditioned* on student performance. That is, these teachers can vary the instructional strategy as the performance of the students varies. Because they are able to use this type of knowledge, they can plan for various contingencies and adapt when contingencies arise.

Can less effective teachers learn to use the strategies employed by more effective teachers? This is a difficult question to answer. On the surface, the answer to this question appears to be yes. However, over the past ten years educational researchers have changed their minds somewhat as to how they define strategies, and that makes it somewhat difficult to interpret the strategy-training studies in an unambiguous way. For example, Good and Grouws (1979) attempted to train teachers in the use of what they called effective strategies (see also Evertson, Emmer, Sanford, and Clements, 1983). Good and Grouws (1979) developed a descriptive list of procedures that had been shown to distinguish more from less effective fourth-grade mathematics teachers. Using this list as a starting point, they developed a 45-page training manual that was intended to teach teachers to use these procedures. Table 17.4 shows some of the key procedures that were described and explained in the manual. These included: (1) having a daily review, (2) developing new material meaningfully and responsively, (3) supervising seatwork efficiently, (4) assigning homework, and (5) having periodic reviews over more content than was covered in daily reviews. Note that some of the procedures listed would be called "management routines" or automated basic skills in today's jargon, while others would qualify as "instructional strategies."

Good and Grouws (1979) attempted to train twenty fourth-grade teachers (volunteers) from schools serving low-socioeconomic-status students to use these procedures. Another twenty teachers served as a control group. The teachers in the training group heard a 90-minute explanation of research on teaching strategies. They were then given the 45-page teaching manual and were told to read it and to begin implementing its ideas in their classrooms. Two weeks later, there was another 90-minute session with the teachers in the training group. During this session the experimenters responded to teachers' questions about specific strategies and gave suggestions for overcoming difficulties in implementing the target behaviors.

Table 17.4 Instructional strategies and management routines that teachers were trained to use (from Good and Grouws, 1979).

Daily review (first 8 minutes except Mondays)
  a. review the concepts and skills associated with the homework
  b. collect and deal with homework assignments
  c. ask several mental computation exercises
Development (about 20 minutes)
  a. briefly focus on prerequisite skills and concepts
  b. focus on meaning and promoting student understanding by using lively explanations, demonstrations, process explanations, illustrations, etc.
  c. assess student comprehension
    1. using process/product questions (active interaction)
    2. using controlled practice
  d. repeat and elaborate on the meaning portion as necessary
Seatwork (about 15 minutes)
  a. provide uninterrupted successful practice
  b. momentum—keep the ball rolling—get everyone involved, then sustain involvement
  c. alerting—let students know their work will be checked at end of period
  d. accountability—check the students' work
Homework assignment
  a. assign on a regular basis at the end of each math class except Fridays
  b. should involve about 15 minutes of work to be done at home
  c. should include one or two review problems
Special reviews
  a. weekly review/maintenance
    1. conduct during the first 20 minutes each Monday
    2. focus on skills and concepts covered during the previous week
  b. monthly review/maintenance
    1. conduct every fourth Monday
    2. focus on skills and concepts covered since the last monthly review

After this session each teacher was observed six times over the next two and a half months. The observers recorded incidences of the targeted procedures. The teachers in the control group were also observed six times during the same period. These observations allowed the experimenters to determine whether or not the teachers in the training group actually implemented the strategies and routines about which they had read. To measure teaching effectiveness, students of both the training- and control-group teachers took a standardized mathematics achievement test before and after the training program.

Table 17.5 shows the percentage of time that the trained and control teachers used each targeted skill. For most of the targeted behaviors, the trained teachers showed a higher frequency than did the control teachers. Some of the largest differences were in conducting reviews (item 1), checking homework (3), working on mental computation (4), and assigning homework (15). However, there were some targeted behaviors that the trained teachers did not exhibit more frequently than controls. These included sum-

marizing the previous day's materials (5), spending at least five minutes on development (7), and using demonstrations during presentation of lessons (9). Note that these behaviors that did not increase in frequency appear to be among the most "strategic," while those that did increase in frequency appear to be more like "routines."

Did the use of the procedures affect student achievement? Yes, it had a substantial effect. Students in the trained teachers' classes had an average percentile gain of 31 from the pre- to the posttest, whereas the control group students had an average percentile gain of 19. Furthermore, several of the targeted teacher behaviors correlated significantly with student achievement. Specifically, conducting a review ($r = .37$), checking homework ($r = .54$), working on mental computation ($r = .48$), holding students accountable for seatwork ($r = .35$), and giving homework assignments ($r = .49$) each correlated signifi-

Table 17.5 The percentage of time that trained and control group teachers used the targeted skills. An asterisk indicates a significant difference (adapted from Good and Grouws, 1979).

	PERCENTAGE OF TIME	
VARIABLE	TRAINED	CONTROL
1. Did the teacher conduct review?	91*	62
2. Did development take place within review?	51*	37
3. Did the teacher check homework?	79*	20
4. Did the teacher work on mental computation?	69*	6
5. Did the teacher summarize previous day's materials?	28	25
6. There was a slow transition from review.	7	4
7. Did the teacher spend at least 5 minutes on development?	45	51
8. Were the students held accountable for controlled practice during the development phase?	33	20
9. Did the teacher use demonstrations during presentation?	45	46
10. Did the teacher conduct seatwork?	80*	56
11. Did the teacher actively engage students in seatwork (first 1½ minutes)?	71*	43
12. Was the teacher available to provide immediate help to students during seatwork (next 5 minutes)?	68*	47
13. Were students held accountable for seatwork at the end of seatwork phase?	59*	31
14. Did seatwork directions take longer than 1 minute?	18	23
15. Did the teacher make homework assignments?	66	13

cantly with student achievement. Thus, the use of the targeted procedures strongly affected student performance.

The results of this study are interesting both because the training was easy and because the gains observed were dramatic. Since the teachers were volunteers, results might be less dramatic for teachers who had less freedom to decide whether or not to take the training. Even so, many teachers are eager to improve, and it appears that this training was effective for motivated teachers.

Another way to look at the results of the study by Good and Grouws is to ask why some of the targeted skills *were not used more frequently* by the trained teachers than by the control group. Is it significant that Good and Grouws did *not* differentiate between instructional strategies (which vary, depending on the situation, and thus require elaborated, well-organized conceptual knowledge as their conditions) and management routines (which typically are standard from day to day and thus become automatic)? Although Good and Grouws referred to all their target behaviors as "strategies," a different interpretation of their findings might result from defining their procedures differently. To understand why, think back again to the discussion of the math educator and Mr. Gene, the fifth grade teacher (Stein, Baxter, and Leinhardt, 1990). Given what we learned about Mr. Gene from the interview, the card sort, and the description of his teaching, it is easy to imagine how he or a teacher like him could acquire and use new management techniques, given the opportunity. Mr. Gene seemed to be very concerned with the effectiveness of his teaching, and he would probably be motivated to improve. On the other hand, given what we know about the importance of well-organized, elaborated conceptual representations to instructional effectiveness, it is hard to imagine how Mr. Gene could change his overall instructional strategies very much without making major

changes in the way he understands the conceptual relation between functions and graphing. The point here is that if a teacher's conceptual understanding of a subject *drives* his strategy for teaching the subject, then one would expect that subtle and complex changes in the knowledge base would be necessary before changes in teaching strategies could occur. In the study reported by Stein et al., no mention was made of attempts to change Mr. Gene's strategies. Nor were his teaching strategies compared to those of the math educator, whose conceptual understanding of functions and graphing was highly integrated. Therefore, we report the results from the study by Good and Grouws here, and we will wait for future studies to report how changes in conceptual understanding might lead to changes in strategic behavior.

THE DYNAMICS OF INSTRUCTION

Effective teachers not only have better management routines and instructional strategies than do ineffective teachers, but these procedures also appear to be better organized and better timed. As we have said, many of the management skills appear to be performed automatically. As for the strategies, the conditions under which particular strategies are appropriate are readily recognized by effective teachers, and this leads to smooth execution of strategic behavior in the classroom. The smooth nature of an experienced teacher's classroom actions has been described in some recent studies (Fogarty, Wang, and Creek, 1983; Housner and Griffey, 1983).

Housner and Griffey (1983) asked sixteen physical education teachers to teach soccer and basketball dribbling skills to groups of four eight-year-old children. Eight of the teachers were experienced, having spent five or more years as elementary PE teachers. The other eight were training to be elementary school PE teachers and so were inexperienced as teachers.

The teachers were given 60 minutes to plan their lessons. They were told that they were to teach two lessons—one on soccer and one on basketball dribbling skills—and that if they wanted more information, they must ask for it. They were told to think aloud while planning, and their protocols were tape recorded. After the planning session the teachers were videotaped while teaching their lessons. They then viewed the videotape with the researchers and reported what cues they were attending to while teaching and what decisions they were making.

Planning

During planning, the experienced teachers asked an average of 6.5 questions of the researchers and the inexperienced teachers asked 4.5. Both groups asked about the number of students they would be teaching, their ages, sex, and ability, and about what equipment was available and the amount of time they would have to teach. However, the experienced teachers asked more questions about the students' prior experience with soccer and basketball dribbling. This result suggests that the experienced teachers planned to teach differently depending on the skill level of their students.

Table 17.6 shows the types of decisions made by experienced and inexperienced teachers during their planning sessions. Activity decisions included what activities the students would engage in (*structure*), the rules for this activity (*procedures*), its spatial arrangement (*formation*), the amount of time, and plans for any adaptations if the students could not do the activity. Instructional decisions included plans for setting rules and motivating students (*management*), observing students and giving feedback, demonstrating a motor skill, moving students from one activity

Table 17.6 Decisions made by experienced and inexperienced teachers during planning. The numbers are percentages of the total number of decisions of a particular class, activity or instructional (adapted from Housner and Griffey, 1983).

	EXPERIENCED	INEXPERIENCED
ACTIVITY DECISIONS		
Structure	42.6%	54.5
Procedures	24.6	28.0
Formations	4.9	1.5
Time	9.0	6.8
Adaptations	18.9	9.1
INSTRUCTIONAL DECISIONS		
Management	13.4%	4.8
Assess/feedback	22.8	15.9
Demonstrate	7.9	7.9
Transitions	5.5	6.4
Focus attention	18.9	19.1
Equipment use	7.9	7.9
Verbal instruction	19.7	34.9
Time	3.9	3.2

to another (*transitions*), focusing students' attention on specific aspects of a motor skill, using equipment, giving verbal explanations or directions, and allocating time.

As you can see, the percentage of thinking-aloud statements related to some of these decisions was different for the two groups. The four types of decisions for which experienced and inexperienced teachers differed significantly were *adaptations, management, assess/feedback,* and *verbal instructions*. In the first three categories the experienced teachers made more decisions. That is, they planned ahead more for contingencies, for establishing rules and motivation, and for assessing students and giving them feedback. In verbal instructions the inexperienced teachers made more decisions, suggesting that they relied more on verbal instructions than did the experienced teachers.

Table 17.7 Types of cues heeded by experienced and inexperienced teachers (adapted from Housner and Griffey, 1983).

CUES	EXPERIENCED	INEXPERIENCED
Student performance	30.1%	19.0
Student involvement	27.4	22.6
Student interest	11.8	27.3
Student verbalizations/ requests	3.2	7.7
Student mood/feelings	3.2	6.5
Teacher's mood/feelings	5.3	1.7
Other	19.0	15.2

Interactive Decision Making

While watching videotapes of their teaching, the teachers reported what cues they heeded during instruction. Table 17.7 shows these results. The experienced teachers were more likely than the inexperienced teachers to heed the students' performance and their own mood and feelings. The inexperienced teach-ers were more likely than the experienced teachers to heed the students' interests, ver-balizations, and moods. Thus the experienced teachers paid attention to the most informa-tive aspect of the students' behavior—their dribbling performance—whereas the inexpe-rienced teachers paid attention to the more salient, but somewhat less informative, aspect of the students' apparent interest. Certainly student interest is important over the long run, but it can fluctuate from minute to minute. Also, what develops interest over the long run is success. Therefore, the experi-enced teachers' focus on student performance was well founded. This difference between expert and novice teachers is reminiscent of the differences between expert and novice physics problem solvers and expert and nov-ice medical diagnosticians (see Chapter 10). That is, the novices attend to an aspect of the problem (student interest) that may not be particularly relevant to solving the problem.

Table 17.8 The percentage of time that a given type of cue resulted in a change of teaching plans during instruction (adapted from Housner and Griffey, 1983).

	EXPERIENCED	INEXPERIENCED
STUDENT BEHAVIOR CUES		
Performance	35.7%	28.1
Involvement	33.3	23.6
Interest	54.5	30.4
Verbalization/request	33.3	76.9
Mood/feeling	50.0	27.2
Interactions	40.0	0.0
Other	44.4	33.3
TEACHER/CONTEXT CUES		
Instructional behavior	20.0%	50.0
Mood/feeling	10.0	33.3
Time	54.5	35.7
Equipment/facility	40.0	0.0
Average percentage of cues that resulted in a change in teaching	37.6%	32.1

Since experts and novices attend to different aspects of the conditions, it is not surprising that their actions differ as they teach.

Table 17.8 shows the percentage of time that a heeded cue resulted in teachers changing their lessons from what they had originally planned. The experienced teachers made changes based on observing cues more often than did inexperienced teachers. This result is similar to a result obtained by Peterson and Clark (1978) for teaching social studies. They found that effective teachers seemed to have more alternatives available when something "went wrong." Less effective teachers were aware that something was wrong but were either less willing or less able to make changes.

Table 17.8 also shows that the inexperienced teachers were far more likely to make changes based on student verbalizations and requests (76.9 percent) than were experienced teachers (33.3 percent). One gets the impression that the students were controlling the inexperienced teachers rather than vice versa. (Of course, there are situations in which teachers should make changes based on stu-

dent verbalizations, but teaching dribbling is probably not one of them.) The experienced teachers more frequently made changes based on cues from the students' performance.

The experienced teachers act as if they have procedural knowledge that is activated by student performance of the motor skills being learned. Table 17.9 shows, in informal production system terms, some of this knowledge. Production 1 applies when students are not quite getting the skill, and its action is that the teacher demonstrates the skill. Production 2 applies when some students are not quite getting the skill but others appear to have it. Its action is that the teacher asks a skilled student for a demonstration rather than demonstrating it herself. Production 3 applies under more drastic conditions, when the students are not even close to performing correctly. Under those conditions the teacher backs up and has the students work on a component skill.

In contrast to the experienced teachers, the inexperienced teachers act as if they are using some procedural knowledge that is relevant to many social situations but is not

Table 17.9 Some procedural knowledge available to experienced teachers that can be activated by poor performance on the part of the students.

	IF	Students are not quite getting skill
P_1	THEN	Stop activity
		And demonstrate skill.
	IF	Some students are getting skill
		And others are not
P_2	THEN	Stop activity
		And have a proficient student demonstrate skill.
	IF	Students are performing very poorly
	THEN	Stop activity
P_3		And select a component skill
		And demonstrate component skill
		And have students practice component skill.

Table 17.10 Some procedural knowledge about social behavior. This knowledge is available to inexperienced teachers and is applied inappropriately in instructional settings.

P_1	IF THEN	Person makes request Try to comply with request
P_2	IF THEN	Other person talks Pay attention Ask followup questions

relevant to teaching. For example, they act as if they have the productions shown in Table 17.10. Production 1 embodies the social norm that when people make requests, one tries to comply. Production 2 embodies the norm that when others talk, it is polite to listen. What inexperienced teachers need to learn is to discriminate general social situations from teaching situations. That is, they need to develop specialized productions for teaching, such as the one shown in Table 17.11. When all its conditions are met, this specialized production overrides the more general production P_1 shown in Table 17.10. Until their domain-specific conceptual knowledge and strategies develop, inexperienced teachers, like novices in other domains, will continue to rely on domain-general procedures.

IMPLICATIONS FOR TEACHER EDUCATION PROGRAMS

A recent study by Livingston and Borko (1989) focused on implications of cognitive analysis for teacher education programs. Livingston and Borko characterized teaching as both a complex cognitive skill and an improvisational performance. This characterization implies that teaching has both its "strategic" aspects, which are conscious and adaptable but executed smoothly by the experienced teacher, and its "routine" aspects, which are drawn automatically from a repertoire of routines or basic pedagogical skills. We would characterize both these aspects of teacher thoughts and actions as sets of productions or procedural knowledge, where the teacher's actions are "driven" by the conditions in the current situation, the teacher's goals, and the teacher's success at matching the current conditions to the existing conditions of procedures in procedural memory.

Livingston and Borko conducted extensive observations of experienced and novice teachers, and also conducted pre- and post-interviews with both groups in which participants were encouraged to reflect on their teaching. These data were analyzed using ethnographic procedures, and case descriptions were prepared, summarizing each participant's planning, teaching, and post-lesson reflections. Based on the differences observed between the groups, Livingston and Borko concluded that teachers only "*begin* to learn to teach during preservice preparation" (p. 41). In addition, they commented that it is common for the practice teaching experience to be overwhelming for the beginners as they attempt to use their limited knowledge and experience to deal successfully with complex problems. According to Livingston and Borko, the perception of many preservice (student) teachers is that the expert teachers "wing it"—that is, the experts deal successfully with the problems in the classroom in an effortless manner. They do not have to plan ahead very much and they always seem to know what to do. When novices perceive that experts appear to succeed without trying very hard, while they (the novices) try extremely hard without nearly as much success, it can be daunting and discouraging for the beginners.

Livingston and Borko make some specific recommendations about how the preservice or practice teaching experience might be enhanced, based on cognitive analysis. First,

Table 17.11 A production that is specific to instructional contexts and that inexperienced teachers need to learn.

IF	Student makes a request And student's safety and health are not at stake And request is irrelevant to instruction.
THEN	Ignore request Or ask student to make the request later Or explain to student that request is irrelevant

they suggest that the full-time teaching responsibility be limited for preservice teachers so that the number of courses or subject areas for which they must plan would decrease at any one time. Since their pedagogical content knowledge is limited and few of their skills are automated, decreasing the amount of full-time teaching responsibility would allow preservice teachers to devote more time and cognitive resources to developing schemas and fine-tuning routines.

A second recommendation is that student teachers teach only in areas where they have strong content preparation. This recommendation also cuts down on the "cognitive burden" of practice teaching. In areas where student teachers have strong content preparation, their content schemas will be well developed and their conceptual understanding of the material will be organized and elaborated. This will mean that they can devote more of their limited cognitive resources to the content's pedagogical aspects (how to make the content comprehensible to the learners), since the content itself is already familiar and well known.

A final recommendation from Livingston and Borko is that student teachers be given multiple opportunities to teach the same content. Given that teaching is a complex cognitive skill, and that learners take many trials to master a complex cognitive skill, this recommendation gives the practice teacher a chance to "learn by doing" and to revise and refine an initial presentation. If the student teacher has a chance to improve a lesson and to observe how one strategy works better than another, and why, then the student teacher can feel that she is progressing towards her goal of becoming an effective teacher. This type of experience will help to allay the perception that expert teaching is "winging it." Expert teachers are effective because they recognize and diagnose instructional problems in the classroom and know how to solve them. If student teachers have opportunities to analyze their teaching, to revise their schemas, and to "fine-tune" their strategies, it will help them to view their practice teaching as a learning experience rather than as an outcome or a culmination.

CHAPTER SUMMARY

The results from many recent studies have begun to provide convincing evidence that the thinking of expert teachers, as well as their behavior, is qualitatively and quantitatively different from the thinking and behavior of beginning teachers. It appears that researchers are on the verge of making significant strides in defining the expert teacher and in determining how one makes the transition from novice to expert. In 1986, the Presidential Address at the annual meeting of the American Educational Research Association was entitled *In Pursuit of the Expert Pedagogue* (Berliner, 1986). In this address Berliner documented and described the many problems that have been encountered in attempts to define expertise in teaching. While a number of these barriers still exist, progress has been made. With continued collaborative efforts among cognitive psychologists, educational researchers, and classroom teachers, progress will continue.

ADDITIONAL READINGS

Berliner, D.C. (1986). In pursuit of the expert pedagogue. *Educational Researcher, 15*, 5–13.

Borko, H., Livingston, C., & Shavelson, R.J. (1990). Teachers' thinking about instruction. *Remedial and Special Education, 11*, 40–49.

Brophy, J. (Ed.) (In Press). *Advances in research on teaching. Vol. 2: Teacher's subject matter knowledge and classroom instruction*. Greenwich, CT: JAI Press.

Leinhardt, G. (1989). Math lessons: A contrast of novice and expert competence. *Journal for Research in Mathematics Education, 20*, 52–75.

Livingston, C., & Borko, H. (1989). Expert-novice differences in teaching: A cognitive analysis and implications for teacher education. *Journal of Teacher Education, 40*, 36–42.

Peterson, P.L. (1988). Teachers' and students' cognitional knowledge for classroom teaching and learning. *Educational Researcher, 17*, 5–14.

Shulman, L.S. (1987). Knowledge and teaching: Foundations of the new reform. *Harvard Educational Review, 57*, 1–22.

Westerman, D.A. (1991). Expert and novice teacher decision making. *Journal of Teacher Education, 42*, 292–305.

References

Adams, L., Kasserman, J., Yearwood, A., Perfetto, G., Bransford, J., & Franks, J. (1988). The effects of facts versus problem-oriented acquisition. *Memory & Cognition, 16,* 167–175.

Adams, M.J. (Ed.) (1986). *Odyssey: A curriculum for thinking (vols. 1–5).* Watertown, MA: Charlesbridge Publishing.

Adams, M.J. (1989a). *Teaching thinking to Chapter I students.* Center for the Study of Reading, Technical Report #473. Champaign, IL: University of Illinois.

Adams, M.J. (1989b). Thinking skills curricula: Their promise and progress. *Educational Psychologist, 24,* 25–77.

Adams, M.J. (1990). *Beginning to read: Thinking and learning about print.* Cambridge, MA: The MIT Press.

Adams, M.J., Buscaglia, J., de Sanchez, M. & Swets, J.A. (1986). *Odyssey: A curriculum for thinking. Volume 1: Foundations of reasoning.* Waterdtown, MA: Charlesbridge Publishing.

Alexander, P.A., & Judy, J.E. (1988). The interaction of domain-specific and strategic knowledge in academic performance. *Review of Educational Research, 58,* 375–404.

Ames, C. (1984a). Competitive, cooperative, and individualistic goal structures: A motivational analysis. In R. Ames & C. Ames (Eds.), *Research on motivation in education: Student motivation,* (Vol. I, pp. 177–207), New York, NY: Academic Press.

Ames, C. (1984b) Achievement attributions and self-instructions under competitive and individualistic goal structures. *Journal of Educational Psychology, 76,* 478–87.

Ames, C.A. (1990). Motivation: What teachers need to know. In S. Tozer, T.H. Anderson, & B.B. Armbruster (Eds.), *Foundational studies in teacher education: A re-examination.* New York, NY: Teachers College, Columbia University.

Ames, R., & Ames, C. (Eds.) (1984). *Research on motivation in education, Vol.1.* New York, NY: Academic Press.

Ames, R., Ames, C., & Garrison, W. (1977). Children's causal ascriptions for positive and negative interpersonal outcomes. *Psychological Reports, 41,* 595–602.

Anderson, J.R. (1976). *Language, memory, and thought.* Hillsdale, NJ: Lawrence Erlbaum Associates.

Anderson, J.R. (1980). Concepts, propositions, and schemata: What are the cognitive units? In J.H. Flowers (Ed.), *Nebraska symposium on motivation* (pp. 121–162). Hillsdale, NJ: Lawrence Erlbaum Associates.

Anderson, J.R. (1982). Acquisition of cognitive skill. *Psychological Review, 89,* 369–406.

Anderson, J.R. (1983). *The architecture of cognition.* Cambridge, MA: Harvard University Press.

Anderson, J.R. (1987). Skill acquisition: Compilation of weak-method problem solutions. *Psychological Review, 94,* 192–210.

Anderson, J.R. (1990). *Cognitive psychology and its implications,3rd Ed.* New York: W.H. Freeman & Company.

Anderson, J.R., Kline, P.J., & Beasley, C.M., Jr. (1980). Complex learning processes. In R.E. Snow, P.A. Federico, & W.E. Montague (Eds.), *Aptitude, learning, and instruction. vol. 2.* (pp. 199–235). Hillsdale, NJ: Lawrence Erlbaum Associates.

Anderson, J.R., Kline, P.J., & Lewis, C.H. (1977). A production system model of language processing. In M.A. Just & P.A. Carpenter (Eds.), *Cognitive processes in comprehension,* (pp. 271–311). Hillsdale, NJ: Lawrence Erlbaum Associates.

Anderson, J.R., & Reder, L.M. (1979). An elaborative processing explanation of depth of processing. In L.S. Cermak & F.I.M. Craik (Eds.), *Levels of processing in human memory* (pp. 385–403). Hillsdale, NJ: Lawrence Erlbaum Associates.

Anderson, J.R., & Thompson, R. (1989). Use of analogy in a production system architecture. In S. Vosniadou & A. Ortony (Eds.), *Similarity and analogical reasoning.* Cambridge, England: Cambridge University Press.

Anderson, R.C. (1977). The notion of schemata and the educational enterprise. In R.C. Anderson, R.J. Spiro, & W.E. Montague (Eds.), *Schooling and the acquisition of knowledge* (pp. 415–431). Hillsdale, NJ: Lawrence Erlbaum Associates.

Anderson, R.C., & Armbruster, B.B. (1989). Some maxims for learning and instruction. In S. Tozer, T.H. Anderson, & B.B. Armbruster (Eds.), *Foundational studies in teacher education.* New York, NY: Columbia Teachers College Press.

Anderson, R.C., & Faust, G.W. (1974). *Educational psychology: The science of instruction and learning.* New York, NY: Dodd Mead.

Anderson, T.H. (1979). Study skills and learning strategies. In H.F. O'Neil, Jr. & C.D. Spielberger (Eds.) *Cognitive and affective learning strategies* (pp. 77–97). New York, NY: Academic Press.

Andrews, G.R., & Debus, R.L. (1978). Persistence and causal perception of failure: Modifying cognitive attributions. *Journal of Educational Psychology, 70,* 154–166.

Applebee, A.N. (1982). Writing and learning in school settings. In M. Nystrand (ed.), *What writers know: The language, process, and structure of written discourse* (pp. 365–381). New York, NY: Academic Press.

Applebee, A.N., Durst, R., & Newell, G. (1984). The demands of school writing. In A.N. Applebee (Ed.), *Contexts for learning to write* (pp. 55–77). Norwood, NJ: Ablex Publishing Co.

Armbruster, B.B., & Anderson, T.H. (1980). *Effect of mapping on the free recall of expository text.* Urbana, IL: Center for the Study of Reading (Tech. Rep. # 160).

Atkinson, R.C., Herrnstein, R.J., Lindzey, G., & Luce, R.D. (Eds.) (1988). *Handbook of Experimental Psychology.* New York: John Wiley.

Atwell, M. (1981). *The evolution of text: The interrelationship of reading and writing in the composing process.* Paper presented at the annual meeting of the National Council of Teachers of English, Boston, MA.

Ausubel, D.P. (1968). *Educational psychology: A cognitive view.* New York, NY: Holt, Rinehart & Winston.

Ayers, T., Davis, G., Dubinsky, E., & Lewin, P. (1988). Computer experiences in learning composition of functions. *Journal for Research in Mathematics Education, 19,* 246–259.

Badian, N.A. (1977). Auditory-visual integration, auditory memory, and reading in retarded and adequate readers. *Journal of Learning Disabilities, 10,* 108–114.

Baker, L. (1987). *Teaching problem solving: Domain-specific versus domain-independent approaches.* Unpublished report, U.S. Army Research Institute, Alexandria, VA.

Baker, L., & Brown, A.L. (1984). Metacognitive

skills in reading. In D. Pearson (Ed.), *Handbook of reading research* (pp. 353–394). Newark, DE: International Reading Association.

Balota, D.A., d'Arcais, G.B.F., & Rayner, K. (Eds.) (1990). *Comprehension processes in reading*. Hillsdale, NJ: Lawrence Erlbaum Associates.

Bandura, A. (1977). *Social learning theory*. Englewood Cliffs, NJ: Prentice-Hall.

Barr, A., & Feigenbaum, E.A. (Eds.) (1982). *The handbook of artificial intelligence, vol. 2*. Los Altos, CA: William Kaufmann.

Barron, F. (1963). The needs for order and disorder as motives in creative activity. In C.W. Taylor & F. Barron (Eds.) *Scientific creativity: Its recognition and development* (pp. 153–160). New York, NY: Wiley & Sons.

Bartlett, B.J. (1978). *Top-level structure as an organizational strategy for recall of classroom text*. Unpublished doctoral dissertation, Arizona State University, Tempe.

Bartlett, E.J. (1982). Learning to revise: Some component processes. In. M. Nystrand (Ed.), *What writers know: The language, process, and structure of written discourse* (pp. 345–363). New York, NY: Academic Press.

Bartlett, F.C. (1932). *Remembering*. Cambridge, England: Cambridge University Press.

Baumann, J.F. (1986). *Teaching main idea comprehension*. Newark, DE: International Reading Association.

Baxter, J. (1987). *Organization of subject matter in computer programming lessons*. Stanford, CA: School of Education, Stanford University.

Bednarz, N., & Janvier, B. (1988). A constructivist approach to numeration in primary school: Results of a three-year intervention with the same group of children. *Educational Studies in Mathematics, 19*, 299–331.

Bell, M.S. (1980). *The relationship between a metaphor and its context: Effects on comprehension of the metaphor and the context*. Unpublished masters thesis, University of Georgia, Athens.

Belmont, J.M., & Butterfield, E.C. (1977). The instructional approach to developmental cognitive research. In R. Kail, & J. Hagen (Eds.), *Perspectives on the development of memory and cognition*. Hillsdale, NJ: Lawrence Erlbaum Associates.

Belmont, J.M., Butterfield, E.C., & Ferretti, R.P. (1982). To secure transfer of training instruct self-management skills. In D.K. Detterman & R.J. Sternberg (Eds.), *How and how much can intelligence be increased* (pp. 147–154). Norwood, NJ: Ablex Publishing Corporation.

Bereiter, C. (1980). Development in writing. In L.W. Gregg & E.R. Steinberg (Eds.), *Cognitive processes in writing* (pp. 73–99). Hillsdale, NJ: Lawrence Erlbaum Associates.

Bereiter, C. (1991). Implications of connectionism for thinking about rules. *Educational Researcher, 20*, 10–16.

Bereiter, C., & Bird, M. (1985). Use of thinking aloud in identification and teaching of reading comprehension strategies. *Cognition and Instruction, 2*, 91–130.

Bereiter, C., & Scardamalia, M. (1987). *The psychology of written comprehension*. Hillsdale, NJ: Lawrence Erlbaum Associates.

Berliner, D.C. (1986). In pursuit of the expert pedagogue. *Educational Researcher, 15*(7), 5–13.

Berlyne, D.E. (1960). *Conflict, arousal, and curiosity*. New York, NY: McGraw-Hill.

Berlyne, D.E., & Frommer, F.D. (1966). Some determinants of the incidence and content of children's questions. *Child Development, 37*, 177–189.

Birnbaum, J.C. (1982). The reading and composing behaviors of selected fourth- and seventh-grade students. *Research in the Teaching of English, 16*, 241–260.

Bloom, B.S. (1976). *Human characteristics and school learning*. New York, NY: McGraw-Hill.

Bond, G.L., & Dykstra, R. (1967). The cooperative research program in first-grade reading instruction. *Reading Research Quarterly, 2*, 5–142.

Borko, H., & Livingston, C. (1989). Cognition and improvisation: Differences in mathematics instruction by expert and novice teachers. *American Educational Research Journal, 26*(4), 473–498.

Borko, H., Livingston, C., & Shavelson, R.J. (1990). Teachers' thinking about instruction. *Remedial and Special Education, 11*(6), 40–49.

Borkowski, J.G., Carr, M., Rellinger, E., & Pressley, M. (1990). Self-regulated cognition: Interdependence of metacognition, attributions, and self-esteem. In B.F. Jones & L. Idol (Eds.),

Dimensions of thinking and cognitive instruction, pp. 53–92. Hillsdale, NJ: Lawrence Erlbaum Associates.

Borkowski, J.G., Johnston, M.B., & Reid, M.K. (1987). Metacognition, motivation and controlled performance. In S. Ceci (Ed.), *Handbook of cognitive, social, and neurological aspects of learning disabilities, Vol. 2,* (pp. 147–174). Hillsdale, NJ: Lawrence Erlbaum Associates.

Bousfeld, W.A. (1953). The occurrence of clustering in recall of randomly arranged associates. *Journal of General Psychology, 49,* 229–240.

Bower, G.H. (1981). Mood and memory. *American Psychologist, 36,* 129–148.

Bower, G.H., & Hilgard, E.R. (1981). *Theories of learning* (5th edition). Englewood Cliffs, NJ: Prentice-Hall, Inc.

Bower, G.H., Black, J.B. & Turner, T.J. (1979). Scripts in memory for text. *Cognitive Psychology, 11,* 177–220.

Bransford, J.D., Franks, J.J., Vye, N.J., & Sherwood, R.D. (1989). New approaches to instruction: Because wisdom can't be told. In S. Vosniadou & A. Ortony (Eds.), *Similarity and analogical reasoning.* Cambridge, England: Cambridge University Press.

Bransford, J.D., Vye, N.J., Adams, L.T., & Perfetto, G.A. (1989). Learning skills and the acquisition on knowledge. In A. Lesgold & R. Glaser (Eds.), *Foundations for a psychology of education* (pp. 199–249). Hillsdale, NJ: Lawrence Erlbaum Associates.

Bransford, J.D., Vye, N., Kinzer, C., & Risko, V. (1990). Teaching thinking and content knowledge: Toward an integrated approach. In B.F. Jones, & L. Idol (Eds.), *Dimensions of thinking and cognitive instruction* (pp. 381–413). Hillsdale, NJ: Lawrence Erlbaum Associates.

Brewer, W.F., & Nakamura, G.V. (1984). The nature and function of schemas. In R.S. Wyer & T.K. Srull (Eds.), *Handbook of social cognition* (pp. 119–160). Hillsdale, NJ: Lawrence Erlbaum Associates.

Briars, D.J., & Larkin, J.H. (1984). An integrated model of skill in solving elementary word problems. *Cognition and Instruction, 1,* 245–296.

Bridwell, L.S. (1980). Revising strategies in twelfth grade students' transactional writing. *Research in the Teaching of English, 14,* 197–222.

Britton, B.K., & Glynn, S.M. (Eds.) (1987). *Executive control processes in reading.* Hillsdale, NJ: Lawrence Erlbaum Associates.

Britton, B.K., Meyer, B.J., Hodge, M.H., & Glynn, S.M. (1980). Effects of the organization of text on memory: Tests of retrieval and response criterion hypotheses. *Journal of Experimental Psychology: Human Learning and Memory, 6,* 620–629.

Britton, J., Burgess, T., Martin, N., McLeod, A., & Rosen, H. (1975). *The development of writing abilities (11–18).* London, England: Macmillan.

Bromage, B.K., & Mayer, R.E. (1981). Relationship between what is remembered and creative problem-solving performance in science learning. *Journal of Educational Psychology, 73,* 451–461.

Brophy, J. (Ed.) (In Press). *Advances in research on teaching: Vol. 2. Teacher's subject matter knowledge and classroom instruction.* Greenwich, CT: JAI Press.

Brown, A.L. (1978). Knowing when, where, and how to remember: A problem of metacognition. In R. Glaser (Ed.), *Advances in instructional psychology* (pp. 77–165). Hillsdale, NJ: Lawrence Erlbaum Associates.

Brown, A.L., Campione, J.C., & Barclay, C.R. (1979). Training self-checking routines for estimating test readiness: Generalizations from list learning to prose recall. *Child Development, 50,* 501–512.

Brown, A.L., & Day, J.D. (1983). Macrorules for summarizing text: The development of expertise. *Journal of Verbal Learning and Verbal Behavior, 22,* 1–14.

Brown, A.L., Kane, M.J., & Echols, K. (1986). Young children's mental models determine analogical transfer across problems with a common goal structure. *Cognitive Development, 1,* 103–122.

Brown, A.L., & Palincsar, A.S. (1989). Guided, cooperative and individual knowledge acquisition. In L.B. Resnick (Ed.), *Knowing, learning, and instruction: Essays in honor of Robert Glaser.* Hillsdale, NJ: Lawrence Erlbaum Associates.

Brown, A.L., & Smiley, S.S. (1977). Rating the importance of structural units of prose passages: A problem of metacognitive development. *Child Development, 48,* 1–8.

Brown, J.S., Collins, A., & Duguid, P. (1989). Situated cognition and the culture of learning. *Educational Researcher, 18*(1), 32–42.

Brown, J.S., & Burton, R. (1978). Diagnostic models for procedural bugs in basic mathematical skills. *Cognitive Science, 2*, 155–192.

Brown, R. (1981). National assessments of writing ability. In C.H. Frederiksen, & J.F. Dominic (Eds.), *Writing: The nature, development, and teaching of written communication* (pp. 31–38). Hillsdale, NJ: Lawrence Erlbaum Associates.

Bruner, J.S., Goodnow, J.J., & Austin, G.A. (1956). *A study of thinking.* New York, NY: John Wiley & Sons, Inc.

Burtis, P.J., Bereiter, C., Scardamalia, M., & Tetroe, J. (1983). The development of planning in writing. In B.M. Kroll & G. Wells (Eds.), *Explorations in the development of writing* (pp. 153–174). Chicester, England: John Wiley & Sons.

Butterfield, E.C., & Nelson, G.D. (1991). Promoting positive transfer of different types. *Cognition and Instruction, 8*, 69–102.

Calfee, R.C., Lindamood, P. & Lindamood, C. (1973). Acoustic-phonetic skills and reading—kindergarten through twelfth grade. *Journal of Educational Psychology, 64*, 293–298.

Carey, L., Flower, L., Hayes, J.R., Schriver, K.A., & Haas, C. (1989). *Differences in writers' initial task representations.* (Tech. Rep. No. 35). Berkeley, CA: Center for the Study of Writing.

Carey, S. (1982). Semantic development: The state of the art. In E. Wanner & L.R. Gleitman (Eds.), *Language acquisiton: The state of the art* (pp. 347–389). New York, NY: Cambridge University Press.

Carpenter, P.A., & Just, M.A. (1981). Cognitive processes in reading: Models based on readers' eye fixations. In A.M. Lesgold & C.A. Perfetti (Eds.), *Interative processes in reading* (pp. 177–213). Hillsdale, NJ: Lawrence Erlbaum Associates.

Carpenter, T.P., & Moser, J.M. (1982). The development of addition and subtraction problem solving skills. In T.P. Carpenter, J.M. Moser, & T.A.Romberg (Eds.), *Addition and subtraction: A cognitive perspective* (pp. 9–24). Hillsdale, NJ: Lawrence Erlbaum Associates.

Carpenter, T.P., & Peterson, P.L. (Eds.) (1988).

Special issue: Learning mathematics from instruction. *Educational Psychologist, 23*, 1–202.

Carraher, T.N., Carraher, D., & Schliemann, A.D. (1985). Mathematics in the streets and in schools. *British Journal of Developmental Psychology, 3*, 21–29.

Carver, R.P., & Hoffman, J.V. (1981). The effect of practice through repeated reading on gain in reading ability using a computer-based instructional system. *Reading Research Quarterly, 16*, 374–390.

Case, R., & McKeough, A. (1990). Schooling and the development of central conceptual structures: An example from the domain of children's narrative. *International Journal of Educational Research, 13*, 835–856.

Cermak, L.S., & Craik, F.I.M., (Eds.) (1979). *Levels of processing in human memory.* Hillsdale, NJ: Lawrence Erlbaum Associates.

Chall, J.S. (1967). *Learning to read: The great debate.* New York, NY: McGraw-Hill.

Chall, J.S. (1983). *Learning to read: The great debate.* Updated edition. New York, NY: McGraw-Hill.

Chall, J., & Feldman, S. (1966). First grade reading: An analysis of the interactions of professed methods, teacher implementation and child background. *Reading Teacher, 19*, 569–575.

Champagne, A.B., Klopfer, L.E., Desena, A.T., & Squires, D.A. (1981). Structural representations of students' knowledge before and after science instruction. *Journal of Research in Science Teaching, 18*, 97–111.

Chance, P. (1986). *Thinking in the classroom: A survey of programs.* Teachers College, Columbia University, New York, NY: Teachers College Press.

Chapin, M., & Dyck, D.G. (1976). Persistence in children's reading behavior as a function of N length and attribution retraining. *Journal of Abnormal Psychology, 85*, 511–515.

Charles, R.I., & Lester, F.K. (1984). An evaluation of a process-oriented instructional program in mathematical problem solving in grades 5 and 7. *Journal for Research in Mathematics Education, 15*, 15–34.

Chase, W.G. (1978). Elementary information processes. In W.K. Estes (Ed.), *Handbook of learning and cognitive processes.* Vol. 5. Hillsdale, NJ: Lawrence Erlbaum Associates.

Chase, W.G. (1983). Spatial representations of taxi drivers. In D.R. Roger, & J.H. Sloboda (Eds.), *Acquisition of symbolic skills* (pp. 391–405). New York, NY: Plenum.

Chase, W.G., & Ericsson, K.A. (1982). Skill and working memory. In G. Bower (Ed.), *The psychology of learning and motivation: Advances in research and theory.* (Vol. 16, pp. 2–58). New York, NY: Academic Press.

Chase, W.G., & Simon, H.A. (1973). Perception in chess. *Cognitive Psychology, 4,* 55–81.

Cheng, P.W., & Holyoak, K.J. (1985). Pragmatic reasoning schemas. *Cognitive Psychology, 17,* 391–416.

Cheng, P.W., Holyoak, K.J., Nisbett, R.E., & Oliver, L.M. (1986). Pragmatic versus syntactic approaches to training deductive reasoning. *Cognitive Psychology, 18,* 293–328.

Chi, M.T.H. (1978). Knowledge structure and memory development. In R.S. Siegler (Ed.), *Children's thinking: What develops?* (pp. 73–96). Hillsdale, NJ: Lawrence Erlbaum Associates.

Chi, M.T.H. (1985). Interactive roles of knowledge and strategies in the development of organized sorting and recall. In S. Chipman, J. Segal, & R. Glaser (Eds.), *Thinking and learning skills: Current research and open questions* (Vol. 2, pp. 457–484). Hillsdale, NJ: Lawrence Erlbaum Associates.

Chi, M.T.H., Feltovich, P.J., & Glaser, R. (1981). Categorization and representation of physics problems by experts and novices. *Cognitive Science, 5,* 121–152.

Chi, M.T.H., Glaser, R., & Farr, M.J. (Eds.), (1988). *The nature of expertise.* Hillsdale, NJ: Lawrence Erlbaum Associates.

Chi, M.T.H., Glaser, R., & Rees, E. (1982). Expertise in problem solving. In R. Sternberg (Ed.), *Advances in the psychology of human intelligence* (Vol. 1, pp. 7–75). Hillsdale, NJ: Lawrence Erlbaum Associates.

Chipman, S.F., Segal, J.W., & Glaser, R. (Eds.) (1985). *Thinking and learning skills, Vol. 2: Research and open questions.* Hillsdale, NJ: Lawrence Erlbaum Associates.

Chomsky, N. (1959). Verbal behavior (a review). *Language, 35,* 26–58.

Clarke, M.S., & Fiske, S.T. (1982). *Affect and cognition: The seventeenth annual Carnegie Symposium on Cognition.* Hillsdale, NJ: Lawrence Erlbaum Associates.

Clay, M.M. (1979). *The early detection of reading difficulties* (3rd edition). Portsmouth, NH: Heinemann.

Clifford, M.M. (1984). Thoughts on a theory of constructive failure. *Educational Psychologist, 19,* 108–120.

Cobb, P., Wood, T., Yackel, E., Nicholls, J., Wheatley, G., Trigatti, B., & Perlwitz, M. (1991). Assessment of a problem-centered second-grade mathematics project. *Journal for Research in Mathematics Education, 22,* 3–29.

Cognition and Technology Group at Vanderbilt University (in press). The Jasper series: A generative approach to improving mathematical thinking. In *This year in school science.* Washington, DC: American Association for the Advancement of Science.

Cohen, E., & Scardamalia, M. (1983). *The effects of instructional intervention in the revision of essays by grade six children.* Paper presented at the annual meeting of the American Educational Research Association, Montreal.

Cohen, P.R., & Feigenbaum, E.A. (Eds.) (1982). *The handbook of artificial intelligence, vol. 3.* Los Altos, CA: William Kaufmann.

Collins, A. (1977). Processes in acquiring knowledge. In R.C. Anderson, R.J. Spiro, & W.E. Montague (Eds.), *Schooling and the acquisition of knowledge* (pp. 339–363). Hillsdale, NJ: Lawrence Erlbaum Associates.

Collins, A., Brown, J.S., & Newman, S.E. (1989). Cognitive apprenticeship: Teaching the crafts of reading, writing, and mathematics. In L.B. Resnick (Ed.), *Knowing, learning, and instruction: Essays in honor of Robert Glaser.* Hillsdale, NJ: Lawrence Erlbaum Associates.

Collins, A.M., & Quillian, M.R. (1969). Retrieval time from semantic memory. *Journal of Verbal Learning and Verbal Behavior, 8,* 240–247.

Collins, A., & Stevens, A.L. (1982). Goals and strategies of inquiry teachers. In R. Glaser (Ed.) *Advances in instructional psychology (Vol. 2).* Hillsdale, NJ: Lawrence Erlbaum Associates.

Collins, J.L., & Williamson, M.M. (1981). Spoken language and semantic abbreviation in writing. *Research in the Training of English, 15,* 23–35.

Cook, L.K. (1983). *Instructional effects of text structure-based reading strategies on the comprehension of scientific prose.* Unpublished doctoral dissertation, University of California, Santa Barbara.

Cooper, G., & Sweller, J. (1987). Effects of schema acquisition and rule automation on mathematical problem-solving transfer. *Journal of Educational Psychology, 79,* 347–362.

Cooper, L.A., & Shepard, A.N. (1973). Chronometric studies of the rotation of mental images. In W.G. Chase (Ed.), *Visual information processing* (pp. 95–176). New York, NY: Academic Press, 1973.

Covington, M.V., & Berry, R.G. (1976). *Self-worth and school learning.* New York, NY: Holt, Rinehart, & Winston.

Cummins, D.D., Kintsch, W., Reusser, K., & Weimer, R. (1988). The role of understanding in solving word problems. *Cognitive Psychology, 20,* 405–438.

Curtis, M.E. (1980). Development of components of reading skill. *Journal of Educational Psychology, 72,* 656–669.

Curtis, M.E., Collins, J.M., Gitomer, D.H., & Glaser, R. (1983). *Word knowledge influences on comprehension.* Paper presented at the annual meeting of the American Educational Research Association, Montreal.

Czepiel, J., & Esty, E. (1980). Mathematics in the newspaper. *Mathematics Teacher, 73,* 582–586.

Daneman, M., & Carpenter, P.A. (1980). Individual differences in working memory and reading. *Journal of Verbal Learning and Verbal Behavior, 19,* 450–466.

Dean, A.L., & Malik, M.M. (1986). Representing and solving arithmetic word problems: A study of developmental interaction. *Cognition and Instruction, 3,* 211–227.

de Groot, A.D. (1965). *Thought and choice in chess.* The Hague, Netherlands: Mouton.

de Groot, A.D. (1966). Perception and memory versus thinking. In B. Kleinmuntz (Ed.), *Problem solving.* New York, NY: Wiley.

Diehl, W.A., & Mikulecky, L. (1980). The nature of reading at work. *Journal of Reading, 24,* 221–227.

Dillon, R.F., & Sternberg, R.J. (Eds.) (1986). *Cognition and instruction.* New York, NY: Academic Press.

diSessa, A. (1987). The third revolution in computers and education. *Journal of Research in Science Teaching, 24*(4), 343–367.

Donders, F.C. (1969). On the speed of mental processes. *Acta Psychologica, 30,* 412–431. (Translated by W.G. Koster from the original in *Onderzoekingen gedaan in het Physiologisch Laboratorium der Utrechtsche Hoogeschool,* 1868, *Tweede reeks, II.* 92–120).

Duke, D. (1975). The student centered conference and the writing process. *English Journal, 64,* 44–47.

Dweck, C.S. (1975). The role of expectations and attributions in the alleviation of learned helplessness. *Journal of Personality and Social Psychology, 31,* 674–685.

Dweck, C.S. (1989). Motivation. In A. Lesgold & R. Glaser (Eds.), *Foundations for a psychology of education* (pp. 87–136), Hillsdale, NJ: Lawrence Erlbaum Associates.

Dyson, A.H., & Freedman, S.W. (1990). *On teaching writing: A review of the literature* (Occasional Paper No. 20). Berkeley, CA: University of California, National Center for the Study of Writing and Literacy.

Egan, D.E. (1983). Retrospective reports reveal differences in people's reasoning. *Bell System Technical Journal, 62,* 1675–1697.

Egan, D.E., & Schwartz, B.J. (1979). Chunking in recall of symbolic drawings. *Memory & Cognition, 7,* 149–158.

Ehri, L.C. (1982). *Learning to read and spell.* Paper presented at the American Psychological Association annual meeting, Washington, D.C.

Ehri, L.C., & Wilce, L.C. (1983). Development of word identification speed in skilled and less skilled beginning readers. *Journal of Educational Psychology, 75,* 3–18.

Elio, R., & Anderson, J.R. (1981). The effects of category generalizations and instance similarity on schema abstraction. *Journal of Experimental Psychology: Human Learning and Memory, 7,* 397–417.

Emmer, E.T. (1982). *Management strategies in elementary school classrooms* (Technical Report No. 6052). Austin, TX: Research and Development Center for Teacher Education, University of Texas.

Emmer, E.T., Evertson, C.M., & Anderson, L.M. (1980). Effective classroom management at the beginning of the school year. *Elementary School Journal, 80,* 219–231.

Ericsson, K.A., & Simon, H.A. (1980). Verbal reports as data. *Psychological Review, 87,* 215–251.

Ericsson, K.A., & Simon, H.A. (1984). *Protocol analysis.* Cambridge, MA: MIT Press.

Estes, W.K. (1972). Reinforcement and human behavior. *American Scientist, 60,* 723–729.

Estes, W.K. (1980). Is human memory obsolete? *American Scientist, 68,* 62–69.

Evertson, C.M., & Anderson, L. (1978). *The classroom organization study: Interim progress report* (Tech. Rep. No. 6002). Austin, TX: Research and Development Center for Teacher Education, University of Texas.

Evertson, C.M., Emmer, E.T., & Brophy, J.E. (1980). Predictors of effective teaching in junior high mathematics. *Journal for Research in Mathematics Education, 11,* 166–178.

Evertson, C.M., Emmer, E.T., Sanford, B.S., & Clements, B.S. (1983). Improving classroom management: An experiment in elementary school classrooms. *Elementary School Journal, 84,* 173–188.

Faigley, L., & Skinner, A. (1982). *Writers' processes and writers' knowledge: A review of research* (Tech. Rep. No. 6). Austin, TX: University of Texas, Writing Program Assessment Project.

Faigley, L. & Witte, S. (1981). Analyzing revision. *College Composition and Communication, 32,* 400–414.

Falbo, T. (1973). The attributional explanation of academic performance by kindergartners and their teachers [summary]. *Proceedings of the 81st Annual Convention of the American Psychological Association, 8,* 122–123.

Feuerstein, R. (1980). *Instrumental enrichment: An intervention program for cognitive modifiability.* Baltimore, MD: University Park Press.

Fisher, C.W., Filby, N.N., Marliave, R.S., Cahen, L.S., Dishaw, M.M., Moore, M.M., & Berliner, D.C. (1978). *Teaching behaviors, academic learning time, and student achievement. Final report of Phase III-B, Beginning Teacher Evaluation Study* (Tech. Rep. No. V-1). San Francisco, CA: Far West Laboratory for Educational Research and Development.

Fisher, K.M. (1990). Semantic networking: The new kid on the block. *Journal of Research in Science Teaching, 27,* 1001–1018.

Fiske, S.T. (1981). Social cognition and affect. In J. Harvey (Ed.), *Cognition, social behavior, and the environment.* Hillsdale, NJ: Lawrence Erlbaum Associates.

Fiske, S.T. (1982). Schema-triggered affect: Applications to social perception. In M.S. Clarke & S.T. Fiske (Eds.), *Affect and cognition: The 17th annual Carnegie Symposium on Cognition.* Hillsdale, NJ: Lawrence Erlbaum Associates.

Fiske, S.T., & Taylor, S.E. (1984). *Social cognition.* Reading, MA: Addison-Wesley.

Fitts, P.M., & Posner, M.I. (1967). *Human performance.* Belmont, CA: Brooks Cole.

Flanagan, J.C. (Ed.), (1978). *Perspectives on improving education.* New York, NY: Praeger.

Flavell, J.H. (1979). Metacognition and cognitive monitoring. *American Psychologist, 34,* 906–911.

Flower, L., & Hayes, J.R. (1981a). A cognitive process theory of writing. *College Composition and Communication, 32,* 365–387.

Flower, L., & Hayes, J.R. (1981b). The pregnant pause: An inquiry into the nature of planning. *Research in the Training of English, 15,* 229–243.

Flower, L., Schriver, K.A., Carey, L., Haas, C., & Hayes, J.R. (in press). Planning in writing: The cognition of a constructive process. In S. Witte, N. Nakadate, & R. Cherry (Eds.), *A rhetoric of doing.* Carbondale, IL: Southern Illinois University Press.

Fogarty, J.L., Wang, M.C., & Creek, R. (1983). A descriptive study of experienced and novice teachers' interactive instructional thoughts and actions. *Journal of Educational Research, 77,* 22–32.

Fong, G.T., Krantz, D.H., & Nisbett, R.E. (1986). The effects of statistical training on thinking about everyday problems. *Cognitive Psychology, 18,* 253–292.

Frase, L.T. (1973). Integration of written text. *Journal of Educational Psychology, 65,* 252–261.

Frederiksen, C.H., & Dominic, J.F. (Eds.) (1981). *Writing: Process, development, and communica-*

tion. Hillsdale, NJ: Lawrence Erlbaum Associates.

Frederiksen, J.R. (1981). Sources of process interactions in reading. In A.M. Lesgold and C.A. Perfetti (Eds.), *Interactive processes in reading.* Hillsdale, NJ: Lawrence Erlbaum Associates.

Frederiksen, J.R. (1982). A componential theory of reading skills and their interactions. In R.J. Sternberg, (Ed.), *Advances in the psychology of human intelligence.* Hillsdale, NJ: Lawrence Erlbaum Associates.

Frederiksen, J.R., Weaver, P.A., Warren, B.M., Gillotte, J.H.P., Rosebery, A.S., Freeman, B., & Goodman, L. (1983). *A componential approach to training reading skills.* (Report No. 5295) Cambridge, MA: Bolt, Beranek, and Newman, Inc.

Frederiksen, J.R., & White, B.Y. (1989). An approach to training based upon principled task decomposition. *Acta Psychologica, 71,* 89–146.

Freedman, S. (1981). Evaluation in the writing conference: An interactive process. In. M. Hairston, & C. Selfe (Eds.), *Selected papers from the 1981 Texas Writing Research Conference* (pp. 65–96). Austin, TX: The University of Texas.

Freedman, S. (1982). The student teacher writing conference: Key techniques. *Journal of English Teaching Techniques, 12,* 38–45.

Freedman, S., & Swanson-Owens, D. (1983) *Metacognitive awareness and the writing process.* Paper presented at the annual meeting of the American Educational Research Association, Montreal.

Gagné, E.D. (1978). Long-term retention of information following learning from prose. *Review of Educational Research, 48,* 629–665.

Gagné, E.D., Weidemann, C., Bell, M.S., & Anders, T.D. (1984). Training thirteen-year olds to elaborate while studying text. *Journal of Human Learning, 3,* 281–294.

Gagné, R.M. (1962). The acquisition of knowledge. *Psychological Review, 69,* 355–365.

Gagné, R.M. (1965). *The conditions of learning.* New York, NY: Holt, Rinehart, and Winston.

Gagné, R.M. (1970). *The conditions of learning* (2nd edition). New York, NY: Holt, Rinehart, and Winston.

Gagné, R.M. (1977). *The conditions of learning* (3rd edition). New York, NY: Holt, Rinehart, and Winston.

Gagné, R.M. (1984). Learning outcomes and their effects. *American Psychologist, 39,* 377–385.

Gagné, R.M. (1985). *The conditions of learning and theory of instruction,* (4th edition). New York, NY: Holt, Rinehart, and Winston.

Gagné, R.M., & Paradise, N.E. (1961). Abilities and learning sets in knowledge acquisition. *Psychological monographs: General and applied, 74,* whole No. 518.

Gallagher, M., & Pearson, P.D. (1989). *Discussion, comprehension, and knowledge acquisition in content area classrooms.* Center for the Study of Reading, Technical Report #480. Champaign, IL: University of Illinois.

Garner, R. (1987). *Metacognition and reading comprehension.* Norwood, NJ: Ablex.

Garner, R. (1990). When children and adults do not use learning strategies: Toward a theory of settings. *Review of Educational Research, 60,* 517–530.

Garner, R., & Reis, R. (1981). Monitoring and resolving comprehension obstacles: An investigation of spontaneous text lookbacks among upper-grade good and poor comprehenders. *Reading Research Quarterly, 16,* 569–582.

Geeslin, W.E., & Shavelson, R.J. (1975a). An exploratory analysis of the representation of a mathematical structure in students' cognitive structures. *American Educational Research Journal, 12,* 21–39.

Geeslin, W.E., & Shavelson, R.J. (1975b). Comparison of content structure and cognitive structure in high school students learning of probability. *Journal for Research in Mathematics Education, 6,* 109–120.

Gentner, D., & Stevens, A. (Eds.) (1983). *Mental models.* Hillsdale, NJ: Lawrence Erlbaum Associates.

Ghatala, E.S., Levin, J.R., Pressley, M., & Lodico, M.G. (1985). Training cognitive strategy monitoring in children. *American Educational Research Journal, 22,* 199–216.

Gick, M.L., & Holyoak, K.J. (1983). Schema induction and analogical transfer. *Cognitive Psychology, 15,* 1–38.

Glaser, R. (1984). Education and thinking: The role of knowledge. *American Psychologist, 9,* 93–104.

Glaser, R., & Chi, M.T.H. (1988). Overview. In

M.T.H. Chi, R. Glaser, & M.J. Farr (Eds.), *The nature of expertise*, (pp. xv–xxviii). Hillsdale, NJ: Lawrence Erlbaum Associates.

Glass, A.L., Holyoak, K.J., & Santa, J.L. (1979). *Cognition*. Reading, MA: Addison-Wesley.

Glucksberg, S., Kreuz, R.J., & Rho, S.H. (1986). Context can constrain lexical access: Implications for models of language comprehension. *Journal of Experimental Psychology: Learning, Memory, and Cognition, 12,* 323–335.

Glynn, S.M. (1989). The teaching with analogies model. In K.D. Muth (Ed.), *Children's comprehension of text* (pp. 185–204). Newark, DE: International Reading Association.

Glynn, S.M. (1991). Explaining science concepts: A teaching-with-analogies model. In S.M. Glynn, R.H. Yeany, & B.K. Britton (Eds.), *The psychology of learning science* (pp. 219–240). Hillsdale, NJ: Lawrence Erlbaum Associates.

Glynn, S.M., Britton, B.K., & Muth, K.D. (1985). Text-comprehension strategies based on outlines: Immediate and long-term effects. *Journal of Experimental Education, 53,* 129–135.

Glynn, S.M., Britton, B.K., Muth, K.D., & Dogan, N. (1982). Writing and revising persuasive documents. *Journal of Educational Psychology, 74,* 557–567.

Glynn, S.M., & DiVesta, F.J. (1977). Outline and hierarchical organization as aids for study and retrieval. *Journal of Educational Psychology, 69,* 89–95.

Glynn, S., Yeany, R.H., & Britton, B.K. (Eds.) (1991). *The psychology of learning science*. Hillsdale, NJ: Lawrence Erlbaum Associates.

Goldberg, F., & Bendall, S. (1992). Computer-video-based tutorials in geometrical optics. In R. Duit, F. Goldberg, S.H. Niedderer (Eds.), *Research in physics learning: Theoretical issues and empirical studies*. Kiel, Germany: IPN.

Goldberg, R.A., Schwartz, S., & Stewart, M. (1977). Individual differences in cognitive processes. *Journal of Educational Psychology, 69,* 9–14.

Goldman, S.R., & Pellegrino, J.W. (1987). Information processing and educational microcomputer technology: Where do we go from here? *Journal of Learning Disabilities, 20,* 144–154.

Goldman, S.R., Pellegrino, J.W., & Mertz, D.L. (1988). Extended practice of basic addition facts: Strategy changes in learning-disabled students. *Cognition and Instruction, 5,* 223–265.

Good, T.L., & Grouws, D.A. (1979). Teaching effects: A process-product study in fourth grade mathematics classrooms. *Journal of Teacher Education, 28,* 49–54.

Goodman, K.S. (1967). Reading: A psycholinguistic guessing game. *Journal of the Reading Specialist, 6,* 126–135.

Graesser, A.C., & Bower, G.H. (Eds.) (1990). *Inferences in text comprehension. The psychology of learning and motivation: Advances in research and theory*. Vol. 25. San Diego, CA: Academic Press.

Graesser, A.C., & Riha, J.R. (1984). An application of multiple regression techniques to sentence reading times. In D.E. Kieras, & M.A. Just (Eds.), *New methods in comprehension research*. Hillsdale, NJ: Lawrence Erlbaum Associates.

Graham, S. (1982). *Communicated sympathy and anger as determinants of self-perception among black and white children: An attributional analysis*. Unpublished doctoral dissertation, University of California, Los Angeles.

Graham, S., & Weiner, B. (1987). Teacher feelings and student thoughts: An attributional approach to affect in the classroom. In R.S. Snow, P.A. Federico, & W. Montague (Eds.) *Aptitude, learning, and instruction (Volume 3)*. Hillsdale, NJ: Lawrence Erlbaum Associates.

Graves, D. (1982). *Children learning to write*. Exeter, NH: Heinemann.

Graziano, W.G., Musser, L.M., Rosen, S., & Shaffer, D. (1982). The development of fair play standards in same- and mixed-race situations: Three converging studies. *Child Development, 53,* 938–947.

Greeno, J. (1987). Instructional representations based on research about understanding. In A.H. Schoenfeld (Ed.), *Cognitive science and mathematics education* (pp. 61–88). Hillsdale, NJ: Lawrence Erlbaum Associates.

Gregg, L., & Steinberg, E. (Eds.) (1980). *Cognitive processes in writing: An interdisciplinary approach*. Hillsdale, NJ: Lawrence Erlbaum Associates.

Groen, G.J., & Parkman, J.M. (1972). A chrVometric analysis of simple addition. *Psychological Review, 79,* 329–343.

Grossman, P.L. (1987). *A Tale of Two Teachers: The Role of Subject Matter Orientation in Teaching.* Paper presented at the annual meeting of the American Educational Research Association, Washington, D.C.

Gudmundsdottir, S., & Shulman, L.S. (1987). Pedagogical content knowledge in social studies. *Scandinavian Journal of Educational Research, 31,* 59–70.

Guthrie, J.T. (1971). Feedback and sentence learning. *Journal of Verbal Learning and Verbal Behavior, 10,* 23–28.

Guyer, B.L., & Friedman, M.P. (1975). Hemispheric processing and cognitive styles in learning-disabled and normal children. *Child Development, 46,* 658–668.

Halliday, M.A.K., & Hasan, R. (1976). *Cohesion in English.* London, England: Longman.

Hansen, R.S., McCann, J., & Meyers, J.L. (1985). Rote versus conceptual emphasis in teaching elementary probability. *Journal for Research in Mathematics Education, 16,* 364–374.

Harari, O., & Covington, M.V. (1981). Reactions to achievement behavior from a teacher and student perspective: A developmental analysis. *American Educational Research Journal, 18,* 15–28.

Harris, A.J., & Sipay, E.R. (1975). *How to increase reading ability.* New York, NY: McKay.

Harris, M.B. (1970). Reciprocity and generosity: some determinants of sharing in children. *Child Development, 41,* 313–328.

Harris, P.L., Kruithos, A., Terwogt, M.M., & Visser, T. (1981). Children's detection and awareness of textual anomaly. *Journal of Experimental Child Psychology, 31,* 212–230.

Hashweh, M.H. (1987). Effects of subject matter knowledge in teaching biology and physics. *Teaching and Teacher Education: An International Journal of Research and Studies, 3*(2) 109–120.

Haviland, S.E., & Clark, H.H. (1974). What's new? Acquiring new information as a process in comprehension. *Journal of Verbal Learning and Verbal Behavior, 13,* 512–521.

Hayes, D.A., & Tierney, R.J. (1982). Developing readers' knowledge through analogy. *Reading Research Quarterly, 17,* 256–280.

Hayes, J.R. (1980). Teaching problem-solving mechanisms. In D.T. Tuma and F. Reif (Eds.), *Problem solving and education: Issues in teaching and research* (pp. 141–147). Hllsdale, NJ: Lawrence Erlbaum Associates.

Hayes, J.R., & Simon, H.A. (1976). The understanding process: Problem isomorphs. *Cognitive Psychology, 8,* 165–190.

Hayes-Roth, B., & Hayes-Roth, F. (1977). Concept learning and the recognition and classification of exemplars. *Journal of Verbal Learning and Verbal Behavior, 16,* 321–338.

Hayes-Roth, B., & Thorndyke, P.W. (1979). Integration of knowledge from text. *Journal of Verbal Learning and Verbal Behavior, 18,* 91–108.

Healy, M.K. (1981). Purpose in learning to write: An approach to writing in three curriculum areas. In C.H. Frederiksen, & J.F. Dominic (Eds.) *Writing: Process, development, and communication,* (pp. 223–233). Hillsdale, NJ: Lawrence Erlbaum Associates.

Heidbreder, E. (1961). *Seven psychologies.* New York, NY: Appleton-Century-Crofts.

Heider, F. (1958). *The psychology of interpersonal relations.* New York, NY: Wiley.

Heller, J.I., & Reif, F. (1984). Prescribing effective human problem-solving processes: Problem description in physics. *Cognition and Instruction, 1,* 177–216.

Herrnstein, R.J., Adams, M.J., Huggins, A.W.F., & Starr, B.J. (1986). *Odyssey: A curriculum for thinking. Volume 2: Understanding language.* Watertown, MA: Charlesbridge Publishing.

Herrnstein, R.J., Nickerson, R.S., deSanchez, M., & Swets, J.A. (1986). Teaching thinking skills. *American psychologist, 41,* 1279–1289.

Hewson, P.W., & Hewson, M.G. (1984). The role of conceptual conflict in conceptual change and the design of science instruction. *Instructional Science, 13,* 1–13.

Hinsley, D.A., Hayes, J.R., & Simon, H.A. (1977). From words to equations: Meaning and representation in algebra word problems. In M.A. Just & P.A. Carpenter (Eds.), *Cognitive processes in comprehension* (pp. 62–68). Hillsdale, NJ: Lawrence Erlbaum Associates.

Hogaboam, T.W., & Pelligrino, J.W. (1978). Hunting for individual differences in cognitive processes: Verbal ability and semantic processing of pictures and words. *Memory & Cognition, 6,* 189–193.

Holley, C.D., Dansereau, D.F., McDonald, B.A., Garland, J.C., & Collins, K.W. (1979). Evaluation of a hierarchical mapping technique as an aid to prose processing. *Contemporary Educational Psychology, 4,* 227–237.

Hollon, R.E., Anderson, C.W., & Roth, K.J. (In Press). Science teachers' conceptions of teaching and learning. In J. Brophy (Ed.), *Advances in research on teaching: Vol. 2. Teacher's subject matter knowledge and classroom instruction.* Greenwich, CT: JAI Press.

Holyoak, K.J., Junn, E.N., & Billman, D.O. (1984). Development of analogical problem-solving skills. *Child Development, 55,* 2042–2055.

Hope, J.A., & Sherrill, J.M. (1987). Characteristics of unskilled and skilled mental calculators. *Journal for Research in Mathematics Education, 18,* 98–111.

Houlihan, D.M., & Ginsburg, H.P. (1981). The addition methods of first- and second-grade children. *Journal for Research in Mathematics Education, 12,* 95–106.

Housner, L.D., & Griffey, D.C. (1983). *Teacher cognition: Differences in planning and interactive decision making between experienced and inexperienced teachers.* Paper presented at the annual meeting of the American Educational Research Association, Montreal.

Houtz, J.C., Moore, J.W., & Davis, J.K. (1972). Effects of different types of positive and negative instances in learning "nondimensional" concepts. *Journal of Educational Psychology, 63,* 206–211.

Hubel, D.H., & Wiesel, T.N. (1962). Receptive fields, binocular interaction, and functional architecture in the cat's visual cortex. *Journal of Physiology, 166,* 106–154.

Hume, A. (1983). Research on the composing process. *Review of Educational Research, 53,* 201–216.

Hunt, E. (1978). Mechanics of verbal ability. *Psychological Review, 85,* 109–130.

Hunt, E.B., Davidson, J., & Lansman, M. (1981). Individual differences in long-term memory access. *Memory & Cognition, 9,* 599–608.

Hunt, E.B., Lunneborg, C., & Lewis, J. (1975). What does it mean to be high verbal? *Cognitive Psychology, 7,* 194–227.

Huss, H. (1970). An international challenge. In D. Braken & S.E. Malmquist (Eds.) *Improving reading ability around the world.* Newark, DE: International Reading Association.

Hyde, A.A., & Bizar, M. (1989). *Thinking in context.* New York, NY: Longman.

Inman, W. (1977). *Classroom practices and basic skills: Kindergarten and third grade.* Raleigh, NC: Division of Research, North Carolina State Department of Public Instruction.

James, W. (1890). *Principles of psychology (Vol. 1).* New York, NY: H. Holt.

James, W., & Rotter, J.B. (1958). Partial and 100% reinforcement under chance and skill conditions. *Journal of Experimental Psychology, 55,* 397–403.

Johnson, D.M., & Stratton, R.P. (1966). Evaluation of five methods of teaching concepts. *Journal of Educational Psychology, 57,* 48–53.

Johnson-Laird, P.N., Legrenzi, P., Legrenzi, M.S. (1972). Reasoning and a sense of reality. *British Journal of Psychology, 63,* 395–400.

Jurgensen, R.C., Donnelly, A.J., Maier, J.E., & Rising, G.R. (1975). *Geometry.* Boston, MA: Houghton Mifflin.

Just, M.A., & Carpenter, P.A. (1980). A theory of reading: From eye fixations to comprehension. *Psychological Review, 87,* 329–354.

Just, M.A., & Carpenter, P.A. (1987). *The psychology of reading and language comprehension.* Newton, MA: Allyn & Bacon.

Just, M.A., & Carpenter, P.A. (1992). A capacity theory of comprehension: Individual differences in working memory. *Psychological Review, 99(1),* 122–149.

Just, M.A., Carpenter, P.A., & Wooley, J.D. (1982). Paradigms and processes in reading comprehension. *Journal of Experimental Psychology: General, 111,* 228–238.

Kahneman, D., Slovic, P., & Tversky, A. (Eds.) (1982). *Judgment under uncertainty: Heuristics and biases.* New York, NY: Cambridge University Press.

Keller, J.M. (1983). Motivational design of instruction. In C.M. Reigeluth (Ed.), *Instructional-design theories and models: An overview of their current status.* Hillsdale, NJ: Lawrence Erlbaum Associates.

Kemeny, J.G. (1955). Man viewed as machine. *Scientific American, 192,* 58–67.

Kerst, S.M., & Howard, J.H., Jr. (1977). Mental comparisons for ordered information on abstract and concrete dimensions. *Memory & Cognition, 5,* 227–234.

Kieras, D.E. (1988). What mental model should be taught: Choosing instructional content for complex engineered systems. In J. Psotka, L.D. Massey, & S.A. Mutter (Eds.), *Intelligent tutoring systems: Lessons learned* (pp. 85–111). Hillsdale, NJ: Lawrence Erlbaum Associates.

King, M.L., & Rentel, V.M. (1981). Research Update: Conveying meaning in written texts. *Language Arts, 58,* 721–728.

Kintsch, W. (1974). *The representation of meaning in memory.* Hillsdale, NJ: Lawrence Erlbaum Associates.

Kintsch, W. (1977). On comprehending stories. In M.A. Just & P.A. Carpenter (Eds.), *Cognitive processes in comprehension.* Hillsdale, NJ: Lawrence Erlbaum Associates.

Kintsch, W. (1979). On modeling comprehension. *Educational Psychologist, 14,* 3–14.

Kintsch, W., & van Dijk, T.A. (1978). Toward a model of text comprehension and production. *Psychological Review, 85,* 363–394.

Klahr, D. (1985). Solving problems with ambiguous subgoal ordering—preschoolers performance. *Child Development, 56,* 940–952.

Klahr, D., Chase, W.G., & Lovelace, E.A. (1983). Structure and process in alphabetic retrieval. *Journal of Experimental Psychology: Learning, Memory, and Cognition, 9,* 462–477.

Klatzky, R.L. (1980). *Human memory: Structures and processes* (2nd Ed.). San Francisco, CA: W.H. Freeman.

Klatzky, R.L. (1984). *Memory and awareness: An information processing perspective.* New York, NY: W.H. Freeman.

Klausmeier, H.J. (1990). Conceptualizing. In B.F. Jones & L. Idol (Eds.), *Dimensions of thinking and cognitive instruction.* Hillsdale, NJ: Lawrence Erlbaum Associates.

Klausmeier, H.J., & Feldman, K.V. (1975). Effects of a definition and varying numbers of examples and nonexamples on concept attainment. *Journal of Educational Psychology, 67,* 174–178.

Koestler, A. (1964). *The act of creation.* New York, NY: Macmillan.

Kosslyn, S.M. (1980). *Image and mind.* Cambridge, MA: Harvard University Press.

Kosslyn, S.M., Ball, T.M., & Reiser, B.J. (1978). Visual images preserve spatial information: Evidence from studies of image scanning. *Journal of Experimental Psychology: Human Perception and Performance, 4,* 47–60.

Krutetskii, V.A. (1976). *The psychology of mathematical ability in children* (J. Teller, Trans.). Chicago, IL: University of Chicago Press.

Kuhl, J. (1985). Volitional mediators of cognition-behavior consistency: Self-regulatory processes and action control versus state orientation. In J. Kuhl, & J. Beckmann (Eds.), *Action control: From cognition to behavior* (pp. 101–128). Berlin & New York: Springer-Verlag.

Kulhavy, R.W. (1977). Feedback in written instruction. *Review of Educational Research, 47,* 211–232.

Kulhavy, R.W., & Stock, W.A. (1989). Feedback in written instruction: The place of response certitude. *Educational Psychology Review, 1,* 279–308.

Kulhavy, R.W., & Swenson, I. (1975). Imagery instructions and the comprehension of text. *British Journal of Educational Psychology, 45,* 47–51.

Kurtz, B.E., Schneider, W., Carr, M., Borkowski, J.G., & Turner, L.A. (In Press). Sources of memory and metamemory development: Societal, parental, and educational influences. In M. Gruneberg, P. Morris, & R. Sykes (Eds.), *Practical aspects of memory, Vol. 2.* New York, NY: Wiley.

LaBerge, D. (1990). Thalamic and cortical mechanisms of attention suggested by recent positron emission tomographic experiments. *Journal of Cognitive Neuroscience, 2*(4), 358–372.

LaBerge, D., & Samuels, S.J. (1974). Toward a theory of automatic information processing in reading. *Cognitive Psychology, 6,* 293–323.

Laird, J.E., & Newell, A. (1983). Universal weak method: Summary of results. In *Proceedings of the Eighth IJCAI*. International Joint Conference on Artificial Intelligence.

Lampert, M. (1986). Knowing, doing, and teaching multiplication. *Cognition and Instruction, 3,* 305–342.

Larkin, J.H. (1981). Cognition of learning physics. *American Journal of Physics, 49,* 534–541.

Larkin, J.H. (1990). What kind of knowledge transfers? In L.B. Resnick (Ed.), *Knowing, learning and instruction: Essays in honor of Robert Glaser* (pp. 283–305). Hillsdale, NJ: Lawrence Erlbaum Associates.

Larkin, J.H., McDermott, J., Simon, D.P., & Simon, H.A. (1980a). Expert and novice performance in solving physics problems. *Science, 208,* 1335–1342.

Larkin, J.H., McDermott, J., Simon, D.P., & Simon, H.A. (1980b). Models of competence in solving physics problems. *Cognitive Science, 4,* 317–345.

Larrick, N. (1987). Illiteracy starts too soon. *Phi Delta Kappan, 69,* 184–189.

Lave, J. (1988). *Cognition in practice.* Boston, MA: Cambridge University Press.

Leinhardt, G. (1983). *Overview of a program of research on teachers' and students' routines, thoughts, and execution of plans.* Paper presented at the annual meeting of the American Educational Research Association, Montreal.

Leinhardt, G. (1989). Math lessons: A contrast of novice and expert competence. *Journal for Research in Mathematics Education, 20*(1), 52–75.

Lepper, M.R. (1988). Motivational considerations in the study of instruction. *Cognition and Instruction, 5,* 289–309.

Lesgold, A.M. (1984). Acquiring expertise. In J.R. Anderson & S.M. Kosslyn (Eds.), *Tutorials in learning and memory,* New York, NY: W.H. Freeman.

Lesgold, A.M., & Perfetti, C.A. (Eds.) (1981). *Interactive processes in reading.* Hillsdale, NJ: Lawrence Erlbaum Associates.

Lesgold, A., Rubinson, H., Feltovich, P., Glaser, R., Klopfer, D., & Wang, Y. (1988). Expertise in a complex skill: Diagnosing x-ray pictures. In M.T.H. Chi, R. Glaser, M.J. Farr (Eds.), *The nature of expertise* (pp. 311–342). Hillsdale NJ: Lawrence Erlbaum Associates.

Levin, J.R., Pressley, M., McCormick, C.B., Miller, G.E., & Shriberg, L.K. (1979). Assessing the classroom potential of the keyword method. *Journal of Educational Psychology, 71,* 583–594.

Lewis, C.H. (1978). *Production system models of practice effects.* Unpublished doctoral dissertation, University of Michigan, Ann Arbor.

Lewis, C.H. (1981). Skill in algebra. In J.R. Anderson (Ed.) *Cognitive skills and their acquisition* (pp. 85–110). Hillsdale, NJ: Lawrence Erlbaum Associates.

Lewis, M.W., & Anderson, J.R. (1985). Discrimination of operator schemata in problem solving: Learning from examples. *Cognitive Psychology, 17,* 26–65.

Liebelt, L.S. (1980). *Knowledge effects in a descriptive task.* Unpublished master's thesis, University of Colorado, Boulder, CO.

Linden, M., & Wittrock, M.C. (1981). The teaching of reading comprehension according to the model of generative learning. *Reading Research Quarterly, 17,* 44–57.

Lindsay, P.H., & Norman, D.A. (1977). *Human information processing.* New York, NY: Academic Press.

Lippett, R.R., Polansky, N., & Rosen, S. (1952). The dynamics power. *Human Relations, 5,* 37–64.

Livingston, C., & Borko, H. (1989). Expert-novice differences in teaching: A cognitive analysis and implications for teacher education. *Journal of Teacher Education, 40,* 36–42.

Luchins, A.S. (1942). Mechanization in problem solving. *Psychological Monographs, 54,* No. 248.

Markle, S.M. (1975). They teach concepts don't they? *Educational Researcher, 4,* 3–9.

Markman, E. (1979). Realizing that you don't understand: Elementary school chldren's awareness of inconsistencies. *Child Development, 50,* 643–655.

Markman, E. (1989). *Categorization and naming in children: Problems of induction.* Cambridge, MA: MIT Press.

Marks, R. (1987). *Those who appreciate: A case study of Joe, a beginning mathematics teacher.* Stanford, CA: School of Education, Stanford University.

Marshall, J.D. (1984). Process and product: Case studies in writing in two content areas. In A.N. Applebee (Ed.), *Contexts for learning to write* (pp. 149–168). Norwood, NJ: Ablex.

Marshall, S.P. (1990). *What students learn (and re-*

member) from word problem instruction. Paper presented at the annual meeting of the American Educational Research Association, Boston, MA.

Martindale, C. (1991). *Cognitive psychology: A neural-network approach.* Pacific Grove, CA: Brooks/Cole Publishing Co.

Martinez, J.L., & Kesner, R.P. (Eds.) (1991). *Learning and memory: A biological view,* (2nd. edition). New York, NY: Academic Press.

Matsuhashi, A. (Ed.) (1987). *Writing in real time: Modeling production processes.* Norwood, NJ: Ablex.

Mayer, R.E. (1975). Different problem-solving competencies established in learning computer programming with and without meaningful models. *Journal of Educational Psychology, 67,* 725–734.

Mayer, R.E. (1980). Elaboration techniques that increase the meaningfulness of technical text: An experimental test of a learning strategy hypothesis. *Journal of Educational Psychology, 72,* 770–784.

Mayer, R.E. (1981). Frequency norms and structural analysis of algebra story problems into families, categories, and templates. *Instructional Science, 10,* 135–175.

Mayer, R.E. (1982). Memory for algebra story problems. *Journal of Educational Psychology, 74,* 199–210.

Mayer, R.E. (1987). *Educational psychology: A cognitive approach.* Boston, MA: Little Brown and Company.

Mayer, R. (1989). Models for understanding. *Review of Educational Research, 59,* 43–64.

Mayer, R.E., & Bromage, B. (1980). Different recall protocols for technical texts due to advance organizers. *Journal of Educational Psychology, 72,* 209–225.

McCombs, B.L. (1987). *The role of effective variables in autonomous learning.* Paper presented at the annual meeting of American Educational Research Association, Washington, DC.

McCombs, B.L. (1989). Self-regulated learning and academic achievement: A phenomenological view. In B.J. Zimmerman & D.H. Schunk (Eds.), *Self-regulated learning and academic achievement: Theory, research and practice* (pp. 51–82). New York, NY: Springer-Verlag.

McCombs, B.L (1991). Motivation and life-long learning. *Educational Psychologist, 26,* 117–127.

McCutchen, D., & Perfetti, C. (1982). Coherence and connectedness in the development of discourse production. *Text, 2,* 113–139.

McGraw, L. (1987). *An anthropologist in the classroom: Chris.* Stanford, CA: School of Education, Stanford University.

McKnight, C.C., Crosswhite, F.J., Dossey, J.A., Kifer, E., Swafford, J.O., Travers, K.J., & Cooney, T.J. (1987). *The underachieving curriculum: Assessing U.S. school mathematics from an international perspective.* Champaign, IL: STIPES Publishing Co.

Means, B., & Gott, S.P. (1988). Cognitive task analysis as a basis for tutor development: Articulating abstract knowledge representations. In J. Psotka, D. Massey, & S.A. Mutter (Eds.), *Intelligent tutoring systems: Lessons learned.* (pp. 59–83). Hillsdale, NJ: Lawrence Erlbaum Associates.

Means, B., Mumaw, R., Roth, C., Shlager, M., McWilliams, E., Gagné, E., Rice, V., Rosenthal, D., & Heon, S. (1988). *ATC training analysis study: Design of the next generation ATC training system* (HII Technical Report). Alexandria, VA: HumRRO International.

Means, B., & Roth, C. (1988). *Some outcomes of a cognitive analysis of troubleshooting.* Paper presented at the American Psychological Association Convention, Atlanta, GA.

Meudell, P.R. (1971). Retrieval and representation in long-term memory. *Psychonomic Science, 23,* 295–296.

Meyer, B.J.F. (1975). *The organization of prose and its effects on memory.* New York, NY: American Elsevier.

Meyer, B.J.F. (1977). The structure of prose: Effects on learning and memory and implications for educational practice. In R.C. Anderson, R.J. Spiro, & W.E. Montague (Eds.), *Schooling and the acquisition of knowledge* (pp. 179–200). Hillsdale, NJ: Lawrence Erlbaum Associates.

Meyer, B.J.F., Brandt, D.M. & Bluth, G.J. (1980). Use of top level structure in text: Key for reading comprehension of ninth grade students. *Reading Research Quarterly, 16,* 72–103.

Meyer, W.U. (1970). *Selbstverantwortlichkeit und Leistungsmotivation.* Unpublished doctoral dissertation, Ruhr Universitat, Bochum, Germany.

Miller, G.A. (1956). The magical number seven, plus or minus two: Some limits on our capacity for processing information. *Psychological Review, 63*, 81–97.

Minsky, M.A. (1975). A framework for representing knowledge. In P.H. Winston (Ed.), *The psychology of computer vision* (pp. 211–280). New York, NY: McGraw-Hill.

Mishkin, M. (1982). A memory system in the monkey. *Philosophical Transactions, Royal Society of London,* B298: 85–95.

Mishkin, M., & Petri, H.L. (1984). Memories and habits: Some implications for the analysis of learning and retention. In N. Butters & L. Squire (Eds.), *Neuropsychology of memory.* New York: Guilford Press.

Monty, R.A., & Senders, J.W. (Eds.) (1976). *Eye movements and psychological processes.* Hillsdale, NJ: Lawrence Erlbaum Associates.

Mook, D.G. (1987). *Motivation: The organization of action.* New York, NY: W.W. Norton.

Moore, J.W., Hauck, W.E., & Gagné, E.D. (1973). Acquisition, retention, and transfer in an individualized college physics course. *Journal of Educational Psychology, 64*, 335–340.

Morales, R.V., Shute, V.J., & Pellegrino, J.W. (1985). Developmental differences in understanding and solving simple mathematics word problems. *Cognition and Instruction, 2*, 59–89.

Moskowitz, G., & Hayman, J. (1976). Success strategies in inner city teaching: A year long study. *Journal of Educational Research, 69*, 283–289.

Moyer, R.S. (1973). Comparing objects in memory: Evidence suggesting an internal psychophysics. *Perception and Psychophysics, 13*, 180–184.

Murdock, B.B., Jr. (1961). The retention of individual items. *Journal of Experimental Psychology, 62*, 618–625.

National Commission on Excellence in Education (1983). *A nation at risk: The imperative for educational reform* (Stock No. 065-000-0017-2). Washington, DC: U.S. Government Printing Office.

Neisser, U. (1967). *Cognitive psychology.* New York, NY: Appleton-Century-Crofts.

Neisser, U. (Ed.) (1982). *Memory observed: Remembering in natural contexts.* San Francisco, CA: W.H. Freeman.

Neves, D.M., & Anderson, J.R. (1981). Knowledge compilation: Mechanisms for the automatization of skills. In J.R. Anderson (Ed.) *Cognitive skills and their acquisition.* Hillsdale, NJ: Lawrence Erlbaum Associates.

Newell, A. (1990). *Unified theories of cognition.* Cambridge, MA: Harvard University Press.

Newell, A., & Simon, H.A. (1972). *Human problem solving.* Englewood Cliffs, NJ: Prentice-Hall.

Newsweek, (1991). The best schools in the world. December 2, 1991, pp. 50–64.

Nicholls, J.G., Cobb, P., Wood, T., Yackel, E., & Patashnick, M. (1990). Assessing students' theories of success in mathematics: Individual and classroom differences. *Journal for Research in Mathematics Education, 21*, 109–122.

Nisbett, R.E., Fong, G.T., Lehman, D.R., & Cheng, P.W. (1987). Teaching reasoning. *Science, 238*, 625–631.

Nolan, S.B. (1988). Reasons for studying: Motivational orientations and study strategies. *Cognition and Instruction, 5*, 269–287.

Nussbaum, J. (1979). Children's conceptions of the earth as a cosmic body: A cross age study. *Science Education, 63*, 83–93.

Nystrand, M. (Ed.) (1982). *What writers know: The language, process, and structure of written discourse.* New York, NY: Academic Press.

Okey, J.R., & Gagné R.M. (1970). Revision of a science topic using evidence of performance on subordinate skills. *Journal of Research in Science Teaching, 7*, 321–325.

Osborn, A.F. (1963). *Applied imagination,* (3rd edition). New York, NY: Scribner's.

O'Sullivan, J.T., & Pressley, M. (1984). Completeness of instruction and strategy transfer. *Journal of Experimental Child Psychology, 38*, 275–288.

Owen, E., & Sweller, J. (1989). Should problem-solving be used as a learning device in mathematics? *Journal for Research in Mathematics Education, 20*, 322–328.

Palincsar, A.S., & Brown, A.L. (1984). Reciprocal teaching of comprehension-fostering and comprehension-monitoring activities. *Cognition and Instruction, 1*, 117–175.

Parnes, S.J. (1961). Effects of extended effort in creative problem solving. *Journal of Educational Psychology, 52*, 117–122.

Parnes, S.J., & Meadow, A. (1959). Effects of

"brainstorming" instructions on creative problem-solving by trained and untrained subjects. *Journal of Educational Psychology, 50,* 171–176.

Pea, R.D., & Kurland, D.M. (1989). Cognitive technologies for writing. *Review of research in education, 14,* 277–326.

Penrose, R. (1989). *The emperor's new mind.* New York, NY: Oxford University Press.

Perfetti, C.A., Finger, E., & Hogaboam, T. (1978). Sources of vocalization latency differences between skilled and less skilled young readers. *Journal of Educational Psychology, 70,* 730–739.

Perfetti, C.A., & Hogaboam, T. (1975). Relationship between single word decoding and reading comprehension skill. *Journal of Educational Psychology, 67,* 461–469.

Perfetti, C.A., & Roth, S.F. (1981). Some of the interactive processes in reading and their role in reading skill. In A.M. Lesgold and C.A. Perfetti (Eds.), *Interactive processes in reading* (pp. 269–297). Hillsdale, NJ: Lawrence Erlbaum Associates.

Perfetto, G.A., Bransford, J.D., & Franks, J.J. (1983). Constraints on access in a problem solving context. *Memory & Cognition, 11,* 24–31.

Perkins, D.N., & Salomon, A. (1989). Are cognitive skills context-bound? *Educational Researcher, 18,* 16–25.

Perkins, D.N., & Simmons, R. (1988). Patterns of misunderstanding: An integrative model for science, math, and programming. *Review of Educational Research, 58,* 303–326.

Perl, S. (1979). The composing processes of unskilled college writers. *Research in the Teaching of English, 13,* 317–336.

Peterson, P.L. (1988). Teachers' and students' cognitional knowledge for classroom teaching and learning. *Educational Researcher, 17,* 5–14.

Peterson, P.L., & Clark, C.M. (1978). Teachers' reports of their cognitive processes during teaching. *American Educational Research Journal, 15,* 555–565.

Peterson, P., Fennema, E., & Carpenter, T.P. (in press). Teachers' knowledge of students' mathematics problem solving knowledge. In J. Brophy (Ed.), *Advances in research on teaching: Vol. 2. Teacher's subject matter knowledge and classroom instruction.* Greenwich, CT: JAI Press.

Peterson, P., & Swing, S. (1988). Elaborative and integrative thought processes in mathematics learning. *Journal of Educational Psychology, 80,* 54–66.

Pflaum, S.W., Walberg, H.J., Karegianes, M.L., & Rasher, S.P. (1980). Reading instruction: A quantitative analysis. *Educational Researcher, 9,* 12–18.

Piaget, J. (1952). *The origins of intelligence in children.* New York: International Universities Press.

Piaget, J. (1967). The mental development of the child. In D. Elkind (Ed.), *Six psychological studies.* New York, NY: Random House. (Original work published in 1940).

Piaget, J. (1980). *Adaptation and intelligence: Organic selection and phenocopy.* Chicago, IL: University of Chicago Press. (Original work published in 1974).

Pianko, S. (1979). A description of the composing processes of college freshmen writers. *Research in the Teaching of English, 13,* 5–22.

Pogrow, S. (1990). Challenging at-risk students: Findings from the HOTS program. *Phi Delta Kappan, 7,* 389–397.

Posner, G.J., Strike, K.A., Hewson, P.W., & Gertzog, W.A. (1982). Accommodation of a scientific conception: Toward a theory of conceptual change. *Science Education, 66,* 211–227.

Potts, G.R. (1972). Information-processing strategies used in the encoding of linear orderings. *Journal of Verbal Learning and Verbal Behavior, 11,* 727–740.

Potts, G.R. (1975). Bringing order to cognitive structures. In F. Restle, R.M. Shriffin, N.J. Castellan, H.R. Lindman, & D.P. Pisoni (Eds.), *Cognitive theory, Vol. 1.* Hillsdale, NJ: Lawrence Erlbaum Associates.

Pressley, M., Borkowski, J.G., & Schneider, W. (1987). Cognitive strategies: Good strategy users coordinate metacognition and knowledge. In R. Vasta, & G. Whilehurst (Eds.), *Annals of child development* (Vol. 4, pp. 80–129). Greenwich, CT: JAI Press.

Pressley, M., Forrest-Pressley, D.L., Elliott-Faust, D., & Miller, G. (1985). Children's use of cognitive strategies, how to teach strategies, and what to do if they can't be taught. In M. Pressley, & C.J. Brainerd (Eds.), *Cognitive learning and memory in children* (pp. 1–47). New York, NY: Springer-Verlag.

Pressley, M., Levin, J.R., & Ghatala, E.S. (1984). Memory strategy monitoring in adults and children. *Journal of Verbal Learning and Verbal Behavior, 23,* 270–288.

Pressley, M., Ross, K.A., Levin, J.R., & Ghatala, E.S. (1984). The role of strategy utility knowledge in children's strategy decision making. *Journal of Experimental Child Psychology, 38,* 491–504.

Pylyshyn, Z.W. (1986). *Computation and cognition: Toward a foundation for cognitive science.* Cambridge, MA: MIT Press.

Raina, M.K. (1984). *Education of the left and right: Implications of hemispheric specialization.* Atlantic Highlands, NJ: Humanities Press.

Raviv, A., Bar-Tal, D., Raviv, A., & Bar-Tal, Y. (1980). Causal perceptions of success and failure by advantaged, integrated and disadvantaged pupils. *British Journal of Educational Psychology, 50,* 137–146.

Rayner, K. (1977). Visual attention in reading: Eye movements reflect cognitive processing. *Memory & Cognition, 4,* 443–448.

Rayner, K. (Ed.) (1983). *Eye movements in reading: Perceptual and language processes.* New York, NY: Academic Press.

Reder, L.M. (1979). The role of elaborations in memory for prose. *Cognitive Psychology, 11,* 221–234.

Reder, L.M. (1982a). Elaborations: When do they help and when do they hurt? *Text, 2,* 211–224.

Reder, L.M. (1982b). Plausibility judgments versus fact retrieval: Alternative strategies for sentence verification. *Psychological Review, 89,* 250–280.

Reed, S.K., Ernst, G.W., & Banerji, R. (1974). The role of analogy in transfer between similar problem states. *Cognitive Psychology, 6,* 436–450.

Reitman, J.S., & Rueter, H.H. (1980). Organization revealed by recall orders and confirmed by pauses. *Cognitive Psychology, 12,* 554–581.

Reitman, W. (1964). Heuristic decision procedures, open constraints, and the structure of ill defined problems. In M.W. Shelly & G.L. Bryan (Eds.), *Human judgments and optimality* (pp. 282–315). New York, NY: John Wiley & Sons.

Resnick, L.B., Nesher, P., Leonard, F., Magona, M., Omanson, S., & Peled, I. (1989). Conceptual bases of arithmetic errors: The case of decimal fractions. *Journal for Research in Mathematics Education, 20,* 8–27.

Resnick, L.B., Siegel, A.W., & Kresh, E. (1971). Transfer and sequence in learning double classification skills. *Journal of Experimental Child Psychology, 11,* 139–149.

Resnick, L.B., & Weaver, P.A. (Eds.) (1979). *Theory and practice of early reading,* (Vols. 1–3). Hillsdale, NJ: Lawrence Erlbaum Associates.

Reys, R.E., Rybolt, J.F., Bestgen, B.J., & Wyatt, J.W. (1982). Processes used by good computational estimators. *Journal for Research in Mathematics Education, 13,* 183–201.

Richardson, J.T.E. (1980). *Mental imagery and human memory.* London: Macmillan.

Rickards, J.P. (1976). Interaction of position and conceptual level of adjunct questions on immediate and delayed retention of text. *Journal of Educational Psychology, 68,* 210–217.

Riley, M.S., Greeno, J.G., & Heller, J.I. (1983). Development of children's problem-solving ability in arithmetic. In H.P. Ginsberg (Ed), *The development of mathematical thinking,* (pp. 153–196). New York, NY: Academic Press.

Robinson, C.S., & Hayes, J.R. (1978). Making inferences about relevance in understanding problems. In R. Revlin & R.E. Mayer (Eds.), *Human reasoning* (pp. 195–206). Washington, D.C.: Winston/Wiley.

Roe, A. (1960). Crucial life experiences in the development of scientists. In E.P. Torrance (Ed.) *Talent and education,* (pp. 66–77). Minnesota: University of Minnesota Press.

Rohwer, W.D., Jr. & Levin, J.R. (1968). Action, meaning, and stimulus selection in paired-associate learning. *Journal of Verbal Learning and Verbal Behavior, 7,* 137–141.

Rosch, E. (1973). On the internal structure of perceptual and semantic categories. In T.E. Moore (Ed.), *Cognitive development and the acquisition of language.* New York, NY: Academic Press.

Rosch, E., & Lloyd, B.B. (Eds.) (1978). *Cognition and categorization.* Hillsdale, NJ: Lawrence Erlbaum Associates.

Rosch, E., Mervis, C.B., Gray, W.D., Johnson,

D.M., & Boyes-Braem, P. (1976). Basic objects in natural categories. *Cognitive Psychology, 8,* 382–439.

Rose, M. (1980). Rigid rules, inflexible plans, and the stifling of language: A cognitivist analysis of writer's block. *College Composition and Communication, 31,* 389–401.

Rosenbaum, R.M. (1972). *A dimensional analysis of the perceived causes of success and failure.* Unpublished doctoral dissertation, University of California, Los Angeles.

Rosenkrans, M.A., & Hartup, W.W. (1967). Imitative influences of consistent and inconsistent response consequences to a model of aggressive behavior in children. *Journal of Personality and Social Psychology, 7,* 429–434.

Roth, K.J. (1986). *Conceptual-change learning and student processing of science texts.* East Lansing, MI: Michigan State University, The Institute for Research on Teaching, Research Series No. 167.

Roth, K.J. (1990). Developing meaningful conceptual understanding in science. In B.F. Jones & L. Idol (Eds.), *Dimensions of thinking and cognitive instruction.* Hillsdale, NJ: Lawrence Erlbaum Associates.

Rouse, W.B. (1982). A mixed fidelity approach to technical training. *Journal of Educational Technology Systems, 11,* 103–115.

Rumelhart, D. (1975). Notes on a schema for stories. In D. Bobrow & A. Collins (Eds.), *Representation and understanding: Studies in cognitive science* (pp. 211–236). New York, NY: Academic Press.

Rumelhart, D.E. (1980). Schemata: The building blocks of cognition. In R.J. Spiro, B.C. Bruce, & W.F. Brewer (Eds.), *Theoretical issues in reading comprehension* (pp. 33–58). Hillsdale, NJ: Lawrence Erlbaum Associates.

Rumelhart, D.E., Hinton, G., & McClelland, J.L. (1986). A general framework for parallel distributed processing. In D.E. Rumelhart & J.L. McClelland (Eds.), *Parallel distributed processing, Vol. 1.* Cambridge, MA: MIT Press.

Rumelhart, D.E., & Norman, D.A. (1978). Accretion, tuning, and restructuring: Three modes of learning. In J.W. Cotton & R. Klatzky (Eds.), *Semantic factors in cognition.* Hillsdale, NJ: Lawrence Erlbaum Associates.

Rumelhart, D.E., & Norman, D.A. (1981). Analogical processes in learning. In J.R. Anderson (Ed.), *Cognitive skills and their acquisition* (pp. 335–359). Hillsdale, NJ: Lawrence Erlbaum Associates.

Rumelhart, D.E., & Norman, D.A. (1983). Representation in memory. In R.C. Atkinson, R.J. Herrnstein, G. Lindzey, & R.D. Luce (Eds.), *Handbook of Experimental Psychology.* New York, NY: Wiley.

Ryle, G. (1949). *The concept of mind.* London: Hutchinson's University Library.

Sabol, M.A., & DeRosa, D.V. (1976). Semantic encoding of isolated words. *Journal of Experimental Psychology: Human Learning and Memory, 2,* 58–68.

Sackur-Grisvard, C., & Leonard, F. (1985). Intermediate cognitive organization in the process of learning a mathematical concept: The order of positive decimal numbers. *Cognition and Instruction, 2,* 157–174.

Salomon, G., & Perkins, D.N. (1989). Rocky roads to transfer: Rethinking mechanisms of a neglected phenomenon. *Educational Psychologist, 24,* 113–142.

Samuels, S.J. (1979). The method of repeated readings. *The Reading Teacher, 32,* 403–408.

Saunders, H. (1980). When are we ever gonna have to use this? *Mathematics Teacher, 73,* 7–16.

Saxe, G.B. (1988). Candy selling and math learning. *Educational Researcher, 17,* 14–21.

Scardamalia, M., & Bereiter, C. (1983). The development of evaluative, diagnostic, and remedial capabilities in children's composing. In M. Martten (Ed.), *The psychology of written language: A developmental approach* (pp. 67–95). London: John Wiley and Sons.

Scardamalia, M., & Bereiter, C. (1985). Written composition. In M.C. Wittrock (Ed.), *Handbook of research on teaching,* Vol. 3.

Scardamalia, M., & Bereiter, C. (1987). Knowledge telling and knowledge transforming in written composition. In S. Rosenberg (Ed.), *Advances in applied linguistics.* New York, NY: Cambridge University Press.

Scardamalia, M., Bereiter, C., & Goelman, H. (1982). The role of productive factors in writing ability. In M. Nystrand (Ed.), *What writers know: The language, process, and structure of written discourse* (pp. 173–210). New York, NY: Academic Press.

Schneider, W. (1985). Training high performance skills: Fallacies and guidelines. *Human Factors, 27*, 285–300.

Schneider, W. (1988). Micro experimental laboratory: An integrated system for IBM PC compatibles. *Behavior Research Methods, Instruments, & Computers, 20*, 206–217.

Schneider, W., & Shriffrin, R.M. (1977). Controlled and automatic human information processing: Detection, search, and attention. *Psychological Review, 84*, 1–66.

Schriver, K.A. (1984). *Revising computer documentation for comprehension: Ten exercises in protocol-aided revision* (CDC TR 14). Pittsburgh, PA: Carnegie Mellon, Communications Design Center.

Schunk, D.H. (1989). Self-efficacy and cognitive skill learning. In C. Ames & R. Ames (Eds.), *Research on motivation in education, Vol. 3: Goals and cognitions* (pp. 13–44). San Diego, CA: Academic Press.

Schwab, J.J. (1978). *Science, curriculum and liberal education.* Chicago, IL: University of Chicago Press.

Searle, J.R. (1990). Is the brain's mind a computer program? *Scientific American, 262*, 26–31.

Segal, J.W., Chipman, S.F., & Glaser, R. (Eds.) (1985). *Thinking and learning skills, Vol. 1: Relating instruction to research.* Hillsdale, NJ: Lawrence Erlbaum Associates.

Shalin, V.L. (1987). *Knowledge of problem structure in mathematical problem solving.* Unpublished doctoral dissertation. Learning Research and Development Center, University of Pittsburgh, Pittsburgh.

Shank, R.C., & Abelson, R.P. (1977). *Scripts, plans, goals, and understanding.* Hillsdale, NJ: Lawrence Erlbaum Associates.

Shannon, C.E. (1962). The mathematical theory of communication. In C.E. Shannon & W. Weaver (Eds.), *The mathematical theory of communication* (pp. 3–91). Urbana, IL: University of Illinois Press. (Reprinted from *Bell System Technical Journal, 47*, 194.)

Sharkey, N., & Mitchell, D.C. (1985). Word recognition in a functional context: The use of scripts in reading. *Journal of Memory and Language, 24*, 253–270.

Shavelson, R.J. (1986). *Interactive decision making: Some thoughts on teacher cognition.* Invited address, I Congreso Internacional, "Pensamientos de los Profesores y Toma de Decisiones," Seville, Spain.

Shavelson, R.J. (1972). Some aspects of the correspondence between content structure and cognitive structure in physics instruction. *Journal of Educational Psychology, 63*, 225–234.

Shulman, L.S. (1986). Those who understand: Knowledge growth in teaching. *Educational Researcher, 15*, 4–14.

Shulman, L.S. (1987). Knowledge and teaching: Foundations of the new reform. *Harvard Education Review, 57*, 1–22.

Shustack, M.W., & Anderson, J.R. (1979). Effects of analogy to prior knowledge on memory for new information. *Journal of Verbal Learning and Verbal Behavior, 18*, 565–583.

Siegler, R.S. (1976). Three aspects of cognitive development. *Cognitive Psychology, 8*, 481–520.

Siegler, R.S. (1988). Individual differences in strategy choices: Good students, not-so-good students, and perfectionists. *Child Development, 59*, 833–851.

Siegler, R.S., & Richards, D.D. (1983). The development of two concepts. In C. Brainerd (Ed.), *Recent advances in cognitive developmental theory* (pp. 51–121). New York, NY: Springer Verlag.

Silver, E.A. (1981). Recall of mathematical problem information: Solving related problems. *Journal for Research in Mathematics Education, 12*, 54–64.

Simon, H.A. (1974). How big is a chunk? *Science, 183*, 482–488.

Simon, H.A. (1978). Information-processing theory of human problem solving. In W.K. Estes (Ed.), *Handbook of learning and cognitive processes* (Vol. 5, pp. 271–295). Hillsdale, NJ: Lawrence Erlbaum Associates.

Simon, J.G., & Feather, N.T. (1973). Causal attributions for success and failure at university examinations. *Journal of Educational Psychology, 64*, 46–56.

Singley, M.K., & Anderson, J.R. (1989). *The transfer of cognitive skill.* Cambridge, MA: Harvard University Press.

Skinner, B.F. (1938). *Behavior of organisms.* New York: Appleton-Century-Crofts.

Slotnick, D.L., Butterfield, E.M., Colantonio, E.S.,

Kopetzky, D.J., & Slotnick, J.K. (1986). *Computers and applications: An introduction to data processing.* Lexington, MA: D.C. Heath and Company.

Smith, E.E., Shoben, E.J., & Rips, L.J. (1974). Structure and process in semantic memory: A featural model for semantic decisions. *Psychological Review, 81,* 214–241.

Smith, F. (1971). *Understanding reading.* New York, NY: Holt, Rinehart, & Winston.

Sneider, C., & Pulos, S. (1983). Children's cosmographies: Understanding the earth's shape and gravity. *Science Education, 67,* 205–221.

Snow, R.E. (1980). Aptitude processes. In R.E. Snow, P.A. Federico, & W.E. Montague (Eds.). *Aptitude, learning, and instruction* (Vol. 1, pp. 27–63). Hillsdale, NJ: Lawrence Erlbaum Associates.

Sowder, J.T. (in press). Making sense of numbers in school mathematics. In G. Leinhardt, R. Putnam, & R. Hattrup (Eds.), *Analysis of arithmetic of mathematics teaching.* Hillsdale, NJ: Lawrence Erlbaum Associates.

Sowder, J.T., & Wheeler, M.M. (1987). *The development of computational estimation and number sense: Two exploratory studies* (Research Report). San Diego, CA: San Diego State University Center for Research in Mathematics and Science Education.

Sowder, L. (1988). Children's solutions of story problems. *Journal of Mathematical Behavior, 7,* 227–238.

Sperling, G.A. (1960). The information available in brief visual presentation. *Psychological Monographs, 74,* Whole No. 498.

Sperling, M. (1991). *High-school English and the teacher student writing conference: Fine-tuned duets in the ensemble of the classroom* (Occasional Report No. 26). Berkeley, CA: National Center for the Study of Writing and Literacy.

Spilich, G.J., Vesonder, G.T., Chiesi, H.L., & Voss, J.F. (1979). Text processing of domain-related information for individuals with high and low domain knowledge. *Journal of Verbal Learning and Verbal Behavior, 18,* 275–290.

Spiro, R.J. (1977). Remembering information from text: The "State of Schema" approach. In R.C. Anderson, R.J. Spiro, & W.E. Montague (Eds.), *Schooling and the acquisition of knowledge* (pp. 137–166). Hillsdale, NJ: Lawrence Erlbaum Associates.

Stallard, C.K. (1974). An analysis of the writing behavior of good student writers. *Research in the Teaching of English, 8,* 206–218.

Stein, B.S., Bransford, J.D., Franks, J.J., Owings, R.A., Vye, N.J., & McGraw, W. (1982). Differences in the precision of self-generated elaborations. *Journal of Experimental Psychology: General, 111,* 399–405.

Stein, M.K., Baxter, J.A., & Leinhardt, G. (1990). Subject-matter knowledge and elementary instruction: A case from functions and graphing. *American Educational Research Journal, 27*(4), 639–663.

Stein, N.L., & Glenn, C.G. (1978). An analysis of story comprehension in elementary school children. In R. Freedle (Ed.), *Multidisciplinary perspectives in discourse comprehension.* Norwood, NJ: Ablex.

Sternberg, R.J. (1979). Stalking the IQ quark. *Psychology Today, 13,* 42–54.

Sternberg, S. (1966). High-speed scanning in human memory. *Science, 153,* 652–654.

Sternberg, S. (1969). The discovery of processing stages: Extensions of Donder's method. In W.G. Koster (Ed.), *Attention and performance II. Acta Psychologica, 30,* 276–315.

Stevens, C.F. (1979). The neuron. *The brain.* San Francisco, CA: W.H. Freeman.

Stigler, J.W., Fuson, K.C., Ham, M., & Kim, M.S. (1986). An analysis of addition and subtraction word problems in American and Soviet elementary mathematics textbooks. *Cognition and Instruction, 3,* 153–171.

Stipek, D.J. (1981). Children's perceptions of their own and their classmates' ability. *Journal of Educational Psychology, 73,* 404–410.

Suchman, J.R. (1962). *The elementary school training program in scientific inquiry* (Project #216, Grant #7-11-038). Washington, DC: Office of Education.

Suppes, P., Jerman, M., & Brian, D. (1968). *Computer-assisted instruction: Stanford's 1965–66 arithmetic program.* New York, NY: Academic Press.

Suppes, P., & Morningstar, M. (1972). *Computer-assisted instruction at Stanford, 1966–68: Data, models, and evaluation of arithmetic programs.* New York, NY: Academic Press.

Surber, J.R., & Anderson, R.C. (1975). Delay-retention effect in natural classroom settings. *Journal of Educational Psychology, 67*, 170–173.

Svenson, O., & Broquist, S. (1975). Strategies for solving simple addition problems: A comparison of normal and subnormal children. *Scandinavian Journal of Psychology, 16*, 143–151.

Sweller, J., & Cooper, G.A. (1985). The use of examples as a substitute for problem solving in learning algebra. *Cognition and Instruction, 2*, 59–89.

Swing, S.R., Stoiber, K.C., & Peterson, P.L. (1988). Thinking skills versus learning time: Effects of alternative classroom-based interventions on students' mathematics problem solving. *Cognition and Instruction, 5*, 123–191.

Taylor, B.M. (1980). Children's memory for expository text after reading. *Reading Research Quarterly, 15*, 399–411.

Tenney, Y.L., & Kurland, L.C. (1988). The development of troubleshooting expertise in radar mechanics. In J. Psotka, L.D. Massey, & S.A. Mutter (Eds.), *Intelligent tutoring systems: Lessons learned.* (pp. 59–83). Hillsdale, NJ: Lawrence Erlbaum Associates.

Tennyson, R.D. (1973). Effect of negative instances in concept learning using a verbal-learning task. *Journal of Educational Psychology, 64*, 247–260.

Tennyson, R.D., & Tennyson, C.L. (1975). Rule acquisition, design strategy variables: Degree of instance divergence, sequence, and instance analysis. *Journal of Educational Psychology, 67*, 852–859.

Tennyson, R.D., Woolley, F.R., and Merrill, M.D. (1972). Exemplar and nonexemplar variables which produce correct concept classification behavior and specified classification errors. *Journal of Educational Psychology, 63*, 144–152.

Thibadeau, R., Just, M.A., & Carpenter, P.A. (1982). A model of the time course and content of reading. *Cognitive Science, 6*, 157–203.

Thompson, M.A. (1992). *Redefining the poor reader: Distinguishing the effects of domain knowledge from aptitude on reading comprehension processes.* Unpublished doctoral dissertation, The Catholic University of America, Washington, DC.

Thompson, P. (1990). *Quantitative concepts as a foundation for algebra: First year progress report.* NSF Grant No. MDR 89-50311.

Thompson, P.W. (in press a). The development of the concept of speed and its relationship to concepts of rate. In G. Harel & J. Confrey (Eds.), *The development of multiplicative reasoning in the learning of mathematics.* Albany, NY: SUNY Press.

Thompson, P.W. (in press b). Quantitative reasoning, complexity, and additive structure. *Educational Studies in Mathematics.*

Thompson, R.F. (1975). *Introduction to physiological psychology.* New York, NY: Harper & Row.

Thompson, R.F. (1985). *The brain: An introduction to neuroscience.* New York, NY: W.H. Freeman.

Thorndike, E.L. (1898). Animal intelligence: An experimental study of the associative processes in animals. *Psychological Review Monographs Supplement, 2*, (8–7), 23–31.

Thorndike, E.L. (1906). *Principles of teaching.* New York, NY: A.G. Seiler.

Thorndike, E.L. (1913). *Educational psychology: The psychology of learning.* (Vol. 2). New York, NY: Teacher's College.

Thorndyke, P.W. (1977). Cognitive structures in comprehension and memory of narrative discourse. *Cognitive Psychology, 9*, 77–110.

Thorndyke, P.W., & Yekovich, F.R. (1980). A critique of schema-based theories of human story memory. *Poetics, 9*, 23–49.

Torshen, K.P. (1977). *The mastery approach to competency-based education.* New York, NY: Academic Press.

Trabasso, T.R., & Riley, C.A. (1975). The construction and use of representations involving linear order. In R.L. Solso (Ed.), *Information processing and cognition.* Hillsdale, NJ: Lawrence Erlbaum Associates.

Tulving, E., Mandler, G., & Baumel, R. (1964). Interaction of two sources of information in tachistoscopic word recognition. *Canadian Journal of Psychology, 18*, 62–71.

Valle, V.A., & Frieze, I.H. (1976). Stability of causal attributions as a mediator in changing expectations for success. *Journal of Personality and Social Psychology, 33*, 579–587.

van Dijk, T.A., & Kintsch, W. (1983). *Strategies in discourse comprehension.* New York, NY: Academic Press.

Venezky, R.L., & Johnson, D. (1973). Development of two letter-sound patterns in grades one through three. *Journal of Educational Psychology, 64*, 109–115.

Vidler, D.C. (1977). Curiosity. In S. Ball (Ed.), *Motivation in education* (pp. 17–43). New York, NY: Academic Press.

Vosniadou, S., & Ortony, A. (Eds.) (1990). *Similarity and analogical reasoning.* New York, NY: Cambridge University Press.

Voss, J. (1987). Learning and transfer in subject-matter learning: A problem-solving model. *International Journal of Educational Research, 11*, 607–622.

Voss, J.F., & Post, T.A. (1988). On the solving of ill-structured problems. In M.T.H. Chi, R. Glaser, M.J. Farr (Eds.), *The nature of expertise* (pp. 261–285). Hillsdale, NJ: Lawrence Erlbaum Associates.

Voss, J.F., Tyler, S.W., & Yengo, L.A. (1983). Individual differences in the solving of social science problems. In R.F. Dillon & R.R. Schmeck (Eds.), *Individual differences in cognition* (pp. 205–232). New York, NY: Academic Press.

Voss, J.F., Vesonder, G.T., & Spilich, G.J. (1980). Text generation and recall by high-knowledge and low-knowledge individuals. *Journal of Verbal Learning and Verbal Behavior, 19*, 651–667.

Walker, C.H. (1987). Relative importance of domain knowledge and overall aptitude on acquisition of domain-related information. *Cognition and Instruction, 4*, 25–42.

Walker, C.H., & Yekovich, F.R. (1987). Activation and use of script-based antecedents in anaphoric reference. *Journal of Memory and Language, 26*, 673–691.

Wang, A.Y. (1983). Individual differences in learning speed. *Journal of Experimental Psychology: Learning, Memory, and Cognition, 9*, 300–311.

Wang, M.C. (1974). *The rationale and design of the self-schedule system.* Pittsburg, PA: University of Pittsburgh, Learning Research and Development Center.

Wanner, H.E. (1968). *On remembering, forgetting, and understanding sentences: A study of the deep structure hypothesis.* Unpublished doctoral disseration. Cambridge, MA: Harvard University.

Wason, P.C. (1968). Reasoning about a rule. *Quarterly Journal of Experimental Psychology, 20*, 273–281.

Waterman, D.A., & Hayes-Roth, F. (Eds.) (1978). *Pattern-directed inference systems.* New York, NY: Academic Press.

Watson, J.B. (1914). *Behavior: An introduction to comparative psychology.* New York, NY: H. Holt.

Wearne, D., & Hiebert, J. (1988). A cognitive approach to meaningful mathematics instruction: Testing a local theory using decimal numbers. *Journal for Research on Mathematics Education, 19*, 371–384.

Webb, N.M. (1991). Task-related verbal interaction and mathematics learning in small groups. *Journal for Research in Mathematics Education, 22*, 366–389.

Weiner, B. (1979). A theory of motivation for some classroom experiences. *Journal of Educational Psychology, 71*, 3–25.

Weiner, B. (1980). *Human motivation.* New York, NY: Holt, Rinehart, & Winston.

Weiner, B., Nierenberg, R., & Goldstein, M. (1976). Social learning (locus of control) versus attributional (causal stability) interpretations of expectancy of success. *Journal of Personality, 44*, 52–68.

Weiner, B., Russell, D., & Lerman, D. (1979). The cognition-emotion process in achievement-related contexts. *Journal of Personality and Social Psychology, 37*, 1211–1220.

Weinstein, C.E. (1978). Elaboration skills as a learning strategy. In O'Neil, H.F., Jr. (Ed.), *Learning strategies.* New York, NY: Academic Press.

Weinstein, R.S. (1983). Student perceptions of schooling. *Elementary School Journal, 83*, 287–312.

Weinstein, R.S., Marshall, H.H., Brattesani, K.A., & Middlestadt, S.E. (1982). Student perceptions of differential teacher treatment in open and traditional classrooms. *Journal of Educational Psychology, 74*, 678–692.

Weiser, M., & Shertz, J. (1983). Programming problem representation in novice and expert programmers. *International Journal of Man-Machine Studies, 19*, 391–398.

Westerman, D.A. (1991). Expert and novice teacher decision making. *Journal of Teacher Education, 42*(4), 292–305.

White, B.Y. (1984). Designing computer games to help physics students understand Newton's laws of motion. *Cognition and Instruction, 1,* 69–108.

White, B.Y., & Frederiksen, J.R. (1986). *Progressions of qualitative models as a foundation for intelligent learning environments.* Tech. Rep. #6277, Boston, MA: Bolt, Beranek, & Newman.

White, R.T., & Gagné, R.M. (1974). Past and future research on learning hierarchies. *Educational Psychologist, 11,* 19–28.

White, R.T., & Gagné, R.M. (1978). Formative evaluation applied to a learning hierarchy. *Contemporary Educational Psychology, 3,* 87–94.

Wickelgren, W.A. (1979). Chunking and consolidation: A theoretical synthesis of semantic networks, configuring in conditioning, S-R versus cognitive learning, normal forgetting, the amnesic syndrome, and the hippocampal arousal system. *Psychological Review, 86,* 44–60.

Williams, M.D., & Hollan, J.D. (1981). The process of retrieval from very long-term memory. *Cognitive Science, 5,* 87–119.

Wilson, S.M. (1988). *Understanding historical understanding: Subject matter knowledge and the teaching of history.* Unpublished doctoral dissertation. School of Education, Stanford University, Palo Alto, CA.

Wilson, T.D. (1985). Strangers to ourselves: The origins and accuracy of beliefs about one's own mental states. In J.H. Harvey & G. Weary (Eds.), *Attribution: Basic issues and applications.* Orlando, FL: Academic Press.

Winston, P. (1984). *Artificial intelligence.* Reading, MA: Addison-Wesley.

Witte, S.P., & Faigley, L. (1981). Coherence, cohesion, and writing quality. *College Composition and Communication, 32,* 189–204.

Wittrock, M.C. (1989). Generative processes of comprehension. *Educational Psychologist, 24,* 345–376.

Yackel, E., Cobb, P., & Wood, T. (1991). Small-group interactions as a source of learning opportunities in second-grade mathematics. *Journal for Research in Mathematics Education, 22,* 366–389.

Yekovich, F.R., & Thorndyke, P.W. (1981). An evaluation of alternative functional models of narrative schemata. *Journal of Verbal Learning and Verbal Behavior, 20,* 454–469.

Yekovich, F.R., & Walker, C.H. (1986). Retrieval of scripted concepts. *Journal of Memory and Language, 25,* 627–644.

Yekovich, F.R., Walker, C.H., Ogle, L.T., & Thompson, M.A. (1990). The influence of domain knowledge on inferencing in low-aptitude individuals. In A.C. Graesser & G.H. Bower (Eds), *The psychology of learning and motivation: Advances in research and theory, vol. 25: Inferences and text comprehension.* San Diego, CA: Academic Press.

Yerkes, R.M., & Dodson, J.R. (1908). The relation of strength of stimulus to rapidity of habit-formation. *Journal of Comparative Neurological Psychology, 18,* 459–482.

Yussen, S.R., Gagné, E.D., Garguilo, R., & Kunen, S. (1974). The distinction between perceiving and memorizing in elementary school children. *Child Development, 45,* 547–551.

Zajonc, R.B. (1980). Feeling and thinking: Preferences need no inferences. *American Psychologist, 35,* 151–175.

Zajonc, R.B. (1984). On the primary of affect. *American Psychologist, 35,* 151–175.

Zhu, X., & Simon, H.A. (1987). Learning mathematics from examples and by doing. *Cognition and Instruction, 4,* 137–166.

Zuker, B. (1985). *Algorithmic knowledge vs. understanding decimal numbers.* Unpublished Master's thesis, University of Haifa, Israel.

Credits

Figure 1-4. From S. P. Marshall, "What students learn (and remember) from word problem instruction." Paper presented at the annual meeting of the American Educational Research Association, Boston, 1990. Adapted by permission of the author. Figure 2-1. From D. E. Rumelhart and D. A. Norman, "Analogical processes in learning," in *Cognitive Skills and Their Acquisition*, ed. J. R. Anderson (Hillsdale, N.J.: Lawrence Erlbaum Associates, 1981). Adapted by permission of the publisher and author. Table 2-1. From W. Kintsch, "On modeling comprehension," *Educational Psychologist* 14 (1979). Reprinted by permission of Lawrence Erlbaum Associates and the author. Figure 2-4. From R. E. Snow, "Aptitude processes," in *Aptitude, Learning, and Instruction*, vol. 1, ed. R. E. Snow, P-A. Federico, and W. E. Montague (Hillsdale, N.J.: Lawrence Erlbaum Associates, 1980). Adapted by permission of the publisher and author. Figure 2-8. From F. R. Yekovich and C. H. Walker, "Retrieval of scripted concepts," *Journal of Memory and Language* 25 (1986). Adapted by permission of Academic Press, Inc. Figure 2-10. From W. Kintsch, "On modeling comprehension," *Educational Psychologist* 14 (1979). Adapted by permission of Lawrence Erlbaum Associates and the author. Figures 3-2, 3-4, and 3-5. From *The Brain: An Introduction to Neuroscience*, by Richard F. Thompson. Copyright © 1985 by W. H. Freeman and Company. Reprinted by permission of the publisher. Table 3-2. From W. K. Estes, "Is human memory obsolete?" *American Scientist* 68 (1980). Reprinted by permission of the publisher. Figure 3-3. From illustration by Carol Donner from Norman Geschwind, "Specializations of the Human Brain," *Scientific American* (September 1979). Adapted by permission. Figure 3-7. From illustration by Albert Miller in Charles F. Stevens, "The Neuron," *Scientific American* (September 1979). Reprinted by permission. Figure 3-8. From Gordon H. Bower/Ernest R. Hilgard, *Theories of Learning*, 5/e, (c) 1981, p. 503. Reprinted by permission of Prentice-Hall, Englewood Cliffs, N.J. Figure 4-3. From H. E. Wanner, "On Remembering, Forgetting, and Understanding Sentences: A Study of the Deep Structure Hypothesis." Doctoral diss., Harvard University, 1968 in J. R. Anderson, *Cognitive Psychology and Its Implications* (New York: W. H. Freeman and Co., 1990). Reprinted by permission of the publisher. Figures 4-6 and 4-7. From A. M. Collins and M. R. Quillian, "Retrieval time from semantic memory," *Journal of Verbal Learning and Verbal Behavior* 8 (1969). Reprinted by permission of the Academic Press, Inc., and the author. Figure 4-9. From P. R. Meudell, "Retrieval and representation in long-term memory," *Psychonomic Science* 23 (1971). Reprinted by permission of the Psychonomic Society, Inc., and the author. Figures 4-10 and 4-11. From S. M. Kosslyn et al., "Verbal images preserve spatial information: Evidence from studies of image scan-ning," *Journal of Experimental Psychology: Human Perception and Performance* 4 (1978). Copyright 1978 by the American Psychological Association. Reprinted by permission. Figures 4-12 and 4-13. From L. Cooper and R. Shepard, "Chronometric studies of the rotation of mental images," *Visual Information Processing*, ed. W. G. Chase (New York: Academic Press, 1973). Adapted by permission of the publisher. Figure 4-14 and Table 4-5. From S. Kerst and J. Howard, "Mental comparisons for ordered information on abstract and concrete dimensions," *Memory and Cognition* 5 (1977). Reprinted by permission of the Psychonomic Society, Inc. Table 5-1. From F. R. Yekovich and C. H. Walker, "Retrieval of scripted concepts," *Journal of Memory and Language* 25 (1986). Reprinted by permission of Academic Press, Inc. Figure 5-2. From E. Rosch et al., "Basic objects in natural categories," *Cognitive Psychology* 8 (1976). Reprinted by permission of Academic Press, Inc. Table 5-2. From F. C. Bartlett, *Remembering* (Cambridge: Cambridge University Press, 1932). Reprinted by permission. Figures 6-2 and 6-6, Table 6-6. Reprinted by permission of the publishers from *The Architecture of Cognition* by John R. Anderson, Cambridge, Mass.: Harvard University Press, Copyright © 1983 by the President and Fellows of Harvard College. Table 7-1. From G. Bower et al., "Scripts in memory for text," *Cognitive Psychology* 11 (1979). Reprinted by permission of Academic Press, Inc., and the author. Table 7-2. From S. Yussen et al., "The distinction between perceiving and memorizing in elementary school children," *Child Development* 45 (1974). Copyright 1974 by the Society for Research in Child Development, Inc. Adapted by permission of the publisher and author. Table 7-4. From R. W. Kulhavy and I. Swenson, "Imagery instructions and the comprehension of text," *British Journal of Educational Psychology* 45 (1975). Adapted by permission of the publisher and author. Table 7-5. From D. A. Hayes and R. J. Tierney, "Developing readers' knowledge through analogy," *Reading Research Quarterly* 17 (1982). Adapted by permission of David A. Hayes and the International Reading Association. Table 7-6. From M. Linden and M. Wittrock, "The teaching of reading comprehension according to the model of generative learning," *Reading Research Quarterly* 17 (1981). Adapted by permission of the author and the International Reading Association. Tables 7-7 and 7-8. From S. M. Glynn and F. J. DiVesta, "Outline and hierarchical organization as aids for study and retrieval," *Journal of Educational Psychology* 69 (1977). Copyright 1977 by the American Psychological Association. Adapted by permission of the publisher and author. Figure 7-9. From A. Y. Wang, "Individual differences in learning speed," *Journal of Experimental Psychology: Learning, Memory, and Cognition* 9 (1983). Copyright 1983 by the American Psychological Association. Reprinted by permission of the publisher and author. Figures 7-12 and 7-13. From J. S. Reitman and H. H. Reuter, "Organization revealed by recall orders and confirmed by pauses," *Cognitive Psychology* 12 (1980). Reprinted by permission of Academic Press, Inc., and the author. Figures 7-14 and 7-15, Table 7-3. From P. Thorndyke, "Cognitive structures in comprehension and memory of narrative discourse," *Cognitive Psychology* 9 (1977). Adapted by permission of Academic Press, Inc., and the author. Figure 7-17 and Table 7-9. From B. Hayes-Roth and P. W. Thorndyke, "Integration of knowledge from text," *Journal of Verbal Learning and Verbal Behavior* 18 (1979). Adapted by permission of Academic Press, Inc. Table 8-2. From B. Hayes-Roth and F. Hayes-Roth, "Concept learning and the recognition and classification of exemplars," *Journal of Verbal Learning and Verbal Behavior* 16 (1977). Reprinted by permission of Academic Press, Inc. Figure 8-4. From M. L. Gick and K. J. Holyoak, "Schema induction and analogical transfer," *Cognitive Psychology* 15 (1983). Reprinted by permission of Academic Press, Inc. Tables 8-4, 8-5, and 8-7. From R. D. Tennyson et al., "Exemplar and nonexemplar variables which produce correct classification behavior and specified classification errors," *Journal of Educational Psychology* 63 (1972). Copyright 1972 by the American Psychological Association. Adapted by permission of the publisher and author. Figure 8-5. From M. W. Lewis and J. R. Anderson, "Discrimination of operator schemata in problem-solving: Learning from examples," *Cognitive Psychology* 17 (1985). Reprinted by permission of Academic Press, Inc. Figures 9-3 and 9-4. From J. R. Anderson, "Acquisition of cognitive skill," *Psychological Review* 89 (1982). Copyright 1982 by the American Psychological Association. Reprinted by permission. Figures 9-5 and 9-6. From L. B. Resnick et al., "Transfer and sequence in learning double classification skills," *Journal of Experimental Child Psychology* 11 (1971). Reprinted by permission of Academic Press, Inc., and the author. Figure 9-7. From M. J. Adams et al., *Odyssey: A curriculum for thinking. Vol. 1: Foundations of reasoning.* (Watertown, M.A.: Charlesbridge Publishing, 1986). Figure 9-8. From R. J. Herrnstein et al., *Odyssey: A curriculum for thinking. Vol. 2: Understanding language.* (Watertown, M.A.: Charlesbridge Publishing, 1986). Table 9-11. From M. J. Adams, "Thinking skills curricula: Their promise and progress." *Educational Psychologist* 24 (1989). Reprinted by permission of the publisher and the author. Table 9-9. From C. H. Lewis, "Production system models of practice effects." Unpublished doctoral dissertation, University of Michigan, Ann Arbor, 1978. Adapted by permission of the author. Table 10-1. From A. Newell and H. A. Simon, *Human Problem Solving* (Englewood Cliffs, N.J.: Prentice-Hall, 1972). Adapted by permission of the publisher. Figure 10-4, Tables 10-2 and 10-3. From A. L. Brown et al., "Young children's mental models determine analogical transfer across problems with a common goal structure," *Cognitive Development* 1 (1986). Adapted by permission of Ablex Publishing. Table 10-4. From G. T. Fong et al., "The effects of statistical training on thinking about everyday problems," *Cognitive Psychology* 18 (1986). Reprinted by permission. Table 11-1. From R. E. Mayer, "Different problem-solving competencies established in learning computer programming with and without meaningful models," *Journal of Educational Psychology* 67 (1975). Copyright 1975 by the American Psychological Association. Adapted by permission. Table 11-2. From R. E. Mayer and B. Bromage, "Different recall protocols for technical texts due to advanced organizers," *Journal of Educational Psychology* 72 (1980). Copyright 1980 by the American Psychological Association. Adapted by permission. Figures 11-4 and 11-5, Tables 11-3 and 11-4. Adapted and reprinted by permission of the publishers from *The Transfer of Cognitive Skill* by Mark K. Singley and John R. Anderson, Cambridge, Mass.: Harvard University Press, Copyright © 1989 by the President and Fellows of Harvard College. Figure 11-6, Tables 11-5, 11-6, 11-7. From R. Gagné and N. Paradise, "Abilities and learning sets in knowledge acquisition," *Psychological Monographs: General and Applied* 75 (1961). Copyright © 1961 by the American Psychological Association. Adapted by permission of the publisher and author. Tables 11-10 and 11-11. From E. S. Ghatala et al., "Training cognitive strategy monitoring in children," *American Educational Research Journal* 22 (1985). Copyright 1985 by the American Educational Research Association. Adapted by permission of the publisher. Tables 11-12 and 11-14. From E. Gagné et al., "Training thirteen-year-olds to elaborate while studying text," *Journal of Human Learning* 3 (1984). Reprinted by permission of John Wiley & Sons, Chichester, England. Figure 12-6. From L. C. Ehri and L. C. Wilce, "Development of word identification speed in skilled and less skilled beginning readers," *Journal of Educational Psychology* 75 (1983). Copyright 1983 by the American Psychological Association. Reprinted by permission of the publisher and author. Table 12-6. From C. A. Perfetti and S. F. Roth, "Some of the interactive processes in reading and their role in reading skill," in *Interactive Processes in Reading*, ed. A. M. Lesgold and C. A. Perfetti (Hillsdale, N.J.: Lawrence Erlbaum Associates, 1981). Adapted by permission of the publisher and author. Figures 12-7, 12-11, and 12-12. From J. R. Fredericksen, "Sources of process interactions in reading," in *Interactive Processes in Reading*, ed. M. A. Lesgold and C. A. Perfetti (Hillsdale, N.J.: Lawrence Erlbaum Associates, 1981). Reprinted by permission. Tables 12-7 and 12-8. From B. J. F. Meyer et al., "Use of top-level structure in text: Key for reading comprehension in ninth-grade students," *Reading Research Quarterly* 16 (1980). Reprinted with permission of Bonnie J. F. Meyer and the International Reading Association. Figure 12-8. From R. C. Calfee, P. Lindamood, and C. Lindamood, "Academic phonetic skills and reading—kindergarten through twelfth grade," *Journal of Educational Psychology* 64 (1973). Copyright 1973 by the American Psychological Association. Reprinted by permission of the publisher and author. Figures 12-9 and 12-10. From R. L. Venezky and D. Johnson, "Development of two letter-sound patterns in grades one through three," *Journal of Educational Psychology* 64 (1973). Copyright 1973 by the American Psychological Association. Adapted by permission of the publisher and author. Table 12-9. From A. Brown and S. Smiley, "Rating the importance of structural units of prose passages," *Child Development* 48 (1977).

Copyright 1977 by the Society for Research in Child Development, Inc. Adapted by permission of the publisher and author. Table 12-10. From C. E. Weinstein, "Elaboration skills as a learning strategy," *Learning Strategies*, ed. H. F. O'Neil, Jr. (New York: Academic Press, 1978). Adapted by permission of the publisher and the author. Table 12-11. From P. L. Harris et al., "Children's detection and awareness of textual anomaly," *Journal of Experimental Child Psychology* 31 (1981). Reprinted by permission of Academic Press, Inc., and the author. Table 12-12. From R. Garner and R. Reis, "Monitoring and resolving comprehension obstacles: An investigation of spontaneous text lookbacks among upper-grade good and poor comprehenders," *Reading Research Quarterly* 16, no. 4 (1981). Reprinted by permission of Ruth Garner and the International Reading Association. Figure 12-13. From M. A. Thompson, "Redefining the poor reader: Distinguishing the effects of domain knowledge from aptitude on reading comprehension process." Doctoral diss., Catholic University of America, 1992. Reprinted by permission of the author. Tables 12-13 and 12-14. From C. W. Walker and F. R. Yekovich, "Activation and use of script-based antecedents in anaphoric reference," *Journal of Memory and Language* 26 (1987). Reprinted by permission of Academic Press, Inc. Table 12-15. From G. J. Spilich et al., "Text processing of domain-related information for individuals with high and low domain knowledge," *Journal of Verbal Learning and Verbal Behavior* 18 (1979). Reprinted by permission of Academic Press, Inc. Table 12-16. From F. R. Yekovich et al., "The influence of domain knowledge on inferencing in low-aptitude individuals," in *Inferences and Text Comprehension* (San Diego: Academic Press, 1990). Adapted by permission of the publisher. Figure 12-18. From A. S. Palincsar and A. L. Brown, "Reciprocal teaching of comprehension-fostering and comprehension-monitoring activities," *Cognition and Instruction* 1 (1984). Reprinted by permission of Lawrence Erlbaum Associates and A. S. Palincsar. Figure 13-1. From L. Flower and J. Hayes, "A cognitive process theory of writing," *College Composition and Communication* 32 (1981). Reprinted by permission of the National Council of Teachers of English. Table 13-1. From L. Flower and J. Hayes, "The pregnant pause: An inquiry into the nature of planning," *Research in the Teaching of English* 15 (1981). Adapted by permission of the National Council of Teachers of English. Figures 13-2, 13-3, and 13-5. From D. McCutchen and C. Perfetti, "Coherence and connectedness in the development of discourse production," *Text* 2 (1982). Reprinted by permission of the authors. Figure 13-4 and Table 13-6. From A. Applebee, R. Durst, and B. Newell, "The demands of school writing," in *Contexts for Learning to Write*, ed. A. Applebee (Norwood, N.J.: Ablex Publishing, 1984). Reprinted by permission of the publisher. Table 13-4. From L. Flower et al., "Planning in writing: The cognition of a constructive process," in *A Rhetoric of Doing*, ed. S. Witte, N. Nakadate, and R. Cherry (Carbondale: Southern Illinois University Press, in press). Reprinted by permission of the publisher. Figure 13-6, Tables 13-2 and 13-3. From M. Atwell, "The author as reader: A comparison of proficient and less-proficient college writers," *New Inquiries in Reading Research and Instruction*, ed. J. Niles. 31st National Reading Conference Yearbook, Washington, D.C., National Reading Conference, 1981. Adapted by permission of National Council of Teachers of English. Table 13-8. From M. Scardamalia and C. Bereiter, "The development of evaluative, diagnostic, and remedial capabilities in children's composing," in *The Psychology of Written Language: A Developmental Approach*, ed. M. Mattern (London: John Wiley & Sons, 1984). Adapted by permission of the publisher. Table 13-9. From E. J. Bartlett, "Learning to revise: Some component processes," *What Writers Know: The Language, Process, and Structure of Written Discourse*, ed. M. Nystrand (Orlando: Academic Press, 1982). Adapted by permission of the publisher. Table 13-10. From J. Voss et al., "Text generation and recall by high-knowledge and low-knowledge individuals," *Journal of Verbal Learning and Verbal Behavior* 19 (1980). Adapted by permission of the Academic Press, Inc., and the author. Tables 13-11, 13-12, and 13-13. From E. Cohen and M. Scardamalia, "The effects of instructional intervention in the revision of essays by grade six children." Paper presented at the American Educational Research Association, Montreal, April 1983. Adapted by permission of the author. Figure 14-1 and Table 14-2. From R. S. Siegler, "Individual differences in strategy choices: Good students, not-so-good students, and perfectionists," *Child Development* 59 (1988). © The Society for Research in Child Development, Inc. Reprinted by permission. Figure 14-2 and Table 14-4. From J. Brown and R. Burton, "Diagnostic models for procedural bugs in basic mathematical skills," *Cognitive Science* (1978). Reprinted by permission of Ablex Publishing. Figure 14-5 and Table 14-5. From W. E. Geeslin and R. J. Shavelson, "An exploratory analysis of the representation of a mathematical structure in student's cognitive structures," *American Educational Research Journal* 12 (1975). Copyright 1975 by the American Educational Research Association. Reprinted by permission of the publisher. Table 14-6. From E. Silver, "Recall of mathematical problem information: Some related problems," *Journal for Research in Mathematics Education* 12 (1981). Adapted by permission of National Council of Teachers of Mathematics. Figure 14-6, Tables 14-7 and 14-8. From R. V. Morales et al., "Developmental differences in understanding and solving simple mathematics word problems," *Cognition and Instruction* 2 (1985). Reprinted by permission of Lawrence Erlbaum Associates and the author. Figures 14-7 and 14-8, Table 14-9. From P. Thompson, "Quantitative concepts as a foundation for algebra: First-year progress reports," NSF Grant No. MDR 89-50311. Reprinted by permission of the author. Figure 14-9. From R. I. Charles and F. K. Lester, "An evaluation of a process-oriented instructional program in mathematical problem solving in grades 5 and 7," *Journal for Research in Mathematics Education* 15 (1984). Reprinted by permission from the *Journal for Research in Mathematics Education*. Figure 14-10. From S. R. Goldman et al., "Extended practice of basic addition facts: Strategy changes in learning-disabled students," *Cognition and Instruction* 5 (1988). Reprinted by permission of Lawrence Erlbaum Associates and the author. Tables 14-10 and 14-11. From

C. Robinson and J. Hayes, "Making inferences about relevance in understanding problems," *Human Reasoning*, ed. R. Revlin and R. E. Mayer (Washington, D.C.: V. H. Winston and Sons, 1978). Reprinted by permission of the author. Figure 14-11 and Table 14-15. From D. Wearne and J. Hiebert, "A cognitive approach to meaningful mathematics instruction," *Journal for Research in Mathematics Education* 19 (1988). Reprinted by permission from the *Journal for Research in Mathematics Education*. Table 14-12. From R. E. Mayer, "Memory for algebra story problems," *Journal of Educational Psychology* 74 (1982). Copyright 1982 by the American Psychological Association. Reprinted by permission. Tables 14-13 and 14-14. From J. A. Hope and J. M. Sherrill, "Characteristics of unskilled and skilled mental calculators," *Journal for Research in Mathematics Education* 18 (1987). Adapted with permission from the *Journal for Research in Mathematics Education*. Table 14-16. From S. R. Swing et al., "Thinking skills versus learning time: Effects of alternative classroom-based intervention on students' mathematics problem-solving," *Cognition and Instruction* 5 (1988). Reprinted by permission of Lawrence Erlbaum Associates and P. L. Peterson. Figures 15-1 and 15-2. From J. Okey and R. Gagné, "Revision of a science topic using evidence of performance on subordinate skills," *Journal of Research in Science Teaching* 7. Copyright © 1970 by John Wiley & Sons, Inc. Reprinted by permission of the publisher. Table 15-2. From B. Bromage and R. E. Mayer, "Relationship between what is remembered and creative problem-solving performance in science learning," *Journal of Educational Psychology* 73 (1981). Copyright 1981 by the American Psychological Association. Adapted by permission of the publisher and author. Figures 15-3, 15-4, 15-11, and 15-12. From M. Chi et al., "Categorization and representation of physics problems by experts and novices," *Cognitive Science* 5 (1981). Reprinted by permission of Ablex Publishing. Figures 15-5 and 15-6. From R. S. Siegler and D. D. Richards, "The development of two concepts," in *Recent Advances in Cognitive Development Theory*, ed. C. Brainerd (New York: Springer-Verlag, 1983). Reprinted by permission of the publisher and author. Tables 15-5 and 15-6. From J. F. Voss et al., "Individual differences in the solving of social science problems," in *Individual Differences in Cognition*, ed. R. Dillon and R. Schmeck (San Diego: Academic Press, 1983). Adapted by permission of the publisher. Figures 15-7 and 15-8, Table 15-3. From R. Siegler, "Three aspects of cognitive development," *Cognitive Science* 8 (1976). Adapted by permission of Academic Press, Inc., and the author. Tables 15-7 and 15-8. From K. J. Roth, "Conceptual change learning and student processing of science texts," Institute for Research on Teaching, Michigan State University, East Lansing, 1986. Reprinted by permission of the author. Figures 15-9 and 15-10. From A. Champagne et al., "Structural representations of students' knowledge before or after science instruction," *Journal of Research in Science Teaching* 19 (1981). Copyright © 1981 by John Wiley & Sons, Inc. Reprinted by permission of John Wiley & Sons, Inc. Figure 15-13 and Table 15-4. From J. H. Larkin, "Expert and novice performance in solving physics problems," *Science* 80 (June 20, 1980).

Copyright 1980 by the American Association for the Advancement of Science. Reprinted by permission of the AAAS and the author. Figure 15-17. From B. Y. White, "Designing computer games to help physics students understand Newton's laws of motion," *Cognition and Instruction* 1 (1984). Reprinted by permission of Lawrence Erlbaum Associates and the author. Figures 15-19 and 15-20, Tables 15-9, 15-10, 15-11, 15-12, 15-13, and 15-14. From L. K. Cook, "Instructional effects of text structure-based reading strategies on the comprehension of scientific prose." Unpublished doctoral dissertation, University of California at Santa Barbara, 1983. Table 16-1. From B. Weiner et al., "The cognition-emotion process in achievement-related contexts," *Journal of Personality and Social Psychology* 37 (1979). Copyright 1979 by the American Psychological Association. Reprinted by permission. Figure 16-4. From R. M. Rosenbaum, "A dimensional analysis of the perceived causes of success and failure." Unpublished doctoral dissertation, University of California at Los Angeles, 1972, as in B. Weiner, *Human Motivation* (New York: Holt, Rinehart and Winston, 1980). Reprinted by permission. Figure 16-5. From W. Meyer, in B. Weiner, *Human Motivation* (New York: Holt, Rinehart and Winston, 1980). Adapted by permission of the publisher and Universitätsbibliothek Bochum. Figure 16-7. From B. Weiner, *Human Motivation* (New York: Holt, Rinehart and Winston, 1980). Adapted by permission of the publisher. Figures 16-9 and 16-10. From S. Graham and B. Weiner, "Teacher feelings and student thoughts," in *Aptitude, Learning, and Instruction*, vol. 3, ed. R. S. Snow, P-A. Federico, and W. Montague (Hillsdale, N.J.: Lawrence Erlbaum Associates, 1987). Reprinted by permission of the publisher and author. Figure 16-12. From W. K. Estes, "Reinforcement and human behavior," *American Scientist* 68 (1972). Adapted by permission of the publisher. Tables 17-1 and 17-2. From E. T. Emmer et al., "Effective classroom management at the beginning of the school year," *Elementary School Journal* 80 (1980). Reprinted by permission of the University of Chicago Press. Figures 17-3 and 17-4. From M. K. Stein et al., "Subject matter knowledge and elementary instruction: A case from functions and graphing," *American Educational Research Journal* 27, no. 4 (1990). Copyright 1990 by the American Educational Research Association. Reprinted by permission by permission of the publisher. Table 17-3. From C. Evertson et al., "Predictors of effective teaching in junior high mathematics," *Journal for Research in Mathematics Education* 11 (1980). Adapted by permission of the author and the National Council of Teachers of Mathematics. Tables 17-4 and 17-5. From T. L. Good and D. A. Grouws, "Teaching effects: A process-product study in fourth-grade mathematics classrooms," *Journal of Teacher Education* 28 (1979). Adapted by permission of the author and American Association of Colleges for Teacher Education.

Tables 17-6, 17-7, and 17-8. From L. D. Housner and D. C. Griffey, "Teacher cognition: Differences in planning and interactive decisionmaking between experienced and inexperienced teachers," *Research Quarterly for Exercise and Sport* 56 (1985). Reprinted by permission of Lynn D. Housner.

Subject Index

Author Index